THE FORGOTTEN BOROUGH

THE FORGOTTEN BOROUGH

Staten Island and the Subway

KENNETH M. GOLD

Columbia University Press
New York

Columbia University Press
Publishers Since 1893
New York   Chichester, West Sussex
cup.columbia.edu
Copyright © 2023 Columbia University Press
All rights reserved

Library of Congress Cataloging-in-Publication Data
Names: Gold, Kenneth M. (Kenneth Mark), 1966– author.
Title: The forgotten borough : Staten Island and the subway / Kenneth M. Gold.
Other titles: Staten Island and the subway
Description: New York : Columbia University Press, [2023] |
  Includes bibliographical references and index.
Identifiers: LCCN 2022027706 (print) | LCCN 2022027707 (ebook) |
  ISBN 9780231208604 (hardcover) | ISBN 9780231208611 (trade paperback) |
  ISBN 9780231557511 (ebook)
Subjects: LCSH: Staten Island (New York, N.Y.)—History—20th century. |
  New York (N.Y.)—History—20th century. | Local transit—Social aspects—
  New York (State)—New York—History—20th century. | Urban transportation—
  New York (State)—New York—History—20th century. | Subways—Social aspects—
  New York (State)—New York—History—20th century. | Staten Island
  (New York, N.Y.)—Politics and government—20th century. | New York (N.Y.)—
  Politics and government—20th century.
Classification: LCC F127.S7 G65 2023 (print) | LCC F127.S7 (ebook) |
  DDC 974.7/26—dc23/eng/20220610
LC record available at https://lccn.loc.gov/2022027706
LC ebook record available at https://lccn.loc.gov/2022027707

Cover design: Julia Kushnirsky
Cover photograph: Shutterstock

ACKNOWLEDGMENTS

In 2004, I was invited to join the Faculty/Staff Research Seminar on the Study of Staten Island and Its Contexts at the College of Staten Island (CSI). The seminar's purpose was to foster scholarship on the college's home borough; my own motivations to participate came from my professional and personal needs at that time. My first book had recently been published, and I was eager to embark on a new project. My first child had recently been born, and I was eager to avoid long research trips out of town. The seminar, ably led by Richard Flanagan and Cindy Wong, provided a wonderful introduction to a fascinating locale and germinated this book.

Nearly twenty years later I have finally managed to finish it. The path to completion was rather circuitous. The direction of the book evolved significantly as I immersed myself in research and continuously discovered stories that required telling and patterns that needed to be understood. Two major detours into academic administration, as department chair and then founding dean of the CSI School of Education, derailed for years my work on the book. Picking up a project after a lengthy hiatus is no easy task; doing it twice is that much more difficult. The acknowledgments that follow are for people who helped me return to this project as well as for those who made this a better book than it otherwise would have been.

Two amazing features of Staten Island that quickly become apparent to me are its notable archival collections and sizeable number of local historians who still know far more than I do about most aspects of Staten Island. In the early years of my research, the Staten Island Historical Society archives at

Richmondtown became a regular destination on Tuesdays as well as on many other days thanks to Carlotta DeFillo. Her good cheer is infectious, and her deep knowledge of the collection led me to many useful sources. More recently, Carli DeFillo has helped me incorporate some powerful images into the book.

When I started this project, the archives of the Staten Island Institute of Arts and Sciences were in the dank basement of the Staten Island Museum on Stuyvesant Place, and I loved going there. The archivist Pat Salmon seemed to know everything about Staten Island, and the late Dottie D'Eletto was a welcoming presence. The archives' move to Snug Harbor and a reading room on the first floor made for a far more picturesque setting to work. There, Cara Dellatte and, more recently, Gabriella Leone ably supported my research by introducing me to multiple items I would not otherwise have found. Gabby also was incredibly helpful in locating many of the maps and images included in this book. Cara relocated to the New York Public Library, where she continued to aid this project, as have numerous others there and at archives across the Northeast. The Staten Island Chamber of Commerce is a place of work and not an archive, so I am especially grateful to Linda Baran for allowing me on multiple occasions to pore over minutes and other documents from the organization's earliest years. Closer to home, Christine McEvilly provided invaluable bibliographic aid in tracking down missing information and correcting anomalies.

Staten Island celebrated its 350th anniversary of European settlement in 2011, an occasion that might have gone unnoticed were it not for Lori Weintrob. Her superb organization of the SI 350 celebration brought together people from a wide array of institutions across the island to plan a series of academic and public events throughout the year, including a wonderful conference at CSI. Thanks to Lori, my involvement included learning much more about local history; meeting Charles Sachs, Phil Papas, Tom Matteo, and many others whose expertise broadened my perspective; and coediting *Discovering Staten Island* with her.

Zachary Schrag read the entire draft as a reviewer for Columbia University Press. I am grateful for his incredibly thorough comments and his willingness to reveal his identity so that we could have additional conversations about the text. Dan Albert, Rich Flanagan, Mary Jane Friedrich, Martin Melosi, and Bethany Rogers read portions of the manuscript, and their observations have made it a better work. At CSI, I have now had more than twenty-five years of conversation about scholarship, and the voices of colleagues in education remained in my head even as the book moved away from a focus on progressive schooling and student life. I did not always heed their recommendations, so I own all the remaining flaws of this book.

At Columbia University Press, I have appreciated Stephen Wesley's interest in the project, patience as it went through numerous revisions, and willingness to heed my voice with regard to how this study should be framed. Christian Winting's eye for images more than compensated for my own lack of discrimination. Michael Haskell has ably supervised the production process, and Annie Barva did a superb job of copyediting. Thanks as well to all the other members of the staff who helped publish this book.

The encouragement I received from my family to complete this work has made all the difference: my brother, Evan, sister-in-law, Sharon, and nephew, Jordan; my sister, Laura, and niece, Raphaela; and especially my mother, Marion. My late father, Robert, has been gone for more than thirty years now but remains a powerful model for my own professional aspirations and growth. This book is dedicated to my wife, Marcy, and sons, Robert, Leo, and Nathaniel. Although data show the nuclear family to be in decline, ours is alive and well even as the kids are starting to depart, and we no longer regularly go camping, watch *SNL*, or play Catan together. It's still the best possible loving environment and more than any other is responsible for nurturing this book.

ABBREVIATIONS

B&O	Baltimore and Ohio Railroad
BRT	Brooklyn Rapid Transit Company
CPC	City Planning Commission
CTC	Citizens Tunnel Committee
ERCA	Emergency Relief and Construction Act
FWIA	Fifth Ward Improvement Association
IRT	Interborough Rapid Transit Company
MRTC	Metropolitan Rapid Transit Commission
NYCTA	New York City Tunnel Authority
PRR	Pennsylvania Railroad
PSC	Public Service Commission
PWA	Public Works Administration
RFC	Reconstruction Finance Corporation
RTB	Board of Rapid Transit Railroad Commissioners
SICC	Staten Island Chamber of Commerce
TBTA	Triborough Bridge and Tunnel Authority
WPA	Works Progress Administration

THE FORGOTTEN BOROUGH

INTRODUCTION

In December 1937, Robert Molinari, a future New York State assemblyman and father of a future borough president, wrote to the master builder Robert Moses in the latter's capacity as the parks commissioner of New York City. Molinari offered words of support mingled with a few suggestions for Moses's projects for the beach and boardwalk on Staten Island. Mindful of past disappointments and overdue improvements, he also wanted to make sure the work was completed: "Staten Island, the forgotten Borough, has long waited for a change for the better. We have seen our transit tunnel started, only to blow up like a dream. We have hoped for cheaper ferry fares only to be set back by technicalities. We have seen the Free Port started, only to be stagnated by red tape."[1] Molinari articulated a sentiment that had steadily gained potency over the nearly forty years since Staten Island joined New York City as Richmond Borough and had seen its transportation needs go unmet. Undeterred by past setbacks, he would continue to work on behalf of a rapid-transit link between Brooklyn and Staten Island during his lone term in the legislature during the early 1940s.

Molinari neither coined the name "Forgotten Borough" nor was the last to use it. A decade earlier, a real estate developer had wondered about the impact of the Port of New York Authority's new bridges on housing prices in the Forgotten Borough, and a generation later locals questioned whether the opening of the Verrazzano Bridge would spur industry to remember it.[2] Over time, "Forgotten Borough" eclipsed other names expressing the same outlook. To some, Staten Island was the "step-child" of the city—that proverbially unloved member of the family.³ Tapping into notions of its abuse, inherent worthiness, and ultimate redemption, others named it "Cinderella" after the literary archetype for stepchildren.⁴ Expressing disappointment with Staten Island's early exclusion from plans for subway expansion, the *Richmond County Advance* dubbed it the "Orphan Borough," and one writer to the paper deemed it the "poor relation" of the city.⁵ But "Forgotten Borough" has evolved into the most common designation for Staten Island by others and the most self-referential description by residents. It is not difficult to discern why.

As Molinari's words suggest, Staten Islanders linked this image to a host of frustrations—policy and otherwise. "It is to be remembered that the City has treated Staten Island shabbily. It has failed to fulfill its promise when it took in Richmond over 50 years ago," one resident wrote to Mayor Fiorello La Guardia in 1941.⁶ Unmet expectations about population growth and economic development thwarted the high hopes of civic boosters and realty interests. Staten Islanders especially bemoaned the failure to obtain desired transportation improvements. Inadequate service by municipal ferries and the Staten Island Railway stymied commuters, but for many the holy grail was a subway connection to the rest of the city. As the *Staten Island Advance* observed of one group working in early 1935 to obtain a rail link, "Their cynicism has a solid foundation on years of sad experience."⁷ Certainly the perception that its needs were ignored by the city was expressed almost from the outset of Greater New York and remained potent as a mentalité of late twentieth-century Staten Islanders.

The notion of mentalité, or shared sensibilities among a defined group of people, grew out of the twentieth century Annales school of French historians. Its use by American historians has always been limited, but Daniel Little's definition—"a shared way of looking at the world and reacting to happenings and actions by others, distinctive from other groups and reasonably similar across a specific group"—holds utility for this book. Little's approach suggests mentalité is formed through reaction, but that reaction may be to material conditions as well as to events—to physical separation and political rebuffs in the case of Staten Island. Identifying mentalité is methodologically similar to defining the related yet distinct notion of ideology—looking for its expression in historical artifacts from an era but also including the analysis of collective behavior. One does not need to scratch very deeply on Staten Island to discover articulations of being forgotten and organized actions around garbage, subways, and secession that expressed it behaviorally.⁸

Despite the varied contexts in which it was asserted, the notion that Richmond was the Forgotten Borough of New York City included some shared understandings. For inhabitants of Staten Island, the key emphasis was on neglect—primarily by the city's government but coming to include any entity, such as New York State and the Port Authority, that had some jurisdiction over Staten Island. There was also a sense of being remembered to its detriment, of mistreatment through unwanted attention that was evident even before the city eyed the borough as a place for its refuse. The signs of its inconsequentiality were unmistakable and ubiquitous to its residents, and Molinari's words capture the sense of grievance inherent in local usage of the phrase. Staten Islanders' resentments became such a common part of its culture that a powerful movement for secession occurred in the late twentieth century. That drive has helped obscure earlier generations who sought connectivity; their efforts with regard to transportation are the focus of this book.

Other New Yorkers acknowledged this perception of the island's unimportance. Their employment of the name "Forgotten Borough" also reflected the social and cultural differences and physical distance associated with it. Staten Island was and remains forgotten because it is neither near nor like the other boroughs—at least in relative terms. In most every manner, Staten Island is closer to Manhattan than to suburban Morristown or rural Minnesota. Staten Island is more typically juxtaposed with the other three outer boroughs, but even they look very different from it, with the exception of their own outskirt areas. That Staten Island is now experiencing changes that began decades earlier in parts of Brooklyn, Queens, and the Bronx does not diminish how much it still stands apart from the rest of New York City.

These fundamental characteristics of Staten Island—social difference and physical distance—are mutually reinforcing and historically determined. Although that may seem like an odd statement to make about Staten Island's geographic location—after all, the mileage to it from the other boroughs has remained unchanged over time—its relative distance from its neighbors has expanded and contracted as a result of developments in transportation and communication. That distance has always mattered, but in some eras it mattered more than in others. The time span covered in *The Forgotten Borough*, the first half of the twentieth century, was such a period of heightened separation for the borough as it alone remained unconnected to Greater New York by the city's subway system.

As for difference, it is far too easy to see the borough ahistorically—that its otherness today is indicative of how it has always been. For much of its pre-twentieth-century history, Staten Island mirrored its neighbors in a number of important ways—from its burgeoning industry to its immigrant population. In 1890, Staten Island was neither so geographically distant nor so socially different from the outer reaches of the future boroughs orbiting around the harbor's two great cities: New York and Brooklyn. After Staten Island joined Greater New York in 1898, it subsequently found that boroughhood did not quite lead to the amenities in transportation that its boosters envisioned. As the other four boroughs became linked by rails going over bridges and through tunnels, Staten Island's relative distance from its counterparts peaked. The central argument of this book is that these crucial years, in which Richmond Borough alone remained physically disconnected from the rest of the city, did much to forge contemporary Staten Island. By the opening of the Verrazzano-Narrows Bridge in 1964, Staten Island differed greatly from the Bronx, Brooklyn, Manhattan, and Queens: primarily by being whiter, wealthier, and less populated. Its politics also became more politically conservative, resembling a number of communities on the periphery or completely outside of many major American cities.[9]

These two seminal events form the chronological bookends for *The Forgotten Borough*, and they should not surprise those who have any familiarity with the city's history. As the new millennium approached in 1999, the *Staten Island Advance* provided its readers with a list of one hundred events from the island's history and polled them on which were the most significant. The highest-rated event was the opening of the Verrazzano-Narrows Bridge in 1964, and ranked second was Staten Island's joining of Greater New York in 1898.[10] Scholarship about Staten Island similarly and rightfully understands these two moments as vital to the island's history.[11] Even histories of New York City, which rarely reference Staten Island, almost always mention Richmond in relation to consolidation and sometimes the bridge.[12] The sixty-plus years that lie between those two events, however, typically receive minimal attention.[13] Much of the historical interest in Staten Island focuses on the eighteenth and nineteenth centuries, and much of its residents' current historicism posits the opening of the Verrazzano-Narrows Bridge as the spark for transformation in the years since 1964. This book is meant as a corrective to both chronological tendencies.

The 1898–1964 period also saw marked change for Staten Island. Richard Flanagan and Dan Kramer have shown how Staten Island's political identity on the center-right emerged in the years following World War II.[14] As Martin Melosi traces in *Fresh Kills*, the opening on Staten Island of a landfill serving the entire city in 1948 created a powerful yet sullied identity for the borough.[15] Ted Steinberg has depicted the rise of conservationism on Staten Island and the subsequent elimination of its common lands, where residents had traditionally hunted.[16] Charles Sachs has shown how Staten Island's nineteenth-century industrial endeavors grew by 1920 into some large-scale enterprises, two with more than 1,000 employees, as industry in Greater New York City took on an increasingly "polynuclear" pattern.[17] The focus here, however, is on a development with arguably the greatest impact on Staten Island during these years, though it was actually a nonevent. For decades, Staten Islanders strove for but did not achieve a rapid-transit or commuter-rail connection to the rest of the city. Because this disappointment helped establish many of Staten Island's modern cultural and demographic features, understanding how and why it transpired becomes imperative. Tracing the most significant of those multiple efforts, explaining their miscarriage, and assessing the impact of their collective failure are this book's primary tasks.

Is there really a story to tell? Is it not easy enough to note that Staten Island's relatively small population made it simply too weak politically to reach its objective to be connected? Or was it too far from Manhattan to become a viable destination for a city always struggling to find funds to build, expand, and operate a subway system without a deficit? Geographic explanations for historical developments, popularized through the work of Jared Diamond, are of great utility provided one avoids overly deterministic interpretations.[18] Historians have increasingly and profitably incorporated spatial analysis into their work, and studies of transportation within metropolitan areas in particular have informed this book.[19] Distance may have dictated that Staten Island would not be the first outer borough linked by rail to Manhattan, but it did not necessarily prevent a route from happening at all—or at least to date. There were multiple moments over a forty-year period when such a line might have been constructed and historically contingent reasons why it wasn't in each case. Dealt a bad hand (five miles by water from Manhattan), Staten Islanders nonetheless played it poorly.[20]

It did not help that sitting around the table with Staten Island were other skilled card players. One set came from the world of business, concerned primarily with turning a profit and disinterested in a subway line that would financially not break even for years. With subways built and operated for the city by private corporations, matters of public transit had to contend with and balance political and economic concerns. To help do so, both the public sector and the private sector increasingly relied on the world of professional expertise. Local civic boosters may have wanted a subway tunnel and businessmen a profit, but the engineers calculated whether either was possible and the managers how it could get done. These experts, too, played a formidable game of cards. A third group comprised the other four boroughs—the Bronx, Brooklyn, Manhattan, and Queens—in competition for resources, in particular those earmarked for public improvements in transportation, recreation, and more. On the powerful New York City Board of Estimate and Apportionment, three citywide elected officials could constitute a voting majority, yet in a political culture where these officials often clashed, the Staten Island Borough president had the same one vote as did the Bronx and Queens Borough presidents. At key moments between 1900 and 1945, players from all of these groups managed to thwart the Staten Islanders' aspirations.

These struggles notwithstanding, far more than a simple pluralist dynamic was at play in Greater New York. Although one incarnation of this dynamic has been the urban center versus its periphery, the field of urban history has evolved from being overly dichotomous between central city and suburb to having much more of a metropolitan focus that emphasizes interplay between them.[21] At the same time, the generalization of poor cities surrounded by affluent suburbs has yielded to a much more nuanced view of both types of spatial organization—finding, for example, a working-class suburban presence in many metropolitan areas in the early twentieth century.[22] Finally, historians have incorporated the lenses of social science—economics, political science, sociology, and geography—to offer a complicated array of factors, including job markets, transportation networks, ethnic cohesiveness, and topography, to explain the centrifugal forces at work in metropolitan areas.

The notion of a forgotten borough implies an underlying assumption that is informed by these scholarly trends. If Staten Island has been overlooked, or even if its residents have just perceived as much, then who or what has been turning away from it? Of the entities and forces—be they cultural, economic, political, or social—that have exerted influence on the borough, New York City emerges as a powerful conduit for them. The history of Staten Island— especially in the twentieth century—cannot be understood in isolation. The island's relationship with New York City, in particular Manhattan, is essential to its experience, central to the approach of recent scholarship on Staten Island, and pivotal to this work as well.[23] The case of Staten Island as part of a larger metropolitan system helps illuminate the growth of political conservatism, heightened resistance to urban annexations, increased reliance on automotive transportation, and other regional and national trends of the mid-twentieth century.

By joining Staten Island to New York City in 1898, island business leaders and civic boosters—by no means mutually exclusive groups—intended to achieve particular outcomes. One of the most important to them was a direct rail connection to the rest of the city. Such an expectation was not unreasonable given the developments in transportation over the previous five decades. New York had commuter steam railroads to Harlem and then Westchester County and New Haven, Connecticut, by the mid-nineteenth century and to Queens shortly thereafter.[24] Streetcars multiplied in the second half of the century, moving on rails and first pulled by horses and then, starting in 1886, running on electricity. They were soon outdone by elevated railroads, which, because they were not mixed with any other type of traffic, had the virtue of becoming the area's first true means of rapid transit. Moreover, streetcars and elevated railways—more commonly known as "trolleys" and "els"—were not limited to Manhattan. Private companies ran streetcars in all four of the future outer boroughs, and all but Staten Island built elevated railroads by 1898. In addition, magnificent new structures facilitated movement within and among the future boroughs of New York City, notably Grand Central Station (1871) and the Brooklyn Bridge (1883). Finally, in 1888 New York mayor Abraham Hewitt challenged the city's business and political interests to build a subway.[25]

By the time Greater New York took shape in 1898, the prospect of putting rapid transit underground and linking the new boroughs was tantalizing. Two years later, August Belmont signed Subway Contract No. 1 with the city to build a route in Manhattan, and for decades afterward diverse constituencies fought over subway expansion.[26] Staten Islanders were no exception. They repeatedly tried to ensure the inclusion of their borough in the plans undertaken, but three periods of possibility stand out most: the negotiations leading up to the formulation of the Dual Contracts (1909–1913), Mayor John Hylan's determination to construct a dual-purpose tunnel under the Narrows (1922–1925), and the possibility of federally funded projects during the early years of the New Deal (1933–1935). City, metropolitan, and national developments, respectively, made these three moments the most propitious for the borough, though with the failure of each one, the likelihood of future success diminished.[27] Islanders were not dormant during the intervening years, but their efforts rarely coincided with broader conditions that fostered opportunity. These slighter episodes receive attention here only when they serve to convey Staten Islanders' long desire for connection with the metropolis they joined and their forty-year persistence in demanding a subway. This mentality is largely forgotten today amid the powerful current assumptions of Staten Islanders' disinterest in and even aversion toward the rest of New York City. Despite the sporadic instances of improved prospects, Staten Islanders fell short of garnering a rail link each time, even as subways sewed much of the rest of the city together socially and economically.

Staten Island's period of physical disconnect from the other parts of New York City was essential to its development. The absence of a means of rapid transit to the other boroughs shaped Staten Island's twentieth-century demographic and physical landscape in ways that highlighted its difference and made it more of an outlier among the boroughs. The fundamental nonevent in its history was that New York City's massive 722-mile subway system failed to extend to Staten Island at a time when the automobile was not yet predominant. *The Forgotten Borough* is careful not to mourn the nonexistent subway or to posit that Staten Island would look like the Bronx, Brooklyn, or Queens if it had obtained one. Counterfactuals rightfully have a dubious reputation among most professional historians, but nonevents can be explanatory or indicative, and some what-if questions are worth pondering.[28] Historians routinely underscore the impact of New York's elevated trains and subway system on the growth of the other outer boroughs as well as the effect of commuter rails on particular suburbs, but a lengthy subway ride—the most likely route starting in Staten Island, traveling under the Narrows, moving through Brooklyn, and finally reaching Manhattan—only *might* have transformed the island or even served its residents better than regular and reliable ferry service.[29] *The Forgotten Borough* is by no means a comparative history, but it does use the other boroughs, most notably the Bronx and Queens, as foils for Staten Island.[30] Although the rims of these two outer boroughs grappled with similar conditions as Staten Island, their centers took on a vastly different look. If rapid transit moved parts of Queens to develop with certain features, then surely the "subway deserts" included not only Staten Island but also Whitestone, Bayside, and Douglaston in Queens.

The Forgotten Borough is divided into three sections. Part 1, "Consolidation and Its Aftermath," contains three chapters focused on the years 1890–1909. Chapter 1 sets the stage for the entire book by assessing whether Staten Island was truly unlike all of the other future outer boroughs of New York City. Census and other data are used to argue that Staten Island was in some fundamental ways as urban—if not more—than the other outer boroughs, with the exception of the heart of Brooklyn. Chapter 2 then narrates the political developments at local, regional, and state levels that led to the formation of Greater New York in 1898. Although opposition to Staten Island's participation in the consolidation was not rampant, some off-island voices questioned why Greater New York would want to include Staten Island, and some island residents resisted joining the city. Chapter 3 addresses why Staten Islanders elected to become a part of Greater New York City. Island voices are presented to reveal a powerful vision—a borough filled with residents, industry, and commerce, well governed and easily reached if only it would join with New York. In the early years after consolidation took effect, efforts to obtain a subway connection became an important conduit through which Staten Islanders continued to articulate this picture of its future.

The narrative heart of *The Forgotten Borough* is part 2, "A Subway for Growth," comprising four chronological chapters that focus on islanders' participation in key moments of transportation development in New York City. Chapter 4 examines the earliest efforts to include Staten Island in the first expansions of the city's nascent subway line, which had opened in 1904. Staten Islanders typically aligned themselves with residents of South Brooklyn and Bay Ridge. As these areas sought to have a line travel down Brooklyn's Fourth Avenue, Staten Islanders pushed to have it continue under the Narrows. Chapter 5 examines the events leading up to the Dual Contracts signed with the Interborough Rapid Transit Company and Brooklyn Rapid Transit Company in 1913 and explains why this relatively unknown moment in Staten Island history was likely the borough's best chance and thus largest missed opportunity to have a subway line reach its shores. The lines awarded through the contracts included several to the outer reaches of Brooklyn, Queens, and the Bronx that spurred their development but not Staten Island's.

The election of John Hylan as mayor of New York City in 1917 set in motion a second moment when a tunnel to Staten Island seemed not only possible but even imminent. Hylan's support for Staten Island during a "garbage war" launched by his predecessor helped forge a powerful working relationship between the mayor and the borough, which is the subject of chapter 6. Hylan's commitment to build a dual-purpose tunnel carrying freight and passengers under the Narrows clashed with past approaches to subway expansion and long-standing economic and nascent regional interests embodied by the Pennsylvania Railroad and the Port Authority. Chapter 7 describes how even with ground broken on a Narrows tunnel in 1923, the demise of the project took place just two years later. Hylan pursued further subway-system extension through new municipal lines to be built and operated independently of the transit companies. Staten Island was not included in this plan as Hylan aggressively undertook his dual-purpose Narrows tunnel. The tunnel would move people during the day and commerce at night, but how it would link to the city's subway system was never certain. While the independent subway lines were constructed, Hylan's Narrows tunnel met with considerable opposition from transit interests and the newly formed Port Authority, whose champion, Governor Alfred E. Smith, ultimately blocked the project.

The final section, part 3, "Subway Persistence and Automobile Emergence," relates the replacement of the subway train by the car and a tunnel by a bridge as the means to connect Staten Island to the city after 1925. This process was intermittent as Staten Islanders continued to argue into the 1940s that a rapid-transit connection made the most sense for the borough. Chapter 8 examines the first impact of motor vehicles, including efforts to make them the basis for a bridge or tunnel to Brooklyn during the years of Mayor James Walker's administration. It ends with renewed local interest in a subway tunnel during the onset of the Great Depression. Chapter 9 then relates the third key (albeit weakest) moment of possibility as Staten Islanders sought to tap into federal funds made available by New Deal agencies. These efforts failed as infrastructure for automobiles elsewhere in the city occupied the thinking of politicians and transit officials during the 1930s and early 1940s. In Richmond Borough, some also leaned toward projects for motor vehicles, but powerful voices for rails continued to be heard during the 1930s. They grew silent by 1945, when a vehicular bridge finally eclipsed the possibility for any type of tunnel.

After 1945, Robert Moses's vision for a Narrows crossing was dominant: a massive span carrying automobiles and trucks but not rails. Chapter 10 traces the years during which this plan was dormant and then burst into the public realm in early 1955 with a joint commitment from Moses's Triborough Bridge and Tunnel Authority and the Port Authority to construct a Narrows crossing by 1960. The crossing was delayed primarily by residents from Bay Ridge in Brooklyn who opposed the uprooting of significant parts of their neighborhood. Moses easily parried the fledgling attempts to include rapid-transit rails on the crossing—or at least a future capacity to add them. By 1959, the bridge was finally approved by all required entities, and it opened in 1964.

Chapter 11 returns to the analytical questions at the heart of this book. What impact did sixty years of rapid-transit privation have on Staten Island? How different from its counterparts in New York City did the borough become? Using census and other data, the chapter considers how Staten Island evolved demographically, politically, economically, educationally, and otherwise from 1900 to 1960, particularly in light of developments in the other four boroughs, all of which had well more than one million residents by 1960, while Staten Island contained only 222,000 inhabitants. It assesses how the island changed, how some of those changes stemmed from the disconnect with the rest of the city, how other changes grew out of the decision to become a part of New York City, and how still others reflected the seepage of regional and national trends that needed neither tunnel nor bridge, subway nor sedan, to reach Staten Island. A brief conclusion offers some concise explanations for why Staten Island failed to obtain a rail link, and an epilogue broadly depicts how Staten Island developed after the bridge opened.

Finally, a few comments on scope, terminology, and audience are warranted. This book is not a comprehensive history of Staten Island from 1898 to 1964. Such a focus would be a profitable enterprise to which this work, publications by Kramer and Flanagan, Melosi, and other scholars and local historians would contribute. As for terminology, the names "Staten Island" and "Richmond" are used interchangeably to refer to the Forgotten Borough. Both "New York City" and "Greater New York" refer to the five boroughs that joined together in 1898. "Manhattan" and at times "New York" indicate the island that formed the original city and is juxtaposed with the outer boroughs—the Bronx, Brooklyn, Queens, and Staten Island. The consolidated city's powerful Board of Estimate and Apportionment is commonly referred to as "Board of Estimate." This clarity will be useful for both general-interest readers and academics. Those with a Staten Island focus will appreciate the book's immersive detail—who did what, when, and where—in tracing multiple successive efforts to obtain better transportation. Its central argument that the absence of a rail link was a key factor in the formation of late twentieth-century Staten Island is particularly aimed at them but may also resonate with those more interested in New York City's development. The latter readers may gravitate toward the connections made with seminal events in the city's transportation politics. Those with a scholarly background may be drawn more to the explanations for why Staten Island's efforts were ultimately futile. Its failure is tied to larger historical questions about the region and nation, about boosters and experts, about business and politics. Whatever purpose or interest the reader brings to it, the text will establish to the benefit of all some key points about the borough's orientation toward and place within the greater city. Staten Island's relationship with New York City was potentially fraught from the outset. Its geographic distance, limited population, and political weakness fed off of one another, posing interrelated obstacles that the repeated failures to obtain a subway only exacerbated. By the mid–twentieth century, those characteristics had solidified enough and created new fissures so that the subsequent opening of the Verrazzano Bridge proved far less transformative than many islanders hoped, feared, or subsequently believed.

PART I
CONSOLIDATION AND ITS AFTERMATH

CHAPTER 1

SETTING THE STAGE

Staten Island in the Late Nineteenth Century

God might have made a more beautiful place than Staten Island, but He didn't.

—George William Curtis

I cannot travel a mile on Staten Island in any direction without observing sources of inconvenience, expense, disappointment and disgust.

—Frederick Law Olmsted to William Butler Duncan, September 22, 1870

What was Staten Island like before it became a part of New York City? Two of its most renowned inhabitants in the latter half of the 1800s offered seemingly divergent depictions. George William Curtis, the influential genteel writer and editor at *Harper's Monthly* and a leading proponent of civil service and other reforms, made the island his home for the last three decades of his life. He was drawn to it for what he saw as its magnificent natural splendor. Frederick Law Olmsted, the landscape designer of New York's Central Park, lived on a different part of the island and only for a few years. His eye gazed at what men had constructed on the island and found it wanting. Olmsted hoped that Staten Island might one day become "the most beautiful suburb of New York" once it engaged in thoughtful planning and eliminated the sources of malaria that damaged its reputation.[1]

The disconnect between its natural and built environments was just one of several discordant juxtapositions found on Staten Island in the late nineteenth century. Its citizens navigated centralized governance at the county level and took care of more localized affairs in its townships and incorporated villages. Richmond, the county seat in the geographic center of the island and the heart of its business, social, and civil life at midcentury, was slowly displaced by areas closer to New York on the island's periphery. With economic activity and population growth on the north shore outpacing the rest of the island, businessmen such as Erastus Wiman intentionally developed infrastructure that further reoriented the island toward New York. Although agriculture on Staten Island remained a potent sector of the economy, industrial establishments started to dot its landscape, and the population clustered in burgeoning communities.

The familiar terms *urban* and *rural* best capture the dichotomies of late nineteenth-century Staten Island. It was both simultaneously: large enough to include bustling towns and sparsely populated farmland but small enough that they were close to each other and to early suburban areas. Its multiple patterns of development and residence enabled people to draw widely different portraits of Staten Island in 1890. The question of what kind of place Staten Island was mattered once the creation of Greater New York became a potent political question in the 1890s. How it was answered might well determine whether the island would participate in the consolidation that took effect in 1898. New York and Brooklyn residents wondered whether Staten Island was sufficiently urban to warrant inclusion in the new metropolis, while Staten Islanders reckoned with what kind of future development they would embrace. Contemporaries framed their understanding of Staten Island in comparison to the other future boroughs and along an urban–rural continuum. Staten Island's subsequent emergence along a trajectory different from that of much of New York City makes it easy to assume today that rural Staten Island made an unlikely match with the rest of Greater New York from its beginning.

Was Staten Island an ill fit with the other entities under consideration for amalgamation with New York? To answer that question, this chapter examines Staten Island's demographic and economic data, presents its institutional patterns in education and governance, and reveals urban features on the island in the 1890s. The Bronx and especially Queens, also future boroughs, serve as the primary comparative foils, but the chapter begins with arguably the most significant manner in which Staten Island was judged during the final decade of the nineteenth century: by its large neighbors that dominated New York Harbor.

The View from the North

Well before consolidation was seriously contemplated, comparisons to New York and Brooklyn framed depictions of Staten Island. This association with Richmond's urban neighbors could lead to both flattery and disparagement. As opposed to the "two great cities" to its north, one late nineteenth-century observer marked Staten Island by its still largely undisturbed natural beauty: "Rising gracefully from its watery depths, its green hills shaded by rich foliage, its slopes covered by an emerald carpet fit for the dainty tread of a queen, its farm houses unostentatious but replete in comfort, its people hardy and industrious, the island was well fitted to fringe the two bays that washed its shores."[2] Drawn to these features, New Yorkers and Brooklynites made Staten Island a place for summer residence or vacation in its large hotels.[3] For many, it became a commuter's home away from a Manhattan workplace, while some business interests lauded its further potential as a suburb. Staten Island could serve as the antidote for a city's less savory aspects, for it was as yet untarnished by the "unthrift, disease, ignorance, vice, and crime [that] go with crowding."[4] Jaundiced by urban machine politics, the editors of the *New York Times* could revel in what they saw in Staten Island: "public spirit and local pride as delicate exotics that cannot exist within a radius of ten or fifteen miles at the nearest from the City Hall."[5]

At the same time, many residents of New York and Brooklyn viewed Staten Island not just as relatively empty or virtuous but also as rather backward. New Yorkers found Staten Island lacking in contrast not just to their own city but to the other suburbs surrounding Manhattan Island. Brooklyn residents could hardly "think of [their] city of 700,000 inhabitants being placed on a par with Staten Island."[6] Indeed, by 1890 Staten Island's population stood at a mere 51,693 compared to more than 800,000 residents in Brooklyn and 1.4 million in Manhattan. Whereas some observers saw great potential for Staten Island, others offered myriad reasons for its lack of growth and development: inaccessibility to its large neighbors, poor internal links, dangers to good health, ineffective local government, and the lassitude of its own populace.[7]

As stark as the contrasts might appear, Staten Island in the late nineteenth century diverged from its neighbors far less than one might imagine. Categorical distinctions between cities and suburbs are in fact often blurred, and Staten Island in some ways varied from Brooklyn and New York only by (albeit considerable) degree.[8] Emphasizing its population density, one contemporary observer noted that "Staten Island has already the characteristics of one continuous city."[9] Staten Island lagged far behind New York and Brooklyn in population and commerce, but its civic and business leaders—like urban boosters of midwestern cities vying with Chicago to make their city the great metropolis of the West—had by no means conceded the race.[10]

A Demographic and Economic Portrait

Staten Island's otherness stemmed primarily from the fact that great swaths of it were sparsely populated and largely agricultural. Of its fifty identifiable communities on the eve of consolidation in 1898, only ten contained populations larger than 1,000. Much more common were the small clusters of one hundred to three hundred residents that dotted the island. Yet Staten Island already possessed several urban areas as defined by the U.S. Census Bureau. In 1890, three-fifths of its population lived in just two incorporated villages: New Brighton (16,423) and Edgewater (14,265), with the latter having grown by 77 percent during the 1880s. Port Richmond experienced similar growth that decade, reaching 6,290 inhabitants.[11] All three of these communities had developed along the north and east shores, areas most proximate to New York and Brooklyn.

Historically, population growth on Staten Island had been spurred by its relationship to New York. The first census in 1790 revealed New York to be the largest city of the new nation, and over the next century it experienced phenomenal growth as it developed into a commercial behemoth and industrial center. Staten Island shared a small portion of that economic activity and population growth, especially prior to the Civil War. Starting in 1790 at a population level (3,827) close to the levels of the other future outer boroughs (see table 1.1), Staten Island's population nearly doubled over the next forty years before it more than tripled between 1830 and 1860, with a particularly explosive 69 percent growth rate during the 1850s. Some of the increase came from migrants from New York, who moved to Staten Island at approximately three times the rate as Richmond County residents moved to Manhattan.[12] The other outlying boroughs rode the same coattails, with Brooklyn becoming a great city in its own right—the nation's third largest in 1860—while Staten Island essentially kept pace with Queens and what would become the Bronx. It would not continue to do so, however.

During the last third of the nineteenth century, population growth on Staten Island fell behind that of the other future boroughs. The Civil War dampened increases nearly everywhere, but Staten Island's pace did not pick up again after the war ended, spurring the state legislature to authorize an investigation of conditions on the island. The ensuing Staten Island Improvement Commission, which included Frederick Law Olmsted, identified insufficient ferry service, limited internal transit, and perceptions of malaria as significant barriers to growth. Other observers contended that memories of the mid-nineteenth-century quarantine station and the diseases associated with it still deterred migration to the island. The consolidation of railway and ferry operations in the 1880s, coupled with expanded rail lines and centralized ferry service at St. George, helped prod an uptick in population growth, but it

TABLE 1.1 Population of the future boroughs of Greater New York, 1790–1890

Year	Richmond	Bronx	Brooklyn	Manhattan	Queens
1790	3,835	1,781	4,495	33,131	6,159
1800	4,564	1,755	5,740	60,515	6,642
1810	5,347	2,267	8,303	96,373	7,444
1820	6,135	2,782	11,187	123,706	8,246
1830	7,082	3,023	20,535	202,589	9,049
1840	10,965	5,346	47,613	312,710	14,480
1850	15,061	8,032	138,882	515,547	18,593
1860	25,492	23,595	279,122	813,669	32,903
1870	33,029	37,593	419,921	942,292	45,468
1880	38,991	51,980	599,495	1,164,673	56,559
1890	51,693	88,908	838,547	1,441,216	87,050

Source: Nathan Kantrowitz, "Population," in *The Encyclopedia of New York City*, ed. Kenneth T. Jackson (New Haven, CT: Yale University Press, 1995), 923.

was not enough for Richmond County to regain the ground it had lost to other parts of the harbor.[13]

A comparison with Queens illuminates how Staten Island was not entirely different from its neighbors, as was commonly imagined. Population size seemed to point toward Queens' more than Staten Island's fitness for Greater New York. Since 1860, Queens' population had grown far more quickly than Staten Island's: its population in 1890 was 68 percent larger, and its most urban community, Long Island City, contained nearly twice the population of New Brighton.[14] However, population growth is hardly the only urban characteristic worth examining, and by many other criteria Staten Island in 1890 was more an urban entity as a whole than Queens. In Richmond County, population density was 891 people per square mile compared to 798 in Queens. The island's greater density served it well in the growth of trolley lines and the development of a riding habit. Despite its smaller population, in 1900 Staten

Island recorded 12,510,890 passengers on its lines compared to 9,545,652 in Queens.[15] Although neither Richmond County nor Queens County experienced the building of tenements and subsequently skyscrapers, New Brighton averaged 6.8 inhabitants per dwelling, and the whole island averaged 6.2 inhabitants per dwelling as opposed to 5.8 in Queens.[16] An examination of economic activity further supports the argument that Staten Island was not that different from the other future boroughs—both large and small.

There was much truth to depictions of Staten Island as rural. Its 342 farms in 1880 averaged forty-eight acres per farm and accounted for more than 44 percent of the island's land. Producing hay had long been the prevailing form of agricultural activity and retained its primacy in 1890, when nearly one-third of the island's 13,662 acreage harvested 6,100 tons. Local farms also branched out into dairy, fruit, and garden vegetables for delivery to nearby markets as wheat and other grains became less competitive. In 1890, fewer than 1,000 acres were devoted to grains and cereals, 61 percent of which were devoted to corn. Apple trees dominated the orchards, but pears and peaches were also grown. Not surprisingly for an island, other residents made a living from the products of the sea, most notably by oystering, which especially occupied the residents of Sandy Ground, originally a free Black community in southwestern Staten Island that thrived after abolition. By the late nineteenth century, oystering became less economically viable for local inhabitants as it was increasingly dominated by large commercial concerns.[17]

The topography of Staten Island prevented large-scale farming. Much of the island's west shore contained wetlands—marsh areas unsuitable for agriculture and reputed to be the source of mosquito-driven illness. The center of the island was marked by hills, forming the highest ground on the Atlantic coast south of Maine. The south shore contained some of the most suitable land for agriculture but was the farthest away from the Brooklyn and New York markets. As Charles Sachs has noted, "Because of its small size, its rocky, hilly, and sandy surface, and its long history of land cultivation, Staten Island was not an easy place to maintain an agricultural existence."[18] Those who did farm grew crops on relatively small plots. In 1890, a majority of the 380 farms contained fewer than 20 acres, only two were larger than 500 acres, and the average size was 36 acres. The average farm in Queens (52 acres) and Westchester County (78 acres) was substantially larger.[19]

Productive life on Staten Island involved far more than agriculture, though. Sachs has uncovered just how much was "made on Staten Island" in the late nineteenth century. West New Brighton, once called Factoryville, housed a textile-dye business that employed approximately five hundred workers in 1900. The area also contained establishments that made cabinets and wallpaper. Kreischerville was named for the owner of the clay-brick factory whose three hundred workers molded 3.5 million bricks yearly in the 1890s. Four hundred workers in a Tompkinsville factory produced "fancy papers." Eight breweries flourished in Clifton and Stapleton during the late 1870s. The S. S. White Dental Manufacturing Company was well established and still expanding in Princes Bay. Its 425 workers in 1896 would increase to approximately 1,850 by 1927. In 1896, the island had twenty-eight industrial establishments with more than 50 employees each.[20]

Data on occupations further depict the prominence of industrial and commercial pursuits. In 1900, Staten Island's labor pool comprised approximately 21,000 men and 5,000 women working in five broadly classified sectors: agricultural, professional, domestic and personal service, trade and transportation, and manufacturing/mechanical pursuits.[21] As table 1.2 indicates, farming was the smallest of these sectors, accounting for 4.8 percent of the male and 0.5 percent of the female workforce.[22] The other nonprofessional sectors were considerably larger, some imprecision of the Census Bureau's categories notwithstanding. A plurality of men (38.6 percent) labored in manufacturing and mechanical pursuits—notably in the making of iron and steel products and in the building trades. Staten Island contained more clerks than farmers and nearly as many merchants, with 29.7 percent of its men working in the trade-and-transportation sector. A majority of women (54.5 percent) worked as domestic laborers, though some were beginning to move into the lower rungs

TABLE 1.2 Occupation sectors of the Staten Island labor force, 1900

Sector	Males	% of Workforce	Females	% of Workforce	Total	% of Workforce
Agriculture	1,007	4.8	26	0.5	1,033	4.0
Professional	1,169	5.6	379	7.3	1,548	5.9
Domestic and Personal Service	4,444	21.3	2,849	54.5	7,293	28.0
Trade and Transportation	6,196	29.7	647	12.4	6,843	26.2
Manufacturing and Mechanical Pursuits	8,045	38.6	1,325	25.4	9,370	35.9
Total	20,851	100.0	5,226	100.1	26,077	100.0

Source: U.S. Department of Commerce and Labor, Bureau of the Census, *Special Report: Occupations at the Twelfth Census 1900* (Washington, DC: U.S. Government Printing Office, 1904), 457.

of white-collar work. Women's presence in the professional sector came largely in their work as teachers, and their role in manufacturing largely involved work with textiles.[23]

In real estate, Staten Island also featured more urban characteristics than Queens. Consider rates of home ownership, as shown on table 1.3. As the nation's largest cities grew immensely and their housing stock expanded skyward, the proportion of residents owning their place of residence plummeted—to 6 percent in New York and 19 percent in Brooklyn in 1890. In Queens, the aggregate figure was 40 percent, with lower rates in its urban areas—32 percent in Long Island City and 38 percent in Flushing. The corresponding rates on Staten Island were uniformly lower: 35 percent for the whole island, 29 percent in New Brighton, and 27 percent in Edgewater.[24] Farmland also became more valuable in urban areas because the space could be more readily used for other purposes. Accordingly, the value per farm acre in New York reached $1,152 in 1890 and $844 in Kings County. Farmland in Richmond County was worth $242 an acre, more than in Queens ($153) or in Westchester ($140). Property values in the built-up areas of Staten Island were also higher than those in Queens. An average-size home in New Brighton was valued at $7,186 compared to $4,207 in Long Island City.[25]

TABLE 1.3 Rates of homeownership by borough and former towns, 1900

Locality	Number of Families	% Owning Homes	% of Unencumbered Homes (No Mortgage)
Staten Island	9,476	35	62
Edgewater	2,814	27	70
New Brighton	3,064	29	60
Queens	24,161	40	59
Flushing	1,667	38	70
Long Island City	6,232	32	68
Brooklyn	176,267	19	63
Manhattan and the Bronx	312,754	6	59

Source: United States Census Office, *Report on Farms and Homes: Proprietorship and Indebtedness in the United States at the Eleventh Census: 1890* (Washington, DC: U.S. Government Printing Office, 1895), 31.

Patterns of debt also suggest that Richmond County's profile looked more urban than that of other outlying areas. In New York, the average mortgage debt per acre from 1880 to 1889 was $361, with $1,022 on average owed for each encumbered acre in 1889. Conversely, in rural Suffolk County the average mortgage debt per acre was only $41, with just $49 owed per encumbered acre. Not surprisingly, Staten Island fell in between these urban/rural extremes but reported more debt than Queens. Residents in Richmond County owed $345 per acre during the 1880s and $273 on each encumbered acre in 1889; the comparable figures for Queens were $134 per acre and $234 per encumbered acre.[26]

The ethnic and racial makeup of Staten Island's population also reflected urban characteristics. In 1890, 62 percent of its residents was either foreign born (33 percent) or the child of someone foreign born (29 percent), and in the 1880s its foreign-born population had grown faster than its native-born population. The dominant immigrant groups remained the German and Irish, who had arrived in large numbers over the previous fifty years. The distribution by nationality of the 14,779 foreign-born Staten Islanders in 1890, presented in table 1.4, indicates that the Irish and Germans respectively accounted for 36 percent and 33 percent of the immigrants. The next largest immigrant groups came from even more traditional sources of immigration in northern and western Europe: 15 percent from England, Scotland, or Wales, another 5 percent from Scandinavia.

By 1900, Staten Island was starting to experience the impact of the wave of "new immigrants" who arrived at Ellis Island from countries in eastern and southern Europe. The island's ethnic distribution in 1900, also included in table 1.4, indicates the early stages of the transition: a decline in the Irish and modest growth in the English, Scottish, and German populations during the 1890s, while the number of Austrians and Russians more than tripled, and the Hungarians and Italians increased fivefold. These newer immigrants settled primarily in New York, Brooklyn, and what would become the Bronx, but some of them also made their way to Staten Island, though not yet in large numbers. Russians composed 2.3 percent of the immigrant population on Staten Island, while Austrians accounted for 1.5 percent in 1900. Italians now constituted 7.7 percent of the island's first-generation immigrant population but were still a much smaller group than the Irish (26 percent) and Germans (29.9 percent). As they did elsewhere, many of these immigrant groups congregated in the island's urban areas. Seventy-seven percent of the population of Edgewater in 1890, which included a German enclave at Stapleton, comprised immigrants or the children of an immigrant.[27]

In the late nineteenth century, many white Anglo-Saxon Protestants understood these differences in nationality as racial. In the past twenty-five years, scholars have shown how the racial categorization of nineteenth-century European immigrants transformed as the "new" immigrants gradually

TABLE 1.4 Origin of the foreign-born population in Richmond County, 1890 and 1900

Nation of Birth	Population 1890	Population 1900	% Growth 1890–1900	% of Foreign-Born Population 1890	% of Foreign-Born Population 1900
Canada	248	617	148.8	1.7	3.3
Ireland	5,269	4,858	−7.8	35.7	26.0
England	1,720	1,790	4.1	11.6	9.6
Scotland	463	493	6.5	3.1	2.6
Germany	4,883	5,589	14.5	33.0	29.9
Austria	81	277	242.0	0.5	1.5
Holland	52	48	−7.7	0.4	0.3
Switzerland	139	238	71.2	0.9	1.3
Norway	255	735	188.2	1.7	3.9
Sweden	349	471	35.0	2.4	2.5
Denmark	135	214	58.5	0.9	1.1
Russia	133	429	222.6	0.9	2.3
Hungary	46	269	484.8	0.3	1.4
Poland	249	510	104.8	1.7	2.7
France	222	310	39.6	1.5	1.7
Italy	262	1,435	447.7	1.8	7.7
Other	262	460	75.6	1.8	2.2
Total	14,779	18,687	26.4	100.0	100.0

Sources: United States Census Office, *Report on Population of the United States at the Eleventh Census: 1890, Part I* (Washington, DC: U.S. Government Printing Office, 1895), 646–47.

became "white" in the twentieth century.[28] Nineteenth-century white Staten Islanders surely shared these commonly held racial notions, which were heightened by an initially large presence of African Americans on the island. In 1790, 23 percent of Richmond County's population were African American, and when the abolishment of slavery took effect in New York State in 1827, nearly 700 slaves were emancipated. Over the course of the century, the African American proportion of the general population diminished. The 964 African Americans recorded on Staten Island in 1890 reflected a gain of less than 100 over the previous one hundred years and now represented less than 2 percent of the island's population.[29]

Staten Island was also a place of considerable religious activity and plurality. In 1890, it contained fifty-four sectarian organizations that used fifty-eight church structures and served 18,793 islanders who identified as religious group members in 1890—a figure to be used with caution.[30] As table 1.5 indicates, 36 percent of Staten Islanders identified as church members, a figure that was

TABLE 1.5 Church membership and facilities by county, 1890

Characteristic	Richmond	Kings	New York	Queens	Westchester	Suffolk
Population in 1890	51,693	838,547	1,441,216	87,050	146,772	62,491
Church membership	18,793	316,164	558,146	36,872	55,813	20,144
Membership percentage	36	38	39	42	38	32
Church organizations	54	398	645	192	237	178
Church edifices	58	426	532	213	252	199
Church capacity	20,110	251,034	354,946	61,864	77,728	48,215
Halls	2	39	162	10	15	8
Hall capacity	100	8,280	26,505	855	2,285	575
Total capacity	20,210	259,314	381,451	62,719	80,013	48,790

Source: United States Census Office, *Report on Statistics of Churches in the United States at the Eleventh Census* (Washington, DC: U.S. Government Printing Office, 1894), 74.

slightly lower than urban counterparts in New York and Brooklyn as well as in the more sparsely settled Queens and Westchester Counties. Another manner in which Richmond County demonstrated some urban characteristics was in how the capacity of its church buildings only slightly exceeded its total church membership: falling in between New York and Brooklyn, where membership far exceeded the seating space in existing structures, and Westchester and Queens, where churches contained many more seats than members. All of these counties reported large numbers of Roman Catholics, as practiced by the Irish and many of the Germans. As table 1.6 indicates, Catholics formed the single largest religious group in Richmond County long before the arrival of substantial numbers of Italians. Among Protestants, there was sizable membership in the Methodist, Lutheran, Episcopal, Baptist, and Dutch Reformed churches. Staten Island had one Orthodox Jewish community as well.

TABLE 1.6 Religious adherents in Richmond County by denomination, 1890

Denomination	Organizations	Halls and Edifices	Membership	% of Island Membership in Churches
Baptists (regular)	4	4	654	3.5
Brethren (Plymouth 3)	1	1	42	0.2
Roman Catholics	9	9	11,385	60.5
Jewish (Orth.)	1	1	125	0.7
Lutheran (all)	3	3	824	4.4
Methodist (all)	15	15	2,244	11.9
Moravians	4	5	266	1.4
Presbyterian	3	3	466	2.5
Episcopal	10	12	1,909	10.2
Dutch Reformed	4	5	907	4.8

Source: United States Census Office, *Report on Statistics of Churches in the United States at the Eleventh Census* (Washington, DC: U.S. Government Printing Office, 1894), 153, 226, 243, 416, 450, 460, 515, 542, 561, 626, 715, 737.

Institutions, Infrastructure, and Identities

The highly localized government was arguably the aspect of late nineteenth-century Staten Island most relevant to any discussion of consolidation. Five townships made up Richmond County: Northfield, Southfield, Westfield, Castleton, and Middletown. Each town government included elected constables, highway and excise commissioners, justices of the peace, a board of assessors, a tax collector, a clerk, and a sealer of weights and measures. Each township also elected a member of the Board of Supervisors, which governed the county along with other county-wide officers, such as the school commissioner, district attorney, and sheriff. Police and fire protection transpired through separate structures. A three-person Board of Police Commissioners oversaw a captain and fifty police officers that served the entire county. In contrast, thirty-three volunteer fire companies existed in 1886, each acting on behalf of a small geographic area. Similarly, there were twenty-eight school districts on the island that year, each one responsible for a single school and run by three elected school trustees. After the Civil War, several of the more thickly settled areas separated from their towns and incorporated as villages, each with a distinct local government, including Tottenville, Port Richmond, New Brighton, and Edgewater, with the latter comprising Tompkinsville, Stapleton, and Clifton.[31] Most residents were thus part of several governing entities at the county, town or village, and school level.

The complexity of these overlapping jurisdictions was compounded by the highly partisan politics that pervaded Richmond County. Staten Island's long-standing tradition of competitive political parties dates to the antebellum, but by the late nineteenth century a powerful Democrat organization had developed that could typically win a county race by a sizeable 1,500-vote margin. In 1885, Nicholas Muller, a former New York congressman steeped in Tammany Hall politics, removed to Staten Island and quickly took control of the local Democratic Party. As in New York's Tammany Hall, the Irish dominated the Democratic Party on Staten Island and were derided by Protestant critics in ways not unlike depictions of New York's corrupt politics. As a result of such scandals, some Democrats chose not to identify with the Muller organization. Staten Island contained enough of these independent Democrats as well as completely nonaligned voters to tip an election periodically in favor of a Republican. In the most notable instance, Republican George Cromwell eked out a victory in the 1897 election to become the island's first borough president.[32]

As elsewhere, inexpensive local newspapers were plentiful and typically linked to a particular political organization. For example, the *Staten Islander* and the *Richmond County Gazette* were Republican organs, though the latter likely aligned with Muller. The *Staten Island Leader* and the *Richmond County*

Democrat were regular Democratic papers. The *Richmond County Standard* and the *Richmond County Herald* were Democratic papers not linked to the Muller organization. The *Staten Island Independent* was founded as a nonpartisan publication in anticipation of the 1894 election. In 1886, the *Richmond County Advance* was established for commercial and not political purposes. Although it initially took an independent editorial stance, in the early twentieth century it too became identified as a Democratic paper. Germans in Stapleton maintained their own paper, the *Deutsche Staten Islander*. In total, there were twelve newspapers serving the island in 1896.[33]

At the time of consolidation, Staten Island had several internal and external transportation networks. The first railroad, opened by Cornelius Vanderbilt in 1860, ran from Clifton to Tottenville. By 1900, the line was owned by the Staten Island Rapid Transit Railway Company, a subsidiary of the Baltimore and Ohio Railroad (B&O), and extended to St. George and then west past Mariner's Harbor. There it connected with the bridge built by Erastus Wiman over the Arthur Kill and used by the B&O to move freight to its new yards on Staten Island. A second passenger spur extended southeast to South Beach (see figure 1.1). Trolley lines started replacing horse cars in the 1890s; the first line ran from Port Richmond to Prohibition Park (Westerleigh) in the island's interior. Ferries had long run to Manhattan; on the east shore, they stopped at Tompkinsville, Stapleton, and Clifton until service was consolidated at St. George in 1886. Shortly thereafter, a ferry from Manhattan to Port Richmond and other north shore destinations also shifted to a St. George terminus. In 1890, ferries ran to New Jersey from Tottenville and Port Richmond; ferries to Brooklyn were reestablished after consolidation.[34]

Historians have long contested the nature of nineteenth-century party affiliation and political conflict. Although some have emphasized social class identity as the basis for political activity, others have focused on the ethnoreligious nature of nineteenth-century politics. Local historians of Staten Island have generally taken the latter approach and have adopted traditional depictions of corrupt political machines serving immigrants countered by upright Protestant reformers.[35] At the same time, these narratives of crusades formulated by local island historians in the late nineteenth and early twentieth centuries highlight a growing middle-class sensibility.

With industry and considerable variations in wealth prevalent on the island, social class identity formed despite the absence of significant class-based parties or unions. This class consciousness is most easily seen in the attitudes and activities of the island's elites. Ira K. Morris reported in 1900 a hearty disdain for the "granting of thousands of dollars annually to chronic alms-seekers."[36] The Good Government Club declined to endorse a candidate for local office because "his occupation of selling milk, although in itself an honorable calling, is not calculated to fit him for the delicate and complicated

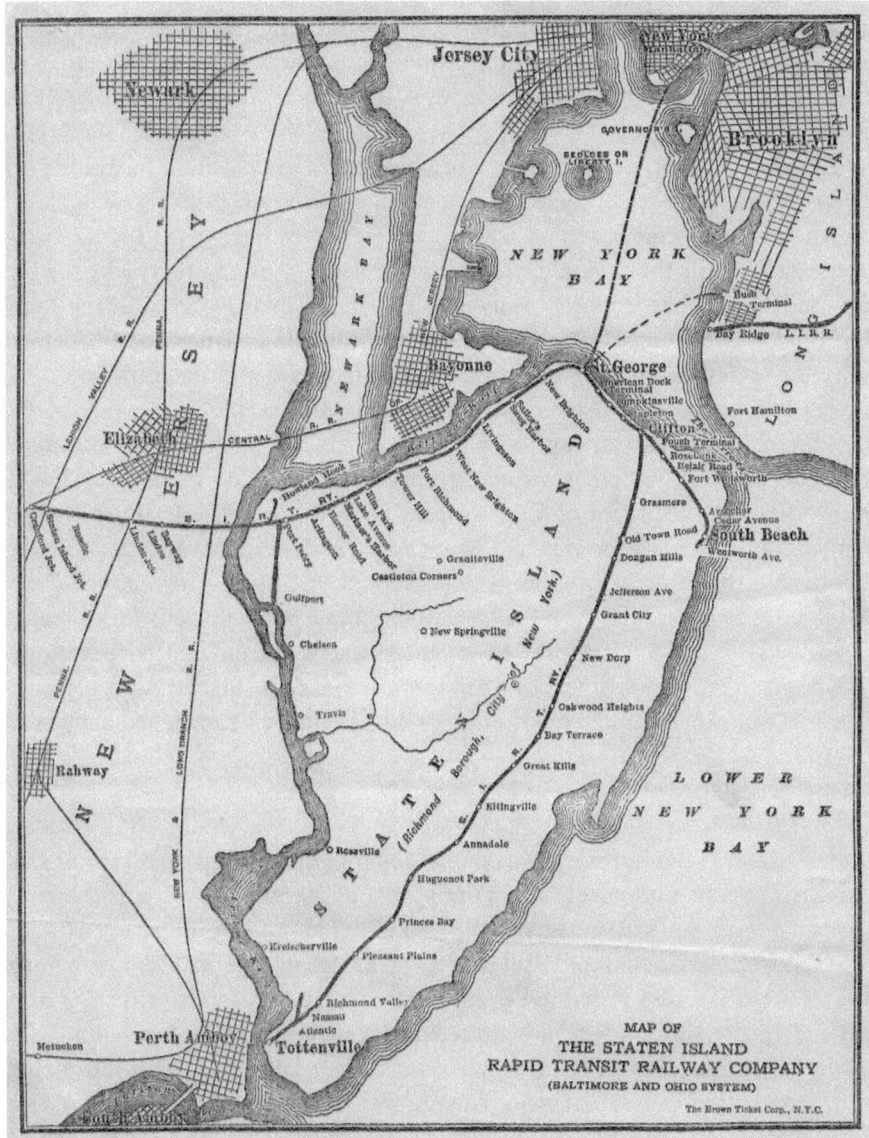

1.1 Map of the Staten Island Rapid Transit Railway Company lines, c. 1907

Staten Island contained a sizable internal railroad system by the 1890s. In addition to trolley lines not shown here, the commuter rails lines went from Tottenville to Clifton and later expanded along the north and east shores of Staten Island. This rail network prompted the consolidation of ferry service to Manhattan and Brooklyn at St. George.

Source: Courtesy of Collection of Historic Richmond Town.

work which our representative is called upon to accomplish next winter."[37] A plethora of propertied and middle-class leisure activities developed on the island in the late nineteenth century. Clubs for cricket, baseball, rowing, tennis, boating, and yachting opened. The Richmond County Country Club formed in 1888. Large hotels such as the St. Marks, the Pavilion, the Bay View, and Peteler's lured more of the comfortable classes to the island for respite. In 1889, the massive New Hotel Castleton opened on the site of the St. Marks.[38]

An incipient working class was also present but harder to discern. One boost came with the arrival of Italian laborers to work laying tracks for the railroads and other initiatives taken by Erastus Wiman, who built the ferry terminal at St. George. Other sites where working-class identity likely formed were the company housing built near several factories and the numerous volunteer fire companies.[39] Staten Islanders also embraced the fraternal societies that swept the nation after the Civil War. There were several lodges of the Ancient Order of United Workmen, a fraternal association most noted for its innovative establishment of a death fund for members. The Junior Order of United American Mechanics had councils in Tottenville and Kreischerville. These fraternal associations were not solely class based, and the American Mechanics in particular had strong nativist underpinnings, but they created "a collectivist counter culture" to growing power of capitalist corporations. The exclusion of people by race or gender only led to the formation of separate organizations that ultimately fostered the agency of disenfranchised peoples.[40]

***

Staten Island in 1890 presented a compelling mix of continuity and change, of industrial bustle and agrarian rhythms. Its population growth was steady if unspectacular, yet urban areas developed along its north and east coasts. Its agricultural sector remained vibrant even as commerce and industry took root. Its old families remained prominent even as thousands of immigrants arrived on its shores. It was engulfed in localized politics that left it with underwhelming governance and public services. Many saw it as backward, but this perception was warped by its proximity to Manhattan and Brooklyn. As a result of these inevitable comparisons, some people on and off the island viewed it as unsuitable for participation in the creation of a great metropolis, yet when it was weighed against other outlying areas, its consideration for consolidation was not unreasonable. Staten Island had greater pockets of population density and less dependence on agriculture than Queens. Politically, economically, and demographically, Staten Island contained sufficient urban characteristics in 1890 to warrant its inclusion in the consolidation project. It also had the geographic advantage of being at the entrance to New York Harbor, a location that appealed to the leaders of the movement to create Greater New York.

CHAPTER 2

JOINING THE CITY

Staten Island and the Consolidation of Greater New York

The future of Staten Island is assured beyond all hazard.

—Andrew Green, 1890

When Andrew Haswell Green spoke before the Municipal Consolidation Commission on December 11, 1890, he did not actually need to persuade the attendees that Staten Island would benefit from a union with Manhattan. His remarks instead addressed the potential skepticism of members who might well wonder what Staten Island could offer New York that it did not already possess. Green, the chairman of the commission and guiding force behind the consolidation movement in the nation's largest city, had just outlined Staten Island's potential as a vital link in the transport of goods through New York Harbor (see figure 2.1). He thus included it in his plans for a Greater New York that would encompass Manhattan, Staten Island, and parts of Long Island and Westchester County. Over the next seven years, considerable political exertion led to the passage of consolidation legislation, the winning of a popular referendum, and the drawing up of a new city charter. Although few citizens outside of Staten Island clamored for its participation, neither did many of them call for its exclusion. When the enlarged city of New York took effect on January 1, 1898, Richmond County became one of its five boroughs.

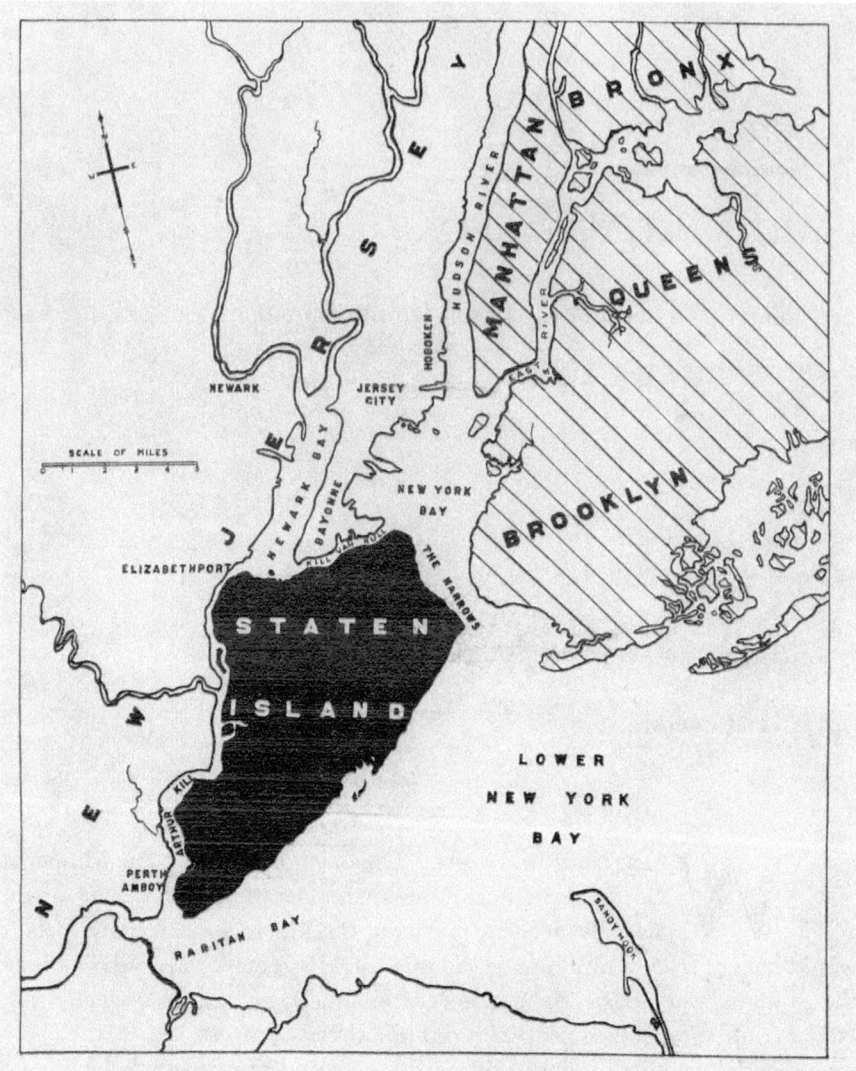

2.1 Staten Island's location at the entrance to New York Harbor

Andrew Green's aspirations for Greater New York centered on the potential economic efficiencies for the movement of freight through a single municipality that encompassed the harbor. Staten Island's location at the Narrows, the entrance to the harbor, led Green to include it in his proposal for consolidation.

Source: *Staten Island, New York City: Its Industrial Resources and Possibilities* (New York: n.p., 1922). Courtesy of the College of Staten Island Library, Archives and Special Collections.

But would Staten Island want to join? The outcome of the nonbinding referendum on consolidation seemingly indicated that it did. On November 6, 1894, its citizens voted overwhelmingly, by a nearly four-to-one margin, to support consolidation. Staten Island's percentage of favorable votes far exceeded those of Manhattan (62 percent), Brooklyn (50.1 percent), Queens (62 percent), and Westchester County (45 percent).[1] Moreover, the margin of victory on Staten Island was evenly distributed geographically, in marked contrast to Westchester, Kings, and Queens Counties, where outlying areas were generally more interested in consolidation than were population centers. The town of Mount Vernon voted not to consolidate and was excluded; the town of Flushing voted not to join but was included anyway; and, most significantly, the residents of downtown Brooklyn soundly rejected union with New York but were undone by voters in recently annexed outlying areas, who provided the slim margin of victory. On Staten Island, no town—no matter how densely or scarcely populated—posted less than a 72 percent vote in favor.

Contemporary observers gave great credence to the results on Staten Island. Buoyant in the aftermath of the 1894 referendum, the *Staten Islander*, a Republican newspaper published in Stapleton, proclaimed, "From the admission of Staten Island into the city of the future, it is impossible now to forecast the favorable consequences."[2] The *New York Times* announced that "all [of] Richmond County is willing to join the city."[3] For the Democratic-leaning but politically unaffiliated *Staten Island Independent*, the referendum results closed the debate over whether to support consolidation and opened the question of the best means of accomplishing it.[4] Likewise, New York State Republican Party boss Thomas Collier Platt now saw consolidation as an "irrepressible movement."[5] This contemporary reaction is echoed in the subsequent historical understanding of Richmond's place in the creation of Greater New York. As the local historian Harlow McMillen wrote of Staten Islanders, "When given the chance to become part of the greatest city in America, they did not hesitate."[6] Historians of Greater New York have shared this assumption, which contributes to the nearly complete omission of Staten Island from accounts of consolidation or to the depiction of it as a rather odd fit with the rest of the city.[7]

The formation of New York's five boroughs is part of a larger national narrative about the growth of municipal boundaries. For many cities in the late nineteenth and early twentieth centuries, annexation represented an effort to retain a middle-class tax base that was headed toward the urban periphery.[8] Concerns about fleeing taxpayers and about losing New York's primacy animated many New Yorkers, but Green offered a relatively early articulation of efficient regional government as an antidote to urban political machines and debilitating capitalist competition.[9] He decried "lawless enterprise" conducted by "colossal and all-pervading monopoly," which undermined his vision for "a grand and cultivated city" that had pervaded his earlier efforts—most notably Central Park—on behalf of the physical improvement of New York.[10] New York's consolidation took place during this era of metropolitan mergers in the United States, and its outlying areas expressed the typical motivations for attaching themselves to an urban center. Suburbs willingly joined large cities to obtain infrastructure and services that they could not yet provide. When cities lost this comparative advantage over suburbs and became associated with crime, poverty, and racial diversity, suburbs outside of those in the Sunbelt no longer aspired to unite with them. Historians thus depict a clear rise and fall of a movement for urban expansion by 1950, and the story tends to be told from the vantage point of the urban center.[11]

Staten Island provides fertile ground for a study of consolidation centered on the periphery's concerns. Richmond County's leading businessmen, realtors, and property owners enthusiastically embraced consolidation and became the island's loudest advocates for it. They envisioned a future in which Staten Island, now a part of Greater New York, would serve as a residential suburb for Manhattan, a commercial hub for New York Harbor, and a manufacturing center for the nation. Unlike boosters in many other communities already linked by commuter rail systems, they imagined a first-class transportation system, with better-paved roads, more railroad lines, improved ferry service, and, for some, a tunnel directly linking Staten Island to the new metropolis.[12] Led by the attorney George Greenfield and the businessman Erastus Wiman, they mobilized a limited but effective campaign for consolidation on the island in the weeks before the 1894 election.

The massive referendum victory nevertheless obscured a more complicated dynamic than simply broad support. Nearly 3,200 people on the island—about one-third of the total number of voters in 1894—left blank the ballot on consolidation. Some local observers assumed that such nonvotes signified consent, but it is also plausible to view them as indicators of confusion or disgust because by election day most expected that the referendum would easily pass in Richmond County.[13] Ira Morris, a local historian writing a few years later, called the outcome "one of those political tidal waves that sweep over the country occasionally, and decide measures of great moment without regard to reason."[14] The considerable support that obviously did exist in 1894 had taken shape only over the previous five years and, despite the civic boosters' lofty vision, probably reflected fairly mundane concerns about the effectiveness and honesty of government. Nor were all residents of Staten Island persuaded that joining New York City would assure the island's future. A small but vocal group of citizens raised a host of concerns about "annexation" by New York. They interpreted the referendum results merely as a decisive rejection of the status quo of overlapping and conflicting local jurisdictions rather than as an affirmation of consolidation. What is more, they offered a different solution to

Staten Island's governmental woes: incorporation of the whole island as an independent city.

Delineating the political and social milieu in which consolidation occurred also exposes the sizable clout of the island's business, professional, and propertied class. Its leading citizens' expectations for joining the city reveal that this decisive moment in Staten Island's history was paradoxically accompanied by both high hopes and deep misgivings. Even before the island became part of the great metropolis, the ambivalence with which many Staten Islanders viewed their larger neighbor to the north was evident in the way they contemplated the virtues of consolidation. In winning the day by tapping into discontent with local governance and into aspirations for new and improved public services, consolidation's civic boosters established a high level of expectations. When the latter went unmet, however, disappointment with and resentment toward New York City followed. The island's consolidation with New York represented and set up the dueling tendencies that marked Staten Island in the twentieth century: simultaneously pulling toward and away from New York City, all while feeling forgotten.

Untangling the complexities of Staten Island's participation in municipal consolidation is crucial to understanding its experience as part of Greater New York in the twentieth century. This chapter treats the politics of the movement, and chapter 3 the aspirations associated with creating and joining Greater New York. This chapter intertwines the regional consolidation movement with the gradual building of support on Staten Island. It then traces the mechanics of turning a positive nonbinding-referendum outcome first into enabling legislation and then into a city. Finally, it analyzes how Staten Island fared in its earliest years as Richmond Borough even as buyer's remorse began to fester. Joining New York City generated concrete expectations by which Staten Islanders' subsequent experience could be measured. Would the desired benefits in public works and services be realized? Would the concerns regarding the diminution of the island's political voice be unwarranted? Before Richmond Borough felt forgotten, it acted on a powerful collective wish to be remembered and heeded in public-policy decisions.

The Advocacy of Consolidation

The consolidation movement is a well-told episode in New York City's history, but one in which Staten Island typically plays a miniscule part. The central story line in the narrative belongs to Brooklyn, where opposition to consolidation was the most heated, where its participation was long in doubt, and where consolidation passed by a mere 277 votes. Andrew Haswell Green, Frederick Law Olmsted, and other advocates for a Greater New York deemed Brooklyn's inclusion as crucial to the success of the enterprise, and the antecedents for consolidation dated at least to early nineteenth-century discussions of the relationship between New York and Brooklyn.[15] After Brooklyn achieved its own city status in 1834, the idea of joining the two major urban areas and other municipalities around New York harbor percolated at several other moments, but without leading either to a concerted movement or to legislative success. In the meantime, New York and Brooklyn began to expand physically on their own as they annexed farmlands and towns on their outskirts.[16]

Staten Islanders did not clamor to join with New York during most of the nineteenth century, but nor did they resist the island's one clear precedent for consolidation. In 1857, the Metropolitan Police Board formed to oversee the law enforcement personnel of New York, Kings, Richmond, and Westchester Counties. On Staten Island, this reform was the first effort to replace a traditional system of town constables and private police that had become "unsatisfactory" as the island's population grew. The Metropolitan Police Board as well as the subsequently created boards for fire and health lasted until 1870, when city charter revisions spurred by the Tweed organization abolished them.[17] As Staten Islanders contemplated a merger with New York more than twenty years later, they drew favorably on this experience. One Staten Island police inspector recalled the municipal police force fondly as a time "when everything worked as smooth as silk."[18] Such memories were offset by other collective experiences—most notably the intentional burning of a quarantine house in 1859—that reflected the islanders' frustration with outside, distant, and unresponsive government agencies.[19]

The political momentum that ultimately culminated in the consolidation of New York, Brooklyn, Queens, Staten Island, and lower Westchester County began in the late 1880s. In 1888, the New York Chamber of Commerce ignited serious discussion with its proposal "to unite New York and all its environs under one general scheme of municipal rule," and some influential entities, including the *Real Estate Record and Builders' Guide* and Mayor Abraham Hewitt, responded favorably. However, this effort at public advocacy was largely ignored on Staten Island, most likely because it did not lead to any concerted drive for the necessary enabling legislation.[20]

The prospect of consolidation met with considerable disdain when it initially garnered attention on Staten Island. In 1889, Green revived his longstanding desire to establish a Greater New York City by petitioning the state legislature to name a commission to study the matter.[21] Fort Hill's John Foord, a critic and writer for *Harper's Magazine* and later a biographer of Green, was proposed as a member of a Greater New York commission and was enthusiastic about the proposition.[22] The idea also found favor with some local political partisans (of both parties), who deemed that consolidation would enhance their prospects for election, though for the most part Staten Islanders responded warily to the pending legislation and largely scoffed at a union with their massive neighbors to the north. The Republican *Richmond County Sentinel* derided the "wicked borough across the river" and dismissed New York's Democratic machine: "No thanks; we don't care to be ruled absolutely by Tammany Hall just yet, as New York is today."[23] In an editorial titled "We'll Annex New York," the *Staten Islander* cited the opposition of "prominent residents" to the idea of joining New York. These naysayers included Eugenius H. Outerbridge, a successful merchant and later the first chairman of the Port of New York Authority; R. Penn Smith, a large property holder on the island; and, most notably, the island's leading civic-minded businessman, Erastus Wiman, who observed, "I am not in favor of the Island being made the tail end of a great place." Acknowledging its own hesitancy to move forward, the paper declared itself "not yet prepared" to become part of New York.[24] Nor was the state Senate prepared for such a union, where the bill died, done in by opposition from Tammany and Brooklyn interests.[25]

Consolidation Commission

In 1890, Green's renewed lobbying for consolidation legislation bore fruit. Playing on concerns about Chicago's ascendancy (Chicago had annexed 133 square miles the previous year) and gaining the support of many New York newspapers, Green persuaded the legislature to authorize the Greater New York Commission. Its membership, including Green as chair, largely shared a predisposition in favor of consolidation.[26] Richmond County was entitled to one representative, but the first choice made by its board of supervisors, George William Curtis, politely declined to serve. Curtis, the influential genteel writer and editor at *Harper's*, a leading proponent of civil service and other reforms, and at the time arguably the most nationally renowned citizen of the island, made public his misgivings about the venture.[27]

Other prominent Staten Island voices also expressed doubt and scorn about the whole proposition. Asked by a reporter if he supported consolidation, the president of Port Richmond's board of supervisors responded bluntly, "No sir, I do not!"[28] The *Richmond County Standard*, a Democratic newspaper, wrote disparagingly of the effort in mid-1890, calling it "a huge joke" and "an absurd movement."[29] The following year, the *Richmond County Advance* published a tongue-in-cheek editorial that offered a list of "benefits" to accompany annexation, such as having "to go up to the City Hall to get a building permit," paying "taxes to support the Central Park menagerie, as well as the one at City Hall," and having to deal with the increased presence of "dime museums, dives, opium joints, and various other accessories of civilization."[30]

Elsewhere on Staten Island, however, the response to the consolidation movement had grown more favorable. The Republican-leaning *Staten Islander* under editor Judson Worrell reversed its initial position and became an active promoter of consolidation. Declaring the union feasible and logical, the paper predicted that most Staten Island residents would support the measure. Worrell hoped that island residents would be "willing and glad" to join the metropolis because "it would be difficult to over-estimate the numerous and substantial advantages" that would arise.[31] For the next six years, his editorials consistently argued for consolidation, and the paper's news coverage was heavily slanted in favor of it, a position taken by many Republicans in the hope that consolidation would dilute the power of Tammany Hall.

Some notable Richmond County citizens also began to favor the bill. The attorney George Greenfield, Staten Island's able and energetic representative on the Greater New York Commission, wanted a thorough consideration of the matter but was committed to the cause.[32] His initial doubts resolved, Wiman became the most prominent spokesman for consolidation and predicted it would contribute to the economic growth of Staten Island and the entire region.[33] Wiman's newfound enthusiasm for consolidation and his exertion on its behalf contributed to the movement's ultimate success on Staten Island.

Several factors likely explain the turnaround by Staten Islanders such as Wiman and Worrell. Foremost was the increase in the chances of Greater New York being formed. In 1889, consolidation remained nothing more than an idea that could be considered on its own terms. Staten Islanders could not see past the fear of being smothered by New York.[34] In 1890, Richmond County residents had to consider consolidation as something that might happen with or without Staten Island. For the local businessman, exclusion rather than participation became the threat to commercial growth; those in real estate looked to a rise in property values. Likewise, many grew to view consolidation as the most politically feasible way of reforming local governance. D. T. Cornell, a large landowner and consolidation supporter by 1894, had previously worked for municipal incorporation within Staten Island but abandoned that position as the chances for consolidation increased.[35] While one's business and social status was not determinative of one's position toward consolidation, Cornell's support for it made sense. So did Wiman's. Wiman was the man who had built the ferry terminal at St. George and the freight railroad to New Jersey, so his energies had long been devoted to forging links off island. Political consolidation with New York only validated the social and economic orientation toward it that already existed among the island's elite and offered a potential boom for its real estate interests.

The Greater New York Commission began meeting in the fall of 1890, but resistance from the Tammany machine and Brooklyn elite stymied it for several years. By April 1891, it had prepared an ambitious bill that called for one city with a single administration, a single property tax rate, an assumption of all public properties and liabilities, and an immediate effective date. Although an amended version of the bill passed out of committee successfully, it was defeated on the Assembly floor, and no action was taken in that legislative session. The Green Commission scaled back its proposals the following year and included a requirement for a nonbinding referendum on the issue. This bill also met with defeat, as did one submitted in 1893 when it died in committee.[36]

With consolidation legislation stalled from 1891 to 1893, Staten Islanders began to consider incorporating as a separate city. Consolidation talk had fueled dissatisfaction with the status quo in local government, and now citizens began to look for an alternative plan for rectifying it. Discussions of the issue swelled in the winter of 1892–1893, and the *Richmond County Standard*, an independent Democratic newspaper, became a leading proponent of incorporation. It bemoaned the "absurdity" of multiple levels of government within a county of 55,000 inhabitants and concluded, "What Staten Island needs is not consolidation with New York but consolidation within itself."[37] Similarly, the *Richmond County Democrat*, an organ of the local Democratic machine, looked for a more politically realistic plan than what "the consolidation dreamers" had to offer. It supported the formation of a city along the island's northern and eastern shores.[38] Even the *Staten Islander*, in a moment of doubt about the likelihood of passing consolidation legislation, was open to the possibility of a city stretching from Mariner's Harbor to New Dorp to reduce taxes and eliminate unnecessary levels of government.[39]

This public sympathy for political consolidation within Staten Island notwithstanding, no formal steps were taken to pursue it when the Greater New York consolidation state legislation was mired in the early 1890s. Any such proposition for a separate city on Staten Island would have encountered strong resistance from Green and other proponents of Greater New York, and the political opening for it was short-lived. In 1893, the rout of the slate of candidates run by Brooklyn boss Hugh McLaughlin, whose opposition to consolidation had been substantial and influential, eliminated many politicians who had previously voted against referendum legislation.[40] On Staten Island, consolidation with New York was becoming increasingly palatable by 1894. The *Richmond County Standard*, satisfied that referendum results would not be aggregated (and thus Staten Island's vote would stand alone as a recommendation for its status), now editorialized in favor of a new consolidation law in December 1893.[41] The *Staten Island Independent*, which was not beholden to the Muller machine, largely reported favorably on the efforts at passage, while reserving judgment on the merits of the issue. The *Staten Islander* returned to its confident position that consolidation with New York was possible and beneficial.

38 CONSOLIDATION AND ITS AFTERMATH

This optimism was well placed as a bill on consolidation passed in 1894, though not without difficulties. Opposition persisted in the legislature, where duplicitous legerdemain in the Senate threatened the passage of any legislation. The bill that ultimately passed was stripped of nearly all of the provisions in the 1891 proposal. Rather than delineate the terms of consolidation, the law provided for a nonbinding referendum on the desirability of consolidation without presenting any plans on how to launch or structure the new city. The particularly divisive issue of taxation was left unmentioned, and the language of the referendum was pared down to a "for" or "against" vote on the idea of consolidation (see figure 2.2).[42] The simplified question was included on the ballot in the November 1894 elections, and after a heated campaign, the results finally placed the consolidation cause in a favorable position.

On Staten Island, the consolidation referendum campaign kicked off in earnest in September. While Green concentrated his efforts on securing a positive outcome in Brooklyn, Greenfield led the effort for a favorable vote on Staten Island. He made the case in an open letter to island residents that was printed in several local newspapers and wrote sharp rebuttals to public expression of misgivings. Working with a group of prominent citizens, he planned two mass meetings, the first of which took place at Prohibition Park on October 9.[43] Hundreds attended the meeting at the 4,000-seat auditorium known as University Temple, and Greenfield presided, introducing to the receptive audience a host of prominent speakers who largely endorsed the proposition.[44] Wiman received "a cyclone of applause"; Worrell introduced supportive resolutions; Cornell sent a letter of support; and the other speakers, including a merchant, a sea captain, a jeweler, and a former county clerk, largely expressed favorable opinions. There were a handful of critics, but the most notable among them, the attorney Sidney Rawson, registered skepticism more than hostility.[45] A similar rally occurred in Clifton two weeks later. At that event, Greenfield predicted with considerable accuracy that 80 percent of the island's

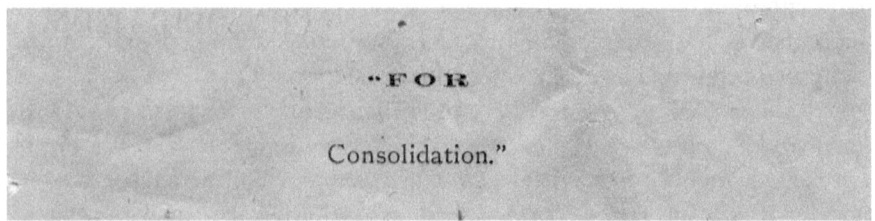

2.2 Consolidation ballot

A simpler referendum question could not have been devised, as voters were asked to submit "for" or "against" the prospect of "consolidation."

Source: Courtesy of Collection of Historic Richmond Town.

voters would favor consolidation. When the referendum achieved a smashing victory on Staten Island on November 6, many residents now saw consolidation as inevitable even though the decision to proceed and to include Staten Island still remained with the state legislature.[46]

The City of Richmond, Greater New York, and the Legislative Process

Neither the Republican landslide nor the referendum victories in 1894 generated the passage of enabling state legislation in 1895. State Republican leaders squabbled, and the questions of who would sit on a committee to devise a charter and what powers would be invested in them proved too divisive to overcome in a few months. On Staten Island, this derailment reignited sentiment to form a separate city.[47] In 1895, the Good Government Club resolved to promote a city charter for Staten Island, and the Staten Island Chamber of Commerce (SICC) and the Richmond County Board of Supervisors jointly established the City Charter Committee to consider a plan of government for the entire island.[48] Assuming that no legislation for Greater New York would be passed in the 1896 legislative session, the organizations determined that Staten Island could not further wait to improve its form of government. George M. Pinney Jr., a prominent lawyer soon to be elected district attorney for Richmond County, chaired the City Charter Committee, which set to work in the fall of 1895.[49]

The City Charter Committee met periodically over the next few months but struggled to navigate the conflicting commitments of its membership. The committee contained both a strong faction of consolidationists such as Greenfield as well as some noted opponents such as Rawson and clashed over their objective and the stalled consolidation movement. Some interpreted the referendum results as an indictment "of the deplorable condition of the county government at that time" rather than as an indication of interest in joining Greater New York.[50] They hypothesized that given a choice between Greater New York and a city of Richmond in late 1895, Staten Island voters would choose the latter. Others disputed any conflict between the two options. One county supervisor contended that moving ahead on a city charter for Richmond County would "in no way affect the Greater New-York [sic] scheme."[51] There was also considerable disagreement over which path—incorporation or consolidation—was the more expedient one for addressing the island's governmental woes.[52] These difficulties notwithstanding, the Charter Committee proclaimed its determination to draw up a charter for an independent city, and the SICC "instructed [members of the committee] to favor the plan of including the whole of Staten Island in the new City."[53]

Was the effort at incorporation intended as a permanent substitution for consolidation or as a temporary improvement until Greater New York could be enacted? The committee membership split over this question, as a 9–7 straw vote in early 1896 revealed.[54] Rancorous meetings of the SICC Board of Directors also indicated the divisiveness of this issue. At the board's meetings in late 1895, a mere announcement of intent to resolve for the organization to pursue a separate city in lieu of annexation to New York generated "an animated discussion." This uncoupling of the separate-city and consolidation issues produced "some oratorial fireworks" when the resolution for incorporation was offered to the board the following month. Greenfield and other proponents of the consolidation plan immediately spoke in opposition to the resolution. Viewing Greater New York as a better solution to Staten Island's governance woes than a city of Richmond, they were concerned that an effort to establish the latter would harm Staten Island's prospects for participation in the former. Even the supporters of the resolution were unwilling to detach the two efforts, describing the city charter "as a temporary measure pending an annexation to New York City." The debate grew protracted, but the strong sentiment for consolidation in the long run led to the SICC's tabling of the motion by a 37–22 margin.[55] The Good Government Club harbored fewer doubts about which approach to follow. In its December 1895 meeting, devoted to considering "whether the Club should favor the 'Greater New York,' or a separate city charter for Richmond County," it chose the latter. Dismayed that the SICC'S City Charter Committee had waivered in its commitment, the club determined to pursue a charter on its own.[56]

The effort to create a separate city of Richmond could not overcome the revival of fortune for the consolidation scheme. In late December 1895, state legislators readied a new Greater New York bill that the *New York Times* expected to pass by mid-February. Already proceeding at a slow pace and chaired by a supporter of consolidation, the SICC City Charter Committee accomplished very little in the aftermath of this news. Still uncertain about the prospects of consolidation, some chamber members pressed for the committee to present "a form of charter" at the January 15, 1896, meeting. Pinney and Greenfield instead reported "that the committee deems it inexpedient to, at the present time, urge the bill in face of the Greater New York measure, and that it would, if the consolidation law passed, put the county in the undignified position of being forced into consolidation." The City Charter Committee affirmed the island residents' unchanged sentiment toward consolidation and so recommended waiting out the legislative process on Greater New York. The committee's fallback measure prevailed, and that victory ended the effort to establish a separate city on Staten Island.[57]

The resuscitation of consolidation stemmed from maneuverings by the state's political powers. Senate leader Thomas Platt and Governor Levi Morton engaged in intense private negotiations over the Greater New York plan, while Platt ally Senator Clarence Lexow guided a consolidation bill through a joint legislative committee. While the prospects for Greater New York were being restored, Staten Islanders faced another significant threat to participation in the scheme. In late January 1896, New York City's corporation counsel, Francis M. Scott, caused an uproar in Richmond when he publicly questioned whether New York needed Staten Island. Scott rightly feared that New York would bear a heavy financial burden for developing such an "inaccessible territory that is sparsely populated."[58] The city comptroller Ashbel Fitch echoed this sentiment, wondering why urban New York needed rural Staten Island (or the farther reaches of Long Island). Noting the great wealth found in New York, Fitch understood well why Staten Island hoped to benefit from joining with it, but he did not think Richmond offered "anything adequate in return."[59] Both men argued pointedly that Staten Island would be a financial "burden" and, more theoretically, that its undeveloped fields simply did not belong in a great city. Their voices represented a large segment of New Yorkers who were not opposed to "political consolidation" but disputed any terms that would include an identical tax rate for all boroughs. The Taxpayers Anti-Equalization League's appearance at the Lexow committee's hearing in Manhattan sparked a heated exchange with the chairman.[60] Staten Island's suitability for Greater New York continued to be questioned at hearings held by New York's mayor William Strong in early April.[61]

Staten Island consolidationists rushed to New York to contest Scott's position. Erastus Wiman once again stepped forward as the island's chief public defender. Issuing statements to the press and testifying at the Lexow committee's final hearing in New York, Wiman reiterated the virtues and opportunities Staten Island offered to New York.[62] Greenfield was equally visible, insisting the future borough would be "thickly settled" and not a financial burden. Ironically, given his earlier role in derailing the movement for a separate city of Richmond, Greenfield emphasized—perhaps a veiled albeit weak threat—that Staten Island would incorporate on its own if excluded from Greater New York.[63] Other proponents of consolidation challenged the long-standing unfavorable image of Staten Island as a haven for disease by citing state data that showed Richmond County with a lower death rate than that of the other three counties under consideration for annexation.[64] Staten Island assemblyman Gustav Barth asserted, "Greater New York is not complete without Richmond County." Though alarmed by Scott and Fitch's sentiment, the *Staten Islander* expressed confidence that Staten Island would remain a part of the Greater New York plan.[65]

In the end, the effort to remove Staten Island was quelled, internal Republican conflicts were contained, and party boss Platt powered a bill through the state legislature that established January 1, 1898, as the effective date for consolidation of all the territories Green wanted. In a compromise with Governor Morton, the bill did not establish new commissions to run police, fire, and other services, nor did it detail any aspect of the governance of the greater city. The legislation instead simply established a new commission to draft a charter for the new city. When the mayors of both New York and Brooklyn vetoed the bill, Platt engineered an override on April 22, 1896, and Governor Morton signed the bill the following month.[66]

Securing a Favorable Charter

The next task for consolidation was devising a charter for the new city. The work of the newly created Charter Commission soon became the focal point for struggles over the terms of consolidation, as the outcome of long-standing debates about tax rates and services ultimately depended on the decisions made by the commission. The membership, appointed by Morton but acceptable to Platt, represented each borough as well as each major party and significant political factions. Its chairman, Benjamin F. Tracy, was a leading Republican figure in New York, and Staten Island's representative was George Pinney, a reform Republican and relative newcomer to Richmond. Not identified with any political machine, Pinney was a noncontroversial choice and became the commission's secretary. The issues confronting the commissioners were considerable: party and borough interests, the financial arrangements of annexation, and the extent of centralized planning and reformist elements present in the new municipal government.[67]

For Staten Islanders invested in consolidation, matters of representation and finance commanded the most attention. Concerned that "Staten Island will get lost in the shuffle," they wanted "as much home rule as we can possibly get" and demanded that the Charter Commission "give Richmond her share."[68] While Staten Islanders often decried their impotency in the overwhelming presence of their larger neighbors, some residents of the other outer boroughs feared that Richmond with its relatively small population would be overrepresented. A commission member from Queens argued for greater representation of some of its towns, noting that Richmond Borough had double the representation but half of Queens' population. An early draft of the charter spurred protest in Brooklyn because it called for a bicameral city legislature, with the upper house comprising two members from each borough. In deriding the idea of giving equal representation, the *Brooklyn Daily Eagle* singled out Richmond County for its extreme variation from Brooklyn in population size and orientation.[69] Concerns about subsidization also remained potent. Some people argued that Brooklyn would lose financially from consolidation by taking on the costs "of the necessary improvements in Flatlands and Staten Island."[70]

Similar sentiment was expressed with greater foresight in Manhattan, where many claimed that the stipulations favored the outer boroughs, especially concerning the debt levels of the various counties, cities, towns and villages, and school districts that would be absorbed by New York.[71]

The SICC took the lead in responding to such assertions and to the terms of the proposed charter. By 1897, the Good Government Club had largely abandoned its political reform agenda, renamed itself the Staten Island Club, and become primarily a social organization. An effort by one county supervisor to sponsor a charter meeting for the general public was thwarted by his colleagues, who assumed he was maneuvering to revive the movement for a separate city of Richmond. The Charter Commission hearings held in New York in January 1897 drew Wiman but few others from Staten Island.[72] In contrast, the SICC established a subcommittee comprising many of its leading members "to examine and report on" the proposed charter. The head start and rushed nature of the charter-drafting process forced the subcommittee to complete a hurried report by February 1897, before a charter was adopted.[73]

Although Greater New York's first charter created a powerful mayoralty and fairly weak borough presidents, Staten Island fared reasonably well overall. The SICC subcommittee described the Charter Commission's process as "creditable," cautioned members not "to be over-critical or fault-finding," and concluded "that the interests of our community were carefully guarded by the charter."[74] Arguably the most favorable clause for Staten Island and the other outer boroughs was that the new city would absorb the debts of all eliminated governing entities. Vested in joining Staten Island to New York City, subcommittee members nevertheless found several aspects of the charter proposal problematic for Staten Island. Greenfield reported that the charter " does not give to Staten Island sufficient home-rule and special powers of local government and improvement."[75] He also asserted that it relied too much on special local assessments for public improvements, an unpalatable feature for a borough trying to tap the great wealth of New York. Another member objected to sharing a parks commissioner with Manhattan, fearing that Richmond's needs would be lost without a commissioner solely devoted to the island. Additional members raised questions about the workability of other charter provisions—such as the pension plan and bipartisan board for the Police Department and the requirements for the issuing of bonds—that did not necessarily undercut Staten Island's interests but that encapsulated their sentiments about larger issues of the day.[76] The few Staten Islanders who attended Charter Commission hearings expressed a sense of unfairness that the island's S. R. Smith Infirmary did not draw a subsidy, as hospitals in other boroughs did.[77]

Symbolic issues loomed as large as technical ones. The question that most animated SICC members was the name of the new borough, which was to be called "Richmond." Many members preferred "Staten Island" because it was far less commonplace, but the discussion revealed the many larger fears and aspirations of Staten Island's business elite. Would the name "Staten Island" reinforce its separateness or "its association with mud, malaria, and mosquitoes"? Might the name afford an opportunity to revise false impressions of the island? Cornelius Kolff, whose business was in real estate and who would remain a civic leader for fifty years, professed astonishment that anyone would find shame in the historic Dutch name "Staten Island." When a vote was finally called, "Staten Island" handily defeated "Richmond" twenty-one to six—although it was a purely symbolic outcome.[78]

The name ultimately selected for the new borough ironically spoke to the qualms many islanders had expressed about being too miniscule to wield power in the greater city. Despite the preference for "Staten Island" among some of the island's most influential citizens, the Charter Commission retained "Richmond" as the borough name.[79] Likewise, the impact of the other concerns raised by the chamber's charter subcommittee was equally negligible. More plausible was the influence wielded by Wiman, who continued to serve as a vocal representative of Staten Island interests—at least those consistent with his vision of commercial and population growth—vis-à-vis the other boroughs. As the entrepreneur behind the ferry terminal at St. George, Wiman wanted regular, reliable, and inexpensive boat service to foster maximum access to Staten Island. He publicly advocated the creation of a Department of Ferries to own and operate the boats to Staten Island and criticized the initial omission of such an office by the Charter Commission, which then quickly addressed the issue to Wiman's satisfaction by creating the Department of Docks and Ferries.[80]

The product ultimately produced by the Charter Commission included features to placate most groups, including Brooklynites, reformers, and commercial interests. As David Hammack has noted, the charter called for "uniform rates of taxes and assessments, and for a strong central government with new if not striking powers to promote 'the complete and rational development of the metropolis.'"[81] The five-borough structure and the twenty-two boards responsible for local improvements (one of which would serve Richmond) attempted to retain the vestiges of home rule. The bicameral municipal assembly, comprising a sixty-member Board of Aldermen (with one member from Richmond) and a twenty-nine-member council (with two members from Richmond), largely relied on proportional representation. The newly created Board of Estimate and Apportionment wielded the considerable power of appropriations, and the borough presidents were added to it in 1901, with Staten Island's incumbent exercising one out of sixteen votes.[82] Although the charter did not offer Staten Island the amount of autonomy many of its residents desired, the *Staten Islander* thought what it did get was enough and counseled its readers to support the charter legislation, which first passed in late March 1897.[83] Platt evaded final legislative efforts to block or delay the charter's passage and easily overrode another veto by New York's mayor William Strong in April 1897. Governor Frank S. Black signed the bill in May, and Greater New York took effect as planned on January 1, 1898.

The Aftermath of Consolidation

Twelve years after joining New York City, Staten Islanders could look back and take note of some immediate changes. Approximately seventy distinct official entities were dismantled, including "supervisors, village trustees, assessors, highway commissioners, and town boards."[84] Public schools gained new buildings, while adding functions as they joined the city's education system. The borough could also revel in the work done on its roads, the improvement of its water supply, and the city's takeover of the St. George ferry. Several fine public buildings were constructed—most notably Curtis High School (1904) and Borough Hall (1906).[85] More than just buildings, these structures sought to convey the significance of their purpose. As the historian François Weil has described, "Everywhere, various municipal services were moved into buildings considered worthy of the civic ideal they were supposed to embody: fire stations, police stations, school buildings constituted so many variations on the theme of municipal grandeur."[86] Both the school building and the municipal building were located in St. George because George Cromwell, the first borough president, shared Wiman's interest in reorienting the island around its closest point to Manhattan.[87] Thus, joining New York City hastened the relocation of the island's civic life to its northern shores, and the "center" of the island would no longer be a geographic position but rather a demographic, economic, and political one.

Amalgamation with New York City by no means settled the debate over whether Staten Island belonged in it. For some, buyer's remorse ensued almost immediately as anticipated results did not materialize. When the real estate boom failed to meet expectations, some developers expressed regret at joining Greater New York rather than holding out for a separate city.[88] One report in the summer of 1898 contended that the island initially had fewer policemen available for public safety than in previous years.[89] Another related early the next year "a Staten Islander's plaint" about a proposed fare hike for electricity, which was attributed to the persistence of monopolies for key services.[90] Other islanders struggled with the changes in taxes. Although the property tax rate of Staten Island residents did indeed decline, the overall tax bill increased because the assessed valuation of property was much higher. Moreover, taxes now had to be paid all at once, whereas prior to consolidation the various jurisdictions to which Staten Islanders paid taxes—county, town, village, schools—staggered their collection over the course of a year. Other areas of unmet expectations included free home delivery of mail, large appropriations for public improvements, and the absence of economies of scale for public schools, whose costs actually rose.[91]

By 1900, the Richmond Borough Separation League had formed to undo the so-called mistake of consolidation. To some extent, the group was seeking to overturn a decision its core members had always fought. Headed by John De Morgan, it weighed in at charter-revision hearings, which occurred because dissatisfaction with insufficient borough autonomy quickly set in across the city. Demonstrable and marked increases in city officials' salaries spurred further discontent, which De Morgan aimed to redirect as support for a separate city of Richmond. The league also sought to tap into broader misgivings about the wisdom of participation and attempted to elect a sympathetic candidate to the state Assembly.[92]

Outside sentiment that Staten Island did not belong in the consolidated city also remained strong. Bird Coler, the expanded city's first comptroller, issued a report that reinvigorated a key misgiving—that Manhattan would subsidize the outer boroughs. In an analysis of the impact of consolidation on taxation submitted in 1899, Coler found that, as expected, Manhattan's taxes had increased significantly, and Brooklyn's had declined slightly. Coler viewed Queens and Staten Island as the real beneficiaries of Manhattan's largesse, for their taxes had remained essentially the same, even while they received new services and paid larger salaries due to the "substitution ... of an expensive, highly developed metropolitan government for rural township." Moreover, Coler noted, New York's assumption of all local debts had pushed the greater city over the state-mandated debt limit of 10 percent of a municipality's real estate valuation, thus reducing its ability to issue bonds for major infrastructure projects.[93] As the economist Edward Dana Durand pointed out at the time, even those who welcomed the consolidated city expected that "the great wealth of the business district ... [would] aid in the improvement of the residence district(s) dependent on it."[94] And so it did. The island's borough presidents often took ribbing from their peers and little credit among their constituents for obtaining so much largesse for Staten Island. Over the next century, partisans and scholars repeatedly showed the disbursement of tax monies collected in Manhattan to the outer boroughs—a reality that did not, however, much dampen Staten Islanders' perception that they contributed more than they received from New York City. Staten Island especially benefited from property tax rates that had historically served homeowners better than owners of rental properties and, arguably, the renters themselves.[95]

Communities in the outer boroughs did not enhance their standing when they went on spending sprees in the months before consolidation took effect.

By one account, expenditures for improvements in Staten Island and Queens were an estimated five times greater than what they would have been in a typical year without consolidation looming. On January 1, 1898, Greater New York assumed nearly $322 million in debt, of which approximately $3.5 million was from Richmond Borough.[96] Comptroller Coler publicly chastised the former towns and villages for running up their debts and held up payments on expenditures he deemed questionable.[97] Whereas critics saw these sprees as greedy and irresponsible, to others they represented a rational calculation of self-interest amid the ongoing concern that Staten Island's needs would go unmet in the huge city. This understanding lay at the heart of the *Brooklyn Daily Eagle*'s applause for the large expenditures on Staten Island in 1897. It framed the issue as a choice between immediate improvements determined locally and carried out expeditiously versus those planned centrally and delayed interminably. In either scenario, the city as a whole would pay the bill.[98]

Even with a greater level of home rule granted by the revised charter of 1901, Staten Islanders soon experienced the frustration of having to accept unwanted municipal institutions. In 1909, the city began building the Sea View Hospital for tubercular diseases on Staten Island despite islanders' protests.[99] Although no concerted secessionist movement materialized over this development, the sentiment that Staten Island had erred in joining New York City had by then become a fault line of political discourse in Richmond Borough. In fact, how Staten Island had fared as Richmond Borough was an important theme in the 1901 electoral campaign for borough presidency. Cromwell defended his record by claiming "the Borough of Richmond got back every dollar paid in *and more.*" To his Democratic opponent, Charles McCormack, "a flood of public funds" on wasteful expenditures was a problem to be attacked.[100] In such a climate, disappointments about particular decisions and about the shortcomings or costs of municipal services quickly became illustrations of a larger mistake in joining New York City. Subsequently at multiple moments during the twentieth century, secessionist sentiment reached a high volume, culminating in the ill-fated effort of the 1990s.[101]

* * *

It is tempting to posit that the creation of Greater New York City could not be understood without a thorough consideration of Staten Island. Richmond County neither held a key place in the plans for consolidation nor played a decisive role in its accomplishment, but the island was no outlier either. Too often the story of consolidation is overly focused on the defeat of resistance in Brooklyn and Manhattan, but the clamor for consolidation among many residents of Long Island, Staten Island, and Westchester requires attention as well. The issues with which Staten Island citizens grappled—taxes, services, and infrastructure—were equally central to the calculations of the residents of outer Brooklyn, Queens, and the Bronx. There was also a moment or two when Richmond took central stage in the consolidation drama. Green included Staten Island as an essential part of New York Harbor, but for others it represented an unwanted appendage and a potential drain on the greater city's finances. Richmond's leading citizens helped halt momentum to detach Staten Island from the scheme, and so it became one of the five new boroughs of Greater New York.

Despite Staten Island's one-sided referendum vote, its participation in consolidation was in no way certain. Islanders contested the very meaning of the landslide vote. To the supporters of union with New York, it was a decisive indication that Richmond County residents strongly favored consolidation. To opponents, the vote simply demonstrated the tremendous dissatisfaction with the status quo in local governance. After the vote, Staten Island's participation grew much more likely, but barriers on the island remained. Many inhabitants who wanted considerable residential, commercial, and industrial development favored incorporation as a separate city as the best means to achieve it. For some, the consolidation movement tapped into a vision for a transformative future, but for many others it simply highlighted a high degree of dissatisfaction with the current state of politics and government. In the short run, consolidation brought the island new facilities and services, but regret set in almost immediately as heightened expectations went unmet and hesitancy to embrace New York City remained a potent political force. In the decades that followed consolidation, the biggest disappointment (the absence of a subway tunnel to Brooklyn) and the largest unintended consequence (the presence of a huge garbage plant at Fresh Kills) would repeatedly generate secessionist sentiment. The power of that panacea only served to highlight the reality that Staten Islanders faced: like it or not, becoming a part of New York City was a seminal development in the island's history.

CHAPTER 3

ENVISIONING THE FUTURE

What Consolidation Would Bring to Staten Island, 1890–1909

With its area of 58 square miles of the most diversified topography and reachable from the Battery for a five-cent ferry fare, a region for workingmen's homes would be added to the city limits by consolidation that would be of the highest importance.

—*New York Times*, February 2, 1896

When in 1896 Erastus Wiman testified before a joint New York State legislative subcommittee examining the prospect of creating a Greater New York, he proffered Staten Island as a solution for three of New York's key problems. Laborers unable to afford the city's exorbitant real estate prices could find accessible, affordable, and beautiful homes in Richmond. As for Gotham's declining share of international commerce and industrial production, the wharves and factories on the island's west shore could well serve the manufacture and movement of goods. Wiman's widely reported testimony was meant to counter a very public denunciation of Staten Island's inclusion in the consolidation plan made just days earlier. It also articulated his vision for Staten Island's future demographic and economic significance, a prospect shared by many other island businessmen and civic boosters.

This chapter explores these and other aspirations for joining Greater New York. What did Staten Islanders hope to accomplish through consolidation? Historians and political scientists alike have grappled with the effectiveness of various kinds of arguments for municipal annexation of outlying areas. Standard interpretations emphasize enlargement and efficiency in providing services, population size and rank, and economic growth.[1] Some of those reasons, however, hold more currency for the center than for the periphery of an expanding metropolis. New York City's greatness mattered little on Staten Island, where boosters were more interested in their own manifest destiny, businesses in their profit and property values, and residents in the quality and quantity of public services. Resisters posited for the island either a different vision steeped in a pastoral identity or of achieving the boosters' vision through different means—a separate city of Richmond. Staten Islanders' arguments for or against joining Greater New York did not likely sway many voters, but they did establish a set of expectations for what would transpire after consolidation and served as a rubric for how their experience as citizens of New York City might be evaluated.

Consolidation and a Vision of Staten Island's Future

In the 1890s, Staten Islanders articulated a host of reasons for and against participation in the consolidation of New York City. At stake in the contest over consolidation were competing aspirations for Staten Island's future. An urban–rural dichotomy only partially captures this divide, which ultimately centered on opposing visions of interconnection and disconnection. One view saw the island as irrevocably linked with its more urban neighbors and envisioned that it would grow more populous, industrial, and commercial as part of Greater New York. The other view celebrated the island's picturesque landscape and sedate lifestyle but more fundamentally wished that Staten Island would remain apart. Some opponents of consolidation did share an urban vision for Staten Island but tapped into a discourse emphasizing independence. Would Staten Island's future be hitched to the great metropolis to its north, or would it determine its own fate? Proponents of consolidation appeared at ease with the interdependence associated with the consolidation plan. That Staten Island was irrevocably linked to New York regardless of its municipal status rarely entered the public discussion.

Staten Islanders clashed over less abstract and more prosaic issues as well. Their discussions of consolidation reveal a number of social, political, and ideological fault lines on Staten Island in the 1890s. They uncover two sets of civic booster images for Richmond—one looking forward to the twentieth century and the other looking backward to the eighteenth. They expose deep concerns about government: the services it provided, the taxes it raised, and the honesty with which it performed its functions. Because both opponents and proponents wanted improved governance and reduced taxes, some debate centered on whether Greater New York would support or undermine those goals. Finally, with respect to not just what was said but who said it, the consolidation debates partially bare the economic and political divisions among the island's populace, exposing fissures but not huge social cleavages. The island's chief proponents of consolidation included large property owners, dealers of real estate, and professionals and businessmen who worked in New York and wanted Staten Island to develop in a similar manner. Many local officials (machine Democrats in particular) opposed consolidation because they felt their positions were threatened, but they did not fight it vociferously.[2] Though consolidation was not strictly a partisan issue, independent Democrats generally supported it but did not enthusiastically promote it. It was instead the island's Republicans and leading civic boosters—represented by the *Staten Islander* and Wiman—who became wildly in favor of consolidation and made the future Borough of Richmond happen.

Staten Island: Suburb, Market, and Factory

Staten Island's consolidationists illustrated an early version of what the sociologists John Logan and Harvey Molotch have called "growth machines." These coalitions of local political and economic elites, seen as "people dreaming, planning and organizing themselves to make money from property," generally favor policies that support economic growth and maximize value.[3] Such policies might dictate nonintervention in markets, but they also include the public provision of services as a way of "making places safe for development."[4] The most enthusiastic local voices for consolidation came from Staten Island's business and propertied class—its own incipient growth machine. Embodied by Wiman, supported by other business and real estate interests, and repeatedly articulated by the *Staten Islander* from 1890 through 1897, this vision depicted bustling wharves, numerous factories, and vibrant neighborhoods as the pathway to civic greatness and prosperity. Wiman argued at length for Staten Island's geographic proclivity as a center of commerce, industry, and residence:

> She [Staten Island] should take her place as the only portion of the city of New York in which the perfection of a terminal is possible, viz: receipt, storage and shipment! That she should take her place as the chief centre of manufactures because all the supplies of raw materials can reach here at the lowest cost and the distribution of finished products is only possible to us with the greatest

economy. But aside from her commercial and manufacturing advantages, her magnificent hills, her splendid residential sites afford the greatest possible attractions. Surrounded as she is with the three great centres of population, in New Jersey, in New York and in Brooklyn, she will with proper encouragement and once a part of the great metropolis spring forward to the fulfillment of a destiny—to form a part of the greatest city of the greatest country under the sun![5]

To Wiman, Staten Island faced the most significant moment in its history, and its residents had the rare opportunity to reach "the possible greatness of our future"—one that contained more business, more production, and more people.[6] These aspirations had long resonated with many of Staten Island's leading citizens, and the campaign for consolidation orchestrated a concerted expression of them.[7] A highly commercialized, industrialized, and populated island appealed especially to owners of major properties who stood to benefit financially. Large landholders such as Daniel Cornell and David Tysen salivated at the prospect of a growth in values that was expected to accompany consolidation. The *Staten Islander* regularly predicted "a marked rise in the price of realty," and even local opponents of consolidation conceded this point.[8]

Supporters of consolidation also posited Staten Island as perfect for trade. George Greenfield declared, "We have the water fronts for miles in extent which ... will furnish room for the commerce of the world."[9] Situated at the entrance to New York's harbor and blessed with plenty of space for wharves and docks, Staten Island was, with good reason, often compared favorably with the current costly and inefficient movement of freight in the harbor. The crux of the problem was that all but one of the major freight lines did not actually reach New York, where most of the area's ocean-going ships docked. Their terminals lay at the New Jersey edge of the harbor, where they relied on a fleet of boats to move goods across the Hudson River. This unwieldy system, coupled with technological developments in shipping and increased competition from other ports, imperiled New York's continued preeminence as a commercial center.[10] Wiman's hyperbolic claim that "the foreign commerce of New York is declining very rapidly" rested in the fact that New York's share of global trade was diminishing, and his suggestion that Staten Island's waterfront more than New York's could be easily linked to railroads heading west offered a solution to the harbor's fundamental limitation.[11] Indeed, he had already played a crucial role in doing just that by introducing the B&O to Staten Island via a bridge constructed over the Arthur Kill in 1889. Cornell argued that consolidation would enable a marked rise in trade because it would bring the necessary improvements in docks and piers. As a result, he opined, "we would have our store houses loading and unloading to the shipping of the world, and Staten Island will be great indeed when this state of affairs comes to pass."[12] The *Staten Islander* reasoned that joining New York would help in "the building up of the trade of the greatest port in the world" by eliminating "an unnecessary amount of handling" of goods in the multiple and unmanaged ports.[13] More than any other, the rationale for more efficient harbor activity led Andrew Green to include Staten Island in his plan for Greater New York.[14]

The promise of greater commerce was often linked to increased industrial activity. The same qualities—a waterfront fit for docks and room to construct connectors to the main railroad lines heading west—made Staten Island "a place of great promise for commerce and industry."[15] Wiman repeatedly linked the two activities, as did leading island businessmen and their new organizational vehicle for the pro-growth interests, the Staten Island Chamber of Commerce. Founded in 1895, the SICC actively promoted consolidation as a means to spur manufacturing on Staten Island.[16] By 1897, even the mere prospect of consolidation, argued the *News Letter*, a Republican weekly published in St. George, had fomented the increase of commercial and manufacturing activity on the island.[17]

Staten Island's boosters also spoke in glowing terms of the population boom that would follow consolidation. As early as 1890, Wiman and others highlighted Staten Island's potential as a suburb of New York, and they projected this image at each stage of the consolidation struggle.[18] Prominent realtors and property owners imagined developing their lands for "an army of new residents" expected to arrive, and they eagerly anticipated a rise in values that would ensue.[19] The *Staten Islander* predicted that consolidation would "turn the mighty currents of the city's [New York's] population and capital to its [Staten Island's] shores."[20] Most observers, including Wiman, posited Staten Island as an ideal place of residence for the working class. As Greenfield argued in 1896, Staten Island offered "a place where thousands upon thousands of thrifty people may find healthful homes."[21]

Greenfield's use of the word *healthful* was no doubt deliberate. Consolidation offered the opportunity for the island to rid itself of a long-standing image as a haven for mosquitos and concomitant fevers. During the 1890s, Staten Island continued to contend with unflattering depictions such as the one by a New Yorker who reported "that he escaped from Staten Island just to avoid having the coat shaken off his back by fever and ague."[22] Its residents aimed for Staten Island to become more than just a place "where the small pox steamships are quarantined."[23] Going even further, many civic and business leaders hoped that these tangible developments would yield "prominence ... in the eyes of the people of New York."[24]

The pro-growth booster image—centering on property, commerce, industry, and population—was not limited to consolidation's ardent supporters. Those who preferred to form a separate city of Richmond spoke and used terms very similar to those Wiman and Greenfield employed. The *Richmond County Standard*, for example, accepted the suburban goal of "striving to attract those looking for healthy and pleasant homes" but argued that "home rule" would serve the island better.[25] The *Richmond County Advance* suggested that "everything essential to growth and prosperity" was already present on the island, which just needed to join its towns under one government.[26] A local attorney suggested that a separate city could generate demand for Staten Island property and presciently argued that consolidation would not eliminate the competition from suburbs in New Jersey and Long Island. In late 1895, SICC members, very much supportive of greater trade, production, and population on the island, debated whether achieving these things would come through consolidation or through incorporation as a separate city.[27]

Staten Island: Favored by God and Geography

Not all Staten Islanders were swayed by the growth-machine vision and instead offered an alternative future for their home. Some of the most prominent residents who publicly expressed doubts or spoke against consolidation infused their arguments with images of the island's natural features. The most vocal of them was John De Morgan, a Westerleigh resident, a minor literary figure, and a former candidate for the state Assembly. In a lengthy letter published in local newspapers during the referendum campaign, De Morgan conveyed his fears for the preservation of Staten Island's idyllic landscape:

> "God made the country, and man made the town," said Cowper, and I shudder to think of the time when our lovely hills and beautiful valleys shall be made as unsightly as the dirty streets of New York, when the neat little cottages with their tasteful gardens shall be swept away, and row after row of brick or stone houses, factories and gin mills occupy their place. Let us retain one place which shall in all its varied picturesqueness [sic] gladden the weary eyes of the workers. Let the bright green of our hills, the lovely tint of our trees, the songs of our birds be retained.[28]

George William Curtis was never quite as direct as De Morgan, but his own concerns about consolidation were linked to his affection for the island's topography. Proponents of consolidation tried to turn De Morgan's argument on its head. Wiman offered that the "peaceful healthfulness of her [Staten Island's] surroundings" was precisely what made it attractive to the other future boroughs.[29] In an pro-consolidation editorial in January 1894, the *Staten Islander* argued that as a "beautiful garden" Staten Island offered a natural setting to the new city.³⁰ For some, though, union with New York would only needlessly tamper with a wonderful creation.

Another line of argument contested the central premise that had led Green to include Staten Island in his plan for Greater New York: Staten Island's place in New York Harbor. Green's position rested on particular answers to two fundamental questions about the island's geography and history. First, was Staten Island too remote from the rest of the city for the union to make sense, or could modern means of transportation forge meaningful links across the water? Doubters stressed "the physical fact that Richmond county is separated from New York city by seven [sic] miles of water" and that such a span "never can be connected by bridges as can Brooklyn and Long Island City."³¹ To Wiman, the distance would not preclude vastly improving ferry service and constructing a tunnel to Brooklyn, both of which he saw as inevitable results of consolidation. Proponents of consolidation posited Staten Island as an essential part of the harbor; the *Staten Islander* explained, "Nature started the consolidation movement by placing three great islands—Manhattan, Staten and Long—where it did."³²

Second, was Staten Island's past and present intricately linked to New York's, or was it truly an independent entity? In advocating for consolidation, the *Staten Islander* reminded residents of the island's historical orientation toward Manhattan: "All the towns, villages and cities which it is proposed to consolidate are offshoots of the first colony established upon Manhattan Island, authority for their establishment emanated thence and to it these dependencies looked for protection and business."³³ Greenfield asserted that the island's interests were strongly associated with New York's and wondered why islanders should put off "a union with which the future inevitably points."³⁴ Wiman emphasized to his neighbors that "our existence as a community depends upon the relation with the city."³⁵ The opposition countered that the miles of water in between New York and Staten Island "made it evident that the two districts have really no coincident interest, and the homogeneity which should be the basis of single municipality is entirely lacking."³⁶ One indicator of these divergent views was the very word used to describe the issue. Proponents discussed plans for "consolidation" with neighbors, whereas opponents often spoke of "annexation" by New York.³⁷

The Cost of Good Government

The most heated debates on consolidation occurred over more immediate and tangible matters rather than long-term growth. Staten Islanders disagreed over the likely impact of consolidation on ferry service, road quality, and judicial proceedings, among other concerns. Underlying the arguments over these specific topics was a larger discussion about the best structure to achieve quality governance and the best means to pay for it. This was no theoretical debate but rather one grounded in the experience islanders had with their existing government and tax entities. The referendum for consolidation coincided with a successful Fusion ticket for reform in the 1894 municipal elections that shared certain assumptions with the movement to create Greater New York. The campaign against Tammany Hall is a well-told story, but on Staten Island reform candidates also toppled Nicholas Muller's regular Democratic organization.[38] Staten Island citizens who voted both to remove party loyalists and to support consolidation likely acted on the same desire to improve government services, an impulse shared in many other outlying communities looking to join larger neighbors.[39]

Consolidationists argued strenuously that joining New York would liberate Richmond County from petty local-machine politics and streamline government. They blamed the numerous and overlapping local jurisdictions for handcuffing the island's development of transportation, education, and commercial facilities. A Brooklyn resident who summered on Staten Island testified that "nothing could be more corrupt than the political rings that rule some of those villages" in Richmond County.[40] The *Staten Island Independent* ridiculed the silly squabbles that pervaded the school districts, and Greenfield assured audiences that annexation would reduce local bickering.[41] The *Staten Islander* derided "hangers on who make a living out of the people for telling them what they may do," reminding readers that New Brighton village sadly paid for all or part of 160 salaries and that the sum of all its local and state taxes rates reached a then whopping 8 percent. Like a winning Fusion slate, annexation would constitute "a revolution in her present government for the better," and its advocates foresaw "a complete release forever from a government of the Boss, by the Boss, and for the Boss."[42] In that government's place, residents would elect better officials who would reduce the number of local posts and island-wide positions. Consolidation would alter the dynamic in which the island's "best citizens" did not participate in local affairs because they already identified with New York over Staten Island.[43] Consolidation would both formalize this association and focus elite attention on the island's affairs.

The irony of this claim was not lost on those who mistrusted consolidation. They doubted that joining with a city long dominated by the Tammany Hall political machine would free Staten Island from bossism; they asserted just the opposite—that joining New York would expose the island to far more corruption and provide it with much less representation than it currently experienced. The *Richmond County Sentinel* warned against affiliation with a city dominated by Tammany Hall.[44] A West Brighton physician, one of the few to speak against consolidation at the 1894 Prohibition Park rally, raised the specter of "blackmailing Tammany hall [sic] police" and wondered, "How do you expect honest administration under corrupt Tammany hall?"[45] Recognizing the defects in Staten Island's current array of jurisdictions, Curtis mused, "I am not aware of any strong conviction that the municipal Government of New York, which, according to the most intelligent authorities, is one of the worst-governed cities in the world, would probably secure such improvement."[46] De Morgan regularly railed against the "jobbery" and "almost open bribery" that permeated New York municipal government.[47] Concerns about the corruption of New York's government resonated even within the pro-consolidation SICC.[48]

Aside from the debate over political vice, Staten Islanders also wrangled over the amount of voice and autonomy they would possess in Greater New York and, more intangibly, whether the island would retain its individual identity and fulfill its distinct destiny. Some residents presciently feared that they would have relatively little representation and would not be able to compete successfully with the other outer boroughs for improvements.[49] The *Richmond County Standard* reasoned as follows: "Staten Island, being an isolated ward, having no closely allied interest with any other, would be the last to secure recognition of her demands for improvements. Meanwhile, taxpayers here would be paying for good sewers and streets on Long Island."[50] The attorney Sidney Rawson worried about the legal system under consolidation. Wondering whether courts in Richmond County would be "wiped out," he decried a potential loss of "control [of] our own business for our clients' benefit." More generally, he continued, would Staten Island become "a tail to a great municipal dog, and so small a tail that its wagging would not even be perceptible?"[51] Individuals affiliated with multiple local institutions feared that larger entities in New York would subsume their organizations.[52]

Consolidation advocates put forth a more optimistic view about the island's authority in a future Greater New York. In June 1890, the *Staten Islander* declared: "[Consolidation] is violative of no legal right, nor does it destroy any profitable autonomy, deprive anyone of a single vestige of the prerogatives which he now justly claims and exercises."[53] Wiman expected "moderate control of local affairs" under a Greater New York plan.[54] Four years later, during the referendum campaign, Greenfield assured Staten Island residents that "the different annexed localities will not lose their individuality."[55] He expected localities to retain their courts but decried the location of Staten Island's courts in the physical center of the island but inconvenient for the bulk of its population, which lived on the northern and eastern shores.[56]

What would the impact of consolidation be on the tax rates paid by the various boroughs? This question animated much of the debate over consolidation throughout the area, and Staten Island was no exception. The most common expectation was that the wealth of Manhattan would subsidize the development of infrastructure and services in the outlying areas, and this perception, which subsequently proved to be correct, accounted for much of the opposition in Manhattan and much of the support in the future outer boroughs.[57] In Brooklyn, consolidation opponents contended that they too would have to pay for the vast improvements needed in Richmond County even though they would also benefit financially from joining with Manhattan.[58] Advocates of consolidation on Staten Island hoped that these off-island naysayers were correct and claimed that the merger would bring material benefits while placing no added burden on and perhaps even offering tax relief to Richmond County. Wiman assured residents that a consolidation plan would come "without increase in taxation."[59] Others even optimistically predicted that taxes would be lowered and, with more accuracy, that Staten Island would still pay less than what it received.[60] The opposite view was still tenable, though. Skeptics expected that "they [consolidationists] . . . [will] make us help to pay New York's bills," that "the island would be entirely neglected, except in the matter of taxation," and that "the claim that taxes would be reduced by consolidation . . . will hardly 'hold water.'"[61]

The issue of taxes was typically linked to considerations about honest and effective government and public services. Proponents found it hard to deny the concerns about Tammany and graft, and so they typically didn't do so. They instead returned to the complaints about the status quo in Staten Island, saying New York's government could not be any worse and would at least offer financial advantages. Shortly before the referendum, Greenfield told voters that "even under the wasteful, corrupt, and extravagant administration of Tammany Hall," the tax rate was still lower in New York.[62] Most opponents did not dispute the value of "obliterat[ing] the local lines of division" even as they contested the plans for consolidation. Their support for a separate city of Richmond stemmed as much from a fear of continued neglect as from a concern about corruption.[63]

Staten Islanders did not relish higher taxes, but they did want improved services and may have been willing to pay for them. Curtis certainly was. Framing consolidation as a trade-off between higher taxes and more effective government, he reasoned that "if the question of consolidation should be submitted to a popular vote in the county and it could be shown that consolidation would lessen the taxes and give us better roads, cheaper water, and a better police and fire department, I am very sure that the scheme would be warmly supported."[64] Others believed that no such trade-off was required. In 1890, for example, New York families paid $15 for piped water compared to $42 in New Brighton and Port Richmond.[65] Islanders were also frustrated with meager sanitation services. While George Waring was revolutionizing street cleaning and garbage removal in New York, complaints on Staten Island included illicit dumping of ashes and garbage at construction sites, on streets, in woods, and in the bay. In 1897, with consolidation legislation passed, sanitation was just one topic in a series of public lectures intended to acclimate Staten Islanders to the coming of Greater New York. Other topics included traffic, schooling, leisure, and finance, and all were indicative of aspirations for improvements once consolidation took effect.[66]

Many Staten Islanders conveyed great confidence that consolidation would improve services. One letter writer to the *Staten Islander* envisioned a plethora of projects underway after consolidation: "It would give us better roads, better police protection, a first class fire department, uniformity in assessments, and a decent and proper place in which our taxes can be paid at a certain fixed date." The writer also predicted boulevards and parks, sewage and water-supply improvements, too, and the editor of the paper expected these "forward public improvements" as well.[67] E. C. Bridgeman, a book publisher and future bank president, was certain that fire protection would improve through the replacement of volunteer fire companies with a paid fire department. He envisioned greater efficiency as strategically located firehouses with well-trained and paid firefighters living in them would require fewer men and engines and entail less squabbling. Moreover, they would fight fires anywhere rather than refusing to cross village borders to respond to fires, as the volunteer companies currently did.[68] Ferry service was another area for which supporters of consolidation had high hopes. Their overarching concern with "ruinous competition" notwithstanding, one proponent predicted that in Greater New York "the monopoly of ferry traffic at present existing will be broken and a field for clear competition thrown open."[69] As a result, Wiman and others predicted the advent of a ten-minute ferry ride to New York that would cost only five cents. Other public improvements posited for Staten Island included new docks, a bridge to New Jersey, and a tunnel to Brooklyn. Opponents scoffed at the likelihood of such projects and services, contending that Staten Island's likely political isolation and New York's inability to keep its streets clean boded poorly for the future.[70] The debate over government services was essentially speculative, but many island residents believed that union with New York would expand and enhance the modern features of living on the island.

Proponents felt that consolidation also offered Staten Islanders a concrete and politically viable solution to its governance woes. In contrast, no single vision united Richmond's opponents of Greater New York, nor did they make much effort to win the referendum. Whereas anticonsolidation rallies took place in other communities grappling with the issue, not one was held on Staten Island; detractors instead attended meetings organized by proponents and spoke before largely hostile crowds. The shock of the referendum outcome spurred a more organized resistance in Brooklyn but not on Staten Island.[71] The landslide in the 1894 referendum suggests proponents for joining Greater

New York clearly won the political battle even though they may not have overwhelmingly prevailed in the war of ideas. Armed with an array of arguments, with an inclination to mobilize politically, and with favorable referendum results, consolidation advocates succeeded in making Staten Island a borough in Greater New York.

* * *

In making an array of arguments for consolidation, its advocates managed to offer people something appealing though unverifiable. For those dissatisfied with highly localized governance and poor quality of public services, consolidation promised good governance. For those unhappy with the level of taxes, annexation secured access to the great wealth on Manhattan. For those frustrated by the slow accrual of worth in one's land, Greater New York offered the prospect of rising property values. For those inspired by the potential of Staten Island, joining New York City would enable it to reach soaring heights in population size, commercial activity, and industrial production. Among the unpersuaded were those who shared these expectations but viewed a separate city of Richmond as a better means of meeting them and those who were especially drawn to Staten Island's natural beauty. Whether Staten Islanders were eager, indifferent, or resigned to joining Greater New York, the positions they took set up a checklist by which to measure satisfaction with membership. High on the list was a rapid-transit connection to the rest of the city, which would serve as both a tangible result of consolidation and the vehicle for reaching the island's aspirations for greatness.

PART II

A SUBWAY FOR GROWTH

CHAPTER 4

HITCHING A RIDE

Early Efforts to Tunnel to Staten Island, 1900–1909

Why should not the City of New York expend the comparatively few dollars which will be necessary to construct this tunnel under the Narrows, and thereby bring the poor man and the cheap land of Staten Island together?

—Staten Island Chamber of Commerce, May 15, 1908

When in 1908 Henry Morrison urged the state's Public Service Commission (PSC) to bring New York City's fledgling subway system to Staten Island, he was not just promoting local real estate. Morrison, an engineer with a long record of public-sector work on roads, political activism in the Democratic Party, and prominence in the Staten Island Chamber of Commerce, was also suggesting that rapid transit to Staten Island would address the underlying rationale for expanding New York's subways.[1] The initial line opened and operated by the Interborough Rapid Transit Company (IRT) enabled passengers to travel within the highly congested areas of Manhattan and Brooklyn. Now planners and politicians alike wanted subways to eradicate Manhattan's crowded tenement neighborhoods by dispersing inhabitants to sparsely populated regions of the outer boroughs. Like Erastus Wiman before him, Morrison contended that Staten Island met that criterion as a potential homestead for the working class.

Morrison was also tapping into the vision that had accompanied Staten Island's joining of Greater New York ten years earlier. Rapid transit was central to the urban future imagined by those Staten Islanders who had embraced consolidation. In the 1890s, prominent businessmen articulated a vision of commercial, demographic, and industrial prowess and had posited better transportation links as the way to achieve it. During the aughts, civic and political leaders such as Morrison mirrored those goals when they pushed hard for a subway. In both decades, Richmond's leading spokespeople hoped that consolidation and then rapid transit would enable the island to develop in the image if not the scale of Manhattan. If consolidation forged a political connection between Staten Island and its neighbors, a subway would economically and socially bind it to Greater New York.

This chapter begins with the arguments made by Staten Islanders who lobbied for a subway. What did they hope to gain from rapid transit? Real estate dealers and property owners expected to make substantial profits. Commuters hoped for an easier, shorter, and/or less expensive route to work and recreation in Manhattan. Civic leaders wanted a fair share of services. Such motivations, however, would not persuade public officials, who instead heard only the arguments for how a rail link would serve the city as a whole by dispersing population outward and moving freight westward.

The remainder of the chapter analyzes the initial attempts to obtain a tunnel to link the island with Brooklyn. The early 1900s were replete with letdowns for Staten Island's subway advocates as substantial developments in rail-transit facilities were often stymied citywide. The hearing before the PSC in 1908 represented Staten Islanders' struggle to set their own terms for a subway and pragmatism in their attempt to hitch on to larger currents in the greater city's transportation politics. Each of these first efforts stood little chance of success, and the themes and dynamics that emerged in these endeavors would continue to dog Staten Island over the next three decades. Financial challenges were arguably the greatest hurdle—both funding the cost of construction and operating a line profitably. Location proved to be a contentious issue that undermined unity among the Staten Islanders organizing for a subway. Disagreement over transit priorities undercut Richmond residents even further because many preferred internal transportation or ferry service improvements to a subway. These impediments aside, the early years of the new century witnessed Staten Island's concerted efforts to join the city's fledgling subway system and make the promise of consolidation come true.

Rapid Transit and the Growth of Staten Island

Staten Islanders may very well have imagined a physical link to New York before they conceived of a political merger with it. In 1869, the *New York Times* reported that some Richmond residents were clamoring for either a bridge or tunnel to Elizabeth, New Jersey, which would then connect to another one entering New York. In 1873, the New York Legislature approved a proposal by the Tubular Transit Company of Staten Island to tunnel under the Kill Van Kull—the tidal straight dividing Staten Island and New Jersey—and some construction reportedly occurred in 1876 before the project faltered. In the 1880s, some residents of Brooklyn opined for a Narrows tunnel to transport goods to the south and west.[2] At a dinner celebrating the takeover of the Staten Island Rapid Transit Railway Company by the B&O in 1885, a letter of regret from Brooklyn (and future New York City) mayor Seth Low expressed his hope for a tunnel under the Narrows.[3] Wiman was responsible for a flurry of talk about a Narrows freight tunnel in the summer and fall of 1890 (see figure 4.1). The following year the U.S. Congress passed a purely symbolic law authorizing the construction of a Narrows tunnel.[4] For both Staten and Long Island, such a route had the advantage of bypassing Manhattan entirely, which remained unconnected to New Jersey in the nineteenth century. By the time the ultimately successful movement for consolidation was under way, proponents viewed a Narrows tunnel as one of the benefits that Staten Island would accrue from joining its more populous neighbors.[5]

Between 1898 and 1910, Staten Islanders regularly articulated reasons for a tunnel connection to Greater New York, but no effort was more notable than the one made before the PSC in 1908. In early May, the leadership of an umbrella organization and about two hundred members of its constituent associations and other assorted Staten Islanders presented their case for a subway tunnel to Richmond Borough. In addition to Morrison, the speakers on the tunnel's behalf included Richmond Borough president George Cromwell, Charles Blair of the SICC, and George Von Kromer of the Citizens Tunnel Committee.[6] At the hearing, Staten Islanders remained atypically and singularly focused on the need for a subway connection. They also were united in their advocacy of a Narrows tunnel link to an extension of the proposed Fourth Avenue subway into Bay Ridge. Finally, unlike any other meeting or hearing from this time, they memorialized the occasion by publishing a transcript, which provides a window into their vision for Staten Island through their rationales for rapid-transit access.

The overt civic boosterism so prevalent during the consolidation referendum campaign of 1894 was more muted fourteen years later before the PSC. Wanting to spark population growth and economic activity, the Staten Island attendees highlighted their borough's qualities as a place of residence and claimed it was "the solution and guarantee of commercial supremacy" for New York City.[7] Industrial prowess was not mentioned at all because the islanders advocated specifically for a rapid-transit tunnel, not for one that would also carry freight. Their line of reasoning was tailored to persuade

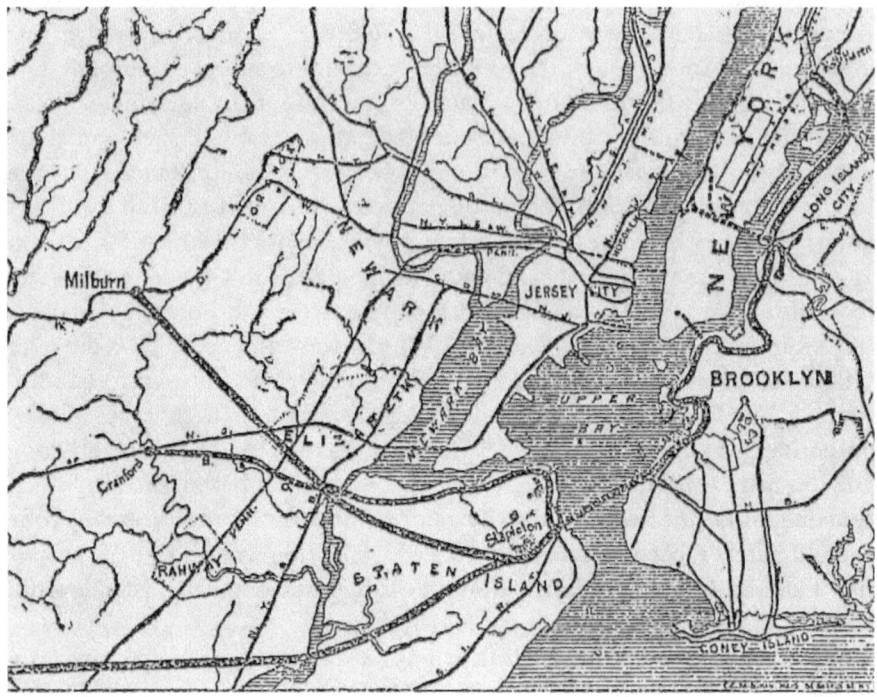

4.1 Narrows Freight Tunnel proposal, 1891

Erastus Wiman, a leading Staten Island businessman and booster, hoped that consolidation with New York would enable the construction of a freight tunnel under that Narrows that would place the island at the center of regional commerce and transportation networks.

Source: *Brooklyn Daily Eagle*, January 14, 1891, 1.

off-islanders of both the viability and the desirability of a subway to Richmond Borough.

One prevalent theme was that the project would benefit not just Staten Island but also Brooklyn, Queens, and Greater New York as a whole. Cromwell, Blair, and Von Kromer suggested that a rapid-transit link to Staten Island would help reduce the congestion in Manhattan by making homes in Richmond Borough accessible to thousands. As another Staten Islander put it, "This tunnel, under the Narrows, however, is of great moment to the citizens of congested New York, to whom it will offer readily accessible, healthful and cheap home sites."[8] Here the island's representatives tapped into the growing understanding of a future subway extension as a means of distributing the city's population more evenly.

The Staten Islanders argued further that the ensuing real estate boom would drive up property values on the island. Yes, profits stood to be made, but they emphasized how the tax base for the city would increase, and the new revenue generated would then cover the expense of construction sooner than expected. Blair presented data that showed a 24 percent increase in property values in Richmond from 1907 to 1908, a figure that was higher than for every other borough except Queens. He argued that "the increase will provide for the cost of the tunnel long before the tunnel reaches the Island."[9] Cromwell, Blair, and Von Kromer then contrasted this outcome with other heralded transit projects that would instead contribute to the loss of taxpayers from the city and state. They noted that the new subway to Brooklyn, which had opened to passengers just days earlier, would take riders directly to the Long Island Railroad Company's terminus at Atlantic Avenue. New Jersey might fare even better because of the still relatively new Hudson and Manhattan north tunnel and the future Pennsylvania Railroad tunnels that would link the Garden State directly to Gotham. The SICC president William Van Clief echoed these arguments, going so far as to emphasize "the cheapness of the extension to the tunnel from Fourth Avenue to Staten Island" owing to the certain rise in property values.[10]

Indeed, almost all of the speakers at the SICC meeting tried to play down the cost of the enterprise. Van Clief contended that the estimated expenditure for the tunnel would be $800 per foot, a rate far lower than construction costs for the initial subway system. The Staten Islanders also had to address concerns about future operating deficits, concerns that were heightened by the new municipal ferry service's financial losses in its first two years. Assuming that the more efficient rapid-transit link would draw greater numbers of patrons, Staten Islanders challenged the notion that the money-losing municipal ferry service was an indicator that future use of a Narrows tunnel would not justify the financial outlays for it. Another speaker argued instead that only with a Staten Island connection could "the Fourth Avenue tunnel [line] . . . be made to pay." He asserted that the Fourth Avenue line by itself would attract largely unprofitable long riders but that a spur to Staten Island would bring in numerous "short riders" in the form of "summer traffic to the beaches."[11] Van Clief also argued that Staten Island's current population could sustain any tunnel project. To that end, he cited a recent meeting with William McAdoo, the lawyer and railroad magnate. Van Clief asked McAdoo, president of the Hudson and Manhattan Railroad Company, which was currently building a south tunnel from Jersey City to lower Manhattan, about extending that tunnel from Bayonne under the Kill Van Kull to Staten Island. The dangling of an option through New Jersey amid talk of lost tax revenues to New York State made one not too subtle point, but Van Clief also used McAdoo to make another even more explicit: that "the fact of the present population was no bar to an enterprise of this kind."[12]

With these arguments, the Staten Islanders aptly recognized that the commissioners were operating from a set of assumptions about projected costs and ridership on a Staten Island line that did not work in their favor. Just three months earlier, the PSC had received a commissioned population report of New York City that included projections for the next forty years. Wildly off the mark, the study expected more than 19 million residents in New York City alone by 1950 (the actual mark reached was just less than 7.9 million). Nevertheless, in 1908 this figure was explicitly cited to justify the importance of expanding the subway system. The breakdown by borough, however, likely hurt Staten Island's chances of benefiting from any expansion because the inaccuracy of the overestimates was not evenly distributed. Brooklyn, Queens, and the Bronx were vastly overprojected to have 7 million, 6 million, and 4 million residents, respectively, by 1950. The report forecasted a population of 250,000 for Staten Island, not a large difference from the 191,555 ultimately recorded for 1950.[13]

In addition to their claims of cost effectiveness and population dispersal, Staten Island's representatives also made an appeal to fairness. Both Blair and Von Kromer observed that because the current subway system was being supported by taxpayers citywide, with Richmond Borough contributing its share, Richmond should be included in the subway system.[14] Another speaker chided that "city officials have been inclined to forget that Staten Island is a part of the City, when distributing public monies for Rapid Transit purposes."[15] Von Kromer reviewed the history of the borough's previous failed efforts to obtain a subway. While demanding Staten Island's fair share of public transit, Van Clief also emphasized that its residents would welcome higher taxes if they were accompanied by a Narrows tunnel-building project.[16] Overall, Staten Islanders centered on overriding objections based on economic grounds and on stoking interest in relieving Manhattan's population density. These arguments would prove insufficient to their task.

The Earliest Movement for a Rail Tunnel: Patterns and Prospects

The consolidation of Greater New York in 1898 immediately enhanced the possibility for massive public projects, but the subway fervor in New York had its genesis a decade earlier when Mayor Abram Hewitt had championed an underground railway in a speech before the city's Board of Aldermen. Interest picked up in the 1890s: first with the work of the Steinway Commission, then with the New York Chamber of Commerce's success in engineering the passage of the Rapid Transit Act in 1894, and finally with the efforts of the Board of Rapid Transit Railroad Commissioners (Rapid Transit Board, or RTB) created by that act. By 1897, the two key elements of the first subway contract were in place: public financing coupled with private operation of the railway and a location that zigzagged across Manhattan. Over the next three years, the RTB shepherded its plan through the complex governmental approval process, drew up a route, and put out a call for bids for a subway contract. In January 1900, it awarded Subway Contract No. 1 to contractor John B. McDonald, who secured financial backing from August Belmont Jr., president of the banking firm established by his father.[17] Largely uninvolved in this course of events, Staten Islanders entered the public discourse on subways as the RTB began considering routes into Brooklyn for Contract No. 2 in 1899, before Contract No. 1 was even signed.[18]

Parties contending over Subway Contract No. 2 included many residents of the outer boroughs, in particular Brooklyn and Staten Island.[19] Their debates encapsulated the tension over how best to relieve population congestion in Manhattan, a conflict that would characterize subsequent subway development. With this contract, Staten Islanders waged and lost their first fight over where in Brooklyn a subway tunnel would go and how far it would extend. The location of the new subway's entrance into Brooklyn would be indicative if not determinative of Richmond Borough's prospects for a tunnel. Staten Islanders aligned with residents of South Brooklyn and Bay Ridge who proposed a tunnel from the Battery to Hamilton Avenue to meet a line that would run south under Fourth Avenue because the Staten Islanders hoped such a line would eventually be extended to and under the Narrows (see figure 4.2).[20] They were countered by the business and shopping centers of downtown Brooklyn, which had the support of some neighborhoods farther north and east in their lobbying for a line to downtown Brooklyn that extended from City Hall to the Battery, went by tunnel under the East River, and reached Flatbush Avenue, under which it would course to a terminus at Atlantic Avenue. The RTB approved such a line in 1901, and the extension to Brooklyn's Borough Hall opened on

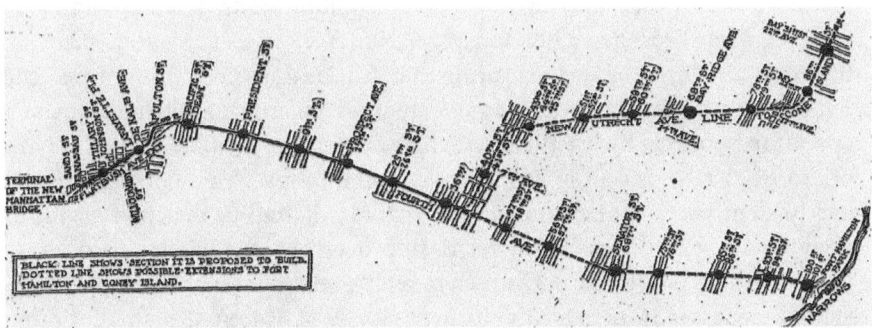

4.2 Proposed route and stations for the Fourth Avenue subway in Brooklyn, 1908

The struggles over Subway Contract No. 2 and later the Triborough plan involved Staten Islanders as allies of South Brooklyn and Bay Ridge residents, who wanted routes to reach their neighborhoods. Staten Islanders hoped that a line reaching the Narrows would soon be extended under it.

Source: New York Times, June 7, 1908.

January 9, 1908, with the final section to Atlantic Avenue ready for passengers on May 1.[21]

Even as the city completed its second subway contract with the IRT, public officials, private investors, and citizens alike were thinking about the system's further enlargement, a process that would culminate with the signing of the Dual Contracts with the IRT and the Brooklyn Rapid Transit Company (BRT) in 1913. Residents of the outer boroughs—Staten Island, Queens, and the farther reaches of the Bronx and Brooklyn—especially desired subway lines that would serve their neighborhoods. Although deadlock over subway expansion largely characterized the years from 1902 through 1910, local citizens groups in all boroughs were active in the pursuit of lines to their areas.[22]

These early subway efforts on Staten Island reveal a number of crucial fault lines that would remain active for decades. First, although many residents shared a desire for a physical connection to Greater New York, they represented disparate localities and social classes and diverged on a number of issues—primarily the connection's function, location, and prioritization. Second, Staten Islanders clearly needed allies from the other boroughs and propitious conditions for rapid-transit action in Greater New York, neither of which was always present. Third, the relatively small size of Staten Island's civic class meant that the appearance of other issues—particularly when the city sought to locate an undesirable facility on the island—easily derailed efforts on behalf of the subway.

Several local Staten Island organizations actively pursued a tunnel during the first decade of the new century. The SICC maintained a Transit Committee, which increasingly became interested in a tunnel leading off island.[23] The Staten Island Board of Trade and Transportation, formed by businessmen in 1904 and focused on Stapleton and other neighborhoods of the island's east shore, regularly broached a link to greater New York in its early years but took little action.[24] The twenty-five leading Staten Island realtors who formed the Richmond Realty Association in 1907 were more vigorous. Aspiring to foster a population boom on the island and recognizing the immediate impact of New York's initial subway on the Bronx's population in just three years, the group quickly identified a tunnel connection with Manhattan as the chief means of achieving its goal.[25] The Fifth Ward Improvement Association (FWIA)—established after consolidation by men in realty, insurance, and other property-related businesses in or near the former village of Tottenville—made transportation one of its top priorities, became a fervid proponent of a Narrows tunnel, and in 1908 launched the first successful umbrella organization focused on a rail link to Greater New York.

Bringing together these and other groups on Staten Island was no easy task. With only a decade of experience as a single political entity, the localism embedded into many of the island's civic organizations separated its residents by geography, ethnicity, and social class. Conflict between good-government businessmen and political party loyalists also remained potent on Staten Island. Two groups, for example, acted separately to push for a South Brooklyn route in Contract No. 2: one was an association filled with professionals and patricians, such as its chairperson David Tysen, a real estate developer and descendent of a long-standing propertied local family; the other was a group loosely tied to the local Democratic organization.[26]

In 1907, an effort to create an umbrella organization to promote a tunnel failed badly. Members of the Richmond Realty Association sponsored a mass meeting and formed the Citizens Tunnel Committee (CTC) of Staten Island, which soon immersed itself in a flurry of activity: gathering 4,500 signatures of support, enlisting borough president Cromwell, raising money for operating expenses, distributing 1,500 letters and circulars, recruiting membership, meeting with the press, and publishing reports.[27] At the same time, the SICC organized the Committee of 100 to push for a subway connection to Staten Island.[28] By establishing its own committee rather than joining the CTC, the chamber may have simply wanted to maintain its preeminent position as the island-wide body focused on creating conditions for good business. The result, however, was two entities that diverged in a number of ways that couldn't be bridged even when Cromwell tried to forge unity.[29]

The SICC's decision to act unilaterally reflected differences in the desired tunnel location, in the tactics adopted, and in the make-up of each tunnel entity. Its leadership was certain that the only practical link to New York must come through Brooklyn because a direct line to Manhattan was financially prohibitive, and a route through New Jersey—in an era before the existence of the Port Authority—would be immensely complicated with multiple municipalities and two states involved. The CTC's position was less definitive. It too would accept a Brooklyn route, but it preferred a direct line to Manhattan and had not ruled out that option. The Committee of 100 eschewed the CTC's active campaigning; it instead operated through social networks to make focused arguments in small meetings with the right officials. These approaches were not mutually exclusive, and the SICC had in fact provided some financial support for the CTC's initiatives, but they reflected the background of each group's participants.[30] The Committee of 100's tactics worked for it because the men in the SICC were better known and more established on the island and in the city at large than were the leaders of the CTC. By midsummer 1907, the potential for disunity among Staten Island's own citizens had thus taken organizational shape.

Consider as indicative the contrasting profiles of the two committees' chairmen: native affluence and immigrant mobility. Charles Blair was born in Ohio, attended Cornell University, and, like his father, practiced law. Moving to New York in 1882, he served in the National Guard, ran for Congress, was active in the SICC, and since 1905 had served as the president of the Hanover Land and Dock Company. He lived on well-heeled Grymes Hill and had previously maintained a home in Ithaca with a cook, a housemaid, and a laundress.[31] George Von Kromer, in contrast, struggled to establish himself. Derided by one local paper as a "disreputable character" with a "questionable past," Von Kromer had come to the United States from Germany in the late 1880s, married in 1895, served in the army (though saw no combat) in 1898, and by 1900 was living in the Rosebank area of Staten Island and working as a druggist. Ten years later he earned a living by teaching music, and by 1920 he had remarried and removed to Roanoke, Virginia, where he owned a sewing machine exchange business; he died in 1958.[32]

The discord over the best route between Brooklyn and Staten Island and whether going directly to Manhattan was a better option was especially pronounced. These questions had not needed resolution during the struggles preceding Contract No. 2, but every subsequent subway initiative during the aughts was marred by disagreement over location. The Staten Island Board of Trade and Transportation had not acted to pursue its desire for a tunnel in part because many members balked at a Narrows route but could not agree on an alternative.[33] The CTC discussed but never decided between two possible placements: directly across New York Harbor or indirectly across the Narrows and through Brooklyn.[34] The SICC favored a Brooklyn route as the most politically feasible option but avoided the still contentious matter of where in each borough the tunnel should surface.

Questions about the tunnel's location became increasingly divisive in the spring and summer of 1908. Some Staten Islanders had always preferred reaching Manhattan through New Jersey, and the opening of the first McAdoo tunnels in February 1908 breathed new life into their cause.[35] For the CTC, this opening gave birth to an independent entity, the Richmond Borough Realty Association, which charged its own subway committee "to agitate and use their best efforts to secure the tunnel" from Staten Island to Manhattan.[36] The group considered routes that passed through Governor's Island, New Jersey, and Robbin's Rest but showed no interest in a Narrows tunnel. Similar plans received favorable comment from the *Richmond County Advance* and its readers as well as from the *Staten Islander*. Communities in New Jersey began expressing interest, and the SICC made overtures to them. By the end of 1908, even Blair had toyed with the idea, as did McAdoo. The opening of the Hudson and Manhattan Railroad Company's tubes to Lower Manhattan in July 1909 would further flame the allure of McAdoo's tunnels.[37]

Moving beyond flirtation with a rail connection to Manhattan through New Jersey was exceedingly difficult, however. A New Jersey route offered less flexibility in the mechanisms for organizing finance and construction than the Fourth Avenue option. The Triborough proposal might engender debate over the merits of a municipally built, owned, and operated subway, but that approach was not available for a project that would involve two states and several localities. Such dilemmas led to discussions of establishing a regional body, but the emergence of the Port of New York Authority was still more than a decade away. Although Staten Islanders such as Blair periodically spoke about raising private capital to build a rail link, that strategy wasn't viable given the connecting tunnel's prospects for profit: poor in the near future and uncertain after that, some local boosters' claims notwithstanding. Nothing came of the SICC's tentative explorations of the New Jersey options.[38]

Once the PSC determined in 1907 to proceed with the Fourth Avenue subway, it had to consider the location for a tunnel to Staten Island. On the Brooklyn side, the question became where on Fourth Avenue the spur to Staten Island should begin, a matter that rested on how far down into Brooklyn the subway would proceed. The initial line approved by the PSC stopped at Fortieth Street, but subsequent proposals placed the end of the Fourth Avenue line at 101st Street, as originally envisioned by the RTB. The PSC's chief engineer Henry Seaman expected a Staten Island branch to start at the 101st terminus.[39] For Staten Island groups, that location meant urging the construction of not two but four tracks for the entire Fourth Avenue subway to enable it to handle commuters from Staten Island. "Without two express tracks there," the FWIA would contend, "this route would be valueless as a future outlet for Staten Island by way of the Narrows tunnel."[40] It remained not at all clear that the Fourth Avenue line would extend that far because the IRT was disinterested in such an extension and other businessmen and politicians continued to oppose it.[41]

On Staten Island, subway advocates imagined a Narrows tunnel connecting with the Fourth Avenue line anywhere from Forty-Third Street to 101st Street. An end at the former would leave commuters much closer to Manhattan; the latter would provide a Fort Hamilton terminus; and one at Sixty-Seventh or Eighty-Sixth Street would transport Staten Islanders to Bay Ridge. The Brooklyn starting point was arguably the least discordant location issue among Staten Islanders because it was largely a matter of how to balance competing priorities. Staten Islanders wanted to shorten the commute to New York, keep the costs of construction manageable by placing the tunnel at or near the Narrows, and maintain the goodwill of the Brooklyn civic and trade groups that continued to offer important support for a Staten Island tunnel. At the same time, the location of the Brooklyn end of a tunnel would have strong implications for where the tunnel would surface on Staten Island.

Staten Islanders had so far largely avoided this logical connection between the placement of each tunnel end. In 1907, the SICC and the CTC agreed that a Brooklyn tunnel should lead to Fort Hamilton but avoided specifying where on Staten Island it would go.[42] In the summer of 1908, the groups working for a subway connection to Staten Island began to address its location. Their ambition forced them to grapple with aspects of the physical and social

74 A SUBWAY FOR GROWTH

environment that were not well aligned. For a tunnel to be viable, the depth and distance in the Narrows mattered greatly, but so did the geology and demography of Staten Island.

In September 1908, Von Kromer and other members of the CTC hand delivered a map (see figure 4.3) to William McCarroll, the PSC member who largely oversaw issues regarding Staten Island. The committee and engineer who had devised the map addressed both internal and external transportation needs with this plan. The map indicated a potential route for the tunnel that aimed to avoid the greatest depth of the Narrows while keeping close to its shortest point. Using Chief Engineer Seaman's own suggested terminus at Fourth Avenue and 101st Street, the tunnel would reach Staten Island near Maple Avenue in Rosebank before splitting in two directions. One would

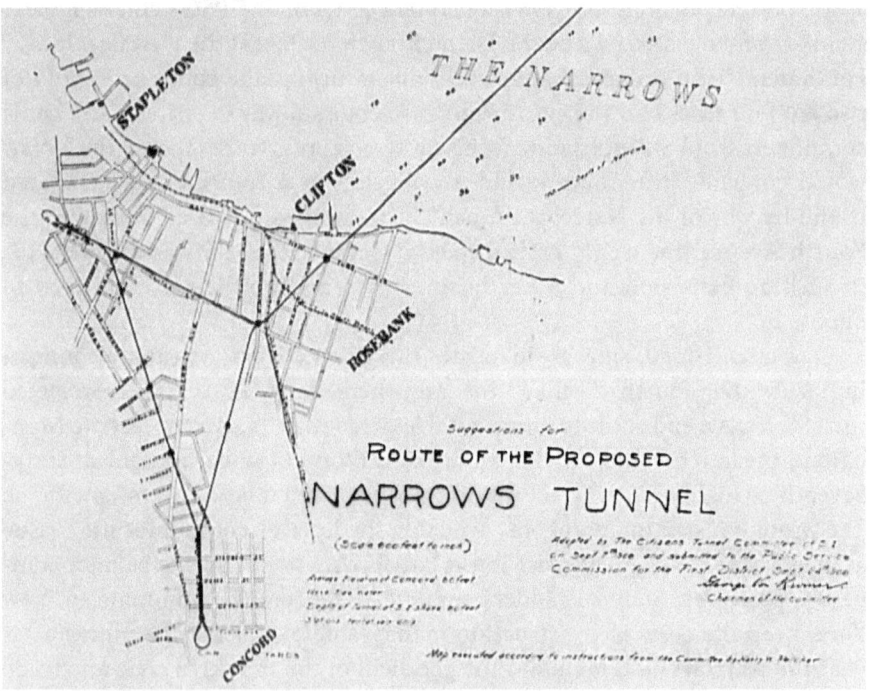

4.3 The Citizens Tunnel Committee proposal for a subway under the Narrows, 1908

In 1908, the CTC presented a plan for a rail link from Fort Hamilton, Brooklyn, to Rosebank, Staten Island. Similar in some respects to the SICC proposal, the CTC's plan diverged over precisely where the link would emerge in each borough and was indicative of how the two groups, though they sometimes collaborated, often worked at cross purposes.

Source: *Richmond County Advance*, September 26, 1908. Courtesy of Collection of the Staten Island Museum.

travel up Center Street, with a station in Stapleton and hopes for a subsequent extension to New Brighton, West New Brighton, and Port Richmond.[43] The other would go southwest to Concord, with a station at Clove Road to facilitate access to the center of the island. The Stapleton and Concord stations would be connected by a separate line that would be positioned to expand to Tottenville in the future.[44] Von Kromer asked for "criticism, and approval or alterations of the route," and although the PSC referred the plan to Chief Engineer Seaman for report, there is no extant record of it resurfacing.[45]

The SICC also identified a possible route for a tunnel in 1908, arguably prodded by the steps taken by the CTC. When the SICC published the transcripts from the PSC hearing in May 1908 as "Tunnel to Staten Island," it included a map showing a route that varied from the CTC's (see figure 4.4).[46] First, the Staten Island spur reached the Fourth Avenue subway at Eighty-Sixth Street. Second, it reached Richmond at Maryland Avenue, still in Rosebank but a few hundred yards closer to Fort Wadsworth. It also split in two directions, but not before the entire line reached Concord. As in the CTC's plan, one branch followed Clove Road, but it would reach Port Richmond, through which it would provide access for the north shore. The other branch followed the route of South Side Boulevard (previously Southfield Boulevard and soon to become a part of Hylan Boulevard), intended to extend to Tottenville. The other major difference was that SICC members did not determine the tunnel's location; they instead used part of a map of the recently proposed Triborough lines for New York City.[47]

Both the SICC and the CTC were highly invested in generating a population and real estate boom on Staten Island. Knowing that a tunnel would spark the desired growth but recognizing that growth would help secure a tunnel, the CTC continued to promote the island's features. In July 1908, it distributed a booklet laying out Staten Island's virtues as a place of residence for the city.[48] Staten Islanders still had to contend with the island's long-standing reputation for mosquito-borne diseases, as indicated in an advertisement describing Grimes Hill in 1908 as "one of the most healthful locations on Staten Island."[49] Fortunately, Richmond Borough received favorable coverage in the real estate news of the city's major newspapers. Dailies such as the *Sun*, the *Evening Post*, and the *Brooklyn Daily Eagle* often reported on growth and development on Staten Island.[50] The *New York Times* determined that the borough's prospects for real estate investment were good and that the only things needed for a real boom was a tunnel from Brooklyn and better internal transportation.[51] The *Times* noted in October 1908 that although "active agitation" for a Narrows tunnel was ongoing, an injunction against proceeding with the Fourth Avenue subway—in place from June 1908 through October 1909—could not but dampen these efforts.[52]

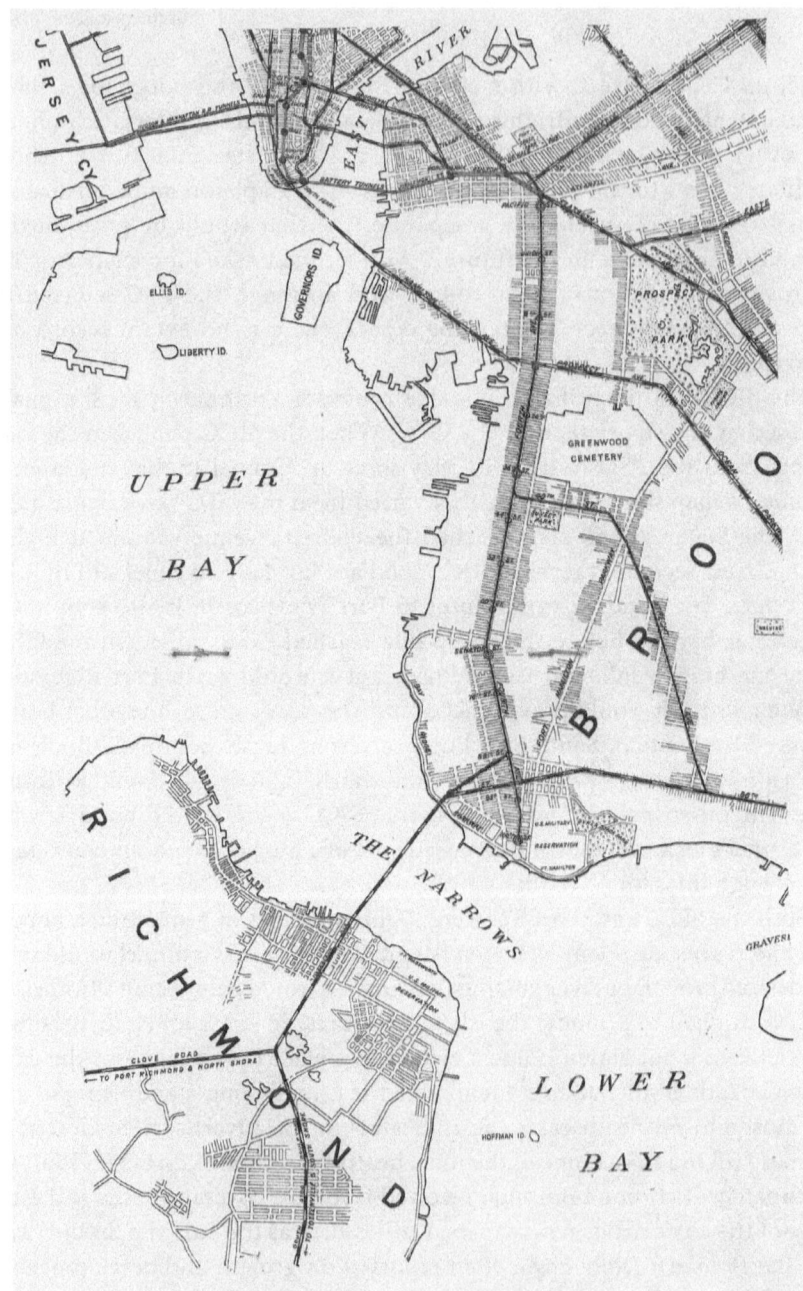

4.4 The Staten Island Chamber of Commerce proposal for a Narrows tunnel, 1908

In 1908, the SICC published a plan for a Narrows tunnel from Bay Ridge, Brooklyn, to Rosebank, Staten Island. Similar in some respects to the Citizen Tunnel Committee's proposal, the SICC's plan diverged over precisely where the tunnel would emerge in each borough and was indicative of how the two groups, though they sometimes collaborated, often worked at cross purposes.

Source: Courtesy of Collection of the Staten Island Museum.

Beyond debilitating disputes over tunnel location, conflict over prioritization among multiple transportation needs on Staten Island regularly squeezed out initiatives for a tunnel. After the island lost out on the subway routes included in Contract No. 2, local attention turned to more immediate shortcomings in external and internal transportation—ferry and trolley service, respectively. These topics arose even at public hearings granted to focus on the subway, as when "every possible sort of complaint was made against the present transit service on the island" at a hearing before the PSC in October 1907.[53] On other occasions, Staten Islanders such as Pascal Harrower, a West New Brighton Episcopal clergyman, and Ira K. Morris, the island's leading historian, publicly and vehemently argued for ferry improvements rather than for a tunnel construction. The quality of ferry service had occupied members of the Staten Island Chamber of Commerce since its founding in 1895.[54] The *Richmond County Advance* repeatedly agitated for better ferries and over the next few years heralded the progress as the city moved toward municipal operation of the ferries, the launching of new boats, and construction of a new terminal in St. George.[55]

Street cars on Staten Island also left many patrons dissatisfied. Numerous trolley franchises granted by the island's towns and villages—emblematic of the extreme localism that had helped spur Staten Islanders' willingness to join Greater New York in the 1890s—had created a patchwork of poorly connected routes, haphazard service, and multiple fares. Even with numerous mergers and acquisitions of these companies, four remained in operation by 1907—two operating by electricity and two by steam.[56] Staten Islanders called for their consolidation, the imposition of a single five-cent fare for regular commuters, and the addition of new routes and night service, among other desired improvements.[57] Reverend Harrower spoke for many when in 1906 he deemed three major "questions of public interest—ferry service, trolley improvement, [and] the agitation for subway communication with Manhattan Borough . . . as of the highest importance."[58]

Choosing a preference among these three "questions" was challenging enough, but pursuing one could actively undermine the other two. For many islanders, a tunnel remained "a rainbow-chasing scheme" that diverted attention from more achievable goals related to ferry service and internal transportation.[59] By 1902, Tysen, participating on a SICC committee that prodded Mayor Seth Low's administration (1902–1904) on ferry issues, argued that the city must serve Staten Island through ferries because it could not build a bridge or tunnel to the island.[60] In 1905, the Staten Island Board of Trade's subway efforts were limited in part because a good portion of that year was spent preparing for the celebration of new ferryboats and agitating for reduced trolley and ferry rates for regular commuters.[61] Overlapping economic interests only made matters even more complicated and contentious. National corporations such as Standard Oil and the B&O held stakes in the island's rail companies, which also owned and operated the island's ferries. A Narrows tunnel might undermine or enhance their profitability depending on its location and function.[62]

News reports also sometimes worked to the detriment of Staten Islanders' push for a rapid-transit tunnel. On Staten Island, coverage was spotty because many local papers did not report on the subway advocates' activities. For example, of the four publications with extant editions from 1907, the *Staten Islander* and the *Staten Island News and Independent* printed no stories about the October 3 hearing before the PSC; the *Staten Island World* included a short blurb; and only the *Richmond County Advance* had a detailed account.[63] Nor were movement leaders such as Blair satisfied with news reports of conflict and stumbles.[64] In Manhattan, the coverage of tunnel efforts sometimes left Staten Islanders looking foolish. The *New York Times* story on the PSC hearing, for example, painted Staten Islanders in an unfavorable light by emphasizing the proposal for a direct line to Manhattan over the steady chorus of Narrows tunnel advocates. In treating the notion as odd, the paper made Blair's assertion "that while the project would doubtless be costly in the first place, it would pay in the end" appear equally absurd.[65] Other off-island factors played even larger roles in denying Staten Islanders their tunnel.

For one, Staten Islanders and their allies faced inhospitable planning and political climates for a Narrows tunnel during the first decade of the twentieth century. The city wasn't reaching any agreement on how new subway lines would be funded and where they would be placed, with the exception that Staten Island would not be reached. Charged with preparing plans for a citywide subway system, William Barclay Parsons, the chief engineer for the RTB, rejected the inclusion of a line to Staten Island in his report to the board in 1903. In justifying this decision, Parsons explained: "I regret to report that the great expense involved is entirely out of proportion to the population to be served."[66] Accordingly, when the RTB released in 1905 a huge plan for subway expansion, it included every outer borough except Richmond. Likewise, a report by the New York Board of Trade and Transportation in August 1905 omitted Staten Island from its recommendations that the city extend the subways into the outer boroughs. Staten Island fared only slightly better with the Municipal Art Society, whose report on rapid transit in 1905 "ultimately" imagined an extension from Fort Hamilton on the island. In 1906, the city's Board of Estimate recommended the invitation of bids for seven new lines—none of which would reach Staten Island, even though one was the by now ubiquitous Fourth Avenue line through Brooklyn to Bay Ridge.[67] In each instance of Staten Island's exclusion from a plan, the chief concern was cost, an issue that the *New York Times* had raised as early as 1890: "It is ... a question of whether its prospective use will justify the outlay for its construction."[68]

Contested transit politics thwarted significant movement on any of these initiatives, but one item of general agreement was that the plan eventually adopted would not include an expensive link to Staten Island.

Finally, the city's propensity for locating unwanted institutions in its least populous and most distant borough would periodically galvanize reaction throughout Richmond Borough and serve to derail proactive tunnel efforts over the next forty years. Facilities for refuse would more famously occupy activists in subsequent decades, but in 1905 the city's plan to build a hospital for tuberculosis patients on Staten Island diverted the Staten Island Board of Trade and Transportation and the SICC from other issues as they organized to block the proposed institution. Concerns about the hospital led to the formation of the Richmond Borough Protective League within a month and occupied groups as disparate as a literary society and a local YMCA. The league's efforts delayed but ultimately did not halt the city's plan, and Sea View Hospital opened in 1913.[69] Together, all these internal and external impediments—disunity, disinterest, derision, and distraction—undercut Staten Island's chances for a subway from 1900 through 1909.

* * *

The repeated failures to obtain a subway connection to Staten Island in the first decade of the twentieth century foreshadowed what lay in wait for Richmond Borough over the next three. In many ways, the failure was part of the political dysfunction that obstructed any further development of subways for several years after 1902. The prospects for a tunnel to Staten Island hinged on the outcome of larger debates in New York City. At the same time, the particular barriers that Richmond Borough faced also became apparent. From the moment Staten Islanders began to envision a subway connection with the city, they had to contend with apprehensions about its projected cost and ridership. Staten Islanders, who had joined New York City with hopes of massive development spurred by public investments in their borough, repeatedly discounted these concerns but could not dispel them.

That there would be too much money spent on too few people was undeniably a leading factor in Staten Island's ultimate exclusion from the subway system, but that reason is too simplistic to stand alone. The lines built through Contract Nos. 1 and 2 largely served densely populated areas, but they also reached and thus transformed considerable open spaces in northern Manhattan and the Bronx.[70] Staten Islanders were well aware of the growth in the Bronx spurred by the opening of the subway. In fact, when they forecast a boom in their island's population and commerce, they often made the comparison to the Bronx explicit.[71] Furthermore, as the RTB and then the PSC began contemplating a comprehensive subway system, their members envisioned serving many outlying areas. The PSC's discovery in 1907 that subway lines were not universally profitable did not dim its hopes for massive expansion but did dictate a strategy for future contracts: the coupling of profitable "short-haul lines" with longer routes to undeveloped areas. The problem for Staten Island was that the Fourth Avenue line in Brooklyn was already predicted to be unprofitable for fifteen years.[72]

Given these formidable financial challenges to achieving a tunnel, Staten Islanders could ill afford to squabble among themselves, but squabble they did. Disagreements arose between companies vying for business, between communities competing over routes, and between boosters arguing over priorities. Tension flared over pursuing a tunnel or a bridge, a link to Brooklyn, Manhattan, or New York. "Transit harmony" between local companies competing for routes and business was a long-standing theme of island newspaper editorials.[73] Ethnic and social class differences, reflected in the SICC and CTC membership, blocked unity.

One collective, unified, and sustained effort proved difficult to achieve, but Staten Islanders recognized its importance. Indeed, the leaders of the various tunnel committees operated with an implicit understanding of the politics of resource distribution and realized that being visible and vocal would help them achieve their goal. Likewise, the editors of local newspapers regularly called their readers to action. The *Staten Island World* put the strategy as follows: "Make the mass meeting so successful, so representative of what Richmond Borough needs in regard to a tunnel, that the result will be such as to cause the proper authorities to give the tunnel to Staten Island their favorable attention."[74] Boosters recognized that civic associations played a vital role in the decision making about public projects: "City officials naturally and properly look to these [civic] organizations for a statement of public sentiment on matters of importance affecting those localities from time to time."[75] And so Staten Islanders organized repeatedly to bring the promise of consolidation to life by working for the approval of a subway line to Richmond Borough. At the same time, they understood that much was decided behind the scenes, which gave them hope during their first major opportunity: the negotiations from 1910 to 1912 that led to the signing of the Dual Contracts in 1913, the largest expansion of New York's subways in its history.

CHAPTER 5

LEAVING THE STATION

The Dual Contracts and Aftermath, 1909–1919

The subway clouds seem rolling by—
Oh such a long delay!
And, maybe, some digging will begin
At some not distant day.
Yes, everything seems lovely now
To get the subways quick—
If present plans are not upset,
And no one makes a kick.

To Staten Island we will go
By way of Brooklyn town
And underneath the Narrows deep,
A hundred fathoms down,
We'll go below at City Hall,
And then some day we will
Pop up again at Stapleton,
Or, maybe, Tottenville.

—Tom W. Jackson, 1912

If Staten Islanders let this opportunity slip by, when the city is using up its credit for years to come, then Richmond must remain a dead end of the city, as it is to-day.

—*Evening World*, September 16, 1911

Tom W. Jackson, a journalist and humor writer for the *New York Press*, liked to compose verse drawn from conditions and events of early twentieth-century New York City. He found an audience, too, as his poetic commentary on political issues and social trends was picked up by newspapers across the state.[1] Launched in 1904, the city's subway system provided much fodder for him. The wrangling over its expansion had made headlines for years, and the "long delay" frustrated citizens throughout the city. The *Staten Island World* picked up the piece of doggerel that starts this chapter for its local context, but the destination in the second stanza could have just as easily been Coney Island or Jamaica. Perhaps Jackson selected Staten Island because the distance and depths to be traversed by a subway made its plight appear especially poignant. Whatever his intention, to those on Staten Island who during the previous decade had worked assiduously for public improvements for their borough, the lack of progress on the subway was no laughing matter.

Substantial improvements in rail-transit facilities, as Jackson well knew, were not easily accomplished. Jackson's image of a train ride from Manhattan to Stapleton or Tottenville was highly contingent upon whether the "present plans," a year away from being concretized as the Dual Contracts, "are not upset, / And no one makes a kick."[2] Looking back from 1912, he had observed plenty of tears and jolts when it came to subways. Staten Islanders certainly experienced them in their earliest efforts to obtain service for their borough, but the first decade of the twentieth century ended with new opportunities for a tunnel under the Narrows. The island's chances for being awarded a line were enhanced by the Triborough plan and grew even stronger with the victory of Fusion candidates across the city in 1909. They peaked in 1911 when Richmond Borough president George Cromwell served on a New York City Board of Estimate subcommittee tasked with working in conference with the Public Service Commission, negotiating with rapid-transit companies, and recommending a course of action for expansion of the system. In what the historian Peter Derrick has termed a "turning point," the subcommittee undertook intricate negotiations with commissioners and businessmen.[3] Morton W. Smith, a descendent of a prominent Philadelphia family and a successful amateur sportsman on Staten Island, recognized the opening and high stakes for his home borough, but by the time he was quoted in the *Evening World* a mere eight months after Cromwell's appointment, Smith likely already recognized that its prospects had slipped away.

This chapter focuses on the crucial five years from 1909 to 1913, when what was arguably Staten Island's greatest window of opportunity for a subway opened and then closed. It begins with the early promise of the Triborough system and the decisive municipal elections of 1909 and continues with the demise of that system in 1910, which fell under the weight of its own ambition for a municipally owned and operated system. Its chief focus is on the momentous year of 1911, when the basic features of the Dual Contracts were determined. The chapter traces the marginalization of a Staten Island subway during negotiations with the Brooklyn Rapid Transit and the Interborough Rapid Transit Companies and examines the chimera that appeared instead: a multipurpose tunnel that would carry shoppers and commuters during the day, freight at night, and water at all hours. Finally, it highlights how Staten Islanders' frustration played out after the contracts were signed in March 1913.

Why did the Dual Contracts hold such promise for Staten Island? The well-understood aim was to disperse the population in congested Manhattan to the city's periphery (i.e., the outer boroughs), and the means of doing so was to grant the rapid-transit companies new profitable short-haul lines coupled with lines to less-developed areas that would need time to build ridership. A comprehensive system based on these principles offered Staten Islanders an opportunity for inclusion that perhaps outstanding stewardship by political leaders and civic boosters could exploit. Instead, Richmond Borough president Cromwell held a seat at the table but was not really present—as Lin Manuel Miranda so memorably phrases it in *Hamilton*—"in the room where it happened." Staten Island's leaders clearly underachieved, but the daunting expense of a Narrows line generated powerful resistance from private enterprise and public officials that likely would have stymied an even more capable effort.

The Triborough Plan, the Municipal Elections of 1909, New Possibilities

As the new century's first decade drew to a close, changing circumstances improved Staten Island's opportunity for rapid transit. First, the PSC united around a comprehensive plan for subway expansion. Originally proposed by the RTB in 1906, the idea for a Triborough system was quickly picked up by the fledgling PSC. Initially just a collection of several small proposals, the plan grew to include 144 miles of new track at a cost of $150 million. With the Triborough system, the PSC members hoped to create competition for the IRT from another privately operated company. Although it did not provide lines for Staten Island or Queens, the Triborough plan embraced the diffusion of the city's population outward from its center. To that end, it included a Fourth Avenue subway in Brooklyn that would start downtown and continue it until it reached the Narrows.[4] Unpopular with both the IRT and the BRT, construction of that specific line was blocked by injunction through most of 1909. More generally, the Triborough plan spawned opposition from a number of groups and politicians, who prevented its adoption.[5]

The municipal elections of 1909 pitted a slate of Democratic candidates against a Republican/Fusion ticket and William Randolph Hearst running as an independent. The campaign centered on plans for rapid-transit expansion, arguably even more so than the previous race of 1905, when Hearst had led a failed Municipal Ownership League ticket. In the earlier election, Hearst's slate of Staten Island candidates did not effectively make their case about rapid transit. The Municipal Ownership nominees from Staten Island did exceedingly poorly in the election, and Hearst was soundly defeated on the island, though only widespread acts of fraud likely prevented his election as mayor in an extremely close citywide election.[6] His reluctance to overpromise in the 1905 elections would not be repeated four years later.

For residents all over New York City in 1909, ample rapid-transit policy issues were at the forefront. Democratic candidate William Gaynor was sympathetic to municipal ownership and distanced himself from Tammany; Fusion candidate Otto Brannard ran directly against Tammany and for progressive approaches to public problems; while Hearst railed against corruption but failed to rekindle his support from 1905. They all spoke enthusiastically about a subway for Staten Island, which was of great concern to the borough's voters. The FWIA sent questionnaires regarding local and city transportation plans to the leading candidates for the major offices. The letter centered on their views regarding a four-track subway along Fourth Avenue (needed to handle additional traffic and allow for express service), a two-track extension to Staten Island, and then the adoption of plans for a tunnel to Staten Island, assuming its feasibility. Most candidates, including all four men running for Richmond Borough president, replied favorably to the changes. Mayoral candidates Gaynor and Bannard championed the Fourth Avenue subway and a subsequent extension to Staten Island.[7]

As the election approached, most candidates overpromised, and some incumbents used their office to pander. With questionable timing just days before the election, the sitting Board of Estimate pressed the PSC on the question of a subway connection to Richmond. In late October, the board passed a resolution asking the PSC to inform it of "what action, if any, has been taken by said Commission to extend the Fourth Avenue Subway beyond Forty-third Street, with a view of its connection with Staten Island."[8] The PSC's response highlighted the contested nature of subway politics as it shifted the onus for inactivity on the Fourth Avenue and other Triborough lines back to the Board of Estimate. It also reaffirmed its intention for the subway to reach "Staten Island should such an extension be found feasible and possible."[9]

The election of almost the entire reform ticket in 1909 upended the subway impasse by placing progressive reformers into many key positions in city government. Although the Democrat Gaynor was triumphant as mayor, the Fusion ticket won nearly everywhere else. Cromwell was reelected as

Richmond Borough president; former City Club president George McAneny became Manhattan Borough president; William Prendergast, city comptroller; and John Purroy Mitchel, president of the Board of Aldermen. These results potentially boded well for subway expansion in general and for Staten Island in particular because the Fusion platform advocated a "comprehensive and adequate system of transit" that would serve "the needs of every section of the city."[10] It did not mean that answers had been found for the questions that had dogged Staten Island for nearly a decade: Who would speak for it? What was its greatest transportation need? If it was a rail connection to the rest of the city, by what route should that link go? If the best route was through Brooklyn, where exactly should the terminus on Staten Island be located?

Over the previous five years, conflict between the RTB and then the PSC with the Board of Estimate had caused much of the delay on subway expansion. The new Board of Estimate members, especially Manhattan Borough president George McAneny, however, shared with the PSC many similar sentiments regarding the subways. After 1909, men committed to dispersing congested populations by building subways to the outer reaches of New York had achieved control over the city's government, and a Narrows tunnel fit into this overall approach to rapid transit. Their unwillingness and inability to provide for a Staten Island connection over the next four years marked the closing of a significant window of opportunity for the Forgotten Borough.

1910: Last Chance for the Triborough System

The municipal elections of 1909 produced a Board of Estimate composed nearly entirely of reform candidates. Newly elected mayor William Gaynor, although a Democrat, quickly and regularly asserted his independence from Tammany. Many on Staten Island recognized that this outcome held much promise for a subway connection. In the weeks following the election, the *Richmond County Advance* editorialized "Now for Subways!" as it heralded the favorable results and urged Staten Islanders to unite around a tunnel. George Von Kromer led a delegation before the PSC and presented a petition with 1,700 signatures urging a quick start to a Narrows tunnel. The PSC chairman William R. Willcox responded approvingly, noting that PSC had already worked out a route from the Fourth Avenue line and that a tunnel under the Narrows could become part of a loop around the Port of New York.[11] Identifying and favoring a route, however, did not necessitate prioritizing or funding it.

In February 1910, the PSC and influential members of the Board of Estimate agreed to move ahead on the Triborough subway lines where the construction or preparatory work was most advanced. They focused on the Lexington

Avenue subway in Manhattan and included the Fourth Avenue route in Brooklyn but excluded an extension to Staten Island.[12] The omission of a Narrows tunnel sparked an outcry that evening at a meeting of the Staten Island Chamber of Commerce. A "full discussion" led to the chamber's forceful articulation of the need to "agitate as promptly and energetically as possible" for a tunnel. Its board moved for President William Van Clief to add ten members to Colonel Charles H. Blair's Subway and Transit Committee. The committee was asked to confer with the PSC and to plan a campaign to promote a subway.[13] The next month, when a resolution urging the preparation and adoption of a comprehensive, five-borough transit plan came to the chamber from the Citizens Rapid Transit Committee, a citywide group that included prominent Staten Islanders, the SICC passed the motion unanimously.[14] Blair's sudden death in April no doubt impaired the work of his committee, and the SICC's efforts on obtaining a tunnel remained largely dormant for the rest of the year.[15]

The absence of Staten Island from the revised Triborough plan also prompted other Staten Island civic groups to react. The FWIA started its own petition for a subway and presented it to the Board of Estimate. Its request was not at all bold: a $25,000 appropriation for the PSC to study the feasibility of a Narrows tunnel that might be built "sometime" in the future.[16] More forcefully, the Concord Property Owners Association urged the PSC "to take immediate action toward the construction of a tunnel under The Narrows [sic] to connect Staten Island with the Fourth Avenue Subway." Throughout the year, additional local groups made singular but not sustained efforts to sway the PSC.[17] The commissioners, not predisposed to service Staten Island in the near future, were preoccupied with the larger challenges facing rapid-transit expansion in Greater New York.

Financing new subway lines remained the greatest obstacle to overcome. Political conditions in the city—in particular suspicions of corporations and of the Tammany organization as well as progressive interest in designing a comprehensive transit system—framed the efforts undertaken. During the previous two years, movement on new subway lines was delayed in large part by political conflict over the actual height of the debt ceiling. For its part, the PSC promoted legislative mechanisms to augment the city's capacity for borrowing. One such approach was the assessment plan, which would ask outlying neighborhoods to help pay for a subway through special tax rates targeted at properties expected to benefit.[18] Once a common method of funding public improvements, the assessment plan had begun to be replaced by the use of general-tax-levied funds as far back as the construction of Central Park in the mid–nineteenth century.[19] Sixty years later, the City Club, a social organization of influential New Yorkers with an interest in efficient government, identified special assessments as the best means to fund a comprehensive subway system that would help decongest the city, and the PSC persuaded the state legislature to pass enabling legislation in 1909.[20] The Citizens Union, a watch group of the municipal government, latched on to the idea, arguing that proposed subway lines could be categorized as either trunk or development lines and that the costs of the latter, such as the Fourth Avenue line, which reached out to sparsely populated sections of the city, should be borne by those areas through special assessments.[21]

Contemporaries and historians alike noted the public's frosty reception of this approach. Special assessments remained routine in New York for improvements such as sewers and water lines but not for large infrastructure projects such as bridges and the incipient subway lines.[22] How to determine and distribute special assessments equitably was a major concern, especially because areas of Upper Manhattan and the Bronx had already benefited from the initial subway lines without being assessed for them. The new Board of Estimate members split on the issue overall: Mitchel and McAneny embraced the idea, Bronx Borough president Cyrus Miller was strongly opposed, Mayor Gaynor was disinclined, and Comptroller William Prendergast was skeptical.[23] Plenty of constituents certainly thought assessments were a poor idea, and civic groups in the Bronx, Brooklyn, and Queens issued resolutions denouncing it. When Mayor Gaynor queried speakers about the approach at a Board of Estimate hearing on April 4, the reaction was largely critical. Looking back a few years later, the former PSC member Edward Bassett recalled the antagonism of property holders that deterred the Board of Estimate and the PSC from pursuing the assessment plan.[24]

Nevertheless, others remained interested in exploring the possibilities of an assessment plan. The PSC interacted with at least two Brooklyn communities willing to fund a subway through special assessments. In September 1909, residents of Brownsville, Brooklyn, petitioned for a subway based on the assessment plan. A line running down Nostrand Avenue to Sheepshead Bay proposed in May 1910 by 150 property owners would also rely on the local community's tax dollars.[25] Vigorous debates in which individuals and organizations spoke of the assessment plan's benefits took place in Brooklyn in early 1910.[26] Important city news organs also examined its potential and reckoned with its complexities. The *Evening Post* saw it as a means of preventing "reckless subway building" of lines to nowhere; the *Brooklyn Daily Eagle* praised communities willing to bear the subway's financial burden in order to develop.[27] In addition to the City Club's and Citizens Union's staunch advocacy, the business periodical *Commercial and Financial Chronicle* looked favorably upon assessments.[28] These supporters considered assessments a reasonable cost to bear in order to gain the benefit of subway-induced growth. Those areas with perhaps little likelihood because they were far down on the priority list for lines might especially be willing for the city to use this means of financing construction. What then of Richmond Borough, which was certainly at the back of the queue?

The possibility of paying for its own subway line was largely ignored on Staten Island during the months the assessment plan was deliberated elsewhere. Unlike his colleagues on the Board of Estimate, who were outspoken in their support or denunciation of special assessments, Richmond Borough president Cromwell appears to have been silent.[29] He may have already recognized the rising disgruntlement on Staten Island about property taxes, which were viewed as too high in part due to special assessments for roads and sewers. This anger led in late 1911 to a formal investigation of his administration's financial transactions. William Mullen, a prominent Staten Island attorney, did not mention assessments at all in extensive remarks he made to advocate for a publicly funded direct subway to Manhattan. In coverage of the Board of Estimate hearing on April 4, 1910, Staten Island newspapers, unlike their counterparts in Manhattan and Brooklyn, did not mention the assessment plan even though it was a major topic of discussion.[30] SICC president Van Clief, apparently the lone speaker from Staten Island, might well have expressed support because the SICC had considered the issue in the previous months. Just two weeks earlier, Colonel Blair had even given a report that recommended the assessment plan be used for half the cost, with the city covering the rest. However, no other Richmond political or civic leader took this small opening for an assessment plan, discouraged perhaps by Blair's coupling of it with a route that directly linked St. George with the Battery, by his unexpected death one week after the hearing, and by the opposition of the borough's allies in South Brooklyn.[31]

Overall, 1910 proved to be another year of inconclusive activity regarding subway expansion in New York. Despite the availability of new mechanisms to generate subway funds and the presence of elected officials on the Board of Estimate and appointed citizens on the PSC who favored developing multiple lines simultaneously and quickly, the efforts to actualize the Triborough system fell short. The city still could not finance the plan even with a raised debt ceiling; private capital showed little interest in participating in the project; and the IRT, which was entirely hostile to the plan, successfully wooed Mayor Gaynor to its own more limited agenda for expansion. In the autumn of 1910, Cromwell remained in favor of the immediate approval of the Triborough plan, but by then support for it on the Board of Estimate had eroded. On November 18, William McAdoo's Hudson and Manhattan Railroad Company submitted to the PSC a proposal for subway expansion that cherry-picked the most profitable lines from the Triborough plan while omitting the lines extending to the outer reaches of the Bronx and Brooklyn. As such, the proposal was not of immediate interest to the PSC, which wanted to place lucrative and money-losing lines together in a single package, as the Triborough scheme did. Although negotiations commenced, the PSC was unwilling to subsidize McAdoo for losses on the unprofitable lines. The discussions likely spurred the IRT to revise its offer from the previous summer and include additional lines. The proposal it submitted on December 5 appealed to Mayor Gaynor but not to most other board members. Nevertheless, the IRT offer—to build lines to Brooklyn and add lines in Manhattan and the Bronx—and the PSC's evasion of a decision by forwarding it to the Board of Estimate ignited a series of developments that culminated in the Dual Contracts signed in 1913.[32]

George Cromwell and a Subway to St. George?

The IRT's December proposal suggested that it recognized but did not embrace the city's chief expectation for future lines: the need to build subways to outlying sections of the city. It wanted lucrative lines serving densely populated areas in Manhattan and had worked quietly with the Pennsylvania Railroad (PRR) to include ample service to that company's newly opened magnificent train station. Railroad and rapid-transit companies were not eager to build lines that would not be profitable for many years.[33] In the IRT's case, it offered to operate the Fourth Avenue line (only to Fortieth Street) but demanded that the city cover the expected deficits. The same requirement—of public dollars for both construction and operating losses—would hold in the future for the areas omitted from the IRT's December proposal, which had excluded all of Queens, Fort Hamilton and Coney Island in Brooklyn, and Staten Island.[34]

Staten Islanders looked skeptically at the IRT proposal because it disregarded a Narrows tunnel. That the IRT accepted the obligation to operate any future subway from Brooklyn to Staten Island that the city might build did not go nearly far enough for Cromwell. The Richmond Borough president urged Mayor Gaynor—both privately and publicly—to include Staten Island in any transit plan, faulted the IRT plan for omitting the island, and chided the PSC for forwarding the IRT proposal to the Board of Estimate unamended. He also reopened local tensions over the tunnel's location by winning passage of a symbolic Board of Estimate resolution calling upon the PSC to consider a Brooklyn–Staten Island subway tunnel route from Sixty-Fifth Street to a new destination: St. George. In response, the PSC scheduled a hearing on a Staten Island tunnel for January 18, 1911. The state of affairs grew more complex in the interim as the BRT made its own proposal to the PSC, one that did nothing for Staten Island but offered South Brooklyn new extensions and connections.[35] The recent spate of events galvanized Staten Islanders to prepare for the upcoming hearing. The *Staten Island World* and *Richmond County Advance* urged residents and civic groups to attend.[36] The SICC needed no prodding: it appointed a delegation that included Van Clief and David J. Tysen, scion of a prominent Staten Island family and a leading landowner on the island, and promoted a mass presence at the upcoming PSC meeting.[37] The clamor, though, suggested more than just anticipation over raised prospects for a tunnel. In the days leading up to the hearing, Staten Islanders jockeyed over the route to be pursued.

In proposing St. George as a terminus, Cromwell forcefully introduced another contender for the Staten Island end of the Narrows tunnel. Rosebank, the closest point to Brooklyn and once the choice of the Citizens Tunnel Committee, was not a well-received location, both because of aspersions cast on those who favored it and because it was not a densely populated part of the island. Subsequent proposals, which had been slowly moving the tunnel terminus to the more heavily populated Stapleton, were buoyed by the initial engineering surveys conducted by the PSC, which indicated that because of the depths and currents involved, the shortest route across the Narrows would not be any less expensive than a tunnel to St. George. Cromwell also intended to maximize ridership by bringing the subway to the island's greatest area of population density and thus to enhance the prestige of its growing civic center.[38] Finally, a subway to St. George could diminish reliance on the municipal ferry service, for which the annual deficit was of concern to Mayor Gaynor and other city officials.[39] Not all islanders, however, responded favorably to a St. George route. The *Staten Island World* reported that Cromwell's plan met with considerable criticism and editorialized that if his route were adopted, "we will be little better off as regards speed than we are today." The *Richmond County Advance* disagreed, observing that "it is a new kink in the subway plan to have the terminus at St. George, but any tunnel is better than no tunnel."[40] Both papers recommended burying any disagreements over location at the hearing and pressing in a single voice for a Narrows tunnel to Staten Island, but unity remained an elusive goal.

A crowd of Staten Islanders came to the PSC hearing on January 18, 1911, in support of a subway tunnel to Richmond Borough. Cromwell spoke forcefully for a route from Bay Ridge at Sixty-Sixth Street in Brooklyn to St. George, but other speakers from civic groups articulated a plethora of proposals. Von Kromer still argued for a much shorter tunnel, from farther south in Bay Ridge to Stapleton. Some islanders spoke in favor of a subway route via Bayonne, and still others emphasized the need for a tunnel but without advocating for a particular route.[41] While the Staten Island papers largely played down the differences among the attendees, the *New York Times* heard "considerable division of opinion" present at the hearing.[42] Nor is it evident from contemporary press reports which views predominated. The *New York Times* and the *Staten Islander* found that most attendees adhered to Cromwell's position, which was buttressed by the civil engineer William Wilgus's estimate of a $6 million price tag. The *Staten Island World*, which remained critical of

Cromwell's plan, claimed that a majority of attendees agreed with Von Kromer's proposal for a Stapleton terminus. The commissioners themselves appeared to be sympathetic to the need for a tunnel but reportedly favored neither Cromwell's nor Von Kromer's preference but rather a third route that reached Staten Island between Stapleton and Tompkinsville.[43] Thus, members of the PSC and the Board of Estimate diverged—as they did on other, more fundamental transit issues—over the best route for a tunnel to Staten Island.

Within the Board of Estimate, Manhattan Borough president George McAneny had emerged as the most influential voice with regard to transit matters. He had immersed himself in transit issues while City Club president, approached them with a progressive's faith in rational planning, and had a clear agenda to disperse the city's population from Manhattan. As Clifton Hood describes him, "With his excellent political and business connections and his belief in rational action and social responsibility, McAneny represented a new breed of dealmaker that arose in the early twentieth-century."[44] McAneny thought the IRT plan worth exploring through negotiation but, like Cromwell, was highly dissatisfied with it. McAneny had myriad reasons for this dissatisfaction and believed that the IRT plan did not "prepare properly for the eventual construction of a tunnel to Richmond."[45] By early 1911, the borough presidents, unwilling to proceed with either the Triborough plan or the IRT proposal and coalescing around McAneny, demanded more time to study the transit issues. In response, the Board of Estimate reconstituted its three-person Transit Committee, appointing Bronx Borough president Cyrus Miller, Cromwell, and, as chair, McAneny.[46] The committee's ostensible purpose was to draft a response to the IRT plan in consultation with the members of the PSC.

Cromwell's presence on the Transit Committee heightened the island's already high expectations that he could deliver a subway tunnel. As one letter writer to the *Richmond County Advance* observed, "It strikes me that there is a splendid chance for our Borough President to distinguish himself by insisting that Richmond be considered."[47] The *Advance* expressed confidence that "with George Cromwell on a committee of three it begins to look as if Staten Island can't get away from a subway."[48] The *Richmond County Democrat*, no friend to Cromwell, still recognized the possibilities of the moment: "Will President Cromwell be the Prince Charming to fit the rapid transit slipper to Cinderella Richmond and lead her out of her lone obscurity to the proud position to which she is entitled? We hope so."[49]

In public, Cromwell certainly sounded ready to deliver. On January 26, he shared his requirements for a contract with the IRT, most of which related to a Staten Island subway. For Cromwell, the project would have to include all five boroughs and simultaneously begin lines to each one. In this way, he aimed to counter the expectation that a subway to Richmond would be built later than sooner. He wanted the IRT to include a four-track extension of the Fourth Avenue line below Fortieth Street to allow for future traffic from Staten Island. To keep fares low for his constituents, he also expected subsequent free transfers to all lines under IRT control after the payment of a single fare of five cents. Most significantly, he was willing to offer some guarantees of profit to the IRT but declined to single out the losses from individual lines. He instead wanted the whole system's operating expenses and earnings to be the basis for the calculation of profit.[50] In this way, a line to Staten Island would not stand on its own financial prospects but would be tied to those of a comprehensive system. These reasonable positions he took publicly did not survive the private deliberations that followed.

The McAneny Subcommittee

Over the next several months, McAneny, Cromwell, and Miller expanded the Board of Estimate Transit Committee's role beyond the examination of the IRT's proposal. More than consulting with the five members of the PSC, they "worked so closely [with them] that they were soon referred to as one entity, 'the conferees,'" in contemporary accounts.[51] The conferees' purview also expanded when in early March 1911 the BRT presented a revised proposal for subway expansion that was far more comprehensive than its January offer. The conferees now intended to coordinate responses to both companies and by late April to make their own plan for subway expansion involving each company.[52]

As the Transit Committee's chairman, McAneny dominated it and with the PSC chairman William Willcox led the conferees. As for Cromwell, most contemporary and scholarly reckonings give him (and Miller) little role or influence, and he appeared to be almost entirely aligned with McAneny.[53] An internal memorandum dated March 5, 1911, that listed the eight conferees' positions on "controverted points" is suggestive of how closely Cromwell's views mirrored McAneny's. Of the ten points identified, Cromwell's position was in each case identical to McAneny's, and both of them were always among the majority (unlike Miller, who was against some of the provisions). The memorandum is also indicative of how little Cromwell shaped the direction of the negotiations in that McAneny didn't even list a Narrows tunnel as a contentious issue.[54] Having already signaled that a Richmond line was at best an eventuality, McAneny did not push for it as part of the next subway contracts. The BRT's revised proposal notwithstanding, by early March Cromwell had acquiesced to the other conferees' and railroad companies' disinclination and failed to keep the construction of a Staten Island tunnel as an outstanding matter.

If the Narrows tunnel project did not embroil the conferees, neither was it entirely neglected in their negotiations with both rapid-transit companies. The BRT's March 2 proposal had included a tunnel to Staten Island that in some regards boded well for the island. First, the tunnel would emanate from the Fourth Avenue line at Forty-Second Street, an advantageous location that required a lengthier tunnel but resulted in a shorter distance to Manhattan. Second, the BRT presented a Narrows tunnel as a priority equal to any other line, but that commitment lasted a mere seven weeks.[55] On April 25, the BRT issued a revised proposal that in some ways moved it closer to the conferees' position and weakened the status of the Narrows tunnel. The route from Staten Island would surface in Brooklyn at Sixty-Fifth Street, farther from Manhattan. It was also now a secondary priority, to be built "on an extension basis— that is[,] [with] losses from operation to be carried by the City, subject to liquidation from the surplus profits of the inner lines."[56] Such a clause for this and other lines left the proposal far short of McAneny's expectation that the private companies would use their own profits from lucrative lines to cover any losses from peripheral lines to the outer reaches of the city. Even as an extension, the Narrows tunnel was left to the city to finance and build. A Narrows tunnel was never going to be part of a proposal from the Manhattan-centered IRT, but the IRT did include Staten Island in its effort to dampen interest in the BRT plan. Contending that its offer would reduce the city's construction costs by $58 million, the IRT suggested that such savings could be used by the city to build a connection to Staten Island.[57]

As the conferees worked, Staten Islanders were largely left unaware of the dismissal of a Narrows tunnel. Although the transit companies made the details of their offers public, the conferees' meetings were neither open nor recorded. Reports of them seeped into the public domain based on comments by participants seeking an edge in the deliberations, but a public leak of Staten Island's dwindling chances served no one, so no such leak occurred. Staten Islanders instead heard optimistic updates from Cromwell, who, for example, expressed great satisfaction with the BRT's proposal for his borough despite the company's unwillingness to fund or construct a tunnel.[58] They digested unsubstantiated reports such as the *Brooklyn Daily Eagle*'s that the IRT would offer to build four tracks to Seventy-Fifth Street with a two-track spur to St. George "as a concession to the demands of Borough President Cromwell of Richmond."[59] They attempted to read into the details that became known, as when the *Richmond County Advance* speculated about the absence of a Narrows tunnel in some financial deliberations, but they generally received optimistic accounts that the "subway to Staten Island is now on the map for sure."[60]

Sanguine or not, Richmond Borough's leading residents understood the significance of the conferees' forthcoming subway report. Staten Islanders gathered on May 5 to rally public support for a subway line and, more importantly, to strategize over how best to pursue a favorable outcome as the conferees' delicate negotiations and deliberations over a comprehensive subway plan grew more protracted. Organized and chaired by a recently reconstituted and enlarged SICC tunnel committee, the meeting expanded beyond the groups that had presented to the PSC in January that year and included representatives from approximately thirty local organizations.[61] The attendees grappled with how publicly and aggressively they should demand a tunnel from the members of the PSC and the Board of Estimate. Whereas Van Clief suggested that at the right moment it might be helpful to go to the Board of Estimate "with flags flying and bands a-playing," most speakers did not think that moment had yet occurred. Louis Tribus, Richmond Borough's long-standing commissioner of public works, counseled that "demonstrative agitation at the present time would be inopportune." Taking a self-serving but concurring position, Cromwell noted that he had already done all that he could to push for a Narrows tunnel and argued that waiting at least until the Board of Estimate hearings had concluded made the most sense. Another speaker urged making a concerted effort by having representatives from each group attend Board of Estimate subway hearings currently taking place, but his plea was not heeded. Instead, the body determined to "make haste slowly."[62] This decision stood in place at a subsequent meeting held one week later, an admonition to "step lively" from the *Advance* notwithstanding.[63] The decision may have stemmed from a false sense of confidence, and it was not one that communities in other boroughs, fearful of being left out of the prospective subway contracts, emulated.[64]

On June 13, 1911, the conferees issued a report that would become the essence of the dual-contract system. The Transit Committee had made significant changes to the two rapid-transit companies' proposals and outlined a municipal system with lines financed by the city, the IRT, and the BRT. Each rapid-transit company would operate the specific lines assigned to it, with the IRT primarily in Manhattan and the Bronx and the BRT largely in Brooklyn (see figure 5.1). Their designated lines balanced highly profitable routes in congested neighborhoods with initially unprofitable lines in outlying areas.[65] As for Richmond Borough, the report called for "provisions . . . [for] an early start upon the Staten Island connection" and requested the Board of Estimate and Apportionment to budget $5 million for its construction, which was to be done by the city (rather than by the BRT).[66] Cromwell had prevailed upon the conferees to locate the Brooklyn terminus at Sixty-Fifth Street rather than Forty-Second, as the BRT had initially proposed, but the report gave no location for the Staten Island end of the tunnel.

The conferees recommended for Staten Island a multipurpose tunnel—one that would accommodate both freight and rapid transit and include a water tunnel as part of the Catskill Water Supply system then under construction. The civil engineer William J. Wilgus had reignited interest in moving freight under the Narrows when he made a tunnel part of his proposed Greater New

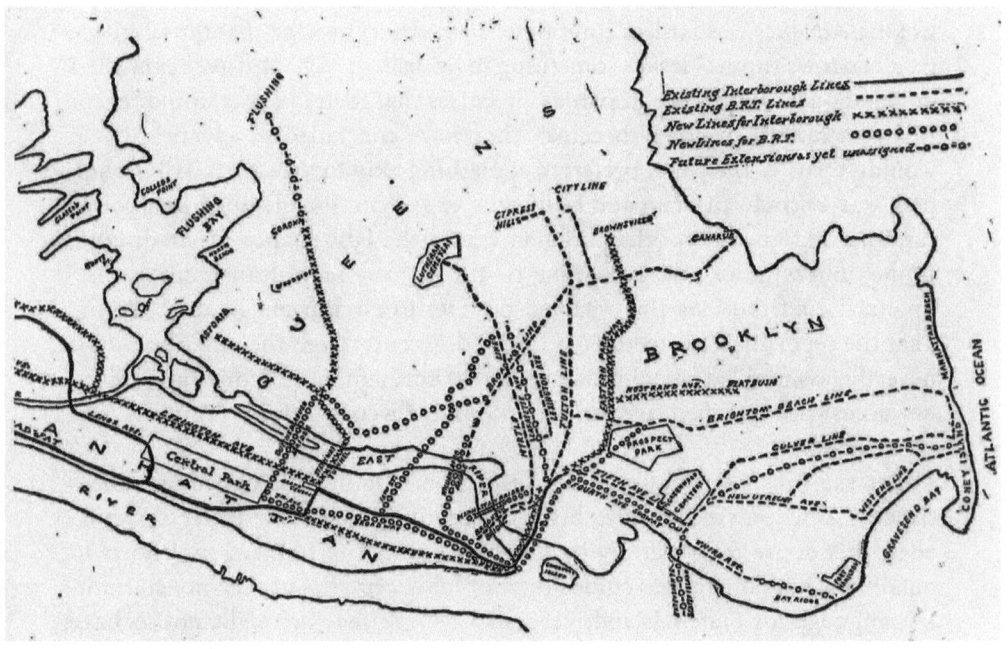

5.1 Proposed subway lines for the dual contracts, 1911

The Dual Contracts outlined multiple new lines for the IRT and BRT alike. Staten Island was left with a possible extension from Sixty-Ninth Street that the BRT had no desire to construct.

Source: *New York Times*, June 14, 1911.

York Belt Line. The prospect intrigued BRT president Timothy S. Williams as a possible means of making a Narrows passenger route financially viable.[67] That the idea required additional participants in an already complicated set of negotiations made it unlikely to occur, but it offered an answer to the vexing finances of a Narrows tunnel. In this way, the conferees hoped to apportion a large part of the estimated cost of $12 million to the railroad companies as well as to tap into funds designated for the water project. The conferees punted on specifying details on the routing and construction of the Narrows tunnel pending further investigation of the freight and water options but promised a supplementary report by August 1. They even suggested delaying work on the South Brooklyn lines until the details of the Staten Island connection could be worked out.[68]

The absence of specifics was one of several reasons why reaction to the report in the Staten Island press was mixed. Newspapers editorialized in ways consistent with their political leanings. The Republican *Staten Islander* called the provisions an "unexpectedly happy outcome for Staten Island" and credited Cromwell for the accomplishment.[69] The Democratic *Richmond County Advance* was far less complimentary, observing that that the language on a Narrows tunnel "leaves something to be desired." The *Advance* expressed doubt about the subway companies' promises that their systems would "eventually include Richmond" because "they have concluded in advance that it wouldn't pay."[70] The paper preferred something akin to the earlier Triborough plan—an entirely city-run and built subway system. It contended that public funding and operation offered Staten Island the best chance of obtaining a tunnel, but without acknowledging that it was the rapid-transit companies' financial contributions that enabled the city to circumvent its debt ceiling. That the report had treated Staten Island differently from the other boroughs nevertheless rankled island residents. Every borough save Richmond received new lines with specified costs and locations and a commitment for immediate construction.

For the *Advance*, the outcome of the report signified Cromwell's ineffectiveness as a conferee. Calling him "George the placid," the paper acknowledged his desire for a subway to Staten Island and recognized his efforts to obtain one but nonetheless chided him for his acceptance of such noncommittal language for Staten Island: "We also believe that he ought not to have signed that report, because it has no saving clause insisting that Staten Island should have a tunnel. If, as we believe, and as he doubtless believes, Staten Island has a right to be connected with Manhattan and every other Borough, he should have refused to sign any report that did not give Staten Island that connection." By acceding to the recommendations of the conference report, Cromwell essentially left in place the consensus reached by the PSC nearly three years earlier: agreement in principle to a Staten Island tunnel but no actual commitment to build it. The *Advance* concluded that despite Cromwell's presence on the conference committee, "Staten Island seems to be still looking on at the game without taking part."[71]

The memoirs of a prominent Staten Islander also suggest the degree of residents' dissatisfaction with Cromwell's actions. David Tysen offered public support when the report came out but years later conveyed his dismay with Cromwell's service on the Transit Committee. In reflecting on the momentous developments of 1911, Tysen recalled his pessimism about Staten Island's chances for a subway tunnel and his determination to pursue instead free transfers from the municipal ferry to the IRT subway lines. After meeting with the IRT president T. P. Shonts and reaching some agreeable terms, Tysen brought Cromwell into the discussions, hoping that he would move ahead on this issue. Tysen's narrative suggests that he didn't:

> Mr. Cromwell was one of the Committee, with Mr. McAneny, and Borough President Miller, of the Bronx, appointed by the Board to arrange with the

Interborough the terms of the dual subway contract. And my object was to get the transfers included in the contract. Mr. Cromwell returned [from vacation] and after a few weeks not hearing from him, I called on him, and he said he had brought the matter up at one of their meetings and that McAneny, Chairman of the Committee, said it was not the psychological time, and that he had not further urged it then.[72]

Although Tysen was speaking of free transfers and not a Narrows tunnel, he was pushing for an arguably easier outcome to obtain for Staten Island but still encountered Cromwell's recalcitrance. In this instance as well as with the tunnel and in most issues placed before the three-person Transit Committee, Cromwell bowed to McAneny's will. Highly dissatisfied with Cromwell, Tysen bemoaned the loss of "an opportunity to help his [Cromwell's] constituents seldom offered to any man" and years later remained bewildered as to why Cromwell had not aggressively pursued this venture.[73]

Cromwell appears to have anticipated his vulnerability to his constituents' adverse reaction. To forestall criticism, he composed the most curious component of the conference report, a letter dated June 5, 1911, to McAneny and the other conferees that was placed in the appendix. In it, Cromwell offered a preemptive defense of his efforts on behalf of a tunnel: "I have consistently and persistently kept to the front the matter of including the Borough of Richmond as territory into which immediate subway construction should be carried, in connection with the main proposition rather than as an extension to be considered at some later date." He then spelled out his efforts to satisfy the needs of Staten Island and reiterated some standard justifications for a connection to Richmond: to provide a fair level of services to the borough and to relieve congestion elsewhere in New York. Finally, he gave details, much of which had made it into the main report, for what he envisioned: a four-track rather than two-track tunnel so that it could serve freight and rapid-transit traffic, a possible use for water-main purposes to save additional money, and an immediate $5 million allocation for the work.[74]

Cromwell's self-justification of his work on the conference Transit Committee no doubt satisfied some but did not persuade the editor of the *Richmond County Advance*. The paper's blistering rejection of the conference report included the following dismissal of Cromwell's missive:

> We have also read with great interest Mr. Cromwell's able letter in the appendix to the report. It is the best presentation of Staten Island's case that has yet been made, and we doubt if any better ever will be made. It is too bad that it is only in the Appendix, and therefore as little likely to be read as if it were the list of Homer's ships or a patent-office report. As to its influence on the subway question, it can of course have none whatever. In this it reminds us of

another letter which we read in the long ago—a letter that was rich in pathos, in eloquence, in pleading. It was written by a rejected suitor to the girl of his choice and received by her—after she had eloped with the other fellow.[75]

In comparing Cromwell to a "rejected suitor," the *Advance* came—apparently unwittingly—very close to the truth.

The appendix with Cromwell's "letter" to the conferees was in fact a calculated and carefully crafted afterthought. An initial list of items for the appendix did not contain this document, and Staten Islanders eventually learned that it surfaced as a "last-minute" attachment. In fact, McAneny had carefully reviewed the letter's language before it was included. Although McAneny's edits of it were not substantive, their very existence suggests the posturing in which Cromwell and the other conferees were engaged. Not willing to provide for Staten Island in the definitive way its citizens had hoped for, the committee intentionally suggested to the readers of its report that Cromwell had been a forceful advocate for a Narrows tunnel.[76] The historical record suggests otherwise. Consider the testimony in 1916 of Bradford Merrill, then publisher of the *New York American*: "Mr. Cromwell was always fascinated by the project of the branch of the subway that should go down opposite Bay Ridge, and they were going to tunnel into Bay Ridge and put his borough on the subway. It was always in the air, it was always a mere plan, but he professed to believe it. No one else believed that it would be carried through."[77] Cromwell's advocacy operated on the level of political theater. He pronouncements on a Staten Island subway neither influenced his colleagues nor forced the issue.

McAneny also made considerable edits to early drafts of the main report, and his changes to language about Staten Island are instructive. Although he offered some revisions that emphasized support for a Narrows tunnel, his changes to earlier versions of the June 5 report overall weakened the committee's commitment to such a project. For example, he wanted to eliminate the request for a $5 million allocation for a Narrows tunnel, though his suggestion went unheeded. He also removed the word *strongly* from the phrase "the conferees are strongly of the opinion [to include Staten Island]," and this edit was reflected in the final text.[78]

If McAneny's marked-up drafts of the conference report are any indication, his tepid support for a Narrows tunnel remained largely in place during the conferees' private deliberations. As a spate of public announcements in January suggest, McAneny unequivocally favored a tunnel to Staten Island, but to be done only at a later stage of subway development, as his initial criticisms of the December 5 IRT proposal had indicated.[79] He told the *Richmond County Advance* that "immediate provision should be made for the continuance of the Fourth avenue line in Brooklyn, either to Fort Hamilton or to a point opposite St. George, in order to permit the earliest practicable start upon the connecting tunnel to SI."⁸⁰ In a January 23 memorandum made public, McAneny presented the composite views of the Board of Estimate members. Regarding Richmond Borough, McAneny expected "the consideration of the practicability of including in the immediate plan the completion of the Fourth Avenue (Brooklyn) line either to Fort Hamilton or to 67th Street, with a view toward proceeding also with the preparation of plans for a tunnel connection with Staten Island from either point."⁸¹ At the same time, he never made a strong public commitment to Richmond Borough as he did to Queens, which had also been omitted from the IRT proposal of December 1910.⁸²

What kept McAneny from exerting greater pressure for a Narrows tunnel? Most likely the resistance from the rapid-transit companies themselves. The negotiations that the conferees undertook with both the IRT and BRT in the winter and spring of 1911 were arduous and protracted. PRR's president Samuel Rea loomed in the background as a confidant of IRT president Shonts and as a member of the B&O Board of Trustees. During these talks, McAneny was forced to give way on several elements he originally demanded. For example, in his January 23, 1911, memorandum, he proposed a "modified assessment plan, under which the city would bear half the cost of construction and the property to be benefited the other half" to pay for the subway additions in Queens, Brooklyn, and the Bronx.⁸³ This approach to funding did not become a part of the conferees' June 5 report. Even more strenuously opposed by the IRT was McAneny's expectation that to operate lines to the far reaches of the outer boroughs, a future contract would guarantee the company a minimum profit if the IRT would combine the revenues from the old and new lines. Although the notion that the highly profitable lines in Manhattan would pay for the operation of less lucrative lines to Richmond and other outer boroughs was embedded in the June 5 report, the IRT succeeded in keeping out of the calculations the lines it had built through the earlier contracts. The BRT demonstrated more sympathy for building to the city's outer reaches than the IRT, but it largely exerted itself to win lines in Queens and Brooklyn.⁸⁴

The IRT and the BRT never publicly rejected building a tunnel to Staten Island, but they clearly had no interest in operating one until a subway would be profitable. More than a year earlier, a BRT executive had identified thirteen extensions of interest to the company, none of which were a link to Staten Island. In subsequent negotiations, calculations of ridership and concerns about deficits weighed heavily on the BRT's president, Timothy Williams.⁸⁵ Just days after the release of the conferees' report, the *Richmond County Advance* wrote to both companies, "asking each company for a concise statement as to what it proposed doing in the way of giving Richmond Borough a subway." Each company offered a perfunctory response to the inquiry. Williams sent over a copy of the BRT's most recent proposal to the PSC (presumably the one dated April 25) and encouraged the *Advance* editors to read the

McAneny report and Cromwell's appendix. The IRT gave the request to its attorney, who sent "a very clever letter" that highlighted the IRT's December 10 offer to operate any additional extensions the city might build. Neither response satisfied the *Advance* and only confirmed its conviction that "Staten Island's only hope is in a city-owned, city-built, and city-controlled subway."[86] As the *New York Times* acknowledged nearly a year later, the Staten Island tunnel proposal "had always been regarded as one of the portions of the general scheme which was not likely to be carried out in the immediate future."[87] Even so, the negotiations among the conferees during the first half of 1911 had afforded the Forgotten Borough its greatest opportunity to date for a subway connection, but by July that moment had passed. Mayor Gaynor confided as much in a letter to Cromwell on July 25: "I fear Richmond is not to get any tunnel or rapid transit connections for some time by the looks of things."[88]

Despite their disappointment with the McAneny report, Staten Islanders responded. A group of residents prepared to bring their case directly to the Board of Estimate, which began reviewing the conferees' report shortly after its release. For the most part, the board accepted the location of the new subway lines, the BRT accepted the conferees' proposal, but the IRT balked. It was the financial arrangements, particularly with the IRT, that extended contract negotiations over the next twenty months.[89] As part of this review process, the Richmond Borough Citizens' Tunnel Committee of Staten Island was granted a one-hour hearing with the Board of Estimate early in the summer of 1911. As chairman of the group, William Van Clief headed the delegation that appeared before the board in July.[90] The hearing moved Staten Island no closer to a subway link, though, and the conferees' follow-up report expected by August 1 never materialized.

The PSC reconsidered the matter of a Staten Island tunnel in February 1912 when it tackled the larger questions of the best lines for outer Brooklyn, which was also unresolved in the June 5, 1911, conferees' report. Cromwell spoke publicly about his vision for a Staten Island freight and rapid-transit tunnel but essentially rehashed his earlier plan. The idea of a freight route through Staten Island had gained new life the previous December, when New York City's dock commissioner, Calvin Tomkins, issued a report proposing a system of tunnels, including one from Brooklyn to Staten Island, to link New Jersey (and thus access south and west) with Long Island and New England but without going through Manhattan.[91] Cromwell's comments accompanied another report by the conferees that was highlighted by a recommendation that an extension of Brooklyn's Fourth Avenue line should contain four tracks and occur underground—in part to facilitate a future tunnel that "can be made" to Staten Island. The conferees further encouraged the Board of Estimate "at the earliest time practicable" to engage the freight railroad companies in discussions about supporting a Narrows tunnel venture—a hollow gesture considering that no such talks had occurred over the previous eight months. Cromwell's Staten Island supporters heaped praise on him for this latest development, but others remained skeptical given that the freight companies had already once declined to participate in a tunnel venture. Perhaps in recognition of the now seemingly fanciful talk of a Staten Island tunnel, Commissioner Milo Maltbie of the PSC voiced opposition to building any addition to the Fourth Avenue line until work on a tunnel to Staten Island had actually begun.[92]

Cromwell continued to promote his ideas among citizens, politicians, and railroad companies into the spring of 1912, even as the state legislature and the courts moved to approve the Dual Contracts in principle and the conferees continued to iron out many of the remaining obstacles with the IRT and BRT. By mid-May, McAneny, Cromwell, Miller, and the members of the PSC had reached agreement, and McAneny outlined the details in a "Supplementary Report" to the Board of Estimate, which approved it on May 24.[93] Although this outcome boded well for subway expansion in New York, it still left Staten Island with little more than favorable but imprecise language about a future tunnel. The "Supplementary Report" contained the principles espoused by Cromwell: a tunnel from the Fourth Avenue line at Sixty-Fifth that would extend to Staten Island and surface at St. George and Stapleton, that would carry freight as well as rapid-transit passengers, and whose $12 million estimated cost would be born in part by the railroad companies and in part by the Board of Water Supply, which would attach water mains to the tunnel. The *New York Times* reported that the agreement "was to give an impetus to the project of a subway to Staten Island," and, indeed, the paper's coverage regularly promoted the likelihood of a Narrows tunnel.[94] Yet no substantive conversations took place with the railroad companies, which had never expressed any interest in the project. As the PRR's Samuel Rea told an inquiring Staten Islander in late 1910, his company had considered and rejected a Narrows route twenty years earlier. The B&O, with its presence on Staten Island, might have looked favorably on the venture, but the PRR wielded a lot of influence as a major shareholder of B&O stock.[95]

Watchful Staten Islanders could note a few positive Narrows tunnel developments in 1912. The PSC approved the basic principles of the "Supplementary Report" on June 14; the Board of Estimate and Apportionment held a hearing on June 27 and then reported favorably on July 11; and the city's mayor approved the resolution on July 16, 1912.[96] Even as the PSC spelled out the route to Staten Island and prioritized the extension of the Fourth Avenue line in Brooklyn, however, its members also made clear that they expected "that it [such an extension] is not likely to be begun for some time." Successful negotiations with the railroad companies and with the city's Department of Water Supply were necessary preconditions to moving ahead on the project for multipurpose tunnels.[97]

Specifications for the Narrows line remained elusive even as the plans for other routes became more concrete. For example, a proposed PSC hearing for May 31 on some recently adopted routes expressly excluded the tunnel to Staten Island on its agenda.[98] Three months later, the *Staten Islander* had to quell rumors that bids had been requested for a Narrows tunnel; the bids had instead gone out for the Fourth Avenue extension in Brooklyn.[99] Perhaps most telling, when the Transit Committee and PSC conferees ordered a study of earning and cost projections of proposed lines, they neglected to include the Staten Island tunnel. Such omissions were detrimental to Staten Island because the drawing up of contracts began in the latter half of 1912—a painstaking process that would take months.[100]

While the *New York Times* sounded sanguine about the Narrows tunnel prospects, voices on Staten Island once again rose to convey alarm over the lack of definitive progress. The *Richmond County Advance* urged Cromwell and Richmond Borough public-works commissioner Louis Tribus, already facing criticisms for promoting unnecessary and costly public improvements, to lay aside those efforts and focus on a tunnel, which "is of infinitely greater importance to Richmond than fancy 'civic centers' and expensive pleasure driveways."[101] The *Advance* was sympathetic to the notion that a commitment from the freight railroads to participate and help finance a tunnel could allay fears of its cost and spur the project forward. The SICC, still concerned by the inactivity on a tunnel, appointed a committee of five "to investigate the status of the subway situation."[102]

The SICC was ultimately not well suited to this task. Having started to organize much too late in the process, this new tunnel committee was soon replaced with another one asked to confer with the PSC and borough president Cromwell on "the subway question."[103] The apparent futility of this halfhearted measure led the Chamber of Commerce to appoint a third tunnel committee in early 1913 as the signing of the Dual Contracts appeared imminent. The committee sent letters decrying the absence of any provision for a Narrows tunnel to the newly appointed PSC chair Edward McCall and to Commissioner J. Sergeant Cram, an outspoken opponent of the Dual Contracts.[104] Nothing came of these inquiries—in part because by then the location of the subways lines was settled.

The Dual Contracts were nearly derailed in the early months of 1913 by continued opposition to the financial terms and by their adversaries' political maneuvering. In the end, though, opponents on the PSC and the Board of Estimate lacked the votes to block the contracts, which were approved by both bodies and signed on March 19, 1913. Together, the contracts provided for the construction of 325 miles of new track construction in Manhattan, Brooklyn, Queens, and the Bronx. A subway tunnel to Staten Island, though still part of the PSC's plans for the future, was not included in the contracts signed that day.[105] On Staten Island, the post mortem on the tunnel's demise lasted for several years.

Fallout from Exclusion

In 1913, George Cromwell was completing his fourth term as Richmond Borough president and once again seeking reelection. The growth of the island's Democratic constituencies and the presence of William Wirt Mills, a third-party Progressive candidate, made the prospect difficult enough, but Cromwell also faced considerable discontent over his record in the subway negotiations.[106] The Democratic nominee, Charles McCormack, was clear in his advocacy for a tunnel, and his criticism of Cromwell's performance on this issue was equally explicit: "After I take my seat in the Board of Estimate, I intend to work for that [the subway tunnel to Staten Island] with all my might. I may not be an orator, but I am a worker. If I had been on the transit committee of which President Cromwell was a member, I would not have agreed to millions for subways in other boroughs and not one cent for Richmond. We want more than a dotted line on an engineer's map."[107]

Throughout the fall, both the McCormack and the Mills campaigns alleged Cromwell's failures and emphasized the need for a subway tunnel. McCormack belittled Cromwell's "unnecessary public improvements" and advocated "better and cheaper transportation facilities between Staten Island and Manhattan," including a tube running directly between them.[108] Mills ran a campaign focused on "local issues" and promoted "'twenty measures' for attracting population to Richmond," including a Narrows connection.[109]

In their campaign visits to Richmond, New York politicians running for citywide positions also gave the tunnel its due in their speeches. Fusion mayoral candidate William Purroy Mitchel, speaking in Stapleton and West New Brighton, promised to aim for a time "when our subway system will no longer be a four-borough but a five-borough system."[110] At the same rallies, McAneny, running as a Fusionist for president of the Board of Aldermen, praised Cromwell and expressed optimism for a tunnel: "Cromwell served with me on the Transit Committee, and we worked out this great dual plan. We could not get to SI, because it would cost too much just at this time; but we did get a route laid out, and I believe in my heart that the work will be done before a great while."[111]

McAneny also directly challenged Staten Islanders' notions that they were shortchanged by New York in general and that Cromwell in particular had failed them. "Now and then in the past several years," he jovially told the gathered crowds, "we have got a little out of patience with Staten Island when we see what you have gotten out of us." Claiming to hold no grudge, McAneny gave credit to Cromwell, "the dean of the Board of Estimate," for securing the generous appropriations.¹¹² In his trip to Staten Island, Democratic mayoral candidate and Tammany place holder Edward McCall made the mistake of acknowledging that Staten Island could not get a tunnel because it was too expensive. Later that day at another stop, McCall quickly reversed himself by announcing that he, too, favored a tunnel and mirrored the argument of local real estate interests: that the tunnel was economically viable because of the huge increase in property values it would spur.¹¹³

On November 4, 1913, Cromwell lost his bid for reelection to McCormack, with Mills coming in a distant third. McCormack won by about 500 votes, but Mills received more than 1,000 votes, and the Republican/Fusion ticket won nearly every other major race in the city, so contemporary accounts explained that the Fusion candidate had pulled the decisive votes away from the incumbent. Cromwell refused publicly to heap blame for his loss on Mills's third-party campaign, instead suggesting that after sixteen years voters were simply ready for a new face.¹¹⁴ Both of these factors no doubt help to explain the outcome, but so too does the public dissatisfaction with Staten Island's exclusion from the Dual Contracts. In a campaign in which "McCormack devoted most of his speeches to this subject [and] Mr. Mills gave it prominence," Cromwell was hard-pressed to stem the disappointment in his representation of Staten Island and to deflect the criticisms flung his way.¹¹⁵ As bids were received, contracts signed, and construction begun on new lines elsewhere, the fallout for Staten Island continued beyond 1913.

A second manner in which Cromwell's failure still reverberated among islanders became apparent in the years that followed: an unwillingness to compromise on a tunnel. Civic leaders unveiled in 1915 a new "to and through" campaign for a direct subway to Manhattan. They had previously pushed for a Narrows route only as a political calculation that stood a better chance of enactment because it was a less expensive alternative. Now they were disinclined to settle for anything less than the service that they most wanted and to which they felt entitled, cost be damned: a direct subway from Staten Island to Manhattan (see figure 5.2).¹¹⁶ In so doing, they reaffirmed their commitment to a New York–centered island, one that would house Manhattan's labor force, handle its trade, and manufacture goods for the greater city and beyond. Their organizing efforts over the next few years proceeded largely free from entanglement in citywide subway politics but encountered three problems that ultimately doomed them and ended the era of fallout. First, the Garbage War of 1916–1918 halted most tunnel activity as islanders organized to prevent and then close a garbage-reduction plant handling refuse transferred from other boroughs.¹¹⁷ Second, New York's mayor John Hylan, who had won local support for his stance on the garbage matter, completely spurned a direct tunnel to Manhattan.¹¹⁸ Third, in the face of the mayor's rejection, the tunnel

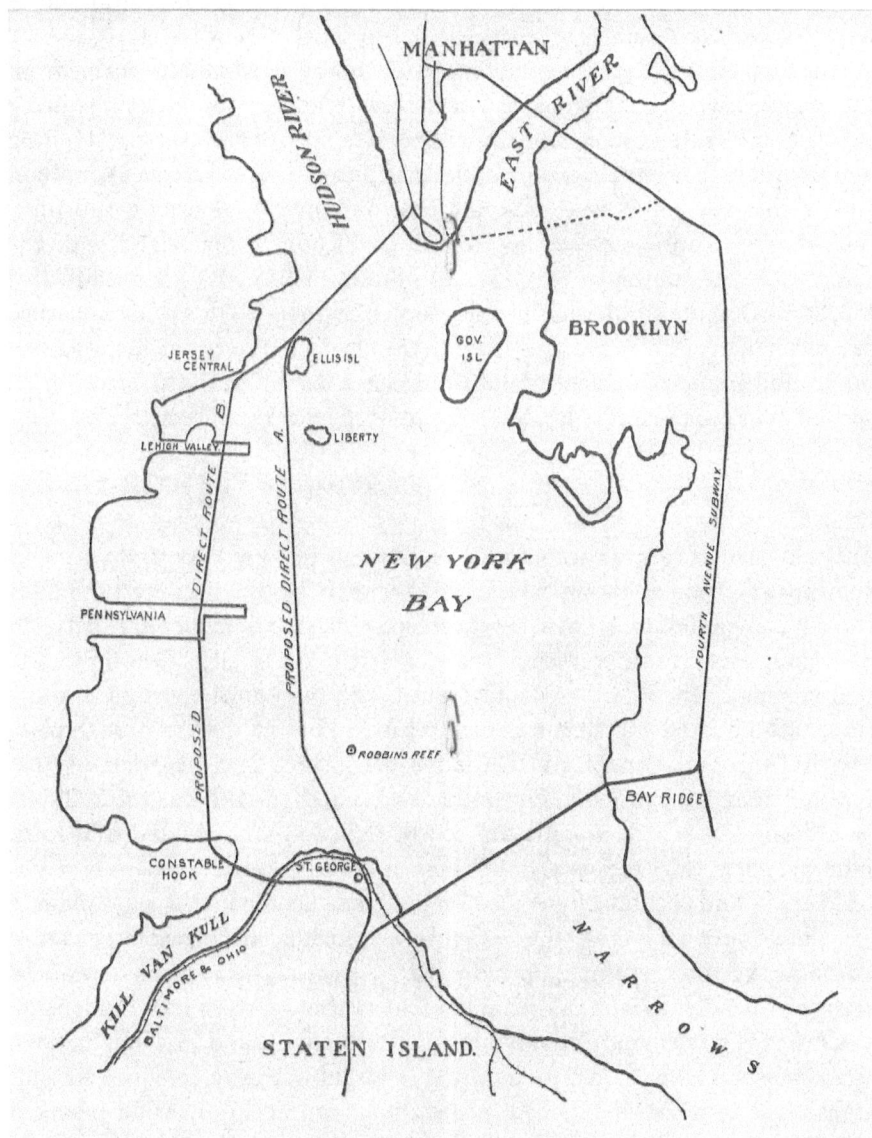

5.2 A direct route to and through Staten Island

The campaign for a direct subway from Manhattan "to and through" Staten Island developed in the wake of the failure to garner a line in the Dual Contracts. Proponents considered two possible routes under the western part of Upper New York Bay and rejected the more circuitous route to and through Brooklyn.

Source: Courtesy of Collection of the Staten Island Museum.

movement split over whether it should maintain a direct-to-Manhattan stance or reconsider compromise routes through Brooklyn or New Jersey.

The final blow to the campaign for a direct tunnel to Manhattan came from the experts. In 1920, the fledgling Transit Construction Commission issued a report that identified six possible subway routes from Staten Island.[119] Finding a direct route to Manhattan unfeasible, the commission selected a $25 million tunnel that reached Brooklyn as the best option: an 8,600-foot, two-tube, dual-purpose tunnel connecting Tompkinsville on Staten Island with the Fourth Avenue subway at Sixty-Seventh Street in Brooklyn. Ironically, this location was quite similar to the one adopted by the PSC in 1912 as a possible extension of the BRT's routes awarded in the Dual Contracts.[120] Having gained no ground since 1913, Staten Island would have to wait until the 1920s for its second major opportunity to obtain the coveted Narrows subway tunnel.

* * *

The year 1911 was a momentous one for subways in New York. It began with subway expansion at an impasse, stalled for years by the disinterest of rapid-transit companies in building unprofitable lines, the squabbling between Tammany and reform politicians (particularly over the city's debt limit), the replacement of the Board of Rapid Transit with the Public Service Commission, and the rapid-transit companies' refusal to bid on the Triborough plan. The IRT's submission of an alternative proposal led to negotiations that resulted in the June proposal for contracts with both the IRT and the BRT. The Dual Contracts, which would ultimately be signed in 1913, would double track mileage, triple rider capacity, build lines in both densely and sparsely populated areas, and cost the city and two rapid-transit companies $366 million.[121] The construction of these lines would—as Morton Smith had predicted—consume the city's resources for more than a decade. Their completion would transform its demographics—bringing tens of thousands of new residents to the Bronx, Queens, and Brooklyn but not to Staten Island. Although Staten Island was not entirely forgotten during these subway developments, a rapid-transit line to it was mentioned in the Dual Contracts only as an intended extension to be completed in an indeterminate future.

A number of factors account for Staten Island's exclusion. The involvement of private businesses generated more borrowing capacity for new lines but posed formidable barriers as well, from the PRR's behind-the-scenes machinations to the BRT's overt reluctance to operate an unprofitable line. Among Staten Islanders, George Cromwell failed to make the most of his advantageous position on the Board of Estimate's Transit Committee, and civic leaders continued to squabble. Staten Islanders navigated differences in social class embedded in institutional affiliation and dissension over goals and tactics: a

Forty-Second or Sixty-Fifth Street terminus? Raise a clamor or quietly exert influence? Hold out for a direct line to Manhattan or settle for an indirect route through Brooklyn? In short, because the economics of a Staten Island line were unsound, the politics of subway expansion to the island would have needed to be flawless to have a chance, and it was not. Unable to resolve these dilemmas, several key players and constituencies grasped at a possibility that ultimately proved to be a costly distraction—the prospect of a joint passenger- and-freight tunnel under the Narrows that also connected the Croton Aqueduct water system to Staten Island. Although this chimera was halfheartedly pursued in 1912, the final negotiations among the PSC, the Board of Estimate, and the IRT and BRT made little mention of Staten Island, and the Dual Contracts were signed in March 1913.

Historians of the New York subway posit that the Dual Contracts are what shaped the New York of the twentieth century. More than the first subway line that opened in 1904 or the independent lines built in the 1920s and 1930s, the hundreds of miles of track built through the Dual Contracts included new lines to underdeveloped areas of the Bronx, Brooklyn, and Queens. By 1917, the city was even formulating plans for some supplementary extensions, but still not the one to Staten Island.[122] The omission cemented Staten Island's physical isolation from the other boroughs for decades to come. This exclusion contributed to its eventual cultural, political, and demographic distinctiveness from the rest of New York.

CHAPTER 6

PLANNING THE REGION

The Hylan Tunnel and the Politics of Commerce, 1920–1922

Don't try to ride two horses at once.

—John Hylan to James S. Graham, 1922

When Mayor John Hylan chided James S. Graham, a civic leader and real estate developer in Brooklyn who owned extensive properties on Staten Island, at a meeting of the Board of Estimate in June 1922, he successfully quelled an effort to induce his administration to cooperate with the state's Transit Commission on a Narrows tunnel. Hylan did not like the Transit Commission, the state organ responsible for subway building in New York City that had replaced the short-lived Transit Construction Commission the previous year. Nor did he approve of George McAneny, the person most responsible for the Dual Contracts and now serving as the commission's chairman. He also distrusted the recently created Port of New York Authority, which he rightly viewed as a serious threat to the city's autonomy. He reviled the Citizens Union, the prominent Manhattan civic organization that was vocal and active on a number of public issues, including a Narrows tunnel. He expected Matthew Cahill, Staten Island's newly elected Democratic borough president, to work solely with the Hylan administration to achieve his Staten Island constituents' long-standing aspirations for a rail link to the rest of the city. As that one testy exchange at a

Board of Estimate meeting suggests, acquiring a Narrows tunnel required Staten Islanders to navigate among competing political interests and cultures that were especially exposed during the early 1920s.

The Borough of Richmond could not escape the central fault lines of governance in early twentieth-century New York. How to characterize those lines has fascinated historians for nearly a century. Contemporaries of that era articulated a divide between political machines with a localist bent and reformers with a more cosmopolitan vision.[1] Urban political campaigns, including those on Staten Island, did in fact often pit a machine Democrat against a Fusion candidate who cobbled together a coalition of Republicans and independent Democrats.[2] Some of the earliest histories written about that era shared the reformers' assumptions and vilified the political machines, an orientation that long held sway.[3] A subsequent generation of scholars reevaluated this pitting of fraudulence against efficiency and found much that was democratic in the "corrupt" urban machines and much that was elitist in the "efficient" social reformers.[4] Over the past few decades, many historians have applied to the city underlying frameworks that sideline or contextualize the politics of urban reform—particularly around the built environment—and find commonalities between supposedly disparate political groups.[5] Recent works of urban history continue to grapple with how to frame efforts—from those by city planner Ed Logue to those by small businessmen in Queens—to shape a city's physical footprint.[6]

In the early years of the twenty-first century, Keith Revell offered an especially fine depiction of urban political conflict over New York's built environment. Revell found on one side both political bosses and corporate leaders blinded by their own parochial self-interest and on the other side a group of technical experts who worked against these two groups and brought their "civic culture of expertise" to bear on the infrastructure problems that linked all New Yorkers. Coming from fields such as economics, engineering, and public health, these experts understood that the modern metropolis produced interconnectedness among its many entities and localities. They looked to formulate centralized and comprehensive solutions to problems such as hauling freight, transporting water, constructing buildings, and moving passengers.[7]

New York in the early twentieth century is too easily straitjacketed in the reform/machine dichotomy. Hylan, who stridently promoted a Narrows tunnel project during his two terms (1917–1925) as mayor, is typically portrayed as a classic career politician beholden to Tammany Hall and unable see beyond political calculations and personal vendettas. New entities established over his opposition (e.g., the Port of New York Authority in 1921) or around his indifference (e.g., the Regional Plan Association in 1922) stood for the cult of the expert.[8] This depiction frames much that is true about New York transportation politics in the first third of the twentieth century yet also obscures it. The limitations of this overall picture become especially clear when examining Staten Islanders' failed efforts to obtain a tunnel to Brooklyn. Many of Richmond Borough's leading citizens obtained positions in the world of business and social science that fostered in them a cosmopolitan vision for their island, an appreciation for the technical expertise that could best help them realize it, and a disdain for the obstructionist local Democratic machine. The episode of failure related here—one that was nearly as significant and more telling than the earlier exclusion from the Dual Contracts—is in part a story of the limitations of expertise when matched against economic and geographic interest. What happens when expert decisions undermine corporate well-being or go against a locality? The culture of expertise was often only skin deep. Lurking inside many Staten Island reformers was a civic booster unwilling to accept the judgment of the experts when their findings appeared beholden to a large company and came at the expense of the reformers' home.

Four strands of thought and action are interwoven through this chapter. First are the tunnel strategies followed by Staten Islanders that eventually coalesced around Hylan's project: a freight-and-passenger tunnel under the Narrows between Staten Island and Brooklyn. Second is the Hylan administration's agenda to resist the power of the "traction" companies and experts and to preserve the city's home rule from the intrusions of New York State and later of the bistate Port of New York Authority. Third are the actions of the railroads, embodied by the gargantuan Pennsylvania Railroad, who were wary and divided over the prospect of market intrusions by public entities. Fourth are the efforts of the Transit Commission and the Port Authority. These organizations saw Staten Island as part of a larger social and economic organism, but the prominence they gave it varied considerably. Although it is tempting to posit the first three strands as the embodiment of traditional—and arguably dysfunctional—politics and the last one as the haven for civic expertise, the narrative that follows reveals a more complex story. Many of the tensions between these disparate orientations existed within single organizations as well as among separate ones. Tracing the interactions of these discrete yet intertwined entities further reveals the complicated plight of Staten Island.

1921: A Year of Momentous Legislation

In January 1921, Nathan Miller became governor of New York as part of a Republican landslide in the 1920 elections at the federal and state level. Having defeated the incumbent Al Smith, he would serve only two years before Smith won a rematch. Despite the short duration of his administration, Miller and the Republican majorities in the state legislature had a profound impact on transportation in New York City. Governor Smith and Mayor Hylan had very different governing styles and priorities but were at least nominally attached as mutual products of the Tammany political organization. Miller had no such connection and in 1921 pushed through legislation that blocked Hylan's effort to establish greater municipal control over rapid-transit development. Miller also revamped the institutional bodies that held authority over the city and supported New York and New Jersey's ongoing attempt to create a regional authority designed to improve the commercial features of the bistate port area. At the same time, though, he inadvertently undermined these efforts by signing legislation that the Hylan administration would use as the basis for its efforts to tunnel under the Narrows. By the end of April 1921, what a contemporary observer called "one of the most remarkable sessions of the New York legislature in the history of the state" had produced three different acts of legislation creating or enabling three distinct entities—all with transportation plans that included or affected Staten Island.[9] Staten Islanders strove to shape all of these legislative outcomes, but once these laws took effect, the islanders found themselves constrained by their impact.

The incoming governor made New York City subway construction and regulation an early legislative priority. Looking to undo the oversight structure of his Democratic predecessor, Miller proposed establishing a new commission that would consolidate and expand the powers of the existing Public Service Commission and replace the Transit Construction Commission with the Transit Commission. The enabling Knight-Adler bill generated much conflict as it wound its way through the legislative process. Vociferously opposed by the Hylan administration, Democratic legislators, and many New York City Republicans for diminishing the home rule of New York City, the terms of the bill ironically grew more unfavorable to New York City as it underwent amendment.[10]

Passing both legislative bodies handily and signed by Governor Miller on March 30, the final bill created the three-member Transit Commission for New York City. The legislature transferred the powers of the Public Service Commission and the Transit Construction Commission to this new entity, and Miller appointed McAneny to chair it.[11] While the Hylan administration mustered a legal challenge to the law (a challenge that would ultimately fail), the new commissioners began to formulate plans for rapid-transit expansion in New York. Their work was soon complemented by a second public entity created by legislation passed in the spring of 1921: the Port of New York Authority.[12]

The establishment of the Port Authority represented the legislative culmination of several years of effort by reformers to maneuver around the debilitating government structures, economic competition, and political culture that made tackling regional issues almost impossible. The idea for a bistate commission substantially insulated from local and state politics and with jurisdiction over the entire port area of metropolitan New York predated Miller's election. With the Chamber of Commerce of New York and its counsel, Julius Henry Cohen, leading the drive, in 1917 the two states established the New York–New Jersey Port and Harbor Development Commission.[13] The report that the new commission issued in 1918 recommended a port entity with considerable responsibility and independence from local municipalities. Facing vocal opposition from Hylan and other New York City officials, the proposal stumbled in the legislatures of both states over the next couple of years.[14]

The passage of bills in both states in early 1921, however, was well assured in light of the Republican landslide of 1920. In this new political landscape, the recalcitrance of local New York City politicians, including Staten Island Borough president Calvin Van Name, actually led to a bill less favorable than the previously rejected version. Legislative bodies in both states passed the bill, and when parties gathered for an elaborate signing ceremony in late April, Hylan, Van Name, and other New York City officials were conspicuously absent. As Jameson Doig observes, "The formal political insulation provided in Cohen's early draft still survived" but with so many powers diminished or eliminated in the final legislation that some thought the new Port Authority to be "a toothless giant."[15] A third piece of legislation unintentionally provided the Hylan administration with the opportunity to test that proposition.

Staten Island's representatives periodically promoted largely symbolic bills to authorize a rapid-transit tunnel. An effort in early 1920 regarding a freight-and-passenger tunnel between Manhattan and Staten Island died quietly but contained three noteworthy features.[16] First, the selection of Manhattan as a terminus reflected the lingering dissension in Richmond over location. Second, its allowance of New York City to build and run the line appealed to Hylan's ambition for municipal ownership of rapid transit. Third, its justification as a means "to maintain the supremacy of the Port of New York" portended a contentious future in light of the concomitant effort to establish the Port Authority.[17] A similar bill was introduced in the Assembly the following year but died in committee when a competing bill from the Senate won favor.[18] Introduced by Senator C. Ernest Smith, a Republican from Staten Island serving his only term in the Senate, the bill in 1921 authorized the Board of Estimate to lease the tunnel to a private entity to operate rather than allow the city to manage the tunnel. With these more palatable terms for a Republican-dominated legislature, the bill soared through both houses with strong votes and little opposition.[19]

One clause of the bill, however, posed a potential snag. The bill more than authorized the construction of a Narrows tunnel; it required the city of New York to build it. This mandate and the absence of a requirement for municipal operation were expected to dissuade Hylan, and home-rule procedures required his approval. Samuel Rea, president of the PRR, believed that legislators had passed the bill in confidence that Hylan would veto it. Hylan did not because he sensed an opportunity for him to pursue an autonomous course for the city. The mayor was also influenced by the large sums the city had recently committed to build public piers on Staten Island that would need railroad access (see figure 6.1).[20]

Governor Miller's support was also uncertain, and threats to the bill circulated Albany. The incipient Transit Commission reportedly looked to reduce the authority granted by the bill to the city's Board of Estimate. The New York–New Jersey Port and Harbor Development Commission, precursor to the Port Authority, rejected the freight function as an impingement on its domain.[21] Ignoring this opposition and his previous clashes with Hylan, Governor Miller signed the bill into law. Staten Islanders rejoiced, but Miller would come to regret the decision. The governor mistakenly viewed the matter as a Staten Island initiative and not a mayoral one. He wrongly assumed that "such a tunnel must necessarily be a part of any comprehensive plan for the development of the port" without interfering with the fledgling Port Authority.[22] Although Miller knew that the bill was imperfect—Rea thought it "a very

6.1 Aerial view of the Stapleton Piers, 1922

The city's new municipal piers at Stapleton on Staten Island were adjacent to an existing B&O freight yard at St. George. They were envisioned as part of a transportation network that would move goods through Mayor Hylan's Narrows tunnel to a proposed port facility at Jamaica Bay. Without the tunnel, however, the piers became an albatross, symbolic of the unprincipled expenditures of the Hylan administration.

Source: Courtesy of Collection of the Staten Island Museum.

crude piece of legislation"—he hoped it would spur a study that would allow an improved bill to be passed in the future.[23]

Staten Islanders, however, quickly used the existing legislation to reignite their long-standing aspirations for a tunnel. Rather than perfect the law and thus risk its demise, proponents urged immediate action by the Board of Estimate to appropriate money and to start the project before the next legislative session. Even before the bill was signed, hundreds of interested Staten Islanders, representatives from the major island civic organizations, and leading businessmen met on April 15 to resuscitate an island-wide committee to bring the subway to Richmond Borough. Speaking to those gathered, Van Name identified the key upcoming task: to get the Board of Estimate to appropriate funds for the project (see figure 6.2).[24] Staten Islanders once again found allies among Brooklyn commercial interests that sought to make their borough a major center for the transport of goods (see figure 6.3).

More significantly, Mayor Hylan also leaped at the opportunity the Smith Act presented. Vehemently opposed to the function of the Port Authority and the Transit Commission and denied injunctions against them by the courts, Hylan looked to use the legislative mandate for a Narrows tunnel to circumvent each entity. He treated the law as a two-year window of opportunity and rushed to begin work on the project. To spearhead the city's efforts, he appointed a special committee chaired by Arthur S. Tuttle, chief engineer of the Board of Estimate. The committee's task was to consult with representatives of the major railroad companies about their interest in developing, financing, and using railroad lines to reach the planned Stapleton piers and the Narrows tunnel, which the city itself would undertake to build. The city needed the trunk lines to use the tunnel to move freight in order to comply with the law, which required that the interest on the bonds issued to finance construction be covered through fees paid by the railroads.[25] The special committee soon recognized that in order to negotiate with the railroads effectively, it needed to have definitive plans and precise cost estimates for the project. As Tuttle assembled a staff, he recruited a prize appointee—William J. Wilgus as consulting engineer.[26]

Wilgus well embodied the cohort of professional expertise that had emerged in the early twentieth century. One of the better-known engineers of his day, he had established his reputation as an engineer and then executive at the New York Central and Hudson River Railroad. After overseeing the construction of Grand Central Terminal, he had set up his own consulting practice in 1907 and worked in France for General Pershing during World War I. Somewhat of an anomaly as a private-sector engineer with a vision for comprehensive planning, Wilgus was uniquely qualified for the task of preparing a public venture that depended on corporate participation. He was intimately involved with determining the specifications for the Narrows tunnel as

CITY NEW YORK
PRESIDENT OF THE BOROUGH OF RICHMOND
BOROUGH HALL, STATEN ISLAND

CALVIN D. VAN NAME
PRESIDENT OF THE BOROUGH

April 28, 1919.

Dear Sir:

There is enclosed to you herewith a printed copy of the written request, dated January 3, 1919, made by me to the Board of Estimate and Apportionment for a Staten Island subway and tunnel. It contains reasons why the Mayor and other city officials, who have charge of the matter, should grant the request and appropriate the funds necessary.

Let me urge every Staten Islander to study the arguments contained in the request, make himself thoroughly acquainted with the subject, and force the same by interviews and letters upon all acquaintances and people in authority in other boroughs.

Now is the time for the greatest activity, and no one should be idle in this matter which is so important to our welfare.

I feel safe in assuring you of success if the support is forcefully given to the movement.

Yours very truly,

CALVIN D. VAN NAME,
President of the
Borough of Richmond.

6.2 Calvin Van Name's appeal to Staten Islanders

Like George Cromwell before him, Richmond Borough president Calvin Van Name sought in vain to bring a subway to Staten Island. In office since 1915, Van Name repeatedly tried to galvanize his constituents and sway his colleagues to act on behalf of a Narrows tunnel. Van Name opted not to seek reelection in 1921 even as tensions heated up between the Hylan administration and the two new entities with which it had to contend: the Transit Commission and the Port of New York Authority.

Source: Courtesy of Collection of the Staten Island Museum.

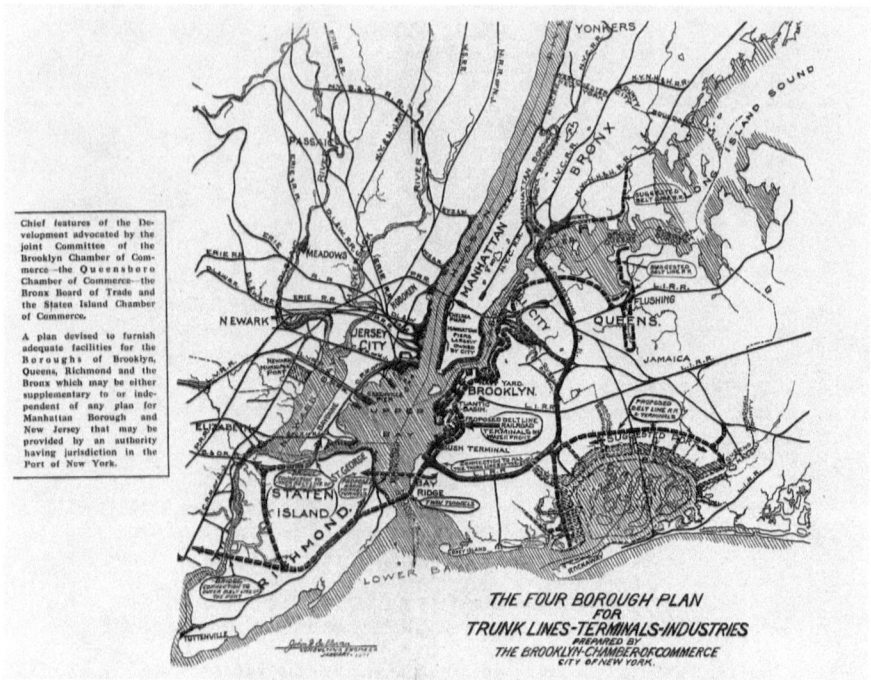

6.3 The Brooklyn Chamber of Commerce's Four Borough Plan, 1921

Staten Islanders sometimes found allies among business interests in Brooklyn and Queens that would also benefit from traffic diverted from Manhattan by a Narrows crossing. Wary of the fledgling Port of New York Authority's plans, the Brooklyn Chamber of Commerce favored the Hylan tunnel for its contribution to the borough's capacity to move freight and help develop Jamaica Bay as a port for the city. It also thought a separate rapid-transit line connected to the Fourth Avenue subway was still feasible. Its support proved to be fickle after the Port of New York Authority proposed an alternative route for a tunnel to Brooklyn.

Source: Courtesy of New York City Hall Library.

well as with the salesmanship it still required.[27] He was also a vocal spokesman for the commercial development of Richmond Borough.[28]

It was not Wilgus's championing of Richmond Borough that won him the gig as consulting engineer but rather his long-standing advocacy of an outer belt rail line for the metropolitan region. Animated by the same conditions of congestion and inefficiency that spurred the creation of the Port Authority, Wilgus had for many years promoted the formation of a series of rail lines that looped through New Jersey, crossed into New York, and, most importantly because the city currently relied on barges to transport goods across the harbor, reached Long Island (whose western part formed Brooklyn and Queens Boroughs).[29] Wilgus did not share Hylan's antipathy for the Port Authority because he was an early proponent of a bistate organization to address matters of the harbor, but he too was immediately intrigued by the possibilities for comprehensive planning created by the Smith law.[30] Over the next nine months, Tuttle looked to Wilgus to help make the public case to engineers, politicians, and reporters for almost all aspects of the Narrows tunnel proposal, and Wilgus did so with great energy.

Tuttle's committee met with the railroads serving the metropolitan area during the summer and fall of 1921. At an initial meeting hosted by Hylan, the railroad presidents insisted that the engineering details be worked out before any pact to use the tunnel could be made but agreed to assign their own engineers to consult separately with Tuttle and his staff.[31] From the outset, many railroad engineers and executives doubted the economic viability of the project and its likely components. The companies operating farther away from Staten Island, such as the New York Central, had never before contemplated a Narrows tunnel and had difficulty imagining how it would serve their interests. Representatives of closer railroad lines still had their freight terminals in New Jersey across from Lower Manhattan (see figure 6.4). Although they conceded that building a tunnel was technically feasible and conceivably useful, they questioned whether the current volume of freight traffic justified building one at the present time, let alone one that went from Staten Island to Brooklyn. Wilgus's tentative route for an outer belt line also met with little enthusiasm, and some disputed the need for one at all.[32]

PRR officials' misgivings were especially damning. As the largest and most prominent of the railroad companies, the PRR was renowned for tunneling under the Hudson and constructing its magnificent railroad station in Manhattan. Tuttle's committee especially courted its support because the PRR also owned the Long Island Railroad Company outright and previously had a controlling majority on the board of the B&O.[33] Unfortunately for the city, the PRR's representatives set a tone of skepticism, dominating the meetings of both railroad executives and engineers.[34]

At a meeting in August 1921, PRR's president Samuel Rea verbally sparred with Wilgus over an outer belt line. He then shared his doubts about the demand for a Narrows tunnel:

> Well, of course, I have realized for a long time that there will have to be a tunnel. We counted ourselves on building one from Greenville [New Jersey] to Bay Ridge. I do not feel that traffic would justify that for some years to come. That is, of course, a more direct route for us. This [the Greenville tunnel] would take the place of that [the Narrows] tunnel. I don't know whether there is enough business in sight to warrant it today. The last time I figured it, as far

118 A SUBWAY FOR GROWTH

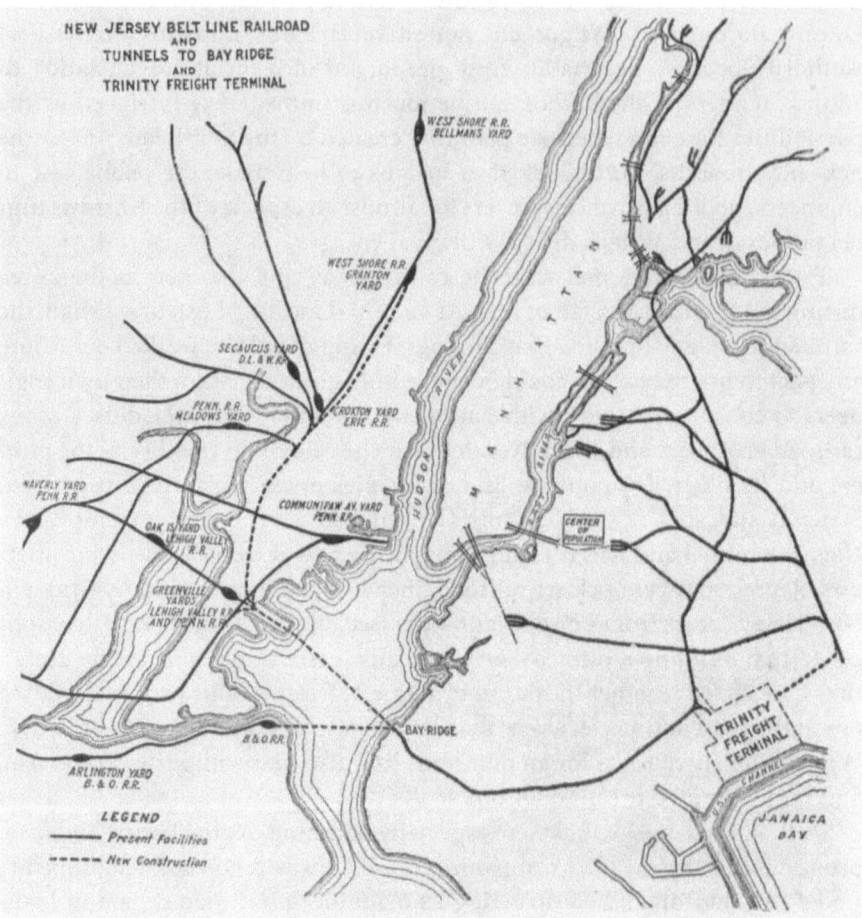

6.4 Freight terminals of the major railroad companies

The Hylan tunnel proposal could never overcome the reality that most of the major trunk lines terminated in Jersey City across from Lower Manhattan. Only the B&O sent its freight through Staten Island.

Source: John H. Ward, "The Trinity of Freight and the Port of New York," in *Port of New York Annual*, ed. Alexander R. Smith (New York: Smith's Port Publishing, 1920), 463. Courtesy of University of Michigan Library.

as our own business is concerned, it wasn't justified. Now, this [Narrows] is a more expensive tunnel.[35]

Given the distances involved for each tunnel, Rea's assessment of costs would not likely withstand scrutiny. Rea was more circumspect regarding his technical concerns about a Narrows tunnel, but they were also considerable.

He drew on the evaluation of one of the PRR's leading experts, Assistant Chief Engineer E. B. Temple, who was equally unenthusiastic about the project from the start. To reduce the gradation necessary, Tuttle's inclination was to locate a Narrows tunnel "as far north as possible," which made it impossible to run the line directly to the Stapleton piers. He observed that a route to Brooklyn through Staten Island, the tunnel's most suitable location, would force the PRR to run more yards, change its usage of current facilities, create an extra route for it to maintain, and in general undermine its recent investment in facilities at Greenville, today the southern part of Jersey City.[36] Temple headed the subcommittee of engineers that drafted a report on the Narrows tunnel, a role that did not augur well for the city's plans.

Also troubling for city officials and Staten Islanders, the B&O never mustered much enthusiasm for the project. City officials, Staten Islanders, and even some other railroads had identified the B&O, with its decades-long history of moving freight over its Arthur Kill Bridge and along the north shore of Staten Island, as a likely supporter of a Narrows tunnel among the trunk lines.[37] When the B&O was freed from PRR's control over it through new placements on its board of directors, Staten Islanders hoped it would chart a more independent course of action, but the railroad nonetheless largely deferred to the PRR's leadership and did not incline the other railroads to support a Narrows tunnel.[38]

Tuttle and his team of engineers began drawing plans for a Narrows tunnel with additional infrastructure in the hopes of assuaging the doubters. Their preliminary report of October 1921 recommended a Narrows tunnel with two tubes, a large rail yard in the center of Richmond Borough, a belt railway that cut across the island, and a new railroad bridge over the Arthur Kill that would connect with an outer belt line in New Jersey from Metuchen to Haworth. The plan included two possible routes for the Narrows tunnel—a northern one from Brooklyn's Owls Head Park to Arietta Street and a southern one from a rail depot in Brooklyn to Maryland Avenue (see figure 6.5). The maximum total cost for the project was placed at $141 million, including a $51 million price tag for the tunnel itself.[39]

The report found favor within the Board of Estimate but less so on Staten Island as its content indicated an important shift in the orientation of the project. The discussions between the city and railroad companies had led Tuttle to alter the intended balance between freight and passenger traffic. Initially, Staten Islanders' conception of a dual-purpose tunnel tended to subordinate freight to the needs of passengers. Since the Dual Contracts, they had envisioned a tunnel serving both freight and passengers but viewed the transport of goods largely as a necessary feature to garner wider support for financing and constructing a passenger tunnel. They saw the Smith bill primarily as an opportunity for Staten Island to be linked to New York's rapid-transit system

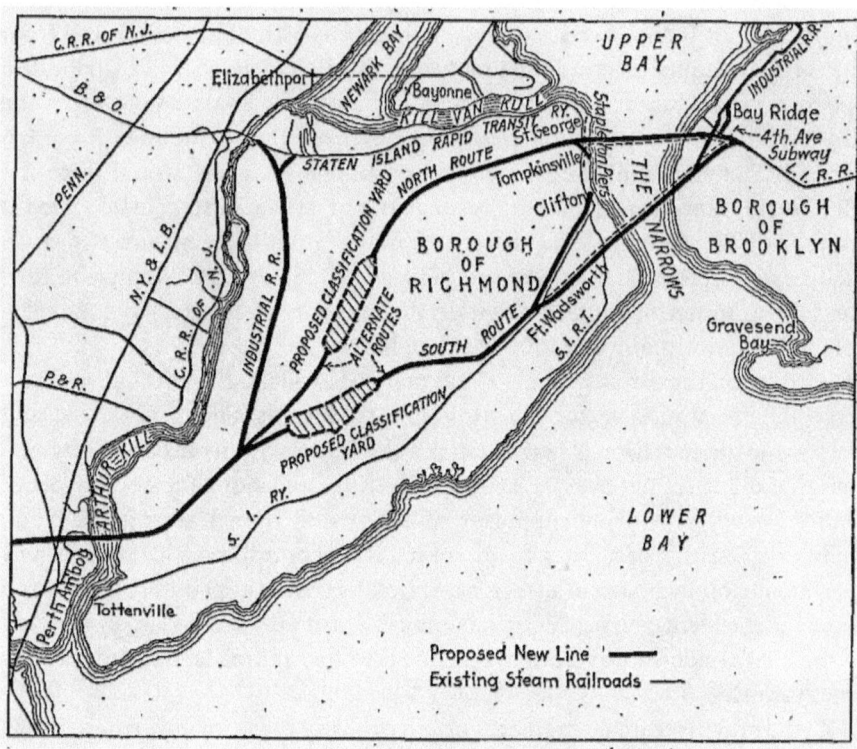

6.5 Two routes under consideration for the Hylan Narrows tunnel

Like Brooklynites, Staten Islanders thought the Hylan tunnel would necessitate new rail lines and transfer facilities in their borough, regardless of whether the northern or southern route were selected.

Source: "Brooklyn–Richmond Freight and Passenger Tunnel," *Railway Age* 70, no. 18 (October 29, 1921): 836. Courtesy of Indiana State University Library.

and assumed that a Narrows tunnel would connect to the Fourth Avenue subway. Some Civic League members even took exception to the inclusion of any freight function.[40]

The city's tunnel subcommittee promoted just the opposite. Tuttle and Wilgus were predisposed to address the larger concerns of the port and grappling with the railroads' reluctance and so focused on preparing a Narrows tunnel to carry freight to an outer belt line. Wilgus argued that such an inclusion was crucial to the success of the project "so as to bring the tunnel a volume of traffic which would justify the expenditure of so much capital on what would otherwise be indefensible."[41] In fact, the city engineers were highly confident that a Narrows tunnel linked to a substantial network of railroads would see heavy use. Tuttle had recommended two separate tubes because he thought the high volume of traffic would preclude the use of the same ones for both freight and passenger service.[42] The subcommittee endorsed the development of new trunk lines to accommodate the anticipated traffic that existing routes were unable to handle. These determinations indicated how the committee had expanded its purview to include "the proper solution of the Port of New York problem."[43] Its report was almost entirely devoted to an economic analysis of the use of the tunnel to transport goods through the region; it hardly mentioned the features for passengers.

The most glaring political problem with defining the project so broadly was that it intruded on the domain of the Port Authority. The authority's precursor, the New York–New Jersey Port and Harbor Development Commission, had preferred a freight tunnel under New York Harbor connecting New Jersey with Bay Ridge, Brooklyn, to a Narrows tunnel linked to tracks spanning the Kill Van Kull. The former route would serve the interests of the PRR and other trunk lines with terminals across from lower Manhattan (see figure 6.6).[44] Adhering to its mandate to address the movement of freight through the port of New York, the Port Authority consulted with railroad executives and engineers at the same time that Tuttle's group did.[45] As Port Authority transportation experts prepared their Comprehensive Plan for the Development of the Port District, they, too, considered a continuous railroad belt line and a harbor crossing going west from Brooklyn as essential items for the port.[46]

Staten Island's leading residents attempted to forestall Port Authority officials from making the same recommendation as its predecessor. The Civic League wrote to Port Authority officials and potential allies from other boroughs. A SICC delegation met with Port Authority officials to promote a route under the Narrows, and Cornelius Kolff brought Eugenius Outerbridge, chairman of the Port Authority and "a former prominent Staten Islander," to speak in Port Richmond, where he highlighted the potential growth of Staten Island through its new piers, a proper waterfront railroad line, and a "large trunk line connecting with all railroads."[47] As for the city's Narrows tunnel, Outerbridge explained that it would not be included in the Port Authority's still forthcoming bistate plan and chided the Board of Estimate for not broaching the Narrows tunnel issue with the Port Authority.[48] Although Cohen believed "a very cordial entente" developed with the SICC members, Outerbridge left dissatisfied with the lack of frank discussion and saw a missed opportunity. He was likely correct as the pending omission of the Narrows tunnel generated rumors across Staten Island that the Port Authority favored the repeal of the legislative authorization of the Narrows tunnel.[49]

By the time the Port Authority released its Comprehensive Plan on December 31, 1921, the details were well known. The centerpiece was a sixty-mile middle belt line, which formed a giant U by using mostly existing rail lines in the Bronx, Long Island, and New Jersey and connecting them with a new five-mile

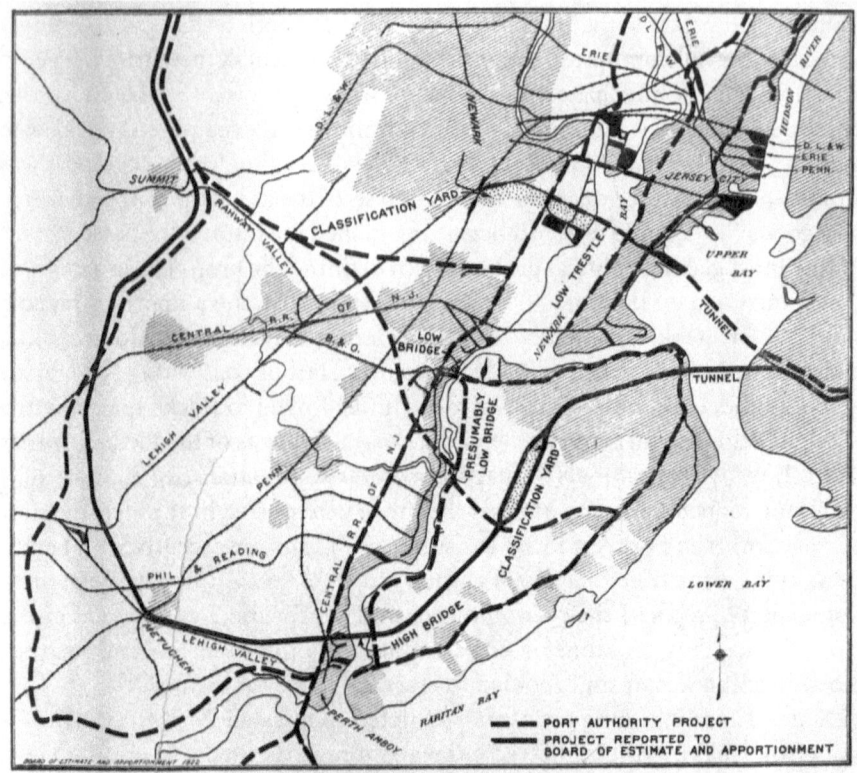

6.6 A comparison of the Port Authority and Hylan administration tunnel proposals, 1922

The key difference between the plans of the City of New York and the Port Authority lay in the proposed means of connecting rail lines between New Jersey and Brooklyn. Adopting the recommendation of the Pennsylvania Railroad, the Port Authority looked to tunnel under New York Harbor directly from Greenville, New Jersey, to Brooklyn. Seeking to preempt the incipient authority's role in harbor development, the city sought to move freight and passengers from New Jersey through Staten Island and under the Narrows to Brooklyn.

Source: New York Board of Estimate and Apportionment, *Progress Report of a Special Committee Consisting of the Chief Engineer of the Board of Estimate and Apportionment, the Commissioner of Docks, the Commissioner of Plant and Structures, and the Engineer of the Borough of Richmond, Concerning the Negotiations with the Trunk Line Railroad Companies with Respect to the Brooklyn-Richmond Freight and Passenger Tunnel Project and the Elements of Difference Between the Narrows Tunnel and Port Authority Plans* (New York: M. Brown Printing and Binding, 1922), 63. Courtesy of Yale University Library.

line tunneling under Upper New York Bay from Greenville, New Jersey, to Bay Ridge, Brooklyn. In addition, there would be inner and outer belt lines in New Jersey, two rail tunnels under the Hudson to Manhattan for electrified rail cars, and twelve terminals for freight. The Port Authority intended to change fundamentally the way commodities moved across these rail lines, so that the twelve major area railroads would operate more harmoniously, and goods would reach their destination more efficiently. Staten Island would be connected to this middle belt line through preexisting tracks from Greenville to Newark to Elizabeth, where the B&O line crossed over the Arthur Kill. The line would be extended to the new city piers being constructed at Stapleton "and to a connection, if the city of New York consent thereto, with the tunnel under the Narrows to Brooklyn provided for under legislation as a municipal project." The existing lines of the Staten Island Rapid Transit Railway Company would be a part of the belt, as would a new line on the west shore that connected with both the middle belt line and, by way of a new rail bridge over the Arthur Kill, the outer belt line.[50]

The reaction to the Port Authority's plan on Staten Island was largely one of outrage, Outerbridge's efforts notwithstanding. The most obvious sore spot was the selection of a tunnel route to Brooklyn that bypassed the island, but there was an overall sense of neglect by the Port Authority despite the improvements it slated for Staten Island. Van Name's critical comments were widely reported, and editorials in the *Staten Island Advance* (formerly the *Richmond County Advance*) and *Staten Islander* derided the report. As one member of the Civic League put it, Staten Island's place in the Comprehensive Plan "is so small as to be almost negligible."[51] The Civic League took the lead in marshaling local opposition to the Port Authority by reconstituting its Tunnel Committee. Before a large crowd representing more than one hundred city organizations, the Tunnel Committee's newly appointed chairman, Max Thaten, excoriated the Port Authority for making Staten Island "the back yard instead of the front door of the Port of New York."[52] Local civic boosters such as Thaten still envisioned an economic and demographic boom for Staten Island, which needed the Narrows tunnel, he contended, because the B&O alone could not meet its rail needs.[53]

Staten Islanders found a sympathetic voice in their mayor. Touting the "impracticality and unworkability" of the Port Authority's plan, Hylan lambasted "the disastrous sidetracking of the Borough of Richmond."[54] Having failed to block the formation of the Port Authority, he now placed his administration in direct and vocal opposition to its agenda. With the construction of the Narrows tunnel for freight and passenger traffic as dictated by the Smith law as its primary goal, the Civic League was in accord with the mayor and formally gave its approval of the city's plans to the Board of Estimate. As for the Port Authority, Thaten recognized that it was not likely to abandon its disposition toward the Greenville tunnel, and so he urged a symbolic gesture: the addition of the city's Narrows tunnel to the Port Authority's maps. Outerbridge countered that the Port Authority could not legally add it without cooperation from the city, which was not forthcoming.[55]

Were two tunnels really viable? For Staten Islanders who had lived through two decades of failure stemming from the low financial prospects of a Narrows tunnel, it surely was not difficult to imagine "that the competition of a tunnel from Brooklyn to Greenville, N.J., would make the other [Narrows] tunnel impractical economically."[56] The Civic League likewise assumed that the Greenridge and the Narrows tunnels were simply too pricy for both to be built. Its leaders argued that the latter would easily enable not just the B&O but all of the major trunk lines to move freight into the city. The *Staten Islander* agreed, praising the Civic League and urging it to maintain pressure on the Board of Estimate.[57] The *Advance* counseled against "trying to hitch up a tunnel issue with the plan of the above commission [the Port Authority] . . . [when] the tunnel is a City affair and the Port Authority plan is a bi-State affair. They have nothing to do with each other."[58] The SICC, mindful of the political thicket into which Staten Island was about to plunge, tried hard to reconcile the two divergent tunnel plans. Businessmen in Staten Island (and other outer boroughs) had long recognized the potential perils of bistate collaboration, which might thwart their hopes to develop their own facilities.[59] Now with the Port Authority's Comprehensive Plan, these fears had come to fruition. After Outerbridge gave "assurance that the Port Authority's plans did not in any way interfere with the construction of the tunnel under the Narrows," the SICC passed a resolution of appreciation that stopped short of endorsing the Port Authority's plan but still triggered vocal criticism of the chamber.[60] By the end of 1921, stung by the way its statement had been received locally, the SICC moved closer to the position staked by the Civic League, and the two organizations began to work together through Thaten's Tunnel Committee.[61]

The net result of this subtle but important shift by the SICC was that Staten Island's leading organizations joined together to support the city's efforts to build the Narrows tunnel and to oppose (or alternatively to amend) the Port Authority's Comprehensive Plan. They tried hard to do so without being hostile to the Port Authority, but their alliance with Mayor Hylan made this task more difficult. The alignment with Hylan also tainted Staten Islanders' interactions with the state Transit Commission, newly charged to consider, among other things, Staten Island's rapid-transit connection with its neighbors.

The Transit Commission also commenced its own investigation of subway expansion in 1921. On Staten Island, the commission was met with much suspicion. Not only was its creation designed to curtail the city's autonomy, but now it appeared to be interfering with the Narrows tunnel project already embarked upon by the city.[62] McAneny had once countenanced a freight-and-passenger tunnel, but he rejected it now.[63] At a hearing in December 1921, he committed to bring rapid transit to Staten Island but reported that Transit Commission engineers had concluded that a dual-purpose tunnel was not feasible, and he essentially admitted his intention to ignore the Smith Act: "It is our present purpose to include a passenger tunnel to Staten Island. We are prepared, if the funds are properly available, to go ahead with the construction of such a tunnel. Whether a freight tunnel is built or not, we are not prepared to put our passenger traffic in a freight tunnel."[64] McAneny did tender the possibility that separate freight and passenger tubes placed side by side and constructed together would considerably reduce the expense of both projects. Nevertheless, he recognized that this approach as well as his general commitment to any rapid-transit expansion depended on the "cooperation" of the Hylan administration. The mayor gave every indication that McAneny was not likely to receive it.[65]

The Clash Over Competing Plans

In early 1922, the conflicting approaches of the three distinct entities weighing in on transportation lines for Staten Island came to a head. The exclusive projects championed by the Port Authority and the Transit Commission—for freight and rapid transit, respectively—did not clash, but each posed a direct challenge to the city's intention to move both goods and people through a Narrows tunnel. In fact, the Port Authority and the Transit Commission generally consulted and cooperated with each other, whereas the Hylan administration readily infringed upon the others' areas of purview.[66] An immediate focal point for the struggle between the Hylan administration and the Port Authority was an upcoming legislative hearing on the latter's Comprehensive Plan scheduled for January 31, 1922. The date became an unofficial deadline for the officials and engineers conferring about the Narrows tunnel as Hylan and Tuttle hoped to have a resolution in their favor that would sway the legislators against the Port Authority's plan.

At stake were the interrelated questions of what entity would chart a course for the movement of cargo through metropolitan New York and by what route. The Hylan administration used the Narrows tunnel to try to smother the fledging Port Authority and to ensure that the city—through the development of Staten Island—would retain the bulk of harbor activity. Speaking before the Municipal Engineers of the City of New York in late December 1921, Tuttle and Wilgus made the case for a freight-and-passenger tunnel connecting Brooklyn and Staten Island in a talk titled "The Narrows Tunnel and Its Relation to the Port of New York Problem." Tuttle leveled charges at the Port Authority while he explained how the tunnel would serve the needs of Staten Island residents, enable the use of the city's new piers at Stapleton, and develop the port to the advantage of the entire region. Wilgus related how the project would profit constituents and communities in both states and in all boroughs but concluded by emphasizing its benefit to Richmond Borough. "Finally," he observed, "in turning the arterial flow of commerce through Staten Island, it will change that potentially rich borough from a vermiform appendix to a healthy and prosperous section of Greater New York." Overall, both Tuttle and Wilgus centered their talk on issues of port development and rebutted the criticisms directed at their plans.[67]

One of the most damning critiques of the Narrows tunnel was its dependence on the major railroad corporations' inclination to make use of it. Wilgus dispelled for the engineers the contention that the enabling legislation required companies to lease the Narrows tunnel prior to its construction, but the point was argued repeatedly. Speaking for (though not officially representing) the Port Authority, Nelson Lewis, the long-serving chief engineer of the Board of Estimate, expressed skepticism that the railroad companies would finance the new lines favored by Tuttle and doubted that they would prefer a Staten Island to a Greenville route. Now employed by the Regional Plan of New York and Its Environs, Lewis wondered how the city could construct its planned facilities without the railroads' participation and (responding directly to Wilgus) asserted that the Port Authority and not the city would be the most suitable entity to bridge the Arthur Kill. Although the railroads' stance was not yet publicly known, Wilgus expressed confidence that an endorsement would soon come.[68]

In actuality, Tuttle and Wilgus knew by the end of 1921 that the railroad companies were not likely to participate in the Narrows tunnel venture and that this rejection mattered. The engineers from the twelve main trunk lines had met three times since October, and their evaluation of the project differed sharply from that of Wilgus and Tuttle. In early December, Temple circulated a draft of a report from the railroad engineers that questioned the economic feasibility of the city's plan. The railroads' engineers disputed many of the city's figures, and their revisions indicated that the tunnel would raise costs for their companies. Over the next few weeks, Temple and Wilgus sparred over the details: the current expense of moving freight, the expenditures required to build the additional lines and a bridge (over the Arthur Kill) needed to service the Narrows tunnel, and the future cost of moving goods through it. Wilgus was determined to receive the railroad companies' support and did not hesitate to make bold requests, including the reversal of their conclusion that there was no justification for the tunnel.[69]

The heart of Wilgus's appeal to Temple was neither technical nor quantitative but rather imaginative. Central to his vision was the industrial and commercial potential of Staten Island. Wilgus was confident that the commerce through the Narrows tunnel would eclipse all current estimates. Thus, he lectured Temple that "the railroads should not deal with this matter exclusively from the standpoint of demonstrated tonnage based on existing conditions. All great projects have been launched more or less on the faith of those who believe in their future rather than through pencil and paper demonstrations."[70] Wilgus appeared perplexed that Temple could so easily dismiss his soaring rhetoric by citing examples of projects "built on this faith" that had not become economically viable and by reminding Wilgus that "we as engineers should not try to make a project appear good by depending too much on its future prospects."[71]

At a final meeting with the railroad engineers on January 19, 1922, Tuttle and Wilgus found themselves on the defensive. They endured criticism of the project from nearly every attendee, as even the B&O representatives continued to express little interest in the Narrows tunnel "as a matter of dollars and cents."[72] In the railroads' analysis, building a Narrows tunnel for freight simply would not sufficiently benefit each individual corporation, most of which had built up freight facilities farther north.[73] From that meeting, the denouement was swift as Temple hastened to complete the railroads' Engineering Committee report. The document that emerged on January 26 contained few alterations from the previously circulated draft. Using the report as its basis, the railroad executives rushed to send Mayor Hylan a rejection letter. On January 30, 1922, just one day prior to the hearing in Albany on the Port Authority's Comprehensive Plan, they wrote to Mayor Hylan that they would not participate in the undertaking for a Narrows tunnel, "which ... is not now, nor in the near future, required for the volume of traffic moving."[74] The project was also panned for high cost and circuitous location, which would require many trunk lines to reroute their freight traffic. Finally, in a point that no doubt especially stung Hylan, the railroad executives suggested that the Port Authority's chosen route from Greenville, New Jersey, to Brooklyn would make more sense in the future.[75]

The railroad companies benefited from other vocal opposition to the Narrows tunnel. Governor Miller, who once preferred the Narrows tunnel to one directly from New Jersey to Brooklyn, could not condone Hylan's recalcitrance. He lambasted the city for failing to consult with the Port Authority and Transit Commission regarding its plans and deemed the tunnel's projected cost as excessive.[76] The *New-York Tribune* reprimanded the Board of Estimate for its "obstructive" stance and labeled the Narrows proposal "a wasteful and harmful project, entered into in a spirit of destructive rivalry."[77] The *New York Morning World*, the *Evening Post*, the *New York Times*, the *Brooklyn Times*, and the *Brooklyn Eagle* leveled similar criticisms. Even the Port Authority waded into the fracas. Former governor Al Smith, now serving as one of its commissioners, praised the Comprehensive Plan and rebuked his fellow Tammany Democrat Hylan for pushing the Narrows tunnel project. Outerbridge kept up his public criticism of the city, and the New York Chamber of Commerce produced a pamphlet that shared the accolades by major civic and commercial organizations and editorial pages for the Port Authority's plan.[78]

The Hylan administration countered this barrage as best it could. The mayor held a one-sided Board of Estimate hearing on the Comprehensive Plan on January 26 at which the Port Authority—invited but rejecting the "belated offer"—was lambasted by nearly all who testified. The star witness was Wilgus, who with Tuttle continued to weigh the technical and economic merits of each plan in multiple venues.[79] They both largely missed the crux of the Narrows tunnel condemnation, though a city attorney did not: "The city's plan is no haphazard political guess . . . but is the mature judgment of competent experts."[80]

The dilemma faced by Staten Islanders was clear as they navigated these political thickets. Who were the experts, where lay the powerful interests, and were these labels even meaningful? Ideally, they would straddle differences and urge negotiation and compromise. They would convey their island's need to any audience, as Tribus informed the city's engineers that the Narrows tunnel needed to carry commuters more than move freight.[81] Despite such forthrightness, the discussion at the municipal engineers meeting likely reminded those Staten Islanders in attendance just how precarious their position was. Although they preferred rapid-transit passenger service, Staten Islanders were aligning themselves with a mayoral administration that was focused on moving freight. They were willing to work with the Transit Commission and the Port Authority, but the city engineers' defensiveness illustrated the increasing isolation of the Hylan administration.[82]

On Staten Island, Thaten and the Tunnel Committee planned their own "aggressive campaign" to get the Narrows tunnel built. Leading citizens become more vocal in their criticism of the Port Authority and more active in their lobbying efforts, reaching out to Governor Miller, the Real Estate Board of New York, and other influential individuals and organizations.[83] Initial statements that spoke well of the Port Authority and expressed hope for coordination between it and the city increasingly gave way to indictments of the bistate authority. Thaten, for example, railed against the authority's "poison propaganda, intended to create a public belief that the Island . . . is not adapted for an ocean steamship terminal, or for industrial development."[84] Meanwhile, the Tunnel Committee remained hostile toward the Greenville tunnel despite two other notable concessions made by the Port Authority: the Narrows tunnel was now included on its maps, and a cross-island railroad line had been restored.[85] Staten Islanders were relatively restrained in their objections; Mayor Hylan displayed no such moderation. As the most vocal though not necessarily most effective critic, Hylan regularly and vociferously denounced the Port Authority. Far more charged accusations came from Charles L. Craig, the city's comptroller. He made headlines with the assertion (articulated by some Staten Islanders for months) that the PRR lay behind the Port Authority's Comprehensive Plan. He would repeat this charge at the January 31 hearing in Albany, calling the Port Authority a puppet of outside forces and its Comprehensive Plan "a railroad proposition, pure and simple."[86] Although most aspects of the plan were undermined by the railroad companies' disinterest, Craig was not so far off from the truth regarding the authority's plans for a Greenville tunnel.[87]

Jockeying for Advantage

In the summer and fall of 1921, the PRR exerted itself with the Port Authority and other railroad companies to block the Narrows tunnel venture. President Rea had a cordial relationship with Outerbridge dating back at least several years, and he took a personal interest in the development of the Port Authority's plans.[88] Eager to solicit the railroad presidents' views on the rail lines under consideration, Port Authority officials began meeting with them in June 1921.[89] Rea attempted but failed to get the twelve trunk lines to respond in unison, but he and Temple took the opportunity to lobby for their own company's interest in a Greenville terminus in New Jersey for a tunnel under the bay to Brooklyn. This effort helped block a freight route under the Narrows and persuaded the Port Authority to abandon its initial route under New York Harbor to propose one from Greenville to Bay Ridge.[90]

The PRR also assisted the Port Authority in its contest with Mayor Hylan over the development of the harbor. Its singular contribution was to stall—at Outerbridge's request—the railroads' deliberations about the Narrows proposal until the Port Authority's Comprehensive Plan was completed.[91] The railroad companies took six months to study and formally respond to Tuttle's proposal even though their presidents and chief engineers were disinclined to participate in the Narrows tunnel venture from the outset. In his private correspondence, Rea readily shared his negative views of the Narrows proposal but appeared willing to let the Engineering Committee run its course, confident that it would "no doubt reach [the] proper conclusion."[92] Once it did, Rea made a special effort to communicate the railroad companies' disinterest in the Narrows tunnel venture to Outerbridge in time for the New York State Legislature's hearing on the Port Authority's Comprehensive Plan.[93]

The joint legislative hearing on January 31 contained few surprises but was filled with drama.[94] The hearing was ostensibly about the Meyer-Mastick bill to approve the Port Authority's Comprehensive Plan in its entirety, but contention over the two proposals for tunnels to Brooklyn dominated the testimony. Before a packed chamber, former (and future) governor Al Smith captivated the crowd with a well-received polemic against the city.[95] Many organizations sent delegations to support the Port Authority plan, and Outerbridge appeared on its behalf.[96] Comptroller Craig headed New York City's delegation, Wilgus testified at length, and Thaten spoke for Staten Island.[97] Representing both the Civic League and the SICC, Thaten argued for the substitution of the Narrows tunnel for the Greenville tunnel.[98] When both branches of the legislature finally voted in late February, the outcome was a resounding endorsement of the Port Authority's Comprehensive Plan, Greenville tunnel included.[99] That decision left Staten Islanders doubtful that two tunnels could be built when just one had long eluded the borough.

* * *

When a freight-and-passenger tunnel under the Narrows had entered the public discourse during the Dual Contracts deliberations, it had garnered neither much enthusiasm nor resistance. Ten years later a similar proposal ignited the passions of businessmen and boosters, politicians and professionals. Its politics was particularly complicated by quarreling governing bodies and outlandish personalities in the city and region, all of which bore upon Staten Island's chances for a physical link to the rest of the city. That Mayor Hylan's warning against straddling sides in large part reflected his own intransigence made his assertion no less true. Staten Island's leading citizens made a choice calculated on the probability and pace of a tunnel's potential for construction. In opting for the joint freight-and-passenger tunnel championed by Hylan, they selected the project they deemed most likely to occur expeditiously—a decided contrast to the indefinite pronouncements they had long heard from politicians, including McAneny. They also sided with a mayoral administration that had served their borough well during the Garbage War and with a major appropriation for new piers at Stapleton. In return, Staten Island rewarded Hylan with his highest percentage of voters in the city during his reelection in 1921.[100] The two other potential partners for the island were new and unproven entities that, from the islanders' perspective, proposed unacceptable (the Port Authority) and unsuitable (the Transit Commission) tunnel locations, respectively.

Staten Islanders themselves had shaped Mayor Hylan's thinking on how to tunnel the Narrows. In 1918, before the mayor had publicly committed to a particular route or function, William J. Welsh, president the Richmond Light and Power Company, directly advised the mayor, "You could make this the one big feature of your administration: to bring all of the western stuff right through Staten Island and right into the Boroughs of Manhattan, Brooklyn and the Bronx—three big boroughs with freight traffic direct from the west."[101] Earlier permutations of a multipurpose tunnel had subordinated the movement of goods to the carrying of passengers; the minimal commercial functions were meant to help defray the costs of building the tunnel. Hylan's tunnel inverted this prioritization by privileging freight in the service of port development. When a Staten Island legislator sought to authorize the city to pursue this vision in 1921, neither Mayor Hylan nor the Smith law's supporters on Staten Island would pass up that opportunity.

The speed with which they undertook the tunnel was quite deliberate. A strategy of fait accompli characterized the approach of both the Hylan administration and the Staten Island business and civic organizations. Embroiled in struggles with the nascent Port Authority and the Transit Commission over the development of the harbor and its transportation networks, the city government intended to assert its control over these areas by building its tunnel before these other entities could construct their conflicting projects. Burned by their experience with the Dual Contracts, Staten Islanders wanted to launch the project before the predictable naysayers could muster their anticipated opposition.

Staten Islanders worked hard to move the Hylan tunnel project forward, but in so doing they undermined their prospects for the long-coveted link to Greater New York. In hindsight, it is easy to conclude that in John Hylan they backed the wrong horse, but in the winter of 1922 it was not at all certain that he would ultimately fail to build the Narrows tunnel. What was evident by then were clear signs of the limits on his power: the city's lack of authority to operate any tunnel it built, its inability to persuade the legislature to empower it to do so, and its failure to interest the leading railroad companies in the project. The strongest contemporary criticism of Staten Island's allegiance to the Hylan tunnel lay not in the standard bearer but in the cause. A freight-and-passenger tunnel service may have fit the vision of the island's business and propertied class, but many thought that the island would be better served by a subway tunnel alone. As a former city official questioned, Why would Richmond residents support the city's plan—"a freight tunnel which will carry no passengers except through passengers? Rapid transit is what Staten Island wants."[102] The answer lay in the pragmatism of Staten Islanders eager to get something rather than nothing.

It is hard, however, to overlook the obvious flaws in backing Mayor Hylan. First, although Staten Island's leading citizens were willing to put their trust in his plans, the business and professional elite of Greater New York were far less confident. They had largely voted against Hylan and distrusted his stance on most matters. The *New York Times* tartly summed up Hylan's approach on the tunnel (and nearly every issue) as "obstruct everything, challenge everybody, defy court orders."[103] Second, the mayor greatly desired the major trunk lines to embrace his tunnel, but his record, most obviously his vilification of the traction companies, undermined his negotiations with them. Hylan could not have known the extent of the PRR's sabotage of his tunnel, but the PRR clearly led an industry that was unenthusiastic about the project. Finally, some Staten Islanders were growing frustrated by the city's unwillingness to cooperate and coordinate with the Port Authority and the Transit Commission. Although the former entity showed relatively little interest in Staten Island, the latter under McAneny appeared committed to tunneling to Richmond, yet Hylan would not work with it.

Civic organizations on Staten Island largely cooperated in support of the Hylan tunnel. Navigating the evolving, fragmented, and largely dysfunctional city, state, and region transportation politics, the island's two leading citizens groups bridged their differences and combined efforts to build a freight-and-passenger tunnel to Brooklyn. The island's local public officials—most of them Democrats—worked with civic leaders but followed the lead of Mayor Hylan, who saw a Narrows tunnel as a means of pursuing home rule in transportation and harbor development. With multiple and overlapping governmental structures all at work planning for New York's future transportation needs, the Hylan administration encountered obstacles that it could initially circumvent as it moved toward the state-imposed deadline for the start of construction.

Staten Islanders faced risks no matter where they placed their allegiance. But the story told here of the manner in which Richmond's leading citizens went about trying to obtain a tunnel suggests that these local civic boosters were challenged by the shifting political terrain, which was marked not only by the rise of expertise but by the expanded lens that saw a single region rather than atomized communities and municipalities. The very arguments that tunnel advocates made, such as keeping citizens and taxpayers living and working within the municipal boundaries or building up the shipping possibilities on Staten Island or in Jamaica Bay, went against the more metropolitan vision of other civic and governmental entities. The very methods the advocates used—appealing to the local city politicians more readily than to the state commissioners overseeing New York's transit development—went against the realignment of power in the governance and management of New York City. The very nature of the city's project—one that included both freight and passengers—triggered resistance by the Port Authority, which ultimately toppled it. As chapter 7 relates, Staten Islanders found themselves tethered to the mayor, and even as some began to question the wisdom of that alliance, the rush of events would sustain the Hylan tunnel coalition for three more years until the swift demise of both his project and his mayoralty in 1925.

CHAPTER 7

GETTING THE SHAFT

The Demise of the Hylan Tunnel, 1922–1925

No one except God can stop the work.

—John Hylan, July 19, 1923

At three in the afternoon of July 19, 1923, New York City's mayor John Hylan and an array of public officials and dignitaries arrived at St. George on the *Theodore Roosevelt* ferryboat. In a festive display of civic pomp, the mayor's party was accompanied by official and civilian vessels as it crossed the harbor, greeted by a delegation of Staten Island's leading citizens and politicians as it landed, and entertained by a police band as it proceeded up the quay and paraded down South and Bay Streets. Thousands of people lined the streets and cheered as the official delegation marched to the foot of South Street, the location of the groundbreaking ceremony for which it had traveled to Richmond Borough in the first place.[1] When Hylan arrived at the site, he briefly addressed the crowd, raised a silver pick, and broke ground on a shaft for a long-awaited and much-anticipated project, a railroad tunnel connecting Staten Island with Bay Ridge, Brooklyn. Declaring the work unstoppable except by divine intervention, Hylan intended this fait accompli to stymie the considerable Narrows tunnel opposition elsewhere in the city, state, and region (see figure 7.1).[2]

7.1 Groundbreaking ceremony on Staten Island for the tunnel to Brooklyn, 1923

Breaking ground for his freight and passenger tunnel between the boroughs of Richmond and Brooklyn, Mayor John Hylan, holding the pick, hoped to preempt the Port Authority from moving ahead on its own plans for moving goods through the region.

Source: Courtesy of Collection of Historic Richmond Town.

Most Staten Islanders were quite supportive of the project. They may have squabbled over where the tunnel would run, what types of transportation it would serve, and how it would be financed, but their desire for a direct physical link to Manhattan or Long Island dated back decades and had percolated for the previous twenty-five years. After consolidation with New York by itself had failed to produce many of the predicted benefits for the island, civic boosters leaped to embrace a tunnel project that would at last bring the forecasted boom in population, commerce, and industry. Bitterly disappointed by their exclusion from the Dual Contracts with the IRT and BRT in 1913 and stymied in their efforts to gain a direct tunnel to Manhattan, Staten Islanders regrouped, organized anew, and aligned themselves with Mayor Hylan's effort to build a joint freight-and-passenger tunnel under the Narrows. It was an uneasy partnership, born of a misguided sense of pragmatism, but in 1923 they appeared finally to be on track to obtain the coveted railroad connection to New York. How they entered that alliance was the subject of the previous chapter; its inherent weakness and ultimate collapse two years later is the focus of this one.

The Hylan tunnel was never completed. Workers broke ground and dug shafts, but in 1925 the state legislature rescinded the city's authority to complete the freight-and-passenger project. Its abandonment served as another reminder for Richmond residents of the city's neglect of their island. Caught up in tensions between Mayor Hylan and Governor Al Smith, a power struggle between New York City and the relatively new bistate Port Authority, disagreement over the proposed tunnel's capacity for carrying freight, and concerns for its immense cost, work on the project halted. The shafts dug at both ends were eventually filled and covered, and subsequent discussions of tunnel projects were forestalled by disunity, economic depression, and world war as well as silenced by the decision to build the Verrazzano Bridge.

While most other failed efforts to tunnel or bridge the Narrows have faded from view, the prospect and demise of the Hylan tunnel have remained a part of public memory and entered into historical scholarship. In an exhibit at the Museum of the City of New York in 2012–2013, Hylan's project served as the example of Staten Island's unfulfilled hopes for a link.[3] Descriptions of the plan, albeit not always accurate, have made it into *Wikipedia* and other online sources of information.[4] Excellent scholarship on the Port Authority, the Regional Plan of New York and Its Environs, the Fresh Kills landfill, and Staten Island politics highlight this episode as the key if not sole instance of thwarted ambition for a tunnel.[5] Implicit in this work is the assumption that the Hylan project was more serious and moved much farther along than any other effort, but popular memory and scholarly work have unfortunately collapsed a forty-year history of foiled tunnel ventures into five. This chapter argues that despite the groundbreaking, the Hylan tunnel is better viewed as a form of political theater than as a proposal with tremendous likelihood for success, its significance stemming from its symbolism more than from its chances for enactment. The demise of the Hylan tunnel may have concluded another episode of dashed hopes and unfulfilled ambition, but it was also caught in the larger dynamic of New York's contentious governing culture failing to grapple with larger economic and social forces shaping the region.

By 1920, municipal governments were increasingly overwhelmed and often incapacitated by large-scale problems with infrastructure and commerce. One response to this economic and political complexity was the formation of public authorities whose focus transcended municipal and in some cases state boundaries. Chapter 6 related how the Port Authority—which evolved from the Comprehensive Plan developed for the city's harbor—was one such entity. A second means of addressing urban conditions—typically chosen by private business and professional leaders—became regional planning. In 1923, a small group of architects and planners formed the Regional Planning Association of America.[6] By then, many such associations had already been established locally. In New York, the Committee on the Regional Plan formed in 1922 and published a massive plan for the tristate area in 1929.[7] The 1920s also saw the formation of the Chicago Regional Planning Association and the Rapid

Transit Commission in Detroit.[8] Planning efforts also extended into other fields such as housing and sewage.[9]

A third context for any discussion of Staten Island's efforts at obtaining a tunnel in this period must consider its place in New York City politics in the twentieth century. Staten Islanders entered New York City in 1898 aware that achieving their agenda would prove challenging given Brooklyn and Manhattan's outsize influence. The island's earlier exclusion from the city's subway system then made formidable rivals out of the Bronx and Queens. With its population now growing much more slowly than that of the other outer boroughs, Staten Islanders feared the further erosion of their borough's already limited political strength. Many histories of twentieth-century New York City politics and governance highlight the roles of Staten Islanders who rose to citywide prominence, from Charles W. Berry in the 1920s to Frederick Zermuhlen in the 1950s. They rarely, however, treat Staten Island or groups within it as distinct constituents with agendas to pursue or with any likelihood of success.[10] This chapter focuses on Staten Islanders' perspective from the periphery and their navigation of the powerful political currents in Greater New York.

Some Distance from Hylan?

The New York Legislature's approval of the Port Authority's proposed tunnel from Greenville, New Jersey, to Bay Ridge, Brooklyn, in February 1922 was widely understood to be a defeat for the Hylan tunnel, but it did not negate the city's fait accompli strategy. Statements to the contrary notwithstanding, city officials and Staten Island boosters understood that there would never be two tunnels enabling freight to move from New Jersey to Long Island; one was unlikely enough. The mayor and his Staten Island constituents continued to move ahead on the Narrows tunnel as quickly as possible in hopes of completing it before the Port Authority could implement its tunnel plan.

For Staten Islanders, the legislative hearing on the Port Authority's Comprehensive Plan provided a stark reminder of the perils of identifying too closely with Mayor Hylan. Even as they supported Hylan's tunnel, they recognized that their island's interests diverged from those of the mayoral administration. They met with Governor Nathan Miller to convey their honest desire for a Narrows tunnel as well as to distance themselves from the mayor, whose position commonly was derided as insincere and obstructionist. In the aftermath of the legislative hearing, some civic boosters looked askance at Hylan's intransigence and thought to bridge differences between the competing public entities. Others suggested abandoning the movement of freight and working with the state's Transit Commission to procure a rapid-transit-only tunnel.[11]

This divergence between borough and city widened over two matters of governance that arose in 1922: legislative authorization and fiscal appropriation for the Narrows tunnel. By late 1921, Arthur Tuttle, the city Board of Estimate's chief engineer, realized that the law authorizing the Narrows tunnel contained ambiguities that could impede its construction. The Hylan administration proposed revisions that would explicitly allow for separate but adjacent tunnels for freight and passengers; permit the acquisition or building of connections from the tunnel to existing rail lines, roads, ferries, and trolleys; sanction the construction of a bridge to New Jersey as well as classification and other railroad yards on Staten Island; and authorize the issuance of bonds to finance these projects, among other corrective measures.[12] This new language would make the city less vulnerable to charges that it lacked the jurisdiction, finances, and freight traffic needed to realize its plans.

Largely supportive of these measures, Staten Islanders nonetheless tacked rather than sailing directly into the prevailing political winds. With the state government controlled by upstate Republicans, local legislators sensed the unfavorable politics and did not press hard for the passage of the proposed amendments.[13] They understood that only a unique set of circumstances had enabled the passage of the enabling Smith Act; there would be no improvements coming from Albany. Calls to delay the required start date by one year were vigorously opposed. Understanding that the two-year time frame would remain intact, Richmond Borough president Matthew Cahill consistently urged a quick start on the tunnel.[14] The city's failure to pass its legislative amendments and engage the railroad companies forced it to recede the tunnel's freight role and emphasize its passenger function.[15] This shift would satisfy many Staten Islanders, but it brought to light another contested issue: the type of passenger service that could be run in a dual-purpose tunnel. Many experts agreed that commuter lines or interstate travel could be accommodated in a combined tunnel but held doubts about rapid-transit passenger service, and that is what Staten Islanders wanted.

Negotiations over appropriations for the tunnel further exposed the wedge between borough leaders and city officials as well as the hollowness of Hylan's adamancy. Tuttle needed funds to move the tunnel work beyond the planning stage, but over the first five months of 1922 the Board of Estimate repeatedly whittled down the amount it would consider. Surprising his colleagues, the newly elected Richmond Borough president, Cahill, audaciously petitioned for an $85 million appropriation for the tunnel shortly after taking office in January 1922. Two months later he tried again, albeit for $65 million.[16] In April, the city's Tunnel Committee requested a $27 million appropriation from the Board of Estimate, primarily to pay for the shafts and to purchase required land.[17] Urged by members of the Board of Estimate to adjust his request, Tuttle returned with a much lower price tag of $4,080,000 by foregoing the funds needed for land condemnation. In each of these cases, Comptroller Charles Craig and other Board of Estimate members recoiled at the price tag. In mid-May, the board finally authorized spending for salaries and supplies with an allocation for $580,000.[18] Despite the heated rhetoric over the past year, city officials were both unwilling and unable to provide the funds to construct the Narrows tunnel, leaving Staten Islanders to question the seriousness of the project.

Many other New Yorkers questioned its integrity. The significantly reduced appropriation was still too much for the Citizens Union. This potent force for reform and good governance went to court and won a temporary injunction against all tunnel work. Most of its claims were familiar—Hylan's blatantly political motives, the infeasibility of a dual-purpose tunnel, and the Hylan tunnel's superfluity given the work of the Port Authority and the Transit Commission—but it also made technical arguments that the Hylan administration had attempted to negate by amending the Smith Act. The crux of its argument was that the scope of the project exceeded the Board of Estimate's authority. The Citizens Union acknowledged that the city could build the tunnel but asserted that it had no independent means of connecting the crossing to the Fourth Avenue subway (the domain of the Transit Commission) or of guaranteeing the tunnel's use by the trunk lines.[19] The lawsuit found a receptive audience in the major newspapers of New York but did not ultimately persuade a judge of the state Supreme Court, which ruled against the Citizens Union.[20]

The efforts to block the Hylan tunnel were buttressed by the Transit Commission's progress on its own plans for subway development. While the Board of Estimate was grappling with the appropriation for the Hylan tunnel, the details of the Transit Commission's $218 million proposal for subway expansion became public. Ranked third among its priorities was a Narrows subway tunnel, which was expected to take five and a half years to construct and at $17 million was projected to cost much less than Hylan's tunnel. The commission identified two possible locations for the Staten Island subway: a southern track from Fort Hamilton, Brooklyn, to Rosebank, Staten Island, and a northern one from Bay Ridge to St. George. Eager to woo Richmond residents, Transit Commission chair George McAneny encountered mostly disinterest or opposition on Staten Island.[21]

Staten Islanders' support for Hylan's Narrows tunnel persisted for several reasons. For many residents, the project appeared on a much faster track than the alternatives. The very newness of both the Port Authority and the Transit Commission meant that timelines and other details of their plans were not yet developed. As former borough president George Cromwell explained to McAneny, an overwhelming majority of people on Staten Island supported the Hylan tunnel "because it was in sight, [and the city was] already working out the borings and preliminary detail problems."[22] Speaking before the Civic League in May 1922, a prominent Staten Islander agreed, suggesting that the Hylan plan offered "the only real, tangible tunnel project at present." In contrast, he dismissed the Port Authority freight-tunnel proposal as "indefinite, uncertain and vague as to the time of its commencement." He described the Transit Commission's plans in similar terms: "As to Rapid Transit, between Staten Island and the other boroughs, through a tunnel under the Narrows to be constructed by the Rapid Transit Commission, what is definitely and concretely known about that? Only the promise of the Rapid Transit Commission that it will begin construction of such a tunnel after it has constructed a subway between Queens and Brooklyn Boroughs. How long will it take to construct the Queens–Brooklyn subway? Who knows? Nobody knows?"[23]

Staten Islanders defended Hylan's Narrows project not necessarily because they favored it on the merits—though many, such as the Civic League Tunnel Committee chair Max Thaten, did—but because they thought it held the best prospects for the speediest completion. Whether the Transit Commission's rapid-transit tunnel was a better fit for the island did not matter to a populace that had begrudgingly learned to compromise on its desires to obtain what it could. As a result, support for Hylan's tunnel was often more faint than fervid.

Many Staten Islanders had doubts about being so thoroughly linked to Hylan's intransigent positions. They grew eager to see the various bodies working together for the benefit of their borough, city, and region. Cromwell, Louis Tribus, and Senator C. Ernest Smith publicly urged the city government to cooperate with the Transit Commission. Borough president Cahill, frustrated by his inability to secure a substantial tunnel allocation, challenged Hylan's public position that the city alone had the authority to work out its transit needs.[24] In a move deemed "unfortunate" by the *Staten Island Advance*, the mayor quickly quashed Cahill's effort to name a special Board of Estimate committee to confer and develop proposals with the Transit Commission.[25] James Graham's pitch for Board of Estimate collaboration with the Transit Commission was similarly rebuffed by the mayor, who warned, "Don't go pussyfooting around the Transit Commission."[26] After the spring of 1922, Staten Islanders rarely tried, in part because Cahill died unexpectedly in July. By the autumn of 1922, both the civic and political leadership of the island had largely accepted that they were wedded to the plans and the prospects of Mayor Hylan.

John A. Lynch, Staten Island's new borough president, epitomized this union with the Hylan administration. Unlike his predecessor, Cahill, the mildly capable and mildly corrupt Lynch functioned as a Hylan loyalist with regard to most matters, including the tunnel. A former insurance salesman and current realty dealer from West New Brighton, Lynch was an active machine Democrat who had previously served one term in the state Senate. As borough president, he ran "a sturdy county [Democratic] organization that had strong ties to the Manhattan political club that dominated New York politics, Tammany Hall."[27] Seeing in Richmond "a potential field for the expansion of the city's commerce" and touting Staten Island's "unrivalled water frontage," Lynch accentuated the Hylan tunnel's capacity for carrying freight.[28] He championed the tunnel and its benefits in his election campaign that fall, earning a victory helped by a second tunnel appropriation of $575,000 for work on the Brooklyn shaft made just days before the voters went to the polls.[29]

Mayor Hylan cemented his Staten Island support with his own proposal for new municipally owned and operated subway lines in August 1922. His $600 million plan included "recapture" of existing lines run by the IRT and BRT and contained thirty-five additional lines, bridges, tunnels, and extensions totaling 126 miles. Staten Island was not neglected. Hylan prioritized a Narrows tunnel from Bay Ridge to Tompkinsville, made the tunnel's connection to the Fourth Avenue subway explicit, and promised "an extensive system of buses" on Staten Island.[30] Most of these details were heralded by Staten Islanders, and local businessmen especially liked that the most recent tunnel plans included lines that went all the way to Arlington and the island's west shore. This connecting link to New Jersey was "believed to be the one feature of the tunnel plan that will bring about an Island boom."[31] Recognizing the competition with other boroughs, these businessmen also urged the city's Board of Estimate not to alter its grouping of projects, which had favored Staten Island.

Hylan's subway plan widened the gulf between the city and the state's Transit Commission. Lambasted by McAneny for this blatantly political move, the mayor usurped the commission's function. Two months later, the Transit Commission signaled its rejection of the Hylan tunnel when it selected the less expensive southern route of the two crossings it had considered. Favoring a tunnel from Fort Hamilton to Rosebank made nearly impossible any reconciliation with the city's tunnel plans from Bay Ridge to St. George.[32] The city's route also entered the most built-up area of the island, which was consistent with the way many lines in Hylan's recent proposal for an independent subway targeted the most congested neighborhoods. The southern route chosen by McAneny recalled his approach for the Dual Contracts, in which he built lines into less-dense areas in the hopes of dispersing population to the outer boroughs. The Transit Commission's plan met with overt hostility by city officials and denunciations by Staten Islanders committed to the Hylan tunnel; it was not funded by the Board of Estimate.[33]

Al Smith's rematch victory over Governor Miller in November 1922 fortified Hylan's resistance to the Transit Commission. The two Tammany Democrats may have disagreed about the need for a Port Authority, but Smith still favored more home rule for the city than had Miller. With Smith back in office,

Hylan encountered reduced pressure to compromise with the Transit Commission because during the campaign Smith had advocated replacing it with a city board. Hylan could reject the commission's plan in the expectation that the city would soon gain control over rapid-transit development. His hopes were initially dashed in the next legislative session as Smith was unable to move the Republican majority in the Assembly to reconfigure transit authority. Nor could Hylan prod the legislature—in a near replay of the previous year—to amend the Smith law to expand the city's authority in connecting its tunnel to existing rail lines.[34]

These legislative failures motivated the Hylan administration and its Staten Island supporters to accelerate the strategy they had enacted upon the passage of the Smith law in 1921. For many months these officials and citizens had attempted to make headway on a tunnel quickly in order to comply with the legislation's requirement that tunnel construction begin within two years. Their haste was also intended to forestall the forces arrayed against the city's Narrows tunnel by getting it underway before the Port Authority or the Transit Commission could build their tunnels or, better yet, to deter these rivals from pursuing their projects. Another potential peril lay in Albany, where the state's failure to amend the Smith law fueled the concern that legislator opposition would alter the law's terms unfavorably or repeal it entirely.[35]

Staten Islanders did their part to move the project along. In early 1923, they began planning for a spring groundbreaking celebration.[36] As the initial start date began to be pushed back into summer, borough president Lynch engaged in parliamentary maneuvers to speed the matter ahead.[37] When a few weeks later the Board of Estimate accepted the bid of a contractor, Thaten praised the body for its quick work: "It was wise to close the contract in order to have work start immediately on this end of the tunnel under the Narrows."[38] Staten Islanders were well represented at each of the public ceremonies held by the Hylan administration to mark each milestone in the Narrows project: the contract signing for the sinking of the Brooklyn shaft on January 4, a groundbreaking in Brooklyn on April 14, the awarding of a contract for the Staten Island shaft on May 19. Thousands were expected at the groundbreaking ceremony on Staten Island eventually scheduled for July 19, 1923.[39] As the day approached, many Staten Islanders no doubt thought that the Narrows tunnel was truly a reality.

The Hylan Tunnel Delayed: 1923–1924

The groundbreaking ceremonies in Bay Ridge and St. George in 1923 culminated the city's two-year effort to launch the Narrows tunnel swiftly in order to preempt competing projects. Even then the project was not viewed as secure because construction would take five or six years, so the Hylan administration continued to press for the completion of enough work on the tunnel that its opponents would see the futility of their position. Arthur Tuttle remained in charge of the project, leading an expanding corps of engineers who worked with contractors to move ahead swiftly on sinking the shafts. This component of the tunnel encountered only minor setbacks and was completed in mid-1924.[40]

Following this initial progress, however, the controversial Narrows project encountered distractions that stalled the subsequent work on the main tunnel. Tuttle continued to spend a considerable portion of his job engaged in the politics and not the engineering of tunnel construction. Under regular assault for pushing the Narrows project, Hylan constantly turned to Tuttle to make the case in its favor. For example, in late 1924 Hylan enlisted Tuttle to fend off growing opposition from interests in Brooklyn and Queens. The fledgling project was troubled as well by early signs of labor strife that Tuttle feared would add cost and length to the project.[41]

A fundamental design dilemma also plagued engineers such that final plans and specifications for the tunnel never materialized. After announcing that the plans would be complete in April 1924, the preparations by Tuttle's staff continued well past that date, with several false starts. Much of the delay stemmed from the city's indecision about which method of tunnel construction to adopt. The traditional technique involved digging a tunnel in the ground underneath the water. In the approach known as the shield method, compartments protected workers as they slowly dug the tunnel, and compressed air was used to withstand the pressure. For the Narrows tunnel, this approach was projected to take six to seven years, but a faster option was available by the mid-1920s. Engineers had developed the trench method, which could shave a year or two off of the project by sinking a deep trench underneath the Narrows and then placing in it tubes that were reinforced with concrete.[42] Utilizing this new innovation was not purely an engineering decision, however, because the trench technique cost more than the shield method, and financing the tunnel was fraught with politics.

The holdup was most evident in Tuttle's stymied efforts to secure an appropriation of additional funds for the construction of the main portion of the tunnel. In April 1924, Tuttle requested $30 million from the Board of Estimate, which would enable him to advertise for bids on the work and purchase the lands on Staten Island necessary for a right-of-way. When contract negotiations with the proprietor of the trench method stalled board action, Tuttle drastically reduced his request to $800,000 to keep his staff working for another six months.[43] Ultimately, $200,000 was made available just days before expiration of the previous allocation. The Board of Estimate intimated that more funds would be forthcoming when this cash was spent, but months went by without another appropriation as the city's coalition in favor of the Narrows tunnel began to crack, while squabbling for limited resources continued to hinder the project.[44]

While construction was largely dormant in 1924, new opponents lined up to ridicule the project. In Brooklyn, where interest in a Narrows crossing had always been greater in its southern reaches than in downtown, key clergymen, businessmen, and newspaper editors publicly voiced strong disagreement. The Brooklyn–Manhattan Transit Corporation, the successor to the BRT and a regular target of Hylan's vitriol, engaged the mayor in a public spat over the delays in subway construction during his administration. Its chairman called the Narrows tunnel a distraction from the more essential question of subway construction and expansion, a stance echoed by the *New York Times*.[45] In Queens, the local chamber of commerce, a rapid-transit committee, and other neighborhood civic groups pressed hard for new subways to their borough.[46] Non-revenue-generating improvements such as new schools were again competing for room under the city's debt ceiling following the demise of a briefly imposed "pay-as-you-go" policy.[47]

Familiar combatants remained disinterested in the Hylan tunnel but evolved their tactics. PRR president Samuel Rea continued to assert that the Narrows tunnel was "a silly proposition" precisely because of its combined freight-and-passenger service, though privately he acknowledged that the Narrows tunnel would give the B&O advantages over his company that it did not currently possess.[48] The Port Authority, under the new though short-lived tenure of Chairman Dewitt van Buskirk, became less vocal in its objections to the Narrows tunnel. In both private conversations and public statements, van Buskirk voiced no opposition to the city's Narrows tunnel. The Port Authority had received legislative authorization to construct two bridges from New Jersey to Staten Island, giving it the potential both to use leverage and to display forbearance in its dealings with the Hylan administration.[49]

The increasing discord between the boroughs over competing demands for large capital projects was made only more complicated by the impasse over subway construction. The Hylan administration constantly demonized and feuded with the subway companies as well as with the Transit Commission. As Clifton Hood has noted, "During his second term, the mayor brought the same strident rhetoric and anti-corporate crusading to rapid transit planning that he had already brought to the nickel fare and fiscal reorganization [of the subways]. The result was that subway expansion became especially competitive and conflict-ridden."[50] Meetings between commissioners and Mayor Hylan yielded much acrimony and grandstanding but no action.[51] The only auspicious moments occurred during Hylan's six-month absence for illness, but when he returned to office in March 1924, he squelched the progress that had been made. Even without Hylan, it was difficult to overcome the deep suspicions about the other's project. Transit commissioner Leroy Harkness thought the city's Narrows tunnel was the worst waste of funds he had seen in twenty years. In June 1924, the Board of Estimate rejected all of the Transit Commission's proposals. This renewed intransigence likely stemmed from the anticipated arrival of city control of rapid transit through a new Board of Transportation.[52]

In trying to recapture the governorship in 1922, Alfred Smith had made home rule a general theme of his campaign and had castigated the Transit Commission as the embodiment of state overreach. By 1924, he had the votes to shift the responsibility for planning new rapid-transit lines to a city Board of Transportation. The new board reported to Hylan and was authorized to plan, construct, and operate subways.[53] Headed by John Delaney, a "hard-nosed Tammany veteran," the Transportation Board came into being on July 1, 1924—right in the midst of the outer boroughs' backlash against the Narrows tunnel.[54] Recognizing that the views of this new entrant into the rapid-transit battles were important, leading Staten Islanders privately urged Delaney to issue a statement of support as part of a broader flurry of effort to secure an appropriation for the Narrows tunnel.[55] Borough president Lynch was especially vocal in his advocacy, and local Staten Island organizations renewed their efforts for the Narrows tunnel in typical ways—making public statements, issuing resolutions, writing letters to officials, launching petition drives, and holding mass meetings.[56]

Staten Island civic leaders recognized the daunting political realities facing the project. Staten Islanders generally favored the tube for its rapid-transit, not freight, features. Promoting the Hylan tunnel in an article in the fall of 1923, the *Staten Island Advance*, for example, included an accompanying "bird's-eye view" of the harbor that inaccurately labeled it a subway (see figure 7.2). Narrows tunnel proponents had to minimize the role of freight to keep the locals happy yet emphasize its necessity for making the project financially and politically viable. A passenger-only tunnel, argued Civic League president Francis Leman, would place Staten Island far behind other boroughs with more pressing rapid-transit needs. With freight remaining a major component, Thaten asserted that the funds to build the Narrows tunnel would not deter other subway projects.[57] Others disagreed with this assessment. Writing to the *Advance*, a local lawyer chided Staten Island's civic leaders for seeing only "old ghosts" and not rising to the seriousness of the threat posed by the Brooklyn opposition, who certainly believed that the expense of the Narrows tunnel would defer the construction of new subways in Brooklyn.[58] The flurry of civic activity in 1924 pointed toward a singular goal: securing a $30 million tunnel appropriation to avoid further construction delays.[59] Behind the political squabbling lay the underlying challenges of financing subway construction. As Keith Revell has observed, "During the 1920s, subways surpassed water supply, schools, streets and sewers as the most expensive municipal infrastructure project."[60] In addition to the pressure of the subways' immense cost, New York continued to operate under the constraints posed by the clause in the state constitution that limited a municipality's indebtedness to 10 percent of the assessed valuation of its property. Although some officials clung to the

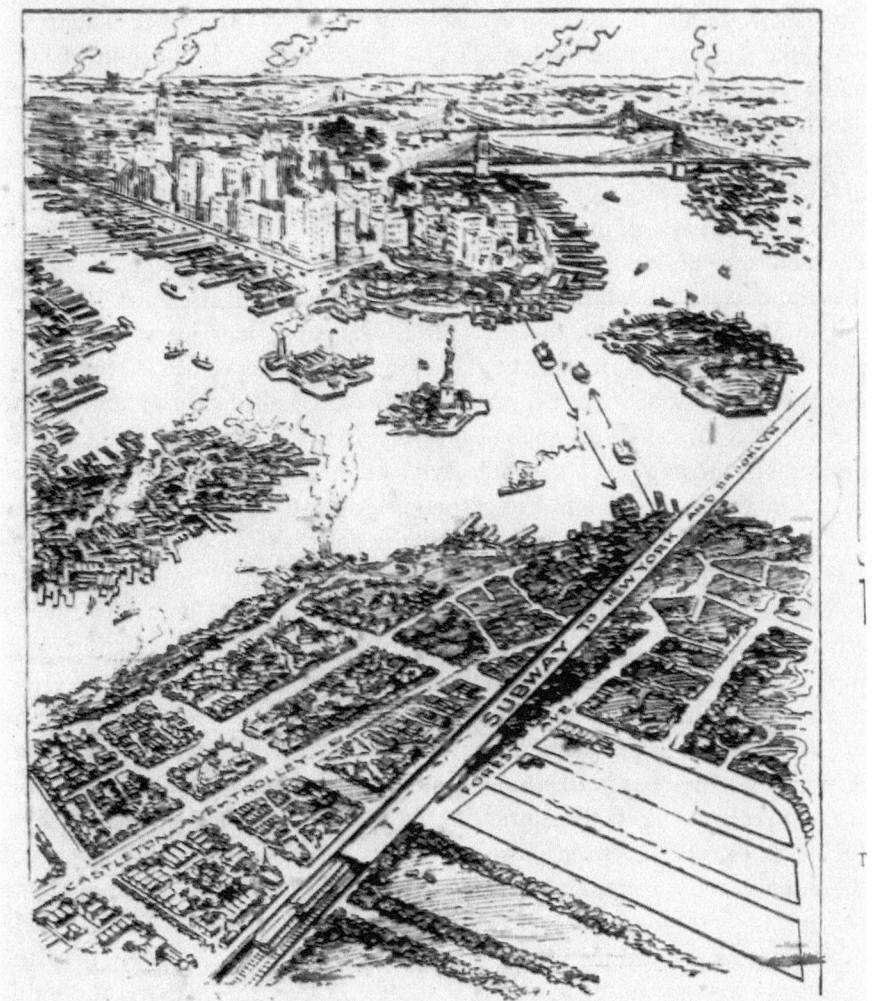

7.2 **A bird's-eye view of New York Harbor with a Narrows tunnel**

This view of the harbor appearing in the *Staten Island Advance* on July 19, 1923, indicated that for many Staten Islanders the Hylan tunnel was fundamentally about providing a subway connection and not about moving freight.

Source: Courtesy of Collection of the Staten Island Museum.

initial expectation that funds used for the Narrows tunnel would not count against the city's legal debt ceiling, that interpretation grew increasingly untenable as challenges to the project mounted. When Staten Islanders organized in 1924 to obtain a $30 million appropriation for the Narrows tunnel, the city had only about $50 million available for all subways and other major projects. Hylan might assure the islanders that the tunnel would be built without holdup, but he also signaled the city's fiscal bind by urging them to help get debt legislation passed that would expand the city's ceiling.[61]

The Hylan administration adopted a two-pronged response to the shortage of funds available for capital projects. First, it again prepared legislation authorizing an expansion of the city's capacity for debt limit by $275 million. Mayor Hylan, despite his swaggering "no delay" rhetoric, acknowledged publicly that the tunnel contracts would be deferred until early 1925 if the state legislature did not pass such a bill on the city's behalf. As in previous years, though, the city's legislative agenda for transit did not muster the votes it needed in Albany, and as a result the Board of Estimate again balked at allocating $30 million for the Narrows tunnel.[62] For much of 1924, a spiral of delay engulfed the tunnel project. The incomplete plans that lacked a firm decision on using the shield or trench method hurt the effort to garner a significant appropriation, yet those very delays in allocating funds was slowing down the pace of the work anyway. Even without a raised debt ceiling, one estimate for 1925 expected an additional $75–125 million in borrowing capacity, but the political problem remained because the Narrows tunnel and existing school construction plans were expected to consume nearly all of the increase.[63]

By 1925, the mayor conceded the political necessity of piecemeal allocations or "installment appropriation" that would allow the city to avoid reaching the debt ceiling. The Board of Estimate would allocate money and solicit bids for the first year of work on the tunnel, with contracts drawn to allow the successful bidder to renew them in subsequent years.[64] Although this policy was not the same as the one imposed on the Mitchel administration, it, too, became referred to (with greater accuracy) as a "pay-as-you-go" policy. The downside of this approach lay in the limitations and extra expenses it imposed on planning and carrying out the project, a point ironically made by Governor Smith when discussing expenditures by the state.[65]

Despite its failure to raise the city's debt ceiling or finalize the tunnel blueprints, the Hylan administration finally moved the project forward in early 1925. A few days after the year began, Hylan and Tuttle jointly announced that the tunnel plans and appropriation would occur within a month.[66] Three weeks later, Richmond Borough president Lynch informed his constituents that on January 29 the Board of Estimate would review plans and specifications for the tunnel, and the mayor would ask for $7 million to start the work.[67] On Friday, January 30, more than 1,000 Staten Islanders turned out to see the

Board of Estimate vote unanimously to appropriate $6.5 million for what Lynch and others suggested should be named the Hylan Tunnel.[68] Unfortunately for the mayor and borough president, by then the project was gravely imperiled by developments in Albany, where long-standing opponents to the dual-purpose Narrows tunnel appeared politically ready to render moot the Board of Estimate's allocation.

The Demise of the Hylan Tunnel, 1924–1925

When the New York City Board of Estimate sent Governor Smith a formal complaint about the Transit Commission in October 1924, it no doubt thought that it was solidifying rather than endangering its stake in new rapid-transit and freight developments. After all, Smith had risen out of Tammany Hall to capture the governor's seat, had regained it in 1922 by excoriating the Transit Commission in his promotion of home rule, and had recently weakened the commission by championing the creation of the New York City Board of Transportation. The Hylan administration greatly miscalculated. Smith, already wary of the Narrows tunnel due to his sympathies for the Port Authority, had grown weary of Hylan's antics and used the petition to appoint a commission to investigate not just the city's complaints about the Transit Commission but also the entire transit situation in an effort to account for the inordinate delays in new construction.[69]

The new commission became a vehicle for undermining Hylan and the Narrows tunnel. Named by Smith to head the commission, Judge John V. McAvoy accepted the broad mandate he was given and held public hearings that garnered considerable attention in the press over several weeks in late 1924 and early 1925. Witnesses clashed over a range of rapid-transit issues, including whether the Narrows tunnel represented rational metropolitan planning or localized politics. Criticism of the Narrows project centered on the unwieldiness of a freight-and-passenger tunnel, the wasting of limited resources, and the superiority of a tunnel used purely for rapid transit.[70] Made public in early February, McAvoy's report vindicated the Transit Commission and offered a damning indictment of the Hylan administration for its diversion from completing construction of the Dual Contracts lines and for obstructionism on subway expansion, but "none [of McAvoy's conclusions] held more public interest than his broad condemnation of the Hylan joint tunnel."[71] Nor did McAvoy view the tunnel as a fait accompli, noting that because only the shafts had been sunk, "it is still possible to change the tunnel plan" to one for rapid transit only. Not surprisingly, Hylan and members of his administration derided the report.[72]

The McAvoy report spurred the Republican-dominated legislature to pounce on the Narrows tunnel. Days after its release, two Manhattan Republicans,

Senator Courtland Nicoll and Assemblyman Samuel Hofstadter, introduced legislation that permitted only the construction of a passenger tunnel between Staten Island and Brooklyn. The bill was an intersection between good policy—curtailing a project dependent on but rejected by the private railroads—and good politics—stirring a split between Governor Smith and Mayor Hylan, the two leading Tammany Democrats. The elimination of freight was vociferously opposed by Mayor Hylan, who rounded up support on the Board of Estimate and urged civic groups from Staten Island to go to Albany to fight the bill.[73]

The leading politicians, civic leaders, and editorial pages on Staten Island needed no such counsel to organize. Both the *Staten Island Advance* and the *Staten Islander* dismissed the McAvoy report and remained staunch in their support for the Narrows tunnel.[74] Borough president Lynch captured the public mood with his expressions of derision for the report and the pending legislation. The sponsor of the original authorizing legislation of 1921, former Republican state senator C. Ernest Smith, promised to lobby his colleagues who remained in the Senate; local Democratic politicians attempted to sway Governor Smith; and a series of bipartisan public gatherings were held. In March, hundreds of Richmond Borough residents attended a sympathetic Board of Estimate hearing, and more than one hundred Staten Islanders representing twenty-two civic groups journeyed to Albany for a legislative hearing. There they cheered local speakers and the mayor, who testified that his plans would, among other accomplishments, "give Staten Island, the Borough which has been marooned for years, its first rapid transit connection with the other boroughs of New York."[75]

Whether the Hylan tunnel would in fact best satisfy Richmond's real need for rapid transit was at the center of the debate in Albany. Its proponents highlighted the freight role for its salutary effect on the efficiency of New York Harbor and the commercial development of Stapleton but also as a necessary feature to provide Staten Island with a transit link. Lynch argued that to remove the freight function would imperil the project because without the revenues from transporting goods the tunnel would incur a loss for many years in the future. Lynch rightly acknowledged that the freight component was what enabled Staten Island to avoid the queue for rapid-transit lines, made the tunnel a city rather than a local project, and generated support from other boroughs. Maurice Connolly, the Queens Borough president, justified the tunnel's freight capacity as the element vital to the success of a proposed development project for Jamaica Bay as a port for commerce.[76] The tunnel's opponents, in contrast, understood the Nicoll-Hofstadter bill as a means of killing the entire enterprise rather than enabling a passenger-only alternative to it.[77]

The bill's supporters viewed the freight component as the crux of the matter, too. Its sponsors, Nicoll and Hofstadter, cited the high cost of constructing a dual-purpose tunnel. They also noted that it infringed on the Port Authority's plans for the transport of goods through the metropolitan area. Finally, they queried whether the tunnel would ever see use by the trunk lines.[78] Transit commissioners launched especially devastating critiques of the tunnel's capacity for freight. Harkness added that the tunnel was neither a wise use of limited credit nor a means of providing rapid transit to Staten Island.[79] McAneny questioned whether even the B&O would use the tunnel, given its interest in acquiring the Central Railroad of New Jersey with its direct connections to Manhattan. Satisfied that the Port Authority had made a superior proposal and convinced that the city could never gain the additional legislation it needed, McAneny urged the passage of the Nicoll-Hofstadter bill.[80]

The divide over freight notwithstanding, the success of the Nicoll-Hofstadter bill depended largely on partisan politics. Upstate Republicans controlled both the Senate and the Assembly and were eager to embarrass and perhaps split Hylan and Smith. Although some New York City Republicans in the Assembly defected, the measure still passed handily in an 83–64 vote. Staten Islanders, knowing they lacked the votes in the Assembly, had focused on the Senate, where the Democrats had a smaller deficit to overcome and might siphon off some local Republican votes. Such hopes were misplaced as the expected Republican votes did not materialize, and the bill passed the Senate 28–22.[81] Now all eyes turned to Governor Smith.

The governor's position on the Nicoll-Hofstadter bill was complicated by his competing priorities. He thought a rapid-transit-only tunnel made the most sense and had agreed with McAvoy's condemnation of the Hylan administration for the inexcusable delays in subway expansion. He was also sympathetic to the city's frustration with many of the impediments to public projects imposed by the state. Smith had long emphasized home rule in transit affairs for New York City, had backed the weakening of the Transit Commission in 1924, and now favored an increase in the city's debt ceiling. Yet as an advocate for home rule, he also decried the original state law of 1921 that mandated a freight-and-passenger tunnel under the Narrows, and he favored legislation to limit the project to just passengers.[82] He held a hearing on the bill that revealed no new arguments or positions but signified how Staten Island found itself caught up in a much larger political drama. Hylan and speakers from his administration dominated the hearing, while representatives from Staten Island were few and limited in their remarks. The 450 Staten Islanders who had traveled to Albany for it were largely along for the ride.[83]

The sidelining of Staten Island was practical as well as symbolic. The developments in Albany in 1925 unleashed local dissent to the Hylan tunnel that had remained largely muted since 1922. E. C. Bridgeman, president of the Staten Island Savings Bank, hailed the findings of the McAvoy report for undermining the political momentum of the Hylan tunnel, for which he believed Staten Islanders were not displaying "their real sentiment." Mary Otis

Gay Willcox, prominent widow of the first Staten Islander to serve as president of the Board of Education of the City of New York, echoed Bridgeman's view that public money would be better spent on improved ferry service than on a tunnel (see figure 7.3).[84] Most officials and organizations on Staten Island still clamored for the Hylan tunnel, but their lobbying efforts did not prevail.[85] Committed to the Port Authority and disenchanted with Mayor Hylan, Smith signed the Nicoll-Hofstadter bill to the accolades from the major New York newspapers and Hylan's vitriol.[86] Hylan's instinct to resist—as evidenced by the steps the Board of Estimate continued to take to construct the tunnel and the threats Hylan made to contest the law through the courts—was quickly tempered by a much more muted reaction on Staten Island.[87]

7.3 Two reasons to prefer improved ferry service to a subway tunnel

This editorial cartoon from the *Staten Island Advance* (c. 1923) gave voice to those Staten Islanders who always preferred improving the island's ferry service to connecting with the New York City subway.

Source: Courtesy of Collection of the Staten Island Museum.

In Richmond, residents and civic leaders conveyed resignation or relief more than outrage regarding the bill's success. The *New York Times* reported that ferry passengers appeared hardly perturbed at all and that some men in real estate also expressed contentment with the decision in the hopes that a true rapid-transit connection could now finally be achieved.[88] The *Staten Islander* did not advocate continuing the fight for a dual-purpose tunnel.[89] The *Staten Island Advance* initially expected "long litigation" for the joint tunnel but within a week reported that sentiment had shifted.[90] The Staten Island Chamber of Commerce, the West New Brighton Board of Trade, and the Kiwanis Club quickly issued resolutions expressing regret at the governor's decision but rejecting protracted litigation, instead calling for immediate rededication to a passenger-only tunnel. With the city no longer mandated to construct a Narrows tunnel, Staten Islanders were anxious to see the Hylan administration stand by its commitment to build a line without freight.[91]

With the Hylan administration veering toward defiance and Staten Islanders advocating compliance, borough president Lynch helped identify a middle-ground position. Lynch's inclinations were aligned with Hylan's, but he recognized that local sentiment was accepting of the outcome. At a meeting with business and civic leaders in early May, Lynch suggested building a passenger-only tunnel but retaining the existing specifications for a tube wide enough to serve freight as well. Prodded by Staten Islanders with Hylan in acquiescence, the Board of Estimate formally adopted this strategy of evasion, but it proved to be no more than a gesture.[92] Hylan tunnel opponents expected that the courts would enjoin such a course of action, and perhaps the mayor did as well. Hylan ultimately declined to contest the law's constitutionality and quickly dispersed the special staff of engineers working on the Narrows tunnel to various city departments.[93] By the summer of 1925, the Narrows tunnel project was dead, though by then Mayor Hylan had more immediate political concerns.

The conflict over the McAvoy report and the Nicoll-Hofstadter Act was accurately perceived to have irrevocably split Governor Smith and Mayor Hylan.[94] With his second term winding down, the mayor hoped to win a third, while the governor took the unusual step to run a challenger against Hylan in a Democratic primary. Tammany Hall sided with Smith and with the governor's approval selected state senator James J. Walker to run against Hylan. The primary divided the city's Democratic organizations and was widely followed for its implications for the presidential race of 1928.[95] Transit matters—including the Narrows tunnel—loomed large in the campaign, with Walker advocating a rapid-transit-only Narrows tunnel.[96] The Democratic Party on Staten Island renominated Lynch and endorsed Hylan, who had fervently championed the borough's causes related to transit and trash. However, many Staten Island Democrats blamed the mayor for the failed Narrows tunnel, and

Richmond became the first borough where an anti-Hylan, Democratic slate of nominees for local positions was formed. In the September primary, Walker handily defeated Hylan, and though the mayor carried Staten Island with 66 percent of the vote, he underperformed relative to Lynch, who garnered 76 percent in his bid for reelection to the borough presidency.[97] Walker went on to become mayor, while Hylan's freight-and-passenger Narrows tunnel initiative would never again be seriously resurrected.

***

The Hylan administration's fait accompli strategy—symbolized by the tunnel groundbreaking ceremony in July 1923—ultimately failed to accomplish the construction of the Narrows tunnel. The strategy was difficult to implement tactically as work proceeded slowly, especially once the shafts were completed. The city encountered delays in formulating precise plans for the project and in allocating funds for it. Competing types of construction—the less expensive shield method versus the more easily built trench method—linked engineering decisions to the politics surrounding the tunnel; the emergence of experts meant that each politicized entity brandished its own experts. The city's legal constraints on financing capital projects exacerbated the competition for limited resources as officials and constituents in other boroughs balked at paying for the tunnel—especially if it meant deferring their own aspirations for public works. Finally, the strategy depended on the construction reaching a point of no return, but the approximately $6 million spent on the tunnel did not prevent its opponents from defying what is now often referred to as the Concorde Fallacy.[98] Staten Islanders largely continued to support the city's plans but found themselves reacting defensively to a number of challenges and challengers.

Less than two years after Hylan proclaimed that only divine intervention could halt the Narrows tunnel project, human hands killed it. Democratic governor Al Smith wielded the knife given to him by the Republican-controlled state legislature in the form of a bill that prohibited a freight-and-passenger Narrows tunnel. In the background lurked many familiar faces and regional organizations pressing for the tunnel's demise, while Staten Islanders struggled to persuade first the legislature and then the governor not to abandon the Narrows rail tunnel. Their efforts were in vain because Hylan's Narrows project was ultimately about staving off a regional approach to metropolitan problems and not about serving Staten Island. In the early 1920s, Staten Islanders had largely rallied around a single project, albeit a highly flawed one. What replaced it over the next eight years was a series of disjointed initiatives for some form of infrastructure linking Staten Island to Brooklyn, New Jersey, or Manhattan (via Governor's Island).

PART III
SUBWAY PERSISTENCE AND AUTOMOBILE EMERGENCE

CHAPTER 8

DRIVING THE NARROWS

New Options for Connection, 1925–1932

Your Transportation committee feels that the Board of Directors should take affirmative action in the matter of the vehicular tunnel to Brooklyn.

—Staten Island Chamber of Commerce, April 23, 1929

When William Wirt Mills introduced in April 1929 a resolution of support for a Narrows vehicular tunnel to the Board of Directors of the Staten Island Chamber of Commerce, he might have hoped that the old aphorism "third time's the charm" would take effect. Weeks earlier the city's Board of Estimate had approved a vehicular tunnel, but when Mills, as chairman of the SICC's Transportation Committee, had first proposed a similarly innocuous resolution, it had generated intense debate in the chamber and failed to pass. Asked to reconsider the matter, his committee then reversed its position and asserted that what the island really needed was completion of the rapid-transit tunnel to Brooklyn. A second resolution in favor of a subway connection passed at the next meeting, but the SICC's leadership, concerned by the apparent lack of support for the city's vehicular tunnel project, backpedaled and brought back a third resolution that would include such a project. It still encountered resistance and passed only when the following sentence was added: "The Staten Island Chamber of

Commerce sincerely hopes that this is but the first step in the construction of a series of connections between the borough and Brooklyn, one of which will be a rapid transit tunnel."[1] These internal SICC discussions indicate a new difficulty in settling upon a single transit approach in the late 1920s. Numerous individuals and organizations now wondered whether the automobile would best connect Staten Island to the rest of the city.

Mayor James J. Walker quickly encountered competing visions for a Staten Island link when he took office in 1926. The city's Board of Transportation had made a public commitment to Staten Islanders to build a subway tunnel under the Narrows in the aftermath of the Hylan tunnel debacle. Now unfettered by the Hylan project, local bank president Edward Bridgeman advocated instead for a spectacular bridge that would serve vehicles, rapid transit, and pedestrians. Other initiatives for a bridge and subway appeared during the Walker administration, but the mayor came to focus on a third proposal—a vehicular tunnel under the Narrows. The city took several early steps toward constructing a tunnel for cars and trucks—including making initial appropriations, obtaining necessary permission from the U.S. War Department, and successfully lobbying for enabling legislation—before the ongoing economic depression halted the project in early 1932.

These fruitless efforts by Staten Islanders and city officials to secure a link to the rest of the city bore much in common with earlier failed campaigns. As Queens and the Bronx boomed, Staten Island's small population was at its lowest point relative to the other boroughs—a mismatch that put it at a great disadvantage in the perennial competition for public works. The debt ceiling imposed by the state constitution capped the availability of funds, a limit soon to be heightened by the Great Depression. Larger entities engaged in planning for future development of the metropolitan area but clashed over the location of new transportation networks and port facilities. Local civic boosters often worked at cross-purposes with each other as well.

At the same time, certain characteristics distinguished the transit developments from 1925 to 1932. As in earlier eras, unanimity over the route and function of a transit connection eluded Staten Islanders, but the very disjointedness of their efforts in these years revealed the arrival of new fault lines for civic boosters to navigate. The debates over tunnels and bridges overlapped with new tensions between trains and automobiles. Staten Islanders did not rally around Walker's vehicular tunnel as they largely had around Hylan's rail tunnel, and even as the city moved ahead on the project, an active civic movement for a subway began anew on Staten Island. While business and real estate interests remained prominent in the campaigns for a subway, the leaders of this movement were ostensibly more disinterested experts: local engineers and architects. These advocates jumped at the opportunity to tap new spigots of funding, and their passion for rapid transit suggests that desire for a subway to

Staten Island was not inaudible nor its decline inevitable. During the seven-year period covered by this chapter alone, the contested nature of transportation politics and blurred lines between business, politics, and expertise were epitomized by the three distinct efforts to join Staten Island to its larger neighbors that garnered serious consideration and momentum before collapsing: a Narrows bridge, a Narrows vehicular tunnel, and a rapid-transit tunnel to South Brooklyn.

The Automobile in the 1920s

Taken together, the three aborted projects share some common traits. Most significantly, they all were part of a growing tension between roads and rails in cities and their suburbs throughout the United States. The automobile came into its own in the 1920s, and its arrival hastened the recession of rail traffic in all its forms (commuter, freight, mass transit). This transition was anything but straightforward or automatic and reflected changing conditions in street use and paving technology already emerging by the turn of the century.[2] It was also more encompassing than just a new dominant mode of transportation, pitting a whole new automotive culture against an urbanism centered on rapid transit.[3] In addition, none of these projects was an isolated idea; all were all strongly linked to the considerable efforts at regional planning that marked the decade. How well a Narrows crossing fit into larger plans for the city and metropolitan area was an essential component of how it would be evaluated. Finally, all three of these projects demonstrated the island's inherent weakness in political struggles between local politicians and officials with a citywide or statewide purview.

Historians have long grappled with how the movement of people and goods shifted from rails to rubber. The decade after World War I witnessed a rise in automobile ownership—there was one car for every 4.5 people in the United States in 1929—and in the rapid construction of roads and highways. One result of these new networks was more decentralized suburban development, away from the linear population dispersal found along commuter rail lines. Trends in transportation were made only more complicated by their impact on development patterns—most notably the spread of suburbs.[4] Within cities themselves, the subway "riding habit" declined in the 1920s, while the automobile "driving habit" soared, as did "car culture."[5] Some changes on Staten Island reflected these national developments, primarily the rise of the automobile and the replacement of internal rapid-transit rail systems with first private and then municipal buses. This period also witnessed the first groups of residents to organize for a motor vehicle link to Greater New York.

Trying to account for the ascendancy of the automobile, scholars have established some important areas of inquiry. Many have shown how federal, state, and local policies privileged the automobile and penalized railroads and mass transit.[6] Others have argued that the automobile represented the free-market choice of a populace increasingly able to buy one and inclined to do so as Americans embraced a consumer culture in the 1920s.[7] Most acknowledge these leading factors while emphasizing a host of others, ranging from technological innovation to precarious economic conditions.[8] This issue has spurred contentious debate—one that teeters uneasily between evidence and values—because of the environmental and cultural impact of the decentralized development that characterized the latter half of the twentieth century.[9] In most metropolitan areas in the United States, including New York, the rise of the automobile eroded cities' centripetal force and magnified suburbs' and ultimately exurbs' pull.

Some factors and actors identified by historians are particularly salient for understanding what transpired on Staten Island. Kenneth Jackson has uncovered the machinations of General Motors in buying up financially struggling street car companies and promoting the adoption of buses. New York City went from having 1,344 miles of trolley lines in 1919 to just 337 miles twenty years later.[10] This rivalry—though not necessarily marked by chicanery—holds some currency for Staten Island. The two modes of transportation engaged in competition and controversy throughout the decade, bus companies opened routes in the 1920s following disruptions in trolley service, and trolleys closed for good in 1934.[11]

Overall, the findings in this chapter caution against placing too much explanatory weight on consumers selecting the automobile to purchase and drive. Most critiques of this interpretation emphasize the numerous factors that no doubt constrained market choices, but other types of evidence are also worth considering. The choice argument relies on a behaviorist assumption—people must have wanted cars because they purchased them—but the aspirations of citizens on Staten Island are also telling. In Richmond Borough, political, economic, and civic elites deliberated over the type of transportation they hoped to see, and many of them chose rail lines over highways. One should not take this point—meant as a corrective and not as a repudiation of motor vehicle preference and culture—too far. Indeed, the Staten Island engineers who rejected a vehicular tunnel and pined for a subway connection to New York probably owned and drove cars.

Two pivotal developments helped secure the eventual dominance of the automobile on Staten Island. First, the exclusion of a Narrows tunnel from the Dual Contracts in 1913 denied Staten Island the development and population density spurred by the subway in the other outer boroughs. Second, the Port Authority's stymied efforts at railroad planning led it to a rather fortuitous long-term success with motor vehicles, building three automobile bridges from Staten Island to New Jersey within a ten-year period. By the late 1920s, managing vehicular traffic had become a great concern of planners and engineers.[12] On Staten Island, regionally minded experts looked to complete a transportation loop that would enable automobile traffic from New Jersey to continue on to Long Island via a Narrows crossing. Even so, the prospects for building a vehicular tunnel, though impossible to quantify, were probably dimmer than earlier efforts for a rail tunnel during the Dual Contract negotiations and for a dual-purpose tunnel during the Hylan administration. The significance of the 1925–1932 era lay not in the strong likelihood of construction but rather in the origins of three key shifts: in structure (from tunnel to bridge), in orientation (from railroad to automobile), and in funding streams (from municipal to federal or tunnel authority).

Tunnel or Bridge, 1925–1928

As the first quarter of the century ended, many prominent politicians, planners, and engineers remained enamored of a rapid-transit tunnel under the Narrows. On Staten Island, leading civic organizations, prominent citizens, and Richmond Borough president John Lynch were on record as favoring a rapid-transit tunnel, though they did not push hard for it.[13] George McAneny, still chair of the now diminished state Transit Commission, appeared ready to honor the commitment he had made nearly fifteen years earlier. Although the Transit Commission was no longer responsible for the planning and construction of new subway lines, commission engineers studied the features of a potential crossing. In a report issued in 1926, they concluded that a shorter tunnel from Fort Hamilton, Brooklyn, to Rosebank, Staten Island, was preferable to a route from Bay Ridge to St. George, which for nearly fifteen years had been the predominant location suggested. When later that year McAneny was not reappointed to the commission, his public valedictory and private correspondence listed a Narrows tunnel as one of four key projects for the Board of Estimate to accomplish.[14] Daniel Turner, who was now working on the Regional Plan, agreed. In a letter to McAneny in January 1926, he observed that "it is futile to talk of not providing rapid transit to Richmond because it has no population to justify it. Transportation must precede the population. Population will follow as soon as adequate transportation is furnished it."[15] This perspective had animated routes articulated in the Dual Contracts and had found a place in the Regional Plan, but it was not to prevail in the deliberations that led to the independent subway lines then under construction.

As mayor of New York, John Hylan had committed himself to building new city-owned and run subway lines that would compete with the IRT and BMT.

His demonization of the "traction interests" and his championing of the five-cent fare were popular and helped him twice win election. He was finally in a position to proceed with an independent subway line when the Board of Transportation superseded McAneny's Transit Commission in July 1924. Through the Board of Transportation, John Delaney immediately set out to devise routes that would improve service in established business and residential districts and replace elevated lines. These guidelines did not bode well for Staten Island, though, nor did the timing of the board's work. The Board of Estimate's Narrows tunnel was still an ongoing project when the Board of Transportation proposed eight new lines in December 1924, none of which extended to Staten Island. To add a subway to Richmond after the Nicoll-Hofstadter law subsequently killed the freight-and-passenger tunnel would have meant adding a component to and contravening the defining parameters for a subway expansion plan already underway in 1925 and already under criticism for its great cost. Of the seven new lines eventually built, only one reached a relatively unpopulated area (in Queens).[16]

The Nicoll-Hofstadter Act placed serious constraints on a Narrows tunnel for rapid transit, its permissive language for a subway to Staten Island notwithstanding. Not only was the city already committed to other routes for its independent subway system, but Hylan thought the law killed the whole Narrows tunnel project by taking away the source of revenue that would make it cost effective. Consumed by the political challenge posed by Walker in the election of 1925 and obligated by the law to let the Board of Transportation and not the Board of Estimate lead any tunnel initiative, Hylan left the matter alone as he completed his term as mayor. Despite an initial public declaration of intent to proceed on a rapid-transit tunnel, Delaney soon signaled his own lack of enthusiasm for a purely passenger tunnel. Most city officials tended to oversell the prospects for a Narrow crossing, but Delaney offered a gloomy public assessment of the project. In an interview with the *Staten Islander* in June 1925, he noted that the cost would be nearly double the $22 million claimed by the McAvoy report released a few months earlier and admitted that his engineers were now focused on the other boroughs' subway needs. Perhaps even more provocatively in a city where the five-cent subway fare remained sacrosanct, Delaney floated the possibility of a one-dollar charge to make it self-supporting.[17] Even with the incoming Walker administration's public record of support for a Narrows tunnel, the Board of Transportation omitted such a tunnel from its latest subway-expansion plans in early 1926.[18]

By 1926, many leading Staten Island businessmen were clamoring for a bridge and not a tunnel to Brooklyn. For years, the idea that a bridge might best link Staten Island with the rest of the city had periodically entered public discussions, but the halting of the Hylan tunnel work gave it new purchase.[19]

Just weeks after the Nicoll-Hofstadter law took effect, Louis Tribus, former commissioner of public works on Staten Island, promoted the idea in a featured article in the *Staten Islander*. A few months later, the suitably named Edward Bridgeman hosted a meeting of bankers, realtors, publishers, and other professionals from Staten Island and Bay Ridge, Brooklyn, out of which came the Narrows Bridge Campaign Committee. The leadership of both the SICC and the Staten Island Civic League spoke favorably of a bridge, and the *Staten Islander* vigorously promoted it.[20] A number of organizations elsewhere in the city favored the idea, ranging from the predictable support from the Brooklyn Chamber of Commerce to the surprising advocacy from the Municipal Art Society.[21]

These proponents argued that a bridge posed several advantages over a tunnel. A bridge would evade the proscriptions of the Nicoll-Hofstadter law and generate revenue by including rails for freight and passengers. It would enhance the usefulness of the planned bridges to New Jersey by including lanes for automobiles. It would make a spectacular entrance to New York Harbor.[22] As Tribus wrote, a Narrows bridge would be "not only a tribute of New York for the vast convenience of an enormously growing traffic, connecting the west with the east, but a monument to engineering skill, esthetic taste, architectural proportion, financial ability and breadth of vision of the whole United States."[23] To accomplish these goals, a privately commissioned engineering study described a massive $50 million bridge: a suspension bridge 11,000 feet long with a 4,000-foot central span; 125 feet wide with room for six to eight vehicular lanes, two to four rail lines, and pedestrian lanes; and 200 feet high to keep the Narrows clear for shipping.[24]

Doubts about the feasibility of a bridge ultimately forestalled any concerted effort to pursue one. Initial speculation that the Board of Transportation liked the idea proved untrue as Delaney adhered to the War Department's reluctance to approve a span over the Narrows. State senator Thomas Walsh recognized that the idea needed considerable backing and urged its advocates to secure the Port Authority's support. Borough president Lynch, though careful to praise the project, cautioned Staten Island civic groups not to act in way detrimental to prospects for a subway tunnel, which he preferred for its lower cost.[25] The *Staten Island Advance* echoed this concern in early December 1925, reminding its readers, "Those who recall the delay of many years, the frequent defeats and the political side-tracking of the Staten Island tunnel plan cannot but fear that this colossal bridge project will serve to jeopardize the bitterly won concession of the tunnel."[26] In the midst of considerable bridge hoopla in New York and Staten Island newspapers, the SICC determined to work primarily for a Narrows subway tunnel, and the city's lame-duck Board of Estimate declined to allocate $100,000 for initial surveys, borings, and cost estimates for a bridge.[27] Thus, the end of 1925 left Staten Islanders stymied in their efforts to obtain any kind of connection with Brooklyn: either a freight-and-passenger tunnel or a rapid-transit tunnel or a suspension bridge.

Advocates continued their efforts to ignite a Narrows bridge movement into the early 1930s. Having encountered little interest from public entities, Bridgeman and other Staten Island and Brooklyn business leaders formed the Narrows Development Corporation in September 1926. Ostensibly a private company with the intention of building a bridge, its real goal was to raise funds for preliminary surveys that might then spur the city to action.[28] Several Brooklyn and Staten Island organizations pressed the Board of Estimate to either grant the company a franchise or to take definitive action on what many now called the Liberty Bridge.[29] Within a year, the corporation had reorganized as the Interboro Bridge Company and had submitted an application to the War Department for permission to construct a bridge.

The Interboro Bridge Company brought together Staten Island boosters with prominent men from other parts of the city, most notably Brooklyn. James S. Graham, a Brooklyn resident and real estate dealer on Staten Island's south shore, served as its president. On its board sat a former U.S. secretary of commerce, a former Brooklyn Borough president, and a former New York City comptroller. The company commissioned the well-established engineering firm of David B. Steinman—who also served on the board—and Holton D. Robinson to produce an engineering study.[30] The SICC, with its former president and current secretary also serving as officers in the company, was intertwined with the bridge company and formed a bridge committee to coordinate with chamber counterparts in Brooklyn, Queens, and Long Island.[31] Their efforts, however, were soon eclipsed by the Walker administration's initiatives in transportation planning.

Rails or Roads, 1926–1929

Mayor James Walker took urban planning seriously. Remembered mostly for his elegant image, active social life, expansive patronage, and the personal corruption that forced his resignation during his second term, Tammany's "Beau" Jimmy Walker became "one of the best friends planning advocates ever had."[32] In his first year in office, Walker established a 472-member City Committee on Plan and Survey to explore all facets of public administration, including transit.[33] His administration repeatedly sought the creation of a New York City Bridge and Tunnel Authority that could investigate a list of long-standing project ideas and issue bonds to construct those found to be worthy.[34] It also cooperated with the Committee on the Regional Plan, the private organization hard at work developing a comprehensive plan for the metropolitan area.[35] In late 1928, the Board of Estimate established a Bridge Committee to review recent communications from civic groups urging a variety of Narrows projects, including a bridge, a vehicular tunnel, and a rapid-transit tunnel.[36] Just weeks later the Board of Estimate engaged the engineering firm Day and Zimmerman to study the city's traffic needs and make proposals for bridges, tunnels, and highways.[37]

The emergence of a vehicular tunnel as the city's favored option for a Narrows connection evolved out of this larger effort to plan bridges, tunnels, and arteries for New York City and its region. In prior years, Staten Island voices had dominated advocacy efforts for a Narrows crossing, while business and political leaders from the other outer boroughs sometimes chimed in support or opposition. By 1926, demands for the linkage of Staten Island and Brooklyn often came from non-Richmond entities. Walker's City Committee and the Interboro Bridge Company exemplified this pattern, as did the actions of the other outer boroughs' chambers of commerce. In particular, the Brooklyn Chamber of Commerce repeatedly asserted the need for a Narrows tunnel and/or bridge that would serve all three major types of traffic: rapid transit, rail freight, and vehicles. By 1929, its focus had narrowed to a vehicular crossing, as did the demands of the Queens Chamber of Commerce, when its confidence that the Port Authority would build its long-proposed New Jersey-to-Brooklyn freight tunnel waned.[38] In the spirit of the abundant regional planning initiatives in the late 1920s, Brooklyn, Queens, and Staten Island business and civic organizations increasingly justified a Narrows vehicular crossing as part of a larger network of other current and future infrastructure projects.

The Regional Plan Association was an especially authoritative off-island voice for a Narrows connection. Viewed on Staten Island with a mix of appreciation and trepidation, the association produced a massive plan in 1929 that proposed major new rail facilities for freight and passenger traffic.[39] Staten Island would be served by an outer belt line, which would reached St. George on the island and then Brooklyn through a tunnel under the Narrows, and three inner belt lines, including one in northern New Jersey with a spur from Jersey City to Staten Island over the Kill Van Kull. Six commuter and long-distance passenger terminals were slated for New Jersey, along with at least one placed in every borough, with Staten Island's to be located south of Port Richmond. Rapid transit would also be expanded, with all rails for passengers in "unified operation." Vehicular traffic would enjoy new parkways and boulevards but would move efficiently on its own system of highway loops. The major loop would pass through Richmond via the Narrows tunnel and Goethals Bridges, with a minor one from Staten Island over what would become the Bayonne Bridge to Fort Lee, where it would connect to the planned span to Upper Manhattan.[40]

The Port Authority's decision to build two (subsequently three) vehicular bridges to New Jersey generated considerable momentum for a similar Narrows crossing. For businesses and residents in Brooklyn and Queens, spanning the Narrows made little sense unless accompanied by roadways to New Jersey. The state legislative approval of the Goethals Bridge and Outerbridge Crossing in 1924 provided a new justification for a Narrows structure that was only enhanced by the opening of these two structures four years later.[41] Albert Goldman, Walker's commissioner of plant and structures, feared the traffic that would ensue when bridges and tunnels from New Jersey to Staten Island and Manhattan were completed without sufficient interborough links.[42] James Graham of the Interboro Bridge Company expected the bridges to revive the prospects for a Narrows crossing, as did the *New York Times*, which surmised that without such a crossing ferries would transport cars from New Jersey into Manhattan or Brooklyn.[43] Robert Moses, speaking before the Parks Association in 1930, literally traced a pointer across a huge map of New York City to show the audience how a motor vehicle could move from his Long Island parkways to what would become the Belt Parkway and then proceed through a tube under the Narrows, across Staten Island, and finally over one of the new bridges to New Jersey. Then, retracing his way over the Narrows, he moved his pointer north and east through Brooklyn to the terminus of the Grand Central Parkway in Queens, where he asked the audience to imagine a series of bridges connecting it to Manhattan and the Bronx.[44]

The city's prospective Triborough Bridge was also influential in spurring developments for a Narrows crossing. First promoted in 1916 and allotted a small planning appropriation nine years later, the project was uniformly championed by civic and business leaders in Queens, Brooklyn, and the Bronx.[45] Like Moses with his pointer, civic boosters imagined it as part of a road network with multiple components, typically including a midtown tunnel, a Narrows tube, and a highway connecting all three crossings. The Brooklyn Chamber of Commerce made these interconnected items the heart of its Four Point Comprehensive Plan, and other chambers of commerce and boards of trade in Brooklyn, Queens, the Bronx, and Long Island advocated for them as well.[46] The city's Citizens Union, which had fiercely opposed the Hylan tunnel, favored action on all of these arteries for vehicles. Mayor Walker included them all in a proposed $500 million program for bridges and tunnels, and a bill to authorize them was introduced by a city alderman in September 1928.[47]

The Walker administration's determination to build a vehicular tunnel under the Narrows doused the nascent movement to span it despite the considerable public wrangling over the best option. The internal dissension in the SICC that began this chapter also occurred in larger forums as bridge and tunnel advocates sparred in the press and at meetings of professional associations. When David Steinman presented the features of his bridge design to the New York section of the American Society of Engineers, Ole Singstad rose to reject it in favor of a Narrows tunnel. Steinman had proposed a structure even more massive than earlier plans, to which Singstad, the originator of the innovative ventilation system of the recently opened Holland Tunnel, raised political and mechanical concerns.[48] Most engineers at the meeting appeared to prefer a span over the Narrows, but most Board of Estimate members lined up against the bridge. While Walker was reported to be ambivalent and Lynch noncommittal, Board of Aldermen president Joseph McKee and comptroller (and Staten Island resident) Charles Berry opposed and blocked the granting of a franchise to the Interboro Bridge Company.[49] The political terrain grew even more treacherous when the U.S. War Department began signaling its disinclination to approve a bridge and subsequently approved a tunnel but not a bridge.[50] The Board of Estimate never ruled out a bridge even after it had the Board of Transportation develop plans for a tunnel, but Staten Islanders surely recognized which structure had emerged victorious. As the *Staten Island Advance* proclaimed in a headline in late 1929, "Vehicular Tunnel Bans Narrows Bridge Plan."[51]

Behind the demand for the Liberty Bridge and the vehicular tunnel lay the inescapable fact that American culture beckoned the automobile and that automobile usage nationwide was flourishing. In 1929, the nation's nearly 27 million motor vehicles traveled about 198 billion miles.[52] In New York City, traffic was both rapidly growing and increasingly portrayed as a problem, and the Liberty Bridge was proposed as a solution (see figure 8.1). The number of motor vehicles registered in the city rose from 379,000 in 1923 to 511,000 in 1926, with the *New York Times* declaring that "the motor car has come into dominance."[53] By 1928, there were 675,000 registered motor vehicles in the city, and trucks and automobiles arriving from Long Island, Westchester, and New Jersey only added to the traffic woes. Newspapers regularly reported on massive traffic jams and hours-long waits at ferry terminals. Much of the information on hot spots came from data compiled by the Committee on the Regional Plan, which was greatly concerned with motor vehicle congestion.[54] To many experts and automobile boosters, the solution was obvious. As Jane Holtz Kay has observed, "When bottlenecks came, planners looked to more roads," and Matthew Dalbey argues the same for boosters.[55] Vehicular bridges to New Jersey, however, did not top the list of transportation improvements wanted by many Staten Islanders, but they were obtainable when others were not. Like the islanders' support for the Hylan tunnel, this sort of realism often permeated Staten Island organizations and led them to back the project deemed most agreeable rather than most desirable. The Staten Island Board of Trade preferred the Narrows bridge but made clear that it would support the project "which appears to the Minute Men [members] to be the line of least resistance."[56] The SICC pushed for completion of a vehicular tunnel (even though many members preferred rapid transit) because politically it was the only viable option in late 1929.[57] The *Staten Island Advance* expressed

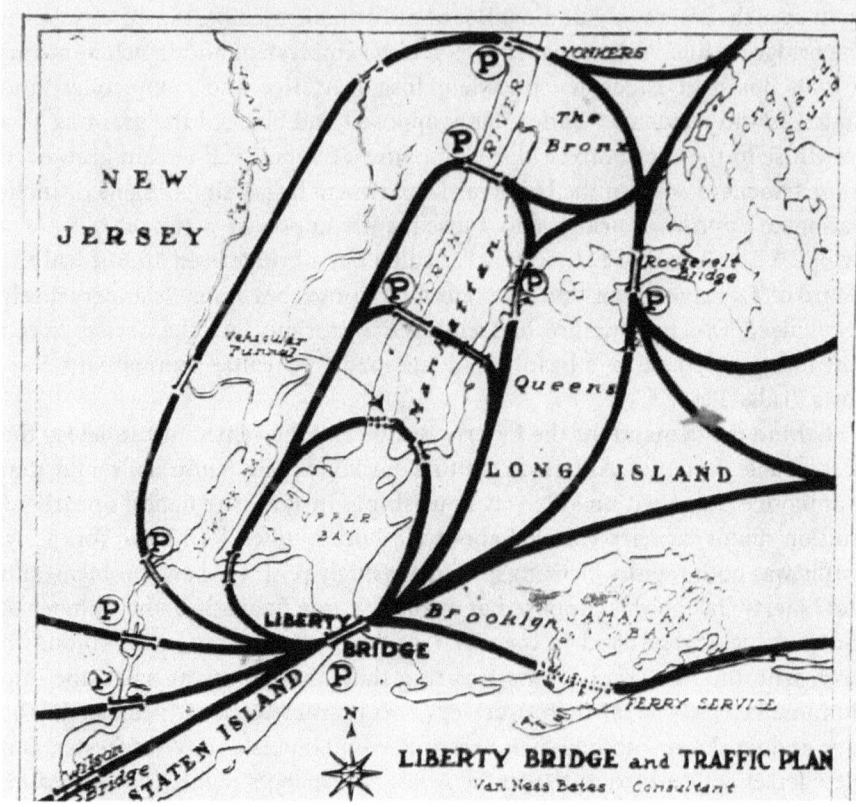

8.1 The Liberty Bridge proposal

Proponents of the Liberty Bridge in the late 1920s posited its fundamental role in automobile transport by generating beltways around Manhattan as well as highways to the rest of the continental United States.

Source: Staten Island Advance, December 9, 1925. Courtesy of Collection of the Staten Island Museum.

heightened enthusiasm for a Narrows bridge when its prospects appeared especially strong and subsequently urged work on a vehicular tunnel even though it found rapid transit the "most alluring" plan.[58] A letter writer to the paper favored a subway to Bayonne, New Jersey, in part because he thought the PRR would continue to block the construction of a Narrows tube. Likewise, the *Advance* rejected criticism that Staten Island didn't really need the Port Authority's bridges to New Jersey. The island, it argued, would simply get what it could.[59]

Even as Staten Island leaders argued for the more important Narrows connection, they had thought for years that a span to New Jersey made sense. They routinely conversed about one with New Jersey politicians and businessmen from Elizabeth to Perth Amboy.[60] The Port Authority may not have been looking to build bridges for vehicles, but its aspirations for a more comprehensive rail system remained at the mercy of railroad companies unwilling or unable to cooperate.[61] The authority's institutional capabilities and political support meshed well with Staten Islanders' dreams. Instead of competing with more populous and politically powerful boroughs for meager city resources, Staten Islanders took advantage of both the rise of the automobile and the new possibilities for interstate cooperation embodied by the Port Authority. The opening of motor vehicle bridges to New Jersey as well as the Walker administration's interest in planning and the strong demand for more highways, tunnels, and bridges in the other outer boroughs had by 1929 considerably improved the borough's chances of obtaining the elusive Narrows connection.

A series of actions in early 1929 demonstrated how favorable Staten Island's position had become for a vehicular tunnel. Even as Mayor Walker awaited his consulting engineers' study, he made a public commitment to build and connect a Triborough bridge and Narrows tunnel and introduced legislation to fund both through bonds and tolls.[62] The Board of Estimate voted unanimously to build them and ordered the Board of Transportation to begin planning and make borings. Certain contours of the tunnel were already known. The tunnel would cross at the shortest point—from Fort Hamilton, Brooklyn, to Rosebank, Staten Island—though the greater depth there required entrances farther from the shore. It would be paid for through the sale of city bonds and the charging of tolls. Moving quickly, the Board of Transportation presented its formal plans in June, projecting two tubes to cost $78 million and take five years to construct. The most significant step came in July, when the Board of Estimate voted to appropriate $3 million for the tunnel.[63] But would Staten Island not just settle for but also embrace an initiative that did not emanate from it? Or, as one local civic leader put it, was the island being "hoodwinked" by the Walker administration?[64]

The emergence of the Narrows vehicular tunnel in late 1928 allowed the tension between rails and rubber to crystallize on Staten Island. In spite of the Walker administration's endorsement of a vehicular tunnel and the SICC's support of a Narrows bridge—or perhaps because of them—the Tompkinsville Board of Trade expanded its lobbying efforts for the completion of the Hylan tunnel to be used only for rapid transit. The group hosted a mass meeting attended by hundreds, at which its leaders argued that finishing the subway tunnel would avoid writing off the $6 million already spent and that doing so quickly would keep reasonable the cost of the land already condemned for it. Some of the other reasons offered for a rail tunnel—such as the island's growing population, overcrowded ferries, and traffic from the bridges to New Jersey—might just have easily been harnessed in support of a vehicular crossing, though.[65]

The editorial page of the *Staten Island Advance* revealed similar tensions over what was the most appropriate connection to Brooklyn. In the aftermath of the Board of Estimate's approval of the vehicular tunnel, many readers asserted that Staten Island needed a rapid-transit and not a vehicular tunnel. As one asked skeptically, "Will a vehicular tunnel to Brooklyn meet the requirements of Staten Islanders or the desire of autoists to pass us by on their way to the Jersey pleasure gardens?"[66] Only the speeding up of travel time from home to business provided by a rapid-transit tunnel, the writer contended, would yield the population growth desired by so many. Without denying the value of a subway, the newspaper acquiesced to a vehicle tunnel, telling readers that the project would provide some local benefits even though the city's interest in building one had little to do with Staten Island's needs. The Staten Island Real Estate Board, recognizing that the city's vehicular tunnel was not intended to build up Richmond Borough, pressed Lynch to commit to a subway and planned yet another mass campaign for rapid transit. At the same time, though, the board's president urged Staten Islanders to accept the city's vehicular tunnel.[67]

Backing the vehicular tunnel did not signify rejection of rapid transit, but it did dampen the likelihood for it. The *Advance* typically offered an optimistic assessment of the island's chances for rapid transit even if the vehicular tunnel were built.[68] Borough president Lynch, the SICC, and other Staten Island civic and political leaders claimed there was no conflict—or at least no harm—in advocating for both vehicular and rail connections to the rest of the city.[69] For other islanders, the notion of receiving two links after years of failure in getting even one Narrows crossing seemed absurd. They instead expected the vehicular tunnel to delay, not hasten, the arrival of rapid transit.[70] One letter to the editor chided the credulity of anyone who "believes that the city will spend another sixty million dollars or more for the other tube 'in a few years.'"[71] Three decades of futility in making just one connection warranted such doubts.

The Subway Reemerges, 1930–1932

One local organization was not at all convinced of a vehicular tunnel's utility or its potential to spur subsequent construction on a rapid-transit crossing. The Richmond County chapter of the New York State Society of Professional Engineers and Land Surveyors (SPE), headed by future New York City commissioner of public works Frederick Zurmuhlen, had completed a study of transit conditions on the island in April 1930. For $61 million, the SPE claimed, the city could provide Staten Island with efficient rapid-transit service for a five-cent fare. The report's most unique feature was its placement of the tunnel, illustrated in figure 8.2. The SPE rejected a route through Bayonne as too lengthy and a direct route to Manhattan as too limited. It argued that earlier proposals through Brooklyn had been undermined by the prospect of a time-consuming commute along the Fourth Avenue line to Manhattan. The SPE advocated instead for service not to Bay Ridge or Fort Hamilton but under the flats off of Red Hook directly to the subway station at Smith and Ninth Streets, a Brooklyn location much closer to Manhattan.[72]

The SPE moved to unify Staten Island around its plans, but its novel tunnel route unleashed the same basic conflict over location that had plagued earlier efforts to form an umbrella organization devoted to a subway. Invited by Zurmuhlen to form a permanent transit council, twenty-eight civic groups founded the Staten Island Transit Conference in April 1930, but members clashed at its very first meeting. While some arguments occurred over the engineering and financial details, many local civic activists remained firm supporters of earlier routes that the SPE report had discarded. Disagreement ensued in part over the projected usefulness of each particular location, but the core of the disharmony was tactical. The discord was not over what route would best serve the island but rather which route would garner the most support on and off the borough. Guest speakers Ole Singstad and Port Authority executive director John Ramsey contended that the Fourth Avenue route gave Staten Island its "best shot." SPE members countered that a route to Red Hook would better attract interests in Brooklyn, Manhattan, and even Queens.[73] The Transit Conference's agenda evolved out of this contentious discussion: to assess multiple subway routes and ultimately recommend one to the island and city.

Staten Islanders deliberated over a subway location into 1931. The Transit Conference conducted its study and ruled out all the formerly considered locations until just one primary alternative to the SPE's proposal remained: a route to Manhattan via Governor's Island. The plan originated from a larger pitch to build an airport on Governor's Island and to link it by subway to Manhattan, Staten Island, and Bay Ridge. Its champions on Staten Island actively promoted it as better serving the majority of commuters heading to Manhattan and as more appealing politically because the airport would serve constituents throughout the city. The plan received favorable coverage in the local newspapers but ultimately failed to sway enough members of the Transit Conference.[74] At a well-attended meeting in April 1931, the SPE proposal took the final vote, 27–15.[75] By mid-May, twenty-seven local groups had passed resolutions of support for the Transit Conference plan, and newspapers including the *Staten Island Advance* and the *Brooklyn Eagle* had commented favorably

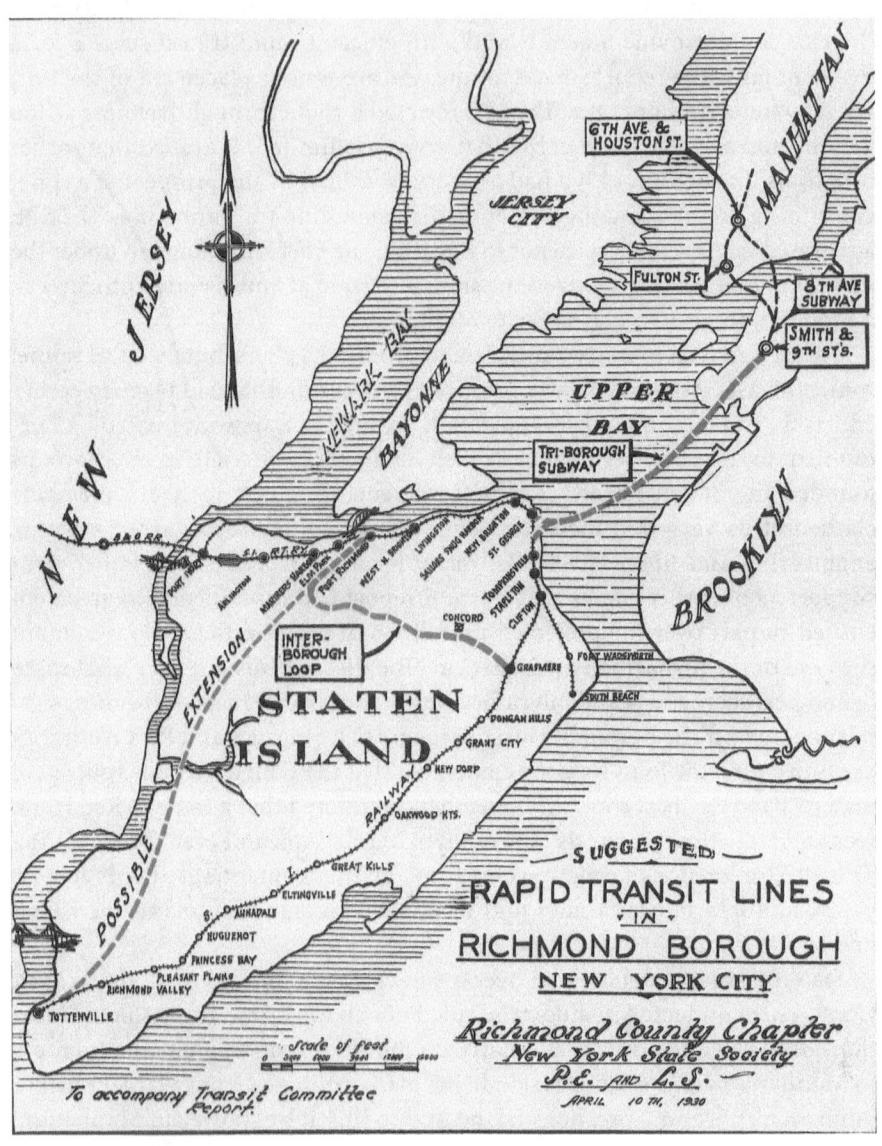

8.2 Staten Island engineers propose a new subway route to Brooklyn

The Richmond County Chapter of the New York State Society of Professional Engineers spearheaded the continued drive for a subway link during the 1930s, but it preferred a longer tunnel that would reach Manhattan more quickly and so settled on a route from St. George, Staten Island, to the Smith and Ninth Street subway station in what was then called South Brooklyn. It also wanted to expand the island's internal network of passenger rails.

Source: Courtesy of Collection of the Staten Island Museum.

on it.[76] That November, the Transit Conference organized three mass rallies for the subway, with one in New Dorp attracting more people than any gathering during the most recent election campaign and demonstrating the continuing potency of Staten Island's interest in a subway.[77]

Despite the momentum for a subway on Staten Island, the Transit Conference's movement faltered when it encountered the intransigence of key city politicians. Locally, Staten Island public officials undermined the Transit Conference's decision to push the SPE's subway proposal. Lynch and Consulting Engineer Theodore Oxholm had demurred from expressing any preference for a particular route during deliberations, but once the Transit Conference voted, Lynch acknowledged that he preferred a plan that would use the Hylan shafts. The borough president had also promised to submit the plan to the Board of Estimate in the immediate aftermath of the Transit Conference vote but subsequently urged the conference to desist from agitation.[78] Had he publicly advocated more forcefully for the Transit Conference's subway tunnel, Lynch still would have had to contend with the sentiment of Mayor Walker, other members of the Board of Estimate, and Delaney, who still chaired the Board of Transportation—all of whom to varying degrees resisted the drive for a Staten Island subway.

The "elusive Delaney," as one local activist called him, was perhaps the most formidable opponent. Certain that the current work on the independent subway routes would keep the city at its debt limit for years, he earned much scorn for telling a Transit Conference delegation that the island had "no chance" for a subway. Perhaps even more frustrating to conference members, Delaney had already spent years delaying a Board of Transportation study of rapid-transit options for Staten Island. He had dropped the matter entirely until begrudgingly agreeing in 1931 to include a discussion on rapid transit as part of his expected report on the Narrows vehicular tunnel, anticipated for early February 1932.[79]

Other Staten Islanders began to undermine the local unity around the Transit Conference's selected route to Brooklyn. Comptroller Berry offered the SICC his support for rapid transit in lieu of a vehicular tunnel to Richmond but saw a line over the Bayonne Bridge and through New Jersey as the most feasible route. The *Advance* also preferred a subway but began inching back toward the position that any plan was better than no plan, a stance that led it directly back to Walker's plans for the Narrows.[80] The Transit Conference insisted its route retain status as the island's choice, but it struggled to address an increasingly important question: How would its transit project fare against the city's many other infrastructure projects also vying for public funds?

The Narrows vehicular tunnel's inclusion in the city's package of motor vehicle projects helped position it to answer that question. Nevertheless, how the Narrows tunnel was prioritized among the various projects in the package mattered a great deal for its prospects of completion. As the project with "the widest support," the Triborough Bridge received a $3 million appropriation before its counterparts received anything, and Mayor Walker broke ground before 10,000 spectators on October 25, 1929.[81] The future Queens–Midtown Tunnel eventually nudged aside the Narrows tunnel as well. In part because the question of vehicular bridge or tunnel remained indeterminate for so long, the city started to study a midtown tunnel before it took any further action on a Narrows crossing. An earlier Board of Estimate resolution had authorized the Narrows tunnel and Triborough Bridge but omitted the tunnel to Queens, spurring intense lobbying from that borough's civic groups. The board subsequently appropriated $2 million for a midtown tunnel on the same day it allocated $3 million for the Narrows tunnel.[82] The Narrows tunnel was then subordinated by the midtown tunnel a few months later when the Day and Zimmerman report for the Board of Estimate listed it and a Triborough bridge but not a Narrows tunnel as top priorities.[83]

The city made some progress on the Narrows tunnel over the next two years despite the tunnel's struggles against competing projects amid the onset of the Great Depression. At the city's bequest, in 1930 the state legislature passed the Steingut bill, which provided the Board of Transportation with the authority it needed to spearhead the tunnel work.[84] Board engineers reviewed plans with interested constituencies and published some details—most notably that the various tunnels would be longer and wider than originally anticipated. The War Department approved the project, and workers began to make borings in late 1930.[85] Nevertheless, planning for the Narrows tunnel lagged behind that of a midtown tunnel. Final blueprints were not yet ready in 1930 because some key engineering decisions remained, primarily how to handle the tricky problem of ventilation, where to place the terminal plazas, whether to accommodate the freight interests of the B&O, and which method of construction to use—shield or trench. In late 1930, the Board of Transportation estimated a July 1932 start date and a four-year construction process.[86] By then, though, it was too late for the city to fend off the severe budgetary constraints posed by the economic crisis that had engulfed the nation following the stock market crash of 1929.

As the condition of the city's finances worsened, it became increasingly untenable to continue many of the major projects underway. Retrenchment occurred in multiple stages. In 1930, the city rescinded the $3 million dollars—most of which had not yet been spent—it had approved for the Narrows tunnel the previous year. It then made smaller appropriations as needed to cover the salaries of the engineers planning the tunnel, the last of which came in November 1931.[87] The midtown tunnel was the first to face the budget axe, with work halted in 1931, but prominent businessmen soon called for additional suspensions, including of the Narrows tunnel.[88] Following a pattern nationwide, New York became mired in the worst phase of the Depression in 1932. Nearly one in four employable New Yorkers was homeless, city revenues reached their low point, and construction expenditures declined by 70 percent between 1931 and 1933.[89] Early that year the city determined that it would continue planning for the Narrows tunnel but without allowing any additional expenditure or accrual of debt. Two months later it rescinded much of the money still appropriated for the tunnel, and work on it all but halted.[90] Neither the Triborough Bridge nor the Queens–Midtown Tunnel fared better, though in the end they rebounded much more quickly, with the former opening in 1936 and the latter in 1940. Their revival occurred in large part because a new entity became crucial to the success of large urban infrastructure projects: the federal government.

* * *

Over a seven-year period, Staten Islanders had pinballed between three distinct connections to Brooklyn and lived through the demise of another mayoral effort to physically link their island to the rest of New York City. Walker's vehicular tunnel, though never built, was an obvious precursor to the Verrazzano Bridge, intended to play the same role in the larger artery of highways being built in New York City. The SPE's plan for a subway indicated the resilience of interest in rapid transit even after the automobile had begun to transform metropolitan space. These unbuilt projects, however, were indicative of the fundamental conflicts embedded in their features. The advocates for the Liberty Bridge literally tried to span the competing options by including them all. These discrete possibilities were thus intertwined, and their interaction revealed new aspects of Staten Island's plight.

The significant issue from the Hylan debacle—Would a link carry freight or passengers?—had diminished but not disappeared. If the link included the former, would it primarily serve short- or long-haul goods? If it served the latter, would it provide rapid transit for Staten Island or another commuter option for New Jersey? The ascension of the freight role in the Hylan tunnel had riled many island residents, and in the years immediately after this project's termination, it was primarily the Interboro Bridge Company that sought a link for the transport of goods as well as people. Local boosters regularly trumpeted both an industrial and a residential future for the island, but these two components were not always compatible. Many Staten Islanders had not mourned the demise of the Hylan tunnel even though they had not actively organized against it and did not aim to include a place for freight in a prospective link.

A second dilemma was whether a crossing would serve trains or automobiles. The increase in automobile ownership and usage, the completion of vehicular bridges to New Jersey, and the planning of a regional system of additional crossings and highways for commerce pointed to making a Narrows link for motor vehicles. Mayor Walker's administration championed a vehicular tunnel and was moving forward until the Great Depression eroded the city's fiscal resources. At the same time, planners still called for a subway tunnel but admitted that it was years away from fruition. With pragmatism as their guide, Staten Islanders largely acquiesced to the vehicular tunnel project, but the SPE and other civic leaders continued to prefer and pursue a subway.

Finally, this period saw the rise of a tension between advocates of a Narrows tunnel and supporters of a bridge. For decades, professionals and citizens alike had debated the relative merits of these two options for numerous locations and would continue to do so, most notably in the 1930s with the rejection of Robert Moses's Brooklyn Battery Bridge proposal.[91] On Staten Island, the conflict that crystallized in the mid-1920s remained in place for two decades. Although the bridge advocates were largely prominent businessmen, the island's tunnel proponents primarily held sway from 1925 to 1932. Only in the mid-1940s would Moses's plan for a Narrows bridge emerge triumphant.

Staten Islanders were no less wracked by these choices and contexts than businessmen, politicians, and experts throughout the region. After 1925, their organizational efforts did not reach the level achieved during the eras of the Dual Contracts and the Hylan tunnel. Civic boosters faced perennial issues—squabbling among Staten Islanders and the city's financial limitations—and new challenges, such as the more overt competition from projects championed by constituents in the other boroughs and rising conflict between the needs of the borough and the needs of the region.[92] As Staten Islanders confronted the shifts affecting most urban areas in the United States during the 1920s, the resilience of their ambitions for a subway is noteworthy. Even as city and regional entities embraced developing modes of transportation for motor vehicles, the Staten Island Transit Conference determined that a subway to Staten Island would best serve the borough. Staten Island engineers and civic leaders continued to urge a rail connection well after the political defeat of Hylan's tunnel in 1925.

CHAPTER 9

FACING THE COMPETITION

Last Gasps for a Subway and a Tunnel, 1933–1945

Now we know who our enemies are.

—*Staten Island Advance*, December 6, 1933

Like many Staten Islanders, Herman W. Ordeman, vice president of the Staten Island Transit Conference, was dismayed to read in December 1933 a damning New York City Board of Transportation report regarding a subway tunnel to Staten Island. An engineer, civic leader, and soon-to-be consulting engineer to the Richmond Borough president, Ordeman was largely responsible for developing the now stalled Transit Conference proposal for a subway route, including its projected costs and anticipated revenues. Having already waited more than two years for the Board of Transportation study to be completed and released, Ordeman was outraged by its findings. The board had not even considered the location recommended by the Transit Conference, had made the four lines it had examined adjacent to but not connected to the Fourth Avenue subway in Brooklyn, and had projected insufficient ridership for every option. Long wary of the board's chairman, John Delaney, but confident after meeting and communicating with the board's engineers prior to the report's release, Transit Conference members and other Staten Islanders now felt "doublecrossed [*sic*]" by Delaney and other board members.[1] Equally frustrated with the "absurd" length of time to produce the report, the *Staten Island Transcript* could only wonder whether "this tunnel plan was drawn by the Board of Transportation with the intent of throwing cold water on the whole tunnel proposition."[2]

Ordeman's observation highlights a shift in the politics enveloping the efforts to connect Staten Island to the rest of the city. For three decades, New York City politicians and public officials had regularly spoken in favor of a Staten Island connection, yet no tunnel was built. With the exception of the Hylan tunnel's demise in 1925, it was often difficult to tell exactly from where the opposition came given that so many public pronouncements were supportive. Staten Islanders came to recognize—quite cynically—that come election season, the promises for a link were especially prevalent and thus particularly hollow. They had learned not to assume that the island's borough presidents—from George Cromwell to John Lynch—would necessarily fight for a tunnel in private meetings outside of the public's view.

The tight budgets of the Depression years made the competition for resources especially fierce, and as a result the political opposition Staten Island faced became more transparent than in the past. The Board of Transportation report confirmed what was long suspected: that Delaney was unequivocally opposed to a subway to Staten Island in the foreseeable future. But in December 1933 an even more significant antagonist was just days away from taking office: Fiorello La Guardia. Although the new mayor at times spoke favorably of a tunnel, he also repeatedly made it clear that a Staten Island tunnel would not be among his administration's priorities for public works. Without mayoral support, civic activists looked to Albany for backing, but at the state level a third antagonist loomed. Robert Moses thought favorably of a Narrows link—albeit one that carried motor vehicles and not rapid transit—but placed many other projects ahead of it. Knowing the antagonists' identity did not diminish their ability to stymie Staten Islanders' aspirations.

This opposition notwithstanding, in one important manner Staten Island's chances for obtaining a tunnel improved in 1933. The Roosevelt administration's New Deal programs provided a novel mechanism for financing the project: federal funding for public works. Most prominently, the Public Works Administration provided a combination of federal grants and loans to states and municipalities nationwide for large-scale projects beyond the reach of local governments alone. This administration and later federal programs expected applicants to work through local governments yet still enabled circumvention of them.[3] With their hopes for a transportation link to the rest of the city once again dashed, Transit Conference members and many other Staten Islanders embraced federal avenues for financing a tunnel. In so doing, they shifted momentum away from the plan for a vehicular tunnel and back toward the project they wanted most: a rapid-transit connection.

This chapter depicts how Staten Islanders attempted to gain access to federal funds for a subway tunnel and why they remained blocked despite these new features of governance and the massive infusion of federal funds into New York City. Looking first to the Reconstruction Finance Corporation, then to the Public Works Administration, and finally to the Works Progress Administration, Staten Islanders made their best case but ultimately fell short—hung up on one key point: they could persuade neither the La Guardia administration nor the New Deal agencies that a Narrows tunnel project would be self-liquidating.

New Opportunities for a Subway: The Great Depression and the Reconstruction Finance Corporation

As the Great Depression eviscerated municipalities' ability to finance many basic government functions, not to mention large-scale public-works projects, new possibilities for funding appeared. In the 1930s, the federal government undertook unprecedented interventions in the private and public sectors to forestall further financial ruin, stimulate economic activity, and create work for the unemployed. Herbert Hoover, whose supposed inactivity during the Depression was only true relative to the scale of the misery and the steps taken by his successor, established the Reconstruction Finance Corporation (RFC) in early 1932 to restart private money markets by infusing them with public funds. Capitalized at $500 million and authorized to borrow $1.5 billion, the RFC was able to provide financial assistance to banks, railroads, credit unions, insurance companies, and other large lenders. By July 1932, the RFC had made 4,000 loans totaling more than $1 billion, but although these funds helped, banks typically fortified their own reserves with them rather than loaned the money.[4]

The Hoover administration eventually turned to options it had long rejected: direct relief and large-scale public-works projects. With no revival of investment, production, and employment in sight, and after the Bonus Army of veterans marched on Washington, the president signed the Emergency Relief and Construction Act (ERCA) in July 1932. Under the ERCA, the RFC was allocated $1.5 billion to make loans on self-liquidating public-works projects, a hefty sum at the time though insufficient for covering the nation's employment and infrastructure needs. Even so, states and localities scrambled for these newly available resources and overwhelmed the RFC with applications, most of which were eventually denied for not meeting the self-liquidating standard. This mandate required extra scrutiny of plans to ensure that the proposed projects could produce income to cover costs, interest, and amortization and was especially burdensome to cities. By the time Hoover left office in March 1933, only ninety-two applications for $197 million had been approved, and only $20 million had actually been disbursed.[5] These figures, of course, were initially unbeknownst to the Staten Islanders, who immediately recognized that the ERCA offered at least two clear local benefits: work for those in need and a mechanism for funding a rapid-transit tunnel.

In 1932, many residents of Richmond embraced the evolving federal approach to public works and looked to the RFC for succor from their physical isolation. During the congressional debate over the Reconstruction Finance Corporation Act, Staten Island congressman Anning Prall offered an unsuccessful amendment to make cities directly eligible for RFC public-works loans. The *Staten Island Advance* praised Hoover for his new flexibility regarding this issue in the spring of 1932, which might at last provide the island a mechanism for funding its rapid-transit tunnel. As the legislation that would become the ERCA inched toward passage in July, Prall, lobbied by the Transit Conference, vowed to his constituents that he would strive to help secure a subway loan from the RFC. Likewise, borough president Lynch informed Richmond residents that he would ask the Board of Estimate to apply for an RFC loan.[6] These reassurances only begged the question whether the city would finally prioritize a Staten Island connection. The prospect of federal funds was not as liberating as it appeared.

Staten Islanders understood that they could not sidestep the municipal and state politics that had long deferred their desires. A report by the American Society of Civil Engineers in 1932 identified hundreds of suspended projects nationwide totaling more than $2.25 billion that would qualify as self-liquidating—with more than $1 billion in projects halted in New York State alone. Multiple constituencies and locales angled to have their projects prioritized. The Fifth Avenue Association of Manhattan vocally championed the Triborough Bridge and Queens–Midtown Tunnel projects, and the Queens Borough president had already written to the RFC about the former. Robert Moses planned to request funds for parkways. The Port Authority looked for aid for its Lincoln Tunnel proposal. Some Brooklynites still clamored for a vehicular rather than rapid-transit tunnel. With so much competition, Staten Islanders feared that Lynch and the Transit Conference were too passive given the immense difficulty of garnering sufficient support from the Board of Estimate.[7] Thus, Staten Island contended with the same urban competition it always had—the other boroughs proposing projects that would inevitably serve far more people—as well as with the need for gubernatorial approval in a state political environment not particularly hospitable to its metropolis.[8]

The Walker administration ultimately did not prioritize a tunnel to Staten Island. Although federal money was not available yet, the administration had included a vehicular Narrows tunnel in a list of projects in late 1930 to provide "constructive help for NYC's unemployed—unskilled and White collar groups."[9] In 1932, Walker still wanted a tunnel for motor vehicles, while strong sentiment remained on Staten Island for a subway tunnel, but neither was considered shovel ready in the same way that other suspended projects were.[10] The Walker administration had not signaled any interest in pursuing a loan for the Narrows crossing, and the *Staten Island Advance* recognized that the proposed Triborough Bridge and Lincoln Tunnel benefited from far more support than a Staten Island tunnel.[11] Mayor Walker appeared to grow more amenable to a Narrows tunnel for rapid transit, but his resignation as mayor in September 1932, stemming from a two-year investigation of his acceptance of bribes and following a public hearing before then governor Franklin Roosevelt, did not fundamentally relieve the political pressures that worked against Staten Island.[12]

Unable to count on mayoral backing, Staten Islanders appealed directly to their elected officials in Washington for support for the tunnel. Heeding neither Lynch's voice of caution nor the vehemence of one civic leader who urged a "march on City Hall, 50,000 strong," the Transit Conference embarked on a letter campaign and personal lobbying.[13] In September 1932, U.S. senator Robert Wagner and congressman Prall of New York met with RFC officials to make the case for a rapid-transit tunnel. They were joined at a second meeting by local leaders, including Lynch, Frederick Zurmuhlen, and Arthur Hedquist of the SICC. These men emphasized fiscal considerations—from the familiar argument about the millions already invested by the city to the RFC's new requirement for a project to be self-liquidating. RFC officials agreed to have their engineers review the plans with an emphasis on the projected costs and revenues rather than on a tunnel's technical feasibility, but they offered little encouragement.[14] How could they, when the RFC was inundated by special requests from numerous legislators? In fact, Senator Wagner himself had engaged in similar tactics on behalf of the Triborough Bridge more than one month earlier.[15]

Staten Islanders continued to press in 1933 for a rapid-transit tunnel. In early May, Lynch arranged for a four-hundred-person delegation to meet with New York City's recently elected mayor, John O'Brien.[16] There, the SICC urged the mayor to commit to a Narrows project, and the Transit Conference lobbied for the particular route it had identified. Zurmuhlen intimated that the RFC was inclined to approve an application if the city would just make it, but Mayor O'Brien, citing complications with the RFC, informed the gathering that the city would not make a loan request. His administration nonetheless consented to a trip to Washington by the Brooklyn and Staten Island borough presidents for another long-shot meeting with RFC officials.[17]

The islanders did not, however, possess a strong case that a Narrows tunnel would cover its costs. This economic reality was not lost on its supporters. Only by stretching the definition of *self-liquidating* could the Transit Conference meet that standard.[18] The conference also dubiously contended that thousands of ferry riders would immediately switch to the subway, making the tunnel solvent nearly from the start. The Transit Conference always acknowledged that tunnel revenues would not cover operating expenses during its first year of operation, but its projections were growing bleaker—by May 1933 it projected that its tunnel would operate in the red for three years.[19] For all of its efforts, the Transit Conference could not claim the tunnel met the RFC's condition, but by then additional avenues for federal support of public works had opened. By the time the latest Staten Island delegation arrived in Washington in late June, the Roosevelt administration was in office, so the delegation's destination was now the recently authorized Public Works Administration.[20]

Last Chance for a Subway: The New Deal and the Expansion of Federal Roles

When Franklin Delano Roosevelt was inaugurated as president of the United States in March 1933, he moved quickly to address various aspects of the Depression within the first hundred days of taking office. His administration declared a national bank holiday and induced Congress to pass bills related to banking, farming, industry, public works, regional planning, and unemployment relief. From these acts arose the earliest of the alphabet agencies that promulgated the work of the New Deal: the Civilian Conservation Corps, the Tennessee Valley Authority, the National Recovery Administration, the Home Owners' Loan Corporation, and, most significantly for the tunnel advocates on Staten Island, the Public Works Administration (PWA).[21]

The PWA marked a massive expansion of the federal government's role in financing public works. Initially empowered to make grants and loans valued at $3.3 billion, it was especially alluring to city officials and civic boosters with idle infrastructure projects. Despite the attractiveness of federal largesse, the PWA also posed a political risk if its considerable funds were distributed unfairly or corruptly. This outcome especially concerned Roosevelt and the man he appointed to head the PWA, Secretary of the Interior Harold Ickes.[22] Ultimately, the PWA's care in weighing the appropriateness of projects trumped its desire to act expeditiously, and so its initial impact on unemployment was minimal. Nevertheless, between 1933 and 1939 the PWA spent $1.4 billion dollars on transportation projects alone. Responsible for the construction of 65 percent of the nation's new school buildings, 65 percent of its sewage plants, and 35 percent of its hospitals during those same years, it left an indelible imprint on the infrastructure of America.[23]

The PWA offered less opportunity for the Forgotten Borough than Staten Islanders had anticipated. A number of factors had boded well for Richmond

Borough, including the PWA's initial reliance on the RFC for staff and proposals, its rejection of the RFC's "self-liquidating" requirement, its tendency to bypass states and establish direct contact with municipalities and contractors, its willingness to prioritize the value of a project over its impact on unemployment, and the potential to override state and local laws as well as constitutional debt limits.[24] Despite the PWA's possibilities, several aspects of its operation worked against any would-be suitor. Heavily indebted states and communities were less likely to obtain support than those in better fiscal health. The expectation of "self-liquidating" projects also remained even if the regulation did not. A large portion ($1.25 billion) of the PWA's $3.3 billion was already slated for existing federal departments such as the army and navy, and much of the discretionary funds went to large hydroelectric projects in the West.[25] Finally, the PWA was never very far removed from political considerations even though it was not necessarily beholden to them.

Politics intruded in several ways that ultimately hampered Staten Island's efforts. First, although the PWA abandoned its initial plan for U.S. senators to name state administrators, the state organizations eventually adopted and appointed by the PWA were often filled through congressional pressure. Many of the appointed "experts" were no such thing.[26] Second, as with the RFC, politicians tried to intervene directly in the PWA's review of proposals. As Jason Scott Smith has observed, "State congressional delegations made it a point to stop by the PWA's offices, to ensure that their states cornered their share of the PWA's $3.3 billion appropriation."[27] Finally, these efforts at intervention contributed to the slowness of PWA decision making. Already grappling with a shortage of lawyers to review requests, the PWA, to Ickes's great frustration, devoted limited human resources to responding to political pressures: "You can't imagine the precious hours that we have to give clamorous members of Congress who come singly, in pairs, in trios and in droves, dinning the same speeches into your ears and demanding that their projects be approved whether they are meritorious or not, and not only approved, but they be given preference over everyone's else [sic] projects," wrote Ickes in October 1933.[28] Staten Island politicians were equally as likely to attempt to sway the PWA as any other area's elected officials. But whether the stage was city hall, Albany, or Washington, the chances that they would succeed were always dampened by the island's political isolation.

Despite its civic activists' best efforts, Staten Island could not circumvent city and state officials. Although PWA spokespersons, legislators, and even President Roosevelt were reported to view the Narrows tunnel favorably, they urged the borough to proceed through proper channels. Congressman Prall assured Staten Islanders that all New York City had to do was apply for a PWA loan, and it would be granted. At a meeting in June 1933, PWA officials gave the Staten Island delegation the same impression, urging it to gain Board of

Estimate approval and make a formal bid for a tunnel. The following day Mayor O'Brien declared that the city would request a federal loan for the Narrows tunnel. Technically keeping his word, O'Brien got the Board of Estimate to include the project in the city's application for PWA funds.[29]

As Staten Islanders could plainly see, however, there was a hitch in the city's effort to obtain federal monies for the tunnel. The Board of Estimate had placed all projects into an A or B category and put the Narrows tunnel in the latter group. O'Brien explained the A group as projects deemed ready rather than preferable, but Staten Islanders were dubious. The Narrows tunnel had survived a significant whittling down from a larger list, but with the projects remaining still estimated to cost $100 million, not all of them would receive funds, and many Staten Islanders suspected that the tunnel's inclusion was meaningless. SICC president Louis Kaufmann called its placement on the list an act of "election smokescreen," irrelevant because PWA funds would be distributed before plans for the tunnel could be completed.[30] The *Advance* expressed similar skepticism, though Zurmuhlen remained confident that the PWA would approve any loan requested by the Board of Estimate. By the autumn of 1933, the city still had not submitted a formal application to the PWA as it awaited the long-pending Board of Transportation report. Without an accompanying application from the city, the PWA declined to consider Staten Islanders' direct request for tunnel funds.[31]

The release of the Board of Transportation's Narrows tunnel study in December 1933 eliminated the small chance that the new Board of Estimate would act on Staten Island's behalf. The report's conclusion could not have been a complete shock to Staten Islanders, but its disregard of the Transit Conference's subway plan was disheartening, and its estimates of ridership were maddening.[32] As the *Advance* sarcastically noted, "Not content with offering [Staten Island] a subway that nobody wants, they ingeniously proved that such a project was a financial impossibility."[33] The Transit Conference charged borough president Lynch with determining why the report was so unsatisfactory and getting it referred back to the Board of Transportation.[34]

An act of political theater further undermined the Transit Conference's proposed tunnel. Admonished by Lynch and the SICC, the Board of Estimate instructed the Board of Transportation to analyze a tunnel route to Smith and Ninth Streets. The hollowness of that gesture was soon revealed when the latter's head, Delaney, released a damning supplemental report on the Transit Conference's preferred location that projected a route to South Brooklyn would save nine and a half minutes per trip and cost an additional $4.7 million, a trade-off the *Advance* thought was warranted.[35] The Board of Transportation disagreed, concluding that the route "would not be in the interest of the city."[36]

In light of the Board of Transportation's negative assessment, Staten Island's civic and political leaders faced a perennial tactical question: Was it time to compromise and accept a more politically viable if not especially suitable tunnel? The *Advance* wanted to continue to press for the Smith and Ninth Street route as the most desirable for the borough. Ordeman, who found all of the routes to Fourth Avenue unsuitable, agreed. Representatives from the Brooklyn and Staten Island Chambers of Commerce were ready to settle for what they could get, as was Lynch, who was approaching his final days in office. The borough president quickly shifted to pursuit of what was arguably the least objectionable routes to Fourth Avenue—a passenger-only tunnel to the express station at Fourth Avenue and Sixty-Ninth Street. The Board of Estimate adopted this route but declined to appropriate money or even to request federal funds to build it. As the *Advance* glumly reported, the result was "a line on a map."[37]

A Board of Estimate hearing in December 1933 revealed just how much Staten Island leaders had already turned to the federal government to circumvent local antipathy. Appearing before city officials who were convinced that Staten Island lacked sufficient population and projected growth to warrant a subway, Lynch was "met with [a] frigid reception" when he asked to circumvent Board of Estimate approval. Asking for permission to take advantage of the "friendly feeling" for the project in Washington, Lynch sought not a commitment to build the tunnel but merely a vote to approve it, which would grant him entrée to federal agencies. This strategy ultimately persuaded George McAneny (briefly back on the Board of Estimate as comptroller) and two other members to vote in favor, but only after making clear that they would not allocate any funds. Although some members of the Transit Conference acquiesced, the *Advance* recognized the vote as the empty gesture of lame-duck politicians. The paper decried Tammany's preelection promises as insincere and pinned its hopes on the new mayor about to take office in 1934: Fiorello La Guardia.[38]

The 1933 election season had included a fair amount of pandering to Staten Island regarding a subway tunnel. Campaigning on Staten Island, Mayor O'Brien highlighted his conversations with President Roosevelt about the proposal and his intention to move forward to obtain federal money. La Guardia proved to be a bit more circumspect, but he derided Democrats for delays in the Narrows project and even declared "that he 'will see to it that a Staten Island tunnel is built as soon as I have the money.'"[39] Within weeks of his election, however, La Guardia made it clear that such a time was not at hand. The new mayor was not especially interested in rapid-transit expansion and instead focused on the financial woes of the three entities (IRT, BRT, the municipality) operating subways in the city.[40]

The La Guardia administration provided the final blow for a federally funded subway tunnel under the Narrows. Embracing the prospect of federal involvement in infrastructure projects, the mayor-elect conferred with Harold Ickes in Washington. Ickes "was impressed with the tough, knowledgeable New Yorker" but still admonished him to "go home and balance your [city's] budget, [its] credit is no good."[41] Indeed, upon taking office, La Guardia's attention was immediately given to the passage of an "economy bill" that would give him broad emergency powers to streamline the city's government. After much wrangling, first with New York governor Herbert Lehman and then with the state legislature, La Guardia was able to get the city's budget bill approved. Even in its compromised form, the mayor was now able to cut hundreds of jobs and reduce numerous salaries.[42] His decisive action put the city in good standing in DC and paved the way for its public-works projects to receive loans from the notoriously slow-moving PWA. A Narrows rapid-transit tunnel would not be one of these projects because La Guardia was acutely aware of the PWA's disinterest in funding projects not likely to be self-liquidating and of the city's inability to pay for a Narrows tunnel.

La Guardia instead revived the idea of moving freight through a Narrows tunnel as the only means of making the project financially sustainable. Shortly after assuming the mayoralty, he began conferring with the Port Authority about a Brooklyn–Staten Island freight link. Still interested two years later, he drafted legislation that would remove any limitation on the size of the Narrows tunnel stemming from the Nicoll-Hofstadter Act.[43] He also proposed a free-trade zone on Staten Island to make use of its Stapleton piers, notoriously built by the Hylan administration and underutilized ever since. Congress passed the enabling legislation in 1934, the New York State Legislature did the same in 1935, and one year later Staten Island was awarded the nation's first free foreign-trade zone.[44] These actions, though potentially beneficial to Staten Island, did not employ the PWA, which funded La Guardia's most favored public-works projects.

During the 1930s, the PWA issued millions of dollars in loans to New York City. The public works immediately prioritized by La Guardia included the completion of the Triborough Bridge, the West Side Highway, and many smaller, nontransit projects. There was even an appropriation for the independent subway lines despite the near universal disinclination to use federal funds for local rapid transit. Before the summer of 1934, the PWA approved nearly $100 million for these and other New York City projects. Like many mayors, La Guardia grew frustrated by the PWA's deliberate pace in reviewing applications, but he also developed a close relationship with its officials and starting in 1935 served as the National Conference of Mayors' representative to the PWA.[45] By the end of the decade, PWA funds had further contributed to the city's infrastructure, with the Queens–Midtown Tunnel, the Lincoln

Tunnel, the Henry Hudson Parkway, and the Belt Parkway intentionally serving motor vehicles. On Staten Island, PWA funds shied away from transportation but contributed to building all or parts of the Franklin D. Roosevelt Boardwalk at South Beach, Bayley Seton Hospital, Sea View Hospital, New Dorp High School, and Tottenville High School.[46]

In the mid-1930s, Staten Islanders still viewed the PWA as a potential source for transportation salvation. Emboldened by Roosevelt's rhetoric and his legislative proposal to establish a $5 billion emergency program for public employment that would become the Works Progress Administration (WPA), the Transit Conference resumed in early 1935 its subway campaign of letter writing, petitions, and meetings. One key target was borough president Joseph Palma, elected in 1933 as part of the La Guardia Fusion slate in a close race over Lynch and a third candidate.[47] A delegation from the SICC pressed Palma, and Palma urged the mayor to sway the Board of Estimate to approve funds for the preparation of an application for federal funds. The United Civic League of Midland Beach held a rally in January 1935 to marshal local rapid-transit advocates, which drew more than two hundred people representing forty-one civic groups.[48]

Concurrent actions by the La Guardia administration at the very least gave the appearance that these voices were heard. The likelihood of a new federal appropriation for public-works relief prodded city officials to move preemptively to access it. As the city was compiling a list of requests for appropriations for transit lines, roads, parks, schools, housing, sewage, hospitals, and water supply, Palma persuaded the Board of Estimate to include a Narrows subway tunnel on the city's application.[49] In February 1935, while Congress was still deliberating new legislation, the city submitted more than $1 billion worth of projects to the PWA. Among the projects identified as self-liquidating were the Sixth Avenue subway line and four tunnels, including the Staten Island subway tunnel, the Brooklyn–Battery Tunnel, the Queens–Midtown Tunnel, and a cross-Manhattan tunnel. Together, the four tunnels would cost more than $200 million, with the price tag on the Narrows tunnel put at $47 million. Its inclusion on the list was a pyrrhic victory, though, for the city would certainly not capture one-fifth of the total funds requested, no matter its great size and its mayor's large clout in DC, nor was the subway route long advocated by the Transit Conference submitted.[50]

In early 1935, the local unity in favor of the Transit Conference subway tunnel to South Brooklyn began to unravel. First came an uptick in the isolationist sentiment that had always held sway with a component of the populace, the business and civic interest in a link notwithstanding. In late January 1935, the *Staten Island Advance* gave voice to rising fears that a tunnel would "bring 'riff raff from Brooklyn' and other boroughs to Staten Island" and corrupt the local real estate market. Although still in favor of a connection, the paper presciently cautioned the island to "guard itself against mushroom growth" and to remain a borough of "small, substantially built houses."[51] Going even further, the *Staten Island Transcript* concluded that efforts on behalf of rapid transit to Manhattan through Brooklyn were ill advised. Given the failures of the past five years and the reality that the borough's population could not currently support subway service, the paper advised securing improvements for the ferries already in place.[52]

Even among those who remained sure of the desirability of a connection, the dominance of the subway eroded. Congressman Prall reignited interest in a bridge by proposing a bill to authorize the Interboro Bridge Company to construct a Narrows span. Palma formed a Committee of Twelve to review six options for a bridge or tunnel to Staten Island.[53] Although Ordeman and other Transit Conference members agreed to serve, leadership on transit matters was moving away from the conference and back toward the borough president. Palma gave the committee a broad charge to consider all possible connections: moving freight or passengers or both either over or under the Narrows and by either motor vehicle or rail. His intent was to influence a special committee on a Staten Island connection recently established by La Guardia.[54]

The Committee of Twelve's report further reflected the Transit Conference's compromised position. For one, the committee concluded that a vehicular bridge over the Narrows was necessary to connect the arterial highways and parkways being planned for the city. It imagined a 100-foot-wide bridge with eight lanes and two pedestrian walkways. While the committee also called for a subway tunnel to Brooklyn, some key details had changed from the Transit Conference's proposal of 1931. Most notably, the Committee of Twelve abandoned the route to Smith and Ninth Streets and selected instead the location espoused by the Board of Transportation fourteen months earlier: to use the Hylan shafts and reach Fifty-Ninth Street in Brooklyn.[55] The city ultimately sent this revised route to the PWA for consideration, but the PWA would soon no longer be the chief dispenser of federal dollars for public works.

The congressional passage and subsequent implementation of the Emergency Relief Appropriations Act of 1935 offered less opportunity to obtain federal support for a Narrows subway tunnel than first appeared. When President Roosevelt proposed a new round of funds for public-works relief, Staten Islanders, like many others, envisioned the PWA distributing these funds. Instead, the act triggered a contest between Ickes's PWA and Brain Truster Harry Hopkins's newly formed WPA. Wanting the funds to have a direct impact rather than indirect benefits, Roosevelt ultimately channeled most of the nearly $5 billion available to the WPA, which would run labor-intensive projects that could be completed quickly and did not require massive expenditures on materials. Roosevelt had concluded that the PWA, which moved slowly and paid union rather than relief wages, had not significantly reduced unemployment. The WPA operated under a fundamentally different rationale (social welfare more than economic development) and used a different procedure (it built projects rather than hiring private contractors) than the PWA.[56] Established as such, the WPA was even less likely than the PWA to take on a massive project such as a Narrows tunnel.

However, New York was especially successful at obtaining WPA funds. Both the city and the State of New York moved expeditiously in proposing projects, and the Roosevelt administration largely viewed them as responsible partners in distributing federal funds. La Guardia cultivated a particularly close relationship with the WPA, which established a separate administration to work with the city. As a result, in July 1935 an initial $77.6 million for projects was approved, and New Yorkers were on the federal payroll by October 1935, when many other cities had yet to apply. By early 1936, nearly a quarter million New Yorkers were employed by the WPA, two-thirds of whom worked on construction and engineering projects.[57] Although some of the WPA infrastructure projects included massive undertakings such as the Triborough Bridge and a new tube for the Holland Tunnel, major highways on the west and east side of Manhattan, and La Guardia Airport, most of them were on a much smaller scale. In New York, bridges were painted and repaired, streets were built or bettered, and trolley tracks were removed. WPA funds paid for labor on sewers, water mains, sewage-treatment plants, piers, parks, pools, playgrounds, hospitals, schools, libraries, firehouses, and police stations.[58] The racial discrimination, indignities, and other limitations associated with these endeavors are now well known, but for public officials of a politically weak borough in a financially strapped city with massive unemployment, the WPA offered another viable approach to land a subway tunnel.[59]

In 1936, Richmond Borough president Joseph Palma tried again to attract federal dollars. As the previous year showed, the WPA could allocate more than a proportionate amount of funds to New York City but still finance only a fraction of the many projects the city submitted. Landing on a wish list of proposals for federal funding was meaningless without significant backing from the city's administration. La Guardia remained discouraging when Palma asked him to use his "great personal influence in Washington" to secure a loan for a rapid-transit tunnel.[60] The mayor surprised observers by agreeing in July 1936 to support a symbolic Board of Estimate resolution in favor of rapid transit to Staten Island, but his public comments on the action dimmed expectations for success. Staten Islanders quickly and accurately concluded that the mayor had intentionally kept the issue on the back burner, and La Guardia privately informed Palma that there was no chance of obtaining federal funds for the project.[61] The borough president began to look anew at other transportation options and for financing them.

Any Tunnel Is Better Than No Tunnel

When it came to a physical link between Staten Island and its neighbors, Palma was a polygamist and a pragmatist. He preferred a subway to Brooklyn, but as his Committee of Twelve indicated, he was willing to consider a bridge, a freight tunnel, and other ideas for linkage that continued to percolate. He hoped for PWA or WPA funds but also recognized that other public initiatives might be able to serve Staten Island's needs. Palma's willingness to champion multiple endeavors simultaneously sometimes gave rise to accusations that he did not wholeheartedly pursue a subway.[62] Even as Staten Island was failing to attract federal dollars for a subway, Palma was not deterred from exploring three other significant ventures: a Port Authority freight tunnel to Brooklyn, a Port Authority suburban rapid-transit system, and a subway or vehicular tunnel funded by a new public authority.

In the mid-1930s, the buzz for the New Jersey–Brooklyn freight tunnel revived. The railroad companies remained disinclined, but renewed interest in the project had arisen in Brooklyn, and Mayor La Guardia offered at least nominal support. In the early 1930s, the Brooklyn Chamber of Commerce had repeatedly urged the Port Authority to tackle this component of its Comprehensive Plan.[63] La Guardia's tunnel committee had conferred with the Port Authority and appeared comfortable with a freight route that bypassed Staten Island. On February 4, 1935, Palma, La Guardia, and other members of the Board of Estimate met with Port Authority officials to consider possible routes for a such a tunnel. William Wilgus, now serving in the La Guardia administration, took the opportunity to push as an alternative his plans for carrying freight by tunnel under the Narrows.[64] The nearly ten years since the demise of the Hylan tunnel hadn't softened Wilgus's position, but it hadn't tempered the Port Authority's either.

The Port Authority's disinterest in a Narrows tunnel reflected familiar technical, political, and economic arguments as well as some new ones. Its officials believed that there was little need for rail movement of freight through Staten Island, that an open cut through a residential section would become a public nuisance, and that "a look at these plans dispassionately" would reveal the superiority of the Greenville route. Three new conditions solidified the Port Authority's resolve. First, the Narrows freight route would require state legislative action to undo the Nicoll-Hofstadter Act of 1925, whereas the Greenville tunnel was already an approved part of the Port Authority's Comprehensive Plan. Second, with all three Staten Island–New Jersey bridges still losing money, the agency was wary of building an additional Staten Island connection.[65] Finally, its relationships with the city and federal governments were especially complicated in the 1930s. The Port Authority was in competition with the La Guardia administration for federal funds for its own projects (e.g., the Lincoln Tunnel) and in conflict with the Roosevelt administration regarding the taxation of municipal bonds.[66]

Despite its continued opposition to a Narrows location, the Port Authority was not prepared to tunnel directly from New Jersey to Brooklyn, either. With the Great Depression and the authority's own shaky finances as a backdrop, the 1930s was a period of uncertainty for the agency. It encountered fresh resistance from politicians and railroad company executives who remained unwilling to address their various economic challenges cooperatively.[67] The Pennsylvania Railroad, still the largest and most powerful of the trunk lines, had no desire to move ahead on the Greenville project that it had instigated. Neither did the Port Authority, which made this position clear in 1937 following hearings and studies on the matter that projected high costs and low usage.[68]

The final abandonment of both the Greenville and the Narrows freight-tunnel plans was not particularly mourned on Staten Island. The Greenville route had remained unpopular on Staten Island because residents viewed the Port Authority as "in control of interests adverse to Staten Island" and believed that bypassing their island by means of this route would only reinforce its isolation and cement its exclusion from the city's transportation networks.[69] A freight route under the Narrows modeled on the old Hylan tunnel also garnered little local support. Transit Conference leaders were interested in the efficient movement of people, not freight. The *Staten Island Advance* also preferred rapid transit and argued that freight passing through Richmond would offer no benefit to the island. Borough president Palma still privileged rapid transit among all the options for a link to the city and region. A Narrows tunnel, however, was not the only way to provide it.[70]

In the mid-1930s, some Staten Islanders looked again to the Bayonne Bridge and New Jersey as a viable route for rapid transit to reach Manhattan. Local interest in a rapid-transit route across or under the Kill Van Kull and through New Jersey predated the Port Authority but took on new weight with the opening of the bridge to Bayonne in 1931. As the Port Authority liked to remind Staten Islanders, the bridge's arch-shaped truss was deliberately designed to accommodate two light-rail lines in the future. While leading citizens and businessmen called for the Port Authority to exercise that option as it was building the bridge, the agency showed little interest until pressed by the New Jersey State Legislature to study the possibilities for metropolitan rapid transit.[71] The report published by the Port Authority in early 1937 identified multiple potential rail extensions from the tubes of the Hudson and Manhattan Railway, including a southern route to Staten Island, but ultimately dismissed them all as non-self-liquidating. The study generated some interest on Staten Island, but the Port Authority's conservative leadership never moved ahead on the plan.[72]

Staten Islanders continued to wonder whether another authority could be created to provide rapid transit to the island. Public authorities became an increasingly common mechanism for building major public works in the fifteen years following the creation of the Port Authority in 1921. Portrayed as organizations steeped in expertise rather than in politics, such authorities were favored for appearing to circumvent dysfunctional municipal political cultures.[73] They were formed to handle all sorts of infrastructure needs, from water supply to transportation projects. By the late 1920s, the Walker administration was considering and Governor Franklin Roosevelt was promoting authorities as a means of funding bridges and tunnels in New York City.[74] Authorities' popularity was further aided by Robert Moses's masterful management of the Triborough Bridge Authority, which was established in 1933 to revive the project halted by the economic crisis. With this example so close at hand, Staten Islanders considered whether they could follow the same route to rescue their Narrows crossing.

Public figures and local activists first advocated for the establishment of a new authority to build a Narrows crossing in the mid-1920s. President Joseph McKee of the New York City Board of Aldermen had proposed in 1926 an authority to build a Narrows bridge—a position that had won the support of the Staten Island Civic League. The *Staten Island Advance* supported the Walker administration's effort to establish such an authority, but the bill died in the Republican-controlled state legislature.[75] Mayor O'Brien likewise favored a city bridge board modeled after the Port Authority but did not advance that agenda during his abbreviated term. La Guardia expressed interest in a public authority for New York City public-works projects, but not if it would apply to a Narrows crossing. In the winter of 1935, the New York State Assembly and Senate passed legislation creating the Queens–Midtown Tunnel Authority. With the mayor's blessing, Governor Lehman signed the law to renew that long-delayed project.[76]

Staten Islanders tried in vain to hitch their tunnel on to the one for Queens, which was favored by both La Guardia and officials in Washington. The new Queens–Midtown Tunnel Authority was hastily recast in 1936 as the New York City Tunnel Authority (NYCTA) to meet certain PWA conditions. Designed to obtain federal funds, the bill to create the NYCTA attracted advocates for other projects as it moved through the legislature. The city's comptroller and Brooklyn's borough president succeeded in adding authorization for the NYCTA to construct a tunnel from Brooklyn to the Battery at the tip of Manhattan. Other Brooklyn interests attempted but failed to tack on a bridge route from Grand Street to Houston in Manhattan. On Staten Island, Palma and the Real Estate Board urged La Guardia—to no avail—to support an amendment to add a Narrows rail tunnel to its purview.[77] Staten Island's legislators then unenthusiastically undertook the difficult task of changing the bill after its passage "to includ[e] in the definition of 'project' a vehicular tunnel or tunnels under the Narrows from the borough of Richmond to the borough of Brooklyn."[78] Failing to do so, they continued to press for the creation of an authority solely dedicated to constructing a link to Staten Island.

Staten Island's efforts at mimicry of Queens also fell short. In 1935, two state legislators had managed to pass a bill to establish the Staten Island Bridge and Tunnel Authority, which La Guardia declined to back.[79] Although a delegation from Staten Island had attempted to sway Governor Lehman, the mayor's rejection proved influential as the governor allowed the act to die by not signing it. La Guardia's opposition reportedly stemmed from terms that undermined home rule and exposed the city to new competition for federal dollars. Staten Islanders couldn't help but wonder whether he thought it a bad bill or a bad project as La Guardia was rumored to have uttered that "if Staten Island ever gets the tunnel it will be over my dead body."[80]

Some Staten Islanders continued to question whether a bridge would fare better. In the spring of 1936, state senator Rae Egbert shepherded through a bill creating a Richmond Bridge Authority. Calling for a three-person commission, with one member from Staten Island and another from Brooklyn, his bill did not include a tunnel, ostensibly because the city already possessed the authority to construct one even if it lacked the funds. The version of the bill in the Assembly included the possibility for rapid transit over the span but faced overwhelming opposition from legislators outside of the five boroughs and vocal hostility from Bay Ridge politicians.[81] Mayor La Guardia was intrigued by a Narrows bridge—perhaps in light of San Francisco's permission from the War Department to build the Golden Gate Bridge—which would be the longest suspension bridge in the world. The mayor also benefited from supportive coverage by the *New York Times* and unanimous Board of Estimate consent to pursue a similar authorization in Washington, but he was unwilling to support the legislation without federal approval in hand. When the War Department reaffirmed its rejection of a Narrows bridge in 1928 but its approval of a Narrows tunnel in 1930, La Guardia was content to watch the Egbert bill die in the Assembly.[82]

Whether a tunnel or a bridge was envisioned for Staten Island, by 1937 either one was increasingly likely to move motor vehicles rather than rapid transit. Sentiment remained for a subway, and spasmodic local efforts on behalf of one would occur over the next ten years—most notably efforts to latch a Staten Island tunnel onto plans for a Governor's Island airport, a renewed interest in a direct tunnel to Manhattan for which two residents wrote and recorded the song "Ten Minutes to Broadway," and a bill introduced by Assemblyman Robert Molinari in 1943 to authorize a subway—but nothing as substantial as the subway movements from the previous four decades occurred.[83] With Delaney still at its helm, the Board of Transportation's inclusion of a Narrows subway tunnel in its capital plans from 1938 to 1945 did not generate local activity. At the same time, the prospects for a vehicular connection gained political momentum. Up for reelection in November 1937, La Guardia surprisingly reversed himself by advocating that the NYCTA expand its purview to include a Narrows vehicular tunnel.[84] Prominent Staten Islanders once again grasped at a viable option as officials in the borough president's office and citizens from the local Civic League and Chamber of Commerce rallied around the idea of a vehicular tunnel.[85] Finally, having La Guardia's support after more than two years of trying, a bill enabling the NYCTA to construct a Narrows vehicular tunnel sailed through the New York State Legislature and was signed by Governor Lehman.[86]

Legislative authorization for a Narrows vehicular tunnel was not accompanied by solid backing from Staten Island's civic leaders. They had offered tepid support for the bill while its outcome was still uncertain and largely expressed resignation once it passed. Supportive of the vehicular tunnel legislation in 1936, the *Staten Island Transcript* now in April 1937 voiced its preference for rails: "The tunnel will bring visitors. A subway would bring residents."[87] The *Staten Island Advance* likewise observed, "And so we shall get a vehicular tunnel, not because we want it (Islanders would much prefer a rapid transit tube) but because traffic conditions in the metropolitan district make it indispensable."[88] Assemblyman Herman Methfessel asserted "that the proposed vehicular tunnel would mean to Richmond 'just about five per cent of the benefit the borough would get from a rapid transit link.'"[89] Many local voices still conveyed the pragmatism that had long guided them, preferring rapid transit but concluding that a vehicular tunnel would be better than nothing. The SICC, for example, shifted its efforts between 1936 and 1940 to the more politically viable vehicular connection.[90] Lack of local enthusiasm could not kill a tunnel that was not primarily intended to benefit Staten Island.

Robert Moses's antipathy for the NYCTA would prove quite detrimental to the success of the Narrows vehicular tunnel. Eager to control the NYCTA from the outset, Moses was thwarted in his initial designs on it by the La Guardia administration's crafting of the enabling legislation to make Moses ineligible to serve as a NYCTA commissioner. Untethered to Moses, the NYCTA focused on building its raison d'être, the Queens–Midtown Tunnel, and, Moses's attacks on the NYCTA's competency notwithstanding, the agency came in under budget when the passageway opened in 1940.[91] As the NYCTA tunneled under the East River, it also began to design a tunnel for under the Battery, but Moses had other plans and nearly took over the latter. His highly unpopular attempt to substitute a Battery bridge for a tunnel, which engendered much opposition due to the impact it would have on Lower Manhattan, cleared all hurdles at the city and state levels only to be halted when the War Department denied permission to construct a bridge. The victory over

Moses, though, belonged not to the NYCTA but to the prominent civic reformers who appealed directly to the Roosevelts for succor.[92] Moses was still gunning for the NYCTA when it finally began to move ahead on the tunnel to Staten Island.

The NYCTA intended to build a vehicular tunnel under the Narrows as its third major initiative. Ole Singstad, the authority's chief engineer, had championed a vehicular tunnel since the 1920s, and the NYCTA began conducting extensive traffic surveys in 1937. Dormancy on this project marked the next few years as the NYCTA focused on its primary (East River) and secondary (Battery) projects.[93] Palma moved to prod action in the autumn of 1940, and the outbreak of war in Europe the previous year offered him a new justification for a vehicular connection to Staten Island: military preparedness. In October 1940, the borough president highlighted the potential need for East Coast troop movements in yet another attempt to sway La Guardia to his cause. Rejecting the rationale for national defense and once again pleading poverty—"As soon as I get my hands on sixty million dollars, we will build the tunnel you want"—the mayor's rebuff sparked a brief spurt of local activism.[94]

In the winter of 1941, Staten Island's civic and political leadership collectively pushed for a vehicular tunnel to a degree not seen since the efforts on behalf of a subway in the early 1930s. The impetus came from the Staten Island Vigilantes, a South Shore civic group dating to the mid-1930s that, among other accomplishments, claimed responsibility for the construction of Tottenville High School. The Vigilantes' efforts—telegrams to key officials, a dinner for members of the NYCTA, and a Tunnel Night at the Paramount Theater in Stapleton—were initially aimed to obtain a federal loan for the whole project. The group soon shifted to a much more achievable step: seeking a $50,000 appropriation from the Board of Estimate to allow the NYCTA to begin surveys for the tunnel. The SICC and the Richmond County Democratic Party rallied around this approach. Republican state senator Robert Johnson introduced a resolution calling on the Board of Estimate to act, and he and Palma similarly urged La Guardia in private correspondence. Sounding exasperated, the mayor rebuffed them, and the proposal for city funds went nowhere. In response, Democratic assemblyman (and future Richmond Borough president) Albert Maniscaclo asked for a state appropriation of $50,000 for a Narrows tunnel survey, and a Manhattan representative made the same request of the U.S. Congress.[95]

The following year, Staten Islanders achieved this minimal objective. Granted a $50,000 appropriation from the New York State Post-War Planning and Capital Reserve Fund in 1942, the NYCTA began planning in earnest a crossing at the Narrows (see figure 9.1). One year later, Singstad issued a preliminary report that pronounced the project feasible and described its location, structure, construction methods, and estimates of costs and traffic.[96] Singstad also presented arguments fitting for a nation that not only was in the middle of a war but also worried about the postwar economy: a tunnel would be good for homeland defense and would provide four years of employment for 2,000 workers and 200 engineers.[97] Singstad envisioned a five-year project: one year to develop final plans and four years to build. He recommended

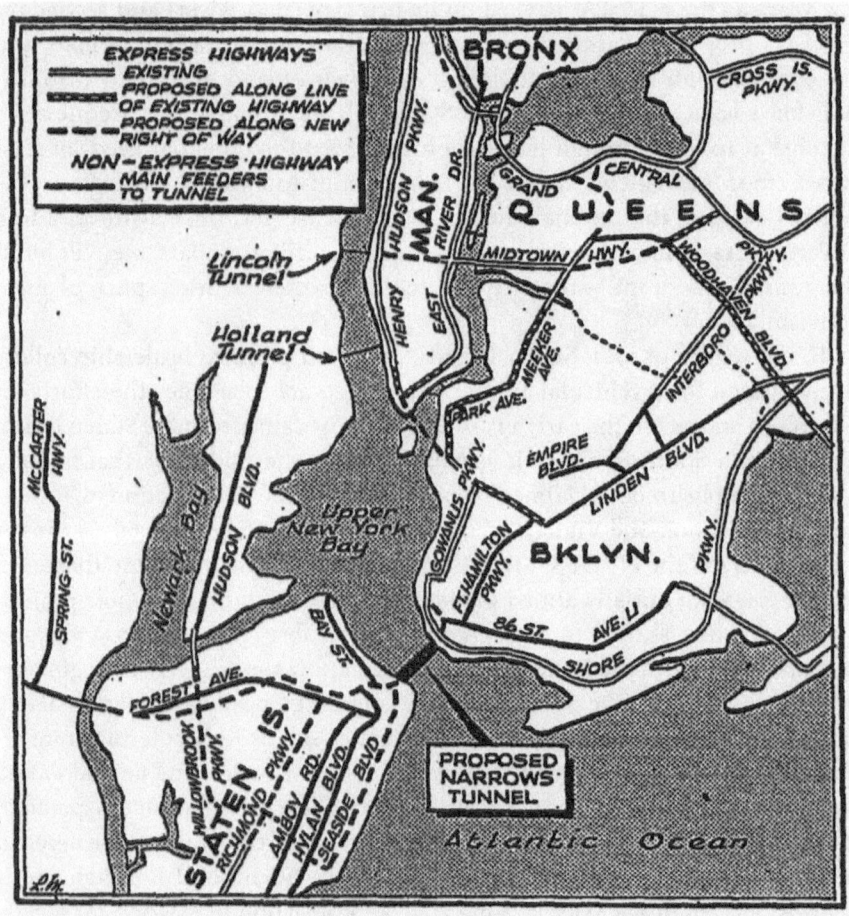

9.1 New York City Tunnel Authority plans for Narrows vehicular tunnel, 1943

The New York City Tunnel Authority's plan for a vehicular tunnel under the Narrows recognized the tunnel's vital role in linking the metropolitan area's growing network of roads and highways. Unlike in the various plans for a rail tunnel, the location for a bridge was always envisioned at the narrowest section of the Narrows.

Source: *New York Times*, March 22, 1943, 1.

completing the plans immediately even though no envisioned construction would take place until after the end of the war.[98]

The NYCTA received mixed reactions to its plans. The *New York Times* identified "cause for satisfaction" in the report's favorable findings. Declaring a tunnel "an important link in the outer belt of the metropolitan highway system" and "a convenient by-pass" for traffic between Long Island and New Jersey, the paper did not highlight any special benefits for Richmond Borough.[99] The *Staten Island Advance* was confident that the project would not be a "white elephant" and basked in the notion that a significant off-island entity, the NYCTA, would become an advocate for its funding.[100] From Moses and his allies, however, only criticism flowed. After failing to block the initial appropriation, Moses now questioned how the NYCTA could finance the project and criticized the proposed sites for the tunnel approaches. Moses and Edwin A. Salmon, chairman of the New York City Planning Commission (CPC), chastised the NYCTA for not consulting with Salmon's commission in accordance with the city charter. Most significantly, both called for a halt to work—a strategy of delay akin to what Moses had recently enacted with the Battery Tunnel.[101]

With Singstad looking to move ahead and Moses to postpone, Richmond Borough president Joseph Palma unwittingly served to help Moses prevail. After failing to halt the state legislature's tunnel appropriation for the NYCTA report, Moses sought to suspend further activity by securing an alternative study. Although lacking influence in the NYCTA, Moses controlled the CPC, which had also committed to a Narrows link but had not determined whether it should be a tunnel or a bridge. The CPC proposed an amended budget that now included $75,000 to be divided between Palma and John Cashmore, borough president of Brooklyn, for additional studies of the Narrows tunnel approaches. When the Board of Estimate failed to act on this recommendation, Moses lobbied La Guardia for months until the board allotted $50,000 for this purpose, with Palma receiving $20,000.[102] With these studies set in motion, Moses called for the NYCTA to defer undertaking its comprehensive report until the borough presidents completed their studies.

The NYCTA had intended to proceed swiftly but ultimately found its work held up as it complied with Moses's demand. To move ahead, Chairman Alfred Jones requested an additional $90,000 from the state legislature for underwater planning, to be followed by another $500,000 to cover detailed plans and specifications and make the project shovel ready for when the war ended.[103] Moses, citing "much more urgent projects" than the Narrows tunnel, was able to block this request through his influence in the state's Department of Public Works.[104] Deprived of the funds enabling it to continue its planning, the NYCTA reluctantly awaited the Staten Island and Brooklyn Borough presidents' findings before finalizing its own report. Essentially completed by

November 1943, the borough presidents' report was not released by the CPC until November 1944 and not approved by the Board of Estimate until April 1945. The NYCTA took just one month after that to finish its own report—one that kept intact the basic features of the tunnel outlined in 1943 and only marginally changed its estimates of costs and revenues.[105]

Despite the simultaneous studies being conducted by opposing entities, there really was minimal disagreement between the two reports. Consider, for example, the location of the Staten Island approaches. A study by the Transit Conference vice president Herman Ordeman in 1937 placed a tunnel at the thinnest part of the Narrows, with a plaza in Shore Acres on Staten Island, just before the intersection of Hylan Boulevard and Bay Street.[106] The NYCTA's chief engineer, Singstad, receiving cooperation from Palma's office, retained the same basic trajectory for the tunnel and only slightly altered the location of the plaza. The borough presidents' study in 1944—conducted by an outside engineering firm—highlighted its "[concurrence] with the opinion of other agencies who have studied the problem as to the general location of the proposed Richmond approaches."[107] While adding and lengthening some connections to the tunnel, it, too, retained the plaza in Shore Acres and included approaches that also reached Hylan Boulevard and Bay Street. In his final report, Singstad likewise noted the very similar recommendation for plazas and acknowledged making some small changes in the local street system in accordance with Palma's preferences.[108] Thus, all in all, the extra time taken to perform an additional study had not yielded a fundamentally different result.

The symmetry between the reports notwithstanding, the NYCTA's report came too late. As the NYCTA began to move ahead on the Narrows vehicular tunnel, Moses finally managed to take over his rival. He assumed effective control of the NYCTA in the summer of 1945 and formally merged it with his own Triborough Bridge Authority to form the Triborough Bridge and Tunnel Authority in 1946. How he pulled off this coup is well related by Robert Caro, who depicts how Moses moved stealthily in engineering a wartime halt on construction of the Battery Tunnel, undermining the NYCTA with Mayor La Guardia, obtaining appointment as a NYCTA commissioner, forcing out its longtime chairman Alfred Jones, and inserting his trusted subordinate George Spargo as general manager until the merger took place.[109] His correspondence with La Guardia about the Narrows tunnel was part of this campaign to undermine the NYCTA. In an especially damning letter, Moses told La Guardia on December 2, 1943, "No one but a madman would suggest even planning it [the Narrows tunnel] in detail at this time," and concluded with the following plea: "Let's not makes ourselves ridiculous at this late stage of the game [of getting federal and state money for arterial connections] by advocating crackpot plans."[110] Despite the recent warm reception for the NYCTA Narrows report, within weeks after Moses assumed control over the agency, both he and the mayor publicly declared the vehicular tunnel project dead.[111] Over the next decade, movement toward a Narrows crossing came to a near standstill, but talk of it continued unabated and shifted from a tunnel to a bridge.

* * *

The subway's hold on Staten Island's civic imagination remained potent in the 1930s. A telling moment occurred in 1933, when the local Kiwanis club passed a resolution urging the sale of the right-of-way property purchased for $5 million in the 1920s to construct the Hylan tunnel. Concerned that these unmaintained lots were sitting idle, dragging down adjacent property values, and denying the city potential revenues, the Kiwanis imagined the sale to be a quick and easy fix. Instead, the resolution met with firm opposition—from the SICC, the *Staten Island Transcript*, and borough president John Lynch, among others—and the Kiwanis declined to pursue the matter.[112] Staten Islanders heeded the cautionary plea from William Wirt Mills: "Don't give up the subway right of way. The shafts and the land are promissory notes given by the City to Staten Island.... Hold fast to the right of way until we get the subway."[113] The memory of the Hylan Tunnel debacle still motivated civic leaders such as Mills, who remained determined to achieve a rapid-transit connection and embraced the potential of federal funding (see figure 9.2).

Federal support proved to be a chimera, but its attraction to Staten Islanders was understandable. Historically stymied by city and state officials, Staten Islanders were drawn to the power of the PWA and later New Deal agencies to bypass existing local political structures and officials. Transit Conference leaders found a far more receptive audience among federal officials than among local ones. Even among the alphabet agencies, however, there were limits to the ability to flank local political entities. Some politicians turned federal funding streams into patronage machines; others managed to exercise veto power—if not direct control—over federal public-works projects. In New York, the La Guardia administration held considerable sway, and Staten Islanders looking for federal funding ultimately could not sidestep the lack of support from their own mayor.

While Staten Island public officials and civic leaders were focused on obtaining subway tunnel funding from a New Deal agency during the 1930s, two significant and all but irreversible changes occurred between 1933 and 1945 regarding a Narrows link. First was the nature of the conduit. On January 1, 1933, efforts on Staten Island still focused on a rapid-transit tunnel. By the end of the 1945, however, subway advocates had largely capitulated and professed their desire for a vehicular bridge (though some hoped such a bridge could carry rapid-transit lines as well). Second was the means for constructing the link. On January 1, 1933, Mayor La Guardia came into office and, unlike his

FOR 12 years, the building pictured here has been waiting for the legend on the sign above it to come true: "On this site will be sunk the Staten Island shaft of the freight and passenger tunnel . . . across the Narrows." The shaft was built in 1923 and 1924, but the tunnel hasn't. The sign has been removed, but the buildings, standing east of the vehicular ramp at St. George terminal, is a daily reminder to commuters, rushing to board the crowded boats, that Staten Island was promised a subway.

9.2 Staten Island Tunnel shaft sign, c. 1928

Even after it deteriorated and was eventually removed, the sign for the Hylan Tunnel shaft on Staten Island remained a potent reminder of unfulfilled aspirations for a subway even though the project was unlikely to connect with the city's rapid-transit system.

Source: Courtesy of Collection of the Staten Island Museum.

recent predecessors, limited the city's efforts to connect Staten Island to the other boroughs. By the end of his third term, the potential for action rested with neither the incoming mayoral administration nor the Staten Island civic activists, but rather with Robert Moses's Triborough Bridge and Tunnel Authority. These transformations in intended purpose (from rapid transit to motor vehicles), product (from tunnel to bridge), and process (from city to public authority) mattered greatly for the ultimate spanning of the Narrows. The considerable but failed effort to receive an allocation from the PWA or the WPA proved to be a sidebar.

Through all these efforts, the rationale for a connection remained constant. As one reader wrote to the *New York Times* in April 1935, "Give Staten Island a tunnel or bridge and in very short time the population would double and continue to multiply."[114] As chapter 10 explores, the prospect of a bridge raised anew a discussion of what the impact on Staten Island would be. Although some bridge advocates continued to promote the now decades-old mantra of residential, commercial, and industrial growth, others recognized that a bridge that functioned as part of a regional transportation system might not have the specific local impact that islanders had long sought. For many Staten Islanders, getting the bridge would become the focus more than identifying or planning for what having it might actually entail.

CHAPTER 10

SPANNING THE NARROWS

The Triumph of the Verrazzano Bridge, 1945–1964

I've watched you pull rabbits out of your hat before.

—Herbert Lynn to Robert Moses, November 20, 1940

And the chances are that, with Moses at the wheel, we'll go somewhere.

—*Staten Island Advance*, August 7, 1945

The summer of 1945 was a moment of celebration nationwide as World War II was on the verge of ending. Staten Islanders had additional reasons for optimism, anxieties about acclimating returning servicemen and avoiding economic depression notwithstanding. For the previous five years, deliberations over a physical connection to Brooklyn presumed that nothing would be built until the war concluded. That time was now. Even more propitious was the emergence of the Triborough Bridge and Tunnel Authority (TBTA). As Staten Islanders experienced decades of recalcitrance from municipal governments and the apparent impotence of the borough president's office, they had also witnessed major infrastructure accomplishments elsewhere by the region's nascent public authorities. Finally, Staten Islanders seemed to have on their side a magician who could "pull rabbits" out of a hat. As they grew particularly frustrated with Mayor Fiorello La Guardia and borough president Joseph Palma, citizens such as Herbert Lynn (who owned a clothing store in Port Richmond and actively participated in the Knights of Pythias) and newspapers such as the *Staten Island Advance* turned to the head of the TBTA, a public official with the reputation for taking projects that stymied all others and getting them done: Robert Moses.

Over the next fifteen years, Staten Islanders tied their dream of a Narrows crossing to Moses. They even did this despite the temporary hit his reputation took in 1946 as Staten Islanders held him largely accountable for the decision to open a landfill at Fresh Kills.[1] That the *Advance* had pilloried Moses in its recent editorials on the city's plans for refuse did not negate its confidence that he could connect the island to the city. Its image of Moses "at the wheel" was particularly apt, for Moses was an aficionado of the motor vehicle and a critic of railroads. He generally preferred bridges to tunnels as well. He also had a dismissive approach to those who questioned his choices or asked for more than he intended to supply. His papers are filled with correspondence advising citizens and public officials to be satisfied with something, be thankful that it was likely more than anyone else would or could have provided, and be patient for the appropriate time to obtain his version of what they wanted to have. Moses was no less blunt with Richmond Borough's elected leaders in discussion of a Narrows crossing. When in early 1937 Palma asked for Moses's support for the inclusion of a Narrows bridge in a Tri-Borough Bridge Authority bill, Moses sent him an atypically genial but nonetheless direct response: "You are moving too fast on the Staten Island bridge matter," he wrote, suggesting that once a crossing at the Battery (and the Belt Parkway that served it) opened, "the pressure for a connection with Staten Island at the Narrows will become irresistible."[2] Moses would deliver the Verrazzano Bridge on his terms.

In a way, Moses was correct as the Verrazzano Bridge emerged out of considerable "pressure" but not the political or civic kind that Staten Islanders had applied to no avail for more than forty years. By 1945, Staten Islanders rightly recognized that Robert Moses was—arguably uniquely—able to complete a Narrows project, and so after World War II they no longer organized a sizeable movement for a Narrows link. They instead found themselves largely marginalized from the developments that finally culminated in the construction of the Verrazzano Bridge. The "pressure" that Moses referred to came not from citizens working to influence political processes but rather from motorists bottlenecked on his highways and parkways on Long Island without an easy means of avoiding the congestion of Manhattan on their way to New Jersey and beyond.

Moses's recognition of motorists' "pressure" is ironic given Robert Caro's influential framing of his legacy. In his tome *The Power Broker: Robert Moses and the Fall of New York* (1974), Caro forged the contemporary image of a domineering man consumed by power and arrogance and largely unhindered in his remaking of New York's built environment. Caro censures Moses for bypassing or steamrolling the elected leadership of the city in his rush to create parks, construct highways and bridges, and clear slums. Subsequent reassessments of Caro's work have focused not on his depiction of Moses's personal characteristics but rather on his conclusion that Moses ultimately had a malignant effect on New York that the city otherwise might have avoided. Historians such as Kenneth Jackson and Joel Schwartz have emphasized national trends and local contexts, respectively—a broader view of Moses's "pressures"—that propelled American cities to follow the trajectory pursued by Moses. As Jameson Doig has suggested, "It is as likely that Robert Moses was as much a captive as he was a shaper of the economic and other social forces that have determined the rise and decline of American cities and suburbs in the twentieth century."[3] As a result of this work, more recent conclusions about Moses have tempered his influence and upgraded his impact.[4]

Staten Islanders' aspirations for better transportation were no less captive of large social forces than Moses's vision. National postwar dynamics—including the reorientation of family life inward, the cultural affinity for the automobile and the single family home, the militarization of American society, the movement of urban populations to suburban peripheries, the rise of trucking and air freight at the expense of the railroad, the expansion of the role of the federal government, and the early stages of deindustrialization—surely privileged a vehicular bridge and made a rapid-transit connection to Staten Island an even less likely proposition than it had been before the war.[5] On Staten Island, the wartime economic boom fueled growth in the manufacturing sector through the early 1950s, but then a gradual yet steady decline in industrial plants began.[6] Many businesses, particularly in growing industries, relocated their factories or built new ones farther out in the metropolitan periphery or eventually decamped for the Sunbelt. Residential expansion occurred—primarily in the form of single-family homes—as Staten Island's population growth picked up again in the 1950s, after the preceding Depression and war had dampened it. The growing population density made internal transportation needs more pressing, and civic and political leaders devoted considerable energy to ferry service and bus routes. They worked with partial success to keep open the internal commuter railroad lines of the Staten Island Railway amid declining revenues. Moreover, the opening of the Fresh Kills landfill in 1948 provided a new civic cause that would preoccupy leading citizens and officials alike. These pressures notwithstanding, Moses remains central to understanding how a Narrows crossing was finally built and why it took shape as the vehicular Verrazzano Bridge.

A Bridge in Waiting, 1945–1953

Robert Moses fancied building bridges, not tunnels. In the years immediately following the bitter outcome of his Battery Bridge proposal, however, he sometimes muted this preference.⁷ When the New York City Tunnel Authority controlled the Narrows crossing project, Moses commented judiciously in public about the viability of a vehicular tunnel, while privately he schemed to block the NYCTA's work.⁸ As chapter 9 related, Moses ultimately thwarted the NYCTA by first taking it over in 1945 and then eliminating it through a merger with his Triborough Bridge Authority in 1946. The city's Board of Transportation, another potential rival, also posed no threat to Moses's plans. That board's chairman, John Delaney, continued to block a Staten Island subway until his retirement in 1945. When the Narrows tunnel appeared in the board's request for appropriations in 1946, it was placed near the bottom of the prioritized list, intended for an unspecified and distant future.⁹ Staten Islanders looking for a politically viable project had already turned toward a Narrows bridge even as Moses was acquiring the means to construct one.

During the 1940s, Staten Islanders gradually began to coalesce around a vehicular bridge. As the previous two chapters related, for twenty years some Staten Islanders had periodically organized to promote a span across the Narrows but were usually overwhelmed by the more numerous and powerful voices for a tunnel. Staten Islanders did not prefer a bridge by the early 1940s, but following the demise of the Transit Conference subway project, a strain of pragmatism reasserted itself into the public debate as many islanders expressed a willingness to embrace any Narrows crossings plan with a chance for approval. Capturing this flexibility, starting in early 1938 the City Planning Commission annually called for a vehicular crossing of the Narrows without specifying which type of structure it favored.¹⁰ Similar adaptability was evident in Palma's report of 1944 on potential tunnel approaches under the Narrows, which acknowledged the sentiment for a bridge and noted that its recommendations could be modified to accommodate a span over it.¹¹

By the mid-1940s, the luster of rapid transit had diminished, and public officials and civic groups turned toward motor vehicles. Throughout the city, ridership was up in the still newly unified municipal subway system, but signs of its shortcomings were evident.¹² On Staten Island, the Richmond County Chapter of the New York State SPE, the most important organizational voice for a rapid-transit tunnel, reassessed its position in 1945 and opted for a bridge. Borough president candidate Cornelius Hall spoke favorably for a vehicular tunnel as he publicly challenged Mayor La Guardia's assertion that such a tunnel was at least twenty to twenty-five years in the future. Shortly after taking office in 1946, the newly elected Hall shifted his position and voiced his partiality for a bridge, as did the SICC a few months later.¹³ Although many Staten Islanders had acquiesced to the vehicular bridge by then, some hoped that a span could also accommodate rapid transit.

When Robert Moses would discuss a Narrows crossing during the late 1940s, he spoke only of building a bridge in some indeterminate future. Palma, however, was not so certain about the form a crossing should take.¹⁴ Nearing the end of his term of office, he became a vocal proponent of a fresh consideration of all options—including whether to pursue a bridge or a tunnel for vehicles and/or rapid transit. He persuaded Mayor La Guardia to appoint a committee to make a comprehensive study of transportation issues on Staten Island, but its appointees arrived with fairly set views: Palma, who looked upon rapid transit favorably; John Delaney, who was nearing retirement as chairman of the Board of Transportation and remained dubious of a rapid-transit tunnel; and the bridge-promoting Moses as chair.[15]

Moses's role on the committee and his subsequent chairmanship of the TBTA appeared favorable to many Staten Islanders. In August 1945, the *Staten Island Advance* expressed confidence in Moses's ability to get things done and his willingness to examine the bridge and tunnel options impartially and concluded that the "merger [of the Triborough Bridge Authority and the NYCTA] may be good."[16] Knowing Moses's predilections, Palma suggested that reviewing the need for arterial highways without considering mass transportation would be senseless. He expected the committee to investigate five key areas, one of which would be a Narrows bridge or tunnel with rapid transit, but Moses steered the group elsewhere.[17]

The report that emerged just three months later proved a great disappointment to Palma but no doubt satisfied Moses, whose views dominated the document. Deriding the making of "slogans and promises of projects and improvements beyond anything which could be accomplished," the report dampened immediate expectations for any Narrows connection.[18] It explicitly disregarded the NYCTA's estimates of building costs, rejected its projections for use of a vehicular tunnel, and subtly privileged a bridge as the least objectionable option for a distant future. The vehicular tunnel was deemed "wholly unthinkable," and a rapid-transit tunnel was declared—at Delaney's insistence—unrealistic for at least ten years after the opening of the Battery Tunnel and likely longer in order to expand Brooklyn's rapid-transit lines to handle additional traffic coming from Staten Island. A Narrows bridge was labeled feasible but likely to be blocked by the military. With seemingly no immediate prospects for a physical link to the rest of the city, the report instead recommended improvements to the island's ferry service—from the terminal to the access roads to the boats themselves. Unhappy with the report's conclusions and discontented with the cursory manner in which the committee—having met just once—completed its work, Palma continued to advocate in vain for a comprehensive study of Staten Island's transit issues after he left office.[19]

Other Staten Island political and civic leaders responded more favorably, if not excitedly, to the prospect of a Narrows vehicular bridge. Alfred Pouch, a third-generation member of a leading Staten Island family in the shipping business, envisioned greater development of harbor facilities in both Staten

Island and in New Jersey south of Bayonne. Frederick Zurmuhlen—one of Staten Island's chief advocates for a subway in the 1930s and now serving as New York City's commissioner of public works, valued the project as a means of linking Long Island to New Jersey. The Staten Island Rotary Club enthusiastically received a proposal for a Narrows span by the noted engineer David Steinman.[20]

Nonetheless, Staten Islanders grew increasingly marginal to the consideration of a link. Uncertainty about the virtue of a bridge remained on Staten Island, and some politicians straddled the issue. During a two-week span in 1946, Staten Island Republican assemblyman Edmund P. Radigan introduced a bill to establish the Richmond–Brooklyn Bridge Authority and another one to create the Richmond and Manhattan Transit Authority.[21] Although Radigan's proposals did not pass, they represented a long-standing Staten Island tradition—the willingness to follow multiple leads simultaneously to see which held merit in the political arena. Staten Islanders had by the late 1940s largely abandoned a more assertive posture and had become primarily reactive to political currents in transportation matters. Thus, the island was at best tangential to the interests that now pushed for a bridge, and its residents were largely peripheral to the events that jump-started the project.

For several years after the end of World War II, the Narrows bridge project remained dormant at the city level and among civic and political leaders on Staten Island. Its absence from a CPC report by Moses in 1946 was indicative of how low a Narrows crossing had fallen as a priority.[22] George Spargo, the first general manager of the TBTA, immediately dampened expectations for the project in terms quite familiar to Staten Islanders: claiming that it would not pay for itself and that it must wait until the completion of more pressing undertakings.[23] Early in his first term as borough president, Cornelius Hall organized the Committee for the Advancement of a Physical Connection between Richmond and the Other Boroughs with the goal of "waging a continuous campaign" on behalf of a link. After an enthusiastic first meeting, competing concerns soon rendered the committee inactive.[24]

In the summer of 1945, Staten Islanders learned of the city's renewed interest in a landfill at Fresh Kills. With the municipal elections approaching in November 1945, the Board of Estimate declined to fund the project, but by mid-1946 it looked to make an appropriation. Newly elected mayor William O'Dwyer and Richmond Borough president Cornelius Hall had campaigned against such a facility but reversed themselves just months later. On Staten Island, "dissent over Fresh Kills turned to fury."[25] The tension over the landfill moved islanders' attention away from the movement of goods and people toward the disposal of garbage. Ironically, the landfill also offered the borough president an opportunity to barter for a link to New York. Hall acquiesced to the landfill in part because of his "horse trading" to gain transportation improvements. Negotiating for an internal parkway and potential airport, not a Narrows crossing, Hall became susceptible to charges of dereliction by his constituents and ultimately felt betrayed when the city neither funded the parkway in 1947 (or for many years to come) nor limited the size and duration of the landfill.[26]

When Staten Islanders exerted themselves on behalf of transportation in the latter part of the 1940s, they often addressed needs other than either subways or bridges. Hall heeded the many complaints and demands of ferry and bus riders, with whom he held several meetings upon taking office. Even as plans for a new ferry terminal were being formulated by the city, a fire in June 1946 destroyed the old building, further drawing local attention away from a Narrows crossing. Similarly, when the city took over operation of the borough's bus lines in February 1947, some islanders chose to contend with the higher fares they paid compared to the rest of the city.[27] One New Dorp resident urged the development of an interior trolley line using the land condemned for the right of way for the old Hylan tunnel—following a route that would serve West New Brighton, Westerleigh, and what would become Willowbrook.[28] With a sense of crisis mounting on numerous fronts, the SICC launched an island-wide advisory council in October 1946, and the group settled on an initial set of priorities that reflected the local preoccupation with these issues: blocking the landfill, restoring the ferry, and improving internal transportation.[29] Over the next few years, the chamber's interest in pursuing a bridge remained fickle. In 1948, the project was one of nine goals for the year; in 1949, a new head of the SICC Transportation Committee paid singular attention to the Brooklyn–Staten Island ferry.[30]

Despite the relative inactivity between 1945 and 1954, three significant developments occurred regarding a Narrows crossing. First, the authority approach became the only foreseeable mechanism for funding a link, and the TBTA had become the only viable authority to do so. Contrary to the discussions from previous decades, no funds would be forthcoming from the city's capital budget, as its commissioner of public works acknowledged. Nor would any be immediately forthcoming from the TBTA, but the TBTA did at least start to lay claim to the project in its maps that projected future arteries and crossings (see figure 10.1).[31] As Moses repeatedly informed people publicly and privately as late as October 1953, "The bridge will be built some day but it's a long way off."[32]

Second, Moses made perfectly clear that he would build only a bridge and finally ended the decades-long flirtation with a Narrows tunnel. After conveying his views through the study of transportation on Staten Island in 1945, Moses began regularly floating the idea for a bridge and to dismiss the viability of a tunnel.[33] As the very public controversy over the Battery crossing showed, Moses simply preferred bridges to tunnels. He claimed—not always

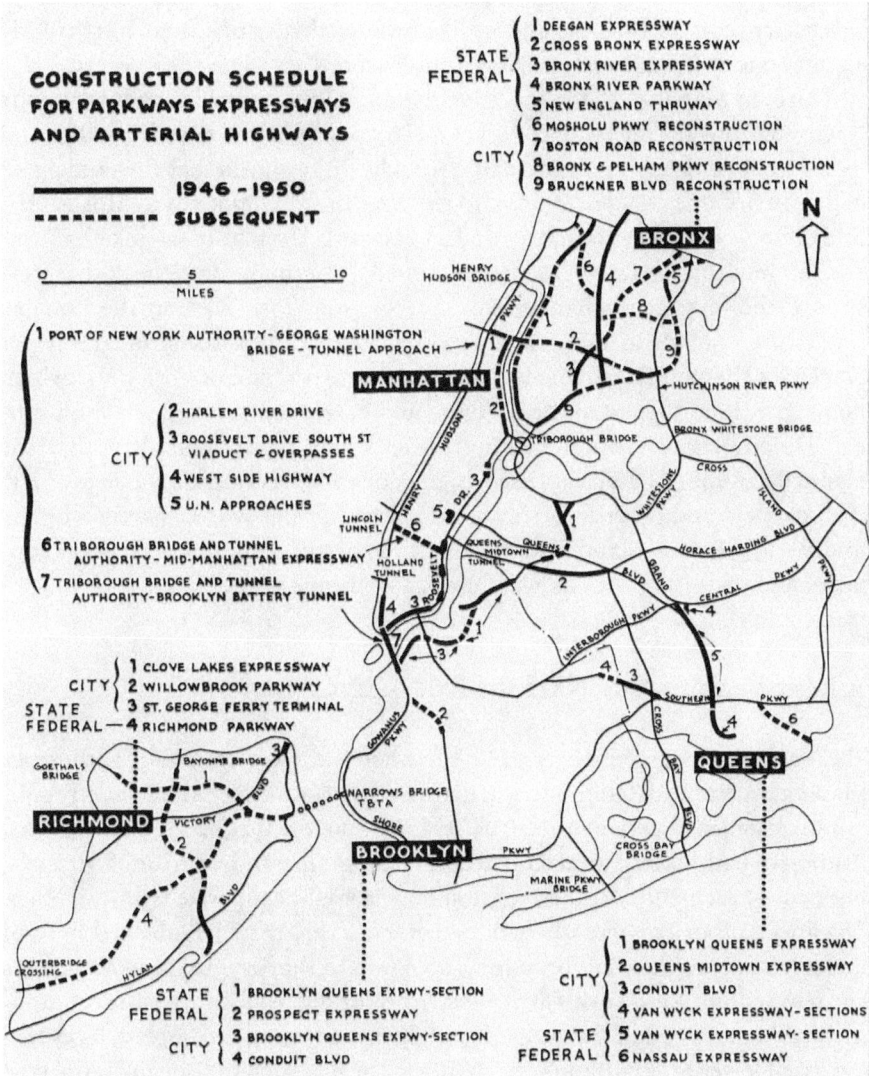

10.1 A Narrows bridge plan for an unspecified future date

The New York Traffic Commission included Robert Moses as a dominant member. This map from its report to Mayor William O'Dwyer in 1949 represented Moses's eventual intention for the TBTA to construct a Narrows tunnel along with an expressway and two parkways on Staten Island.

Source: City of New York Traffic Commission, *Report to Mayor William O'Dwyer* (New York: The Commission, 1949), 13. Courtesy of Harvard University Library.

accurately or truthfully—that the overall economics of bridge construction was better than for tunnels, and he liked the aesthetics of a span, particularly a grand one at the entrance to New York Harbor.[34]

Third, in May 1949 the War Department finally approved a bridge over the Narrows. Considering its rejection of a Narrows span two decades earlier and its very public quashing of the Battery Bridge in 1939, whether it would agree had been of some concern, at least to the *New York Times* if not to Moses: "If a bridge between Forts Hamilton and Wadsworth were to be wrecked in war and fall into the Narrows," the paper argued, "a veritable bottleneck that constitutes the only deep-channel entrance to New York Harbor, the possible results are enough to make one shudder."[35] Given this scenario, the paper braced for the War Department to reject the construction of a bridge, at which point its editors suggested the TBTA would have to return to plans for a tunnel. Despite the *Times*'s misgivings, Moses was rightly confident that the planned 228-foot underclearance—high enough to easily allow passage of aircraft carriers and other fleet ships—would satisfy the War Department.[36] By midcentury, Staten Island's only realistic chance at obtaining a physical connection to the rest of the city was a bridge by means of the TBTA.

A Joint Venture for a Narrows Bridge, 1954–1955

The Narrows bridge project came to life when the two great public authorities shaping the transportation infrastructure of New York City and its metropolitan area joined together to pursue it. In the 1940s, the TBTA and the Port Authority had clashed over construction programs and control of airports, but by 1953 each entity could envision how it might cooperate with the other. The Port Authority currently had the revenues that the TBTA lacked to fund massive new projects, but only the TBTA was authorized to build structures entirely within New York City. A Narrows bridge was an essential component of Moses's vision for vehicular highways forming a complete loop that bypassed lower Manhattan. As such, it had the potential to transform the Port Authority's three bridges connecting Staten Island and New Jersey from money losers to revenue generators.[37] After several months of delicate negotiations, in February 1954 the two authorities announced a joint $750,000 undertaking of a "comprehensive study of all major phases of the arterial traffic problem in the New York–New Jersey metropolitan area," one that would look to divert the through traffic from Manhattan. As an endeavor of two nonpartisan entities, there was minimal geographic or political consideration for participation; thus, although some authority employees conceivably lived on Staten Island, no one expressly represented the borough.[38]

The report from the Port Authority and the TBTA in January 1955 prominently featured a Narrows bridge. In the *Joint Study of Arterial Facilities: New York–New Jersey Metropolitan Area*, the bridge was the major component of a wide-ranging construction-program proposal that included the addition of a second deck for the George Washington Bridge, the building of the Throg's Neck Bridge, and the construction of connecting expressways and parkways in all five boroughs. At $220 million, the Narrows bridge was the most expensive piece of a total package estimated to cost $600 million. Lest the public or politicians balk at the price tag, the report made clear that federal and state funds authorized by the Interstate Highway Act (then being championed by President Dwight Eisenhower and subsequently passed by Congress in 1956) would heavily subsidize the expected $200 million cost of the new roads between the bridges. On Staten Island, the six-lane Clove Lakes Expressway and the Willowbrook Parkway would connect the massive bridge to the Goethals and Bayonne Bridges, respectively (see figure 10.2).[39]

The Narrows bridge immediately caught the public eye as the "most exciting" recommendation of the *Joint Study*. Its scale was massive: two 700-foot towers, a length of 2.5 miles, including approaches, and a 237-foot clearance above the Narrows at its middle. With a 4,400-foot center span, the Narrows Bridge would become the longest suspension bridge in the world. With a double-decked structure carrying six lanes of vehicular traffic on each level, it would handle a large volume of traffic: 14.5 million vehicles were expected to cross it in its first year of operation, with that number projected to more than triple within twenty years. The funding mechanisms for the projects described in the *Joint Study* reflected the TBTA's relatively weak financial position at the time. The proposal called for the Port Authority to fund and build the Narrows crossing, then lease it to the TBTA to operate the span and within ten years to purchase it.[40]

The Narrows bridge may have been the centerpiece of the recommended projects, but Staten Island was not at the forefront with it. The impetus for conducting the study—the diversion of traffic from passing through Manhattan—remained the most potent rationale for its recommendations. There were specific expected outcomes for the borough—most notably a tripling of its population by 1975 and an expanding economy that would grow more intertwined with New Jersey's and Long Island's—but these changes also assumed that Staten Island was now part of the existing metropolitan fabric.[41] Turn-of-the-century civic boosters had imagined that a Narrows crossing would reorder Greater New York's spatial hierarchy so that Staten Island would join the center stage as a beacon of commerce and industry with a massive population to support it. By the 1930s, those fanciful hopes were more muted but still apparent in local discussions of a connection to Greater New

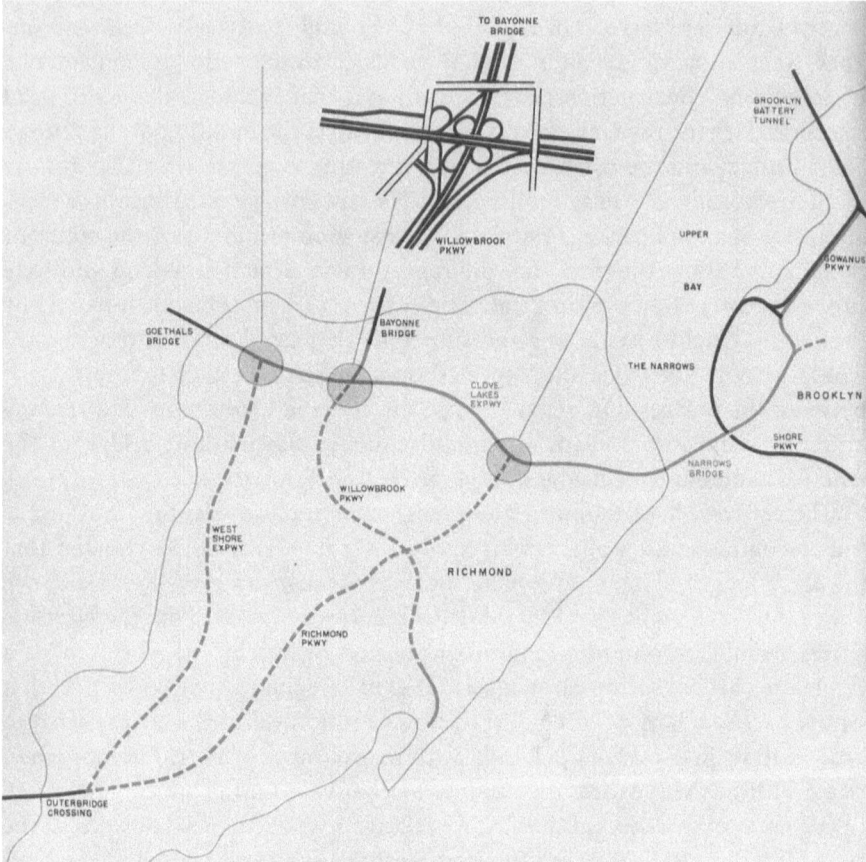

10.2 The Narrows bridge in the *Joint Report*, 1955

A Narrows bridge was the centerpiece of the plan produced together by the Port Authority, which would fund and build, and the TBTA, which would operate the structure. Robert Moses's plans for Staten Island now included a West Shore Expressway as well as the long-envisioned Cloves Lake and Willowbrook Expressways and the Richmond Parkway.

Source: Port Authority of New York and Triborough Bridge and Tunnel Authority, *Joint Study of Arterial Facilities: New York–New Jersey Metropolitan Area* (New York: n.p., 1955), 24. Courtesy of Lehman College, City University of New York.

York, particularly among those who held out for a direct route to Manhattan. As late as 1949, when the TBTA first obtained permission from the War Department to construct a bridge over the Narrows, Moses highlighted access for Staten Island residents. Newspaper coverage, however, framed the need for the bridge around traffic congestion in the metropolitan area.[42] By the 1950s, the larger vision for a metropolitan network of highways had diminished the local rationale for the project, and Staten Island and its residents were mostly on the shelf. As they considered the bridge, they also collectively sat on the fence much more than was understood at the time or since.

Many contemporaries assumed that Staten Islanders in general welcomed the proposal for the bridge and highways, in large part because its leading citizens and institutions were vocally in favor of its construction from the outset. In January 1955, the *Staten Island Advance* proclaimed in a headline "Progress Beckons Island Into New World of New Opportunities" and called for "a bold acceptance by the Borough of Richmond."[43] The SICC immediately passed a resolution in support of the proposal. Borough president Albert Maniscalco regularly lauded the project, and state senator Edward Curry quickly moved to introduce enabling legislation. Real estate interests both on and off the borough salivated at the prospect of a massive increase in demand for property and homes on the island. They all placed the proposal in the multigenerational effort to forge a physical link to the rest of the city: the culmination of decades of exertion, observed the SICC president Frank Mulvihill.[44] In fact, however, a vehicular bridge was only loosely similar to the rail tunnel that had animated islanders for the first four decades of the twentieth century, but it shared one inescapable characteristic: a physical link to the rest of Greater New York.

The initial reaction on Staten Island to the *Joint Study* also included skepticism and resentment. As noted regarding consolidation in chapter 1, immediacy to the news is a useful occasion to gauge dissent—a time before an idea gains traction or a project momentum. "Heaven forbid," one letter writer to the *Advance* opined. Recognizing Staten Island's marginalization, another observed that the plan "is designed not to help Staten Island but to relieve traffic congestion in the Lincoln and Holland Tunnels and lower Manhattan."[45] Others expected the island to become a "turnpike" or "stepping-stone" between Long Island and New Jersey. Echoing that sentiment, the *Advance* reported that there was a local perception that future traffic would go *through* and not *to* the island and at moments expressed its own uncertainty that travelers would come and remain. Still more residents doubted that a bridge was a more pressing need than new schools and better roads and believed that booster claims of a fifteen-minute express bus ride or a population of 400,000 by 1975 were exaggerated.[46] An *Advance* report in February 1955 that "there has been no outspoken opposition to the bridge-building scheme on Staten Island" was accurate only in the sense that the dissent was not vociferous.[47] The paper soon tempered that assertion, admitting that "Staten Island is not sure about the whole thing."[48] The *New York Times* reported similarly that there was confusion on the island about both the prospects and the merits of the bridge. Residents asked for greater voice on the matter, with one insisting that the proposal would not pass a referendum.[49]

The terms of dissent were also familiar. Louis Tribus had wanted the inclusion of a Narrows line in the Dual Contracts and had subsequently headed the SICC Subway and Transit Committee in the 1920s to transform Staten Island. His son Lucien had other thoughts. In opposing the Narrows bridge, he articulated a pastoral idyll for Staten Island that harkened back to the 1890s and to those who preferred that it remain apart from New York:

> Gone will be the woods, the green fields, the wild life, the streams and the brooks. Instead up will go multiple dwellings; up will go the taxes; down will go the trees, and in addition our streets will become congested with traffic, the pure air will be fouled by the exhaust from more decrepit and broken down buses (twice as many will be stalled on Victory Boulevard hill); carpet baggers with the intent solely of making money (after taxes, of course) will come in from the north and flood the Island with jerry-built homes sold on terms of nothing down and the balance in thirty years. If this is progressive civilization, I personally want none of it![50]

At the same time, the younger Tribus showed how the shape of the island's otherness had evolved over sixty years. He had a notion of how the rest of the outer boroughs had developed and of the people of lesser means who had presumably gone to live in those boroughs, and he wanted "none of it" for Staten Island. His words resonated with subsequent correspondents to the *Advance*, who raised similar themes.[51] Others addressed a graver concern for the built environment of Staten Island—it would become a borough filled with apartment buildings, not homes.[52]

Advocates for the Narrows bridge had a common answer to the worries about growth: manage and shape it. Austin Tobin, executive director of the Port Authority, knew his audience when he warned the SICC about Richmond becoming "indistinguishable from the other four boroughs." His positive vision for the impact of the bridge matched the chamber members' own optimism, but Tobin's caveat was that the island needed to plan for the future. "Healthy urban development," he told the chamber, could be Staten Island's if it took advantage of the five-year window it now had to address defects in zoning regulations, ill-advised subdivisions of property, and poorly conceived plans for new streets.[53] Moses offered a similar message in describing Staten Island's good fortune for being "the only one [borough] which can still be planned intelligently."[54]

Staten Islanders appeared interested in the opportunity to chart the borough's growth but ultimately failed to do so. Maniscalco announced early on that he would form a group of business and civic leaders to plan for the future, but he neither moved expeditiously on the matter nor imagined a particularly ambitious effort. The *Advance* wanted a more extensive initiative from the borough president, a larger advisory group with multiple subcommittees tackling individual issues such as schools, real estate, and commuting.[55] Maniscalco's committee eventually met periodically but offered nothing substantive or of lasting consequence to the island even though suggestions were not in short supply. The *Advance*, for example, promoted the provision of parking for commuters taking buses over the bridge; the *Times* wanted to see rapid transit as well as vehicles move over the new bridge.[56]

Rapid Transit on a Narrows Bridge?

Robert Moses had long rejected the notion of placing rapid-transit facilities on a vehicular bridge spanning the Narrows. His general disdain for New York's subways and buses dated back decades, and he typically took positions or made decisions at odds with multiple forms of rapid transit.[57] As early as 1950, Moses privately spelled out his engineering and financial arguments against the inclusion of rail lines on a Narrows bridge: given the necessary height of the bridge, the approaches for automobiles would not suit rapid transit, and making accommodations for the rail lines would cause the costs to skyrocket; Brooklyn's current subway lines could not handle the increase in passenger traffic; and, finally, the experience of the Hylan tunnel suggested the futility of such an overly complex and ambitious proposal.[58] The Port Authority's perspective on this issue was less predictable. Although its overall record showed great success in planning arteries and building crossings for automobiles but failure in working with the railroad corporations, bridge designer Othmar Ammann's early plans for what would become the George Washington Bridge included four tracks for rapid transit on a lower level. The Bayonne Bridge was also built with the possibility of adding a second deck that could accommodate rail lines, and the Port Authority recommended doing so in a report in 1937.[59] In this collaborative endeavor, Robert Moses's position was not certain to prevail. The *Joint Study* retained the original idea for the George Washington Bridge, in which a lower level with rapid-transit capability would be built.[60] Might it also have included rail lines on the Narrows bridge, despite Moses's proclivities?

The *Joint Study* heeded Moses and recommended omitting all kinds of rails from the Narrows Bridge. It articulated arguments against subway, commuter, and freight trains that Moses had offered in the past. The report ruled out a subway by noting that the Fourth Avenue subway line in Brooklyn was already operating at capacity, so that an expensive subway expansion through Brooklyn would have to be included in the price tag. Fighting the ghost of the Hylan tunnel, the report explained that a railroad required an easier grade that would necessitate a much longer approach using elevated tracks through the adjacent neighborhoods—highlighting the adverse impact on Bay Ridge in particular. It did not explicitly mention a factor of which Moses was certainly aware—that Staten Island did not have the necessary concentration of population necessary to generate enough revenue to cover the operating expenses of a rail link—but its opposition was at bottom based on financial considerations rather than on technical feasibility.[61]

The omission of rapid transit from the Narrows bridge generated further criticism of the proposal from Staten Islanders who might otherwise have been inclined to favor the intended span. Although hardly a torrent, letters to the *Staten Island Advance* saw a missed opportunity in the exclusion of rapid-transit lines on the bridge. One resident of Stapleton saw an island largely stagnant since consolidation with the city "due in greatest measure to our complete isolation" and questioned by implication whether true growth would really come from a vehicular bridge alone.[62] Others thought a monorail to Bay Ridge would make sense, with one advocate including a route around the island as well as over the proposed bridge. The *Advance* reported a number of residents wondering why there would not be rapid-transit lines on the Narrows bridge. Its editorial voice, however, gave only lukewarm support for a new effort to study rapid-transit options for Staten Island.[63]

More than such tepidness constrained rapid transit; by 1955, new organizational and political contexts discouraged it as well. One factor was the absence of any well-established group on the island that prioritized or fully engaged in making a connection to the New York City subway. The lack of a constituency for rails was a significant dynamic in the entire metropolitan area, and Staten Island was no exception.[64] The Richmond County Chapter of the SPE had long abandoned its efforts for a subway. No business or civic group sought to create an island-wide rapid-transit committee, nor would the borough president lend his office to such an effort. The relatively new Civic Congress of Staten Island was sympathetic to rapid transit but did not undertake a popular or political campaign.[65] The SICC would have let the matter drop entirely but for its longtime executive secretary, Art Hedquist. Without working through the chamber's membership, Hedquist proposed a "Loop Rapid Transit System" with links on both the Bayonne Bridge and the Narrows bridge. In early 1955, he persuaded the SICC leadership to sponsor his proposal, but such backing was a hollow gesture because it was up to Hedquist alone to move his idea forward.[66]

Hedquist's subsequent efforts on behalf of the Loop Rapid Transit System nicely illustrates a second important change: the target of any initiative was no longer just a democratically elected person or body but rather two public authorities intentionally buffered from popular outcry. Hedquist understood this reality and sent his plan to the Metropolitan Transit Authority, the Regional Plan Association, and the TBTA as well as to the governors of New

Jersey and New York.[67] His correspondence with Moses illustrated the TBTA chairman's insularity as much as his imperiousness. Moses rejected Hedquist's assertion that the Loop Rapid Transit System would cut expenses and wondered how the city could handle the project when it could not build the Second Avenue subway.[68] Hedquist responded with the trope that introduced this chapter: that only someone with Moses's ability and vision could turn this challenging idea into reality, but flattery did not succeed. In a second letter, Moses reminded Hedquist of other rapid-transit priorities and elaborated on the costly longer approaches that were required for rails. Moses finished by scornfully observing that "many of the 'worthwhile ideas' scratched on tablecloths at lunch conferences end up where they belong, in the laundry."[69] The Loop Rapid Transit proposal failed to gain traction locally either—the *Advance* thought the plan was overly ambitious—but elsewhere in the region there were entities and individuals not yet deterred by the intentional absence of rapid transit on the Narrows bridge. Hedquist had also submitted his loop proposal to the most significant of these bodies, the recently formed Metropolitan Rapid Transit Commission (MRTC).[70]

In 1954, the states of New York and New Jersey had established the MRTC to study the region's rapid-transit needs. Spurred by the financial troubles of private commuter railroad companies, each state had previously created a body to study rapid transit, and both had concluded that the issues were regional. The two states gave the MRTC a huge task with a pittance of resources, but into the financial void stepped the Port Authority, which provided $500,000 to the MRTC to conduct its study but also extracted an agreement that placed limits on the study's focus and its independence overall.[71] The MRTC announced its work in January 1955 just four days before the *Joint Study* was made public. Its cochair from New York, Charles Tuttle, immediately took a stance at odds with Moses's report.[72]

Tuttle responded with skepticism to the *Joint Study*'s near total rejection of rapid transit. He believed in "tying Staten Island into the greater rapid transit system of metropolitan NY" and saw minimal commercial and residential development for the island without it. The MRTC would examine two possible bridge connectors for train lines: the prospective Narrows bridge and the existing Bayonne Bridge. Because adding rail lines to the latter was technically feasible but a highly speculative enterprise, Tuttle did not want to miss the opening presented by the Narrows bridge to include rapid transit.[73] His commitment and vigorous promotion won praise from the *New York Times*, whose editorial board feared missing the "opportunity of a lifetime" and urged the city's Board of Estimate to challenge the rejection of rails for the Narrows bridge.[74] His promotion also initially intrigued the *Advance*, but the paper soon soured on the endeavor, fearing that the MRTC study was pointless, given funding challenges and the position already taken by the two authorities. It was well aware of and concerned that Moses was not swayed by the arguments for including rapid transit on the bridge and along the expressway.[75]

In the winter and spring of 1955, Moses and Tuttle jousted over rapid transit. They had tussled before, with the attorney Tuttle challenging on the stand Moses's assertions of fact in two earlier cases from the 1920s and 1930s.[76] Decades later Tuttle did the same in the press and before audiences on Staten Island. Speaking before the Staten Island Real Estate Board, Tuttle emphasized the rapid transit of the future—not the old locomotive model but the high-speed, single-rail model. He also asserted that without better rapid transit Staten Island would not develop, and Greater New York would suffer from "vehicular strangulation." He attributed Staten Island's relatively slow growth in population and industry—12 new factories on Staten Island from 1946 to 1950 compared to 226 in Queens, 250 in Bergen County, and even 91 in Suffolk County—to the island's historic failure to obtain a rapid-transit link to the rest of the city.[77] Thinking Tuttle "a jack ass [sic]" and the issue moot, Moses initially ignored him but then went on the offensive when he could not make the challenge disappear. Opposed to rails on the bridge in the present and unwilling even to prepare for them in the future, he asserted to Tuttle in January 1956 that "if the bridge is to be strengthened for this purpose, some other agency will have to supply the additional funds. The [Triborough Bridge and Tunnel] Authority will not."[78] The contretemps had spilled into 1956 when the MRTC engaged Day and Zimmerman, the Philadelphia firm that had studied a vehicular tunnel for Mayor Walker in the late 1920s, to assess the viability of rapid transit on the Narrows bridge.[79]

Three major issues underlay the arguments about rapid transit on the Narrows bridge. First, there was little agreement on basic facts about capacity and cost. Could Brooklyn's Fourth Avenue subway handle additional riders from Staten Island? The MRTC had for months publicly discounted Moses's claim that the line already operated at capacity by citing Metropolitan Transit Authority figures to the contrary.[80] Moses simply doubled down on his assertion, suggesting to Tuttle that $750 million for an additional subway line in Brooklyn and a new tunnel to Manhattan would be needed to provide rapid transit to Staten Island.[81] Tuttle yielded nothing in his response to Moses, spelling out how, in lieu of a new tunnel and line, the Metropolitan Transit Authority would lengthen platforms and make other improvements at key stations to accommodate the additional riders.[82] Moses resorted to public invective of the MRTC for its "preposterous" ideas and the Metropolitan Transit Authority for its ineptness. He also dialed back to $500 million his initial price tag for a new Brooklyn subway and East River tunnel.[83] A few months later his estimate for strengthening a Narrows bridge for rail capacity increased fivefold from $10 million to $50 million when he corresponded with New York's governor Averill Harriman.[84] The opponents' acceptance of the same set of numbers proved impossible when one party routinely adjusted and wielded them like clubs.

Second, the combatants offered or presumed vastly different assessments of the automobile's impact on the built environment. Tuttle was not opposed to vehicular traffic but was simply wary of overreliance on it. He envisioned a comprehensive transportation system with multiple components. For him, rapid transit would complement the automobile in opening up the metropolitan area: "The future development of the vast potentials of Staten Island and the adjoining territory in New Jersey can scarcely be kept dependent upon vehicular transportation solely and the limited and time-consuming ferries, but requires in all prudence and foresight that mass transportation by rapid transit also be considered, particularly as to whether comparatively small expenditure now would save vastly greater expenditure later or prevent denial of rapid transit travel to and from Staten Island at all."[85]

For Moses, such language sounded at odds with the trends in transportation over the past twenty years or more. He noted that the original plan for rapid transit on the lower level of the George Washington Bridge was not being implemented; that the city's commissioner of public works, Frederick Zurmuhlen, favored removing rail lines from the Manhattan Bridge; and that no "responsible organization" had yet approached him with any interest in constructing rails on the Narrows bridge.[86] Moses's read was that the era of expanding the subway system was stalled if not over in New York City, a point that Tuttle ultimately acknowledged in his memoir.[87] Because the *New York Times*, among others, thought "Mr. Moses could be wrong," Governor Harriman at the very least wanted the MRTC to complete its work before the two authorities reached a decision regarding rapid transit on the Narrows bridge. Moses's discouragement did not sway Harriman from taking this position.[88]

The emergence of a new vision for Staten Island's future was a third important factor illustrated by the contention over rapid transit on the Narrows bridge. Local boosters had once viewed a subway as the prerequisite for tremendous population, commercial, and industrial growth akin to what had occurred in Queens and the Bronx. Citywide officials often articulated a similar image for Richmond—for example, when they constructed piers in Stapleton. After World War II, the kind of development planned for Staten Island no longer anticipated much population density or economic activity. Consider the CPC's expectations—penned by one of its leading members, Robert Moses—for Staten Island regarding density and commuting:

> SI in the future as envisioned by the City Planning Commission and controlled by zoning laws will be a community of one-family homes with extensive industrial development along Arthur Kills. The new residents will be employed to a great extent on SI and their wish for rapid transit will

be limited to occasional visits to the City rather than daily commuting. The low density of population will make it impossible to provide a satisfactory rapid transit system to serve all areas on the Island except as a tremendously expensive deficit operation.[89]

In a direct appeal to Staten Islanders, Moses called for "proper planning" for the island's vast areas of open land, committed to an upgrading of zoning requirements, and offered resistance to "attempts to create business and industrial areas where they do not belong."[90]

This vision for a future of single-family homes had plenty of support on Staten Island. Opponents of the bridge raised the specter of unwanted growth, but even those who favored the Narrows span sought to retain the island's current patterns of development. Speaking before the Staten Island Real Estate Board in 1955, Richmond Borough president Maniscalco assured his audience that Richmond would remain a "borough of homes."[91] SICC president Mulvihill likewise expressed confidence that the population projections were overdrawn and that Staten Island would remain a single-family residence. The *Advance*, recognizing the anxiety that gripped some residents regarding the future, insisted the island keep what was feared might be lost: "The garden-within-a-city tradition must be maintained . . . the small homes . . . the residential sections . . . the open spaces to play and breath[e] fresh air."[92] Austin Tobin, the longtime executive director of the Port Authority, cautioned an appreciative gathering of SICC members about the perils of growing too quickly and too haphazardly. He urged serious planning for the newcomers and warned against current zoning regulations that permitted "the erection of six-story apartment houses in residential areas now dotted with only one and two-family homes. If allowed, these structures would make Richmond indistinguishable from the congested residential areas of Brooklyn and the Bronx."[93]

The powerful desire for a borough of homes helps explain why Staten Islanders largely stayed on the sidelines or supported Moses during his public spats with Tuttle and the *New York Times*. At the SICC meeting in April 1956, its leadership determined not to involve itself in the rapid-transit issue but resolved to support the TBTA's request for an extension of its permission from the U.S. Army to construct the bridge.[94] The *Advance*, which the previous year had signaled both support for the *Joint Study* and a willingness to see the MRTC engage in its work, had by 1956 fully embraced Moses and distanced itself from the voices clamoring for rapid transit on the bridge. Frustrated by the seeming inactivity in the year since the publication of the *Joint Study*, the paper blamed rapid-transit advocates as one of five reasons for delays.[95] Calling for "one project at a time," the *Advance* now derided the work of the MRTC and cautioned against jeopardizing the bridge by insisting on the inclusion of rapid transit.[96]

The demise of the prospects for rapid transit on the bridge was surprisingly anticlimactic. In November 1956, the Day and Zimmerman report concluded that although the Fourth Avenue subway could handle the additional commuter traffic for ten to twenty years, the route would not save much time compared to the ferry and would operate at an annual $2 million deficit. Accepting the engineers' findings, the MRTC executive director omitted rapid transit on the bridge and along the expressway in his own report issued on January 1957 and instead recommended bus service, which "would have nearly equal public convenience" as rails and would cost far less. As for a Bayonne connection, a separate study released later that year concluded that no current demand existed for such a line but that it could be considered in the future.[97]

When the MRTC released its final report in 1958, it made a compelling case for rail transit in general but offered none for Richmond Borough. Staten Islanders appeared unruffled. The MRTC drew few Staten Islanders to hearings on its report. With Hedquist having stepped down as the SICC's executive secretary, the chamber did not raise any concerns. The *Advance* noted that the MRTC "seems to have concluded, almost sadly, that rails across the Narrows are not likely in our time," but it did not share this disappointment and instead pronounced Moses the victor.[98] The MRTC ultimately marked a failure to coordinate a regional rapid-transit solution, a failure that included but was hardly limited to Staten Island.[99]

The Triumph of the Verrazzano-Narrows Bridge

Even after Robert Moses prevailed regarding rapid transit, other issues still delayed groundbreaking on the Narrows project until 1959. Planning for the bridge proceeded for four years, but obtaining needed funding and approvals took longer than anticipated. Three major issues accounted for the holdup. The most prominent and controversial of them was the sustained opposition to the project emanating from Brooklyn, the Bay Ridge neighborhood in particular. There were also negotiations to be completed with the U.S. Army for use of its land belonging to Forts Wadsworth and Hamilton on either side of the Narrows. Finally, there were significant issues related to governance and jurisdiction because the New York City Board of Estimate was especially eager not to cede total control over the project to the two authorities.

The prospect of a Narrows bridge and new expressways triggered opposition over the inevitable dislocation of homes and businesses that would occur. On Staten Island, the release of the *Joint Study* in January 1955 prompted dozens of property owners to flood the phone lines and clog the hallways at Borough Hall.[100] Their fears that the proposed routes for the bridge, its approaches, and the expressway would force them to move were not easily assuaged. Although Staten Island's business, civic, and political leaders asserted that some routes would change and assured property owners of their vigilance on the matter, they recognized that for some the price would be steep: "Progress will gouge a great highway across the widest part of the Island, from Fort Wadsworth to the Goethals Bridge, leveling hillocks, widening or bridging roads, moving or destroying ... [,] and this is the saddest part of the picture[,] ... scores, perhaps, they say, hundreds of homes."[101]

Some dislocation was an acceptable cost for the benefits these leaders believed the bridge would bring, but they sought to minimize the damage. The obligation to limit the dislocation to "scores" rather than to "hundreds" fell especially on Albert Maniscalco. A firm supporter of the project, the borough president made it clear to Staten Islanders that he could not dictate terms to the authorities and would not make "unreasonable demands" of them.[102] Maniscalco struck the right chord by moving Moses to find a less disruptive route yet forestalling the development of strong opposition to the bridge.[103] The TBTA had determined that a route that sliced across the corners of the U.S. Army forts located on each side of the Narrows (Wadsworth and Hamilton) would require a shorter bridge and save housing units.[104] Maniscalco persuaded the TBTA to locate the expressway in a more southerly route largely near Victory Boulevard, preserving neighborhoods and cutting housing dislocation by one-third, though one casualty would be Sunnyside Hospital.[105] Eventually, about three hundred buildings were destroyed for the approaches, requiring approximately 3,500 residents to move.[106] Despite the considerable dislocation, potent homeowner resistance never materialized on Staten Island.

In Brooklyn, the antagonism in Bay Ridge was sustained and pronounced. The struggle is a well-told story of grandstanding, litigating, lobbying, protesting, and stalling that lengthened the approval process to nearly four years.[107] Bay Ridge was largely united in opposition to the disruption and dislocation that would come with construction, particularly of the approaches to the bridge. The neighborhood received support from several politicians and organizations across Brooklyn, first in an attempt to defeat the entire project and then, bowing to the superior forces arrayed against them, in an effort to alter the location of the approaches from the Seventh Avenue route selected by the planners. The protestors did not garner much sympathy in the other four boroughs, and leaders on Staten Island feared that the Brooklyn neighborhood's opposition might derail the project.[108] As the conflict over the Seventh Avenue approaches dragged into the summer of 1958, Maniscalco pressed Mayor Robert F. Wagner Jr., with whom he was closely aligned, not to delay any longer.[109] Staten Islanders attended Board of Estimate hearings on the matter and were one of the many constituencies that held firm for the bridge. After four contentious years, the Brooklyn approaches stayed as the Port Authority and

TBTA had planned, and 7,000 residents of Bay Ridge were forced to relocate during construction.

Negotiations with the U.S. Army over the acquisition of its land on either side of the Narrows were neither public nor heated but took longer than expected. Moses initially assumed the army would readily renew the permission it had already granted to bridge the Narrows, but as the expiration date in 1956 approached, the ask became more complicated when the proposed location shifted to include military property from Forts Wadsworth and Hamilton. There was no fundamental principle at stake: the army had already determined that a bridge would not be or become an impediment during war, and it was willing to release the land Moses wanted. The army and the TBTA simply haggled over the price as the army insisted that it be compensated for the cost of replacing military structures that would need to be destroyed. Agreement on the anchorage sites, easements, and $24 million in compensation for the construction of new military facilities took two years of negotiations. In May 1957, the TBTA was granted permission to build the bridge in the location it wanted with the condition that construction begin by June 17, 1959.[110]

Passing enabling legislation in both states took little time but presented complications. In New York, questions of home rule for New York City and some partisan wrangling arose, but the most divisive issues stemmed from the city's intent to retain autonomy over matters the two authorities believed to be in their domain. Mayor Wagner expected any legislation to allow the city approval over any condemnation of land for the three major bridge projects. The city council delayed passing a home-rule message—a constitutionally required mechanism to indicate a city's support for special legislation that targets it alone—while the Wagner administration negotiated with the two authorities. They all quickly reached an agreement in principle that the legislation would include financial relief to pay for condemned properties and approval of final routes for the city as well as language on the relocation of displaced families.[111]

Wagner's certitude was tested in late March 1955 when the Port Authority balked at the actual language the mayor's administration wanted to insert in the bill. The city sought the power to amend the routes after the authorities completed the final mapping and to limit its own liability for the cost of compensating relocated landowners.[112] The Port Authority's chief interest was with the second deck for the George Washington Bridge, but its insistence on proceeding with the comprehensive plan in its entirety and not in a piecemeal manner imperiled the Narrows bridge. In a letter to the mayor, Port Authority chairman Howard Cullman charged the city with an attempt "to gain control over responsibilities that are properly and legally those of the Port Authority."[113] With the state legislature scheduled to adjourn the next day, Cullman and Moses reached resolution with Wagner on April 1, 1955. The city largely ceded to the Port Authority the power of land condemnation for the new approaches to the George Washington Bridge. In exchange, the Port Authority agreed to limit its power of condemnation to a specified area in northern Manhattan and dropped its last-minute haggling over the Narrows bridge condemnations.[114] With a settlement in place, the necessary authorizations from the Board of Estimate, the City Council, and the state Assembly and Senate followed rapidly, with the only significant votes against them coming from Brooklyn politicians.[115] Similar concerns about dislocation arose in New Jersey, where legislation stalled for a year but then passed in March 1956.[116]

Other hurdles had to be jumped in order to break ground on the project. President Eisenhower had encouraged congressional action on interstate highways in 1954, but the legislation did not become law until 1956. By then, Moses had already secured the inclusion of the new connecting expressways in the federal highway system, ensuring that 90 percent of the anticipated $200 million cost would be funded by Washington. New York's effort to cover the remainder was stymied by the electorate. Bombarded by the New York State Automobile Association's campaign against passage and objecting to an accompanying two-cent increase in the state gas tax, voters turned down a $750 million bond authorization for highway construction in November 1955. One year later a reduced request that omitted a gas tax and garnered the support of the Automobile Association was passed easily by more than a two-to-one margin.[117]

Moses wielded the prospect of massive federal highway funds like a cudgel during the final approval process for the bridge and its approaches. Brooklyn opponents could and did challenge his assertions on technical and financial details of any project, but his authoritative statements about politics and governance could not be easily overcome.[118] In the conflict over rapid transit on Staten Island in 1956, he insisted that federal funds could not be used to acquire land for rapid transit alongside the Clove Lakes Expressway.[119] This argument was also crucial to Moses's intransigence on the TBTA's planned Seventh Avenue approach to the Narrows bridge. As the approach locations slowly moved through the approval process during 1957 and 1958, Brooklynites proposed alternative routes; the CPC stuck with the TBTA's choice. The Brooklynites maneuvered the passage of legislation forbidding the use of the Seventh Avenue approach to the bridge; Governor Harriman vetoed it. They clamored for an alternative link across New York Harbor to New Jersey, drawing Staten Islanders to Board of Estimate hearings throughout the summer and fall of 1958; courts refused to delay the project so that this alternative could be studied. The Brooklynites grew unruly and acted out of order at meetings, postponing a final decision for weeks and then months. In all of these instances, Moses and TBTA officials maintained that their approach was the most feasible—which could easily be contested—and that it was the only one eligible for federal funds—which was hard to negate. On December 30, 1958, the Board of Estimate finally voted to approve the routes for the Narrows bridge. Although some last-gasp efforts to block the project continued into 1959, all the required authorizations were now in place, and ground was broken on Staten Island on August 14, 1959.[120] Later that year, with its financial position looking much better than it had in 1955, the TBTA took over the entire project from the Port Authority—eight years earlier than intended.[121] Construction took the anticipated five years, and the Verrazzano-Narrows Bridge opened for traffic on November 21, 1964.

What's in a Name?

One issue that for five years had animated citizens on Staten Island and throughout the city remained unsettled in 1959: what to name the new bridge. This chapter has referred to it as the "Narrows bridge," as it was described at the time, but people offered alternatives almost immediately upon the release of the *Joint Study* in 1955. Letter writers to the *New York Times* suggested, among many other names, "Neptune Bridge" for the Roman god of the seas, "New World Bridge" for its gateway location, and "Freedom Bridge" as a doorway to the Statue of Liberty. The *Times* editorial page echoed the latter sentiment and suggested "Liberty Bridge," while the *Advance* recommended sticking with "Narrows Bridge," but a different name soon rose to prominence.[122]

The name "Verrazzano Bridge" was an early contender, promoted by the city's fledgling Italian Historical Society.[123] Its leaders lobbied officials to draw greater attention to Italian explorer Giovanni da Verrazzano through an annual day in his honor and the name of the new span. Governor Harriman, in acknowledgment of the voyager's arrival at what would be New York Harbor in 1524 and of the increased visibility and prominence of Italian Americans, publicly committed to the name at the Verrazzano Day festivities in 1958. So did his successor, Governor Nelson Rockefeller, speaking at the same event one year later.[124] The *New York Times*, Robert Moses, and many Staten Islanders still preferred an alternative. An *Advance* survey indicated a fondness for "Narrows Bridge" and limited support for "Verrazzano Bridge."[125] The SICC favored the name "Staten Island Bridge." In a letter to Rockefeller, the chamber articulated the frustrations of the Forgotten Borough, wondered why the other boroughs had bridges with their names, and asked him "to let Staten Island get in the limelight for a change."[126]

The local effort to influence the name of the bridge came too late, however, and was too weak to reframe the discussion around Staten Island's wishes. Rockefeller forged a compromise with officials from both authorities and political leaders: the bridge was named the "Verrazano-Narrows Bridge." The

Italian Historical Society accepted the settlement, while the SICC did not. Chartering an airplane to fly over the groundbreaking ceremony with a banner reading "Name it the Staten Island Bridge," the SICC continued its efforts through the fall of 1959.[127] It won some civic support but could not undo the resolution that had been reached by public officials. A bill to approve the hyphenated name with one z was passed during the 1960 legislative session.[128]

* * *

The rejection of the name "Staten Island Bridge" was indicative of the larger sidelining of the borough in the series of events that led to the construction of the Verrazzano-Narrows Bridge. This link to the city appeared decades later than Staten Islanders had desired and expected. Arriving without rapid transit, the outcome was still not what many Staten Islanders had craved. Coming as part of a massive highway system that used Staten Island as a connector rather than treating it as a destination, the bridge was not at all what many Staten Islanders had imagined. Rapid transit remained the "rainbow dream of the Island" for some, but many others increasingly sought to keep their distance from the other boroughs and began to resent the newcomers who did arrive on the island after 1964.[129]

In a span of fifteen years, Staten Islanders acquiesced to the abandonment of a rapid-transit connection, the elimination of a tunnel as an option, and, most fundamentally, the removal of Staten Island's development as the primary motive for the bridge. Population growth was certainly anticipated, and industrial and commercial development hoped for, but the Verrazzano Bridge was built to serve expanding motor vehicle traffic by creating a bypass of Manhattan for cars and trucks bound for Long Island and New England. To get the bridge done, Staten Islanders were relegated to minor roles in a process largely housed in the increasingly autonomous Port Authority and TBTA, in which even the city and state struggled to assert themselves. Creating a regional transportation network for motor vehicles had trumped the local aspirations of Staten Islanders.

CHAPTER 11

ASSESSING THE DISCONNECT

What the Distance Wrought

Nothing changes here except the date on the daily paper.

—Attributed to the poet and Staten Island resident Edwin Markham, c. 1938

Once, merely by crossing Cedar Avenue, one would know without being told that he was in another community.

—Attributed to Richmond Borough president Albert Maniscalco, 1957

When reporter Gilbert Millstein profiled Staten Island for the *New York Times* in October 1957, he framed what he encountered through the lens of the past. The late 1930s adage of poet Edwin Markham, who had lived in Westerleigh for nearly forty years, spoke to the strong continuity Millstein had found in the island's rural landscape and local identities. Yet twenty years later Richmond Borough president Albert Maniscalco saw those individualized community characteristics dimming as the island developed and homogenized. Neither Markham nor Maniscalco was native to Staten Island, but they had grown—Markham as an adult and Maniscalco as a child—to identify strongly with their adopted home and had become wary of unwanted developments. By 1957, perspectives on continuity and change in the past especially lived in the shadow of the future.

Growing rapidly was a third perception on which Maniscalco and Markham could likely agree: significant transformations would come with the construction of the bridge across the Narrows.

In what ways and to what degree had Staten Island evolved from 1890 to 1960? How had the successful effort to join New York City and then the failed efforts to obtain a rapid-transit link to it shaped the island's trajectory? To answer the first question, this chapter assesses shifts and stasis on Staten Island over time and relative to the other boroughs. In 1960, Staten Island looked starkly different from what it was in 1890—Markham's observation notwithstanding—but its changes were made less obvious by the implicit comparison found in the "Forgotten Borough" moniker. The juxtaposition with the Bronx, Brooklyn, Manhattan, and Queens heightened the notion of Richmond as a place neglected by time. Compared to its siblings, Staten Island appeared little altered over the decades, and in some sense it was. Yet profiles of housing, land use, occupations, nativity, education, and religion indicate several ways in which by 1960 Staten Island had indeed changed significantly.

The reality of consolidation followed by the absence of a rail link shaped much of the island's development to 1960. For nearly fifty years, Staten Islanders tried and failed to obtain a rail connection to Manhattan. The repeated disappointment to garner a link to the subway contributed mightily to residents' self-identity as the Forgotten Borough. That link's absence—when rapid transit soon reached every outer borough—exacerbated Richmond's natural distance from the rest of the city. This chapter uses demographic and economic data from 1890 to 1960 to convey the impact of the island's heightened geographic isolation, which influenced who resided there, where they lived, and how they made a living. The disconnect with the rest of New York had profound cultural and material effects on Staten Island.

Other factors in addition to the absence of a rail tunnel help account for Staten Island's trajectory in the twentieth century. Most notably, the consolidation with New York in 1898 also shaped the island's subsequent history. Sixty years after the political union, many contemporaries still found being a part of New York City meaningful despite major setbacks in transportation and sanitation. The island's business and civic leaders remained largely approving of the decision to join Greater New York. Their efforts to capitalize on new commercial opportunities and their relative satisfaction with services and amenities that had appeared after consolidation continued through most of the twentieth century.

Large economic structures and political developments also propelled evolving conditions on Staten Island. Regional and national trends in agriculture, deindustrialization, immigration, and suburbanization were already reshaping the entire metropolis by 1960 and would continue to do so in subsequent decades. Staten Island farms would decline, factories would close, and social identities would shift even if the island had not consolidated with New York or had gained a rapid-transit connection. In short, this chapter explores continuity and change on Staten Island through three broad lenses: physical isolation, political consolidation, and socioeconomic penetration. The place to begin is with population growth, which reflected all three factors but was especially related to the level of connectivity to the city's rapid-transit system.

Population Growth

Historians of urban transportation have readily and persuasively shown how the arrival of a new rail line stimulated an increase in inhabitants. As population grew in each New York borough, larger numbers clustered around transit routes, while less densely populated neighborhoods remained in areas lacking easy access to rapid transit. The arrival of the subway and its extension deep into Brooklyn, Queens, and the Bronx preceded an especially powerful surge in the size and pace of population growth in each borough. As Clifton Hood has suggested, the Bronx is the most telling example. It was the beneficiary of being reached by the first subway line opened in 1904, and its population more than doubled from 1900 to 1910, grew by another 68 percent in the 1910s, added another 500,000 people in the 1920s, and totaled 1,424,815 in 1960.[1] Subway lines came later to Queens, which had healthy growth during the first twenty years of the new century but whose population doubled to more than one million in the 1920s and reached 1,809,578 in 1960. Brooklyn, already a massive city with more than one million people in 1900, nonetheless grew by approximately 500,000 over each of the next three decades as subways arrived and extended to its lesser-populated outer regions. Its 2,627,319 residents made it the most populous borough in 1960.[2] The expansion of the New York subway, in particular the lines built through the Dual Contracts, had a substantial impact on the boroughs that received it.

Staten Island experienced a consistent rise in population from 1890 to 1960 but not at the same scale as its counterparts. Consolidation certainly helped prod the growth, which was particularly strong from 1890 to 1930 and peaked in the 1920s. As the data in table 11.1 indicate, over these forty years its population increased by about a third in each decade and tripled overall, from just less than 52,000 to more than 158,000. Its solid rate of growth, however, did not come close to the meteoric gains elsewhere; Staten Island (referred to as "Richmond" in this chapter's tables), unlike Queens and the Bronx, never approached one million residents or doubled its population in any decade. Its population reached 221,991 in 1960, making Staten Island a decidedly urban environment from a demographic perspective. In 1960, the U.S. Census Bureau defined urban areas as having a density of greater than 1,000 people

TABLE 11.1 Population of New York City and its boroughs (in thousands), 1890–1960

Year	Richmond Pop.	Growth (%)	Brooklyn Pop.	Growth (%)	Queens Pop.	Growth (%)	Bronx Pop.	Growth (%)	Manhattan Pop.	Growth (%)	New York City Pop.	Growth (%)
1890	51.7	32.6	838.5	39.9	87.0	52.6	88.9	71.2	1,441.2	23.7	2,507.4	31.2
1900	67.0	29.7	1,166.6	39.3	153.0	75.9	200.5	125.8	1,850.1	28.4	3,437.2	37.1
1910	86.0	28.3	1,634.4	40.0	284.0	85.6	431.0	114.4	2,331.5	26.2	4,766.9	38.7
1920	116.5	35.6	2,018.4	23.5	469.0	65.1	732.0	69.8	2,284.1	-2.1	5,620.0	17.9
1930	158.3	35.9	2,560.4	26.9	1,079.1	130.1	1,265.3	72.8	1,867.3	-18.3	6,930.4	23.3
1940	174.4	10.2	2,698.3	5.4	1,297.6	20.2	1,394.7	10.3	1,889.9	1.2	7,455.0	7.6
1950	191.6	9.9	2,738.2	1.5	1,550.8	19.6	1,451.3	4.0	1,960.1	3.7	7,892.0	5.9
1960	222.0	15.9	2,627.3	-4.1	1,809.6	16.7	1,424.8	-1.8	1,698.3	-13.4	7,782.0	-1.4
1970	295.4	33.1	2,602.0	-1.0	1,986.4	9.8	1,471.7	3.3	1,539.2	-9.4	7,894.8	1.5

Source: Compiled from "City of New York & Boroughs: Population & Population Density from 1790," 6 tables, Demographia, http://www.demographia.com/dm-nyc.htm.

per square mile; Richmond County had 3,700 per square mile, larger than nearly every other New York county but small in comparison to the other four boroughs.[3] At 16,014 people per square mile, Queens was more than four times as dense as Staten Island but still half as dense as the Bronx (33,135) and Brooklyn (34,570). Manhattan topped them all with a population density of 77,195 people per square mile.[4] Other factors affected population trends throughout the city, both before and after the arrival of the city's subways. The prospect and then the fact of consolidation, the bridging of the Harlem River, and growing economic interdependence generated growth rates in the Bronx (126 percent) and Queens (76 percent) that strongly outpaced Staten Island's 30 percent increase during the 1890s. Making the case for a subway grew harder every year in the early twentieth century as Staten Island's population fell farther behind these two boroughs. As the Dual Contracts were negotiated in 1912, the Bronx had more than five times and Queens more than three times as many residents as Staten Island. After that, two major deterrents—World War I and federal legislation in the 1920s—vastly reduced European immigration. Internal migrations—primarily second-generation immigrants outward from Manhattan and African Americans upward from the South—initially sustained expansion in the 1910s and 1920s. Then growth plummeted with the onset of the Great Depression and World War II in the 1930s and 1940s. Postwar suburbanization saw Staten Island's population increase by 15.9 percent at a time when the other boroughs save Queens began to experience loss. The city's overall population decline in the 1950s signaled the growing difficulties that many northern and midwestern cities faced in the second half of the twentieth century. New York ultimately met these challenges more successfully than many lesser cities, and Staten Island avoided or experienced them less acutely than the other boroughs.

Housing

Varied housing patterns developed between and within each borough to accommodate the concentration of newcomers. Richmond County neither grew so rapidly nor reached such densities that generated a market for many residences other than single-family homes. In 1960, most of its housing units were detached single-family homes; together with attached single-family homes and two-unit buildings, they accounted for 86.4 percent of the island's housing units. As the data in table 11.2 indicate, buildings with three or more units—typically in the form of tenements or large apartment buildings—were not especially common. Manhattan of course—with more than 96 percent of its structures containing five or more units—provides the most extreme contrast, but other boroughs mirrored it: 78 percent in the Bronx and 50 percent

TABLE 11.2 Size and type of housing structures in 1960 by borough: number and percentage

Housing- unit type	Richmond		Bronx		Brooklyn		Manhattan		Queens	
	Number	%	Number	%	Number	%	Number	%	Number	%
Detached single-family homes	35,294	54.2	21,812	4.6	41,618	4.8	3,319	0.5	143,408	23.3
Attached single-family homes	2,572	4.0	11,900	2.5	50,362	5.8	7,264	1.0	50,024	8.1
2-unit structures	18,378	28.2	41,334	8.7	190,027	21.7	3,386	0.5	143,071	23.2
3- and 4- unit structures	3,204	4.9	30,695	6.5	153,738	17.6	12,852	1.8	41,746	6.8
5-or-more-unit structures	5,621	8.6	367,092	77.6	439,293	50.2	700,684	96.3	238,134	38.6
5–9 units	1,078	20.6	18,832	5.3	122,304	29.8	55,681	8.6	31,283	15.4
10–19 units	647	12.4	38,080	10.8	50,363	12.3	147,699	22.8	17,757	8.8
20–49 units	2,255	43.1	164,609	46.7	118,621	28.9	205,522	31.7	59,912	29.6
50 or more units	1,249	23.9	131,293	37.2	118,467	28.9	239,533	36.9	93,723	46.2
Total housing units	65,069	99.9	472,833	99.9	875,038	100.1	727,325	100.1	616,383	100.0

Source: U.S. Bureau of the Census, "Advance Reports—Housing Characteristics," in *1960 Census of Housing* (Washington, D.C.: U.S. Government Printing Office, 1962), sec. 4 (New York), 20.

in Brooklyn. All the outer boroughs had their share of detached single-family homes, but only in Queens did such homes comprise a double-digit percentage (23) of housing structures. Looking more granularly at the apartment buildings with greater than five units, among the five boroughs Staten Island had the lowest percentage (24) of buildings with 50 or more units, and Queens had the highest (46). The number of units in a home was also indicative of residents' proprietary relationship to it. As presented in table 11.3, 60 percent of housing units were occupied by their owner on Staten Island. In every other borough, the majority of domiciles were occupied by renters, ranging from 55 percent in Queens to 94 percent in Manhattan. Though other areas would claim the moniker, Staten Island's relatively slow population growth enabled it to become the city's true borough of homes.

Much unoccupied space remained on Staten Island despite its high proportion of single-family homes. A report in 1960 indicated that 40.4 percent of the borough's acreage was vacant. Of the land in use, a plurality of 23.5 percent was occupied by streets or highways. Residences took up only 12.6 percent of the island, with the remaining land distributed among parks and recreation (10.6 percent), community facilities such as Wagner College and the Sailor's Snug Harbor (6.9 percent), industry (4.2 percent), and means of transportation other than roads (1.8 percent). Although farmland and parking lots were treated as vacant land, the report still identified 15,606 completely empty acres

TABLE 11.3 Occupancy of housing structures in 1960 by borough: number and percentage

Housing status	Richmond		Bronx		Brooklyn		Manhattan		Queens	
	Number	%	Number	%	Number	%	Number	%	Number	%
Owner occupied	37,249	59.7	59,133	12.6	198,342	23.0	25,310	3.6	256,337	43.2
Renter occupied	24,482	39.3	404,268	86.1	652,394	75.5	670,456	94.1	326,810	55.1
Vacant	631	1.0	5,919	1.3	13,191	1.5	16,998	2.4	10,358	1.7
Total	62,362	100.0	469,320	100.0	863,927	100.0	712,764	100.1	593,505	100.0

Source: U.S. Bureau of the Census, "Advance Reports—Housing Characteristics," in *1960 Census of Housing* (Washington, D.C.: U.S. Government Printing Office, 1962), sec. 4 (New York), 20.

on Staten Island, more than twice as many as on Queens despite being roughly half its size.[5]

Agriculture

Staten Island's rural identity was still powerful in 1960. A strong proponent of the bridge, Richmond Borough president Maniscalco nonetheless cautioned that "we have to watch out that it won't engulf the island so that we will lose our rural communities."[6] That fear, however, was probably more indicative of the past rather than predictive of the future because farms on Staten Island were disappearing well before the bridge opened. As table 11.4 demonstrates, the number of farms, average farm size, and total farm acreage on Staten Island had steadily declined since 1890. Some farms failed—the 1920s and 1930s were a particularly treacherous time for farmers when foreclosures spiked.[7] Others were sold to developers, who built new tracts of housing. Still more gave way to alternative economic uses—primarily industrial or commercial. These trends were hardly unique to Staten Island, and they led to a loss of

TABLE 11.4 Agriculture on Staten Island, 1890–1964

Year	Number of farms	Percentage of land used for agriculture	Average number of acres per farm
1890	380	35.6	36.0
1900	290	30.5	40.4
1910	163	17.3	32.6
1925	159	9.6	22.1
1935	91	3.6	14.3
1945	65	3.3	18.5
1954	72	3.2	17.2
1964	52	0.7	5.4

Source: For each of the years listed, U.S. Bureau of the Census, *Census of Agriculture* (Washington, DC: U.S. Government Printing Office), https://www.nass.usda.gov/AgCensus/ or https://agcensus.library.cornell.edu/census_parts/1964-new-york/.

farmland throughout the eastern part of the United States from 1900 to 1960. In New York, every single county experienced a net decline in farmland during those six decades.[8] The gradual disappearance of agriculture on Staten Island continued after the Verrazzano-Narrows Bridge's opening in 1964 but had long preceded it.

This larger pattern of decline notwithstanding, Staten Island retained its agricultural sector longer than the other four boroughs. In 1964, the 52 farms found on Staten Island were just eleven fewer than the 63 farms located in the remainder of the city. Manhattan unsurprisingly contained no farms in 1964; the agricultural census of 1925 was the final one to identify some on the island. With 360 farms, Brooklyn had more than Staten Island's 290 in 1900, though they covered far less of the borough. The decline in Brooklyn was more precipitous in the subsequent twenty-five years, and by 1964 only 14 farms remained there. Agriculture in the Bronx also vanished faster than on Staten Island, and only 8 farms averaging 1.2 acres in size existed by 1964. Queens was more rural than Staten Island before consolidation and even after its eastern portion became Nassau County in 1899. With nearly 1,200 farms in 1900, more than one-third of its land was devoted to farming compared to 30.5 percent on Staten Island. Yet agriculture on Queens also disappeared more rapidly than on Staten Island, and by 1964 its 43 farms averaged 2.7 acres and composed only 0.2 percent of the borough's land. In every borough but Staten Island, agriculture was further undermined by the massive pre–World War II population growth precipitated by the arrival of the subway.[9]

Work

Without a subway to Brooklyn or Manhattan, Staten Islanders also developed work and commuting habits that looked different from those of the other boroughs. Far more than the image of ferry commuters to Lower Manhattan would suggest, 53 percent of Staten Islanders stayed in the borough for work in 1960, whereas most residents of Queens and the Bronx commuted elsewhere to work (see table 11.5). Not surprisingly, Staten Islanders relied minimally on the subways or railroads to reach their place of employment—just 7 percent of them, whereas buses served 15 percent and automobiles 37 percent of residents. In the other four boroughs, between 44 percent and 55 percent relied on the subways and the remaining elevated railroads to reach their place of employment, and only in Queens did the percentage of workers using automobiles approach the figure for Staten Island. The nearly 27 percent of Staten Islanders who identified an unspecified mode of transport were largely referring to the ferries that took them to Manhattan and—until the Verrazzano Bridge opened—to Brooklyn. Walking to work was not common in any of the

TABLE 11.5 Place of work and means of transportation to work by borough, 1960

Place of work	Richmond		Bronx		Brooklyn		Manhattan		Queens	
	Number	%	Number	%	Number	%	Number	%	Number	%
In county of residence	42,588	52.8	215,963	37.8	548,142	53.4	640,848	82.0	285,772	36.9
Outside county of residence	33,703	41.8	317,062	55.4	408,431	39.8	74,002	9.5	447,596	57.9
Not reported	4,413	5.5	39,012	6.8	69,848	6.8	66,906	8.6	39,753	5.1
Totals	80,706	100.1	572,037	100.0	1,026,421	100.0	781,756	100.1	773,121	99.9
Means of transportation	Number	%	Number	%	Number	%	Number	%	Number	%
Private automobile or car pool	29,674	36.8	102,631	17.9	198,766	19.4	52,246	6.7	227,817	29.5
Railroad, subway or elevated	5,484	6.8	312,777	54.7	515,021	50.2	349,485	44.7	359,498	46.5
Bus or streetcar	12,203	15.1	62,582	10.9	127,266	12.4	152,127	19.5	77,541	10.0
Walked to work	5,596	6.9	42,950	7.5	95,908	9.3	109,383	14.0	51,851	6.7
Other means	21,610	26.8	4,689	0.8	8,557	0.8	21,659	2.8	6,842	0.9
Worked at home	1,739	2.2	8,810	1.5	17,080	1.7	30,594	3.9	10,471	1.4
Not reported	4,400	5.5	37,598	6.6	63,823	6.2	66,262	8.5	39,101	5.1
Totals	80,706	100.1	572,037	99.9	1,026,421	100.0	781,756	100.1	773,121	100.1

Note: The data did not account for commuters who took more than one mode of transportation.

Source: U.S. Bureau of the Census, *Census of Population: 1960*, vol. 1: *Characteristics of the Population* (Washington, D.C.: U.S. Government Printing Office, 1963), pt. 34 (New York), 352–56.

boroughs but roughly correlated with a borough's population density and size. As the most densely populated borough, 14 percent of Manhattan residents walked to work; the equivalent figure for Staten Island was still 7 percent.

The duration of a Staten Islander's commute depended on the distance between place of home and work as well as on the nature of transportation options available. Those who worked on the island likely had a reasonably short commute, while those who worked off island without a rapid-transit option faced a lengthy trip to work. A study in the 1930s found that after Manhattan, Staten Island had the largest percentage (28 percent) of commuters with less than a twenty-minute commute. Conversely, arriving at work took one-third of its commuters more than sixty minutes each way, many of whom lived along the route of the Staten Island Railway and traveled by train and then ferry to Manhattan. New York residents living in the outer edges of the Bronx and Queens experienced lengthy commutes at a similar proportion, and between 27 and 32 percent of these three outer boroughs had twenty- to forty-minute commutes. The real difference between them lay in forty- to sixty-minute commutes, which only 7 percent of Staten Islanders faced compared to 27 percent and 20 percent in the Bronx and Queens, respectively.[10] For many Staten Islanders, the advantage of having a relatively short commute was more than offset by the difficulty in taking advantage of economic opportunities in Manhattan.

Consolidation with New York had an impact on aspects of Staten Island's already diverse occupation structure. As presented in table 11.6, manufacturing provided significant employment options for more than a quarter of island residents in 1900. Equally as sizeable were sectors in trade and transportation as well as in domestic and personal service, while agriculture had already begun to diminish. Several trends are noticeable over the next sixty years—not the least of which is the more nuanced classifications adopted by the Census Bureau (as explained in table 11.6). The manufacturing sector grew smaller but remained a prominent source of employment for Staten Islanders through 1960, notwithstanding a blip in 1920 as the economy remained geared up from World War I. The growth of the professions and the rise of the financial/insurance/real estate labor force—to 15 percent and 11 percent, respectively, in 1960—was likely helped by Staten Island's borough status and, for people of means, less hindered by its relative inaccessibility. The public sector, which also grew during these years, was buttressed even more by the municipal residency requirements that were the norm for public employees. These developments stemmed not from consolidation alone because Staten Island's occupation structure increasingly diverged from the other boroughs from 1900 to 1960.

By 1960, Staten Island disproportionately housed workers in a number of fields. Sixty years earlier, few characteristics distinguished its workforce from

TABLE 11.6 Occupations by sector on Staten Island, 1900–1960

Sector	1900* (%)	1920** (%)	1940 (%)	1960 (%)
Agriculture, forestry, fishing, mining	4.0	1.3	0.6	0.4
Building trades/construction	9.4	NT	5.8	5.7
Manufacturing	26.5	40.1	22.8	20.3
Transportation and trade	26.2	NT	NT	NT
Transportation, communication, and other public utilities	NT	12.0	13.0	13.4
Wholesale and retail trade	NT	10.0	16.0	14.2
Finance, insurance, and real estate	NT	NT	8.2	11.1
Domestic and personal service	28.0	8.3	6.2	3.0
Professional service	5.9	7.2	11.4	15.2
Other services	NT	NT	2.6	3.1
Government	NT	7.3	11.7	8.6
Clerical	NT	13.8	NT	NT
Not reported	NT	NT	1.7	5.0
Totals	100.0	100.0	100.0	100.0

* In 1900, the transportation-and-trade category included police and firefighters; hotel workers, restaurant workers, and saloon keepers; and nurses—jobs that would be found elsewhere in subsequent census categories.

** Building trades and construction are included in manufacturing in 1920.

NT = Not tabulated as such.

Note: This table presents just the broad designations the Census Bureau used to group the dozens of very specific job types. As the American economy grew more complex, the Census Bureau added countless more job classifications and subdivided the general categories so that the six used in 1900 became twelve for 1960. The table retains the original classifications of 1900 when possible and uses the newer labels when they yield greater clarity. Both the older and newer classification for trade and transportation are used because disaggregating the data was not feasible.

Sources: U.S. Bureau of the Census, *Census of Population: 1900*, vol. 2, *Population* (Washington, DC: U.S. Government Printing Office, 1902), part 2; *Census of Population: 1920*, vol. 4: *Population, Occupations* (Washington, DC: U.S. Government Printing Office, 1923), 131; *Census of Population: 1940*, vol. 2: *Characteristics of the Population* (Washington, DC: U.S. Government Printing Office, 1943), pt. 5 (New York–Oregon), 196; *Census of Population: 1960*, vol. 1: *Characteristics of the Population* (Washington, DC: U.S. Government Printing Office, 1963), pt. 34 (New York), 377.

those of the other boroughs. As the data in table 11.7 indicate, manufacturing, transportation and trade, and service were the three largest sectors in every borough in 1900. Staten Island's service workforce was a bit larger and its manufacturing and transportation-and-trade labor force smaller than the other boroughs but not drastically so. The size of its professional class was slightly larger than average and corresponded closely to Manhattan's. By 1920, greater variation from the other boroughs was evident, as shown in the data presented in table 11.8. Most noticeably, the island's burgeoning population of government workers was not matched in the other boroughs, as an astonishing 7.3 percent of the island's workforce identified as public employees compared to the city's average of 2.4 percent.[11] As Mike Wallace relates in *Greater Gotham*, the new metropolis expanded the scope of its activities in myriad ways during the first two decades of the twentieth century, and its pursuits required labor.[12] Staten Island's professional sector had also grown and

TABLE 11.7 Occupations by sector and borough, 1900

Category	Richmond (%)	Brooklyn (%)	Manhattan and the Bronx (%)	Queens (%)	New York City (%)
Agriculture, forestry, fishing, mining	4.0	0.5	0.3	7.2	0.7
Building trades/construction	9.4	6.7	6.0	9.9	6.4
Manufacturing	26.5	32.3	30.8	28.7	31.2
Transportation and trade	26.2	33.9	31.7	23.8	32.0
Domestic and personal service*	28.0	21.1	25.3	25.2	24.0
Professional service	5.9	5.4	5.8	5.2	5.7
Totals	100.0	99.9	99.9	100.0	100.0

* In 1900, this category included police and firefighters; hotel, restaurant, and saloon keepers; and nurses—jobs that would be found elsewhere in subsequent census categories.

Source: U.S. Bureau of the Census, *Census of Population: 1900*, vol. 2, *Population* (Washington, DC: U.S. Government Printing Office, 1902), part 2, 578–81.

TABLE 11.8 Occupations by sector and borough, 1920

Category	Richmond (%)	Bronx (%)	Brooklyn (%)	Manhattan (%)	Queens (%)	New York City (%)
Agriculture, forestry, fishing, mining	1.3	0.3	0.2	0.1	1.2	0.3
Manufacturing*	40.1	39.0	40.5	34.2	42.2	37.6
Transportation, communication, and other public utilities	12.0	8.0	9.9	9.6	9.2	9.5
Wholesale and retail trade	8.6	16.3	14.0	13.9	11.4	13.9
Finance, insurance, and real estate	1.4	1.5	1.6	1.6	1.5	1.6
Domestic and personal service	8.3	6.6	7.5	18.3	6.8	12.1
Professional service	7.2	6.4	5.6	7.7	5.8	6.6
Government	7.3	2.4	2.8	1.7	3.4	2.4
Clerical	13.8	19.5	17.9	13.0	18.4	15.9
Totals	100.0	100.0	100.0	100.1	99.9	99.9

* Building trades and construction are also included in manufacturing in 1920.

Source: U.S. Bureau of the Census, Census of Population: 1920, vol. 4: Population, Occupations (Washington, DC: U.S. Government Printing Office, 1923), 131.

remained the largest in the outer boroughs. In other sectors, Staten Islanders were only somewhat underrepresented (trade) or overrepresented (transportation), and the financial, insurance, and real estate sectors combined formed a small part (1.6 percent) of the overall city's labor force, with little divergence by borough.

When the Great Depression struck after the stock market crash of October 24, 1929, Staten Island withstood the onslaught somewhat better than its counterparts. There was of course much suffering. In early 1933, the *New York Times* identified Mariners Harbor and Tottenville as the hardest-hit areas on Staten Island, describing some residents as living in their own subsistence shelters: "little huts on muddy lanes. Their homes lack modern improvements and people are using kerosene lamps for light and wood stoves for heat."[13] At the same time, relief and other public programs alleviated some of the hardships wrought by unemployment. By early 1934, agencies at all levels of government employed 19,000 people on Staten Island.[14] Staten Island may even have benefited disproportionately from public programs, for in 1940 nearly 5 percent of its labor force remained on work relief compared to a citywide average of 3 percent.[15]

Finally, Staten Island's occupation structure also helped to protect the borough. Sectors of the New York economy hit hard at the start of the Great Depression, such as manufacturing and recreation, were underrepresented on Staten Island. Conversely, Staten Islanders were overrepresented in the three sectors with the lowest recorded unemployment rates in 1930—finance, insurance, and real estate; professional service; and government. To take the starkest case as an example, the public sector—with a citywide unemployment rate of 1.1 percent in 1930—did not contract in the first year of the Depression. This essential stability especially benefited Staten Island, where nearly 8 percent of employment was with government compared to a little more than 2 percent citywide.[16]

Staten Island's occupation structure in 1940 indicated further solidification of white-collar jobs. In 1940, nearly 12 percent of its population was now employed in government, almost six percentage points higher than second-ranked Queens (see table 11.9). The transportation sector also remained sizable, and the island had a greater proportion of professionals than did the other outer boroughs. The relative heft of its labor force in construction and finance had diminished, and it continued to attract disproportionately fewer workers into wholesale and retail trade. Although manufacturing was still the island's largest sector, the proportion of its workers in manufacturing was the smallest among the city's outer boroughs. Workers in middle-class occupations still maintained their employment more readily than those in industry. As in 1930, Staten Islanders in 1940 were overrepresented in the three sectors with the city's lowest unemployment rates.[17]

TABLE 11.9 Occupations by sector and borough, 1940

Category	Richmond (%)	Bronx (%)	Brooklyn (%)	Manhattan (%)	Queens (%)	New York City (%)
Agriculture, forestry, fishing, mining	0.6	0.1	0.1	0.1	0.2	0.1
Building trades/construction	5.8	5.6	4.7	3.1	5.8	4.6
Manufacturing	22.8	27.5	32.1	18.8	25.8	26.3
Transportation, communication, and other public utilities	13.0	8.9	8.6	7.4	11.0	8.9
Wholesale and retail trade	16.0	24.4	21.9	21.8	20.2	21.9
Finance, insurance, and real estate	8.2	7.5	6.4	9.1	9.4	7.9
Domestic and personal service	6.2	7.0	7.8	17.8	7.6	10.4
Professional service	11.4	7.8	7.6	11.6	7.0	8.7
Other services	2.6	4.0	3.4	5.0	4.3	4.1
Government	11.7	4.9	4.1	3.2	5.9	4.5
Not reported	1.7	2.2	3.2	2.1	2.6	2.6
Totals	100.0	99.9	99.9	100.0	99.8	100.0

Source: U.S. Bureau of the Census, Census of Population: 1940, vol. 2: Characteristics of the Population (Washington, DC: U.S. Government Printing Office, 1943), pt. 5 (New York–Oregon), 161, 168, 175, 182, 189, 196.

These pronounced Staten Island workforce characteristics remained in place in 1960. As table 11.10 relates, professional positions, although more prevalent throughout the city, now occupied 15.2 percent Staten Island's workforce, tied with Manhattan for the largest rate in the city. As for government jobs, the prevalence of government workers on Staten Island remained unrivaled, though at 8.6 percent the sector was proportionally smaller than in 1940 in light of the post-Depression retrenchment in the public sector. Transportation (13.4 percent) retained while finance (11.1 percent) and construction (5.7 percent) restored their relative hold on the borough's labor force compared to its four counterparts. Manufacturing (20.3 percent) and trade (14.2 percent) remained important on the island but still drew smaller pools of labor than in the other boroughs. What is most remarkable overall about Staten Island's occupation structure is how quickly patterns appeared and how stable they remained. The absence of a subway may have exacerbated these trends, but the catalyst appears to be Staten Island's joining with New York in 1898.

Certain contours of the area's occupation structure became apparent to much of the public in the wake of the September 11 attacks in 2001. With just 5.5 percent of New York City's population at the time, Staten Island accounted for 16 percent of its casualties and contained the third- and fourth-highest death tolls by zip code areas. In particular, many of these victims were firefighters and other first responders, who disproportionately lived on Staten Island.[18] It is instructive to look more closely at when these jobs came to hold an emphatic place in Staten Island's occupation structure as well as at other jobs that were pervasive in New York but did not heavily penetrate the Borough of Richmond. Table 11.11 presents the distribution of firefighters, police officers, and restaurant/saloon proprietors and employees among the five boroughs and compares each borough's share of workers in these fields with its overall portion of the city's employed workers. In 1900, Staten Island's 1.8 percent share of city police officers and firefighters was identical to its portion of all workers, and not one borough was greatly over- or underrepresented in the precinct and fire houses. By 1920, members of both services were much less inclined to live in Manhattan and instead congregated in the outer boroughs, though much more so in the Bronx and Queens than on Staten Island. In 1940, Staten Island's share of police officers (4.1 percent) and firefighters (4.8 percent) showed another incremental increase relative to its overall labor pool. In the postwar era, police and especially firefighters became even more prevalent on Staten Island. The borough accounted for a mere 2.5 percent of the city's workforce but contained 6.1 percent of the city's police and a whopping 11.8 percent of its firefighters in 1960. These protective-service personnel also still disproportionately lived in the Bronx and Queens, but except for in the case of police officers in the Bronx, their shares did not grow at the pace of the overall pool of labor after 1920.

TABLE 11.10 Occupations by sector and borough, 1960

Category	Richmond (%)	Bronx (%)	Brooklyn (%)	Manhattan (%)	Queens (%)	New York City (%)
Agriculture, forestry, fishing, mining	0.4	0.2	0.2	0.2	0.3	0.2
Building trades/construction	5.7	4.4	4.0	2.3	4.3	3.8
Manufacturing	20.3	26.1	30.0	22.0	26.6	26.3
Transportation, communication, and other public utilities	13.4	8.8	8.9	6.6	9.8	8.7
Wholesale and retail trade	14.2	20.0	18.5	18.2	20.0	18.9
Finance, insurance, and real estate	11.1	8.1	8.5	7.5	8.4	8.2
Domestic and personal service	3.0	5.1	4.9	9.2	4.6	5.8
Professional service	15.2	10.6	10.0	15.2	10.4	11.6
Other services	3.1	4.5	4.1	6.9	4.9	5.0
Government	8.6	5.6	4.7	3.6	5.6	4.9
Not Reported	5.0	6.7	6.4	8.4	5.0	6.6
Totals	100.0	100.1	100.2	100.1	99.9	100.0

Source: U.S. Bureau of the Census, Census of Population: 1960, vol. 1: Characteristics of the Population (Washington, DC: U.S. Government Printing Office, 1963), pt. 34 (New York), 373–77.

TABLE 11.11 Share of workforce in protective services and food/drink establishments by borough

Year	Category	Richmond (%)	Bronx (%)	Brooklyn (%)	Manhattan (%)	Queens (%)
1900*	Watchmen, police, firefighters / all job sectors	1.8/1.8	NA/NA	30.9/32.2	63.7/61.9	3.6/4.0
1920	Police / all job sectors	2.8/1.9	20.1/12.2	34.5/34.0	25.8/44.1	16.8/7.8
1920	Firefighters / all job sectors	3.5/1.9	18.7/12.2	36.0/34.0	24.7/44.1	17.1/7.8
1940	Police / all job sectors	4.1/2.1	20.6/18.0	29.3/34.7	10.2/27.6	35.8/17.7
1940	Firefighters / all job sectors	4.8/2.1	21.4/18.0	27.0/34.7	7.8/27.6	39.0/17.7
1960	Police / all job sectors	6.1/2.5	20.9/17.7	27.5/31.6	9.0/24.3	36.4/23.8
1960	Firefighters / all job sectors	11.8/2.5	18.6/17.7	24.6/31.6	5.8/24.3	39.2/23.8
1900*	Restaurant workers and saloon keepers / all job sectors	2.3/1.8	NA/NA	30.6/32.2	61.6/61.9	5.4/4.0
1920	Restaurant workers, waiters, saloon keepers, and bartenders / all job sectors	1.0/1.9	8.3/12.2	20.9/34.0	65.8/44.1	4.0/7.8
1940	Workers at eating and drinking places / all job sectors	1.1/2.1	14.6/18.0	23.9/34.7	46.2/27.6	14.1/17.7
1960	Workers at eating and drinking places / all job sectors	1.4/2.5	17.0/17.7	24.3/31.6	36.2/24.3	21.2/23.8

*The 1900 census combined data for Manhattan and the Bronx and did not allow for the inclusion of waiters and bartenders.

Sources: U.S. Bureau of the Census, *Census of Population: 1900*, vol. 2, *Population* (Washington, DC: U.S. Government Printing Office, 1902), part 2, 578–81; *Census of Population: 1920*, vol. 4: *Population, Occupations* (Washington, DC: U.S. Government Printing Office, 1923), 131; *Census of Population: 1940*, vol. 2: *Characteristics of the Population* (Washington, DC: U.S. Government Printing Office, 1943), pt. 5 (New York–Oregon), 161, 168, 175, 182, 189, 196; *Census of Population: 1960*, vol. 1: *Characteristics of the Population* (Washington, DC: U.S. Government Printing Office, 1963), pt. 34 (New York), 373–77.

Staten Island began the twentieth century with a slightly greater total of restaurant and saloon keepers than one might expect. In 1900, as noted in table 11.11, the island contained 2.3 percent of the city's proprietors, making up only 1.8 percent of the city's total employed labor force, and no borough stood out disproportionately. By 1920, Manhattan had undergone "cultural consolidation" and established itself as the city and nation's center for myriad entertainments that went well with a good meal and a stiff drink.[19] With lengthy and late working hours, many employees stayed close by, and Manhattan's share increased to 65.8 percent even as its overall labor pool in the sector declined to 44.1 percent of the city's. Conversely, the workers in this sector formed a relatively smaller proportion of the labor pool in the four outer boroughs, with Staten Island's being nearly half (1 percent) the size of its total share of job holders (1.9 percent) in the city. The other boroughs, however, started to close the gap after 1920 as increased transit options running all hours enabled workers to reach residences in the outer boroughs. By 1960, the Bronx's and Queens' shares of workers in these establishments had not only grown substantially—from 8 percent to 17 percent in the Bronx and 4 percent to 21 percent in Queens, but the rate of increase had outstripped their concomitant growth in population. Not so in Staten Island, which contributed only 1.4 percent of the city's workers in the industry, whose total number of employed workers had increased to 2.5 percent.

The occupation structure on Staten Island had its peculiarities, but it was also a healthy indicator of the island's deep connection to its city, region, and nation. Staten Islanders may have labored disproportionately for the fire department or finance companies, but that work—as in many other fields—typically took them to Manhattan. The industrialization that made New York a "factory town" in the early twentieth century reached Staten Island, albeit at a much smaller scale than in the other boroughs. The rise of industry in Bayonne and Elizabethport, New Jersey, spurred early twentieth-century industrial establishments across from them on the Kill Van Kull. The subsequent and gradual movement of the region's great port facilities from New York to New Jersey further encouraged the rise of Staten Island industrial sites along its west shore waterways.[20] Nor did the war economy bypass Staten Island. During World War II, a former marine repair dock in Mariner's Harbor became a major builder of ships for the navy, and government contracts enabled the island's largest industrial establishments to expand. After the war, the deindustrialization that spread through the Northeast and Midwest over the next six decades began to be felt on Staten Island as long-standing factories relocated or closed.[21]

Staten Island's critical mass of workers in fields that afforded comfort or even affluence contributed to its status as a middle-class enclave within the larger city. The borough was already viewed that way by midcentury, when data on income became readily available. Table 11.12 presents median family incomes for the boroughs for 1950 and 1960.[22] In both years, Staten Island ranked only (and closely) behind Queens in family median income. In 1960, nearly 21 percent of its families reported incomes greater than $10,000, while fewer than 10 percent had incomes that fell lower than $3,000, and the gap separating Staten Island and Queens from the Bronx and Brooklyn had grown wider since 1950. Manhattan was an anomaly. Its median incomes were low because its many pockets of wealth were nonetheless dwarfed by its great swaths of urban poor, but on a per capita basis it was (and remains) the wealthiest of the boroughs. In 1959, its per capita income (in 1989 dollars) was $11,423; Staten Island ranked third among the boroughs at $8,056.[23]

An Immigrant Presence

Staten Island's ethnic makeup embodied nineteenth-century urban diversity and movement. In 1890, its population was 33 percent foreign born and 29 percent children of someone foreign born, and, as elsewhere in the future Greater New York, most of its immigrants came from Ireland and Germany, though many still arrived from England, Scotland, and Scandinavia. By 1960, Staten Island's population reflected the impact of the two primary trends in immigration to the United States over the previous seventy years: the predominance of "new immigrants" arriving from southern Europe (principally Italians) and eastern Europe (primarily Russian Jews) through World War I and the decline of newcomers overall during the war and following the passage of restrictive immigration laws in the 1920s.[24] Because of the latter of these two developments, the proportion of immigrants grew smaller in all five boroughs from 1900 to 1960. Staten Island, however, experienced the most precipitous drop of the four outer boroughs. As noted on table 11.13, Staten Island began the century with 28 percent foreign born—the smallest percentage in the city but one nonetheless huddling closely to its peers' percentages: the Bronx and Brooklyn at 31 percent and Queens at 29 percent. By 1960, foreign-born residents remained about 20 percent of the population in all four other boroughs, whereas they had decreased to 11.5 percent on Staten Island. Including second-generation immigrants further highlights the tremendous reach of nonnative communities and corroborates the picture for the 1900–1960 period. Immigrants and their children made up a strong majority of each borough's population, with the smallest percentage (64.3 percent) on Staten Island and the greatest (80.9 percent) in Manhattan. Over the first sixty years of the century, these figures declined for all five boroughs, but more steeply on Staten Island than in all boroughs except Manhattan. The drop is not surprising, but the data beg the question of why it was especially pronounced on Staten Island.

TABLE 11.12 Median family income, by borough, 1950, 1960

Families	Year	Richmond	Bronx	Brooklyn	Manhattan	Queens	New York City
Median family income	1950	$3,845	$3,612	$3,447	$3,073	$4,121	$3,526
% with income less than $3,000	1950	29.5	33.7	36.8	45.1	24.9	35.6
% with income higher than $10,000	1950	3.6	3.1	3.5	7.2	5.4	4.3
Median family income	1960	$6,836	$5,930	$5,816	$5,338	$7,176	$6,091
% with income less than $3,000	1960	9.6	15.9	16.0	22.1	8.6	15.2
% with income higher than $10,000	1960	20.7	15.1	15.0	19.3	25.0	18.5

Sources: U.S. Bureau of the Census, *Census of Population: 1950*, vol. 2: *Characteristics of the Population* (Washington, DC: U.S. Government Printing Office, 1952), pt. 32 (New York), 116, 168–69; *Census of Population: 1960*, vol. 1: *Characteristics of the Population* (Washington, DC: U.S. Government Printing Office, 1963), pt. 34 (New York), 202, 207.

TABLE 11.13 Immigrants in borough population, 1900–1960

Year	Richmond	Bronx	Brooklyn	New York	Queens
	Percentage of first-generation immigrants				
1900	27.9	30.7	30.5	42.7	29.3
1920	27.3	36.6	33.0	41.6	23.9
1940	20.2	33.2	28.8	30.8	21.5
1960	11.5	21.5	19.7	22.1	18.5
	Percentage of first- and second-generation white immigrants in total population				
1900	64.3	73.7	71.7	80.9	70.1
1920	65.9	81.2	75.7	78.0	67.0
1940	53.7	75.6	69.6	57.2	55.8
1960	40.0	50.6	50.2	42.4	51.7
	Ratio of first-generation to second-generation population				
1900	0.76	0.71	0.73	1.10	0.70
1920	0.70	0.82	0.76	1.07	0.55
1940	0.60	0.75	0.69	1.00	0.62
1960	0.40	0.74	0.64	1.08	0.56

Note: The Census Bureau tabulated data on first- and second-generation immigrants—what it labeled as "foreign stock"—only for white (defined as European) immigrants. The first-generation immigrants included both foreign-born whites and people of color, the latter accounting for less than one percent of the total population for each outer borough in each census year.

Source: U.S. Bureau of the Census, *Census of Population: 1910*, vol. 1: *Population, General Report and Analysis* (Washington, DC: U.S. Government Printing Office, 1912), 948; *Census of Population: 1920*, vol. 2: *Population, General Report and Analytical Tables* (Washington, DC: U.S. Government Printing Office, 1922), 941–42; *Census of Population: 1940. Nativity and Parentage of the White Population* (Washington, DC: U.S. Government Printing Office, 1943), 74; *Census of Population: 1960*, vol. 1: *Characteristics of the Population* (Washington, DC: U.S. Government Printing Office, 1963), pt. 34 (New York), 393–96.

All four outer boroughs shared a role as a destination for immigrants leaving the crowded neighborhoods of Manhattan. This dynamic is captured by the ratios between first- and second-generation immigrants also presented on table 11.13. With a ratio at or higher than 1.0 for all four years, Manhattan's foreign-born population almost always remained larger than its number of residents with at least one immigrant parent.[25] This constancy is noteworthy given that the relative size of the borough's foreign-born population declined precipitously from 1900 to 1960, falling from nearly 43 percent to a little more than 22 percent of its total population. With new immigrants tailing off, only the departure of second-generation immigrants kept Manhattan's ratios stable for sixty years. The out-migration from Manhattan during the decades before World War II included hundreds of thousands of residents—both first and second generation—relocating to Brooklyn and especially the Bronx. The arrival of these newcomers is reflected in the ratios for the outer boroughs. In 1900, all four exhibited ratios of around 0.73—much lower than Manhattan's but comparable to each other's. The subsequent changes in their ratios varied, roughly reflecting each borough's relative strength as a magnet for out-migration from Manhattan as well as for immigrants directly arriving in New York. As a key destination, the Bronx saw its ratio increase to 0.82 in 1920 and remain higher than its 1900 level through 1960. Brooklyn's ratio also increased initially, though by 1960 it had fallen somewhat below its 1900 level. In Queens, the ratio fluctuated—declining to 0.55 in 1920, rebounding to 0.62 in 1940 before landing at 0.56 in 1960—suggesting that considerably more of its residents were second-generation immigrants. Despite the variation, all three outer boroughs experienced a decade after 1920 when their first-generation communities grew at a faster rate than their population as a whole: the Bronx and Queens in the 1920s and Brooklyn in the 1930s.[26] Not so Staten Island.

Staten Island presented a stark shift in its immigrant population from 1900 to 1960. In 1900, Staten Island's ratio of first- to second-generation immigrants, 0.76, was second only to Manhattan's, and the increase of new immigrants outpaced its overall population growth during the aughts. Over the next fifty years, a comparatively large decline in foreign-born residents as a proportion of its population as well a rise in second-generation Americans produced a ratio that fell to 0.40 in 1960. Staten Island was the only borough with an increase in its actual second-generation population from 1940 to 1960. Admittedly, the scale of the population changes on Staten Island was much smaller than elsewhere in the city, but it is clear that the island increasingly diverged from the other boroughs as the relative presence of newcomers from foreign lands grew much smaller. At first, the size of Staten Island's immigrant population reflected that of Greater New York, but its growing inaccessibility as the other outer boroughs became linked by bridges and tunnels prevented it from becoming a primary recipient of Manhattan's outgoing population and new immigrants alike.

Staten Island's lack of subway access to the other boroughs appears less relevant to which particular nationalities arrived on its shores. The mass arrival of immigrants from southern and eastern Europe in 1885–1915 fundamentally altered the makeup of New York City's population. Table 11.14 traces this change from 1900 to 1920 by presenting the percentages of the foreign-born population by region of Europe.[27] Staten Island's foreign-born population, like the rest of the city's, reflected heavy nineteenth-century immigration from England, Scotland, Ireland, Germany, and Scandinavia—nations of northwestern and central Europe. By 1900, immigrants from these regions accounted for 70 percent of the city's foreign-born population, but some variation by borough was already in place. For example, nearly 50 percent of Staten Island's immigrant population had originated from northern and western Europe, and 34.5 percent—primarily Germans living in Stapleton and other areas—from central Europe. In Queens and the Bronx, these two figures were nearly reversed, but, overall, the traditional nineteenth-century immigrant groups remained dominant. The regional shift in European immigration was most evident in Manhattan. Whereas nearly 65 percent of its immigrant population in 1900 originated from the British Isles, Scandinavia, and Germany, more than 32 percent of its immigrants already hailed from countries in southern and eastern Europe—primarily Italy and Russia.[28] That figure was much lower for the outer boroughs, with a high of 20 percent in Brooklyn and a low of 12 percent on Staten Island.

By 1920, the huge influx of immigrants from Russia and Italy had significantly altered the ethnic complexion of the city's outer boroughs. Like its counterparts, Staten Island saw a marked increase in the proportion of residents from eastern and southern Europe, who now accounted for 35 percent of its first- and second-generation immigrant population. Meanwhile, its population from northern/western and central Europe had declined to 32.1 percent and 27.8 percent, respectively. This turnover continued to be even more precipitous in Manhattan and the Bronx (less so in Queens), but on Staten Island the transformation was marked by the island's particular attraction for Italians. The southern Europe category, overwhelmingly comprising Italians during these years, ably serves as an indicator of their growth from 1900 to 1920—during which they started at 7.8 percent and ended at 28.1 percent of the island's foreign-born population.[29]

The Italian presence on Staten Island dated back decades not centuries. The Italian nationalist Giuseppe Garribaldi briefly lived on the island in the mid–nineteenth century before he returned to Europe to help create a unified Italy.[30] By 1900, there were 1,435 native-born Italians living on Staten Island, but southern Europeans were better represented in every other borough save

TABLE 11.14 Region of origin of first- and second-generation immigrant population, 1900–1920: percentage distribution by borough

Region	Year	Richmond	Bronx	Brooklyn	Manhattan	Queens	New York City
Northern and Western Europe	1900	49.4	35.9	42.3	30.5	33.9	34.5
	1910	38.7	24.0	26.0	21.7	25.1	23.5
	1920	32.1	14.6	19.8	20.9	24.0	20.0
Central Europe	1900	34.5	43.9	33.5	34.3	50.8	35.1
	1910	29.7	35.6	23.1	28.3	47.3	28.0
	1920	27.8	31.8	23.0	27.7	46.2	27.7
Eastern Europe	1900	4.1	3.9	9.6	19.8	6.0	15.5
	1910	9.9	20.7	29.8	28.1	11.1	27.3
	1920	6.6	36.5	31.5	23.0	8.3	26.6
Southern Europe	1900	7.8	12.9	10.7	12.4	6.8	11.7
	1910	17.9	17.1	17.9	18.7	14.2	18.1

	1920	28.1	15.2	21.7	22.1	18.2	20.9
Asia	1900	0.5	0.4	0.4	0.7	0.4	0.6
	1910	0.3	0.2	0.5	0.7	0.3	0.6
	1920	0.5	0.4	0.9	1.1	0.6	0.9
Americas	1900	3.5	2.7	3.2	2.0	1.9	2.4
	1910	3.3	2.2	2.5	2.4	1.9	2.4
	1920	4.1	1.4	2.9	4.9	2.5	3.6
Other	1900	0.2	0.2	0.2	0.1	0.2	0.2
	1910	0.3	0.1	0.1	0.1	0.1	0.1
	1920	0.2	0.1	0.2	0.2	0.2	0.2

Note: Northern and western Europe includes England, Scotland, Wales, Ireland, Norway, Sweden, Denmark, the Netherlands, Belgium, Luxembourg, Switzerland, and France. Central Europe includes Germany, Poland, Czechoslovakia, Austria, Hungary, and Yugoslavia. Eastern Europe includes Russia, Lithuania, Finland, Rumania [sic], Bulgaria, and European Turkey. Southern Europe includes Greece, Italy, Spain, and Portugal. Asia includes Armenia, Syria, Asian Turkey, China, and Japan. The Americas include Canada, Mexico, the West Indies, Central and South America.

Source: U.S. Bureau of the Census, *Census of Population: 1910*, vol. 1: *Population, General Report and Analysis* (Washington, DC: U.S. Government Printing Office, 1912), 856–57; *Census of Population: 1920*, vol. 2: *Population, General Report and Analytical Tables* (Washington, DC: U.S. Government Printing Office, 1922), 735.

Queens, with the Bronx leading the way at 12.8 percent. By 1910, this gap was nearly closed, as Italians on Staten Island had tripled to 4,260. Only the Bronx surpassed this rate of increase, but it also experienced the arrival of numerous immigrants from eastern Europe.[31] Over the next ten years, Staten Island's Italian population doubled again to 8,772, and the growth accounted for 63 percent of the total increase in the borough's foreign-born population. Italians were still moving to the Bronx in far greater numbers than to Staten Island but were not increasing at as high a rate (57 percent) as on Staten Island or even at the pace of the island's total foreign-born population. The Russian community had more than tripled in the Bronx during the 1910s, while the Russian-born population declined on Staten Island, as did the proportion of eastern European immigrants (see table 11.14). In short, Italians came in sufficient numbers that, coupled with the relative absence of newcomers from eastern Europe, gave Staten Island a distinctively Italian presence by 1920.

Staten Island's relative distance to the rest of the city had not yet reached its full extent when large numbers of Italians settled in the borough. The rail lines generated by the Dual Contracts of 1913 took years to construct, but as they came into service in the years after 1915, the other outer boroughs' advantage in accessibility was compounded. The means of reaching Staten Island had not changed but nonetheless had grown more difficult relative to traveling to the Bronx, Brooklyn, and Queens. Over the next forty years, groups choosing to exit Manhattan or starting to arrive in New York were less likely to make Staten Island their home than immigrants were from 1900 to 1920. The sizable exceptions were those groups that already had a foothold in Staten Island by 1920. Connected to the borough through family and community, the absence of rails did not deter Italians and to a much lesser extent Norwegians from continuing to move to Staten Island.[32]

Staten Island's ethnic communities were marked by demographic stability after 1920. Table 11.15 indicates that the diminished proportions of earlier arriving groups from Germany, Ireland, and the United Kingdom and the corresponding rise in immigrants from Italy were already largely complete by 1920. Four other countries—Norway, Poland, Russia, and Austria—had by then also established a presence on the island. Remarkably, immigrants from these eight nations accounted for 82 percent of all immigrants on Staten Island in 1920 and 1960. The proportion of Poles and Russians peaked in 1920 but then only declined somewhat. The population from Norway continued to grow through the 1950 census. By 1960, no other borough came close to having 6 percent of its immigrants from Norway, and there were more Norwegians living on Staten Island than in Manhattan, the Bronx, and Queens combined. The largest growth, again, was with the Italians, who in 1960 numbered a little less than 33,000 and constituted 37 percent of the island's immigrant population and 15 percent of its total population.[33]

TABLE 11.15 Percentage of foreign-born residents on Staten Island by country of origin, 1900–1960

Country	1900	1910	1920	1930	1940	1950	1960*
Germany	29.9	21.6	13.8	12.6	11.8	9.8	9.7
Ireland**	26.0	16.5	11.8	10.7	9.9	9.0	9.7
United Kingdom	12.5	10.1	8.4	10.1	9.5	9.2	8.1
Norway	3.9	5.6	5.0	8.9	8.5	8.3	6.0
Austria	1.5	3.2	2.6	2.0	2.5	2.5	2.2
Italy	7.7	17.5	27.5	27.9	30.7	32.6	37.1
Poland	2.7	7.5	7.7	5.5	5.2	5.1	5.8
Russia/USSR***	2.3	3.3	5.2	3.7	4.1	4.2	3.5
All eight countries	86.5	85.3	82.0	81.4	82.2	80.7	82.1

* The distributions for 1960 are for what the Census Bureau labeled "foreign stock," which includes the children of immigrants as well as the foreign born.

** Includes Northern Ireland even after it remained a part of the United Kingdom.

*** Includes Latvia and Lithuania when they were independent in 1930 and 1940.

Sources: U.S. Bureau of the Census, *Census of Population: 1910*, vol. 1: *Population, General Report and Analysis* (Washington, DC: U.S. Government Printing Office, 1912), 856–57; *Census of Population: 1920*, vol. 2: *Population, General Report and Analytical Tables* (Washington, DC: U.S. Government Printing Office, 1922), 735; *Census of Population: 1940*, vol. 2: *Characteristics of the Population* (Washington, DC: U.S. Government Printing Office, 1943), pt. 5 (New York–Oregon), 194; *Census of Population: 1950*, vol. 2: *Characteristics of the Population* (Washington, DC: U.S. Government Printing Office, 1952), pt. 32 (New York), 158; *Census of Population: 1960*, vol. 1: *Characteristics of the Population* (Washington, DC: U.S. Government Printing Office, 1963), pt. 34 (New York), 394.

Despite Staten Island's attraction to particular immigrant communities, its relative isolation made it a less likely destination than the other outer boroughs. As the numbers on table 11.16 demonstrate, by 1960 the new southern and eastern European immigrants and their children accounted for 53.8 percent of Staten Island's total foreign population, a figure lower than that of Queens (59.8 percent), the Bronx (66.6 percent), and Brooklyn (73.7 percent); other Italians and Jews had migrated out of the city and headed to Nassau and Suffolk Counties.[34] As immigrants increasingly came from non-European

TABLE 11.16 Region of origin of foreign-born residents and their children in 1960: percentage distribution by borough

Region	Richmond	Bronx	Brooklyn	New York	Queens
Northern and Western Europe	38.0	24.7	16.6	29.4	31.9
Southern and Eastern Europe	55.1	66.6	73.7	51.3	59.8
Non-Europe	6.5	8.3	8.7	18.8	8.1
Not reported	0.4	0.4	1.1	0.5	0.3
Total	100.0	100.0	100.1	100.0	100.1

Note: Northern and Western Europe includes the United Kingdom, Ireland, Norway, Sweden, Denmark, the Netherlands, Germany, Switzerland, and France. Southern and Eastern Europe includes Poland, Czechoslovakia, Austria, Hungary, Yugoslavia, the Soviet Union, Lithuania, Finland, Rumania [sic], Greece, Italy, Portugal, and the rest of Europe. Non-Europe includes Canada, Mexico, and other regions.

Source: U.S. Bureau of the Census, Census of Population: 1960, vol. 1: Characteristics of the Population (Washington, DC: U.S. Government Printing Office, 1962), pt. 34 (New York), 393–94.

countries, many found their way to Manhattan, composing nearly 19 percent of its immigrant population in 1960. Few made it to Staten Island, whose small immigrant population was only 6.5 percent non-European, the lowest proportion among the five boroughs. Puerto Ricans also began migrating to New York City in large numbers after World War II; they too avoided Staten Island in comparison to the other boroughs. Staten Island's Puerto Rican population grew from 190 in 1930 to 2,505 in 1960, but its portion of New York City's total Puerto Rican population remained at 0.4 percent, much lower than the island's overall share of the city's population.[35] Out-migration of more established immigrant groups was also typically lower for Staten Island. For example, as New York City's Irish population declined as a whole from 1910 to 1960, it increased in the Bronx and Queens as thousands left Manhattan and Brooklyn. On Staten Island, the number of Irish-born residents also shrank because they stopped migrating there. In 1930, nearly half of Staten Island's Irish-born population had arrived between 1901 to 1910, a disproportionality not shared by any of the other boroughs, whose Irish residents came more steadily over the entire thirty-year period.[36] Two aspects of the century's first decade offer some context for that Irish surge: Staten Island's presence in newly consolidated Greater New York and the near absence of subways to any of the outer boroughs at that time.

African Americans were also unlikely to choose Staten Island as a destination. Blacks made up about 20 percent of late colonial Staten Island's population, but as chapter 1 demonstrated, their slowly growing numbers failed to keep pace with those of whites over the course of the nineteenth century. This pattern pervaded Kings, Queens, New York, and Westchester Counties as well, so that—as the data in table 11.17 indicate—by 1900 African Americans constituted between one and two percent of the population in all five boroughs. Even as the number of Blacks continued to increase throughout the city, in the outer boroughs the percentages largely declined or stagnated through 1920 as European immigrants continued to arrive in mass numbers through the start of World War I. After the Great Migration from the South began during the war, the African American population surged in Manhattan and, to a lesser extent, in Brooklyn during the 1920s. After growth slowed down during the Great Depression, wartime employment opportunities lured and continued oppression at home drove thousands of southern Blacks to the city in the 1940s. More now settled in the outer boroughs of Brooklyn and the Bronx, as did many of the 40,000 Blacks who migrated from Manhattan in that decade. In the 1950s, Queens' Black population nearly tripled and Staten

TABLE 11.17 African Americans in New York City, 1900–1960: number (in thousands) and percentage of borough population

	Richmond		Bronx		Brooklyn		Manhattan		Queens		New York City	
Year	No.	%	No.	%	No.	%	No.	%	No.	%	No.	%
1900	1.1	1.6	2.4	1.2	18.4	1.6	36.2	2.0	2.6	1.7	60.7	1.8
1910	1.2	1.4	4.1	1.0	22.7	1.4	60.5	2.6	3.2	1.1	91.8	1.9
1920	1.5	1.3	4.8	0.7	31.9	1.6	109.1	4.8	5.1	1.1	152.4	2.7
1930	2.6	1.6	12.9	1.0	68.9	2.7	224.7	12.0	18.6	1.7	327.7	4.7
1940	3.4	1.9	23.5	1.7	107.3	4.0	298.4	15.8	25.9	2.0	458.5	6.2
1950	5.4	2.8	97.8	6.7	208.5	7.6	384.5	19.6	51.5	3.3	845.5	10.7
1960	9.7	4.4	163.9	11.5	371.4	14.1	397.1	23.4	145.9	8.1	1,088.0	14.0

Source: Edward F. Bergman and Thomas W. Pohl, *A Geography of the New York Metropolitan Region* (Dubuque, IA: Kendall/Hunt, 1975), 91.

Island's nearly doubled as the migration continued. Nevertheless, the lag in growth until then left Staten Island's African American community disproportionately small in 1960.[37] By then, Blacks constituted 14 percent of city's total population but only 4.4 percent of Staten Island's; African Americans on Staten Island constituted less than 1 percent of the city's total Black population. Heading North when Staten Island's relative distance from the rest of the city was at its greatest, Blacks on Staten Island were starkly underrepresented by 1960.

Religion

The permutations of Staten Island's immigrant population also shaped its religious identity. Determining that makeup, however, is difficult because population data on religious groups are far from precise.[38] Data from U.S. census surveys are more approximate than actual; comparisons between denominations must be made with strong qualifications and are largely avoided here. The data are useful for tracing the presence of a single group across the city's boroughs. They reveal some truths about the religious makeup of Staten Island and whether particular denominations were inclined to locate there or not.

Staten Island was exceedingly Catholic from the moment it joined New York City, but not more so than any of the other boroughs. Its 11,385 church-identified Catholics in 1890 constituted 1.8 percent of the city's Catholic population, while the borough as a whole made up 2 percent of the city's total population (see table 11.18). The other boroughs' Catholic populations were also dispersed in a manner consistent with their overall size—either slightly less than (Brooklyn and Queens) or greater than (Manhattan) their fraction of the city's total population. That balance was lost over the next fifteen years as Italians and other Catholic immigrants from Europe poured into New York and largely settled in Manhattan. In 1906, Catholics were overrepresented in Manhattan by 5 percent and underrepresented in Brooklyn by 5.4 percent. Staten Island continued to attract its share of Catholics, containing exactly 1.9 percent of the city's Catholics and its total population.

By 1906, Staten Island's identified Catholic population had at least doubled. The U.S. Census of Religious Bodies in 1906 (see table 11.19) identified 27,613 Catholics on the island, but the survey's limitations—for example, no data were reported for the Moravian communities known to exist on the island—suggests that they were overcounted relative to other religious groups. In 1900, a better though still flawed survey put the distribution for the entire city at 46 percent Protestant, 37 percent Catholic, and 17 percent Jewish. For Staten Island, it is likely that Catholics were a plurality and possibly a majority of its citizens. In contrast, New York City's ample Jewish population had not arrived

TABLE 11.18 Borough share of Catholics over time, 1890–1952

Year		Richmond	Bronx	Brooklyn	Manhattan	Queens
1890	% of city's Catholic population	1.8	NA	32.9	62.1	3.1
1890	% of city's total population	2.0	NA	33.1	59.8	5.1
1890	Differential	−0.2	NA	−0.2	2.3	−2.0
1906	% of city's Catholic population	1.9	NA	31.3	61.8	5.0
1906	% of city's total population	1.9	NA	36.3	56.4	5.3
1906	Differential	0.0	NA	−5.0	5.4	−0.3
1926	% of city's Catholic population	2.5	10.9	39.6	35.4	11.6
1926	% of city's total population	2.4	14.8	37.5	33.1	12.2
1926	Differential	0.1	−3.9	2.1	2.3	−0.6
1952	% of city's Catholic population	3.7	20.9	30.7	21.8	22.9
1952	% of city's total population	2.4	18.4	34.7	24.8	19.7
1952	Differential	1.3	2.5	−4.0	−3.0	3.2

Sources: Data compiled from U.S. Bureau of the Census, *Report on Statistics of Churches in the United State at the Eleventh Census* (Washington, DC: U.S. Government Printing Office, 1890); *Census of Religious Bodies, 1906* (Washington, DC: U.S. Government Printing Office, 1910); *Census of Religious Bodies, 1916* (Washington, DC: U.S. Government Printing Office, 1919); *Census of Religious Bodies, 1926* (Washington, DC: U.S. Government Printing Office, 1928); *Census of Religious Bodies, 1936* (Washington, DC: U.S. Government Printing Office, 1940).

TABLE 11.19 Religious bodies on Staten Island, 1906, 1926, and 1952

Denomination	1906		1926		1952	
	No. of affiliated members	% of all NYC denominations	No. of affiliated members	% of all NYC denominations	No. of affiliated members	% of all NYC denominations
Roman Catholic	27,613	2.0	43,476	2.5	79,317	3.7
Jewish	798	0.1	5,502	0.3	8,000	0.3
Lutheran	943	1.9	5,117	5.1	7,174	5.3
Methodist	2,603	3.4	3,580	5.0	3,879	6.9
Presbyterian	495	1.0	805	1.2	1,126	2.9
Episcopalian	3,211	3.5	6,790	4.8	5,023	3.9
Reformed	770	3.0	1,165	5.3	1,284	6.9
Moravian	NA	NA	NA	NA	2,769	68.0
Baptists	976	2.2	1,016	1.7	NA	NA
Other Protest.	1,348	5.3	305	0.9	1,052	1.1
Total Protest.	10,346	2.7	18,778	3.8	22,307	4.5
Other	NA	NA	3,663	6.6	NA	NA
Total	38,757	NA	71,419	NA	109,624	NA

Sources: U.S. Bureau of the Census, *Census of Religious Bodies, 1906* (Washington, DC: U.S. Government Printing Office, 1910); U.S. Bureau of the Census, *Census of Religious Bodies, 1926* (Washington, DC: U.S. Government Printing Office, 1928); National Council of Churches, *Churches and Church Membership in the United States: An Enumeration and Analysis by Counties, States, and Regions* (New York: National Council of Churches, 1956).

on Staten Island in any large numbers, with approximately only 800 Jews living there in 1906.[39] Staten Island's Protestant communities—of which there were chiefly Methodists and Episcopalians—likely constituted well more than 26.7 percent of the borough's populace. Protestants were overrepresented on the island by 1.3 percent, while Staten Island's Jewish community accounted for a mere one-tenth of one percent of the city's Jews, well lower than the island's 1.9 percent share of the city's total population. These differentials may seem small, but with 1.9 percent of the city's population and 2.7 percent of its Protestants, Staten Island's Protestant population was nearly 50 percent larger than it would be with a distribution proportional to population size.

By 1926, Staten Island appeared to be considerably more Catholic than most of the other boroughs and yet internally it was growing more religiously diverse. As shown in table 11.19, the island's 43,476 Catholics continued as its largest religious group, and probably constituted a majority of its total population even with the likely undercounts of other groups. They were also now slightly overrepresented on the island. Among the Protestants, the island's Lutheran population had grown considerably, reflecting the arrival of immigrants from Norway and elsewhere in Scandinavia. The number of Episcopalians and Methodists also increased, and the size of all three groups was at least twice that of the island's 2.4 percent share of the city's total population. Protestants as a whole remained overrepresented as well; although the Jewish population had grown, it remained underrepresented.[40]

Staten Island's religious diversity was maintained in 1952. A National Council of Churches survey identified about one hundred different churches and synagogues on the island and nearly 110,000 people affiliated with them.[41] As seen in table 11.19, a clear majority of inhabitants were identified as Catholics, though once again a likely undercount of Protestants meant that the Catholic share of the island's populace was probably smaller than it appeared. The more telling data point remains the island's percentage of an individual denomination within New York. With Staten Island's 2.4 percent share of the city's total population, the groups with a higher number—such as the Catholics at 3.7 percent—were overrepresented. Conversely, although the borough's Jewish population had grown since 1926, it continued to be vastly underrepresented on Staten Island; its approximately 8,000 adherents constituted a mere 0.3 percent of the city's total. Staten Island's Lutheran and Episcopalian populations continued to have sizable numbers and were overrepresented in the borough. The members of Methodist and Reformed Churches, though with fewer members, each composed 6.9 percent of the city's total population of that denomination. Finally, the 1952 survey is useful for its statistics on Staten Island's celebrated Moravian community, which comprised 2.5 percent of the borough's population but a startling 68 percent of the Moravians throughout New York City.

In short, the religious profile of Staten Island remained surprisingly stable over the first sixty years of boroughhood. Predominantly Catholic at the outset, so it remained. Disproportionately without Jewish residents, so it stayed. It retained its considerable pockets of Protestant denominations as well. Consolidation does not appear to have much altered the borough's religious makeup, but to what extent is it reasonable to link this constancy to the absence of a direct rapid-transit link? Decades of multidisciplinary research indicates that interpersonal relationships among kin, ethnic, and religious groups strongly affect subsequent migrations, whether across an ocean or a river or a bay.[42] Patterns of movement can thus be followed for years as more and more newcomers arrive at a locale holding shared identities if not actual kinship with its inhabitants. For Staten Island and the other outer boroughs in the early twentieth century, immigrants and migrants found relatively open land and did not necessarily displace previous residents. In looking at the disposition of Catholics in New York City, for whom the data are more reliable than for Jews or Protestants and for whom the connection to Staten Island is most relevant, there nevertheless is a small but meaningful momentum over time. As with ethnic groups, the absence of easy access would be less of a deterrent to a religious group already well established on the island. For Jewish communities with minimal presence on Staten Island and no easy commute to garment industry jobs in Manhattan, the borough held little draw.

Politics and Education

Staten Island's relative physical isolation shaped its political leanings as much as its built and social environments. Its turn toward political conservatism—highly visible in the electoral boost it gave to the Republicans Rudy Giuliani and Mike Bloomberg in the mayoral elections of the 1990s and 2000s—also predated the opening of the Verrazzano Bridge but not consolidation. In the first few decades after Staten Island joined New York, its electoral results continued to mirror what had existed before 1898 and what was also found elsewhere in the city: a powerful Democratic organization winning most elections but at times defeated by a reform or Fusion candidate supported by independent Democrats and Republicans. In this manner, Staten Islanders elected George Cromwell as borough president in 1897, supported Seth Low for mayor in 1901 and 1903 and John Purroy Mitchel in 1913 (before abandoning him in 1917), and elected Joseph Palma as borough president in 1933. However, as Dan Kramer and Richard Flanagan have shown, aspects of the conservative leanings of Staten Island politics were "locked into place" by the time the Verrazzano Bridge was built—placing Staten Island in the vanguard of the larger suburban conservatism uncovered by Lisa McGirr.[43] The twenty years following the end of World War II witnessed the overwhelming support for President Dwight Eisenhower in 1956, an infusion of new energy into the local party organization by young Republicans, and the movement of political leaders from the Democratic to the Republican Party. Kramer and Flanagan observe that with more registered Democrats than Republicans both then and now, Staten Island was not and is not decidedly conservative; rather, they emphasize that its critical mass of rightward-leaning voters has resulted in many competitive elections since 1956 and that its distinctiveness from the other four boroughs makes it appear more conservative than it really is.[44] That feature of Staten Island was in evidence a decade before the bridge opened.

Staten Island's growing conservatism coincided with an increasing percentage of its residents opting to send their children to Catholic rather than public schools. Early in the century, this growth reflected patterns across the city. The island's number of parochial schools had expanded from four in 1900 to eighteen educating more than 5,000 children in 1927, nearly 20 percent of the students enrolled in public schools.[45] By 1961, its Catholic school population of 18,633 students totaled 57 percent of its public-school population of 32,655. By comparison, the Bronx parochial-school to public-school enrollment fraction was 40 percent, and the city's as a whole was 37 percent.[46] Staten Island's robust parochial system gave it the highest borough-wide percentage of students attending nonpublic schools in 1960. In 1962, more than 30 percent of Staten Island's K–12 student population attended a Catholic school.[47] These concomitant leanings in Catholic education and conservative politics were mutually reinforcing.

Twentieth-century trends in public education needed neither a subway tunnel nor a vehicular bridge to reach Staten Island. Consolidation instead helped to spur the rapid infusion of progressive education into the island. Most immediate was the centralization of the island's twenty-eight independent school districts into a single borough unit that was part of Greater New York's school system. By joining New York, Staten Island averted "the great school war" over centralization that might have occurred with the creation of a separate city of Richmond.[48] The centralized system created the context in which leading reformers took over leadership posts in the school system, expenditures for schooling rose, the capacity of school buildings was enlarged, the curriculum and extracurricular activities were expanded, and the opening of separate high schools on the island was hastened.

The transition of the secondary school from an elite institution to a mass one was one of the key developments in American public education from roughly 1890 through 1940. The high school as a public institution distinct from the common school originated in antebellum cities and steadily expanded to sizable towns in the latter half of the nineteenth century. To foster such growth, New York State passed the Union Free School Act in 1853 to encourage the consolidation of smaller district schools and organize the curriculum around sequential grades. On Staten Island, several communities—first Port Richmond in the 1880s and then Tottenville and Stapleton by 1898—attached secondary grade levels, or high school departments, to their existing common schools. Housed on the upper floors of common schools, these added levels enabled children to continue learning but did not function as distinct institutions, offer a four-year program, or attract many students.[49]

One of the first tangible benefits of joining Greater New York was the opening of Curtis High School in 1904. Housed in a magnificent Collegiate Gothic structure near the St. George ferry, Curtis gave Staten Island its own cathedral of learning for its adolescents. Early attendance trends comported with two long-standing patterns in secondary education: more girls were enrolled than boys, and most students did not stay long enough to graduate. For example, in 1910 girls made up 58 percent of the 699 students registered at the school, 242 of whom were in their first year of study and only 37 in their fourth.[50] Even with most students not staying through graduation, Curtis was quite popular. It quickly reached capacity and thrice underwent expansion during the 1920s and 1930s. During those same decades, four more high schools opened to accommodate the swelling demand for secondary education: Port Richmond High in 1927, the Staten Island Vocational High School (soon renamed McKee) in 1935, New Dorp and Tottenville High Schools in 1936.

High school attendance became normalized for Staten Island adolescents from 1920 to 1940. As the data in table 11.20 indicate, fourteen- and fifteen-year-old Staten Islanders already typically attended school, but the percentage rose from 79 percent to 97.4 percent. The increase for sixteen- and seventeen-year-olds was far more precipitous, climbing from 24.4 percent to 81.5 percent in attendance.[51] Some of that growth stemmed from the arrival of more boys, who by 1930 outnumbered girls at every age level. Variations in high school attendance and race remained. In both 1930 and 1940, U.S.-born whites enrolled at higher rates than immigrants and African Americans (see table 11.21). Nevertheless, high school attendance became a common experience for most Staten Island adolescents in each of these groups by 1940. This development occurred in all five boroughs of the city, with only small differences between them initially but greater variation in educational attainment in the postwar years, reflecting the more pronounced patterns in the ethnic, racial, and social class composition of their residents. In 1930, for example, the percentage of sixteen- and seventeen-year-olds in school ranged from 55.2 percent in Brooklyn to 62.4 percent in the Bronx, with Staten Island's 59.5 percent the second highest. In 1940, the average number of school years attained by borough ranged from 8.1 to 8.5 years, with Staten Island reporting 8.4 years. Adolescents throughout the city were even more likely to be enrolled by 1960, but the range of length of attendance by borough had widened from 9.4 years in the Bronx to 10.9 years in Queens, with an average of 10.7 years for Staten

TABLE 11.20 School attendance of adolescents on Staten Island, 1920, 1930, 1940

Year	Age group	Female Number	%	Male Number	%	Total Number	%
1920							
	14–15	NA	NA	NA	NA	3,062	79.0
	16–17	NA	NA	NA	NA	878	24.4
	18–20	NA	NA	NA	NA	432	7.7
1930							
	14	1,406	97.2	1,429	97.8	2,835	97.5
	15	1,380	92.5	1,451	93.8	2,831	93.2
	16–17	1,616	57.8	1,665	61.4	3,281	59.5
	18–19	521	18.8	588	21.3	1,109	20.1
1940							
	14	1,482	97.5	1,525	97.4	3,007	97.4
	15	1,539	97.6	1,536	97.3	3,075	97.5
	16–17	2,508	80.0	2,675	82.9	5,183	81.5
	18–19	796	25.0	1,115	30.5	1,911	27.9

Sources: U.S. Bureau of the Census, *Census of Population: 1920. State Compendium, New York* (Washington, DC: U.S. Government Printing Office, 1924), 40; *Census of Population: 1940*, vol. 2: *Characteristics of the Population* (Washington, DC: U.S. Government Printing Office, 1943), pt. 5 (New York–Oregon), 193.

TABLE 11.21 School attendance of adolescents by race and ethnicity, 1930 and 1940

Year	Age group	U.S. born white		Foreign-born white		Black		Total	
		Number	%	Number	%	Number	%	Number	%
1930									
	14	2,722	97.6	84	98.8	29	85.3	2,835	97.5
	15	2,677	93.3	127	90.7	26	89.7	2,831	93.2
	16–17	3,078	60.1	162	50.0	40	63.5	3,281	59.5
	18–19	1,034	20.6	66	15.3	8	9.8	1,109	20.1
1940									
	14	2,897	97.5	56	96.6	49	96.1	3,007	97.4
	15	2,961	97.5	66	98.5	48	94.1	3,075	97.5
	16–17	4,933	81.7	169	80.9	75	72.1	5,183	81.5
	18–19	1,788	28.0	103	30.3	19	17.6	1,911	27.9

Source: U.S. Bureau of the Census, *Census of Population: 1940*, vol. 2: *Characteristics of the Population* (Washington, DC: U.S. Government Printing Office, 1943), pt. 5 (New York–Oregon), 193.

Island.⁵² The split between these outer boroughs reflected school attendance patterns associated with southern and eastern Europeans, southern African Americans, and Puerto Ricans, all of whom constituted a larger portion of the population in the Bronx and Brooklyn than in the more middle-class Queens and Staten Island.⁵³

* * *

Not surprisingly, Staten Island in 1960 was a place fundamentally shaped by its decision to join New York, its relative isolation from the other boroughs, and other pervasive developments in the region and nation. Subway or no subway, changes in the U.S. political economy reached Staten Island. Its farms were disappearing, factories closing, and newspapers folding. Its schools embraced many progressive innovations and expanded as high school attendance became a norm. Its population shifted, first becoming more ethnically diverse to reflect the inflow of new immigrants from southern and eastern Europe and then homogenizing into a racialized "white" as war, quotas, and depression stifled immigration. African Americans and Puerto Rican migrants also generally steered clear of Staten Island even as they arrived in New York City in large numbers. By 1960, Staten Island was a vastly different place than the island that had joined the city nearly seventy years earlier.

At the same time, Staten Island looked unchanged when juxtaposed with the other outer boroughs. In 1890, Staten Island was on a similar track as Queens County and what would become the borough of the Bronx, if perhaps behind in total population than comparable in areas of urban density. They all had populations of less than 100,000, a few towns, small villages, and abundant farmland coupled with incipient industries. By 1960, the Forgotten Borough was on a trajectory more akin to suburbs than to vast parts of the other four boroughs. Queens's population underwent a twenty-fold increase between 1890 and 1960; the Bronx's population a sixteen-fold increase. Staten Island's population had grown by less than five times, from 51,693 to 221,991. The divergence was already evident in 1910 as population growth in the Bronx and Queens accelerated with consolidation. The variance was even more pronounced by 1925 as the subways enabled thousands of Manhattans to reach those outer boroughs. Contemporaries certainly understood how transportation factored into Staten Island's less than spectacular growth. A *Scientific American* article in 1927 heralding the arrival of the three Port Authority bridges to New Jersey easily identified "an adequate reason for the sparsely-populated condition of [Staten Island]. . . . Staten Island has been treated as the 'poor relation,' and not a rapid-transit bridge or tunnel crosses its encircling waterways."⁵⁴

With sharp population growth stifled, several concomitant characteristics appeared on Staten Island. The island never developed the same population density as wide swaths of the Bronx, Brooklyn, and Queens, at less than one-fourth of Queens' and a tenth of the Bronx's.[55] The relative lack of population density made expanding outward more feasible than building upward. Staten Island remained mostly empty of large apartment buildings as single-family homes continued to fill its landscape. The island failed to attract many of the more diverse immigrant and migrant populations arriving in New York City during the twentieth century, leaving it whiter than all the other boroughs and wealthier than most by 1960. Its political leanings shifted away from the other boroughs as well, its flirtation with the Republican Party was already in evidence by then. In short, many powerful trajectories for Staten Island were well in place by the time the Verrazzano-Narrows Bridge opened in 1964. "Before the bridge" is an understandable marker of time for lifelong residents of the borough, but the automobile access that the bridge brought was not a fundamental catalyst for change in the same way or to the same degree as the subway was to the Bronx, Brooklyn, and Queens. Yet the bridge was not inconsequential, and what it wrought is considered in the book's epilogue that follows a brief conclusion.

CONCLUSION

On Saturday, November 21, 1964, political, civic, and business luminaries gathered to open the Verrazzano-Narrows Bridge. Arriving in a motorcade of fifty-two limousines, they first met in Brooklyn to cut the ribbon, then crossed to Staten Island to hear speeches, and finally returned to Brooklyn for a reception. Robert Moses served as the master of ceremony for the dignitaries—including Governor Nelson Rockefeller, Mayor Robert Wagner, and Richmond Borough president Albert Maniscalco—who spoke to a crowd of 1,500. Maniscalco, among others, expressed the sentiment that had long permeated discussions of Staten Island's future: that a physical link to the rest of the city—what he labeled a "pathway to progress"—would portend a great makeover of the island. The first twenty-four hours of operation did not disappoint: 100,000 cars crossed the bridge, and real estate advertisements heralded the expected boom by highlighting a property's proximity to the bridge or, more generally, the "substantial acreage" available on Staten Island. Even those who were not eager for the bridge nonetheless acknowledged that it would have a transformative effect.[1]

The Verrazzano-Narrows Bridge seemed to culminate decades of efforts by Staten Islanders to obtain a physical connection to the rest of the city. Seventy years earlier, residents frustrated by the inefficiencies of highly localized government, intrigued by the fire, police, sanitation, and other services afforded by New York, and drawn to the prospect of raised property values in turn readily responded favorably to the overtures of Andrew Haswell Green's consolidation movement. Staten Island's civic boosters voted to become a part of

Greater New York in the expectation that consolidation would lead to a bustling and productive economy and burgeoning population. Better governance and fuller services would help realize this vision of greatness, but a rail tunnel to move people and/or products to the enlarged city's other boroughs was also a crucial component. A connection did not happen in the form or timespan these Staten Islanders anticipated, and that delay mattered greatly to the way their borough developed.

This book's central argument is that Staten Island's distinctiveness emerged in large part due to its decades of disconnect, while the subway significantly (though not completely) threaded the other four boroughs together. The book adopted an atypical structure to demonstrate this thesis, using quantitative social history in the opening and closing chapters to explore the economic, political, and social continuities and changes on the island between the 1890s and the 1950s. In addition to this linear analysis, those chapters presented spatial comparisons with the other boroughs to make two major points: first, that Staten Island was not fundamentally different from many other areas of what would become the outer boroughs in 1890, when consolidation was first seriously contemplated; and, second, that by the time the Verrazzano-Narrows Bridge opened in 1964, Staten Island had in important ways grown apart from its four counterparts.

Significant developments *had* occurred on Staten Island in the seventy years preceding the opening of the bridge. Some, such as the closing and departure of factories, were early signs of deindustrialization in the region. Others, such as the expansion of secondary schooling, were evidence of national movements in progressive education. The experience of consolidation hastened the reorientation of the island's civic center to its northern shore and spurred some demographic variation from the other outer boroughs. These trends did not need to catch a subway to reach Staten Island, but others did. Rapid transit brought massive population growth in early twentieth-century Brooklyn, Queens, and the Bronx and generated a denser built environment and a more heterogeneous population in those boroughs than what occurred on Staten Island. The absence of rapid transit is not the only reason that Staten Island looked so different by midcentury, but it is the formidable one with which the heart of this book engaged. If the absence of a subway significantly accounts for Staten Island's divergent trajectory, then why didn't the borough obtain one?

Chapters 2–10 tell the story of multiple efforts to build a physical link to New York. The political union of 1898 took place amid New York's initial foray into subway planning, and Staten Islanders aspired for inclusion once lines would expand beyond Manhattan and downtown Brooklyn. For more than forty years, residents would mobilize for a subway again and again. They worked through established organizations such as the local chamber of commerce and civic league, through new ad hoc umbrella groups bringing together dozens of community associations, or under the auspices of the current borough president. Sometimes they initiated the conversation with city and state officials—a movement for a direct tunnel from Manhattan "to and through Staten Island" from 1915 to 1918 being the most notable instance. More often they strove to take advantage of the outside circumstances of the moment: the deliberations over routes specified in Contract No. 2 with the Interborough Rapid Transit Company in the aughts; the alliance with Mayor John Hylan in his push for the city's transit independence in the 1920s; the efforts to obtain New Deal funds for a tunnel during the 1930s; and, most significantly, the negotiations leading up to the Dual Contracts of 1913.

So what went wrong? It is easy to discount these and other efforts by Staten Island's civic boosters. Too often they clashed with powerful outside entities, such as the Pennsylvania Railroad and the Port Authority, which masked their institutional interests behind impartial expertise. Too often the competition from the Bronx, Brooklyn, or Queens could make a more compelling case for the allocation of scarce funds for subway construction. Too often Staten Islanders undermined their own struggle. They could not agree among themselves about the location for the route or the type of link: Manhattan or Brooklyn? St. George or Stapleton? Tunnel or bridge? Roads or rails? Passengers or products? Nor could they even settle on whether a bridge or tunnel was a more pressing transportation need than better ferry or internal railroad service. Too often the pronouncements of support from office holders in need of future votes rang hollow. Most significantly, the economic challenge of Staten Island's geographic distance and demographic limitations could not be overcome: experts' projections for ridership and costs always discouraged private enterprises and public officials from making an investment in Staten Island's future.

These factors created long odds for even the most powerful local exertions for a subway. The outcomes of such exertions, however, were still contingent on the specific choices and actions made in moments of time—none more so than the negotiations leading up to the Dual Contracts of 1913. Animated by a philosophy of disbursing Manhattan's population to the outer boroughs, buoyed by a financial plan that could satisfy the public and private entities involved, and well positioned by its borough president's placement on a key subcommittee, Staten Island might have with a small twist of fate ended up with a subway instead of vague commitments that were never realized. This work has detailed these attempts for rapid transit in part because they might have worked out but in larger part because their failure to do so had such a profound impact on Staten Island's development.

Staten Islanders' unsuccessful efforts are important for another reason as well: they highlight the pervasiveness and strength on Staten Island of those who saw New York City as a beacon, not a warning light. The civic boosters who promoted consolidation first and then a rapid-transit connection understood the central premise of this entire book: that Staten Island's history is fundamentally shaped by its relationship with the great city to its north. For sixty years, the island remained uniquely untethered, a time when its relative distance from the rest of the city was maximized. This period of heightened isolation nurtured what is arguably the most important change of all: a cultural and ideological reorientation away from Manhattan and the rest of the city. That disconnection caused Staten Island to forego the kind of urbanization engendered by the subway system and increased its sense of otherness. As European immigrants morphed into whiteness by the 1960s, many in this still largely white borough associated the city with people of color and urban unrest. Staten Islanders had always felt some ambivalence about their relationship with New York City, but over the years the negatives seemed to counterbalance the positives for many residents. Expected to house the great city's residents with medical illnesses and developmental disabilities, required to store its refuse, and fearful of its perceived crime and corruption, Staten Islanders both appreciated their own oasis in the city and resented the forgetfulness that helped create it.

For many islanders, calling their home the "Forgotten Borough" articulated a frustration at being either neglected or targeted by the city's municipal government—no subway tunnel to the island but a garbage dump on it. For some, the moniker highlighted its alternative path of development—a result of its long disconnect from the rest of the city—that gave it a sense of being a place that time forgot. This sense of otherness also underscored references to it by non–Staten Islanders, though their language was tinged less with marvel and more with condescension for the island's perceived backwardness and conservatism in a cosmopolitan, liberal city. The continued prevalence of these meanings suggests that the book's underlying assumption of the island's powerful relationship with New York City retains its potency today. Staten Island's economic links to metropolitan New York remain strong even as the location of work continues to grow more decentralized. Staten Island's transportation fate can also be understood only through a regional lens. Staten Island appears set to remain a part of New York City in the future even as regional demographic shifts may alter its political profile. Perhaps the strongest bond for now is its cultural one as the Forgotten Borough, and the island will be seen as such until material conditions generate a new image and identity. Until then, Staten Islanders will continue to grapple with the nature of their connection to New York City as they try to chart their future.

EPILOGUE

What the Bridge Wrought

Did the opening of the Verrazzano-Narrows Bridge have the transformative impact that many residents and regional planning experts expected? Nearly sixty years later, those predictions have been echoed in a powerful narrative among longtime residents of the island. Typically tinged with nostalgia and often with resentment, the phrase "before the bridge" serves to convey the changes attributed to the spanning of the Narrows: the elimination of the vestiges of a rural countryside and small-town lifestyle, the appearance of unwanted subdivisions and unwieldy traffic, and the arrival of residents from Brooklyn who were of a lower social class and/or nonwhite.[1] To the extent that these sentiments hinge on population growth, there is some truth to the notion that developments spurred by the Verrazzano-Narrows Bridge altered the island. In absolute numbers, Staten Island experienced its greatest growth in the 1960s, when its population rose by 70,000, driven by a surge in migration of whites from the other boroughs.[2] Overall, the number of residents has doubled since 1964, approaching 500,000 for the 2020 census. With this growing population and the finite space of an island, density increased, open fields were converted into housing developments, and blighted areas appeared.

One implication of this book's argument is that the bridge's impact could not have been too extreme because so many patterns were established before its construction as a result of the island's previous disconnect. At times, attributing such influence to the Verrazzano-Narrows Bridge obfuscates more than it illuminates. First, the actual population growth fell far short of projections.

The TBTA and Port Authority's *Joint Study* predicted that the island's population would triple by 1975. A more hyperbolic estimate forecast that it would reach 750,000 by 1980. Richmond Borough president Albert Maniscalco's scaled-back prediction in 1963 still suggested the population would double by 1975. The careful projections in the New York Metropolitan Region Study, conducted from 1956 and 1959 for the Regional Plan Association, conveyed caution rather than confidence about the impact of the planned Narrows bridge, yet even its intentionally conservative population projection of 485,000 in 1985 overestimated what transpired. Despite its considerable rise in the 1960s, the island's population remained less than 300,000 in 1970, and by 2000 its population still had not reached 450,000.[3] The vehicular bridge built fifty years after Manhattan's population had begun to disperse elsewhere simply did not have the same demographic impact on Staten Island as the earlier arrival of subways had on the other outer boroughs.

Second, some of the changes attributed to growth spurred by the bridge long preceded its opening. Consider the disappearing farmland on Staten Island. Memories of the years "before the bridge" rightly recall the presence of local farms because in 1964 there were fifty-two in Richmond County. Not large, they averaged 5.4 acres, accounted for less than one percent of the island's land, and, as depicted in chapter 11, were the remnant of a much larger agricultural economy present on Staten Island in the nineteenth century.[4] The bridge indeed proved to be not a cause but an accelerant of that decline; the island lost thirty-eight farms in the decade between 1964 and 1974, the largest drop since the Great Depression. Even more tellingly, there was an 83 percent reduction in farm acreage, which soon accounted for just one-tenth of one percent of land on the island in 1970.[5]

Likewise, Staten Island's middle-class identity was well established by 1960, but it did solidify even more after the bridge opened. In its occupation structure, the workforce in jobs likely to offer a middle-class or higher lifestyle showed a modest overall increase from 33.7 percent of all workers in 1960 to 35.6 percent in 1970. This proportional increase came in its professional class, which rose from 11.6 percent to 14.2 percent of all employed workers. This slight growth, however, did not entirely reflect the occupations of many new arrivals because at the same time service-sector and white-collar jobs associated with the continued deindustrialization of the city also increased on Staten Island. Clerical positions grew from 23.5 percent to 27.4 percent of the workforce; employees in sales rose from 5.4 percent to 6.6 percent; and nondomestic service jobs increased from 11.4 percent to 14.0 percent during the 1960s.[6]

Growing income levels after the bridge opened also contributed to Staten Island's middle-class status. Staten Islanders had reported greater levels of income compared to most other parts of the city since data began to be collected in the 1930s, and the disparities grew in the postwar years. In 1950, its median family income was 9.0 percent higher than the city average but by 1960 it grew to 12.2 percent higher. The 1960s saw an even greater leap in income by the borough, and in 1970 the island's median family income was 22.8 percent higher than the city's average. Moreover, Staten Island had passed Queens to post the highest average income as well as the lowest poverty rate in the city. This rapid growth likely reflected both the arrival on Staten Island of some new residents with means and the departure from the other boroughs of far more residents heading for Long Island, Westchester, and New Jersey. Here, as with its occupation structure and racial makeup, the opening of the Verrazzano-Narrows Bridge functions as a symbolic marker of time on Staten Island more than as a material cause of its change.

A similar argument for the bridge as fuel rather than as catalyst can be made for politics on the island. As Daniel Kramer and Richard Flanagan have shown, Staten Island's conservatism incubated in the postwar years, continued to gain strength after the bridge opened, and soon manifested in electoral victories. In the campaign for borough president in 1965, the Republican Robert Connor defeated Maniscalco and would hold the post for twelve years. The Democrats regained the office through appointment in 1977 and won the next three elections until Guy Molinari defeated the incumbent in 1989. No Democrats have served since then. In the U.S. Congress, Molinari had previously defeated a nine-term Democrat in the Reagan landslide of 1980, and until 2018 only one other Democrat was elected, which was only in the aftermath of a personal scandal that forced the retirement of the six-term Republican incumbent.[7]

These points are meant to undermine, not invalidate, the notion of "before the bridge." Two episodes in the island's late twentieth-century political history are telling indicators and determinants of how it evolved after the bridge. First was the fate of the South Richmond Plan. As a span across the Narrows looked increasingly likely in the 1950s, many Staten Islanders cautioned against unfettered growth and called for Maniscalco to initiate planning efforts for the undeveloped land on the island—estimated in 1957 at two-thirds of the total acreage of the island and accounting for 62 percent of all undeveloped land in the city.[8] Elected mayor of New York City in 1965, John Lindsay embraced urban design, and his administration quickly identified the Staten Island communities of Annadale and Huegenot, already approved as potential urban-renewal locations and experiencing haphazard market forces, as prime areas for planned development. Lindsay's centralized approach alienated Richmond Borough president Connor, however, and the proposal's scale, reliance on eminent domain, and inclusion of affordable housing raised the ire of the Conservative Party on Staten Island. Local hearings on a state Senate bill to create the South Richmond Development Corporation became newsworthy for the heated opposition they attracted. White homeowners expressed outrage over the perceived domination by outsiders, infringement of their property rights, and the prospect of poor people of color arriving in large numbers. The bill never made it through the State Assembly, the plan died, and piecemeal development on the south shore continued unabated.[9] The absence of planned growth and the ravages of the real estate market have left Staten Islanders with some of their thorniest late twentieth and twenty-first century problems: a road system unable to handle the traffic, neighborhoods pockmarked by teardowns and subdivisions, onerous commute times, and tensions exacerbated by the vastly different profiles of the island's geographic regions—a northern tier with a large population of people of color, new immigrants, and white progressives and a south shore dominated by white conservatives.

A decade after the demise of the South Richmond Plan came a secession movement with real staying power. Talk of secession had often entered the public discourse throughout the century, particularly in instances of heated political battles or of disappointing outcomes. It came up during frustrating moments over a tunnel link, at times when the city considered or actually transported its garbage to the island, or in disgust over myriad seminal citywide events. But such talk never triggered a serious movement until a judicial decision that rendered the Board of Estimate unconstitutional resulted in the diminishment of Staten Island's representative power in the city government. A secession movement gained followers in the late 1980s and early 1990s and culminated in a referendum in 1993 in which islanders voted in favor of separation by a 65–35 percent margin. Among the reasons why Staten Islanders wanted to leave was the belief that they were not receiving the public services to which they were entitled. Secession was ultimately blocked by the majority leader of the state Assembly.[10] Since then, secessionism has been submerged in the political discourse. Staten Island's pivotal role in mayoral races from 1993 through 2009 generated a high level of attention from Republican mayors Rudy Giuliani and Mike Bloomberg that led to the removal of two sore spots: the ferry fare was eliminated, and the Fresh Kills landfill was closed.

Staten Island will never reach the population levels of the other boroughs, but its demographic profile is shifting in ways that mirror what transpired in other boroughs in the twentieth century. While its white population is declining and its African American population is stable, its international population is steadily climbing. The absence of a subway tunnel and the appearance of the bridge had considerable impact on Staten Island but nothing necessarily permanent. Physical and social structures make outcomes likely but not destined. If there's any usable past to be found in the experiences narrated here, it's that individuals and communities should strive through democratic processes to create the kinds of environments they desire, as Staten Islanders of all stripes have done for generations.

A NOTE ON STATEN ISLAND'S HISTORIC NEWSPAPERS

This book draws from the news coverage and editorial stance of numerous Staten Island newspapers. Like most areas filled with towns and villages in the late nineteenth century, Staten Island had various publications that typically reflected a particular locality and/or political affiliation. Usually printed biweekly or weekly, most of these publications folded as the twentieth century progressed. By 1950, the *Staten Island Advance* dominated what had dwindled to a very small field. Thus, most of the journalistic variety here appears in the earlier chapters, which can better speak to the partisan and geographic permutations of support for consolidation and a rapid-transit link. The later chapters increasingly rely on the *Advance* as the island's imperfect but functional paper of record.

For thorough treatments of the history of the printed press on Staten Island, see Charles W. Leng and William T. Davis, *Staten Island and Its People: A History, 1609–1929*, 5 vols. (New York: Lewis Historical, 1929–1933), 2:757–68, and Charles L. Sachs, "The Press on Staten Island, 1800–1986," *Staten Island Historian* 4 (new series), nos. 1–2 (Summer–Fall 1986): 1–19. For a full listing of historic Staten Island newspapers with microfilm location by repository, see the data compiled through the New York State Newspaper Project (https://www.nysl.nysed.gov/nysnp/all/443.htm). Several of these papers are available online through the New York State Historic Newspapers Project (https://nyshistoricnewspapers.org/). For the purposes of this book, brief synopses of the papers consulted will suffice.

The *News Letter* was a short-lived (1896–1903) Republican weekly published in St. George. The College of Staten Island (CSI) Archives Collection holds issues from 1896 to 1897 on microfilm.

The *Richmond County Democrat* was started in 1880. The following decade it was beholden to the Democratic political machine of Nicholas Muller. After its demise, it merged with the *Richmond County Herald* and was published from Tompkinsville as the *Democrat-Herald* through at least the 1920s. The Staten Island Historical Society at Richmondtown has an incomplete run of the *Democrat* from 1881 to 1895 as well as some issues of the *Democrat-Herald*. The New York State Historic Newspaper Database has issues of the *Democrat* from 1890 to 1892 online.

The *Richmond County Sentinel* was a Republican paper owned briefly by Erastus Wiman in the 1880s, when it merged with the older *Staten Island Gazette*. By the 1890s, it was believed to be beholden to the Democratic political machine of Nicholas Muller. The Staten Island Museum holds issues from 1885 to 1889 on microfilm.

The *Richmond County Standard* was a Democratic newspaper independent of the Muller organization. The local historian Ira K. Morris served as its editor in the 1890s, and it ceased publication around 1900. The CSI Archives hold issues from 1881 to 1900 on microfilm.

The *Staten Island Advance* began as the *Richmond County Advance* in 1886. Published in West New Brighton as an independent paper without partisan affiliation, the paper's name briefly changed to the *Daily Advance* to commemorate its new publication schedule. It took its current name midway through 1921 following its purchase by S. I. Newhouse. In the text and notes here, the different names are used depending on when the paper is cited. Its availability on microfilm is limited to 1945 in most metropolitan locations, but the Staten Island Museum's microfilm collection has much earlier editions. The New York State Historic Newspaper Database has issues from 1886 to 1910 online.

The *Staten Islander* was a Republican paper started in 1889. It became one of the more established papers on the island, with its own building in the heart of St. George on the corner of Bay Street and Central Avenue. It ceased publication in 1928 due to financial difficulties. Microfilm reels of issues from 1889 to 1927 are available at the CSI Archives.

The *Staten Island Independent* was a short-lived paper started in 1893. Published in Port Richmond and affiliated with independent Democrats, it focused on the election of 1894 and provided ample coverage of the consolidation effort. The CSI Archives hold issues from 1893 to 1895 on microfilm, and the New York State Historic Newspaper Database has issues from 1894 to 1895 online.

The *Staten Island Leader* was a Democratic paper started in 1866 and published at least through the 1920s. In the 1890s, it was affiliated with the Muller organization. The CSI Archives hold issues from 1868 to 1907 and 1924 to 1928 on microfilm. The New York State Historic Newspaper Database has scattered issues but a good run from 1924 to 1925 online.

The *Staten Island Light* was a monthly publication begun by the Staten Island Chamber of Commerce in 1926 and ran for several years. The New York Public Library holds issues from 1926 to 1929 on microfilm.

Formed in 1927 following the merger of two independent local papers, the *Staten Island Times-Transcript* was published out of Tottenville and gave special attention to issues affecting the southern part of the island. By 1930, it had shortened its name to the *Staten Island Transcript*, which is how it is referred to and cited in this book. Microfilm reels from 1927 to 1941 (inclusive) are available at the New York Public Library.

The *Staten Island World* was an independent Democratic paper published weekly out of Stapleton for eight years, 1901–1908. The CSI Archives hold issues from 1902 to 1920 on microfilm.

SOURCE ABBREVIATIONS

AES	Alfred Smith Papers, New York State Archives, Albany
AH	Arthur Hollick Papers, Staten Island Institute of Arts and Sciences, Staten Island Museum, Staten Island, NY
AHG	Andrew Haswell Green Papers, New York Historical Society, New York
CL	Charles Leng Collection, Staten Island Institute of Arts and Sciences, Staten Island Museum, Staten Island, NY
CSI	College of Staten Island Archives Collection, College of Staten Island, Staten Island, NY
CWL	Clarence W. Lexow Papers, Historical Society of Rockland County, NY
FLG	Fiorello La Guardia Papers, Municipal Archives, New York
GM	George McAneny Papers, Seeley G. Mudd Library, Princeton University, Princeton, NJ
JFH	John Francis Hylan Papers, Municipal Archives, New York
JJW	James John Walker Papers, Municipal Archives, New York
JPM	John Purroy Mitchel Papers, Municipal Archives, New York
NLM	Nathan L. Miller Papers, New York State Archives, Albany
PCRR	Penn Central Railroad Records, Pennsylvania Railroad Company Papers, Series: President, Samuel Rea, Pennsylvania State Archives, Harrisburg
RFW	Robert F. Wagner Papers, Municipal Archives, New York

RM	Robert Moses Papers, Manuscript and Archives Division, New York Public Library, New York
SICCHS	Staten Island Chamber of Commerce Collection, MS 90, Staten Island Historical Society, Richmondtown, Staten Island, NY
SICCR	Staten Island Chamber of Commerce Records, Staten Island Chamber of Commerce Building, Staten Island, NY
SIHS	Staten Island Historical Society Collection, Richmondtown, Staten Island, NY
SIIAS	Staten Island Institute of Arts and Sciences Collection, Staten Island Museum, Staten Island, NY
SR	Pennsylvania Railroad Company, department records, Executive Department, Acc. No. 1810 VP (Samuel Rea), Hagley Museum and Library, Wilmington, DE
TSW	Timothy S. Williams Papers, Manuscript and Archives Division, New York Public Library, New York
WJG	William J. Gaynor Papers, Municipal Archives, New York
WJW	William J. Wilgus Papers, Manuscript and Archives Division, New York Public Library, New York
WOD	William O'Dwyer Papers, Municipal Archives, New York

NOTES

Introduction

1. Robert Molinari to Robert Moses, December 3, 1937, series 6, box 97, 1936–1937 folder, RM.
2. *New York Times*, July 15, 1928, RE1; October 19, 1950, 35; and November 23, 1958, R1.
3. George H. Nulty to John Purroy Mitchel, March 15, 1916, Subject Files, box 30, folder 276, JPM; *Staten Islander*, January 25, 1922, 1.
4. *Richmond County Advance*, December 31, 1910, 1; *Staten Island Transcript*, June 30, 1931, 3; Vernon B. Hampton, *Staten Island in Transition: An Environmental Review* (Richmondtown, NY: New York Board of Education and Staten Island Historical Society, 1970), n.p.
5. *Richmond County Advance*, December 8, 1906, 4, and May 8, 1909, 3.
6. M. Glauber to Fiorello La Guardia, c. April 1941, Subject Files, roll 248, FLG.
7. *Staten Island Advance*, February 23, 1935, 3.
8. The concept "mentalité" poses questions regarding historical methodology and interpretation: How can a mentalité be formed, identified, and used to explain change? Understanding the connection between mentalité and change is the most difficult aspect of the notion and is not taken up here, though anyone writing the history of Staten Island from 1964 to the present would do well to consider it. For a classic case of the use of this concept, see Emmanuel Le Roy Ladurie, *Montaillou: The Promised Land of Error* (New York: Vintage, 1979). For a short but useful treatment, see Daniel Little, *New Contributions to the Philosophy of History* (Dordrecht: Springer Netherlands, 2010), 195–216, quote on 196. For an example of social and economic conditions producing mentalité on American soil, see James A. Henretta, "Families and Farms: Mentalité in Pre-industrial America," *William and Mary Quarterly* 35, no. 1 (January 1978): 3–32. For recent uses of the concept, see Jean-Marc Hill,

"Identity and *Mentalité*: British Naval Sailors and Encounter During the 'Scientific' Voyages, 1764–1803," *Journal for Maritime Research*, March 13, 2022, https://www-tandfonline-com.csi.ezproxy.cuny.edu/action/showOpenAccess?journalCode=rmar20, 1–33; and Michael John Williams, "The Enduring Culture of Restraint in Modern Germany: German *Mentalités* on the Use of Force as Portrayed in Contemporary Television Narratives," *German Politics* 30, no. 1 (2021): 87–105.

9. Over the past two decades, a number of fine studies have explored this dynamic: Dan T. Carter, *The Politics of Rage: George Wallace, the Origins of the New Conservatism, and the Transformation of American Politics*, 2nd ed. (Baton Rouge: Louisiana State University Press, 2000); Matthew D. Lassiter, *The Silent Majority: Suburban Politics in the Sunbelt South* (Princeton, NJ: Princeton University Press, 2007); Lisa McGirr, *Suburban Warriors: The Origins of the New American Right*, rev. ed. (Princeton, NJ: Princeton University Press, 2015); and Richard Moss, *Creating the New Right Ethnic in 1970s America: The Intersection of Anger and Nostalgia* (Lanham, MD: Fairleigh Dickenson University Press, 2017).

10. *Staten Island Advance*, December 26, 1999, M1. The complete list can be found at http://sites.rootsweb.com/~nyrichmo/history.shtml. More recently, the *Advance*'s Tom Wrobleski offered his list of top-ten events in Staten Island history: the opening of the Verrazzano Bridge remained number one, while joining Greater New York came in at number nine. See *Staten Island Advance*, posted February 20, 2016, updated May 16, 2019, https://www.silive.com/opinion/columns/2016/02/the_10_biggest_events_in_state.html.

11. Michael Rosenfeld, "Staten Island Historians and the Arcadian Myth," in *Community, Continuity, and Change: New Perspectives on Staten Island History*, ed. Michael Rosenfeld and Charles LaCerra (New York: Pace University Press, 1999), 33–41; Daniel C. Kramer and Richard M. Flanagan, *Staten Island: Conservative Bastion in a Liberal City* (Lanham, MD: University Press of America, 2012), 51–56; Martin V. Melosi, *Fresh Kills: A History of Consuming and Discarding in New York City* (New York: Columbia University Press, 2020), 87–91, 232–36; and Joseph Borelli, *Staten Island in the Nineteenth Century: From Boomtown to Forgotten Borough* (Charleston, SC: History Press, 2022).

12. Edward Robb Ellis, *The Epic of New York City: A Narrative History* (1966; reprint, New York: Kodansha America, 1997), 451–52; George J. Lankevich, *American Metropolis: A History of New York City* (New York: New York University Press, 1998), 132–35; Thomas Kessner, *Capital City: New York City and the Men Behind America's Rise to Economic Dominance, 1860–1900* (New York: Simon and Schuster, 2003), 324–26. Edwin Burrows and Mike Wallace provide some coverage of Staten Island in their Manhattan-centric volumes. See Edwin G. Burrows and Mike Wallace, *Gotham: A History of New York City to 1898* (Oxford: Oxford University Press, 1999); and Mike Wallace, *Greater Gotham: A History of New York City from 1898 to 1919* (Oxford: Oxford University Press, 2017).

13. Those who write the history of Staten Island routinely observe considerable inattention to it. See, for example, Amy Stempler, "Communal Reflections: The Jewish Historical Society of Staten Island Oral History Project," *New York History* 96, no. 1 (Winter 2015): 67–83.

14. Kramer and Flanagan, *Staten Island*, 39–56.

15. Melosi, *Fresh Kills*, 2–3.

16. Ted Steinberg, *Gotham Unbound: The Ecological History of Greater New York* (New York: Simon and Schuster, 2014), 230–37.

17. Charles L. Sachs, *Made on Staten Island: Agriculture, Industry, and Suburban Living in the City* (Richmondtown, NY: Staten Island Historical Society, 1988), 67. The term *polynuclear* comes from Richard Harris and Robert Lewis, "The Geography of North American Cities and Suburbs, 1900–1950: A New Synthesis," *Journal of Urban History* 27, no. 3 (2001): 263.
18. Although Jared Diamond's most recent works have elaborated his emphasis on geography, *Guns, Germs, and Steel: The Fates of Human Societies* (New York: Norton, 1997) remains the place to begin. Other important works in the field include Wilbur Zelinsky, *The Cultural Geography of the United States*, rev. ed. (Englewood Cliffs, NJ: Prentice Hall, 1992); and Colin Gordon, *Mapping Decline: St. Louis and the Fate of the American City* (Philadelphia: University of Pennsylvania Press, 2009).
19. For a fine transportation study with a metropolitan focus, see Jameson W. Doig, *Empire on the Hudson: Entrepreneurial Vision and Political Power at the Port of New York Authority* (New York: Columbia University Press, 2001).
20. Alternatively, one could see Staten Island's location at the doorway of New York Harbor as its good fortune. Even though it sits physically closer to New Jersey, separated by the narrow Kill Van Kull and the Arthur Kill, Staten Island's placement in the harbor made it a part of New York State from the outset and led it to be included in Greater New York in 1898.
21. Kara Murphy Schlichting, *New York Recentered: Building the Metropolis from the Shore* (Chicago: University of Chicago Press, 2020). For a cultural and intellectual focus, see Thomas Bender, *The Unfinished City: New York and the Metropolitan Idea* (New York: New Press, 2002). Race remains a major fault line in both cities and suburbs. See David M. P. Freund, *Colored Property: State Policy and White Racial Politics* (Chicago: University of Chicago Press, 2007).
22. See, for example, Robert Lewis, ed., *Manufacturing Suburbs: Building Work and Home on the Metropolitan Fringe* (Philadelphia: Temple University Press, 2004).
23. Martin Melosi's book *Fresh Kills* is an outstanding recent model of the vitality of a relational approach. Beginning with a chapter on consumption, land use, and waste in Manhattan in a study ostensibly about Staten Island, Melosi demonstrates that one simply cannot explain the landfill on Staten Island without understanding consumption and waste throughout the city. For a recent exploration of Staten Island during the nineteenth century that contextualizes its place in the region, see Adam Zalma, "Staten Island in the Harbor Metropolis," PhD diss., Rutgers University, 2015. Rosenfeld and LaCerra's edited collection *Community, Continuity, and Change* is tied together by a similar emphasis on interconnectivity.
24. Kenneth T. Jackson, *Crabgrass Frontier: The Suburbanization of the United States* (New York: Oxford University Press, 1985), 35–37.
25. Wallace and Burrows, *Gotham*, 931–45; Clifton Hood, *722 Miles: The Building of the Subways and How They Transformed New York* (Baltimore, MD: Johns Hopkins University Press, 1993), 21–28, 37–55; Erica Judge, Vincent Seyfried, and Andrew Sparberg, "Elevated Railways," and Mark H. Rose and Vincent Seyfried, "Streetcars," in *The Encyclopedia of New York City*, ed. Kenneth T. Jackson (New Haven, CT: Yale University Press, 1995), 368–69, 1127–28; Richard Dickenson, ed. and comp., *Holden's Staten Island: The History of Richmond County: Revised Resource Manual Sketches for the Year Two Thousand Two* (New York: Center for Migration Studies, 2002), 141–42.
26. Hood, *722 Miles*, 69–71.
27. Scholars have typically recognized only the middle of these three episodes. The Dual Contracts episode is rather surprisingly somewhat lost, and some Staten Islanders'

continued insistence on a subway into the 1940s meshes poorly with narratives that highlight the advent of the automobile. See Darl Rastorfer, *Six Bridges: The Legacy of Othmar H. Ammann* (New Haven, CT: Yale University Press, 2000), 135–37; Kramer and Flanagan, *Staten Island*, 206–7.

28. For example, Douglas Rae posits the nonevent of early development of automotive technologies as crucial to the early twentieth-century heyday of industrial cities such as New Haven, Connecticut. Erik Conway's history of this country's failure to build a supersonic airplane superbly blends the impact of politics, economics, and environmentalism. Kenneth Jackson, a leading historian of New York City, has imagined a much lesser city without the subway, albeit not in a formal, academic sense. Niall Ferguson's work is a notable exception to the avoidance of counterfactuals. See Douglas Rae, *City: Urbanism and Its End* (New Haven, CT: Yale University Press, 2003), 11–15; Erik M. Conway, *High-Speed Dreams: NASA and the Technopolitics of Supersonic Transportation, 1945–1999* (Baltimore, MD: Johns Hopkins University Press, 2005); Kenneth T. Jackson, "If the Subway Had Never Been," *New York Times*, March 28, 2004; and Niall Ferguson, *Virtual History: Alternatives and Counterfactuals* (London: Picador, 1997).

29. See, for example, Hood, *722 Miles*; Sam Bass Warner, *Streetcar Suburbs: The Process of Growth in Boston, 1870–1900* (Cambridge, MA: Harvard University Press, 1962); Robert C. Reed, *The New York Elevated* (South Brunswick, NJ: A. S. Barnes, 1978); Peter Derrick, *Tunneling to the Future: The Story of the Great Subway Expansion That Saved New York* (New York: New York University Press, 2001); and Roger P. Roess and Gene Sansone, *The Wheels That Drove New York: A History of the New York City Transit System* (New York: Springer, 2013).

30. As Michael Mandelbaum has noted, all history is loosely comparative ("Some Forms and Uses of Comparative History," *American Studies International* 18, no. 2 [Winter 1980]: 21). Comparative history has its own ample share of criticism, but for an argument of its utility, see Philippa Levine, "Is Comparative History Possible?," *History and Theory* 53, no. 3 (October 2014): 331–47.

1. Setting the Stage: Staten Island in the Late Nineteenth Century

1. Staten Island Improvement Commission, *A Letter Introductory from Messrs. Olmsted, Harris, Trowbridge, and Richardson* (New York, 1871), 28.
2. *Brooklyn Daily Eagle*, December 19, 1897, 15.
3. *Brooklyn Daily Eagle*, February 10, 1884, 12; August 10, 1888, 2; and September 11, 1888, 4.
4. *New York Times*, September 18, 1881, 6.
5. *New York Times*, November 19, 1888, 4.
6. *New York Times*, June 6, 1872, 6; *Brooklyn Daily Eagle*, May 16, 1885, 6.
7. Nathan Kantrowitz, "Population," in *The Encyclopedia of New York City*, ed. Kenneth T. Jackson (New Haven, CT: Yale University Press, 1995), 923; *New York Times*, May 13, 1872, 4, July 30, 1874, 4, and November 10, 1874, 3.
8. For scholarship that moves away from static categorization, see a fine collection of essays in Kevin M. Kruse and Thomas J. Sugrue, eds., *The New Suburban History* (Chicago: University of Chicago Press, 2006). For an argument that neither "urban" nor "rural" nor "suburban" captures the late nineteenth-century built environment, see John R. Stilgoe, *Metropolitan Corridor: Railroads and the American Scene* (New Haven, CT: Yale University Press, 1983).

1. Setting the Stage 285

9. David Van Pelt, *Leslie's History of Greater New York*, vol. 2 (New York: Arkell, 1898), 492.
10. William Cronon, *Nature's Metropolis: Chicago and the Great West* (New York: Norton, 1991), 23–45.
11. Richard Dickenson, ed. and comp., *Holden's Staten Island: The History of Richmond County* (New York: Center for Migration Studies, 2002), 306; United States Census Office, *Abstract of the Eleventh Census: 1890*, 2nd ed. (Washington, DC: U.S. Government Printing Office, 1896), 34, 36.
12. Nadia H. Youssef, *Population Dynamics on Staten Island: From Ethnic Homogeneity to Diversity* (New York: Center for Migration Studies, 1991), 3–4; Edward F. Bergman and Thomas W. Pohl, *A Geography of the New York Metropolitan Region* (Dubuque, IA: Kendall Hunt, 1975), 11–15; Ira Rosenwaike, *Population History of New York City* (Syracuse, NY: Syracuse University Press, 1972), 15–16, 65.
13. Youssef, *Population Dynamics on Staten Island*, 4–5; Charles W. Leng and William T. Davis, *Staten Island and Its People: A History, 1609–1929*, 5 vols. (New York: Lewis Historical, 1929–1933), 1:303; Staten Island Improvement Commission, *Report of a Preliminary Scheme of Improvements* (New York: James Sutton, 1871); *Richmond County Democrat*, May 5, 1891, n.p.
14. Rosenwaike, *Population History of New York City*, 60. The data from Queens come only from the portion that would subsequently join Greater New York and exclude the section that would become Nassau County.
15. Board of Rapid Transit Railroad Commissioners, *Report of the Board of Rapid Transit Railroad Commissioners for and in the City of New York for the Year Ending December 31, 1902* (New York, 1903), 311, https://catalog.hathitrust.org/Record/008301975.
16. United States Census Office, *Report on Population of the United States at the Eleventh Census: 1890, Part I* (Washington, DC: U.S. Government Printing Office, 1895), 924–25.
17. Charles L. Sachs, *Made on Staten Island: Agriculture, Industry, and Suburban Living in the City* (Richmondtown, NY: Staten Island Historical Society, 1988), 17, 23, 29; U.S. Department of the Interior, Census Office, *Report on the Statistics of Agriculture in the United States at the Eleventh Census: 1890* (Washington, DC: U.S. Government Printing Office, 1895), 221, 377–78, 444, 523; Ted Steinberg, *Gotham Unbound: The Ecological History of Greater New York* (New York: Simon and Schuster, 2014), 167–70. For discussions of Sandy Ground, see William V. Askins, *Sandy Ground: Historical Archaeology of Class and Ethnicity in a Nineteenth Century Community on Staten Island* (Ann Arbor, MI: University Microfilms International, 1990); and Lois A. H. Mosley, *Sandy Ground Memories* (Staten Island, NY: Staten Island Historical Society, 2003).
18. Sachs, *Made on Staten Island*, 20.
19. U.S. Department of the Interior, *Report on the Statistics of Agriculture*, 166.
20. Sachs, *Made on Staten Island*, 35, 41, 46–47, 52–53, 59–62, 64, 76–79; Henry G. Steinmeyer, *Staten Island, 1524–1898* (Staten Island, NY: Staten Island Historical Society, 1950), 74. See also *Industries of Staten Island Before Consolidation* (New York: Richmond, 1898); Charles LaCerra, "Some Industries on Staten Island in the Nineteenth Century," in *Community, Continuity, and Change: New Perspectives on Staten Island History*, ed. Michael Rosenfeld and Charles LaCerra (New York: Pace University Press, 1999), 7–16.
21. County data were not provided in the 1890 census, but in 1900 the New York City data were disaggregated by borough.

286   1. Setting the Stage

22. These figures underestimate the reach of the agricultural sector. With 290 farms on Staten Island, surely more than twenty-six women labored in ways that were not counted as work. Similarly, a fair number of businesses serviced the agricultural sector—for example, nearly another five hundred workers engaged in making food products.
23. U.S. Department of Commerce and Labor, Bureau of the Census, *Special Report: Occupations at the Twelfth Census 1900* (Washington, DC: U.S. Government Printing Office, 1904), 456–59; *Agriculture Part I: Farms, Live Stock, and Animal Products* (Washington, DC: US Government Printing Office, 1902), 108.
24. United States Census Office, *Report on Farms and Homes: Proprietorship and Indebtedness in the United States at the Eleventh Census: 1890* (Washington, DC: U.S. Government Printing Office, 1895), 31.
25. United States Census Office, *Report on Real Estate Mortgages in the United States* (Washington, DC: U.S. Government Printing Office, 1894), New York map between pp. 153 and 154; United States Census Office, *Report on Farms and Homes*, 452. Per capita property value in Queens' Long Island City ($424), however, was more than double the valuations in New Brighton ($203).
26. United States Census Office, *Report on Real Estate Mortgages*, 146 and map between pp. 153 and 154. Richmond County residents took on debt for several reasons. On January 1, 1890, they owed about $9.2 million for nearly 3,400 mortgages. The largest portion of the debt—nearly $4.2 million—was for the purchase of buildings, while the nearly 1,400 mortgages undertaken for improvements to property already owned accounted for another $3 million in debt. People also received mortgages for taxes, land purchases, and family expenses. The largest mortgages tended to be taken to support manufacturing, with twelve such debts averaging $12,600. The other 326 business ventures supported by a mortgage reflected the breadth of the Staten Island economy, ranging from manufacturing dyes to cutting lumber, bottling, and wagon making (United States Census Office, *Report on Real Estate Mortgages*, 930).
27. United States Census Office, *Report on Population*, 470–71.
28. See, for example, Noel Ignatiev, *How the Irish Became White* (New York: Routledge, 1995); David R. Roediger, *Working Toward Whiteness: How America's Immigrants Became White: The Strange Journey from Ellis Island to the Suburbs* (New York: Basic, 2005); Karen Brodkin, *How Jews Became White Folks and What That Says About Race in America* (New Brunswick, NJ: Rutgers University Press, 1998); Nell Irvin Painter, *The History of White People* (New York: Norton, 2010).
29. Kantrowitz, "Population," 922; Ira K. Morris, *Morris' Memorial History of Staten Island, New York*, vol. 2 (New York: Memorial, 1900), 2, 46.
30. United States Census Office, *Report on Statistics of Churches in the United States at the Eleventh Census* (Washington, DC: U.S. Government Printing Office, 1894), 74. Census figures relied on clerks within the hierarchy of each religious group to report its membership and may reflect the degree of centralization of each organization, accounting for extremely high percentages of Roman Catholics.
31. Dickenson, *Holden's Staten Island*, 97–100, 137.
32. Morris, *Memorial History of Staten Island*, 2:249, 258–59, 436–38; Leng and Davis, *Staten Island and Its People*, 1:306, 309, 420–21; *New York Times*, October 21, 1887, 8.
33. Morris, *Memorial History of Staten Island*, 2:358–59; Leng and Davis, *Staten Island and Its People*, 2:760–64; "List of Staten Island Newspapers," c. 1895, Good Government Collection, bound volume, SIHS; Steinmeyer, *Staten Island*, 74.

34. Staten Island Rapid Transit, or SIRT, as it is commonly known, has had many names over its long history. When Erastus Wiman took over the line from the Vanderbilts in 1880, he chartered it as the Staten Island Rapid Transit Railroad Company (Dickenson, *Holden's Staten Island*, 140–41; Morris, *Memorial History of Staten Island*, 2:461–67).
35. Morris, *Memorial History of Staten Island*, 2:242–43; Leng and Davis, *Staten Island and Its People*, 1:306, 419–20. David Hammack also finds that New York's late nineteenth-century elite and emergent middle class were also distinguished by their ethnoreligious identities. See David C. Hammack, *Power and Society: Greater New York at the Turn of the Century* (New York: Russell Sage Foundation, 1982), 65–89.
36. Morris, *Memorial History of Staten Island*, 2:436.
37. *Staten Island Independent*, October 30, 1895, n.p., in Good Government Club, Correspondence and Clippings, SIHS.
38. Leng and Davis, *Staten Island and Its People*, 1:311–14, 326; Morris, *Memorial History of Staten Island*, 2:483–85; Dickenson, *Holden's Staten Island*, 113–17.
39. Leng and Davis, *Staten Island and Its People*, 1:321, 353; Morris, *Memorial History of Staten Island*, 2:485–86; Amy S. Greenberg, *Cause for Alarm: The Volunteer Fire Department in the Nineteenth Century City* (Princeton, NJ: Princeton University Press, 1998); Susan G. Davis, *Parades and Power: Street Theater in Nineteenth Century Philadelphia* (Philadelphia: Temple University Press, 1986), 115–16, 143–47. A study of mid-nineteenth-century fire companies on Staten Island reveals strong rivalries but offers no class analysis of them. See "Going to Blazes: Staten Island's Volunteer Fire Department, 1837–1872," *Staten Island Historian* 31, no. 19 (July–September 1974): 171.
40. Mary Ann Clawson, "Fraternal Orders and Class Formation in the Nineteenth-Century United States," *Comparative Studies of Society and History* 27, no. 4 (October 1985): 672–95, David Montgomery's turn of phrase "a collectivist counter culture" quoted on 673; David T. Beito, "'To Advance the Practice of Thrift and Economy': Fraternal Societies and Social Capital, 1890–1920," *Journal of Interdisciplinary History* 29, no. 4 (Spring 1999): 587.

2. Joining the City: Staten Island and the Consolidation of Greater New York, 1898

1. Ira K. Morris, *Morris's Memorial History of Staten Island New York*, vol. 2 (New York: Memorial, 1900), 489.
2. *Staten Islander*, November 10, 1894, 1.
3. *New York Times*, November 8, 1894, 1.
4. *Staten Island Independent*, November 16, 1894, 1.
5. Thomas Collier Platt and Louis Jay Lang, *The Autobiography of Thomas Collier Platt* (New York: B. W. Dodge, 1910), quoted in David Hammack, *Power and Society: Greater New York at the Turn of the Century* (New York: Russell Sage Foundation, 1982), 216.
6. Harlow McMillen, "Consolidation: How Staten Island Became Part of Greater New York," *Staten Island Historian* 31, no. 2 (April–June 1970): 9.
7. Edwin G. Burrows and Mike Wallace, *Gotham: A History of New York City to 1898* (New York: Oxford University Press, 1999), 1232. See also Mike Wallace, *Greater*

Gotham: A History of New York City from 1898 to 1919 (New York: Oxford University Press, 2017), 49–60; Hammack, *Power and Society*, 185–229; John A. Krout, "Framing the Charter," in *The Greater City: New York, 1898–1948*, ed. Allan Nevins and John A. Krout (New York: Columbia University Press, 1948), 41–60; Edward Robb Ellis, *The Epic of New York City: A Narrative History* (1966; reprint, New York: Kodansha America, 1997), 452.

8. Gerald Frug, "The Legal Technology of Exclusion in Metropolitan America," in *The New Suburban History*, ed. Kevin M. Kruse and Thomas J. Sugrue (Chicago: Chicago University Press, 2006), 216–17; David Rusk, *Cities Without Suburbs*, 2nd ed. (Washington, DC: Woodrow Wilson Center Press, 1995); Robert A. Beauregard, *When America Became Suburban* (Minneapolis: University of Minnesota Press, 2006), 48–50; Jon C. Teaford, *City and Suburb: The Political Fragmentation of Metropolitan America, 1850–1970* (Baltimore: Johns Hopkins University Press, 1979), 32–63.

9. Rusk, *Cities Without Suburbs*, 18–19. Mike Wallace especially emphasizes "ruinous competition" in *Greater Gotham*, 51–52.

10. Andrew Green to the New York Legislature, March 4, 1890, in *Municipal Consolidation Inquiry* (New York: Stettiner, Lambert, 1893), 15–16; Anita Klutsch, "Andrew Haswell Green: The Father of Greater New York and His Dual Vision of a Cultivated and Consolidate Metropolis," PhD diss., Ludwig-Maximilians University, Munich, Germany, 2012, 85.

11. Kenneth Jackson, *Crabgrass Frontier: The Suburbanization of the United States* (New York: Oxford University Press, 1985), 138–56; Peter R. Gluck and Richard J. Meister, *Cities in Transition: Social Changes and Institutional Responses in Urban Development* (New York: New Viewpoints, 1979), 132–34, 163–68; Teaford, *City and Suburb*, 76–104. One study with considerable emphasis on the outer boroughs (except for Staten Island) is Richardson Dilworth, *The Urban Origins of Suburban Autonomy* (Cambridge, MA: Harvard University Press, 2005).

12. Dilworth, *The Urban Origins of Suburban Autonomy*, 6.

13. *Staten Islander*, October 24, 1894, 1; November 14, 1894, 4.

14. Morris, *Memorial History of Staten Island*, 2:488. Writing more than 120 years after Morris, Joseph Borelli regrets consolidation as a bipartisan mistake that failed to deliver. See Joseph Borelli, *Staten Island in the Nineteenth Century: From Boomtown to Forgotten Borough* (Charleston, SC: History Press, 2022), 14, 133, 149–52.

15. Hammack, *Power and Society*, 187–88; Krout, "Framing the Charter," 47; John Foord, *The Life and Public Services of Andrew Haswell Green* (Garden City, NY: Doubleday, Page, 1913), 178; Albert Fein, introduction to *Landscape Into Cityscape: Frederick Law Olmsted's Plan for a Greater New York*, ed. Albert Fein (Ithaca, NY: Cornell University Press, 1967), 39–40.

16. New York annexed three Westchester County towns to its north in what is now the western Bronx in 1874. Brooklyn's physical growth started even earlier when in 1855 it absorbed Williamsburg and Bushwick. New York added all of the remaining land that would become the Bronx in 1895, and Brooklyn annexed the towns of New Lots in 1886, Flatbush, Gravesend, and New Utrecht in 1894, and Flatlands in 1896, making Brooklyn coterminous with Kings County. The growth spurts of the 1890s occurred simultaneously to the coordinated movement for consolidation (Burrows and Wallace, *Gotham*, 719, 1222, 1231; *Brooklyn Daily Eagle*, May 18, 1886, 1).

17. Charles W. Leng and William T. Davis, *Staten Island and Its People: A History, 1609–1929*, 5 vols. (New York: Lewis Historical, 1929–1933), 1:306; Richard M. Bayles, *History of Richmond County (Staten Island), New York: From Its Discovery to the Present*

Time (New York: L. E. Preston, 1887), 660; Hammack, *Power and Society*, 188; Burrows and Wallace, *Gotham*, 1220. There is a discrepancy in these Staten Island histories regarding the inception of the Metropolitan Police Board, but on June 1, 1857, the *New York Times* reported on the commission's early activity (p. 5).

18. *Staten Islander*, March 20, 1889, 4. For a less sanguine recollection of the metropolitan police force, see Morris, *Memorial History of Staten Island*, 2:479.
19. In 1890, Green offered a common understanding that the burning of the quarantine house "resulted from the circumstances that these persons had no voice in the counsels which inflicted the nuisance upon them" (Andrew Green to the New York Legislature, March 4, 1890, in *Municipal Consolidation Inquiry*, 12). For a recent treatment of the conflict over the quarantine facility, see Martin V. Melosi, *Fresh Kills: A History of Consuming and Discarding in New York City* (New York: Columbia University Press, 2020), 78–86.
20. The New York Assembly and Senate retained authority to pass legislation specific to a single locale even as—in the name of home rule—this practice had abated in many other states. See Hammack, *Power and Society*, 193; Burrows and Wallace, *Gotham*, 1222–23; David Scobey, "Real Estate Record and Builder's Guide," in *Encyclopedia of New York City*, ed. Kenneth Jackson (New Haven, CT: Yale University Press, 1995), 990; and Teaford, *Cities and Suburb*, 28.
21. Burrows and Wallace, *Gotham*, 1220; Hammack, *Power and Society*, 192. Green's vision for consolidation grew from his service and leadership on the Central Park Commission, whose area of focus grew in 1865 and 1866 to include northern Manhattan and Westchester County. Green first wrote down his ideas about consolidation in 1868, when in his capacity as a park commissioner he proposed that "the City of New York and the County of Kings, a part of Westchester County and a part of Queens and Richmond, including the various suburbs of the City, [combine] under one municipal government, to be arranged in departments under a single executive head" (quoted in Burrows and Wallace, *Gotham*, 1220).
22. *Staten Islander*, March 20, 1889, 4.
23. *Richmond County Sentinel*, March 16, 1889, 1.
24. *Staten Islander*, March 20, 1889, 4, 5.
25. Hammack, *Power and Society*, 193–94.
26. Hammack, *Power and Society*, 194–95; Burrows and Wallace, *Gotham*, 1224.
27. *Staten Islander*, June 28, 1890, 1, and October 4, 1890, 6; Edward Cary, *George William Curtis* (Boston: Houghton Mifflin, 1894), 294–307; Gordon Milne, *George William Curtis and the Genteel Tradition* (Bloomington: Indiana University Press, 1956), 231–40. In a letter penned in mid-1890, Curtis observed, "I am very sure that it must be a pretty badly governed rural community that would gain by being subjected to the control of Tammany Hall" (*Richmond County Herald*, quoted in the *Richmond County Advance*, July 12, 1890, 1). "In common with other taxpayers," Curtis noted the following year, "I should gladly see the reasons for anticipating these good results stated with a little more definite detail than I have yet observed" (*Staten Islander*, April 8, 1891, 1). Curtis died in 1892 and so played no role in the referendum campaign of 1894.
28. *Staten Islander*, August 6, 1890, 2.
29. *Richmond County Standard*, June 21, 1890, 4.
30. *Richmond County Advance*, April 25, 1891, 4. The *Advance* remained hostile to the proposition over the next few years. See *Richmond County Advance*, January 23, 1892, 4; January 28, 1893, 4; and February 24, 1894, 4.

31. *Staten Islander,* June 14, 1890, 4, and December 27, 1890, 4.
32. Borelli, *Staten Island in the Nineteenth Century,* 129; *Staten Island Independent,* October 5, 1894, 2; *Staten Islander,* December 16, 1893, 1, and January 31, 1894, 8. Many saw Greenfield as "the man most responsible for bringing Staten Island into the Greater City" (McMillen, "Consolidation," 11; see also Albert E. Henschel, *Municipal Consolidation: Historical Sketches of Greater New York* [New York: Stettiner, Lambert, 1895], 18). Years later, Edward C. Bridgeman, president of Staten Island Savings Bank, implied that he had helped persuade Greenfield, but no records from the 1890s support his assertion (Edward Bridgeman to John Mitchel, March 9, 1916, Subject Files: Protests: Garbage Disposal, box 30, folder 276, JPM).
33. *Staten Islander,* June 11, 1890, 2.
34. Some proponents of consolidation viewed the initial criticisms as a reflexive obstructionism that would gradually subside (*Staten Islander,* August 6, 1890, 2, and April 15, 1891, 1).
35. *Richmond County Democrat,* April 9, 1892, 4.
36. *Staten Islander,* April 8, 1891, 1; January 20, 1892, 5; and November 11, 1893, 4.
37. *Richmond County Standard,* March 19, 1892, 4, and February 4, 1893, 4.
38. "For a Staten Island City," *Richmond County Democrat,* reprinted in *Staten Islander,* March 2, 1892, 2.
39. *Staten Islander,* March 12, 1892, 4.
40. *Staten Islander,* November 11, 1893, 4; *Brooklyn Daily Eagle,* November 8, 1893, 1; Hammack, *Power and Society,* 204.
41. *Richmond County Standard,* December 16, 1893, 4. How votes were counted was key to interpreting the results. Queens' totals were typically reported in aggregate, thus downplaying that Flushing had voted against consolidation. To say that Brooklyn barely voted in favor of consolidation is also misleading because residents of the dense downtown area voted solidly against the proposition, and only the votes of outlying areas just recently annexed by the city accounted for the positive result. For a more modern discussion of this issue, see Mark Toma, "The Impact of Institutional Structures on City–Country Consolidation Outcomes," *Public Choice* 34, no. 1 (1979): 117–22.
42. Hammack, *Power and Society,* 204; *Staten Islander,* December 16, 1893, 1, February 17, 1894, 3, and March 3, 1894, 2; *Richmond County Standard,* March 10, 1894, 4.
43. Krout, "Framing the Charter," 48; *Staten Island Independent,* October 5, 1894, 1; *Staten Islander,* September 26, 1894, 7, and October 3, 1894, 8; *Richmond County Advance,* October 27, 1894, 4.
44. *New York Times,* October 10, 1894, 5; *Staten Islander,* October 10, 1894, 1; Richard Dickenson, ed. and comp., *Holden's Staten Island: The History of Richmond County* (New York: Center for Migration Studies, 2002), 111. The estimated number of attendees varied widely.
45. *Staten Island Independent,* October 12, 1894, 1; *Richmond County Advance,* October 13, 1894, 1; and *Staten Islander,* October 10, 1894, 1. The other speakers included Reed Benedict, Edward D. Clark, former county clerk Cornelius A. Hart, Captain Jacob J. Housman, and Dr. I. K. Funk.
46. *Staten Islander,* September 26, 1894, 7, October 24, 1894, 2, October 27, 1894, 1, November 7, 1894, 1, and November 10, 1894, 1; *Staten Island Independent,* October 30, 1894, 3; *New York Herald,* January 13, 1895, 2.
47. Hammack, *Power and Society,* 209–17; Burrows and Wallace, *Gotham,* 1233–34; Krout, "Framing the Charter," 50–52.

48. William A. Shortt to Governor Levi P. Morton of New York, December 19, 1895, published in the *Brooklyn Daily Eagle*, December 26, 1895, 6. The Good Government Club had formed in 1894 as part of the government-reform movement that arose in Manhattan. In both New York and Staten Island, these movement clubs supported Fusion tickets that swept to victory in the 1894 elections.
49. *Staten Islander*, September 7, 1895, 1, and November 30, 1895, 1.
50. *Brooklyn Daily Eagle*, December 26, 1895, 6.
51. *New York Times*, December 31, 1895, 8.
52. Greenfield and Rawson debated this question in the *Staten Islander* prior to the 1894 referendum vote. See *Staten Islander*, October 6, 1894, 1, and October 10, 1894, 1.
53. *Staten Islander*, September 7, 1895, 1; Staten Island Chamber of Commerce (SICC), *Minutes of the Board of Directors*, July 29, 1895, 13, and August 20, 1895, 18, SICCR. Edward P. Doyle, a charter member of the Chamber of Commerce and a Democrat who served the town of Northfield on the Richmond County Board of Supervisors, forged the unified effort. Doyle later became a leader of local resistance in the Garbage War of 1916–1918.
54. *New York Times*, January 15, 1896, 8.
55. SICC, *Minutes*, November 19, 1895, 36, and December 17, 1895, 42–43; *New York Times*, December 21, 1895, 8; *Staten Islander*, December 21, 1895, 1; *Richmond County Advance*, December 21, 1895, 5.
56. "[Good Government Club] Meeting Announcement," December 18, 1895, and January 3, 1896, box 38, folder 21, AH; Shortt to Morton, December 19, 1895.
57. *Staten Islander*, November 30, 1895, 1, December 28, 1895, 2, and January 18, 1896, 1; *New York Times*, December 21, 1895, 8, December 31, 1895, 8, and January 11, 1896, 8.
58. *New York Times*, January 23, 1896, 9. The *Times* expressed sympathy with Scott's position—noting the "incongruity" of adding such a relatively distant "insular and isolated territory"—without affirming his rejection of Staten Island (*New York Times*, January 24, 1896, 4).
59. *New York Times*, January 24, 1896, 9, and February 6, 1896, 3.
60. *New York Times*, February 2, 1896, 9.
61. *New York Herald*, March 27, 1896, 3; *New-York Tribune*, April 4, 1896, 12, April 7, 1896, 4, and April 8, 1896, 14. Francis Scott again testified against Staten Island's participation, as did former Brooklyn congressman S. V. White, who asked sarcastically, "What man in Brooklyn cares for the erection of lampposts in New Dorp, Staten Island?" (*New-York Tribune*, April 8, 1896, 14). Mayor Strong opposed the terms of consolidation but professed indifference to Staten Island's (and Flushing's) presence in Greater New York.
62. *Staten Islander*, January 29, 1896, 3, and February 5, 1896, 1; *New York Herald*, February 2, 1896, 2.
63. George Greenfield to Clarence Lexow, February 15, 1896, unprocessed box, "Correspondence 1896" folder, CWL; *Staten Islander*, April 8, 1896, 1.
64. *Staten Islander*, April 11, 1896, 3; *New York Times*, April 7, 1896, 8.
65. *Staten Islander*, April 25, 1896, 1.
66. Hammack, *Power and Society*, 217–23; Burrows and Wallace, *Gotham*, 1233–34; Krout, "Framing the Charter," 56–60.
67. Hammack, *Power and Society*, 223–24; *Brooklyn Daily Eagle*, June 26, 1896, 6; *New-York Tribune*, June 10, 1896, 1.
68. *Staten Islander*, December 2, 1896, 4; January 2, 1897, 4; and January 23, 1897, 4.
69. *Brooklyn Daily Eagle*, January 7, 1897, 11, and August 2, 1896, 1.

70. *Brooklyn Daily Eagle*, January 18, 1895, 8.
71. *New York Times*, January 6, 1897, 4, and March 14, 1897, 22; *New-York Tribune*, April 6, 1897, 7.
72. *News Letter* (St. George, NY), December 12, 1896, 1, December 26, 1896, 1, January 9, 1897, 1, and January 16, 1897, 1; *Staten Islander*, December 5, 1896, 4, January 6, 1897, 4, and January 13, 1897, 4.
73. Chaired by Howard Bayne, a reform Democrat and future state senator, the SICC subcommittee included Greenfield, W. A. Shortt and De Witt Stafford (previous vocal supporters of a separate city, the former being soon replaced by real estate dealer David Tysen), and future borough president George Cromwell (*New York Times*, June 10, 1896, 1; SICC, *Minutes*, December 15, 1896, 42–43).
74. SICC, "Report of the Committee on the Greater New York Charter," in *Minutes*, February 16, 1897, 11; SICC, "Annual Report of the Board of Directors," January 18, 1898, 4, box 1, folder 5, SICCHS.
75. SICC, "Report of the Committee," 8.
76. SICC, "Report of the Committee," 9–11; Joseph Viteritti, "The Tradition of Municipal Reform: Charter Revision in Historical Context," *Proceedings of the Academy of Political Science* 37, no. 3 (1989): 20–22.
77. SICC, "Report of the Committee," 8; *Brooklyn Daily Eagle*, January 7, 1897, 11. In response, Staten Island's Assembly and Senate representatives succeeded in passing legislation that granted the infirmary an annual contribution of up to $10,000 (SICC, "Annual Report of the Board of Directors," January 18, 1898, 4).
78. *Staten Islander*, January 20, 1897, 1, and January 23, 1897, 1.
79. The borough's name was officially changed to "Staten Island Borough" in 1975.
80. *Staten Islander*, January 2, 1897, 1, and January 13, 1897, 4. Wiman's luster had been briefly tarnished in 1894 when he ran into financial and legal difficulties and was briefly jailed, but he was clear and free by 1896.
81. Hammack, *Power and Society*, 223.
82. Mark Ash, *The Greater New York Charter as Enacted in 1897* (Albany, NY: Weed-Parsons, 1897), iii–iv, cvii, 10–12; Mark Ash, *The Greater New York Charter as Enacted in 1897 and Amended in 1901* (New York: Voorhis, 1901), 90; Philemon Tecumseh Sherman, *Inside the Machine: Two Years in the Board of Aldermen, 1898–1899* (New York: Cooke & Fry, 1901), 22–23.
83. *Staten Islander*, March 2, 1897, 4.
84. Morris, *Memorial History of Staten Island*, 2:488.
85. Leng and Davis, *Staten Island and Its People*, 1:355–62, 505; Henry George Steinmeyer, *Staten Island, 1524–1898* (Staten Island, NY: Staten Island Historical Society, 1950), 75.
86. François Weil, *A History of New York*, trans. Jody Gladding (New York: Columbia University Press, 2004), 170.
87. *Richmond County Advance*, May 12, 1900, 1. After the heated municipal campaigns of 1894 resulted in victory for reform candidates and consolidation alike, the election of 1897—its date changed to accommodate the enactment of Greater New York on January 1, 1898—produced an extremely close result on Staten Island. Republican George Cromwell, an attorney and former New York assemblyman, bested the Democrat John L. Feeny after more than six months of legal wrangling about the election outcome. In 1899, the Democrats stormed back and won positions handily across the island (Morris, *Memorial History of Staten Island*, 2:258–59; *The Brown Book: A Biographical Record of Public Officials of the City of New York for 1898-9* [New York:

Martin Brown, 1899], 52–54; Loring McMillen, *Staten Island: The Cosmopolitan Era* [Richmond, NY: Staten Island Historical Society, 1952], 3; Borelli, *Staten Island in the Nineteenth Century*, 139-47).
88. *Brooklyn Daily Eagle*, April 16, 1899, 24.
89. *New-York Tribune*, July 28, 1898, 14.
90. *New York Times*, January 16, 1899, 6.
91. *New York Times*, August 8, 1899, 12; *Brooklyn Daily Eagle*, July 12, 1898, 13, August 7, 1899, 8, and February 20, 1900, 15.
92. *New York Times*, August 8, 1899, 12; *Brooklyn Daily Eagle*, June 5, 1900, 17, and October 24, 1900, 16.
93. Bird S. Coler, *The Financial Effects of Consolidation: An Address Delivered Before the People's Institute at Cooper Union on November 17, 1899* (New York: De Vinne Press, 1899), 5, 7.
94. Edward Dana Durand, *The Finances of New York City* (New York: Macmillan, 1898), 169.
95. "The Borough of Richmond Got Back Every Dollar Paid In AND MORE," Political Parties, box 1, "Wendall Willkie" folder, SIHS; New York Commission on Government Operations in the City of New York, *New York City in Transition: The February 1, 1960, Interim Report* (New York: n.p., 1960), 43; Douglas Muzzio, *Staten Islanders on Secession: A Report Submitted to the New York State Charter Commission for Staten Island* (New York: New York State Charter Commission, 1992), 29–31; Robert Berne, Dick Netzer, and Leanna Stiefel, *Status Quo Fiscal Study: An Analysis of New York City Expenditures and Revenues on Staten Island* (New York: Robert F. Wagner Graduate School of Public Service, New York University, 1992), 3; Joseph Viteritti, "Municipal Home Rule and the Conditions of Justifiable Secession," *Fordham Urban Law Journal* 23, no. 1 (1995): 59–60, 66; Vicki Been, Sam Dastrup, et al., *State of New York City's Housing & Neighborhoods* (New York: Furman Center for Real Estate and Urban Policy, New York University, 2011), 12, 24–25; Glynis Daniels and Michael H. Schill, *State of New York City's Housing & Neighborhoods* (New York: Furman Center for Real Estate and Urban Policy, New York University, 2011).
96. *New York Times*, April 12, 1897, 2, and December 4, 1908, 10; *Brooklyn Daily Eagle*, December 29, 1897, 6; City of New York, Department of Finance, *Comptroller's Monthly Report for December 1914 and from January 1, 1914, to December 31, 1914* (New York: M. B. Brown, 1915).
97. A dispute over such expenditures led to a brief suspension of public electricity in the fall of 1899. Coler initially intended to levy a special tax to cover the costs (*New-York Tribune*, January 8, 1898, 11; *Brooklyn Daily Eagle*, August 19, 1898, 9, September 28, 1899, 9, and October 4, 1899, 2, 17).
98. *Brooklyn Daily Eagle*, December 29, 1897, 6.
99. Leng and Davis, *Staten Island and Its People*, 1:362.
100. Flyer, c. 1909, emphasis in original, Political Parties Collection, box 1, "Wendall Wilkie" folder, SIHS; Charles McCormack to Richmond County, October 21, 1909, Political Parties Collection, box 1, "Democratic Party" folder, SIHS.
101. Daniel C. Kramer and Richard M. Flanagan, *Staten Island: Conservative Bastion in a Liberal City* (Lanham, MD: University Press of America, 2012), 119–33; Viteritti, "Municipal Home Rule"; Raphael Sonenshein, *The City at Stake: Secession, Reform, and the Battle for Los Angeles* (Princeton, NJ: Princeton University Press, 2004), 256–58.

3. Envisioning the Future: What Consolidation Would Bring to Staten Island, 1890–1909

1. On expansion and efficient services, see Jon C. Teaford, *City and Suburb: The Political Fragmentation of Metropolitan America, 1850–1970* (Baltimore: Johns Hopkins University Press, 1979), 39–40; Walter M. Rosenbaum and Gladys M. Kammerer, *Against Long Odds: The Theory and Practice of Successful Governmental Consolidation* (Beverly Hills, CA: Sage, 1974). For population rank, see Michael P. McCarthy, "The Philadelphia Consolidation of 1854: A Reappraisal," *Pennsylvania Magazine of History and Biography* 110, no. 4 (October 1986): 531–48; and Bernard J. Sauers, "A Political Process of Urban Growth: Consolidation of the South Side with the City of Pittsburgh, 1872," *Pennsylvania History* 41, no. 3 (July 1974): 264–87. On economic growth, see David Hammack, *Power and Society: Greater New York at the Turn of the Century* (New York: Russell Sage Foundation, 1982), 185–86; and Suzanne Leland and Kurt Thurmaier, "When Efficiency Is Unbelievable: Normative Lessons from 30 Years of City-County Consolidations," *Public Administration Review* 65, no. 4 (July–August 2005): 475–89. For a critique of this emphasis on ideology over the legal process for joining jurisdictions, see Richard C. Feiock, Jered B. Carr, and Linda S. Johnson, "Structuring the Debate on Consolidation: A Response to Leland and Thurmaier," *Public Administration Review* 66, no. 2 (March–April 2006): 274–78.
2. *Staten Islander*, April 15, 1891; September 26, 1894, 7; October 10, 1894, 1; and November 14, 1894, 2.
3. John R. Logan and Harvey L. Molotch, *Urban Fortunes: The Political Economy of Place* (Berkeley: University of California Press, 1987), 12; see pages 50–98 for an extended discussion of growth machines. Although Logan and Molotch examine a number of ways growth machines interact with municipal efforts at zoning, planning, and other activities, they do not explore movements to create or expand a local governing entity through annexation or consolidation. Political scientists became more drawn to Clarence Stone's regime theory, which amplifies the role of the public sector through its focus on coalitions of government officials with private interests. See Clarence N. Stone, "Urban Regimes and the Capacity to Govern: A Political Economy Approach," *Journal of Urban Affairs* 15 (1993): 1–28. They are less so now, as exemplified by the trenchant critique of regime theory by G. William Domhoff in "The Shortcomings of Rival Urban Theories," *Who Rules America?*, posted 2005, https://whorulesamerica.ucsc.edu/power/rival_urban_theories.html.
4. Logan and Molotch, *Urban Fortunes*, 13.
5. *Staten Islander*, October 13, 1894, 5.
6. *Staten Islander*, October 13, 1894, 5.
7. Leo C. Evans, "A Century Hence," *Staten Island Magazine* 1, no. 2 (September 1888): 70–76; George M. Root, "Commercial Supremacy of Staten Island's Water Front," *Staten Island Magazine* 1, no. 3 (October 1888): 116–20.
8. *Staten Islander*, October 10, 1894, 1, and December 27, 1894, 2.
9. *Staten Islander*, April 8, 1896, 1.
10. Josef W. Konvitz, "The Crises of Atlantic Port Cities, 1880–1920," *Comparative Studies in Society and History* 36, no. 2 (April 1994): 303–5. For a comprehensive history, see Carl W. Condit, *The Port of New York*, vols. 1–2 (Chicago: University of Chicago Press, 1981).
11. *Brooklyn Daily Eagle*, February 1, 1896, 1.
12. *Staten Islander*, October 13, 1894, 5.

13. *Staten Islander*, June 11, 1890, 2.
14. Years later David Tysen, a prominent Richmond County property holder and real estate dealer, recalled that he had persuaded an initially reluctant Green to add Staten Island to his scheme for Greater New York. Some local historians have repeated Tysen's claim, but its accuracy is highly unlikely in the absence of any corroborating evidence. In fact, Green clearly included Staten Island in one of his earliest public articulations of Greater New York and again in his petition to the legislature in 1890. See David Tysen, *Happenings Before and After Staten Island Became Part of Greater New York* (Staten Island, NY: Staten Island Chamber of Commerce, 1924), 13–14; New York (NY) Board of Commissioners of the Central Park, *Twelfth Annual Report of the Board of Commissioners of the Central Park for the Year Ending December 31, 1868* (New York: n.p., n.d.), 163; "Honorable Andrew H. Green and Greater New York" (undated and unattributed [likely John Foord]), 1, 14, 29, 34, box 1, folder 9, AHG; Andrew Green to the New York Legislature, March 4, 1890, in *Municipal Consolidation Inquiry* (New York: Stettiner, Lambert, 1893), 8, 23.
15. *Staten Islander*, May 7, 1892, 1.
16. *Staten Islander*, August 6, 1890, 2; *New York Times*, January 24, 1896, 9, and April 3, 1896, 1; *Staten Island Independent*, October 12, 1894, 1; *News Letter* (St. George, NY), December 19, 1896, 4.
17. *News Letter*, January 2, 1897, 4.
18. *World*, n.d., reprinted in *Staten Islander*, August 6, 1890, 2; *Staten Islander*, April 8, 1891, 4; *Richmond County Standard*, December 27, 1890, 1; *New York Times*, January 24, 1896, 9.
19. *Staten Islander*, October 13, 1894, 5.
20. *Staten Islander*, December 27, 1890, 4.
21. *Staten Islander*, April 8, 1896, 1.
22. *Brooklyn Daily Eagle*, April 4, 1897, 7.
23. *Staten Islander*, October 13, 1894, 5.
24. *Staten Islander*, December 27, 1894, 2.
25. *Richmond County Standard*, February 4, 1893, 4.
26. *Richmond County Advance*, February 24, 1894, 4.
27. *Staten Islander*, October 10, 1894, 1; Staten Island Chamber of Commerce (SICC), *Minutes of the Board of Directors*, November 19, 1895, 36, and December 17, 1895, 42–43, SICCR.
28. *Staten Islander*, October 13, 1894, 5.
29. *Staten Islander*, May 7, 1892, 1.
30. *Staten Islander*, January 31, 1894, 8.
31. *Brooklyn Daily Eagle*, December 26, 1895, 6; *Richmond County Standard*, March 10, 1894, 4.
32. *Staten Islander*, December 28, 1895, 2.
33. *Staten Islander*, December 13, 1890, 1.
34. *Staten Islander*, October 6, 1894, 1.
35. *Staten Islander*, October 13, 1894, 5.
36. *Brooklyn Daily Eagle*, December 26, 1895, 6.
37. *Staten Islander*, March 20, 1889, 5; *Richmond County Advance*, June 28, 1890, 1.
38. Hammack, *Power and Society*, 148–51; Edwin G. Burrows and Mike Wallace, *Gotham: A History of New York City to 1898* (Oxford: Oxford University Press, 1999), 1192–94.
39. Teaford, *City and Suburb*, 60–63; Albert E. Henschel, *Municipal Consolidation: Historical Sketches of Greater New York* (New York: Stettiner, Lambert, 1895), 18.

40. Testimony, Sub-Committee of the Joint Committee on the Affairs of Cities, *In the Matter of the Hearing in Relation to "the Greater New York"* (Albany, NY: Wynkoop Hallenbeck Crawford, 1896), 318.
41. *Staten Island Independent*, September 7, 1894, 2.
42. *Staten Islander*, April 4, 1891, 1; March 12, 1892, 4; and November 10, 1894, 1.
43. *New York World*, n.d., cited in *Staten Islander*, October 1, 1890, 2; *Staten Islander*, April 8, 1891, 1.
44. *Richmond County Sentinel*, March 16, 1889, 1.
45. *Staten Islander*, October 10, 1894, 1; *Staten Island Independent*, October 12, 1894, 1.
46. *Richmond County Standard*, April 11, 1891, 1.
47. *Staten Islander*, June 25, 1890, 4.
48. *Staten Islander*, March 7, 1896, 3.
49. *Brooklyn Daily Eagle*, April 23, 1896, 4.
50. *Richmond County Standard*, March 10, 1894, 4.
51. *Staten Islander*, September 29, 1894, 5.
52. *New York Herald*, February 25, 1896, 12; *Staten Islander*, March 7, 1896, 3.
53. *Staten Islander*, June 14, 1890, 4.
54. *Staten Islander*, June 11, 1890, 2.
55. *Staten Islander*, October 4, 1890, 6.
56. *Staten Islander*, October 6, 1894, 1.
57. David Hammack, "Reflections on the Creation of the Greater City of New York and Its First Charter," *New York Law School Law Review* 42, no. 3 (1998): 706–7; *New York Times*, March 2, 1903, 8.
58. *Brooklyn Daily Eagle*, January 18, 1895, 8, and March 4, 1897, 7.
59. *Staten Islander*, June 11, 1890, 2.
60. *Staten Islander*, April 8, 1891, 1, and November 14, 1894, 2.
61. *Richmond County Standard*, March 10, 1894, 4; *Richmond County Advance*, February 24, 1894, 4.
62. *Staten Island Independent*, October 23, 1894, 1.
63. *Richmond County Democrat*, June 27, 1891, 4, and April 18, 1891, 4.
64. *Staten Islander*, April 8, 1891, 1.
65. Arthur Hollick, "A Few Words About Our Water Supply," *Staten Island Magazine* 1, no. 1 (August 1888): 13; Teaford, *City and Suburb*, 59. For an excellent discussion of how water supply framed considerations of consolidation in Westchester, Queens, and Kings Counties, see Richardson Dilworth, *The Urban Origins of Suburban Autonomy* (Cambridge, MA: Harvard University Press, 2005), 68–90.
66. *Richmond County Advance*, April 5, 1890, 1, April 25, 1891, 8, September 24, 1892, 1, July 27, 1895, 1, 4, and January 11, 1896, 1; *Staten Islander*, April 3, 1897, 2; Martin V. Melosi, *Fresh Kills: A History of Consuming and Discarding in New York City* (New York: Columbia University Press, 2020), 53–61.
67. *Staten Islander*, April 4, 1891, 1, and April 8, 1891, 4.
68. *Staten Islander*, October 20, 1894, 6.
69. Mike Wallace, *Greater Gotham: A History of New York City from 1898 to 1919* (Oxford: Oxford University Press, 2017), 51–52; *Brooklyn Daily Eagle*, April 23, 1896, 4.
70. *Staten Islander*, June 25, 1890, 4, August 6, 1890, 2, December 13, 1890, 1, October 10, 1894, 1, and November 10, 1894, 1; *Richmond County Standard*, March 10, 1894, 4; *Brooklyn Daily Eagle*, July 22, 1894, 12.
71. Teaford, *Cities and Suburbs*, 45–46, 55; *Brooklyn Daily Eagle*, November 21, 1894, 12.

4. Hitching a Ride: Early Efforts to Tunnel to Staten Island, 1900–1909

1. Morrison would become Richmond Borough's commissioner of public works in 1915 and serve until his sudden death in 1918. See *Brooklyn Daily Eagle*, July 8, 1901, 6, and January 30, 1902, 16; *Sun* (New York), December 18, 1918, 7.
2. *New York Times*, July 24, 1869, 2; Herbert B. Reed, "The Planning and Building of Staten Island's Bridges," *Staten Island Historian* 26, no. 2 (April–June 1965): 12; *Brooklyn Daily Eagle*, October 8, 1881, 2, May 4, 1884, 9, and September 7, 1884, 10.
3. "Who Were There and What They Said," December 16, 1885, Ferries and Railroads Collection, box 1, SIIAS; *New York Times*, December 17, 1885, 1. The takeover enabled Wiman to construct a railroad bridge over the Arthur Kill to New Jersey, the first span connecting Staten Island to another land mass.
4. In Albany, the state legislature declined to take up the issue. Wiman's plan called for twin tunnels under the Narrows, estimated to cost $6 million. He continued to advance the idea in public remarks over the next few years, but other than the conducting of borings and soundings along the Bay Ridge shoreline, his promotion of the project did not lead to any significant developments. The departure of Robert Garrett II from the presidency of the B&O derailed Wiman's efforts, as did Wiman's own bankruptcy in 1893. See *Richmond County Standard*, August 9, 1890, 1; *New York Times*, August 5, 1890, 2; *Brooklyn Daily Eagle*, April 20, 1884, 10, February 15, 1891, 6, February 22, 1894, 4, and February 10, 1904, 4; *New York Times*, February 10, 1904, 7; *Congressional Record* 21 (September 29, 1890): 107, 22 (December 18, 1890): 646, and 22 (February 16, 1891): 2761; Richard Harris, "Industry and Residence: The Decentralization of New York City, 1900–1940," *Journal of Historical Geography* 19, no. 2 (1993): 175.
5. *Staten Islander*, August 6, 1890, 2; October 4, 1890, 2; and December 13, 1890, 1.
6. Additional speakers included William Van Clief, president of the SICC; Henry Morrison of the Tax Payers Alliance and North Side Board of Trade; Pliny E. Davis of the FWIA; and Daniel Moynahan of the West End (Brooklyn) Board of Trade. See *Sun*, May 16, 1908, 11; *Richmond County Advance*, May 6, 1908; Fifth Ward Improvement Association (FWIA), *Minutes*, May 18, 1908, SICCR; FWIA, "Annual Report of the Secretary," December 8, 1908, SICCR.
7. Staten Island Chamber of Commerce (SICC), "Tunnel to Staten Island: Arguments Before the Public Service Commission," May 15, 1908, transcript of meeting, 2, 8, 10, Black Box Collection, Tunnels, SIIAS; *Richmond County Advance*, May 16, 1908, 2.
8. SICC, "Tunnel to Staten Island," 2, 15. The quoted phrase came from David Tysen, who was not present at the hearing but whose written testimony was included in the SICC transcript of the meeting.
9. SICC, "Tunnel to Staten Island," 7.
10. SICC, "Tunnel to Staten Island," 3, 4, 6; *Richmond County Advance*, May 16, 1908, 2; *New York Times*, May 3, 1908, 7.
11. SICC, "Tunnel to Staten Island," 4, 9.
12. SICC, "Tunnel to Staten Island," 4. McAdoo eventually concluded that the line "would not be sufficient to warrant capital to engage in an enterprise of this kind" (SICC, *Eighteenth Annual Report* [Staten Island, NY, 1913], 12).
13. *New York Times*, February 23, 1908, C5. The populations of Brooklyn, Queens, and the Bronx in 1950 were 2,738,175; 1,550,849; and 1,451,277, respectively (Nathan

298   4. Hitching a Ride

     Kantrowitz, "Population," in *The Encyclopedia of New York City*, ed. Kenneth T. Jackson [New Haven, CT: Yale University Press, 1995], 921).

14. In fact, Blair and Van Clief, the SICC representatives, were also participating in a larger, citywide civic effort to get the PSC to commit to a "comprehensive and complete rapid-transit system for the entire City of New York" (SICC, "Tunnel to Staten Island," 4; *Richmond County Advance*, May 16, 1902, 2).
15. SICC, "Tunnel to Staten Island," 8.
16. SICC, "Tunnel to Staten Island," 5. Another argument raised but not reiterated was that a tunnel would serve well in time of war by easily allowing troops to move between the two forts at the entrance to New York Harbor (Fort Wadsworth and Fort Hamilton).
17. James Blaine Walker, *Fifty Years of Rapid Transit* (New York: Law Printing, 1918), 128–75; Clifton Hood, *722 Miles: The Building of the Subways and How They Transformed New York*, centennial ed. (Baltimore, MD: Johns Hopkins University Press, 2004), 26–28, 56–71. Hood's book is the best single volume on the developments leading to New York's first subway.
18. The Board of Rapid Transit commissioners indicated that there was some opposition on Staten Island to Subway Contract No. 1, a claim contradicted by James Blaine Walker in 1918 and the author's own investigation. See New York Board of Rapid Transit Railroad Commissioners, *Report of the Board of Rapid Transit Railroad Commissioners in the City of New York for the Year Ending December 31, 1901* (New York: Irving Press, 1902), 41; and Walker, *Fifty Years of Rapid Transit*, 152.
19. Subway Contract No. 2, signed in 1902, is the least studied of the formative New York City subway contracts. Two main factors account for its disregard. First, it had a limited scope: completion of the H layout in Manhattan and an extension into Brooklyn of the initial Manhattan-to-Bronx subway line provided for in Contract No. 1. Second, it followed so closely on the heels of Contract No. 1 and was signed with the same partner (Belmont's IRT) that the two are easily viewed as a single episode. See Peter Derrick, *Tunneling to the Future: The Story of the Great Subway Expansion That Saved New York* (New York: New York University Press, 2001), 33–43; Hood, *722 Miles*, 93–94, 119.
20. *Brooklyn Daily Eagle*, December 5, 1899, 2; December 23, 1899, 18; and January 9, 1900, 2.
21. Derrick, *Tunneling to the Future*, 42–43; Brian J. Cudahy, *A Century of Subways: Celebrating 100 Years of New York's Underground Railways* (New York: Fordham University Press, 2003), 31–32.
22. Derrick, *Tunneling to the Future*, 46–47, 54–56; Hood, *722 Miles*, 119–32.
23. SICC, *Minutes of the Board of Directors*, March 26, 1908, SICCR.
24. *Richmond County Advance*, November 19, 1904, 1. The North Shore Board of Trade was formed shortly thereafter, and the Tottenville Board of Trade and Village Improvement dated to 1896. Although some boards of trade were organized by industry, on Staten Island they functioned as local community subsets of the Chamber of Commerce, which maintained an island-wide focus. Both the chamber and the boards had overlapping members with similar backgrounds and concerns. See *Richmond County Advance*, January 7, 1905, 1, and January 21, 1905, 1; *New York Times*, January 10, 1896, 8.
25. The subway's impact on the Bronx became apparent within a few years of its opening in 1904. The Bronx was already growing by 35 percent between 1900 and 1905, and its rate of population growth increased by 59 percent over the next five years; that

meteoric growth continued through 1930 (Kantrowitz, "Population," 921; *Brooklyn Daily Eagle Almanac* [Brooklyn, NY: Brooklyn Daily Eagle, 1907], 166).
26. *Staten Islander*, May 9, 1900, 1.
27. The CTC was initially called and often referred to as the "Tunnel Committee" (*Staten Island World*, May 18, 1907, 1).
28. SICC, *Minutes*, March 26, 1908; *Richmond County Advance*, June 29, 1907, 1; *Staten Island News and Independent*, August 10, 1907, 1; *New York Times*, July 26, 1907, 6.
29. *Staten Island News and Independent*, August 10, 1907, 1; *Richmond County Herald*, July 27, 1907, 1.
30. *Richmond County Advance*, July 27, 1907, 1; *Brooklyn Daily Eagle*, May 24, 1907, 11, and July 2, 1907, 10; *Staten Island World*, July 27, 1907, 5.
31. Blair chaired the SICC's Committee on Parks, whose report for 1902 recommended that thousands of acres be set aside for parks. By 1908, Blair was the chamber's vice president, but he died at age sixty in 1910 ("Blair, Charles H.," in *Men and Women in America: A Biographical Dictionary of Contemporaries* [New York: L. R. Hammersly, 1909], 172; Charles P. Blair, 1900, "United States Census, 1900," database with images, FamilySearch, https://www.familysearch.org/ark:/61903/1:1:MSGL-B1Q; *New York Times*, April 9, 1910, 11).
32. *Richmond County Herald*, August 3, 1907, 4; George Von Kromer, 1900, "United States Census, 1900," database with images, FamilySearch, https://www.familysearch.org/ark:/61903/1:1:MSLY-6R7; George Von Kromer, Richmond Ward 4, Richmond, NY, "United States Census, 1910," database with images, FamilySearch, https://familysearch.org/ark:/61903/1:1:M5SK-R24, citing enumeration district (ED) ED 1323, sheet 10B, family 194, microfilm publication T624, 1982, roll 1073, FHL microfilm 1,375,086, National Archives and Records Administration, Washington, DC; George Von Kromer, 1920, "United States Census, 1920," database with images, FamilySearch, https://www.familysearch.org/ark:/61903/1:1:MJJF-R57.
33. *Richmond County Advance*, January 14, 1905, 1; *Staten Island News and Independent*, December 22, 1906, 1.
34. *New York Times*, May 2, 1907, 11; *Staten Islander*, May 4, 1907, 1, and May 11, 1907, 1; *Staten Island World*, May 11, 1907, 1, and May 18, 1907, 1.
35. These trains connected Jersey City with the West Village before turning northward under Sixth Avenue and ending at Thirty-Third Street. Today they are known as the PATH lines and are operated by the Port Authority of New York and New Jersey.
36. *Richmond County Advance*, March 21, 1908, 1.
37. *Richmond County Advance*, April 4, 1908, 1, May 16, 1908, 12, October 3, 1908, 8, and December 12, 1908, 2; *Staten Islander*, August 5, 1908, 4; *Brooklyn Daily Eagle*, December 6, 1908, 4; *New York Times*, March 13, 1909, 6; SICC, *Minutes*, December 18, 1908; FWIA, "Annual Report of the Secretary," December 8, 1908.
38. *Staten Islander*, August 5, 1908, 4; SICC, *Minutes*, December 18, 1908, as well as January 19, March 25, and April 23, 1909.
39. *New York Times*, June 28, 1907, 4; *Brooklyn Daily Eagle*, September 23, 1908, 2.
40. FWIA, *Minutes*, June 25, 1909.
41. *New York Times*, February 15, 1906, 2, and April 12, 1907, 18.
42. SICC, "Tunnel to Staten Island," 2–14.
43. Maple Avenue is now Lynhurst Avenue, and Center Street is currently Tompkins Avenue.
44. *Brooklyn Daily Eagle*, September 23, 1908, 2, and September 24, 1908, 4; *Richmond County Advance*, September 26, 1908, 1.

45. Public Service Commission (PSC), *Proceedings* 3 (1908): 1602.
46. Beyond the divergent maps, the collected transcript of the PSC meeting was suggestive of the ongoing strain between the participants because Von Kromer's testimony was not included in it (SICC, "Tunnel to Staten Island," 2–14).
47. SICC, "Tunnel to Staten Island," map after p. 10.
48. *Richmond County Advance*, February 1, 1908, 4; *Brooklyn Daily Eagle*, July 11, 1908, 6. The CTC booklet, featuring the voices of residents interviewed, "gives several hundred reasons why Staten Islanders believe their section of the greater city [is] the very best in which to live" (as quoted in the *Daily Eagle*).
49. *Brooklyn Daily Eagle*, September 3, 1908, 6.
50. *Sun*, January 26, 1908, 25; *Evening Post* (New York), September 17, 1908, 8; *Brooklyn Daily Eagle*, September 3, 1909, 38.
51. *New York Times*, August 9, 1908, C5, and September 25, 1908, 16.
52. *New York Times*, October 11, 1908, SM7.
53. *New York Times*, October 4, 1907, 7.
54. SICC, *Minutes*, August 15 and September 17, 1895, as well as February 18, 1896, and March 16, 1897; *New York Times*, February 21, 1902, 16.
55. *Richmond County Advance*, July 26, 1902, 4; January 3, 1903, 4; December 5, 1903, 1; February 25, 1905, 2; and May 12, 1906, 1.
56. The Richmond Light and Railroad Company and the Staten Island Midland Railway Company ran electric lines that largely operated as one. The steam railroads of the Staten Island Rapid Transit Railway Company and the Staten Island Railway Company were controlled by the B&O and operated jointly (PSC, *Report of the PSC for the First District of the State of NY, 1907*, vol. 1 [Albany, NY: J. B. Lyon, 1908], 118; PSC, *Report of the PSC for the First District of the State of NY, 1909*, vol. 1 [Albany, NY: J. B. Lyon, 1910], 352–88).
57. *Richmond County Advance*, November 23, 1901, 1; January 17, 1903, 1; February 18, 1905, 4; May 13, 1905, 1; and February 3, 1906, 1. Staten Islanders' dissatisfaction with issues related to service and conditions on the local lines led to a series of hearings before the PSC in November and December 1907 that resulted in orders for improvements by Richmond Light and Railroad Company and the Staten Island Rapid Transit Railway Company. See *New York Times*, November 9, 1907, 8, and December 28, 1907, 16; *Staten Island World*, December 14, 1907, 5; *Richmond County Advance*, December 21, 1907, 2, and January 4, 1908, 3; and PSC, *Proceedings* 1 (1907): 58, 93, 408–10.
58. *Richmond County Advance*, March 10, 1906, 4.
59. *Richmond County Herald*, October 12, 1907, 4.
60. David Tysen, *Happenings Before and After Staten Island Became Part of Greater New York* (Staten Island, NY: Staten Island Chamber of Commerce, 1924), 17, 27.
61. *Richmond County Advance*, May 13, 1905, 1, and September 30, 1.
62. *New York Times*, July 2, 1902, 16.
63. *Staten Island World*, October 4, 1907, 5; *Richmond County Advance*, October 5, 1907, 1.
64. *Richmond County Advance*, September 28, 1907, 2.
65. *New York Times*, October 4, 1907, 7.
66. *New York Times*, March 13, 1903, 7.
67. Hood, *722 Miles*, 120; Walker, *Fifty Years of Rapid Transit*, 199–200; *New York Times*, May 16, 1902, 3; Executive Committee of the New York Board of Trade and Transportation, *Report*, August 31, 1905, box 70, 1905 folder, GM; Municipal Art Society of New York, *A Discussion of the Rapid Transit Problem in and About New York by the City*

Plan Committee of the Municipal Art Society (New York: Municipal Art Society of New York, 1905), 40.
68. *New York Times*, October 2, 1890, 4.
69. *Richmond County Advance*, December 16, 1905, 1, and January 20, 1906, 1, 5; Charles W. Leng and William T. Davis, *Staten Island and Its People, a History, 1609-1929*, 5 vols. (New York: Lewis Historical, 1929–1933), 2:581.
70. Hood, *722 Miles*, 105–12.
71. *Staten Islander*, May 4, 1907, 1; *Staten Island World*, December 3, 1910, 2.
72. Derrick, *Tunneling to the Future*, 73–79.
73. *Staten Islander*, December 10, 1898, 4; *Staten Island News and Independent*, February 2, 1907, 4; *Staten Island World*, May 18, 1907, 4.
74. *Staten Island World*, May 18, 1907, 4.
75. FWIA, "Annual Report of the Secretary," December 8, 1908.

5. Leaving the Station: The Dual Contracts and Aftermath, 1909–1919

1. See, for example, *Ithaca Daily Journal*, August 18, 1911, 5; *Watertown Daily Times*, November 25, 1911, 3; *Fayetteville Bulletin*, August 11, 1911, 7; *Buffalo Times*, November 18, 1911, 2.
2. Tom W. Jackson, *New York Press*, undated but printed in *Staten Island World*, May 20, 1912, 1.
3. Peter Derrick offers the most authoritative treatment of the Dual Contracts in *Tunneling to the Future: The Story of the Great Subway Expansion That Saved New York* (New York: New York University Press, 2001). The essentials are also well conveyed in Clifton Hood, *722 Miles: The Building of the Subways and How They Transformed New York*, centennial ed. (Baltimore, MD: Johns Hopkins University Press, 2004).
4. Hood, *722 Miles*, 136–42; Derrick, *Tunneling to the Future*, 65–80; James Blaine Walker, *Fifty Years of Rapid Transit, 1864–1917* (New York: Law Print, 1918), 217–18.
5. *New York Times*, March 21, 1908, 13, and June 13, 1908, 11; *Sun* (New York), May 27, 1908, 1; *Brooklyn Life*, May 30, 1908, 8; *Richmond County Advance*, June 20, 1908, 4.
6. Mike Wallace, *Greater Gotham: A History of New York City from 1898 to 1919* (New York: Oxford University Press, 2017), 126–29; *Richmond County Advance*, November 4, 1905, 1, and November 11, 1905, 4.
7. Wallace, *Greater Gotham*, 136. See also *New York Times*, October 15, 1909, 3; October 22, 1909, 2; October 24, 1909, 2; October 25, 1909, 2; and October 27, 1909, 3.
8. Public Service Commission (PSC), *Proceedings* 4 (1909): 831.
9. PSC, *Proceedings* 4 (1909): 853.
10. Derrick, *Tunneling to the Future*, 86. Fusion/Republican candidates won every position on the powerful Board of Estimate and Apportionment except the borough presidency of Queens and the city mayoralty. Hearst's candidacy diverted votes from the Fusion candidate, enabling Gaynor to win. Gaynor's position on subways was critical of all players: the IRT, the old RTB, and the PSC. For a concise discussion of Gaynor as mayor, see Kenneth Finegold, *Experts and Politicians: Reform Challenges to Machine Politics in New York, Cleveland, and Chicago* (Princeton, NJ: Princeton University Press, 1995), 45–53. For a full-length biography, see Lately Thomas, *The Mayor Who Mastered New York: The Life & Opinions of William L. Gaynor* (New York: Morrow, 1969).

11. PSC, *Proceedings* 4 (1909): 913; *Richmond County Advance*, November 6, 1909, 4, and December 4, 1909, 1; *New York Times*, December 5, 1909, 5.
12. The leading Board of Estimate members were Mayor William Gaynor, Comptroller William Prendergast, and Board of Aldermen president John Purroy Mitchel, all of whom had entered office at the beginning of the year and been appointed by the board as members of the Transit Committee (*New York Times*, February 17, 1910, 1; *Sun*, February 17, 1910, 3).
13. Staten Island Chamber of Commerce (SICC), *Minutes of the Board of Directors*, November 29, 1909, and February 17, 1910, SICCR.
14. Both SICC president William Van Clief and secretary Cornelius Kolff served on the Citizens Rapid Transit Committee.
15. SICC, *Minutes*, March 24, 1910, and April 9, 1910.
16. Frederick Cozzens to William Gaynor, William Prendergast, and John Purroy Mitchel, February 28, 1910, in Fifth Ward Improvement Association (FWIA), SICCR; NYC Board of Estimate, *Journal of Proceedings: Financial and Franchise Matters*, January–March 1910, 967.
17. These groups included the Staten Island and Bayonne Development Company and the Taxpayers' Alliance of the Borough of Richmond. See PSC, *Proceedings* 5 (1910): 235, 421, 433, 562.
18. Keith D. Revell, *Building Gotham: Civic Culture & Public Policy in New York City, 1898–1938* (Baltimore: Johns Hopkins University Press, 2003), 106; Derrick, *Tunneling to the Future*, 77–79.
19. Roy Rosenzweig and Elizabeth Blackmar, *The Park and the People: A History of Central Park* (Ithaca, NY: Cornell University Press, 1992), 81–87.
20. Derrick, *Tunneling to the Future*, 78, 310–11; Robert M. Fogelson, *Downtown: Its Rise and Fall, 1880–1950* (New Haven, CT: Yale University Press, 2001), 91.
21. Henry DeForest Baldwin, "Charter Revisions Commission's Report," *Municipal Affairs* 4, no. 4 (December 1900): 771; Citizens Union, *In the Matter of the Method of Financing Certain Branches of the Triborough Subway* (New York: s.n., 1911), 2–6.
22. In 1896, preconsolidated New York generated about $3 million through special assessments (Wilson L. Gill, *City Problems* [New York: Patriotic League, 1909], 48).
23. Derrick, *Tunneling to the Future*, 336; *New York Times*, February 17, 1910, 11; *Sun*, February 17, 1910, 3; *Brooklyn Daily Eagle*, April 5, 1910, 5; *Evening Post* (New York), August 1, 1910, 4.
24. PSC, *Proceedings* 4 (1909): 839; *Brooklyn Daily Eagle*, January 25, 1910, 1, January 26, 1910, 6, 15, and April 5, 1910, 25; *New York Times*, February 27, 1910, C7, and April 5, 1910, 20; *Richmond County Advance*, April 9, 1910, 1; Edward M. Bassett, "Remarks," in *Proceedings of the Sixth National Conference on City Planning* (Boston: University Press, 1914), 253, cited in Derrick, *Tunneling to the Future*, 336.
25. PSC, *Proceedings* 4 (1909): 667–68; *Evening Post*, August 6, 1909, 1, and May 4, 1910, 3; *Brooklyn Daily Eagle*, September 9, 1909, 24, and June 12, 1910, 64.
26. *Brooklyn Daily Eagle*, February 10, 1910, 5, March 3, 1910, 7, and April 5, 1910, 8; *New York Times*, February 13, 1910, X10.
27. *Evening Post*, March 10, 1908, 6; *Brooklyn Daily Eagle*, June 2, 1910, 4, and September 29, 1910, 4.
28. *Brooklyn Daily Eagle*, July 26, 1910, 2.
29. A search through several local Staten Island newspapers, the *Brooklyn Daily Eagle*, the *New York Times*, the *Evening World* (New York), the *Evening Post*, and the *Sun* yielded no indication of any public comments made by Cromwell.

30. *Richmond County Advance*, January 29, 1910, 3, April 9, 1910, 1, and December 30, 1911, 1; *Staten Islander*, April 6, 1910, 4; *Brooklyn Daily Eagle*, December 27, 1911, 4, and January 3, 1912, 2; *New York Times*, December 27, 1911, 11.
31. SICC, *Minutes*, March 24, 1910. South Brooklyn was strongly opposed to special assessments in large part because its line to Forty-Third Street was already underway, and discussions of extensions to Fort Hamilton and Coney Island were so far along that to expect those areas to pay for them was viewed as a "breach of faith" (*Brooklyn Daily Eagle*, March 3, 1910, 9, and April 6, 1910, 3).
32. Derrick, *Tunneling to the Future*, 123–49; Hood, *722 Miles*, 145–50; Walker, *Fifty Years of Rapid Transit*, 221–24.
33. Ralph Peters to William Gaynor, October 5, 1910, Subject Files, box 19, folder 201, WJG; Samuel Rea to James McCrea, November 22, 1910, box 142, folder 1, SR; Samuel Rea, "New York Subway Situation," August 7, 1911, box 142, folder 5, SR; *New York Times*, April 26, 1911, 1.
34. Derrick, *Tunneling to the Future*, 150–51.
35. George Cromwell to William Gaynor, December 21, 1910, Subject Files, box 19, folder 201, WJG; *New York Times*, December 22, 1910, 1; *Staten Islander*, December 24, 1910, 1; SICC, *Minutes*, January 13, 1911; PSC, *Proceedings* 6 (1911): 6; *New York Times*, January 11, 1911, 2; Derrick, *Tunneling to the Future*, 151–52; Hood, *722 Miles*, 150–51.
36. *Staten Island World*, January 14, 1911, 1; *Richmond County Advance*, January 14, 1911, 1.
37. SICC, *Minutes*, January 13, 1911.
38. *Richmond County Herald*, August 3, 1907, 1; *Richmond County Advance*, January 29, 1910, 3, and July 30, 1910, 2; *Brooklyn Daily Eagle*, January 20, 1911, 2.
39. Mayor Gaynor, "Minority Report," January 11, 1911, in New York State, Joint Legislative Committee to Investigate the Public Service Commission, *Complete Report*, vol. 6 (Albany: New York State, 1917), 244.
40. *Staten Island World*, January 14, 1911, 4; *Richmond County Advance*, January 14, 1911, 1.
41. Tysen, Van Clief, Cornelius Kolff, and Henry Morrison spoke for the SICC, P. C. Davis for the FWIA, Max Ruttenau for the Grasmere Improvement Association, and Max Thaten likely for the Stapleton Business Men's League. The Taxpayer's Association, the Concord Property Owners' Association, and the Stapleton Business Men's League were also represented. See *Staten Islander*, January 21, 1911, 1; *Staten Island World*, January 21, 1911, 1, and January 28, 1911, 2; *New York Times*, January 19, 1911, 2; PSC, *Proceedings* 6 (1911): 32.
42. *Staten Islander*, January 21, 1911, 4; *New York Times*, January 19, 1911, 2.
43. *New York Times*, January 19, 1911, 2; *Staten Islander*, January 21, 1911, 1, 4; *Staten Island World*, January 21, 1911, 1, 4.
44. Hood, *722 Miles*, 153.
45. *New York Times*, January 19, 1911, 1.
46. Derrick, *Tunneling to the Future*, 123–58.
47. *Richmond County Advance*, December 17, 1910, 4.
48. *Richmond County Advance*, January 28, 1911, 4. See also the optimism in the *Staten Islander*, January 25, 1911, 4.
49. *Richmond County Democrat* quoted in *Richmond County Advance*, December 31, 1910, 2.
50. *Brooklyn Daily Eagle*, January 26, 1911, 2; *Staten Islander*, January 28, 1911, 1.
51. Derrick, *Tunneling to the Future*, 159.
52. Derrick, *Tunneling to the Future*, 151–52, 161–62, 166–69; Hood, *722 Miles*, 150–51.

53. Derrick, *Tunneling to the Future*, 158, 169; Hood, *722 Miles*, 154; *New York Times*, January 28, 1911, 6, February 8, 1911, 18, March 16, 1911, 18, and March 22, 1911, 10.
54. George McAneny to "conferees" (Transit Committee members and PSC members), March 5, 1911, box 72, 1911 (3) folder, GM.
55. *Brooklyn Daily Eagle*, March 2, 1911, 1–2.
56. New York City Board of Estimate and Apportionment and New York State Public Service Commission, First District, *Report of a Committee with Relations to Pending Proposals for Construction, Equipment, and Operation of Rapid Transit Lines, and Upon the General Transit Situation in the City of New York* (New York: M. B. Brown Printing and Binding, June 5, 1911), 8–9; hereafter cited as Conferees, *Report*.
57. *Brooklyn Daily Eagles*, May 25, 1911, 7.
58. *Brooklyn Daily Eagle*, March 2, 1911, 2. For the South Brooklyn criticism of Cromwell's location for the spur to Staten Island, see *Brooklyn Daily Eagle*, March 7, 1911, 7, and March 17, 1911, 7.
59. *Brooklyn Daily Eagle*, February 2, 1911, 12.
60. *Richmond County Advance*, February 18, 1911, 4, and April 22, 1911, 4.
61. SICC, *Minutes*, April 28, 1911. The SICC's Subway and Transit Committee now included Gugy Irving, A. L Schwab, Charles A. Drucklieb, Thomas A Fulton, Charles A. Bruns, Louis Tribus, Charles E. Griffith, Cornelius Kolff, Fred Cozzens, David Tysen, and A. B. Pouch as chair.
62. *Richmond County Advance*, May 13, 1911, 2.
63. *Richmond County Advance*, May 20, 1911, 1, 4. The SICC remained disinclined to speak forcefully to the conferees as the report was readied for release. At its June 9 meeting, the SICC Board of Directors buried in committee a motion by Max Ruttenau to file "a protest . . . with the Board of Estimate and Apportionment against the letting of any contract for the building of a subway which does not recognize SI" (SICC, *Minutes*, June 9, 1911).
64. At its May 11, 1911, meeting, for example, the Board of Estimate heard communications from eleven individuals and organizations in the three other outer boroughs who were promoting "additional rapid transit facilities." On May 18 another four and on May 25 another ten wrote with similar requests (Board of Estimate and Apportionment, *Minutes: Financial and Franchise Matters*, part 1, vol. 2 [April 1, 1911–June 30, 1911]: 1888–89, 1945, 2046).
65. Hood, *722 Miles*, 155. The amounts of financing provided by the city, the IRT, and the BRT were $123 million, $75.8 million, and $50.4 million, respectively.
66. Conferees, *Report*, 24.
67. William J. Wilgus, "Preliminary Study for a Greater New York Belt Line," 1913, box 48, "Greater NY Belt Line" folder, WJW; Timothy S. Williams to Calvin Tomkins, June 2, 1911, box 4, folder 2, TSW; Benjamin Miller, *Fat of the Land: Garbage in New York, the Last Two Hundred Years* (New York: Four Walls Eight Windows, 2000), 151–52.
68. Conferees, *Report*, 23–25, 28; *Staten Islander*, June 14, 1911, 1; *New York Times*, June 14, 1911, 1.
69. *Staten Islander*, June 14, 1911, 1, 4.
70. *Richmond County Advance*, June 17, 1911, 4.
71. *Richmond County Advance*, June 17, 1911, 4.
72. David Tysen, *Happenings Before and After Staten Island Became Part of Greater New York* (Staten Island, NY: Staten Island Chamber of Commerce, 1924), 29–30.

73. Tysen, *Happenings*, 29–30; Derrick, *Tunneling to the Future*, 158. Derrick reports that "in all accounts of the Committee's actions the two other members, Cromwell and Miller, are seldom mentioned and, in fact, had very little impact on the eventual plan that was devised."
74. George Cromwell to George McAneny et al., June 5, 1911, Correspondence of the Richmond Borough President, vol. 30 (March 16, 1911–August 5, 1911), SIIAS; Conferees, *Report*, 85–88.
75. *Richmond County Advance*, June 17, 1911, 4.
76. *Staten Island World*, May 23, 1912, 4; New York City Board of Estimate and Apportionment and New York State Public Service Commission, First District, "Report of a Committee with Relations to Pending Proposals for Construction, Equipment, and Operation of Rapid Transit Lines, and upon the General Transit Situation in the City of New York," drafts, New York, June 5, 1911, box 72, 1911 (2) and 1911 (3) folders, GM, hereafter cited as McAneny Drafts.
77. Merill spoke before what became known as the Thompson Committee, which was investigating the developments leading to the Dual Contracts (New York State, Joint Legislative Committee Appointed to Investigate the Public Service Commission, *Minutes and Testimony*, vol. 6 [Albany: New York State, 1916], 704–5).
78. McAneny Drafts; Conferees, *Report*, n.p.
79. *New York Times*, January 19, 1911, 1.
80. *Richmond County Advance*, January 21, 1911, 4. The *Advance* assumed in its calculation of votes on the Board of Estimate that McAneny would vote in favor of any proposal for a Staten Island tunnel. McAneny did not weigh in on Cromwell's push for a route to St. George in that interview.
81. George McAneny, "Memorandum of Modifications in the Pending Proposition of the Interborough Rapid Transit Company Suggested by Members of the Board of Estimate and Apportionment," January 23, 1911, box 43, "Subway Construction, ca. 1909–1914" folder, JPM.
82. *Brooklyn Daily Eagle*, February 17, 1911, 6.
83. McAneny, "Memorandum of Modifications."
84. McAneny, "Memorandum of Modifications"; Derrick, *Tunneling to the Future*, 157, 164–69.
85. J. F. Calderwood to Mr. Kingsley L. Martin, April 27, 1910, Subject Files, box 19, folder 200, WJG; Timothy S. Williams to George McAneny, June 6, 1911, box 4, folder 2, TSW; Timothy S. Williams to Travis Whitney, March 12, 1912, box 4, folder 1, TSW.
86. *Richmond County Advance*, June 24, 1911, 4.
87. *New York Times*, May 16, 1912, 7.
88. William Gaynor to George Cromwell, July 25, 1911, Correspondence Sent, box 2, folder 54, WJG.
89. Derrick, *Tunneling to the Future*, 186; Hood, *722 Miles*, 157. The BRT accepted the McAneny Report a few days after its release, whereas the IRT, taking exception to financial guarantees offered to its rival but not to itself, rejected the proposal and continued to negotiate with McAneny and the PSC.
90. *Staten Islander*, June 21, 1911, 1; *Richmond County Advance*, July 15, 1911, 3.
91. *New York Times*, December 4, 1911, 7.
92. *New York Times*, February 16, 1912, 7; *Richmond County Advance*, February 17, 1912, 1; *Staten Islander*, February 17, 1912, 4, and February 24, 1912, 4; Conferees Report to Board of Estimate and Appropriation, February 13, 1912, and Board of Estimate and

Appropriations Resolution, February 21, 1912, box 72, folder 1912, GM; PSC, *Proceedings* 7 (1912): 146–48, 152.
93. *Staten Islander*, May 18, 1912, 4, and May 22, 1912, 4; *Staten Island World*, May 15, 1912, 1, May 17, 1912, 4, and May 21, 1912, 1; *New York Times*, May 16, 1912, 7; Derrick, *Tunneling to the Future*, 206–10.
94. *New York Times*, May 16, 1912, 7.
95. Samuel Rea to William W. Mills, December 20, 1910, box 141, folder 6, SR; John F. Stover, *History of the Baltimore and Ohio Railroad* (West Lafayette, IN: Purdue University Press, 1987), 199–201.
96. *New York Times*, May 15, 1912, 1, May 16, 1912, 7, May 21, 1912, 3, and June 15, 1912, 6; PSC, *Proceedings* 7 (1912): 443–45, 469, 566–67.
97. *New York Times*, June 14, 1912, 6.
98. *New York Times*, May 23, 1912, 6.
99. *Staten Islander*, August 31, 1912, 1; September 14, 1912, 4; and September 18, 1912, 2.
100. Cost and earnings projections of proposed subway lines, April 10 and 12, 1912, and undated, box 72, 1912 folder, GM; Derrick, *Tunneling to the Future*, 211.
101. *Richmond County Advance*, May 18, 1912, 4.
102. SICC, *Minutes*, December 29, 1911, and May 23, 1912.
103. SICC, *Minutes*, May 23, 1912, and September 19, 1912. This tunnel committee retained Morrison, Ruttenau, and William J. Welsh and added Kolff.
104. SICC, *Minutes*, January 16, 1913, and February 20, 1913.
105. Derrick, *Tunneling to the Future*, 213–22, 367; Walker, *Fifty Years of Rapid Transit*, 232–41.
106. *New York Times*, August 3, 1913, 2.
107. *Richmond County Advance*, October 31, 1913, 1, and October 24, 1913, 1; *Staten Island World*, October 25, 1913, 1.
108. *Staten Island World*, October 25, 1913, 1, and November 4, 1913, 1.
109. *New York Times*, November 2, 1913, 8.
110. *Staten Islander*, October 29, 1913, 1.
111. *Staten Islander*, October 29, 1913, 1.
112. *Staten Islander*, October 29, 1913, 1; *Richmond County Advance*, October 31, 1913, 1.
113. *Richmond Country Advance*, October 24, 1913, 1; *New York Times*, October 25, 1913, 1. See also *Staten Islander*, October 29, 1913, 1. As the *Advance* rightly observed before the partisan squabbling began over taking credit for the idea, free transfers were essentially a "bone to Staten Island" in light of the abandonment of the tunnel plan (*Richmond County Advance*, September 12, 1913, 4).
114. *Richmond County Advance*, November 5, 1913, 1, and November 7, 1913, 1; *New York Times*, November 6, 1913, 1.
115. *Richmond County Advance*, November 7, 1913, 4.
116. *Richmond County Advance*, October 22, 1915, 1; *Staten Islander*, October 23, 1915, 1. For an especially useful discussion of a direct route to Manhattan, see "Transcript of Conference on a Staten Island Subway," October 9, 1918, 2, 3, 9, Subject Files, box 37, folder 375, JFH.
117. The Dual Contracts debacle likely contributed to the virulence and vigilantism of the resistance to the plant. For a full account of the Garbage War, see Martin V. Melosi, *Fresh Kills: A History of Consuming and Discarding in New York City* (New York: Columbia University Press, 2020), 87–119.
118. "Transcript of Conference on a Staten Island Subway," 6.

119. In early 1919 at newly elected governor Al Smith's request, the state legislature had created the TCC to oversee the development of new subway lines for New York City. Smith's intent was to eliminate the squabbling that pervaded the PSC and slowed completion of the Dual Contract routes by adopting a one-person organizational structure used by the federal government during World War I. Under the new law, the PSC retained its regulatory role in matters of rates and service of existing means of transit but with a clear hierarchy of one commissioner and three deputies. The Transit Construction Commission would also have a single commissioner with just one deputy and would assume the PSC's responsibility for new construction. See Alfred Smith, "The Governor's Message," January 1, 1919, in *Documents of the Senate of the State of New York; Documents of the Assembly of the State of New York* (Albany, NY: J. B. Lyon, 1921), 7–8; *New York Times*, January 10, 1919, 13; "Documents, Reports, and Legislation," *American Economic Review* 11, no. 3 (1921): 544.
120. James Nolan, "Subway Report to the Borough President's Advisory Committee," January 4, 1921, printed in *Richmond County Advance*, January 8, 1921, 3; *New York Times*, May 15, 1920, 26; *Richmond County Advance*, May 15, 1920, 1; New York Board of Estimate and Apportionment, *Minutes* 2 (April–May 1920): 2110–18. The widely reported price tag for the TCC-proposed tunnel was misleading because the project was identified as a dual-purpose tunnel but did not include the additional $10 million needed to construct a tube large enough to handle freight.
121. Derrick, *Tunneling to the Future*, 1.
122. Walker, *Fifty Years of Rapid Transit*, 242–52, 260–61.

6. Planning the Region: The Hylan Tunnel and the Politics of Commerce, 1920–1923

1. For classic articulations from the respective vantage point of reformers and machine politicians, see Lincoln Steffens, *The Shame of the Cities* (New York: McClure, Phillips, 1904); and George Washington Plunkitt and William L. Riordan, *Plunkitt of Tammany Hall: A Series of Very Plain Talks on Very Practical Politics* (New York: McClure, Phillips, 1905).
2. For the premier history of politics on Staten Island, see Daniel C. Kramer and Richard M. Flanagan, *Staten Island: Conservative Bastion in a Liberal City* (Lanham, MD: University Press of America, 2012).
3. See, for example, Clifford W. Patton, *Battle for Municipal Reform* (Washington, DC: 1940); and Charles Garrett, *The LaGuardia Years: Machine and Reform Politics in New York City* (New Brunswick, NJ: Rutgers University Press, 1961). For the staying power of this perspective, see, for example, Robert Caro, *The Power Broker: Robert Moses and the Fall of New York* (New York: Knopf, 1974).
4. For an early and seminal example of this approach, see Samuel P. Hays, "The Politics of Reform in Municipal Government in the Progressive Era," *Pacific Northwest Quarterly* 55, no. 4 (October 1964): 157–69.
5. See, for example, the application of cultural geography in David M. Scobey, *Empire City: The Making and Meaning of the New York City Landscape* (Philadelphia: Temple University Press, 2002); the mechanisms through which each group operated to preserve its own power in Jessica Trounstine, *Political Monopolies in American Cities:*

The Rise and Fall of Bosses and Reformers (Chicago: University of Chicago Press, 2008); the competition between laissez-faire business leaders and governments in Robin L. Einhorn, *Property Rules: Political Economy in Chicago, 1833–1872* (Chicago: University of Chicago Press, 1991); and the notion of "the people" in James J. Connolly, *An Elusive Unity: Urban Democracy and Machine Politics in Industrializing America* (Ithaca, NY: Cornell University Press, 2010).

6. Lizabeth Cohen, *Saving America's Cities: Ed Logue and the Struggle to Renew Urban America in the Suburban Age* (New York: Farrar, Straus and Girou, 2019); Kara M. Schlichting, *New York Recentered: Building the Metropolis from the Shore* (Chicago: University of Chicago Press, 2019).

7. Keith Revell, *Building Gotham: Civic Culture & Public Policy in New York City, 1898–1938* (Baltimore: Johns Hopkins University Press, 2003), 4–7. Kenneth Finegold highlights the importance of experts and relies less on rigid class and ethnic lines of conflict in *Experts and Politicians: Reform Challenges to Machine Politics in New York, Cleveland, and Chicago* (Princeton, NJ: Princeton University Press, 1995).

8. Jameson W. Doig, *Empire on the Hudson: Entrepreneurial Vision and Political Power at the Port of New York Authority* (New York: Columbia University Press, 2001), 47–73; David A. Johnson, *Planning the Great Metropolis: The 1929 Regional Plan of New York and Its Environs* (London: E & FN Spon., 1995), 48–69; Clifton Hood, *722 Miles: The Building of the Subways and How They Transformed New York* (Baltimore, MD: Johns Hopkins University Press, 1993), 195–96.

9. F. G. Crawford, "The New York State Legislative Session of 1921," *American Political Science Review* 15, no. 3 (August 1921): 384.

10. *New York Times*, January 25, 1921, 1; February 8, 1921; February 17, 1921, 1; February 22, 1921, 1; March 3, 1921, 1; March 9, 1921, 14; and March 17, 1921, 1. Democrats feared that these changes masked an effort to raise the subway fare higher than five cents—a signature issue for Hylan, who faced reelection that fall. Even the Citizens Union, typically at odds with the Hylan administration on public issues, expressed concern for the bill's reduction of local authority, as did the Republican Fiorello La Guardia, president of the Board of Aldermen. Most Republican members of the Assembly and Senate from New York City, however, ultimately did not choose to oppose Governor Miller.

11. *New York Times*, March 13, 1921, 5, March 17, 1921, 1, March 23, 1921, 1, and March 31, 1921, 1; Peter E. Derrick, "The New York City Transit Crisis of 1918–1925," MA thesis, Columbia University, 1967, 35; "Public Service Commission Law (1921 Amendments)," in *Annotated Consolidated Laws of the State of New York as Amended to January 1, 1918, Containing Also the Federal and State Constitutions with Notes of Board of Statutory Consolidation, Tables of Laws, and Index*, vol. 1, ed. New York State, Clarence F. Birdseye, Robert C. Cumming, Frank B. Gilbert, John T. Fitzpatrick, Harold N. Eldridge, and Minor Bronaugh (New York: Banks Law, 1917–1925), 817–19. Miller also appointed Leroy Harkness, a Brooklyn attorney long associated with the PSC, and General John F O'Ryan, a Tammany Hall Democrat, as the other two members. The bill passed with a 33–18 margin in the Senate and a 91–56 tally in the Assembly, and Staten Island Republicans Senator C. Ernest Smith and Assemblyman Ernest V. Frerichs voted for it.

12. *New York Times*, April 1, 1921, 15, April 17, 1921, 1, April 26, 1921, 1, and May 18, 1921, 1; Hood, *722 Miles*, 193–94.

13. Doig, *Empire on the Hudson*, 27–46; Mike Wallace, *Greater Gotham: A History of New York City from 1898 to 1919* (New York: Oxford University Press, 2017), 1050. Cohen

was appointed as counsel to the New York–New Jersey Port and Harbor Development Commission, for which William R. Wilcox served as chairman.
14. Doig, *Empire on the Hudson*, 48–66.
15. *New York Times*, April 13, 1920, 21, February 17, 1921, 13, March 17, 1921, 1, and May 1, 1921, 19; Doig, *Empire on the Hudson*, 65–73; Jameson Doig, "Joining New York City to the Greater Metropolis: The Port Authority as Visionary, Target of Opportunity, and Opportunist," in *The Landscape of Modernity: New York City, 1900–1940*, ed. David Ward and Olivier Zunz (Baltimore, MD: Johns Hopkins University Press, 1992), 82–85; Carl W. Condit, *The Port of New York: A History of the Rail and Terminal System from the Beginnings to Pennsylvania Station* (Chicago: University of Chicago Press, 1980), 130. The Port Authority could not interfere with certain municipal projects, was required to follow due process to acquire property, needed to obtain legislative authorization to use the state's credit for expenses and improvement costs, and lacked any real regulatory power. However, it did have, as Doig suggests, plenty of areas for potential focus. The Port Authority could act as a corporate body "with full power and authority to purchase, construct, lease, and/or operate any terminal or transportation facility within said District" (Condit, *The Port of New York*, 130). The facilities within the purview of the authority included bridges, tunnels, trucks, harbor craft, docks, piers, ferries, as well as railroads.
16. The Staten Island legislators were Thomas Cosgrove of West New Brighton and George Reynaud of New Dorp, both Democrats and veterans of World War I. Cosgrove was an attorney who served two terms in the Assembly; Reynaud worked in insurance and served just one year.
17. *Richmond County Advance*, February 12, 1920, 1; New York State, *Journal of the Assembly of the State of New York, 1920*, vol. 1 (Albany, NY: J. B. Lyon, 1920), 182.
18. *Richmond County Advance*, April 19, 1921, 1.
19. *New York Times*, April 22, 1921, 28; New York State, *Journal of the Assembly*, 1:255, 717, 875, 1012, 1285, 1605. C. Ernest Smith also initially proposed a Staten Island–Manhattan tunnel but soon amended the bill to establish the more politically palatable Richmond–Brooklyn route.
20. *Richmond County Advance*, April 15, 1921, 1, April 19, 1921, 1, and April 22, 1921, 1; Samuel Rea, "Memorandum on the Staten Island–Brooklyn Tunnel," August 18, 1921, box 87, folder 105/90, PCRR.
21. *Richmond County Advance*, April 26, 1921, 1, and May 13, 1921, 1. The PRR also worked against the bill, though Rea later claimed that the Port Authority did not contest its passage (Rea, "Memorandum on the Staten Island–Brooklyn Tunnel").
22. State of New York, *Public Papers of Governor Nathan L. Miller, 1921* (Albany, NY: J. B. Lyons, 1924), 171; *New York Times*, May 15, 1921, 103. Governor Miller explained his decision by noting that the mandatory nature of the bill was of less concern now that the city administration had indicated it would willingly build the tunnel.
23. *New York Times*, May 13, 1921, 22, and May 15, 1921, 103; *Richmond County Advance*, May 13, 1921, 1, and May 14, 1921, 1; State of New York, *Public Papers of Governor Nathan L. Miller, 1921*, 170–72, 442–55; Rea, "Memorandum on the Staten Island–Brooklyn Tunnel."
24. *Richmond County Advance*, April 16, 1921, 1, and April 18, 1921, 4. Van Name had already traveled to Washington, DC, to secure the approval of the War Department for a Narrows tunnel (*Richmond County Advance*, February 2, 1921, 1).
25. *Richmond County Advance*, May 14, 1921, 1, May 19, 1921, 1, May 20, 1921, 1, and May 21, 1921, 1; *Staten Island Advance*, July 29, 1921, 1, and August 17, 1921, 1; New York City

Board of Estimate and Apportionment, *Minutes* 3 (May 20, 1921): 2947–51; Arthur Tuttle et al. to Mayor John Hylan, October 15, 1921, SI/Richmond Borough President Collection, box 5, folder 55, SIIAS. The special committee's other three members were Murray Hulbert, commissioner of docks; Grover Whalen, commissioner of plant and structure; and Theodore S. Oxholm, chief engineer of the Borough of Richmond.

26. The other two core members of the committee staff were Jesse B. Snow as tunnel engineer and Major John F. Sullivan as consulting engineer. Snow came to the project with more than twenty years of employment on municipal engineering projects, most recently serving as the principal assistant engineer for the Hudson tunnel project. Sullivan had similar experience, having served as an engineer in the navy and for the PSC. Tuttle remained in charge of the day-to-day operations and often reported directly to the full Board of Estimate. See New York City Board of Estimate, *Minutes* 4 (June 3, 1921): 3331, and 4 (June 17, 1921): 3634–36; *Engineering News-Record* 87, no. 6 (August 11, 1921): 254, box 55, WJW.

27. Josef W. Konvitz, "William J. Wilgus and Engineering Projects to Improve the Port of New York, 1900–1930," *Technology and Culture* 30, no. 2 (April 1989): 399. Wilgus served as a consulting engineer for less than one year, but his involvement in the project continued after his departure.

28. See, for example, William J. Wilgus, "Preliminary Study for a Greater New York Belt Line," 1913, box 48, WJW; William J. Wilgus, "The Narrows Tunnel and Its Relation to the Port of New York Problem, Part II," report presented to the Municipal Engineers of the City of New York, December 28, 1921, box 48, WJW; William J. Wilgus (presumably), "The Narrows Tunnel Controversy," December 8, 1921, box 54, WJW.

29. Wilgus, "Preliminary Study," 6–7; Konvitz, "William J. Wilgus," 401–3. Wilgus first made a similar proposal in 1906 to the New York Central and Hudson River Railroads, published the idea in 1910, urged the BRT to build a Narrows tunnel and to consider freight possibilities during the years before the Dual Contracts, promoted the idea to federal officials during his military service in World War I, and renewed his promotional efforts in an address to the New York section of the American Society for Civil Engineers in 1920.

30. Wilgus was not enamored of the enabling legislation or of the eventual form the Port Authority took. See William J. Wilgus to F. A. Molitor, May 23, 1921, box 48, WJW; Benjamin Miller, *Fat of the Land: Garbage in New York, the Last 200 Years* (New York: Four Walls, Eight Windows, 2000), 161–62.

31. Arthur Tuttle (presumably), untitled memorandum, c. August 13, 1921, box 53, WJW; New York City Board of Estimate, *Minutes* 6 (October 21, 1921): 5916; *Staten Island Advance*, July 29, 1921, 1; *New-York Tribune*, July 29, 1921, 20.

32. "Minutes of the Meeting of the Engineering Committee," August 9, 1921, 19–23, 31, 49, box 53, WJW; "Minutes of the Conference of the Mayor of the City of New York and the Executives of Trunk Line Railroads Entering the Metropolitan District," August 16, 1921, 3, 11, box 53, WJW; E. B. Temple, "Memorandum of Meeting in Office of Chief Engineer A. S. Tuttle, Board of Estimate & Apportionment—New York, Tuesday August 9, 1921," box 87, folder 105/90, PCRR.

33. At his initial meeting with the railroad engineers, Tuttle was particularly solicitous of the views of E. B. Temple, the PRR's representative. After the meeting, Wilgus informally lobbied Temple, who reported that "[Wilgus] said that he hoped the P.R.R. would take this proposition up in a big way, as he felt the whole New York situation would never be cleared up unless our Company agreed to go along with something big" (Temple, "Memorandum of Meeting").

34. PRR president Rea became chairman of the railroad executives' committee.
35. "Minutes of the Conference of the Mayor . . . and the Executives of Trunk Line Railroads," August 16, 1921, 34. Wilgus knew of Rea's lack of enthusiasm from their exchange of letters in 1919. See Samuel Rea to William J. Wilgus, April 2, 1919; Wilgus to Rea, November 10, 1919; Rea to Wilgus, November 13, 1919: all in box 48, WJW.
36. Rea believed that even an enlarged B&O bridge across the Arthur Kill could not handle all of the freight slotted for Brooklyn and beyond. As for the Narrows tunnel, he argued that it would require too "heavy grades on the approaches" to be practical (Rea, "Memorandum on the Staten Island–Brooklyn Tunnel"; E. B. Temple to Samuel Rea, July 8, 1921, box 87, folder 105/90, PCRR; "Minutes of the Meeting of the Engineering Committee," August 9, 1921, 3–6).
37. *Richmond County Advance*, May 19, 1921, 1. Temple expressed surprise at the railroads' uniform disinterest in the Narrows tunnel because both he and Rea thought that the Narrows project could benefit the B&O and other trunk lines while drawing some of the PRR's business that went through Manhattan (E. B. Temple to Samuel Rea, September 30, 1921, box 87, folder 105/90, PCRR; *Richmond County Advance*, May 19, 1921, 1; *Staten Island Advance*, August 17, 1921, 1).
38. John F. Stover, *History of the Baltimore and Ohio Railroad* (West Lafayette, IN: Purdue University Press, 1987), 190–214; Daniel Willard to Samuel Rea, September 20, 1921, box 48, folder 72/28, vol. 4, pt. 2, PCRR. Willard was president of the B&O.
39. A new bridge over the Kill Van Kill was also needed to bear the weight of heavy freight. See New York City Board of Estimate, *Minutes* 6 (October 21, 1921): 5916–18; *Staten Island Advance*, October 22, 1921, 1; *Evening World* (New York), October 21, 1921, 3; *New York Times*, October 22, 1921, 22, December 28, 1921, 1, and December 29, 1921, 8.
40. *Richmond County Advance*, May 13, 1921, 1, and May 27, 1921, 1; Charles W. Leng and William T. Davis, *Staten Island and Its People: A History, 1609–1929*, 5 vols. (New York: Lewis Historical, 1929–1933), 1:377–78.
41. William J. Wilgus, "Preliminary Study for a Greater New York Belt Line Including the Narrows Tunnel," 1933, box 48, WJW.
42. Arthur Tuttle et al. to John Hylan, October 15, 1921, in New York City Board of Estimate, *Minutes* 6 (October 21, 1921): 5916–18.
43. New York City Board of Estimate, *Minutes* 6 (October 21, 1921): 5918. The proposals said very little about rapid transit, explaining that "it has not seemed practicable to develop the local passenger service feature of the project beyond the stage of insuring [sic] the line a position suitable to meets the needs of the Borough of Richmond, nor, would it seem advantageous to do so until after the trunk-line railroads have been given an opportunity to join the City in carrying out the belt-line portion of the plan."
44. New York, New Jersey Port, and Harbor Development Commission, *Joint Report with Comprehensive Plan and Recommendations* (Albany, NY: J. B. Lyon, 1920), 22, 285; Eugenius H. Outerbridge, "Development of Staten Island in Connection with the Comprehensive Plan for the Port of New York," December 2, 1921, 3–4, box 1, folder 150-37, NLM; Doig, *Empire on the Hudson*, 66, 92, 414, 430; *New York Times*, January 24, 1921, 20; Miller, *Fat of the Land*, 163.
45. Condit, *The Port of New York*, 128; Doig, *Empire on the Hudson*, 79.
46. *New York Times*, January 30, 1921, E1; Condit, *The Port of New York*, 126–29; Doig, *Empire on the Hudson*, 79–80. The first public articulation of a New Jersey–Brooklyn tunnel had occurred as early as 1869 and reappeared periodically in subsequent years.

47. *Staten Island Advance*, November 18, 1921, 1, November 28, 1921, 1, and December 1, 1921, 1; *Staten Islander*, November 26, 1921, 1, and December 3, 1921, 1. Outerbridge did float the notion of a vehicular tunnel under the Narrows, an early indicator of where the Port Authority was carving out its jurisdiction (see Doig, *Empire on the Hudson*, 108–9).
48. *New York Times*, December 5, 1921, 30, and December 6, 1921, 35.
49. Julius H. Cohen to Nathan L. Miller, December 12, 1921, 2, box 1, folder 150-37, NLM; Eugenius H. Outerbridge to Nathan L. Miller, December 5, 1921, box 1, folder 150-37, NLM.
50. *New York Times*, December 1, 1921, 15, December 8, 1921, 6, and January 1, 1922, 23; Port of New York Authority, *Report with Plan for the Comprehensive Development of the Port of New York* (Albany, NY: J. B. Lyon, 1921), 28–32 (quotation from 29); Doig, *Empire on the Hudson*, 88–92.
51. *Staten Islander*, December 3, 1921, 4; *Staten Island Advance*, November 29, 1921, 1, December 5, 1921, 4, December 8, 1921, 1, and December 9, 1921, 4.
52. *Staten Islander*, November 26, 1921, 1, December 3, 1921, 4, December 14, 1921, 1, and May 13, 1922, 1; *Staten Island Advance*, December 3, 1921, 1, December 5, 1921, 4, and December 13, 1921, 1. William Wirt Mills selected Thaten, a terminal manager for the local American Dock Company, for his strong background in statistics and long interest in transportation. Neither a native Staten Islander nor from a privileged background, Thaten had moved to Staten Island in 1900 and started as a messenger before rising up through the company's ranks.
53. *Staten Island Advance*, December 8, 1921, 1, and December 10, 1921, 1; *Staten Islander*, December 7, 1921, 1.
54. *New York Times*, December 12, 1921, 12.
55. *Staten Island Advance*, December 8, 1921, 1; Outerbridge, "Development of Staten Island," 6.
56. *Staten Island Advance*, December 16, 1921, 1; *Staten Islander*, December 10, 1921, 1.
57. *Staten Island Advance*, December 5, 1921, 4; *Staten Islander*, December 14, 1921, 4.
58. *Staten Island Advance*, December 14, 1921, 4.
59. Doig, *Empire on the Hudson*, 38.
60. *Staten Islander*, December 10, 1921, 1; "Resolution of the Special Committee," December 10, 1921, included in Staten Island Chamber of Commerce (SICC), *Minutes of the Board of Directors*, December 15, 1921, SICCR. The divergence between the SICC and the Staten Island Civic League was perhaps most clear in their representatives' comments to Outerbridge at a public meeting on December 12. The former conveyed its preference for the cross-island line proposed by the former Bi-State Commission. The latter offered a much broader critique of the Port Authority's plan for ignoring the Stapleton piers, relegating Staten Island to service only by the B&O, and omitting a classification yard from Staten Island (William J. Wilgus, untitled memorandum, December 12, 1921, box 54, WJW). For examples of the condemnation the chamber faced, see the *Staten Islander*, December 14, 1921, 4; and *Staten Island Advance*, December 6, 1921, 4.
61. Louis Tribus penned an angry letter to the *Staten Islander* that essentially accused it of missing the nuance in the chamber's statement, which "*did not approve* the Port Authority's plan as to Staten Island … [and] *did in principle* approve the Civic League's criticisms." Tribus implied that the difference between the two groups was a matter of style and not substance. When the chamber "*demanded* (of course politely) … the restoration of the Trans-Staten Island route of the By-State's [sic]

scheme," Tribus reminded the paper, it was pursuing a railroad line that would clearly connect to the Narrows tunnel, making it more viable (Louis Tribus to the Editor of the *Staten Islander*, December 15, 1921, included in SICC, *Minutes*, December 15, 1921, emphasis in the original). The *Staten Islander* rejected Tribus's clarification and reaffirmed the need for the municipal tunnel without any regard for the Port Authority plan (*Staten Islander*, December 17, 1921, 1, 4). For the joint efforts of the Civic League and SICC, see *Staten Island Advance*, January 16, 1922, 1, and January 21, 1922, 1.

62. *Richmond County Advance*, May 4, 1921, 1.
63. During the Dual Contracts negotiations in 1912–1913, McAneny had been open to the movement of freight through a Narrows tunnel and had even spoken more favorably of the possibility in 1919. At the time, he had speculated that the railroad companies might support such a project, but it is likely that by late 1921 he knew that most of them were not interested in the Hylan tunnel (*Richmond County Advance*, April 20, 1919, 1).
64. *New York Times*, December 22, 1921, 5; *Staten Island Advance*, December 22, 1921, 1. McAneny's role in guiding the city through the Dual Contracts without a concrete provision for a Richmond subway appeared to leave him feeling beholden to the borough. That sense of obligation came through in his public pronouncements, which now not only favored a Staten Island tunnel but prioritized it. See, for example, *New York Times*, December 25, 1921, 82; and *Staten Island Advance*, March 27, 1922, 1.
65. *Staten Island Advance*, November 19, 1921, 4, December 22, 1921, 1, and December 23, 1921, 1; *New York Times*, December 22, 1921, 5; Derrick, "The New York City Transit Crisis," 47–49.
66. *New York Times*, October 8, 1921, 8; December 25, 1921, 5; and December 28, 1921, 1. In late 1921, the Port Authority and the Transit Commission considered but rejected the possibility of moving freight on subway lines between 1:00 a.m. and 5:00 a.m. They also agreed about the flaws of the Smith Act, about the limitations of a dual-purpose tunnel, and about how the city's present plans would not transpire.
67. Arthur S. Tuttle, William J. Wilgus, John F. Sullivan, and Jesse B. Snow, "The Narrows Tunnel and Its Relation to the Port of New York Problem," report presented to the Municipal Engineers of the City of New York, December 28, 1921, box 48, WJW; *New York Times*, December 29, 1921, 5. The evening gathered together most of the key experts engaged in the Narrows tunnel controversy—including Chief Engineer Robert Ridgeway of the Transit Commission—which led to a remarkable discussion with the audience following the speeches by the city engineers.
68. Tuttle et al., "The Narrows Tunnel," 7–13, 18–19; *New York Times*, December 29, 1921, 5.
69. E. B. Temple to H. A. Lane et al., December 2, 1921; William J. Wilgus to Temple, December 8, 1921; and Temple to Lane, December 14, 1921: all in box 87, folder 105/90, PCRR.
70. Wilgus to Temple, December 8, 1921.
71. Temple to Lane, December 14, 1921.
72. "Minutes of the Meeting of the Engineering Committee," January 19, 1922, 21, box 53, WJW; E. B. Temple to Samuel Rea, January 21, 1922, box 87, folder 105/90, PCRR.
73. "Minutes of the Meeting of the Engineering Committee," January 19, 1922, 26.
74. Samuel Rea to John Hylan, January 30, 1922, box 87, folder 105/90, PCRR.
75. Rea to Hylan, January 30, 1922. Only Daniel Willard of the B&O declined to sign the letter from the railroad presidents to Hylan. He privately acquiesced but publicly

abstained from the decision "owing to the peculiar relation which the B&O sustains to SI [Staten Island]" (Daniel Willard to Samuel Rea, January 28, 1922, box 87, folder 105/90, PCRR).

76. State of New York, *Public Papers of Governor Nathan L. Miller, 1921*, 376–77; *New-York Tribune*, January 14, 1922, 7.
77. *New-York Tribune*, January 11, 1922, 12, and May 3, 1922, 12.
78. *Staten Island Advance*, December 31, 1921, 1, and January 14, 1922, 1; *Evening Post* (New York), December 28, 1921, 6; *New York Times*, February 1, 1922, 1, and February 5, 1922, 92; New York Chamber of Commerce, "The Plan of the Port Authority of New York for Future Port Development," January 1922, 19–21, 27–28, 30–37, https://babel.hathitrust.org/cgi/pt?id=coo1.ark:/13960/t9v12mk1p&view=1up&seq=3&skin=2021. The relative cost of the two tunnel projects was one of the major areas of contention. Outerbridge charged that the Board of Estimate's plan was in fact more expensive overall than the proposed Greenville–Bay Ridge line. He estimated the total cost of the Port Authority's middle belt line at $329 million, with an additional $65 million for the actual tunnel, and claimed that the annual savings in freight charges would be nearly ten times larger than from the Narrows tunnel. Wilgus repeatedly accused Narrows tunnel detractors of exaggerating the expense, which he put at $141 million, not $225 million, and claimed that price tag included all features of the proposal, not just the tunnel.
79. William J. Wilgus, "Remarks Before the Board of Estimate and Apportionment," January 26, 1922, box 53, WJW; *New York Times*, January 26, 1922, 10. See also William J. Wilgus, "New York's Proposed Belt Railway," *Scientific American* 126 (January 1922): 40–41, 63–74, 140–55.
80. *New York Times*, February 19, 1922, 94.
81. "The Narrows Tunnel," transcript of the meeting of the Municipal Engineers of the City of New York, December 28, 1921, 5–6, 14–15, 22–25, box 53, WJW.
82. "The Narrows Tunnel," transcript, 18. In early February, the municipal engineers voted to ask the legislature to include Tuttle's tunnel in the Port Authority plans. See Joseph Strachen to Brooklyn Engineers Club, undated (c. February 1922), memorandum, box 53, WJW.
83. *Staten Islander*, January 14, 1922, 1; *Staten Island Advance*, January 25, 1922, 1.
84. *Staten Island Advance*, January 7, 1922, 1; *Staten Islander*, January 7, 1922, 1, and January 14, 1922, 1.
85. New York City Board of Estimate, *Minutes* 2 (April 7, 1922): 2077; *Staten Island Advance*, January 16, 1922, 1.
86. *New York Times*, January 24, 1922, 15, and February 1, 1922, 1. Craig often clashed with Hylan on a variety of municipal matters but agreed with him that the Port Authority threatened the city's interests.
87. On the lack of railroad company cooperation on the Port Authority's plans for coordinated freight transport, see Doig, *Empire on the Hudson*, 97–119.
88. Sheppard to Robert C. Wright, October 2, 1917, box 48, folder 72/28, vol. 4, pt. 1, PCRR; B. F. Cresson to Engineering Committee of the Railroads, July 28, 1921, and Samuel Rea to Eugenius Outerbridge, September 21, 1921, box 48, folder 72/28, vol. 4, pt. 2, PCRR. The Port Authority plans did not contain a Narrows tunnel but did include east shore and west shore lines on Staten Island as well as a major belt line that contained east–west track across the heart of Staten Island. Rea did not think current traffic warranted any of these lines, provided the B&O handled all traffic "on reasonable terms" and improved its current tracks and bridge over the Arthur Kill.

89. The PRR's position mattered especially to the Port Authority. See, for example, Eugenius Outerbridge to Samuel Rea, September 8, 1921, box 48, folder 72/28, vol. 4, pt. 2, PCRR; and E. B. Temple, "Memorandum of Rail Trip from Weehawken Terminal, West Shore R.R., to South Amboy," September 20, 1921, box 48, folder 72/28, vol. 4, pt. 2, PCRR.
90. Temple described to Rea a conversation with his Port Authority counterpart as follows: "I told Mr. Cresson confidentially at the last meeting that we could work out a very good tunnel line under Newark Bay from Greenville to Bay Ridge that might possibly appeal to the Port Authority, and, if so, could be used by all Railroads in place of such a tunnel from Staten Island to Bay Ridge. He said that the Commission desired to adopt a tunnel route and would be very glad to work with us along the above lines. I told him of your suggestion about this" (E. B. Temple to Samuel Rea, September 19, 1921, box 48, folder 72/28, vol. 4, pt. 2, PCRR).
91. Outerbridge used language that was guarded rather than explicit, but the meaning was clear to Rea and the other railroad men (Eugenius Outerbridge to Samuel Rea, July 29, 1921, box 48, folder 72/28, vol. 4, pt. 2, PCRR; E. J. Pearson to Rea, August 3, 1921, box 48, folder 72/28, vol. 4, pt. 2, PCRR; E. B. Temple to Rea, August 12, 1921, box 48, folder 72/28, vol. 4, pt. 2, PCRR; Temple and C. S. Krick to W. W. Atterbury, June 5, 1924, box 26, folder 47/22, vol. 3, PCRR).
92. Samuel Rea to W. G. Bexler, September 21, 1921, box 48, folder 72/28, vol. 4, pt. 2, PCRR. Bexler was president of the Central Railroad of New Jersey, one of the twelve trunk lines involved in discussions with both the Port Authority and New York City. Two years later, Daniel Turner of the Transit Commission presented to the railroad executives a massive $700 million proposal for a Metropolitan Transit System. Here, too, PRR leaders were dubious of the plan's value for their company. Following Rea's leadership, the railroad officials of the major trunk lines agreed "that the question be handled similarly to that of the Narrows Tunnel project of NYC, which was recently considered." Organizationally, that meant the executives would appoint an engineering committee to study the details and report back to them with recommendations. But for the PRR, the Narrows model was also a matter of control; Temple recalled that "this work was practically all done by our representatives, and we were at all times in a position to be sure that the matter was being considered from our standpoint" (Samuel Rea to W. H. Truesdale, June 20, 1924, box 26, folder 47-22, vol. 3, PCRR; Temple and Krick to Atterbury, June 5, 1924).
93. Samuel Rea to Eugenius Outerbridge, January 31 and February 1, 1922, box 87, folder 105/90, PCRR.
94. The hearing was conducted jointly by the New York Senate Finance Committee and the Assembly Ways and Means Committee (*New York Times*, February 1, 1922), 1.
95. Outerbridge described the hearing to Rea in a letter dated February 2, 1922. His depiction of Smith's speech was laudatory: "His address was the most masterly, as it was the most entertaining that I have ever heard.... I have never heard the art of good-natured ridicule so adroitly and effectively handled, and the large delegations who went from New York and all over the State in support of the Port Authority's Bill universally said that they would have travelled a great many miles further to hear such a thrilling and entertaining proceeding." Regarding the large crowd, Outerbridge wrote that "even a sign 'Standing Room Only' would not have been truthful as there was no more standing room" (Eugenius Outerbridge to Samuel Rea, February 2, 1922, box 48, folder 72/28, vol. 4, pt. 3, PCRR).
96. *New York Times*, February 1, 1922, 1, and February 19, 1922, 94. The Brooklyn and Queens Chambers of Commerce had previously expressed a preference for the

316   6. Planning the Region

Narrows tunnel, but, believing the tunnel to Greenville would serve them well, they sent a representative in support of the Port Authority.

97. Mayor Hylan remained in Manhattan but sent a statement in which he derided a Port Authority plan that "leaves Staten Island marooned" and aids New Jersey "at the expense of the City of New York." He also implied that the Port Authority, by declining the invitation to participate in the Board of Estimate hearing on January 26, was a disinterested party in coordinating efforts. Responding to this accusation of noncooperation, Al Smith reviewed Hylan's antagonistic position during the lengthy creation of the Port Authority and concluded that "you can't co-operate with a man who has a blackjack in one hand and a slungshot [sic] in the other" (both Hylan and Smith quoted in *New York Times*, February 1, 1922, 1).

98. Two weeks later the Staten Islanders' scaled-back request—to add tunnels to Brooklyn and Bayonne to the existing plan without replacing the Greenville proposal—was also rebuffed (*Staten Islander*, February 4, 1922, 1, and February 8, 1922, 1; *Staten Island Advance*, February 1, 1922, 1).

99. The bill for the Comprehensive Plan passed 37–11 in the Senate and 97–47 in the Assembly (*Staten Island Advance*, February 22, 1922, 1).

100. "Returns of Mayoral Elections in New York City by Borough, 1897–1993," in Charles Brecher, "Mayoralty," in *The Encyclopedia of New York*, ed. Kenneth Jackson (New Haven, CT: Yale University Press, 1995), 738.

101. "Conference on the Matter of a Subway to Staten Island Held at the Mayor's Office," Wednesday, October 19, 1918, 12, box 37, folder 375, JFH.

102. Charles D. Drew for Jesse Snow, memorandum, January 10, 1922, box 53, WJW.

103. *New York Times*, June 10, 1922, 7.

7. Getting the Shaft: The Demise of the Hylan Tunnel, 1922–1925

1. Local businesses had been asked to release their employees from two to six in the afternoon, and given the turnout, estimated at 15,000 by the *Staten Islander* (July 20, 1923, 1), it seems likely that some complied.

2. Nearly 1,000 citizens willing to pay five dollars joined the officials for a reception on a nearby pier. See *Staten Islander*, July 11, 1923, 1, July 14, 1923, 1, July 18, 1923, 1, and July 21, 1923, 1; *New York Times*, July 20, 1923, 28; Narrows Tunnel Groundbreaking Program, 1923, folder 53, CL; Max Thaten to Citizens Committee, July 23, 1923, folder 53, CL.

3. The exhibit *From Farm to City: Staten Island 1661–2012* ran at the Museum of the City of New York from September 13, 2012, through February 10, 2013. See https://www.mcny.org/exhibition/farm-city.

4. A search on Google for "Staten Island Tunnel Project" revealed the following sites among many: "Staten Island Tunnel," *Wikipedia*, last updated October 15, 2022, http://en.wikipedia.org/wiki/Staten_Island_Tunnel; "The Narrows Rail Tunnel (the Brooklyn–Richmond Freight & Passenger Tunnel," Brooklyn Historic Railway Association, n.d.,http://www.brooklynrail.net/verrazano_rail_tunnel.html; and Benjamin Kabak, "A Subway Tunnel to Staten Island, 80 Years in the Making," Second Avenue Sagas, November 13, 2007, https://secondavenuesagas.com/category/staten-island/page/5/.

5. Jameson W. Doig, *Empire on the Hudson: Entrepreneurial Vision and Political Power at the Port of New York Authority* (New York: Columbia University Press, 2001),

81–82, 112–14; David A. Johnson, *Planning the Great Metropolis: The 1929 Regional Plan of New York and Its Environs* (London: E & FN Spon, 1996), 202–12; Martin V. Melosi, *Fresh Kills: A History of Consuming and Discarding in New York City* (New York: Columbia University Press, 2020); Daniel C. Kramer and Richard M. Flanagan, *Staten Island: Conservative Bastion in a Liberal City* (Lanham, MD: University Press of America, 2012), 24–25.

6. Founders of the Regional Planning Association of America included Lewis Mumford, Clarence Stein, and Henry Wright. For relatively recent treatments of planning as a national movement and development, see Matthew Dalbey, *Regional Visionaries and Metropolitan Boosters: Decentralization, Regional Planning, and Parkways During the Interwar Years* (Boston: Kluwer Academic, 2002); and Edward K. Spann, *Designing Modern America: The Regional Planning Association of America and Its Members* (Columbus: Ohio State University Press, 1996). For a useful early history of the organization, see Roy Lubove, *Community Planning in the 1920s: The Contribution of the Regional Planning Association of America* (Pittsburgh, PA: University of Pittsburgh Press, 1963).
7. Johnson, *Planning the Great Metropolis*, 1, 75.
8. Paul Barrett, *The Automobile and Urban Transit: The Formulation of Public Policy in Chicago, 1900–1930* (Philadelphia: Temple University Press, 1983), 73–81, 146; Johnson, *Planning the Great Metropolis*, 48–55; Charles K. Hyde, "Planning a Transportation System for Metropolitan Detroit in the Age of the Automobile: The Triumph of the Expressway," *Michigan Historical Review* 32, no. 1 (2006): 63–75.
9. Joel Schwartz, *The New York Approach: Robert Moses, Urban Liberals, and the Redevelopment of the Inner City* (Columbus: Ohio State University Press, 1993), 1–24; Keith Revell, *Building Gotham: Civic Culture & Public Policy in New York City, 1898–1938* (Baltimore, MD: Johns Hopkins University Press, 2003), 183–226.
10. See, for example, George Lankevich, *American Metropolis: A History of New York City* (New York: New York University Press, 1998); and Edward Robb Ellis, *The Epic of New York City: A Narrative History* (1966; reprint, New York: Kodansha America, 1997). Edwin Burrows and Mike Wallace's magisterial book *Gotham* pays considerable attention to Staten Island in what is still a Manhattan-driven history that ends in 1898, but Staten Island recedes somewhat in Wallace's sequel, *Greater Gotham*. See Edwin G. Burrows and Mike Wallace, *Gotham: A History of New York City to 1898* (New York: Oxford University Press, 1999); and Mike Wallace, *Greater Gotham: A History of New York City from 1898 to 1919* (New York: Oxford University Press, 2017).
11. *Staten Island Advance*, January 18, 1922, 1, January 21, 1922, 1, January 25, 1922, 1, and February 6, 1922, 1; *Staten Islander*, February 8, 1922, 1, and May 24, 1922, 4.
12. New York City Board of Estimate and Apportionment, *Minutes* 8 (December 9, 1921): 7335; *New York Times*, September 30, 1921, 1, and October 4, 1921, 3.
13. *Staten Island Advance*, December 29, 1921, 1, December 30, 1921, 1, January 11, 1922, 1, and March 14, 1922, 8.
14. In a legislative sleight of hand, late amendments to the bill took responsibility for building the Narrows tunnel from the city and placed it with the Transit Commission. These unfriendly amendments passed despite Staten Islanders opposition to the change. Hylan ironically ended up vetoing legislation that he had initially set in motion (*Staten Islander*, March 22, 1922, 1, March 25, 1922, 1, and April 1, 1922, 1; *Staten Island Advance*, January 7, 1922, 1, January 11, 1922, 1, February 4, 1922, 1, and March 23, 1922, 1).
15. Tuttle had adjusted numerous features "to facilitate the use of the tunnel for passenger purposes" without precluding a future possible use for freight (New York City

Board of Estimate, *Minutes* 2 (April 7, 1922): 2079; *Staten Islander*, June 7, 1922, 1). One casualty from the altered orientation of the project was William Wilgus, whose resignation had become public the previous month. Long frustrated by conflict with Tuttle and others, Wilgus now chafed at the reorientation of the project from freight to rapid transit. His tenure as consulting engineer had lasted less than a year (William J. Wilgus to Arthur S. Tuttle, October 31, 1921, as well as January 13, February 10, March 30 (draft), and April 10, 1922, box 54, WJW).

16. *Staten Islander*, March 8, 1922, 1; *Staten Island Advance*, January 20, 1922, 1, January 21, 1922, 1, February 4, 1922, 1, and March 13, 1922, 1; New York City Board of Estimate, *Minutes* 1 (January 20, 1922): 407.
17. New York City Board of Estimate, *Minutes* 2 (April 7, 1922): 2079; G. P. Farley to L. V. Morris, April 25, 1922, box 48, folder 72/28, vol. 4, pt. 2, PCRR.
18. New York City Board of Estimate, *Minutes* 2 (April 7, 1922): 2079; 3 (May 5, 1922): 2529; and 3 (May 12, 1922): 2961–66.
19. Thus, the "waste" to which the Citizens Union's representatives referred was not an early twentieth-century clamor over a tunnel to nowhere. The Citizens Union favored the Port Authority plan for the New Jersey to Brooklyn freight tunnel and preferred to let the Transit Commission develop a Narrows tunnel only for subways, which "will afford Staten Island the relief which it deserves and demands." The Citizens Union also argued that the legislation creating the Port Authority had in effect repealed the Smith Act and that the Board of Estimate's plans for terminals were so far inland that they amounted to street railroads, which the legislation did not permit it to build (*New York Times*, May 20, 1922, 12, May 24, 1922, 18, and June 20, 1922, 2).
20. *Staten Islander*, May 20, 1922, 1; *Staten Island Advance*, July 7, 1922, 1; *New York Times*, May 16, 1922, 14, and June 20, 1922, 2; *New-York Tribune*, May 3, 1922, 12; *Evening World* (New York), May 26, 1922, 34. Judge Lewis Fawcett ruled that the Smith Act bound the Board of Estimate to build the tunnel and allowed the work to continue. The duration of the injunction gave the Board of Aldermen time to work out members' doubts about the finances of the tunnel plans, and the full board moved forward on the expenditure after the injunction was lifted.
21. McAneny held sparsely filled hearings to poll Staten Islanders on the two routes under consideration—to Rosebank and St. George—but most attendees spoke in favor of the Hylan tunnel and declined to identify a preference between the Transit Commission's two options (*New York Times*, May 2, 1922, 1, and June 9, 1922, 14; *Staten Island Advance*, March 27, 1922, 1, and May 12, 1922, 1; *Evening World*, May 25, 1922, 10).
22. *Staten Islander*, June 10, 1922, 1; *Evening World*, May 25, 1922, 10.
23. Alexander R. Smith, "Speech at the Civic League Meeting," May 22, 1922, SICCR.
24. *Staten Islander*, June 10, 1922, 1; *New York Times*, June 9, 1922, 4; *Staten Island Advance*, June 9, 1922, 1. Cahill was also willing for the BRT to run the subway from its Fourth Avenue line in Brooklyn to Staten Island despite the mayor's avowed aversion to the traction companies.
25. *New York Times*, June 10, 1922, 10; *Staten Island Advance*, June 10, 1922, 1, and June 12, 1922, 4. Hylan delivered a "fiery speech" against cooperation; convinced of certain defeat, Cahill withdrew his motion to form a committee.
26. *New York Times*, June 10, 1922, 10; *Staten Island Advance*, June 9, 1922, 1; *Staten Islander*, June 3, 1922, 1, and June 10, 1922, 1. McAneny was willing to consult with the city about subway lines but indicated that the Transit Commission's unwillingness to run rapid-transit trains through the Narrows tunnel was nonnegotiable.

27. *New York Times*, July 18, 1922, 8, and November 8, 1922, 5; Kramer and Flanagan, *Staten Island*, 24, 29. Initially appointed to replace Cahill, Lynch won handily in a special election that November, garnering nearly 70 percent of the vote. He served the remainder of Cahill's term as well as two terms of his own before losing the Democratic nomination and the election (as an Independent) in 1933. He became tainted by corruption as a result of the Seabury investigations in the early 1930s but was never charged with criminal activity.
28. *Staten Islander*, June 6, 1923, 6.
29. *Staten Island Advance*, October 27, 1922, 1, and October 28, 1922, 1.
30. *New York Times*, August 28, 1922, 2; *Staten Island Advance*, August 28, 1922, 1; *Staten Islander*, August 30, 1922, 1; Clifton Hood, *722 Miles: The Building of the Subways and How They Transformed New York* (Baltimore, MD: Johns Hopkins University Press, 1993), 203. The mayor had placed the Narrows tunnel in a group of projects to be built first.
31. *Staten Island Advance*, October 7, 1922, 1, October 10, 1922, 1, and October 11, 1922, 1; *New York Times*, October 10, 1922, 19.
32. *New York Times*, August 29, 1922, 1, and October 14, 1922, 1; *Staten Island Advance*, October 14, 1922, 1. The Transit Commission's plan called for spurs to St. George and South Beach.
33. *Staten Islander*, October 21, 1922, 1; *Staten Island Advance*, November 9, 1922, 1, and November 10, 1922, 1. A large contingent from Staten Island went to a Board of Estimate hearing on the Transit Commission plan to contest an appropriation for the commission's subway tunnel to Staten Island.
34. *New York Times*, November 10, 1922, 1; *Staten Island Advance*, January 15, 1923, 1, April 4, 1923, 1, and April 9, 1923, 1; Hood, *722 Miles*, 204–5.
35. *Staten Island Advance*, November 7, 1922, 1, and April 12, 1923, 1; *Staten Islander*, November 4, 1922, 1.
36. *Staten Island Advance*, January 11, 1923, 1.
37. The *Staten Island Advance* reported on April 12, 1923 (p. 1) that "Lynch has rules set aside to rush plan to final vote." These changes included discarding the practice of holding over resolutions for several weeks before voting, requiring bids to be advertised for three weeks instead of four, and allowing the Committee of the Whole to approve the plans for bids and contracts.
38. *Staten Island Advance*, May 22, 1923, 1; *Staten Islander*, May 26, 1923, 1. All bids came in higher than the $710,000 appropriation the Board of Estimate had previously made, but without acrimony the board revised its appropriation to $850,000.
39. *Staten Islander*, January 3, 1923, 1, and April 14, 1923, 1; *New York Times*, July 20, 1923, 28.
40. Arthur Tuttle to John Hylan, October 18, 1923, Correspondence Received, roll 43, folder 520, JFH; *Staten Island Advance*, March 31, 1924, 1; New York City Board of Estimate, *Minutes* 6 (September 19, 1924): 6534. The tunnel shaft in Brooklyn was finished under budget in late March 1924. The completion of the shaft on Staten Island—first targeted for June 1, 1924—took place in mid-July.
41. Workers who would dig the tunnel, known as "sand hogs," feared a repetition of the high rates of caisson disease—more commonly known as "the bends"—they had encountered while constructing the Holland Tunnel. Represented by the Compressed Air Workers Union, they sought to win—through either negotiation or legislation—shorter hours because, they contended, lengthy work days contributed to a high number of cases ("The Narrows Tunnel in Relation to the Boroughs of Brooklyn and

Queens," in Arthur Tuttle to John Synott, December 21, 1924, Correspondence Received, roll 44, folder 523, JFH; *Staten Island Advance*, January 7, 1925, 1).
42. *Staten Island Advance*, January 21, 1925, 1.
43. *Staten Island Advance*, April 9, 1924, 2.
44. *Staten Island Advance*, April 5, 1924, 1; May 5, 1924, 1; and May 29, 1924, 1.
45. *New York Times*, July 15, 1924, 8, and August 9, 1924, 6; *Staten Island Advance*, July 24, 1924, 1, and August 1, 1924, 1; *Staten Islander*, July 30, 1924, 1. See also N. B. Killmer, *The Authorized Freight and Passenger Tunnel Under the Narrows Between Brooklyn and Staten Island* (Brooklyn, NY: Collison & Klingman, 1925), 13; and Hood, *722 Miles*, 189.
46. *New York Times*, August 2, 1923, 1; February 3, 1924, E1; and August 4, 1924, 5.
47. As Keith Revell notes, the pay-as-you-go policy was imposed in 1914 by private-sector financiers led by J. P. Morgan Jr. in exchange for a fiscal bailout of the city. The policy limited the city to fund only revenue-generating projects through borrowing and any other capital improvements through tax levies. The Mitchel administration did not initially implement the policy, and although his mayoralty had made the city much more adept at financial management, it did not corral the spending levels that pay-as-you-go was meant to curtail. In 1918, Hylan's new comptroller, Charles Craig, vowed to abolish the pay-as-you-go policy to avoid relying on unreasonably high tax rates to generate the money needed for the considerable improvements that Mayor Hylan had promised or that the city desperately needed, such as more schools. The pay-as-you-go policy became ineffective after the city was granted an exception for a $170 million school construction program and after other interests—museums and waste-disposal plants, for example—successfully garnered exemptions for their own projects. The limitation of borrowing only to fund revenue-generating projects completely broke down during Hylan's second term (Revell, *Building Gotham*, 167–78).
48. Samuel Rea to G. LeBoutillier, May 14, 1925, box 87, folder 105/90, PCRR; E. B. Temple to Rea, July 5, 1923, and Rea to LeBoutillier, July 6, 1923, box 48, folder 72/28, vol. 4, pt. 2, PCRR. Confident that the courts and legislature would ultimately block the Hylan administration, Rea did not direct his executives and engineers to intervene as forcefully as they had a few years earlier. While keeping the PRR in the background, Rea had employees monitor both the city's slow progress on the tunnel and the other railroad companies' stance toward it. Rea regularly made this argument in his correspondence with LeBoutillier, who appeared less hostile to the city's plans because the Narrows tunnel offered more promise for the Long Island Railroad Company than for the PRR.
49. *New York Times*, June 8, 1924, XX12; E. J. Pearson to Eugenius Outerbridge, October 4, 1921, box 48, folder 72/28, vol. 4, pt. 2, PCRR; Samuel Rea to Outerbridge, July 12, 1922, box 48, folder 72/28, vol. 4, pt. 3, PCRR; E. B. Temple to Rea, November 28, 1922, box 48, folder 72/28, vol. 4, pt. 3, PCRR; Temple to Rea, December 22, 1922, box 48, folder 72/28, vol. 4, pt. 3, PCRR; Doig, *Empire on the Hudson*, 97–119, 139–40; Erwin Wilkie Bard, *The Port of New York Authority* (New York: Columbia University Press, 1942), 63–74. As events unfolded in 1925, this brief period of relative silence would end, and Port Authority officials served as key witnesses against the Narrows tunnel in the upcoming legislative battle. Although these officials had yet to move ahead on their rival Greenville–Bay Ridge tunnel, they still hoped to build it. Aware of the railroad companies' lack of enthusiasm, they nevertheless had not yet encountered the heavy railroad company resistance that ultimately doomed the Greenville project.
50. Hood, *722 Miles*, 197.

51. Mayor Hylan berated McAneny for never answering questions, swaggered his control of the public purse, and attempted to delay McAneny's testimony (Board of Estimate, "Minutes of Meeting of June 1, 1923," box 73, 1923 folder, Transit Miscellaneous, GM).
52. Johnson, *Planning the Great Metropolis*, 205; *New York Times*, September 14, 1923, 21, and November 13, 1924, 23; Peter E. Derrick, "The New York City Transit Crisis of 1918–1925," MA thesis, Columbia University, 1967, 52–54. The short-lived cooperation, brought about in part by considerable public pressure applied by the Merchants Association and other groups, led to the approval of a Washington Heights and a crosstown Brooklyn subway line by the Board of Estimate and by Hylan, who as the mayor possessed the legal authority to weigh in individually. The larger issue of who—the IRT, the BMT, or the city—would build and operate new lines remained unsolved. Peter Derrick suggests that Hylan was initially willing to cooperate with the Transit Commission because he hoped it would be abolished in 1924, and the city could take over the lines. As the Board of Transportation came closer to assuming some of the responsibilities of the Transit Commission, Hylan hoped to avoid dealing with the commission entirely.
53. Hood, *722 Miles*, 204–5; Derrick, "New York City Transit Crisis," 52–54. The Transit Commission would continue to oversee existing lines, rendering one of Hylan's central goals, the recapture of the existing IRT and BMT lines, nearly impossible.
54. Hood, *722 Miles*, 205.
55. *Staten Island Advance*, July 21, 1924, 1, and July 24, 1924, 1. Both Thaten and Fred Cozzens of the SICC wrote to Delaney, and Cozzens met with him and Tuttle. They could not be heartened by Delaney's public comments, which were ambiguous enough that the *New York Times* viewed him as sympathetic to the cries for more subways in lieu of constructing the Narrows tunnel (*New York Times*, July 15, 1924, 8).
56. *Staten Island Advance*, July 15, 1924, 1, July 16, 1924, 1, July 17, 1924, 1, July 22, 1924, 1, and August 7, 1924, 1; *Staten Islander*, July 23, 1924, 1. For example, the Port Richmond Board of Trade sent Mayor Hylan a letter and launched a petition; the Grant City Improvement Association voted on a resolution opposing the cessation of work on the Hylan tunnel; the Staten Island Chamber of Commerce hosted a planning meeting for all civic groups, and at that meeting Cornelius Kolff was named chairman of a citizens tunnel committee representing thirty civic groups, including the Civic League, the Lions and Rotary Clubs, several local boards of trade, and the Chamber of Commerce.
57. *Staten Island Advance*, October 19, 1923, 1, April 21, 1924, 2, July 11, 1924, 1, July 17, 1924, 1, and July 18, 1924, 1; *Staten Islander*, October 20, 1923, 1, and July 26, 1924, 1.
58. *Staten Island Advance*, July 22, 1924, 1, and July 24, 1924, 2.
59. *Staten Island Advance*, July 24, 1924, 1, August 4, 1924, 1, and August 7, 1924, 1; *Staten Islander*, July 30, 1924, 1.
60. Revell, *Building Gotham*, 114.
61. *Staten Island Advance*, August 14, 1924, 1; *Staten Islander*, August 16, 1924, 1.
62. The Hylan administration remained stymied in its efforts to pass amenable transit bills. In 1923, its proposal to allow $275 million in subway bonds to be exempt from the ceiling, as had been the case for water-tunnel construction, became deadlocked in the legislature and died. Hylan encountered continued resistance in 1924 and 1925. When the legislature finally expanded New York's debt capacity in 1926, Hylan was no longer its mayor, and his Narrows tunnel project no longer had legislative authorization (*New York Times*, February 14, 1923, 4, 16, April 4, 1924, 3, April 9, 1924, 1, April 24, 1924, 21, December 31, 1924, 3, February 18, 1925, 1, and March 12, 1926, 31;

Staten Island Advance, February 26, 1924, 1, July 31, 1924, 1, and August 1, 1924, 1; *Staten Islander*, August 16, 1924, 1).

63. *New York Times*, December 7, 1924, XX3; *Staten Islander*, March 7, 1925, 1.
64. *Staten Island Advance*, January 21, 1925, 1, and March 7, 1925, 1.
65. *New York Times*, February 8, 1925, 20.
66. *Staten Island Advance*, January 7, 1925, 1.
67. This amount, which Tuttle reduced to $6.5 million, would pay for one year of work. The total cost for the four years was now estimated at $28 million (*Staten Island Advance*, January 21, 1925, 1, and January 23, 1925, 1; *Staten Islander*, January 24, 1925, 1, and January 28, 1925, 1).
68. *Staten Island Advance*, January 27, 1925, 1, and January 30, 1925, 1; *Staten Islander*, January 31, 1925, 1. The size of the crowd reflected the results of a concerted effort in which 1,500 letters were sent out to citizens, phone calls were made to real estate interests, and speakers visited every theater two nights before the meeting to urge participation.
69. *New York Times*, December 7, 1924, XX3, and February 17, 1925, 6; Derrick, "New York City Transit Crisis," 55. Although Governor Smith was directly responding to the Board of Estimate's complaints, he was certainly aware of the Transit Commission's displeasure with the Hylan administration. See Transit Commission, "Open Letter from Transit Commission to Governor," c. 1923, box 73, "1923 Transit Miscellaneous" folder, GM.
70. *New York Times*, December 16, 1924, 1, December 20, 1924, 1, December 25, 1924, 1, and January 9, 1925, 1. See also Derrick, "New York City Transit Crisis," 56–57.
71. Joseph P. Raskin, *The Routes Not Taken: A Trip Through New York City's Unbuilt Subway System* (New York: Fordham University Press, 2016), 130–31; Derrick, "New York City Transit Crisis," 57–58; *Staten Island Advance*, February 9, 1925, 1; *New York Times*, February 17, 1925, 6, and May 10, 1925, XX12. McAvoy determined that rapid transit would suffer in a dual-purpose tunnel, while the prospects for freight were limited given the Port Authority's hostility, the railroad trunk lines' disinterest, and the B&O's disinclination to lease the tunnel at the high price required by the city.
72. *Staten Island Advance*, February 9, 1925, 1 (quote), February 10, 1925, 1, and March 7, 1925, 1; Derrick, "New York City Transit Crisis," 58.
73. Johnson, *Planning the Great Metropolis*, 206–7; *Richmond County Advance*, February 11, 1925, 1; *New York Times*, March 10, 1925, 2.
74. *Staten Island Advance*, February 11, 1925, 4, and February 12, 1925, 4; *Staten Islander*, April 1, 1925, 1.
75. *Staten Island Advance*, February 10, 1925 (extra ed.), 1, February 14, 1925, 1, March 6, 1925, 1, March 7, 1925, 1, 2, and March 9, 1925, 1; *Staten Islander*, February 18, 1925, 1, and March 14, 1925, 1; *New York Times*, March 11, 1925, 10.
76. *Staten Island Advance*, March 7, 1925, 1, March 11, 1925, 1, April 4, 1925, 1, and April 8, 1925, 2; *New York Times*, April 21, 1925, 1; Johnson, *Planning the Great Metropolis*, 206; Killmer, *The Authorized Freight and Passenger Tunnel*, 9, 12, 19.
77. There were other familiar arguments as well: the perfidious violation of home rule, the grossly underestimated costs of the Transit Commission's tunnel, and, with a public investment of $5 million already made, the wiping out of the "tremendous amount of work [already] accomplished." The bulk of the opposition came from the Hylan administration and Staten Island (*Staten Island Advance*, February 16, 1925, 1, March 6, 1925, 1, March 10, 1925, 1, and April 4, 1925, 1; *Staten Islander*, February 14, 1925, 1, and April 15, 1925, 1).

78. Three years after the initial rejection by the railroads, Hylan could report that the B&O had committed to use the tunnel and predict that the other lines would scramble to follow suit once it opened (*Staten Island Advance*, March 11, 1925 [extra ed.], 1; *Staten Islander*, March 14, 1925, 1).
79. Leroy Harkness to John Knight, March 21, 1925, box 74, "1925 Legislation on Tunnel" folder, GM. Knight was an upstate Republican state senator who had sponsored the legislation creating the Transit Commission in 1921.
80. George McAneny, "Memorandum Relating to SI Tunnel," April 2, 1925, box 74, "1925 Legislation on Tunnel" folder, GM; *Staten Island Advance*, March 7, 1925, 1, and March 12, 1925; *New York Times*, May 5, 1925, 23.
81. *Staten Island Advance*, March 14, 1925, 1, March 18, 1925, 1, March 25, 1925, 1, and March 26, 1925, 1.
82. *Staten Island Advance*, February 11, 1925, 1, and February 17, 1925 (extra ed.), 1; Alfred Smith to New York State Legislature, February 16, 1925, in *Public Papers of Governor Alfred E. Smith, 1925* (Albany, NY: J. B. Lyon, 1925), 129–33; *New York Times*, February 17, 1925, 1; *Staten Islander*, February 25, 1925, 1.
83. *New York Times*, April 21, 1925, 1; *Staten Island Advance*, April 21, 1925, 1; *Staten Islander*, April 22, 1925, 1. Recognizing the Staten Islanders' marginality, the Staten Island Civic League retained Murray Hulbert, former president of the Board of Aldermen and dock commissioner, to speak at the governor's hearing on its behalf. Other speakers in favor of a veto included Hylan, Tuttle, Queens Borough president Maurice Connolly, Corporation Counsel George Nicholson, as well as the following Staten Islanders: former state senator C. Ernest Smith, Max Thaten, and Cornelius Kolff. Speakers in favor of Governor Smith's signature included Transit commissioners Harkness and McAneny, Citizens Union counsel Leonard M. Wallstein, Port Authority chairman Julian A. Gregory, chief counsel Julius H. Cohen, and consulting engineer General George W. Goethals. No one from the PRR testified, but Hylan invoked the company as a stealthily self-interested party. For other public accusations against the railroad, see also *Staten Island Advance*, February 14, 1925, 1, March 11, 1925, 4, and March 18, 1925, 5.
84. Bridgeman was never enthusiastic about any tunnel. He contended that it would upset rather than bolster local property values and put Richmond realtors at a comparative disadvantage with competing interests in Brooklyn and Queens. Writing to Governor Smith, Bridgeman reported that he once randomly queried five hundred Staten Islanders about transportation needs. Of the eighty-three respondents, only seventeen wanted any tunnel, the rest preferring enhanced ferry service (*Staten Island Advance*, February 11, 1925, 4; *Staten Islander*, March 7, 1925, 1; E. C. Bridgeman to Alfred Smith, April 24, 1925, box 61, folder 200-488, AES).
85. Unwavering supporters included Lynch, the *Staten Island Advance*, the *Staten Islander*, the Civic League, and the SICC. See *Staten Island Advance*, March 21, 1925, 1, March 27, 1925, 1, April 4, 1925, 1, April 6, 1925, 1, April 16, 1925, 1, April 20, 1925, 1, and April 21, 1925, 1. See also *Staten Islander*, March 14, 1925, 5, March 21, 1925, 1, April 8, 1925, 1, April 15, 1925, 1, and April 18, 1925, 1.
86. "Construction of a Tunnel for Freight and Passenger Purposes Under New York Bay Between Staten Island and Brooklyn," in *Public Papers of Governor Smith*, 380–85. The *Wall Street Journal* (April 24, 1925, 1) deemed the whole project to be "absurd," and the *New York Times* (April 23, 1925, 20) praised Smith for bucking the political incentive of party unity with Hylan. One exception was the *Evening Journal* (New York), which hoped for a veto (April 18, 1925, box 55, WJW).

324   7. Getting the Shaft

87. *Staten Islander*, March 7, 1925, 1, and March 14, 1925, 1; *Staten Island Advance*, March 4, 1925, 1, March 12, 1925, 1, March 14, 1925, 1, and April 23, 1925, 1; *New York Times*, April 22, 1925, 5, and May 3, 1925, 22.
88. *New York Times*, April 24, 1925, 2. The realtors named by the *Times* were John B. Cornell, John Hamilton, George Klingeibiel, Walter Simons, Thomas Hall, and William Morton, none of whom had been directly involved with the tunnel efforts of the 1920s.
89. *Staten Islander*, April 25, 1925, 4.
90. *Staten Island Advance*, April 23, 1925, 1, and April 27, 1925, 1.
91. Staten Island Chamber of Commerce (SICC), "Special Meeting of the Executive Committee," in *Minutes of the Board of Directors*, April 25, 1925, SICCR; *Staten Islander*, May 2, 1925, 1, and May 6, 1925, 1; *New York Times*, May 1, 1925, 10, and May 3, 1925, 22. The Civic League did not rush to make a similar statement, but its president, Francis Leman, signed the SICC resolution.
92. *Staten Island Advance*, April 23, 1925, 1, April 24, 1925, 1, April 30, 1925, 1, May 2, 1925, 1, and May 6, 1925; *New York Times*, April 22, 1925, 5, May 3, 1925, 22, and May 10, 1925, XX12. One reason why a rapid-transit tunnel would cost far less than a freight tunnel was that the bore's diameter could be reduced from 24 to 18 feet.
93. *Staten Island Advance*, April 24, 1925, 1; *New York Times*, May 10, 1925, XX12; New York City Board of Transportation, *Proceedings* 2 (January–June 1925): 885, 1016; F. LeBoutillier to Samuel Rea, May 14, 1925, box 87, folder 105/90, PCRR.
94. Memoirs by New York City political insiders abound. For a treatment of the Smith–Hylan relationship sympathetic to the mayor, see Henry H. Klein, *My Last Fifty Years: An Autobiographical History of "Inside" New York* (New York: Isaac Goldman, 1935), 211, 309–14. For a view favorable to the governor, see Grover A. Whalen, *Mr. New York: The Autobiography of Grover A. Whalen* (New York: Putnam's, 1955), 74–76. Smith's biographers have generally pilloried Hylan, who lacks a full-scale biography of his own. See, for example, Christopher M. Finan, *Alfred E. Smith: The Happy Warrior* (New York: Hill and Wang, 2002), 109, 131–32, 191; and Robert A. Slayton, *Empire Statesman: The Rise and Redemption of Al Smith* (New York: Free Press, 2001), 221–24.
95. The Manhattan and Bronx organizations supported Walker; Brooklyn and Queens endorsed Hylan. Observers and scholars have thought the primary reflected long-standing tension between Smith and William Randolph Hearst, whose newspapers strongly favored Hylan. See "The Smith Hylan Battle," *Literary Digest*, September 1925, 8–9; Herbert Mitgang, *Once Upon a Time in New York: Jimmy Walker, Franklin Roosevelt, and the Last Great Battle of the Jazz Age* (New York: Free Press, 2000), 70; Kramer and Flanagan, *Staten Island*, 25; and *New York Times*, May 6, 1925, 2, May 10, 1925, XX1, XX12, and August 16, 1925, XX5. For an account of the primary campaign from a Hearst newspaper insider, see Gene Fowler, *Beau James: The Life and Times of Jimmy Walker* (New York: Viking Press, 1949), 136–48.
96. *New York Times*, September 12, 1925, 5, and September 15, 1925, 3. The Republican candidate for mayor, Frank Waterman, also pledged support for a passenger-only tunnel to Staten Island.
97. *New York Times*, August 9, 1925, XX5, August 10, 1925, 1, August 11, 1925, 1, September 16, 1925, 3, and September 17, 1925, 2. Harry Tiernan, a county judge and surrogate, headed the ticket as a challenger to Lynch, and the race was heated though ultimately not very close.
98. The Concorde Fallacy is that sunk costs require the allocation of additional resources regardless of an investment's current merit. Economists, however, can demonstrate

the rationality of abandoning a project regardless of past expenditures if future revenues are not foreseeable.

8. Driving the Narrows: New Options for Connection, 1925–1932

1. Staten Island Chamber of Commerce (SICC), *Minutes of the Board of Directors*, March 12 and 26, April 9 and 23, 1929, SICCR.
2. New York City, where subway ridership did not peak until 1947 and remained an essential means of transportation for millions of residents, is actually less illustrative of this pattern than are many other cities in the United States. At the same time, New York held a special place in the rise of automobility. See Clay McShane, *Down the Asphalt Path: The Automobile and the American City* (New York: Columbia University Press, 1994), 104–5.
3. McShane, *Down the Asphalt Path*, 73–80, 119–24.
4. Kenneth Jackson's masterful study *Crabgrass Frontier* depicts a nearly two-century trend of population dispersal. Other historians focus on specific eras of suburbanization and the interwar years, and the 1920s in particular are certainly a distinct period. See Kenneth Jackson, *Crabgrass Frontier: The Suburbanization of the United States* (New York: Oxford University Press, 1985), 163–68, 172–77; Robert A. Beauregard, *When America Became Suburban* (Minneapolis: University of Minnesota Press, 2006), 32–33, 44, 54; Jon C. Teaford, *The Metropolitan Revolution: The Rise of Post Urban America* (New York: Columbia University Press, 2006), 3–4; James J. Flink, *The Automobile Age* (Cambridge, MA: MIT Press, 1988), 139–44, 147–51; Dan Albert, *Are We There Yet? The American Automobile Past, Present, and Driverless* (New York: Norton, 2019), 84.
5. Robert Fogelson, *Downtown: Its Rise and Fall, 1880–1950* (New Haven, CT: Yale University Press, 2001), 250–51; Jon C. Teaford, *The Twentieth-Century American City: Problem, Promise, and Reality* (Baltimore, MD: Johns Hopkins University Press, 1986), 66–67; Albert, *Are We There Yet?*, 77. As Dan Albert relates, one aspect of that cultural shift was the phenomenally popular car show (*Are We There Yet?*, 57), and another was the reliance on loans to purchase an automobile (84–85).
6. Jackson, *Crabgrass Frontier*, 166–71; Jane Holtz Kay, *Asphalt Nation: How the Automobile Took Over America and How We Can Take It Back* (New York: Crown, 1997), 166–67, 175–76; Paul Barrett, "Public Policy and Private Choice: Mass Transit and the Automobile in Chicago Between the Wars," *Business History Review* 49, no. 4 (Winter 1975): 473–97; Peter Dreier, John Mollenkopf, and Todd Swanstrom, *Place Matters: Metropolitics for the Twenty-First Century*, 2nd ed. (Lawrence: University Press of Kansas, 2004), 103–51; McShane, *Down the Asphalt Path*, 112–19.
7. For example, Jameson W. Doig's masterful account of the Port Authority dispels the notion that it switched from rails to roads to ensure its political survival. Doig suggests instead that "the initiatives that took the Port agency into the automotive age came more from *outside* demands than from the Authority's own inclination" (*Empire on the Hudson: Entrepreneurial Vision and Political Power at the Port of New York Authority* [New York: Columbia University Press, 2001], 98, emphasis in original). See also Robert Bruegmann, *Sprawl: A Compact History* (Chicago: University of Chicago Press, 2005), 11, 109–12; Carlton Basmajian, "Transportation and Power," *Journal of Urban History* 38, no. 6 (November 2012): 1114–20; and Albert, *Are We There Yet?*, 68–73.

8. Martha J. Bianco, "Technological Innovation and the Rise and Fall of Urban Mass Transit," *Journal of Urban History* 25, no. 3 (March 1999): 348–78; David W. Jones, *Mass Motorization and Mass Transit: An American History and Policy Analysis* (Bloomington: Indiana University Press, 2008), 52; Charles K. Hyde, "Planning a Transportation System for Metropolitan Detroit in the Age of the Automobile: The Triumph of the Expressway," *Michigan Historical Review* 32, no. 1 (April 2006): 94–95; Teaford, *The Metropolitan Revolution*, 5.
9. See, for example, John D. Fairfield, *The Public and Its Possibilities: Triumphs and Tragedies in the American City* (Philadelphia: Temple University Press, 2010); James Howard Kuntsler, *Geography of Nowhere: The Rise and Decline of America's Man-Made Landscape* (New York: Simon and Schuster, 1993); David T. Beito, Peter Gordon, and Alexander Tabarrok, eds., *The Voluntary City: Choice, Community, and Civil Society* (Ann Arbor: University of Michigan Press, 2002); and Edward Glaeser and David Cutler, *Survival of the City: Living and Thriving in an Age of Isolation* (New York: Penguin, 2021). For a theoretical effort to move past debates between urbanism and sprawl, see Thad Williamson, "Beyond Sprawl and Anti-sprawl," in *Critical Urban Studies: New Perspectives*, ed. Jonathan S. Davies and David L. Imbroscio (Albany: State University of New York Press, 2010), 165–82.
10. Jackson, *Crabgrass Frontier*, 170. For a critique of this finding in New York and Chicago, see Scott C. Bottles, *Los Angeles and the Automobile: The Making of the Modern City* (Berkeley: University of California Press, 1987), 1–4, 7.
11. Richard Dickenson, ed. and comp., *Holden's Staten Island: The History of Richmond County: Revised Resource Manual Sketches for the Year Two Thousand Two* (New York: Center for Migration Studies, 2002), 233; Charles W. Leng and William T. Davis, *Staten Island and Its People: A History, 1609–1929*, 5 vols. (New York: Lewis Historical, 1929–1933), 1:375, 1:319, 2:718.
12. Albert, *Are We There Yet?*, 83.
13. *Staten Island Advance*, December 3, 1925, 1; *Staten Islander*, October 28, 1925, 6, and February 19, 1926, 1. Lynch did not make the tunnel a large part of his campaign for reelection in 1925.
14. Transit Commission Memorandum from Chief Engineer, February 5, 1926, 1–2, box 76, first folder, GM; George McAneny to James Walker, April 29, 1926, Correspondence Received, Transit Commission, roll 61, folder 834, JJW; *New York Times*, May 18, 1926, 12. Not only was the shorter southerly route less costly to build, but it was also in keeping with McAneny's long-standing commitment to using rapid transit to disperse population.
15. Daniel Turner to George McAneny, January 11, 1926, box 77, 1927 folder, GM. Turner agreed with McAneny that a Narrows tunnel was a top priority for subway expansion.
16. See Clifton Hood, *722 Miles: The Building of the Subways and How They Transformed New York*, centennial ed. (Baltimore, MD: Johns Hopkins University Press, 2004), 203–7; *New York Times*, December 10, 1924, 1, and December 11, 1924, 22.
17. *Staten Island Advance*, May 6, 1925, 1; *Staten Islander*, June 20, 1925, 1, and June 24, 1925, 4.
18. *Staten Island Advance*, December 3, 1925, 1; *Map Showing Relation Between Rapid Transit Routes Proposed by the Transit Commission and the City Subway System of the Board of Transportation*, January 8, 1926, box 76, folder 2, GM; *New York Times*, April 30, 1926, 6.
19. *New York Times*, May 25, 1870, 4; *Staten Island World*, July 13, 1907, 4; *Staten Islander*, December 20, 1922, 1.

20. *Staten Islander*, November 21, 1925, 1, 4, and January 30, 1926, 7; *Staten Island Advance*, November 19, 1925, 1; *New York Times*, December 1, 1925, 1.
21. *Staten Island Advance*, December 7, 1925, 7; Staten *Islander*, January 23, 1926, 1.
22. *New York Times*, November 30, 1925, 1; *Staten Island Advance*, November 30, 1925, 1.
23. *Staten Islander*, June 6, 1925, sec. 3, 1.
24. *Staten Islander*, November 21, 1925, 1; *Staten Island Advance*, November 19, 1925, 1.
25. *Staten Island Advance*, November 19, 1925, 1, December 3, 1925, 1, and December 4, 1925, 1; *New York Times*, December 1, 1925, 1.
26. *Staten Island Advance*, December 4, 1925, 4.
27. SICC, *Minutes*, November 30 and December 16, 1925, and June 9, 1926; SICC, *31st Annual Report* (1926), 9, SICCR; New York City Board of Estimate and Apportionment, *Proceedings* 8 (December 4, 1925): 9467.
28. *New York Times*, September 21, 1926, 48; *Staten Island Advance*, October 6, 1927, 1, and August 17, 1928, 13.
29. *Staten Island Advance*, November 5, 1926, 1; October 1, 1927, 1; and October 6, 1927, 1. The Brooklyn organizations included groups in Fort Hamilton but not Bay Ridge. Already wary of how a bridge might disrupt their community, the Bay Ridge Chamber of Commerce and the Bay Ridge Citizens Association urged the completion of a passenger tunnel under the Narrows instead (*Brooklyn Daily Eagle*, November 17, 1926, 4, and April 15, 1926, 7; *Staten Island Advance*, November 20, 1926, 1).
30. *Staten Island Advance*, May 2, 1928, 1, and August 17, 1928, 13; *Staten Island Light*, May 1928, 126, and October–November 1928, 254. As young engineers, Robinson had worked on the Williamsburg Bridge, and Steinman on the Hell Gate Bridge. They formed a partnership in 1920, and their firm subsequently built many bridges, including the Henry Hudson Bridge and the Mackinac Bridge.
31. SICC, *Minutes*, October 26, November 22, and December 13, 1927; *Staten Island Transcript*, August 19, 1927, 1; *Staten Island Advance*, November 1, 1928.
32. Keith Revell, *Building Gotham: Civic Culture & Public Policy in New York City, 1898–1938* (Baltimore, MD: Johns Hopkins University Press, 2003), 247.
33. The City Committee's membership included many prominent Staten Islanders: E. C. Bridgeman, Fred Cozzens, Judge William T. Fetherston, Cornelius Kolff, Anning S. Prall, Max Thaten, and Louis Tribus, while George Cromwell, Eugenius Outerbridge, and Theodore Oxholm declined to serve. Two years later its recommendations centered on the creation of a city planning board, which was successfully resisted by the borough presidents ("To the Members of the City Planning and Survey Committee," c. June 1926, Subject Files, box JJW 231, "City Planning Committee, 1926–1928" folder, no. 1, JJW; "Regrets and No Answers," c. June 1926, Subject Files, box JJW 232, "City Planning Committee, Correspondence, 1926–1928" folder, no. 1, JJW; *New York Times*, June 20, 1926, XX1, and June 6, 1928, 1; Revell, *Building Gotham*, 247–51).
34. *New York Times*, December 16, 1926, 11; May 10, 1927, 34; March 20, 1928, 16; February 7, 1929, 4; March 27, 1929, 3; and April 1, 1929, 19.
35. *New York Times*, June 6, 1928, 1.
36. *Staten Island Advance*, September 27, 1928, 10, and October 8, 1928, 1. The three-person Bridge Committee did not include Richmond Borough president Lynch.
37. *New York Times*, February 12, 1929, 27, and June 12, 1929, 23.
38. *New York Times*, May 3, 1926, 5, October 4, 1926, 16, January 22, 1928, 31, April 1, 1928, 169, August 19, 1928, 139, and January 2, 1929, 23; *Brooklyn Daily Eagle*, September 26, 1928, 19.

39. David A. Johnson, *Planning the Great Metropolis: The 1929 Regional Plan of New York and Its Environs* (London: E. & F. N. Spon, 1996), 147–66.
40. Regional Plan Association, *A Close-up of the Regional Plan of New York and Its Environs: What the Plan Is and Does for the Communities and Citizens of the Region, Illustrated with Maps and Diagrams* (New York: Regional Plan Association, 1929), 7–12; *Staten Island Advance*, April 16, 1925, 1, and June 25, 1929, 4; *Staten Island Light* 1, no. 3 (June 1926): 41.
41. *New York Times*, May 3, 1926, 5, and March 17, 1929, XX3; *Staten Islander*, May 4, 1926, 1; *Staten Island Advance*, August 2, 1928, 4, and October 13, 1928, 11.
42. *Staten Island Advance*, July 18, 1928, 1.
43. *New York Times*, February 26, 1925, 20, and August 29, 1926, X4; see also *Staten Island Transcript*, July 13, 1928, 2.
44. Robert A. Caro, *The Power Broker: Robert Moses and the Fall of New York* (New York: Random House, 1974), 341–42.
45. Darl Rastorfer, *Six Bridges: The Legacy of Othmar H. Ammann* (New Haven, CT: Yale University Press, 2000), 93.
46. SICC, *Minutes*, January 22, 1929; *Staten Island Advance*, January 2, 1929, 1; *New York Times*, October 4, 1926, 16, December 11, 1927, RE10, January 20, 1929, XX1, and March 17, 1929, RE12.
47. *New York Times*, September 11, 1928, 29, September 18, 1928, 6, and April 4, 1929, 16; *Staten Island Advance*, September 7, 1928, 1.
48. *Staten Island Advance*, December 20, 1928, 1; *New York Times*, December 20, 1928, 3. Steinman proposed towers 800 feet taller than the Woolworth Building, with observation decks, carillons, and beacon lights on top. Between them would lie a 4,500-foot steel bridge with 45-inch cables and a 235-foot clearance above the water. Unlike earlier plans for a bridge, his did not include any rails (*Staten Island Transcript*, May 11, 1928, 2). Singstad thought that neither would the War Department approve of the span, nor would the city fund its great cost. He also believed there was insufficient bedrock and a span too lengthy to be viable, but he was understandably confident that the ventilation challenges of a tunnel could be addressed. Finally, Singstad thought a tunnel would require less invasive approaches than a bridge (*Staten Island Advance*, January 3, 1929, 1).
49. *Staten Island Advance*, July 31, 1928, 1; August 1, 1928, 4; and January 3, 1929, 1.
50. *Brooklyn Daily Eagle*, January 26, 1928, 3, and May 2, 1928, 3; *Staten Island Advance*, February 13, 1930, 1.
51. *Staten Island Advance*, November 18, 1929, 15.
52. Flink, *The Automobile Age*, 188.
53. *New York Times*, August 8, 1926, XX4.
54. *New York Times*, May 10, 1926, 23; January 9, 1927, A4; April 1, 1928, 141; May 30, 1929, 12; and January 5, 1930, A24.
55. Holtz Kay, *Asphalt Nation*, 149; Matthew Dalbey, *Regional Visionaries and Metropolitan Boosters: Decentralization, Regional Planning, and Parkways During the Interwar Years* (Boston: Kluwer Academic, 2002), 76–80.
56. *Staten Island Transcript*, June 1, 1928, 4.
57. *Staten Island Transcript*, December 6, 1929, 1.
58. *Staten Island Advance*, November 2, 1928, 4, and February 18, 1930, 4.
59. *Staten Island Advance*, January 5, 1929, 1, and February 4, 1929, 4.
60. *Staten Islander*, September 9, 1922, 1; Doig, *Empire on the Hudson*, 112.
61. Doig, *Empire on the Hudson*, 114–19; *Staten Island Advance*, September 26, 1928, 9.

62. *New York Times*, January 30, 1929, 18, and February 16, 1929, 8.
63. "Transportation Board Starts Narrows Tunnel Preliminary Survey," March 13, 1929, Correspondence Received, Board of Transportation, roll 64, folder 870, JJW; *Staten Island Advance*, March 13, 1929, 1, and June 10, 1929, 1; *New York Times*, March 12, 1929, 1, April 7, 1929, RE2, and July 27, 1929, 8. The existing 24-foot shafts could not be used because a vehicular tunnel required a 30-foot diameter and a 3 percent grade. The toll plaza would be placed on the Staten Island side, with portals located at Hylan Boulevard, Clove Road, and Tompkins Avenue.
64. *Staten Island Transcript*, March 19, 1929, 1. The speaker was George J. Houtain, chairman of the Better City Government League on Staten Island.
65. *Staten Island Advance*, October 11, 1928, 13; October 13, 1928, 11; and October 18, 1928, 1.
66. *Staten Island Advance*, March 23, 1929, 4.
67. *Staten Island Advance*, November 29, 1929, 17; December 19, 1929, 8; and September 22, 1930, 1.
68. *Staten Island Advance*, March 21, 1929, 4; April 2, 1929, 4; and April 11, 1929, 4.
69. *Staten Islander*, February 23, 1926, 4; *Staten Island Transcript*, July 13, 1928, 2, and January 11, 1929, 1; *Staten Island Advance*, July 11, 1928, 1, and January 28, 1929, 1.
70. *Staten Island Advance*, April 6, 1929, 4.
71. *Staten Island Advance*, April 12, 1929, 4.
72. Richmond County Chapter of the New York State Society of Professional Engineers and Land Surveyors, "Suggested Rapid Transit for Richmond Borough," April 10, 1930, MS233, box 6, folder 9, SIHS; *Staten Island Advance*, April 11, 1930, 1.
73. *Staten Island Advance*, April 19, 1930, 2; April 25, 1930, 1; and April 26, 1930, 4.
74. *New York Times*, December 8, 1919, 12, and May 9, 1930, 19; *Staten Island Advance*, October 12, 1929, 2, October 31, 1929, 1, November 15, 1929, 1, September 29, 1930, 1, December 23, 1930, 24, and April 6, 1931, 4; *Staten Island Transcript*, August 22, 1930, 4, and December 15, 1931, 2. The Community Councils of New York was the leading proponent of the Governor's Island airport. Daniel De V Harned, a lawyer and Eltingville resident who served as the councils' vice chairman and counsel, spearheaded efforts on Staten Island.
75. *Staten Island Advance*, April 10, 1931, 1. Approximately 175 citizens attended the meeting, at which thirty organizations—with two votes each—were represented. Some delegates did not vote, claiming that they had no instructions to do so. The Staten Island Real Estate Board split its two votes, and the SICC members elected not to vote at all but expressed a willingness to work for the winning plan. The organizations that voted for the SPE plan included Grant City Board of Trade, Kiwanis, Lions, West Brighton Board of Trade, Stickholm Club, Beauvais Post of the American Legion, North Shore Veteran Firemen's Association, Hugh T. Cuff Association, United Civic League of Midland Beach, Westerleigh Improvement Society, Ocean Breeze Welfare Association, and United Steuben Society of Tottenville. The groups that voted for the Governor's Island route included the Midland Beach Colony Club, New Dorp Board of Trade, New Dorp Beach Board of Trade, New Dorp Political Club, Citizens and Taxpayer's Association of Staten Island, Annadale Democratic Club, and the Stapleton Community Council.
76. See, for example, *Staten Island Advance*, April 11, 1931, 4; May 5, 1931, 2; and May 12, 1931, 4.
77. *Staten Island Advance*, November 13, 1931, 1, and November 16, 1931, 4. The other two rallies were in Port Richmond and St. George.

330   8. Driving the Narrows

78. *Staten Island Advance*, October 24, 1930, 1; April 11, 1931, 1; and December 15, 1931, 1.
79. *Staten Island Advance*, November 13, 1931, 1, and December 15, 1931, 1; *New York Times*, March 28, 1928, 3. Local discontent over Delaney's "pending" subway report went back to 1925, when Delaney promised to pursue a rapid-transit-only tunnel in the aftermath of the Nicoll-Hofstadter law but never delivered. For subsequent postponement of the report release date, see the *Staten Islander*, February 19, 1926, 1; *Staten Island Advance*, June 4, 1927, 1, March 28, 1928, 1, and May 17, 1929, 5. It would be nearly another two years before the report was finally completed and made public (*Staten Island Advance*, December 5, 1933, 1).
80. *Staten Island Advance*, April 19, 1932, 4, and April 21, 1932, 4; *New York Times*, April 19, 1932, 13.
81. *New York Times*, February 12, 1929, 27; February 13, 1929, 22; June 28, 1929, 16; October 4, 1929, 24; and October 26, 1929, 1.
82. *New York Times*, May 27, 1927, 25; May 13, 1928, 153; April 4, 1929, 16; June 11, 1929, 3; and July 27, 1929, 8. The initial exclusion of the midtown tunnel may have stemmed from contention over its location as Brooklyn groups favored a structure farther south than what Queens interests wanted. Once the midtown tunnel was approved, the Board of Transportation proceeded with borings for it prior to those for the Narrows tunnel.
83. The Day and Zimmerman report privileged projects that would relieve congestion. The report spoke favorably of a Narrows vehicular tunnel, but only as a means of "convenient access to Staten Island with its large areas suitable for housing, industry and shipping" and as a link between a Triborough bridge and the Goethals Bridge. It found that the tunnel would not be even close to self-sustaining. Assuming a fifty-cent toll, nearly 34,000 daily users would be required to cover costs, and the consultants predicted less than 5,500 daily users upon opening, with no immediate increase envisioned (Dan Zimmerman, "Report No. 2739 on Highway Traffic Conditions and Proposed Traffic Relief Measures for the City of New York," October 22, 1929, 6–9, Subject Files, box 276, "Transit Affairs" folder, JJW; *New York Times*, October 24, 1929, 1; *Staten Island Advance*, October 25, 1929, 2).
84. *New York Times*, January 8, 1930, 9, and April 9, 1930, 16; *Staten Island Advance*, March 28, 1930, 4.
85. New York City Board of Transportation, *Proceedings* 14 (July–September 1930): 3151, and 15 (October–December 1930): 3277–79; *New York Times*, February 8, 1930, 31, and November 23, 1930, 129. The Board of Transportation anticipated 32-foot-diameter tunnels. There would be 5,000 feet between shafts and 11,000 feet between portals.
86. *New York Times*, April 21, 1930, 22, July 11, 1930, 3, and April 25, 1931, 24; *Staten Island Advance*, September 22, 1930, 1. By April 1930, plans for a midtown tunnel were nearly ready, whereas those for the Narrows tunnel were barely underway and would not be completed that year.
87. New York City Board of Transportation, *Proceedings* 13 (January–June 1930): 1828–29, and 17 (July–December 1931): 2000.
88. *New York Times*, July 12, 1931, RE2, and September 30, 1931, 21.
89. Edward Robb Ellis, *The Epic of New York City: A Narrative History* (1966; reprint, New York: Kodansha America, 1997), 531–34; Hood, *722 Miles*, 228.
90. *New York Times*, January 9, 1932, 1, and March 9, 1932, 4.
91. *New York Times*, May 9, 1902, 7; Caro, *The Power Broker*, 639–77.

92. As Lynch reminded the SICC in April 1926, "All other portions of the city are clamoring for increased rapid transit facilities, and unless Staten Islanders do their part, they will be left out in the cold" (*New York Times*, April 4, 1926, RE2).

9. Facing the Competition: Last Gasps for a Subway and a Tunnel, 1933–1945

1. New York City Board of Transportation, *Proceedings* 21 (July–December 1933): 1530–39; *Staten Island Advance*, November 16, 1933, 12, December 5, 1933, 1, December 16, 1933, 4, and December 28, 1933, 1.
2. *Staten Island Transcript*, December 8, 1933, 4. Off-island coverage of the report completely missed this angry sentiment on Staten Island. See, for example, *Brooklyn Daily Eagle*, December 5, 1933, 2; and *New York Times*, December 6, 1933, 47.
3. Mark I. Gelfand, *A Nation of Cities: The Federal Government and Urban America, 1933–1965* (New York: Oxford University Press, 1975), 65–70.
4. James S. Olson, *Saving Capitalism: The RFC and the New Deal, 1933–1940* (Princeton, NJ: Princeton University Press, 1988), 11–15; Anthony J. Badger, *The New Deal: The Depression Years, 1933–1940* (New York: Hill and Wang, 1989), 48–49.
5. James S. Olson, *Herbert Hoover and the RFC, 1931–1933* (Ames: Iowa State University Press, 1977), 68–79; Olson, *Saving Capitalism*, 16–21; Udo Sautter, "Government and Unemployment: The Use of Public Works Before the New Deal," *Journal of American History* 73, no. 1 (June 1986): 83–85; Gelfand, *A Nation of Cities*, 40.
6. *New York Times*, January 15, 1932, 8; *Staten Island Transcript*, July 22, 1932, 1, and August 5, 1932, 4; *Staten Island Advance*, May 17, 1932, 4, July 7, 1932, 1, and July 20, 1932, 1; Gelfand, *A Nation of Cities*, 52–53.
7. *Staten Island Advance*, July 8, 1932, 4, July 19, 1932, 1, August 2, 1932, 4, and September 14, 1932, 1, 4; *New York Times*, August 5, 1932, 15. Staten Islanders counted on Lynch's and the Brooklyn Borough president's votes and held out some hope that Comptroller Charles Berry, a Staten Island resident who had publicly favored a subway just a few months earlier, might supply some key support.
8. Gelfand, *A Nation of Cities*, 40.
9. "Memorandum for Mayor Walker," December 15, 1930, Subject Files, box 232, "City Planning 1930–1932" folder, JJW.
10. *New York Times*, August 5, 1932, 15.
11. *Staten Island Advance*, July 8, 1932, 4; July 13, 1932, 1; and August 18, 1932, 4.
12. Staten Island Chamber of Commerce (SICC) Transportation Committee, *Minutes*, August 17, 1932, SICCR; Edward Robb Ellis, *The Epic of New York City: A Narrative History* (1966; reprint, New York: Kodansha America, 1997), 540–48.
13. *Staten Island Advance*, August 9, 1932, 14. The vehement speaker was Robert S. Molinari.
14. *Staten Island Advance*, August 9, 1932, 14, August 16, 1932, 14, August 24, 1932, 1, August 26, 1932, 2, and September 22, 1932, 1; *New York Times*, September 14, 1932, 2, and September 22, 1932, 10.
15. Olson, *Saving Capitalism*, 20–21; *New York Times*, August 5, 1932, 15.
16. Upon Walker's resignation, Joseph V. McKee served as acting mayor until John P. O'Brien won a special November election and took office in 1933 to complete Walker's

term. Fiorello La Guardia defeated both McKee and O'Brien in the election of November 1933 (Mason Williams, *City of Ambition: FDR, La Guardia, and the Making of Modern New York* [New York: Norton, 2013], 116, 123–29).
17. *Staten Island Advance*, April 29, 1933, 1, and May 4, 1933, 1; *Staten Island Transcript*, May 2, 1933, 1; *New York Times*, May 3, 1933, 2, and May 14, 1933, 20.
18. *Staten Island Advance*, September 15, 1932, 1, and September 22, 1932, 1; *Staten Island Transcript*, May 2, 1933, 1. The Transit Conference included indirect revenues generated by post-tunnel increases in employment and development.
19. *Staten Island Advance*, September 22, 1932, 1, and May 4, 1933, 1.
20. *Wall Street Journal*, June 21, 1933, 5; *Staten Island Advance*, June 23, 1933, 1.
21. William E. Leuchtenberg, *Franklin D. Roosevelt and the New Deal: 1932–1940* (New York: Harper and Row, 1963), 141–62.
22. Badger, *The New Deal*, 66; Jason Scott Smith, *Building New Deal Liberalism: The Political Economy of Public Works, 1933–1956* (Cambridge: Cambridge University Press, 2006), 29–33, 49–50, 62–65.
23. Smith, *Building New Deal Liberalism*, 95; Leuchtenberg, *Franklin Roosevelt and the New Deal*, 70, 133.
24. James T. Patterson, *The New Deal and the States: Federalism in Transition* (Princeton, NJ: Princeton University Press, 1969), 56; Kerwin Williams, *Grants-in-Aid Under the Public Works Administration: A Study in Federal-State-Local Relations* (New York: Columbia University Press, 1939), 103; Smith, *Building New Deal Liberalism*, 36, 45–46, 55, 86.
25. Smith, *Building New Deal Liberalism*, 24–26, 44–48, 86.
26. Smith, *Building New Deal Liberalism*, 42; William D. Reeves, "PWA and Competitive Administration in the New Deal," *Journal of American History* 60, no. 2 (September 1973): 368–70.
27. Smith, *Building New Deal Liberalism*, 60.
28. Harold Ickes to Lawrence Houghteling, October 28, 1933, quoted in Smith, *Building New Deal Liberalism*, 61–62.
29. *Staten Island Advance*, June 23, 1933, 1, June 24, 1933, 1, and July 13, 1933, 1; *New York Times*, June 22, 1933, 21.
30. *Staten Island Advance*, July 14, 1933, 1.
31. *Staten Island Advance*, July 15, 1933, 4, October 4, 1933, 2, and December 22, 1933, 1; SICC, *Minutes of the Board of Directors*, October 3, 1933, SICCR. On December 29, 1933, the Board of Estimate did vote to submit a loan request to the PWA for the subway to Staten Island. Coming two days before the arrival of a new mayor, this act was recognized on Staten Island as a symbolic gesture not likely to sway the incoming La Guardia administration. In August 1935, the PWA formally denied the Staten Island "application" from 1933 but sent no rejection letter because there was no authority to whom to send it. The PWA described the so-called application as follows: "This document was transferred to the PWA by the RFC in August, 1933, but does not strictly constitute an application. No definite amount of money was requested and no plans and specifications or terms relative to the proposed loan were given. The document does not show that it was filed by a legally authorized body and it appears it is simply a collection of endorsements without pretense of authority" (*Staten Island Advance*, December 27, 1933, 1; December 30, 1933, 1; March 27, 1936, 1 [quote]).
32. *Staten Island Transcript*, December 8, 1933, 4; *Wall Street Journal*, December 7, 1933, 5; *Staten Island Advance*, December 16, 1933, 1. The Board of Transportation estimated 14 million passengers in the Narrows tunnel in year one (and 42 million passengers

in year ten), a far cry from consultant Arthur Tuttle's projected 45 million passengers in its first year of operation. The board believed that revenues would more than cover operating expenses from the beginning but would leave only $202,000 available for interest and amortization charges. By year ten, the board predicted $1,279,000 would be generated to service the debt.
33. *Staten Island Advance*, December 5, 1933, 1,
34. *Staten Island Advance*, December 7, 1933, 1.
35. *Staten Island Advance*, December 13, 1933, 1, 4; SICC, *Minutes*, December 15, 1933.
36. *Staten Island Advance*, December 15, 1933, 1.
37. *Staten Island Advance*, December 16, 1933, 1.
38. *Staten Island Advance*, December 16, 1933, 4, and December 22, 1933, 1. At a pre-inauguration banquet for the new La Guardia administration, Richmond Borough president elect Joseph Palma's claim that Richmond received few public works and his call for a subway for Richmond met with laughter from his Republican colleagues. The Bronx Borough president, observing that Staten Island had gotten piers and the Bronx had received a market, quipped, "Want to trade?" Humor was found in the perception that Staten Island was forever crying "no fair" and in the realization that the La Guardia administration would surely economize, not spend (*Staten Island Advance*, December 20, 1933, 1).
39. *Staten Island Advance*, October 20, 1933, 3; *New York Times*, October 6, 1933, 1, and October 18, 1933, 1; Daniel C. Kramer and Richard M. Flanagan, *Staten Island: Conservative Bastion in a Liberal City* (Lanham, MD: University Press of America, 2012), 26.
40. Clifton Hood, *722 Miles: The Building of the Subways and How They Transformed New York*, centennial ed. (Baltimore, MD: Johns Hopkins University Press, 2004), 226–37. La Guardia achieved unification into a single municipally owned and operated system in 1940.
41. Williams, *City of Ambition*, 131–32, 148–53; Thomas Kessner, *Fiorello H. La Guardia and the Making of Modern New York* (New York: McGraw Hill, 1989), 295; Leonard Chalmers, "The Crucial Test of La Guardia's First Hundred Days: The Emergency Economy Bill," *New York Historical Society Quarterly* 57 (1973): 239–40, cited in Alyn Brodsky, *The Great Mayor: Fiorello La Guardia and the Making of the City of New York* (New York: St. Martin's Press, 2003), 294. La Guardia also met with Harry Hopkins, who headed the short-lived Civil Works Administration, which provided millions of dollars in grants for federal improvements and proved to be a precursor to the WPA.
42. Williams, *City of Ambition*, 139–42; Kessner, *Fiorello H. La Guardia*, 262–69; Brodsky, *The Great Mayor*, 294–300; August Heckscher, *When La Guardia Was Mayor: New York's Legendary Years* (New York: Norton, 1978), 37–42.
43. Raymond Ingersoll to Fiorello La Guardia, December 6, 1934; La Guardia to Board of Estimate, January 11, 1934; John Ramsey to La Guardia, January 13, 1934: all in Subject Files, roll 248 "Tunnels—Staten Island," FLG. See also La Guardia to Paul Windels, January 21, 1935, Departmental Correspondence, box 60, NYCTA folder, FLG; and *Staten Island Advance*, November 24, 1933, 1.
44. *New York Times*, January 11, 1934, 41; February 20, 1934, 22; March 19, 1934, 35; June 28, 1934, 4; February 27, 1935, 6; March 1, 1935, 41; March 13, 1935, 9; July 9, 1935, 14; and January 30, 1936, 1.
45. Williams, *City of Ambition*, 178–88; Gelfand, *A Nation of Cities*, 47–48; Hood, *722 Miles*, 230; *New York Times*, September 11, 1935, 18.

46. Smith, *Building New Deal Liberalism*, 79; Leuchtenberg, *Franklin D. Roosevelt and the New Deal*, 133; Dan Albert, *Are We There Yet? The American Automobile, Past, Present, and Driverless* (New York: Norton, 2019), 100; Living New Deal, n.d., http://livingnewdeal.berkeley.edu/us/ny/. Additional public facilities on Staten Island were built through other New Deal programs; for example, the Civilian Conservation Corps constructed the Staten Island Zoo.
47. *Staten Island Advance*, January 5, 1935, 2, January 14, 1935, 9, and April 3, 1935, 3; SICC Transportation Committee, *Minutes*, February 21, 1935; Leuchtenberg, *Franklin D. Roosevelt and the New Deal*, 124; Kramer and Flanagan, *Staten Island*, 30–32.
48. SICC, *Minutes*, March 19, April 2, May 7, and May 21, 1935; Joseph Palma to Fiorello La Guardia, January 11, 1935, Subject Files, roll 248 "Tunnels—Staten Island," FLG; *Staten Island Advance*, January 10, 1935, 10, and January 15, 1935, 11.
49. *Staten Island Advance*, February 11, 1935, 1. The Board of Estimate also resolved, echoed by La Guardia in a private letter to Delaney, to ask the Board of Transportation to restudy a Narrows tunnel, including its projected revenue. Given Delaney and the board's well-known doubts about the project, it is unclear whether the intent was to buttress or torpedo the proposed project (Fiorello La Guardia to John Delaney, March 19, 1935, Departmental Correspondence, box 44, folder 9, FLG).
50. *New York Times*, February 11, 1935, 1; *Staten Island Advance*, January 26, 1935, 1, February 2, 1935, 1, February 6, 1935, 1, and February 8, 1935, 13.
51. *Staten Island Advance*, January 31, 1935, 4.
52. *Staten Island Transcript*, January 18, 1935, 4.
53. *New York Times*, April 20, 1934, 20, and January 7, 1935, 19.
54. *Staten Island Advance*, January 10, 1935, 10, January 15, 1935, 1, and May 8, 1935, 1; *Staten Island Transcript*, January 18, 1935, 4. Members of Palma's Committee of Twelve included the borough's commissioner of public works and its assistant engineer. In addition to Ordeman, the other civic and business leaders included Art Hedquist, M. James Hughes, Louis Kaufmann, Robert Molinari, Alfred Pouch, the former state senator C. Ernest Smith, Theodore Spratt, James Talbot (manager of S. S. White Dental Works factory in Princes Bay), and the architect James Whitford. The mayor's special committee included Palma, Brooklyn Borough president Raymond Ingersoll, Corporation Counsel Paul Windels, and Comptroller Frank Taylor.
55. *Staten Island Advance*, January 23, 1935, 1.
56. Smith, *Building New Deal Liberalism*, 2, 5; Badger, *The New Deal*, 200–201; Williams, *City of Ambition*, 188–204; Barbara Blumberg, *The New Deal and the Unemployed: The View from New York City* (Lewisburg, PA: Bucknell University Press, 1979), 135–39; Milton Derber, "The New Deal and Labor," in *The New Deal: The National Level*, ed. John Braeman, Robert H. Bremner, and David Brody (Columbus: Ohio State University Press, 1975), 124; Leuchtenberg, *Franklin D. Roosevelt and the New Deal*, 124–25.
57. *New York Times*, July 6, 1935, 3; Williams, *City of Ambition*, 189; Mike Wallace, *A New Deal for New York* (New York: Bell and Weiland, 2002), 74; Patterson, *The New Deal and the States*, 76–77; Badger, *The New Deal*, 81. The WPA, the PWA, and the short-lived Civil Works Administration together provided more than $1.15 billion for public works in New York City between 1934 and 1938 (Jon C. Teaford, *The Twentieth-Century American City: Problem, Promise, and Reality* [Baltimore, MD: Johns Hopkins University Press, 1986], 84).
58. Wallace, *A New Deal for New York*, 75–77.

59. For an early treatment of the New Deal's impact on particular sectors and groups, see Braeman, Bremner, and Brody, *The New Deal*, and Joe William Trotter, *From a Raw Deal to a New Deal? African Americans, 1929–1945* (New York: Oxford University Press, 1996). For a more recent critique from the left, see Ira Katznelson, *Fear Itself: The New Deal and the Origins of Our Time* (New York: Liveright, 2013). For a critique from the right, see Robert Eden, *The New Deal and Its Legacy: Critique and Reappraisal* (New York: Greenwood Press, 1989).
60. Joseph Palma to Fiorello La Guardia, May 28, 1936, and La Guardia to Palma, June 18, 1936, Departmental Correspondence, box 60, "President Richmond Borough" folder 3, FLG. For a discussion of La Guardia's "special relationship" with Roosevelt, see Williams, *City of Ambition*, 205–8. Palma's influence with the mayor, though, was questionable at best given his own periodic unreliability as a member of La Guardia's coalition (*Staten Island Advance*, July 15, 1936, 1; Kramer and Flanagan, *Staten Island*, 33; Heckscher, *When La Guardia Was Mayor*, 109, 172).
61. *Staten Island Advance*, July 15, 1936, 1, July 16, 1936, 1, and August 1, 1936, 8; Frederick Sturm to Fiorello La Guardia, July 28, 1936, Subject Files, roll 248 "Tunnels—Staten Island," FLG; Joseph Palma to La Guardia, July 2, 1936, Departmental Correspondence, roll 504, FLG. The WPA passed on a subway tunnel under the Narrows but ultimately funded a number of significant projects on Staten Island, including the South Beach Boardwalk, which cost more than $2 million. It also constructed the George Cromwell Recreation Center and the adjacent Joseph H. Lyons Pool in Tompkinsville, made improvements to the Arbutus Woods Park, renovated the museum of the Staten Island Historical Society, and commissioned the Frederick Charles Stahr murals at Borough Hall (*New York Times*, September 8, 1935, N2; Jay Price, "Sports," in *Discovering Staten Island: A 350th Anniversary Commemorative History*, ed. Kenneth M. Gold and Lori R. Weintrob [Charleston, SC: History Press, 2011], 112; James Kaser, "Civic and Political Life," in *Discovering Staten Island*, ed. Gold and Weintrob, 140–44; Living New Deal, n.d., http://livingnewdeal.berkeley.edu/us/ny/).
62. See, for example, critiques of Palma by Assemblyman Herman Methfessel, Congressman James O'Leary, and Transit Conference president Frederick Zurmuhlen in the *Staten Island Advance*, January 31, 1936, 1, March 27, 1936, 1, and April 8, 1936, 3.
63. Jameson W. Doig, *Empire on the Hudson: Entrepreneurial Vision and Political Power at the Port of New York Authority* (New York: Columbia University Press, 2001), 183–87; *New York Times*, December 6, 1933, 47; Joseph Palma to Fiorello La Guardia, January 15, 1935, Departmental Correspondence, box 60, NYCTA folder, FLG.
64. *New York Times*, February 5, 1935, 40, and September 11, 1935, 13; *Staten Island Advance*, February 5, 1935, 1.
65. *Staten Island Advance*, February 5, 1935, 1, and February 7, 1935, 1.
66. Angus K. Gillespie, *Crossings Under the Hudson: The Story of the Holland and Lincoln Tunnels* (New Brunswick, NJ: Rutgers University Press, 2011), 61; Doig, *Empire on the Hudson*, 192–244. The perception that the Port Authority undermined Staten Island's interests certainly remained strong during the 1930s. See, for example, Herman Methfessel and Charles Robillard to Fiorello La Guardia, c. April 1935, Subject Files, roll 248, FLG.
67. Doig, *Empire on the Hudson*, 181–91. Doig calls this lack of cooperation "agency adrift" (189).
68. Doig goes as far as to suggest that the Port Authority's actions on the Greenville–Bay Ridge tunnel were more likely disingenuous than delusional (*Empire on the Hudson*, 420). In fact, General George R. Dyer, its chair, privately professed disinterest in

reviving the Greenville-to-Brooklyn tunnel in correspondence with William Wilgus in 1933 (William Wilgus to George Dyer, December 18, 1933, and Dyer to Wilgus, December 9, 1933, and January 5, 1934, box 48, "Greater NY Belt Line" folder, WJW; *New York Times*, April 29, 1933, 24, December 10, 1936, 55, and June 2, 1937, 47).

69. *New York Times*, September 11, 1935, 13; *Staten Island Advance*, September 11, 1935, 3.
70. *Staten Island Advance*, February 5, 1935, 1; February 8, 1935, 13; and June 8, 1937, 4.
71. Darl Rastorfer, *Six Bridges: The Legacy of Othmar H. Ammann* (New Haven, CT: Yale University Press, 2000), 81; *New York Times*, October 4, 1927, 20, April 1, 1928, 184, and April 26, 1929, 34.
72. *New York Times*, August 15, 1936, 36, and March 7, 1937, 175; *Staten Island Advance*, January 5, 1937, 1; SICC, *Minutes*, February 16, 1937; Joseph Palma to Fiorella La Guardia, April 6, 1937, Departmental Correspondence, roll 514, FLG; La Guardia to Palma, c. April 1937, Departmental Correspondence, roll 523, FLG; Doig, *Empire on the Hudson*, 190–91. The route to Staten Island would require a link from the Hudson tubes to the New Jersey Central Railroad and then from that railroad over the Bayonne Bridge to the internal Staten Island Rapid Transit. Palma persuaded La Guardia to form a special committee to explore rail transit over the Bayonne Bridge, but the mayor urged patience, and the special committee's efforts faltered.
73. By the late twentieth century, the appeal of such authorities began to give way to a critique of their insularity and antidemocratic nature. Robert Caro makes this point about Robert Moses in *The Power Broker: Robert Moses and the Fall of New York* (New York: Random House, 1974), but for a more universal and concise statement of the issue, see Gerald Frug, "The Legal Technology of Exclusion in Metropolitan America," in *The New Suburban History*, ed. Kevin M. Kruse and Thomas J. Sugrue (Chicago: University of Chicago Press, 2006), 214–15. Gail Radford downplays the influence of ideology and political culture in her work, arguing in *The Rise of the Public Authority: Statebuilding and Economic Development in Twentieth-Century America* (Chicago: University of Chicago Press, 2013) that "the authority evolved as a result of preexisting institutional arrangements, ad hoc choices, and political conflicts" (9). In her essay "From Municipal Socialism to Public Authorities: Institutional Factors in the Shaping of American Public Enterprise," *Journal of American History* 90, no. 3 (December 2003): 863–90, Radford suggests that socialist principles became embedded in public authorities, albeit in still limited ways. In *New York: The Politics of Urban Regional Development* (Berkeley: University of California Press, 1982), Michael N. Danielson and Jameson W. Doig appropriately caution against making too many generalizations about such authorities because the latter took so many different forms.
74. *Staten Island Advance*, October 8, 1928, 1, and January 26, 1929, 4.
75. *Staten Island Advance*, December 28, 1926, 1, January 3, 1929, 4, March 11, 1929, 1, March 14, 1929, 4, and March 28, 1929, 4; *New York Times*, February 16, 1929, 5.
76. *New York Times*, March 29, 1935, 17.
77. *Journal of the Assembly of the State of New York* 1 (January 6, 1935): 38, 3 (April 9, 1935): 2981, and 1 (February 26, 1936): 718; *New York Times*, January 8, 1936, 21, January 10, 1936, 21, and January 12, 1936, N3; Harry S. Clark to Fiorello La Guardia, January 17, 1936, Subject Files, roll 248 "Tunnels—Staten Island," FLG; *Staten Island Advance*, January 30, 1936, 2.
78. *Staten Island Advance*, January 18, 1936, 1; *Journal of the Assembly of the State of New York* 1 (February 5, 1936): 280–81. As La Guardia subsequently made clear to Palma, the law as passed could not be interpreted broadly to include a Narrows tunnel

(Joseph Palma to Fiorello La Guardia, August 18, 1936, and La Guardia to Palma, August 25, 1936, Departmental Correspondence, roll 504, FLG).

79. Senator Rae Egbert initially had proposed two separate bills to create a bridge and a tunnel authority, each of which had parallel legislation championed by Assemblyman Charles Robillard. These two Staten Island Democrats moved the final bill through tumult rather than merit on the final day of the legislative session, at which bills passed at a rate of one per minute at some points (*Journal of the Senate of the State of New York* 1 [March 11, 1935]: 744; 1 [March 13, 1935]: 810; 2 [April 10, 1935]: 1751).

80. *Staten Island Advance*, February 13, 1935, 5, April 2, 1935, 11, May 11, 1935, 1, May 14, 1935, 5, May 16, 1935, 1, 4, and May 18, 1935, 1; *New York Times*, April 18, 1935, 2; Kramer and Flanagan, *Staten Island*, 26. See also Herman Methfessel and Charles Robillard to Fiorello La Guardia, c. April 1935, and Harry S. Clark to La Guardia, January 17, 1936, Subject Files, roll 248 "Tunnels—Staten Island," FLG.

81. *Journal of the Assembly of the State of New York* 3 (May 13, 1936): 3413–14; *New York Times*, May 15, 1936, 1; *Staten Island Advance*, January 18, 1936, 1, January 31, 1936, 1, May 1, 1936, 1, and May 13, 1936, 1.

82. *New York Times*, April 18, 1936, 3, and May 17, 1936, E11; *Staten Island Advance*, April 14, 1936, 1, and April 17, 1936, 1; G. B. Pillsbury to Fiorello La Guardia, April 14, 1936, Departmental Correspondence, roll 504, FLG.

83. *New York Times*, January 30, 1936, 21, March 6, 1936, 4, March 17, 1936, 45, April 1, 1936, 51, and June 16, 1936, 27; *Staten Island Advance*, January 11, 1936, 4, August 26, 1936, 4, January 13, 1937, 1, February 10, 1937, 1, March 17, 1937, 3, and June 18, 1938, 3; *Staten Island Transcript*, April 26, 1938, 1, and July 15, 1938, 1; flyer, 1938, Black Box Collection, "Tunnels" folder, SIIAS; Robert Molinari to Fiorello La Guardia, March 11, 1943, Subject Files, roll 248, FLG; Kramer and Flanagan, *Staten Island*, 49. War Department and corporate opposition had essentially killed the proposal for an airport at Governors Island before Staten Islanders came to appreciate the opportunity it would have afforded.

84. Joseph P. Raskin, *The Routes Not Taken: A Trip Through New York City's Unbuilt Subway System* (New York: Fordham University Press, 2016), 135; Alfred B. Jones to Fiorello La Guardia, February 8, 1937, Departmental Correspondence, box 60, folder 16, FLG; Office of the Mayor, New York, press release, February 8, 1937, Subject Files, roll 248, FLG. La Guardia knew that a vehicular tunnel would have less impact on the local neighborhoods anchoring the link.

85. "Staten Island Civic League Resolution," November 29, 1937, Subject Files, roll 248, FLG; Office, President, Borough of Richmond, "Vehicular Connection: Boroughs of Richmond and Brooklyn, NYC," c. February 1937, Subject Files, roll 248, FLG; SICC, *Minutes*, April 21, 1936; *New York Times*, February 9, 1937, 25. A report from Palma envisioned a two-lane tube using the shield method of construction. It would cost $36 million and extend from Rosebank to Ninety-Seventh Street with open-cut approaches: 800 feet in Brooklyn and 1,600 feet on Staten Island, where toll collection would occur.

86. Joseph Palma to Fiorello La Guardia, January 11, 1935, Subject Files, roll 248, FLG; *New York Times*, April 14, 1937, 2, and May 8, 1937, 10. La Guardia's support did not fundamentally stem the dissatisfaction many Staten Islanders felt toward the mayor. La Guardia's backing of proportional representation in a charter-revision proposal and the "independent" Palma's association with Tammany added to the mutual wariness between the mayor and Richmond Borough. La Guardia still won the borough in his landslide reelection in 1937 but not in 1941. By 1940, his standing on Staten

Island was low enough for Robert Moses to mention it to the mayor and recommend that he lower ferry fares in part to salve the wounds (*Staten Island Transcript*, May 11, 1937, 1; Robert Moses to Fiorello La Guardia, May 2, 1940, box 98, 1940 folder, RM; Kramer and Flanagan, *Staten Island*, 33–34).

87. *Staten Island Transcript*, February 4, 1936, 4, and April 16, 1937, 4.
88. *Staten Island Advance*, April 14, 1937, 4.
89. *Staten Island Advance*, April 14, 1937, 1.
90. SICC, *Minutes*, October 6, 1936; April 4, 1939; and February 20, March 5, and March 19, 1940.
91. Caro, *The Power Broker*, 607–10, 668.
92. Caro, *The Power Broker*, 639–77. One of the leaders of the effort to block a Battery bridge was none other than George McAneny.
93. *New York Times*, December 20, 1928, 3; New York City Tunnel Authority (NYCTA), *Final Report of the New York City Tunnel Authority on Proposed Narrows Vehicular Tunnel Between the Boroughs of Brooklyn and Richmond* (New York: The Authority, May 17, 1945), 8.
94. Joseph Palma to Fiorello La Guardia, October 11, 1940, and La Guardia to Palma, December 6, 1940, Departmental Correspondence, roll 541, FLG; David Rockefeller to M. Glauber, April 14, 1941, Subject Files, roll 248, FLG.
95. Leonard Sutter to Fiorello La Guardia, February 17 and March 3, 1941, and Robert Johnson to La Guardia, March 5, 1941, Subject Files, roll 248, FLG; Johnson to La Guardia, February 12, 1941, La Guardia to Johnson, March 3, 1941, Joseph Palma to La Guardia, February 13, 1941, La Guardia to Palma, February 18, 1941: all in Departmental Correspondence, roll 551, FLG; SICC, *Minutes*, March 4 and 18, 1941; *Staten Island Transcript*, January 24, 1941, 1, February 4, 1941, 1, February 18, 1941, 1, March 4, 1941, 1, and March 11, 1941, 1; *Staten Island Advance*, January 31, 1941, 6, February 12, 1941, 1, March 1, 1941, 1, and March 4, 1941, 1; *Brooklyn Citizen and Eagle*, July 10, 1941, box 73, "Miscellaneous Communications" folder, RM.
96. This Narrows crossing would cost $70 million to build and initially $620,000 to operate annually. Two lanes in each direction were expected to carry 6 million vehicles per year, rising over time to 16 million. A toll plaza on Staten Island would be placed just north of Evelyn Place between Bay and Tompkins Streets, with links to Bay Street, Hylan Boulevard, and an expected island-wide parkway system (*New York Times*, May 16, 1942, 15; NYCTA, *Progress Report: Narrows Tunnel* [March 9, 1943], box 73, "postwar planning" folder, RM).
97. NYCTA, *Progress Report*. The report also included long-standing justifications for a tunnel: its place in the city's master plan for arterial highways, its enabling of a sixteen-minute trip to Manhattan by car, and its relief of congestion in Manhattan by spurring residential and commercial growth on Staten Island.
98. NYCTA, *Progress Report*.
99. *New York Times*, March 24, 1943, 22.
100. *Staten Island Advance*, March 23, 1943, 4.
101. Robert Moses to Fiorello La Guardia, September 23, 1942, box 98, 1942 folder, RM; Robert Moses to John E. Burton, March 22, 1943, and Edwin A. Salmon to the NYCTA, March 29, 1943, box 73, "Postwar Planning" folder, RM. Salmon owed his position to Moses.
102. Robert Moses to Fiorello La Guardia, September 23 and October 15, 1942, box 98, 1942 folder, RM; *New York Times*, April 16, 1943, 42.

103. Alfred Jones to Edwin Salmon, April 1, 1943, and Jones to New York State Postwar Public Works Planning Commission, September 17, 1943, box 98, 1943 folder, RM.
104. Joseph Darcy to Robert Moses, November 1, 1943, and Moses to Darcy, November 3, 1943, box 98, 1943 folder, RM.
105. Robert Moses to Joseph Darcy, November 3, 1943, box 98, 1943 folder, RM; NYCTA, *Narrows Tunnel Report*.
106. Borough of Richmond, "Proposed Vehicular Tunnel Richmond to Brooklyn and Arterial Highway Connections," 1937, MS 233, folder 7, SIHS.
107. Madigan-Hyland, "Narrows Tunnel Studies of Location, Traffic, and Approaches in the Boroughs of Brooklyn and Richmond," 1944, MS 233, folder 8, SIHS; Alfred Jones to Edwin Salmon, April 1, 1943, box 98, 1943 folder, RM.
108. NYCTA, *Narrows Tunnel Report*, 31.
109. *New York Herald Tribune*, August 1, 1945, 15B; Caro, *The Power Broker*, 689–98.
110. Robert Moses to Fiorello La Guardia, December 2, 1943, box 91, "City Planning Commission" folder, RM.
111. *Staten Island Advance*, July 4, 1945, 4, and August 11, 1945, 4; *New York Herald Tribune*, August 1, 1945, 15B; *New York Times*, June 27, 1945, 18, and November 11, 1945, 81.
112. SICC Transportation Committee, *Minutes*, March 1, 16, and 20, 1933; SICC, *Minutes*, March 21, 1933; *Staten Island Transcript*, February 24, 1933, 4; *Staten Island Advance*, February 22, 1933, 4.
113. SICC Transportation Committee, *Minutes*, March 20, 1933; SICC, *Minutes*, March 21, 1933.
114. *New York Times*, April 20, 1935, 12.

10. Spanning the Narrows: The Triumph of the Verrazzano Bridge, 1945–1964

1. Martin V. Melosi, *Fresh Kills: A History of Consuming and Discarding in New York City* (New York: Columbia University Press, 2020), 180–82.
2. Joseph Palma to Robert Moses, February 17, 1937, and Moses to Palma, February 18, 1937, series 6, box 98, 1940 folder, RM. Moses often reminded correspondents of their mistakes, and Palma was no exception. Still smarting from arguably the greatest defeat of his career, Moses chided Palma for not supporting his Battery Bridge legislation in 1939. A bridge, Moses claimed, would have left funds for a Narrows tunnel, but now, he told Palma, the island would have to wait four years until the Battery Tunnel was completed (Moses to Palma, October 16, 1940, series 6, box 98, 1940 folder, RM).
3. Robert Caro, *The Power Broker: Robert Moses and the Fall of New York* (New York: Knopf, 1974); Hilary Ballon and Kenneth T. Jackson, eds., *Robert Moses and the Modern City: The Transformation of New York* (New York: Norton, 2007); Joel Schwartz, *The New York Approach: Robert Moses, Urban Liberals, and the Development of the Inner City* (Columbus: Ohio State University Press, 1993); Jameson Doig, "Some Reflections on Moses and His Biographer," in *Robert Moses: Single Minded Genius*, ed. Joann Krieg (Hempstead, NY: Long Island Studies Institute, 1989), 32.
4. One notable exception is Roberta Brandes Gratz, *The Battle for Gotham: New York in the Shadow of Robert Moses and Jane Jacobs* (New York: Nation Books, 2010).

5. Joshua B. Freeman, *American Empire: Rise of a Global Power, Democratic Revolution at Home, 1945-2000* (New York: Penguin, 2012), 113–42; David L. Rigby, "Urban and Regional Restructuring in the Second Half of the Twentieth Century," in *American Place/American Space: Geographies of the Contemporary United States*, ed. John A. Agnew and Jonathan M. Smith (Edinburgh: Edinburgh University Press, 2002), 150–83. See also Elaine Tyler May, *Homeward Bound: American Families in the Cold War Era* (New York: Basic, 1988); and Edgar M. Hoover and Raymond Vernon, *Anatomy of a Metropolis: The Changing Distribution of People and Jobs Within the New York Metropolitan Region* (Cambridge, MA: Harvard University Press, 1959).
6. Daniel C. Kramer and Richard M. Flanagan, *Staten Island: Conservative Bastion in a Liberal City* (Lanham, MD: University Press of America, 2012), 6–7; Charles L. Sachs, *Made on Staten Island: Agriculture, Industry, and Suburban Living in the City* (Richmondtown, NY: Staten Island Historical Society, 1988), 105–6. Sachs identifies 252 factories with more than 12,238 employees in 1952; by 1979, there were only 118 factories, of which just 9 employed more than 100 people.
7. For the supplanting of Moses's Battery Bridge project by a tunnel, see Caro, *The Power Broker*, 639–77.
8. Robert Moses to Joseph Palma, February 18, 1939; Palma to Moses, October 11, 1940; and Moses to Palma, October 16, 1940: all in series 6, box 98, 1940 folder, RM. In 1941 Moses also wrote but never released a highly critical statement on the Bay Ridge–Narrows tunnel. "Bay Ridge–Narrows Tunnel," July 14, 1941, series 1, box 73, "Miscellaneous Correspondence" folder, RM.
9. *Staten Island Advance*, August 24, 1945, 1; *New York Times*, October 23, 1945, 14. The city's Board of Transportation still envisioned a longer route that would connect in Brooklyn at Fourth Avenue and Sixty-First Street and surface in New Brighton and Tompkinsville on Staten Island—with an estimated cost of $50,610,000.
10. New York City Planning Commission and Department of City Planning, *Annual Report*, 1938, 64, Planning Collection, box 16, SIIAS; New York City Planning Commission and Department of City Planning, City of New York, *Annual Report*, 1940, 47, Planning Collection, box 2, SIIAS; Eugenie Ladner Birch, "City Planning," in *The Encyclopedia of New York*, ed. Kenneth T. Jackson (New Haven, CT: Yale University Press, 1995), 232–33; Caro, *The Power Broker*, 659. Twenty years after the CPC's creation, Wallace S. Sayre and Herbert Kaufmann underscored its "two decades of frustrations and disappointments" and failure to produce a master plan. They depicted a CPC mired in the politics from which it was intended to be insulated and vulnerable to pressure from the Board of Estimate. They decried Moses's "membership on the Commission [as] one of the major claimants in the capital budget process and an articulate critic of comprehensive planning" (Wallace S. Sayre and Herbert Kaufman, *Governing New York City: Politics in the Metropolis* [New York: Russell Sage Foundation, 1960], 372–80).
11. City Planning Commission and Department of City Planning, City of New York, *Annual Report*, 1940, 47, Planning Collection, box 2, SIIAS; Madigan-Hyland, "Narrows Tunnel Studies of Location, Traffic, and Approaches in the Boroughs of Brooklyn and Richmond," 1944, MS 233, folder 8, SIHS.
12. Clifton Hood, *722 Miles: The Building of the Subways and How They Transformed New York* (Baltimore, MD: Johns Hopkins University Press, 2004), 240–48.
13. *Staten Island Advance*, June 27, 1945, 4, October 23, 1945, 3, and January 4, 1946, 1; Staten Island Chamber of Commerce (SICC), *Minutes of the Board of Directors*, July 30, 1946, SICCR.

14. *New York Herald Tribune*, August 1, 1945, 15B; *Staten Island Advance*, April 1, 1946, 1.
15. *Staten Island Advance*, August 10, 1945, 11.
16. *Staten Island Advance*, August 7, 1945, 4.
17. *Staten Island Advance*, August 10, 1945, 11.
18. *Staten Island Advance*, November 17, 1945, 1; *New York Times*, November 17, 1945, 19.
19. *New York Herald Tribune*, November 17, 1945, 13A; *Staten Island Advance*, November 15, 1945, 1, and November 17, 1945, 1.
20. *New York Times*, July 20, 1948, 26, June 19, 1950, 39, and February 11, 1954, 31; *Staten Island Advance*, April 1, 1946, 1, and May 1, 1946, 18; SICC, *Minutes*, March 30, 1948, and January 25, 1949. Pouch was president of Pouch Terminal and vice president of the American Dock Company. Cornelius Kolff, the longtime secretary of the Staten Island Chamber of Commerce, was excited by Steinman's proposal, which made a case based not just on cost or expediency but on lofty aesthetic terms. To him, a bridge "is more than a thing of steel and stone ... [and] symbolizes the ideals and aspirations of humanity" (*Staten Island Advance*, May 1, 1946).
21. *Staten Island Advance*, February 5, 1946, 1, and February 20, 1946, 1. The proposed bridge authority was based on preexisting models, with members appointed by the New York City mayor and the authority to issue bonds up to $100 million. The transit authority was to build a subway tunnel to Bayonne, New Jersey, that would connect to Central Railroad of New Jersey and then to the PRR and pass through the Hudson tubes to Cortland Street. The bridge authority would also be empowered to issue bonds for a rapid-transit tunnel direct to Manhattan that would rather optimistically take residents of Tottenville just a little more than thirty minutes to reach Manhattan.
22. City Construction Co-ordinator, "Report to the Mayor, Board of Estimate, CPC, and City Council on Progress and Proposed Revision in the Program of Essential Postwar Public Improvements," April 15, 1946, 40, 43, Subject Files, box 147, folder 1567, WOD. Moses had placed projects in three categories: (1) those that were funded and underway, (2) those that were urgent and could be built by the city without exceeding its debt limit, and (3) those that were in planning but indefinitely deferred until funds became available. The Narrows bridge was not listed even under the third category, nor did it appear in annual memos conveying the current activities of the newly formed TBTA.
23. *Staten Island Advance*, April 1, 1946, 1.
24. *Staten Island Advance*, February 4, 1946, 1, and March 7, 1946, 5; SICC, *Minutes*, March 26, 1946. The Advancement Committee was composed of one member from each of the following—the SICC, the Richmond County Bankers Association, the Staten Island Savings and Loan League, and five service clubs (Rotary, Kiwanis, Staten Island Lions, Central Lions, and South Shore Lions)—and three members from the local chapter of the SPE. Richmond Borough president Hall was an ex officio committee member, and O. G. Pouch, president of the Staten Island Chamber of Commerce, served as chair. Despite the indeterminacy of the committee's name, at its very first meeting its members expressed a preference for a bridge rather than a tunnel.
25. Melosi, *Fresh Kills*, 181.
26. Melosi, *Fresh Kills*, 181–82; Cornelius Hall to Robert Moses, November 6, 1946, box 98, 1946 folder, RM. Moses was sympathetic to Hall's outrage, scribbling, "I don't blame him. The whole thing is lousy" on a letter to Moses from Arthur Hodgkiss dated November 2, 1946 (box 98, 1946 folder, RM).
27. Staten Island Ferry Commuters' Committee to Mayor O'Dwyer, February 14, 1946, and Cornelius Hall to William O'Dwyer, February 21, 1946, Departmental

Correspondence, box 1, folder 7, WOD; *New York Times*, December 31, 1946, 15; SICC, *Minutes*, March 25, 1947.
28. *Staten Island Advance*, November 18, 1946, 1, and November 20, 1946, 4. Frederick Spender, an attorney and civic leader, argued that such a line would spur population growth in the heart of the northern part of the island, which may have accounted for his willingness to wait for a Narrows tunnel. The *Advance*, although sympathetic to the proposal, rightly expected that it would not generate interest from either the city or private railroads.
29. SICC, *Minutes*, October 29 and November 26, 1946; *Staten Island Advance*, October 25, 1946, 1.
30. SICC, *Minutes*, March 30, 1948, and March 29, 1949.
31. See, for example, City Planning Commission, "New York City's 1950–1954 Requirements for Capital Funds," 1949, Subject Files, box 96, folder 1018, WOD; Triborough Bridge and Tunnel Authority (TBTA), *NYC Construction, 1946–1949*, Departmental Correspondence, box 45, folder 420, WOD; *New York Times*, February 11, 1954, 31.
32. Robert Moses to Edgar Stockton, October 6, 1953, box 75, "1954 Correspondence" folder, RM.
33. *Wall Street Journal*, September 24, 1947, 9; *New York Times*, September 25, 1947, 28, and January 13, 1949, 46.
34. Caro, *The Power Broker*, 641.
35. *New York Times*, July 20, 1948, 22.
36. *New York Times*, October 5, 1947, X15, and May 29, 1949, E2; Darl Rastorfer, *Six Bridges: The Legacy of Othmar H. Ammann* (New Haven, CT: Yale University Press, 2000), 137. In the Battery Bridge conflict, Moses was privately assured by the Army Corps of Engineers that the approval was coming. Interference by President Roosevelt at the behest of prominent New York reformers prevented the approval (Caro, *The Power Broker*, 671–74).
37. Caro credits Moses with planning a system of arterial routes—including a Narrows bridge—and then selling the plan to Port Authority officials in late 1953 and early 1954 (*The Power Broker*, 920–26). Doig persuasively contests this view, showing how the Port Authority's traffic studies in the early 1950s pointed to new routes outside of Manhattan and how Austin Tobin, the Port Authority's executive director, presented to Moses in November 1953 plans that Tobin's agency had developed (*Empire on the Hudson*, 376–78).
38. *New York Times*, February 15, 1954, 22, and February 21, 1954, X17; Port Authority of New York and TBTA, *Joint Study of Arterial Facilities: New York–New Jersey Metropolitan Area* (New York: s.n., 1955), 9, 61–62; "Catalog of Built Work and Projects in New York City, 1934–1968," in *Robert Moses and the Modern City*, ed. Ballon and Jackson, 223.
39. Port Authority and TBTA, *Joint Study of Arterial Facilities*, 7–9; Andrews, Clark & Buckley, Consulting Engineers, "Narrows Bridge SI Approaches," October 15, 1954, Subject Files, box 87, folder 115, RFW; *New York Times*, January 17, 1955, 1, 18–19; *Staten Island Advance*, January 17, 1955, 1. The proposed Clove Lake Expressway would eventually expand to a whopping twelve lanes. Additional projects included in the study but not recommended and never built were a new cross-Hudson bridge at 125th Street and elevated expressways across mid- and Lower Manhattan.
40. Port Authority and TBTA, *Joint Study of Arterial Facilities*, 18–19; *Staten Island Advance*, January 17, 1955, 1; "Catalog of Built Work and Projects in New York City, 1934–1968," 239.

41. Port Authority and TBTA, *Joint Study of Arterial Facilities*, 6–7, 17, 21–25.
42. "New Projects for SI," March 13, 1954, box 75, series 2, RM; *New York Times*, May 25, 1949, 1.
43. *Staten Island Advance*, January 17, 1955, 4.
44. SICC, *Minutes*, January 25, 1955; *Staten Island Advance*, January 17, 1955, 4, January 18, 1955, 1, and January 29, 1955, 1.
45. *Staten Island Advance*, February 16, 1955, 4, and February 17, 1955, 4.
46. *Staten Island Advance*, January 15, 1955, 4; January 18, 1955, 1; January 22, 1955, 1; February 15, 1955, 4; February 22, 1955, 4; March 4, 1955, 4; March 11, 1955, 4; and April 4, 1955, 4.
47. *Staten Island Advance*, February 22, 1955, 1.
48. *Staten Island Advance*, March 11, 1955, 4.
49. *New York Times*, January 24, 1955, 25; *Staten Island Advance*, March 4, 1955, 4, and March 11, 1955, 4.
50. *Staten Island Advance*, February 14, 1955, 4.
51. *Staten Island Advance*, March 4, 1955, 4, and March 12, 1955, 4.
52. *Staten Island Advance*, January 18, 1955, 1; January 21, 1955, 4; and January 22, 1955, 4. Proponents and opponents of the Narrows bridge shared this vision of Staten Island as a borough of homes.
53. *Staten Island Advance*, February 15, 1955, 1.
54. *Remarks of Robert Moses at the Celebration of the Seventy-Fifth Anniversary of the Staten Island Institute of Arts and Sciences*, pamphlet, April 13, 1957, New York City Hall Library.
55. *Staten Island Advance*, January 18, 1955, 1; January 21, 1955, 4; and March 23, 1955, 2.
56. *Staten Island Advance*, February 19, 1955, 4; *New York Times*, March 24, 1954, 26, and April 12, 1954, 28.
57. Caro, *The Power Broker*, 319, 519, 546–47, 897–98, 907–9; Hood, *722 Miles*, 246.
58. Robert Moses to John McGrath, March 15, 1950, box 99, 1950 folder, RM.
59. "Cass Gilbert: Twelve Projects," in *Inventing the Skyline: The Architecture of Cass Gilbert*, ed. Margaret Heilbrun (New York: Columbia University Press, 2000), 154–60; Francis E. Griggs Jr., "Bridge Across the Hudson," *Journal of Bridge Engineering* 14, no. 5 (September–October 2009): 403–4; Doig, *Empire on the Hudson*, 161, 191; Rastorfer, *Six Bridges*, 80; Port of New York Authority, *Suburban Transit for Northern New Jersey* (New York: The Authority, 1937), 13–15.
60. *New York Times*, January 17, 1955, 19.
61. Port Authority and TBTA, *Joint Study of Arterial Facilities*, 30; T. T. Wiley, Commissioner of Traffic, "Review of Traffic Proposals," c. February 1955, series 2, box 75, "TBTA 1953" folder, RM.
62. *Staten Island Advance*, February 9, 1955, 1.
63. *Staten Island Advance*, January 19, 1955, 1; January 31, 1955, 4; February 23, 1955, 4; and March 12, 1955, 20.
64. Jameson W. Doig, *Metropolitan Transportation Politics and the New York Region* (New York: Columbia University Press, 1966), 103–4; Hood, *722 Miles*, 253.
65. The Civic Congress would prove more active on matters of zoning for South Richmond and Fresh Kills in subsequent decades.
66. SICC, *Minutes*, March 29, 1955; *Staten Island Advance*, April 7, 1955, 4.
67. *New York Times*, April 5, 1955, 15; *Staten Island Advance*, April 15, 1955, 1.
68. "Loop Rapid Transit System," Art Hedquist to Robert Moses, April 4, 1955, and Moses to Hedquist, April 8, 1955, box 76, "Coordinator Correspondence, 1955" folder,

RM. Although Moses scribbled to Spargo about Hedquist, "Should we answer this nut?," he had corresponded with Hedquist in the 1940s over the Fresh Kills site for garbage.
69. Art Hedquist to Robert Moses, April 16, 1955, and Moses to Hedquist, April 25, 1955, series 2, box 76, "Coordinator Correspondence, 1955" folder, RM.
70. *Staten Island Advance*, April 8, 1955, 4, and April 15, 1955, 1; *New York Times*, April 5, 1955, 15.
71. Port of New York Authority and Metropolitan Rapid Transit Commission, "MOU on Cooperation Between the Two Agencies on Studies Designed to Determine Means of Improving Interstate Rapid Transit Service Between NJ and NY," January 4, 1955, Departmental Correspondence, box 107, folder 1248, RFW; Doig, *Metropolitan Transportation Politics*, 47–79. The scope of the study would be confined to just the New Jersey–Manhattan area, would involve the Port Authority in its enactment, would exclude discussions of roads, and would include a proposal for meeting the inevitable deficits, which essentially ruled out a role for the Port Authority. Members of the MRTC begrudgingly accepted these conditions for funding. For a more concise treatment of the MRTC, see Joan B. Aron, *The Quest for Regional Cooperation: A Study of the New York Metropolitan Regional Council* (Berkeley: University of California Press, 1969), 84–85; and Gerald Benjamin and Richard P. Nathan, *Regionalism and Realism: A Study of Governments in the New York Metropolitan Area* (Washington, DC: Brookings Institution Press, 2001), 135–37.
72. *New York Times*, March 5, 1954, 1, and January 14, 1955, 20, 23; *Staten Island Advance*, January 14, 1955, 1. Tuttle was a lawyer, civic activist, and former Republican candidate for governor of New York in 1930.
73. *Staten Island Advance*, February 8, 1955, 1, and February 21, 1955, 1; *New York Times*, February 9, 1955, 29.
74. *New York Times*, January 17, 1955, 22, and January 20, 1955, 30.
75. *Staten Island Advance*, February 18, 1955, 4, and March 16, 1955, 4. Port Authority officials also stuck by and publicly defended the decision not to include rapid transit on the Narrows bridge. See, for example, *Staten Island Advance*, January 24, 1955, 5, and April 7, 1955, 1; and *New York Times*, March 3, 1955, 26.
76. Caro, *The Power Broker*, 398–99; Charles H. Tuttle, *Life Stories of a Celebrated Lawyer in New York and Lake George* (Clinton Corners, NY: College Avenue Press, 2002), 80.
77. "Address by Honorable Charles H. Tuttle, Chairman of the Metropolitan Rapid Transit Commission at the Fortieth Annual Dinner Meeting of the SI Real Estate Board on Saturday, March 26, 1955," 6-7, Departmental Correspondence, box 142, folder 1640, RFW; *Staten Island Advance*, March 28, 1955, 1.
78. George Spargo to Robert Moses, March 3, 1955, box 75, "TBTA Correspondence 1955" folder, RM; Roger Gilman to Arthur S. Hodgkiss, January 18, 1956, George E. Spargo to Moses, January 20, 1956, and Moses to Charles Tuttle, January 24, 1956, box 76, "1956 Library Correspondence" folder, RM.
79. Charles H. Tuttle to Robert Moses, March 15, 1956, and Moses to Tuttle, March 28, 1956, box 76, "1956 Library Correspondence" folder, RM; Robert Moses to Jonathan B. Bingham, July 10, 1956, box 76, "1956 Library Correspondence" folder, RM; Doig, *Metropolitan Transportation Politics*, 110–11.
80. The MRTC acknowledged that construction would need to be done to eliminate a bottleneck at DeKalb Avenue in downtown Brooklyn and hedged its assertion by noting that even if capacity were reached in the future, expansion of the subway lines in Brooklyn was a worthy project (*Staten Island Advance*, February 21, 1955, 1).

81. Robert Moses to Charles Tuttle, January 24, 1956, box 76, "1956 Library Correspondence" folder, RM.
82. Tuttle's conclusion was based on the Metropolitan Transit Authority's calculation that station improvements would allow the Fourth Avenue subway to handle Staten Island passengers—up to 31,200 in peak times, when only 16,075 took the ferry (Charles H. Tuttle to Robert Moses, March 15, 1956, box 76, "1956 Library Correspondence" folder, RM).
83. *New York Times*, April 9, 1956, 29; *Staten Island Advance*, April 9, 1956, 1.
84. Robert Moses to Averill Harriman, June 8, 1956, box 76, "1956 Library Correspondence" folder, RM. In subsequent correspondence with the governor's secretary, Moses contended that his estimate was conservative based on the 4 percent grade he used (Robert Moses to Jonathan B. Bingham, July 10, 1956, Bingham to Moses, July 13, 1956, and Moses to Bingham, July 17, 1956, box 76, "1956 Library Correspondence" folder, RM).
85. Charles H. Tuttle to Robert Moses, March 15, 1956, box 76, "1956 Library Correspondence" folder, RM.
86. Robert Moses to Charles Tuttle, January 24, 1956, box 76, "1956 Library Correspondence" folder, RM; *New York Times*, April 13, 1956, 24, and April 19, 1956, 29.
87. Tuttle, *Life Stories*, 256–59. This new political and fiscal environment was epitomized by the planned Second Avenue Subway, which was already delayed and would not open until 2017.
88. *New York Times*, April 13, 1956, 24; Averill Harriman to Robert Moses, April 27, 1956, Harriman to Donald Lowe, April 27, 1956, and Moses to Harriman, June 8, 1956, box 76, "1956 Library Correspondence" folder, RM. For Moses's relationship with Harriman, see Caro, *The Power Broker*, 707–9.
89. Robert Moses to Jonathan B. Bingham, July 10, 1956, box 76, "1956 Library Correspondence" folder, RM.
90. *Staten Island Advance*, April 29, 1956, 1.
91. *Staten Island Advance*, January 29, 1955, 1.
92. *Staten Island Advance*, April 29, 1956, 4.
93. *Staten Island Advance*, January 18, 1955, 1, and February 15, 1955, 1.
94. SICC, *Minutes*, April 24, 1956. At this and the subsequent SICC meeting in May, Hedquist again appeared interested in pursuing rapid transit but was unable to sway the SICC members. At both meetings, he reported on inquiries he had made regarding Moses's claims that a 4 percent grade was unsuitable and provided an engineer's conclusion that Moses was wrong: a 4 percent grade could work and was in fact often in use. He also read into the minutes an excerpt from a Charles Tuttle editorial in favor of rapid transit over the bridge. The SICC Board of Directors took no action (SICC, *Minutes*, May 22, 1956).
95. *Staten Island Advance*, January 10, 1956, 4, and April 9, 1956, 1. The other reasons given for the delays were the New Jersey Legislature's concerns about the Port Authority; the opposition in Bay Ridge, Brooklyn; negotiations between Albany and Washington, DC, over funding for the new highways; and Staten Islanders not wanting their bucolic island changed.
96. *Staten Island Advance*, April 11, 1956, 1, 4; April 18, 1956, 4; April 19, 1956, 4; April 29, 1956, 1; and June 11, 1956, 4. The *Advance* wanted what the *New York Times* articulated as a "large future" for the island (April 19, 1956, 29), but not a huge one. The *Advance* recognized its shift from its past insistence on rapid transit and continued to provide a platform for Moses. By mid-1956, Moses saw no need even to use the paper to condemn the push for rapid transit to the island.

97. Metropolitan Rapid Transit Survey, *Report of the Project Director to the Metropolitan Rapid Transit Commission* (New York: n.p., May 23, 1957), 8; Doig, *Metropolitan Transportation Politics*, 114, 133–34, 280; *Staten Island Advance*, February 6, 1957, 1. Day and Zimmerman did predict a doubling of commuter traffic from Staten Island over the next twenty years. The firm also found that rails on the Narrows bridge would reduce commute time for 93 percent of commuters to Midtown or beyond and for 55 percent of those going downtown or to Brooklyn. These improvements were simply deemed not worth the cost or significantly more advantageous than buses (*New York Times*, November 20, 1964, 24).

98. *Staten Island Advance*, February 6, 1957, 1, and February 7, 1957, 4; Caro, *The Power Broker*, 742, 757, 872, 977. Indeed, Moses was victorious, perhaps more than the *Advance* realized. The cost estimates that Day and Zimmerman used in its Narrows bridge rail study were based on assumptions made by the City Planning Commission, a body on which Moses had long served and dominated. The study relied on the commission's expectation that employment for Staten Islanders would grow in the borough and in New Jersey and Brooklyn rather than in Manhattan. The CPC did not envision rail-induced population growth at such a level that annual operating costs would be more than matched by increased property taxes and other revenues. Thus, it did not project a level of traffic intensity that would give the MRTC its "only justification for the large expenditure for rail transit" (*Staten Island Advance*, February 6, 1957, 1).

99. Metropolitan Rapid Transit Commission, *Rapid Transit for the New York–New Jersey Metropolitan Area* (New York: n.p., January 1958), xi, 2–7; Doig, *Metropolitan Transportation Politics*, 166–90.

100. *Staten Island Advance*, January 17, 1955, 1; January 18, 1955, 1; January 19, 1955, 1; and January 22, 1955, 1.

101. *Staten Island Advance*, January 17, 1955, 4. See also *Staten Island Advance*, January 19, 1955, 1.

102. *Staten Island Advance*, January 12, 1955, 16; January 18, 1955, 1; January 27, 1955, 1; February 17, 1955, 4; March 4, 1955, 4; and April 4, 1955, 1.

103. Three years later, Maniscalco proved less deft. His grandstanding rankled Moses, who wrote to Spargo, "He can't keep our support and do any more pre-election stunts" (Robert Moses to George Spargo, January 9, 1958, box 77, "1958 Coordinator File" folder, RM). Two months after Moses made this comment to Spargo, Maniscalco's public questioning of the handling of the official notices to vacate property prompted Moses to scold him: "You know the steps that we are taking to help in the relocation of people within the right of way and you have approved them. They won't be kicked around by us and you know it. You either want the bridge and its approaches or you are against it. You can't have it both ways" (*Staten Island Advance*, March 1, 1958, clipping, box 77, "1958 Coordinator File" folder, RM; Robert Moses to Albert Maniscalco, March 10, 1958, box 77, "1958 Coordinator File" folder, RM).

104. The revised bridge site would allow for the reduction of the span by 220 feet—leading to a savings of $15 million and the preservation of 1,600 housing units in Brooklyn and 80 on Staten Island (Robert Moses to Charles E. Wilson, November 8, 1954, box 75, "1954 Correspondence" folder, RM; Othmar Ammann and Charles Whitney, "Memorandum on Location of Narrows Bridge," November 8, 1954, box 75, "1954 Correspondence" folder, RM; *Staten Island Advance*, January 26, 1955, 1, and January 27, 1955, 1).

105. *New York Times*, January 17, 1955, 1; *Staten Island Advance*, March 26, 1955, 4, April 2, 1955, 1, and April 8, 1955, 1. The *Joint Study* did not indicate the route for the Clove Lakes Expressway with any precision, but the expressway would roughly be parallel to Forest Avenue and apparently cut through the heart of the Castleton Corners and Westerleigh neighborhoods. By April 1955, the TBTA had agreed to consider keeping the highway south of Victory Boulevard for most of its seven-mile stretch and not cross it until west of Meier's Corner.
106. *New York Times*, November 22, 1964, 80. Figures for the expressway are more difficult to ascertain. Gay Talese estimated that about 14,000 Staten Islanders were moved to build the Verrazzano Bridge and its highways (Gay Talese and Lili Réthi, *The Bridge: The Building of the Verrazano Narrows Bridge* [New York: Harper & Row, 1964], 16).
107. See, for example, Talese and Réthi, *The Bridge*, 15–26; and Caro, *The Power Broker*, 927–28.
108. *Staten Island Advance*, March 8, 1955, 4, and February 14, 1957, 4; SICC, *Minutes*, February 25, June 17, and September 23, 1958.
109. Robert Moses to Albert Maniscalco, August 18, 1958, box 77, "1958 Coordinator File" folder, RM; Kramer and Flanagan, *Staten Island*, 54; *Staten Island Advance*, September 26, 1958, 1.
110. Robert Moses to Robert T. Stevens, June 14, 1955; Stevens to Moses, June 27, 1955; Moses to Stevens, July 5, 1955; Stevens to Moses, July 21, 1955; Moses to Wilber Brucker (new secretary of the army), August 2, 1955; Brucker to Moses, September 9, 1955; Moses to Brucker, September 15, 1955: all in box 75, "TBTA Correspondence 1955" folder, RM. See also *Staten Island Advance*, October 10, 1956, 1; *New York Times*, May 1, 1957, 34, and May 28, 1959, 33; and Rastorfer, *Six Bridges*, 137.
111. *Staten Island Advance*, February 1, 1955, 1, February 23, 1955, 1, March 5, 1955, 1, and March 16, 1955, 1; *New York Times*, February 21, 1955, 1, and March 22, 1955, 1. There would also be provisions specifically for Staten Island—most notably that the CPC would review the location for the Clove Lakes Expressway.
112. The initial bill split the condemnation costs evenly between the city and the state; the Wagner administration wanted the state to assume 95 percent of the financial burden. Additional financial concerns were raised about the estimated loss in property tax revenue and the new expenditures needed for utilities and other services.
113. *New York Times*, April 1, 1955, 1, 16; *Staten Island Advance*, April 1, 1955, 1.
114. Howard Cullman to Robert Wagner, March 30, 1955, Departmental Files, box 107, folder 1248, RFW; *New York Times*, April 1, 1955, 1; *Staten Island Advance*, April 2, 1955, 1. The problematic language was replaced with something more benign: "The Port Authority will have to submit its plans for street connections with bridge approaches, and for use of the city's park property, for Board of Estimate approval" (*New York Times*, April 2, 1955, 1). The city retained its long-standing function in approving plans and routes but gave up its demand for a precise role in the condemnation procedure.
115. *New York Times*, April 1, 1955, 1; April 2, 1955, 1; April 3, 1955, 1; and May 1, 1955, 60. In the Board of Estimate, the lone dissenting vote came from the Brooklyn Borough president. The New York City Council issued its home-rule message of approval by a 14–9 vote, and the enabling legislation passed 124–22 in the Assembly and 41–12 in the Senate, with the negative votes coming largely from Brooklyn.
116. Because of its bistate status, the Port Authority needed approval by both states even for the bridges entirely in New York. See Borough President of Staten Island, *Annual Report* (Staten Island, NY: s.n., 1956), 15–16; *New York Times*, February 5, 1956, 61,

348 10. Spanning the Narrows

March 13, 1956, 37, and April 4, 1956, 31; *Staten Island Advance*, March 5, 1956, 1, and March 6, 1956, 1.
117. *New York Times*, November 9, 1955, 1, May 31, 1956, 29, and November 7, 1956, 22; *Staten Island Advance*, February 2, 1957, 1.
118. Caro, *The Power Broker*, 704–11.
119. *Staten Island Advance*, April 19, 1956, 1.
120. *New York Times*, March 27, 1957, 1; April 2, 1957, 28; April 17, 1957, 33; May 18, 1957; 12; June 20, 1957, 31; February 19, 1958, 58; April 11, 1958, 1; May 23, 1958, 25; August 25, 1958, 1; December 31, 1958, 1; September 22, 1958, 23; and August 14, 1959, 1. See also *Staten Island Advance*, July 1, 1958, 1; August 15, 1958, 1; and December 19, 1958, 1.
121. "Catalog of Built Work and Projects in New York City, 1934–1968," 239.
122. *New York Times*, February 17, 1955, 26, February 22, 1955, 20, February 23, 1955, 26, and March 11, 1955, 24; *Staten Island Advance*, February 5, 1955, 4, and March 12, 1955, 4.
123. *Staten Island Advance*, April 11, 1955, 12; *New York Times*, April 17, 1956, 30.
124. *New York Times*, April 17, 1958, 44; April 18, 1959, 25; and August 4, 1959, 29. Harriman also agreed to spell "Verrazzano" with a double *z* in accordance with the Italian spelling. Rockefeller, however, preferred the Americanized spelling with one *z* in the name. New York State officially reinserted the second *z* in 2018.
125. *New York Times*, August 4, 1959, 26, and September 13, 1958, 18; *Staten Island Advance*, February 1, 1958, 1; Italian Historical Society of America, "The Naming of the Verrazzano Bridge," n.d., http://www.italianhistorical.org/verrazzano_bridge.html.
126. SICC, *Minutes*, June 22 and September 21, 1959; *New York Times*, August 3, 1959, 27. The SICC also challenged the appropriateness of the name "Verrazano," citing other ways in which the city had honored the explorer and questioning whether he actually sailed up the Hudson. The chamber's crude attack led to the public resignation of Dr. Natale Colosi, the chair of its public-health committee (*New York Times*, August 6, 1959, 10).
127. *New York Times*, August 7, 1959, 48.
128. *New York Times*, September 27, 1959, 66; October 8, 1959, 17; October 24, 1959, 21; and March 10, 1960, 15.
129. *Staten Island Advance*, February 23, 1955, 4.

11. Assessing the Disconnect: What the Distance Wrought

1. In fact, rapid growth in the Bronx predated consolidation and the subways because the towns closest to Manhattan had joined New York in 1874, and the first elevated railroad linking them to Manhattan opened in 1886. See Clifton Hood, *722 Miles: The Building of the Subways and How They Transformed New York* (Baltimore, MD: Johns Hopkins University Press, 1993), 108–12; Marion R. Casey, "From the East Side to the Seaside: Irish Americans on the Move in New York City," in *The New York Irish*, ed. Ronald H. Bayor and Timothy J. Meagher (Baltimore, MD: Johns Hopkins University Press, 1996), 400; Peter Derrick, *Tunneling to the Future: The Story of the Great Subway Expansion That Saved New York* (New York: New York University Press, 2001), 30.
2. Hood, *722 Miles*, 168–80; Roger Sanjek, *The Future of Us All: Race and Neighborhood Politics in New York City* (Ithaca, NY: Cornell University Press, 1998), 24–25.
3. Edward F. Bergman and Thomas W. Pohl, *A Geography of the New York Metropolitan Region* (Dubuque, IA: Kendall/Hunt, 1975), 67; Nathan Kantrowitz, "Population," in

The Encyclopedia of New York City, ed. Kenneth T. Jackson (New Haven, CT: Yale University Press, 1995), 921–23; U.S. Bureau of the Census, *Geographic Areas Reference Manual* (Washington, DC: U.S. Government Printing Office, November 1994), chap. 12, p. 4, https://www2.census.gov/geo/pdfs/reference/GARM/Ch12GARM.pdf. Nassau County was the sole exception outside of New York City.
4. U.S. Bureau of the Census, *Census of Population: 1960*, vol. 1: *Characteristics of the Population* (Washington, DC: U.S. Government Printing Office, 1963), pt. 34 (New York), 13.
5. Community Council of Greater New York, *Staten Island Communities: Population Characteristics and Neighborhood Social Resources* (New York: Bureau of Community Statistical Services, Research Department, Community Council of Greater New York, May 1960), xii.
6. *New York Times*, October 20, 1957, SM42.
7. Lee J. Alston, "Farm Foreclosures in the United States During the Interwar Period," *Journal of Economic History* 43, no. 4 (December 1983): 885–903.
8. John Fraser Hart, "Loss and Abandonment of Cleared Farm Land in the Eastern United States," *Annals of the Association of American Geographers* 58, no. 3 (September 1968): 421. For an exploration of the dynamics in a particular region of New York, see Grey Osterud, "Farm Crisis and Rural Revitalization in South-Central New York During the Early Twentieth Century," *Agricultural History* 84, no. 2 (Spring 2010): 141–65.
9. U.S. Bureau of the Census, *Census of Agriculture* (Washington, DC: U.S. Government Printing Office), for various years, https://www.nass.usda.gov/AgCensus/ or https://agcensus.library.cornell.edu/census_parts/1964-new-york/; Ira Rosenwaike, *Population History of New York City* (Syracuse, NY: Syracuse University Press, 1972), 131–37.
10. John K. Wright, "The Diversity of New York City: Comments on the Real Property Inventory of 1934," *Geographical Review* 26, no. 4 (1936): 620–39.
11. In 1920, positions within this category included employees of the Fire, Police, and Sanitation Departments; laborers and inspectors for all levels of government; and military personnel. It did not include public-school teachers or members of other professions employed in the public sector.
12. Mike Wallace, *Greater Gotham: A History of New York City from 1898 to 1919* (Oxford: Oxford University Press, 2017).
13. *New York Times*, January 13, 1933, 8.
14. Charles Sachs, *Made on Staten Island* (Staten Island, NY: Staten Island Historical Society, 1988), 99.
15. U.S. Bureau of the Census, *Census of Population: 1940*, vol. 2: *Characteristics of the Population* (Washington, DC: U.S. Government Printing Office, 1943), pt. 5 (New York), 160, 195.
16. U.S. Bureau of the Census, *Census of Population: 1930. Population, Unemployment*, vol. 1 (Washington, DC: U.S. Government Printing Office, 1931), 715.
17. These three sectors were government; professional service; and finance, insurance, and real estate (U.S. Bureau of the Census, *Census of Population: 1940*, vol. 2: *Characteristics of the Population*, pt. 5 (New York–Oregon), 161, 197; U.S. Bureau of the Census, *Census of Population: 1940*, vol. 3: *The Labor Force* (Washington, DC: U.S. Government Printing Office, 1943), pt. 4 (Nebraska–Oregon), 460–65.
18. *New York Times*, August 21, 2002, sec. B, p. 1.
19. Wallace, *Greater Gotham*, 341–43, 426–27.

350   11. Assessing the Disconnect

20. Wallace, *Greater Gotham*, 305–9; Martin V. Melosi, *Fresh Kills: A History of Consuming and Discarding in New York City* (New York: Columbia University Press, 2020), 172.
21. Sachs, *Made on Staten Island*, 105.
22. The Census Bureau began collecting data on income for the 1940 census, but neither it nor the Bureau of Labor Statistics or other early entities studying income published data that allowed for a borough-level study.
23. U.S. Bureau of the Census, "Historical Income Tables," last revised October 8, 2021, https://www.census.gov/data/tables/time-series/dec/historical-income-counties.html.
24. Nancy Foner, *From Ellis Island to JFK: New York's Two Great Waves of Immigration* (New Haven, CT: Yale University Press, 2000), 10, 146–47.
25. In 1940, the ratio rounded to 1.0, but second-generation immigrants slightly outnumbered first-generation immigrants.
26. Rosenwaike, *Population History of New York City*, 131–32; Foner, *From Ellis Island to JFK*, 147.
27. During these years, the Census Bureau altered its classification of regions as well as the countries it placed in each one. The classifications used for table 11.14 are consistent for all three years reported, with country-level data being used to recalculate regional percentages when necessary.
28. These data underestimate the transition underway in Manhattan because the Census Bureau's "central Europe" category included both long-standing sources of immigration in Germany and newer places of origination, such as the soon-to-be nation-states of the Austro-Hungarian Empire. In 1900, Germans still composed 90 percent of the immigrants from Central Europe in the four outer boroughs, but in Manhattan that figure had dropped to 61 percent by 1920 as thousands of immigrants from Austria-Hungary now lived in the borough. The presence of new immigrants in this category also helps explain why the drop in the proportion of northern and western Europeans was larger than that of central Europeans after 1900. This pattern was particularly noticeable on Staten Island.
29. On Staten Island in 1900, for example, Italians accounted for 98.1 percent of the southern Europe group (U.S. Bureau of the Census, *Census of Population: 1910*, vol. 1: *Population, General Report and Analysis* (Washington, DC: U.S. Government Printing Office, 1913), 856–57.
30. The Census Bureau first began asking about the country of birth in 1850 and compiling the response by 1870, when it reported no Italians living on Staten Island.
31. U.S. Bureau of the Census, *Census of Population: 1910*, vol. 1: *Population, General Report and Analysis*, 856.
32. Rosenwaike, *Population History of New York City*, 167.
33. The percentage of residents of Italian descent was considerably higher given the presence of third-generation immigrants not counted by the Census Bureau. An estimate in 1953 held that up to 25 percent of the island's population was of Italian descent (*New York Times*, October 31, 1953, 32).
34. U.S. Bureau of the Census, *Census of Population: 1960*, vol. 1: *Characteristics of the Population*, pt. 34 (New York), 393–96.
35. These figures are based on census counts and estimates compiled in Rosenwaike, *Population History of New York City*, 139.
36. Before the influx of the new immigrants, the Irish constituted between 14.7 percent and 18.7 percent of Staten Island's population in three successive state censuses from

1855 to 1875 (Marion R. Casey, "From the East Side to the Seaside: Irish Americans on the Move in New York City," in *The New York Irish*, ed. Bayor and Meagher, 395–96, 557, 560).

37. The 1960 census recorded 9,674 African Americans on Staten Island following an 80 percent growth in the number of African Americans there in the 1950s, a rate that surpassed the 78 percent and 68 percent growth, respectively, of Brooklyn and the Bronx. Out-migration continued to limit the increase in the Black population in Manhattan to 3 percent, but Queens far exceeded them all with an upsurge of 183 percent (U.S. Bureau of the Census, *Census of Population: 1960. Negro Population by County, 1960 and 1950* [Washington, DC: U.S. Government Printing Office, 1966], 39–40).

38. The U.S. Census Bureau long refrained from asking Americans directly about their religious affiliation. Its periodic census of religious bodies—in which each denomination provided the number of its members—was plagued by inconsistencies in the rate of response and the definition of membership. See U.S. Bureau of the Census, *Report on Statistics of Churches in the United States at the Eleventh Census* (Washington, DC: U.S. Government Printing Office, 1890); U.S. Bureau of the Census, *Census of Religious Bodies, 1906* (Washington, DC: U.S. Government Printing Office, 1910); U.S. Bureau of the Census, *Census of Religious Bodies, 1916* (Washington, DC: U.S. Government Printing Office, 1919); U.S. Bureau of the Census, *Census of Religious Bodies, 1926* (Washington, DC: U.S. Government Printing Office, 1928); U.S. Bureau of the Census, *Census of Religious Bodies, 1936* (Washington, DC: U.S. Government Printing Office, 1940). Other bodies and researchers have tried direct surveys or indirect calculations (e.g., using reported deaths or school absences on holidays) to estimate totals or have offered useful commentary and adjustments to earlier studies. See National Council of Churches, *Churches and Church Membership in the Unites States: An Enumeration and Analysis by Counties, States, and Regions* (New York: National Council of Churches, 1956); Walter Laidlaw, Robert E. Chaddock, Neva Ruth Deardorff, and Haven Emerson, *Population of the City of New York, 1890–1932* (New York: Cities Census Committee, 1932); Paul Ritterband, "Counting the Jews of New York, 1900–1991: An Essay in Substance and Method," in *Papers in Jewish Demography, 1997: Selected Proceedings of the Demographic Sessions Held at the 12th World Congress of Jewish Studies, Jerusalem, June, 1997* (Jerusalem: Avraham Harman Institute of Contemporary Jewry, Hebrew University of Jerusalem, 2001), 199–228; Robert Wuthnow and Clifford Nass, "Government Activity and Civil Privatism: Evidence from Voluntary Church Membership," *Journal for the Scientific Study of Religion* 27, no. 2 (1988): 157–74; William M. Newman, Peter L. Halvorson, and Jennifer Brown, "Problems and Potential Uses of the 1952 and 1971 National Council of Churches' 'Churches and Church Membership in the United States' Studies," *Review of Religious Research* 18, no. 2 (1977): 167–73; Wilbur Zelinsky, "An Approach to the Religious Geography of the United States: Patterns of Church Membership in 1952," *Annals of the Association of American Geographers* 51, no. 2 (June 1961): 139–93.

39. The 1906 religious census counted 30,414 Jews in New York City and 35 on Staten Island—each figure an obvious undercount. A more likely estimate of 798 Jews on Staten Island was calculated by following Ritterband's methodology for the city's total Jewish population and using estimates of proportions for each borough derived from other studies (Ritterband, "Counting the Jews of New York, 1900–1991," 204; Rosenwaike, *Population History of New York City*, 111, covering the survey).

40. The 1926 Census of Religious Bodies is widely considered the most accurate of the five conducted by the Census Bureau. One notable exception was the complete nonparticipation of Jewish institutions throughout New York City; Ritterband's methodology was again used here to compute an estimate of the population on Staten Island ("Counting the Jews of New York, 1900–1991").
41. The 1936 Census of Religious Bodies, the final in that series, is largely discredited. The National Council of Churches' study, which also relied on surveying religious denominations and using their self-reported membership totals, is preferable, especially when its data are understood to count affiliations rather than members. See Wuthnow and Nass, "Government Activity and Civil Privatism," 165; Newman, Halvorson, and Brown, "Problems and Potential Uses," 168; Zelinsky, "An Approach to the Religious Geography of the United States," 143–44.
42. For a contemporary and international example of similar dynamics at work, see Marcel Fafchamps and Forhad Shilpi, *Determinants of Choice of Migration Destination* (Washington, DC: World Bank, 2008).
43. Daniel C. Kramer and Richard M. Flanagan, *Staten Island: Conservative Bastion in a Liberal City* (Lanham, MD: University Press of America, 2012), 55; "Returns of Mayoral Elections in New York City by Borough," in Charles Brecher, "Mayoralty," in *The Encyclopedia of New York*, ed. Jackson, 739; Lisa McGirr, *Suburban Warriors: The Origin of the New American Right* (Princeton, NJ: Princeton University Press, 2001). See also Becky Nicolaides, *My Blue Heaven: Life and Politics in the Working-Class Suburbs of Los Angeles, 1920–1965* (Chicago: University of Chicago Press, 2002); Matthew D. Lassiter, *The Silent Majority: Suburban Politics in the Sunbelt South* (Princeton, NJ: Princeton University Press, 2007); Robert O. Self, *American Babylon: Race and the Struggle for Postwar Oakland* (Princeton, NJ: Princeton University Press, 2003); Paul H. Mattingly, *Suburban Landscape: Culture and Politics in a New York Metropolitan Community* (Baltimore: Johns Hopkins University Press, 2001).
44. Kramer and Flanagan, *Staten Island*, 12–19, 48–51, 55.
45. Charles W. Leng and William T. Davis, *Staten Island and Its People: A History, 1609–1929*, 5 vols. (New York: Lewis Historical, 1929–1933), 1:521–22; Board of Education of the City of New York, *Thirtieth Annual Report of the Superintendent of Schools for the Year Ending July 31, 1928* (New York: n.p., 1928), 447.
46. *New York Times*, September 2, 1961, 17; New York (N.Y.). Board of Education of the City of New York, *Sixty-Fifth Annual Report of the Superintendent of Schools, 1962–63, Statistical Section* (Brooklyn, NY: n.p., 1964), 5.
47. Richard Dickenson, ed. and comp., *Holden's Staten Island: The History of Richmond County* (New York: Center for Migration Studies, 2002), 220; U.S. Bureau of the Census, *Census of Population: 1960*, vol. 1: *Characteristics of the Population*, pt. 34 (New York), 359–63.
48. Diane Ravitch, *The Great School Wars: A History of the New York City Public Schools* (New York: Basic, 1974).
49. In 1895, Port Richmond, with the largest of the three high school departments on Staten Island, enrolled fifty-six scholars. The following year only eight students graduated from all three high school departments combined (Maurice Denzil Hodgen, "Public Secondary Education in Staten Island: A Perspective," *Staten Island Historian* 21, no. 1 [January–March 1960]: 3–10).
50. Department of Education of the City of New York, *Twelfth Annual Report of the City Superintendent of Schools for the Year Ending July 31, 1910* (New York: n.p., 1910), 145, 148.

51. With age-based grades increasingly well established, these U.S. census figures are highly indicative of but are not identical to school enrollment data, which city superintendents did not disaggregate by grade and borough. The fourteen- to fifteen-year-old students were largely but not entirely attending high school.
52. U.S. Bureau of the Census, *Census of Population: 1930*, vol. 2: *Population, General Report of Statistics by Subjects* (Washington, DC: U.S. Government Printing Office, 1931), 1144–45; U.S. Bureau of the Census, *Census of Population: 1940*, vol. 2: *Characteristics of the Population*, pt. 5 (New York–Oregon), 166, 173, 180, 187, 194; U.S. Bureau of the Census, *Census of Population: 1960*, vol. 1: *Characteristics of the Population*, pt. 34 (New York), 359–63.
53. For an exploration of ethnic group variations in schooling, see Joel Perlmann, *Ethnic Differences: Schooling and Social Structure Among the Irish, Italians, Jews, and Blacks in an American City, 1880–1935* (Cambridge: Cambridge University Press, 1990). For the argument that educational attainment followed social mobility more than generated it, see Stephen Steinberg, *The Ethnic Myth: Race, Ethnicity, and Class in America*, 3rd ed. (Boston: Beacon Press, 2001).
54. J. Bernard Walker, "Placing Staten Island on the Map," *Scientific American* 137, no. 4 (1927): 306.
55. U.S. Bureau of the Census, *Census of Population: 1960*, vol. 1: *Characteristics of the Population*, pt. 34 (New York), 13.

Conclusion

1. *New York Times*, November 22, 1964, 1, 81, R6, R34, and November 23, 1964, 1; Triborough Bridge and Tunnel Authority (TBTA), "Spanning the Narrows," 1964, CSI; "Verrazano-Narrows Bridge Dedication," November 20, 1964, New York Public Radio Archive Collections, https://www.wnyc.org/story/verrazano-narrows-bridge-dedication/.

Epilogue: What the Bridge Wrought

1. For example, see Eddie Joyce, "Before the Bridge: The Verrazano-Narrows at 50," *n+1*, November 2014, https://nplusonemag.com/online-only/city-by-city/before-the-bridge/; *Staten Island Advance*, June 6, 2010, https://www.silive.com/memories_column/2010/06/growing_up_on_staten_island_before_the_bridge.html; *New York Times*, November 20, 1988, SMA48. A column called "In Days Gone By" started appearing in the *Staten Island Advance* as early as 1965.
2. Ira Rosenwaike, *Population History of New York City* (Syracuse, NY: Syracuse University Press, 1972), 137.
3. Port Authority of New York and Triborough Bridge and Tunnel Authority (TBTA), *Joint Study of Arterial Facilities: New York–New Jersey Metropolitan Area* (New York: s.n., 1955), 9, 61–62; *New York Times*, November 20, 1963, 45; Edgar M. Hoover and Raymond Vernon, *Anatomy of a Metropolis: The Changing Distribution of People and Jobs Within the New York Metropolitan Region* (Cambridge, MA: Harvard University Press, 1959), 244, 252; Raymond Vernon, *Metropolis 1985: An Interpretation of the Results of the New York Metropolitan Region Study* (Cambridge, MA: Harvard

University Press, 1960), 222, 239; Nathan Kantrowitz, "Population," in *The Encyclopedia of New York City*, ed. Kenneth T. Jackson (New Haven, CT: Yale University Press, 1995), 921. The Region Study was directed by Harvard's Raymond Vernon, who quickly recognized that the growth would be substantially slower than even he predicted once the preliminary figures for the 1960 census were released.

4. U.S. Bureau of the Census, *Census of Agriculture, 1964*, vol. 1: *Statistics for the State and Counties* (Washington, DC: U.S. Government Printing Office, 1966), pt. 7 (New York), 262; Charles L. Sachs, *Made on Staten Island* (Richmondtown, NY: Staten Island Historical Society, 1988), 20–23.
5. U.S. Department of Agriculture, *Census of Agriculture, 1974* (Washington, DC: National Agricultural Statistics Service, U.S. Department of Agriculture, 1974), https://www.nass.usda.gov/AgCensus/.
6. U.S. Bureau of the Census, *Census of the Population: 1970*, vol. 1: *Characteristics of the Population* (Washington, DC: U.S. Government Printing Office, 1973), pt. 34 (New York), 629.
7. Daniel C. Kramer and Richard M. Flanagan, *Staten Island: Conservative Bastion in a Liberal City* (Lanham, MD: University Press of America, 2012), 58–60, 87–105, 166–70.
8. *New York Times*, October 20, 1964, SM42.
9. Jeffrey Kroessler, "The Limits of Liberal Planning: The Lindsay Administration's Failed Plan to Control Development on Staten Island," *Journal of Planning History* 16, no. 4 (November 2017): 263–84; Kramer and Flanagan, *Staten Island*, 58–61, 68–73.
10. Kramer and Flanagan, *Staten Island*, 121–33.

INDEX

abolition, 18, 23
accessibility, 44, 49, 60, 66, 210, 227, 330n83; of education, 260–262; of outer boroughs, 252
African Americans, 18, 155, 229, *255*, 255–256, 262, *264*, 274, 351n37
agriculture/agricultural sector, 226–227, 272, 286n22; decline in, *232*, 232–233; employment, 235, *236–238*, *237*, *240*; pre-consolidation, 14, 16, 19, *19*, 28. *See also* farms/farmland
airports, 169, 191, 206, 208, 329n74, 337n83
Albert, Dan, 325n5
allies, 114, *116*; in South Brooklyn, 69–70, 88
American Mechanics, 28
American Society of Civil Engineers, 164, 178, 310n29
Ammann, Othmar, 213
annexation, 6, 31–32, 35, 40–42, 50, 55–56, 60, 288n16
appropriations, fiscal, 86, 156, 164, 186–187, 203, 322n76; Board of Estimate, 193–194, 205, 319n38; Hylan/Narrows dual-purpose tunnel, 137–138, 140, 142, 144, 146; Narrows vehicular tunnel, 172–173; for NYCTA, 193; PWA, 181, 184–185; for Stapleton piers, 130; Triborough Bridge, 172
Army, U.S., 181, 218–221
arterial highways, 126, 186, 204, 338n97; New York–New Jersey, 208–213, 218, 342n37; traffic and, 208–213, *210*, 342n37. *See also Joint Study* (TBTA and Port Authority)
Arthur Kill Bridge, 26, 52, 119, 123, 297n3, 311n36, 314n88
Arthur Kill, 26, 119, 123, 126, 217, 283n20, 297n3, 311n36, 314n88
Assembly, New York State, 46, 54, 149, 190, 222, 274, 289n20
assessment plans, 99, 303n31; special, 86–88, 302n22, 303n31
attendance, school, 262, *263–264*, 265
Austria/Austrian immigrants, 252, *253*, 350n28
Automobile Association, New York State, 165, 222
automobiles, 7, 167, 217, 233, *234*, 284n28, 325n2, 325n5; rapid-transit impacted by, 9, 157–159. *See also* traffic, vehicular

Baltimore and Ohio Railroad (B&O), 65, *113*, 172, 297n4, 300n56, 313n75; Arthur Kill Bridge used by, 26, 52, 119, 123, 311n36; on Hylan/Narrows dual-purpose tunnel, 124, 127, 149, 313n75, 322n71, 323n78; on Narrows rail tunnel, 77–78; Rea/PRR influencing, 99, 101, 117, 143, 199, 311nn36–37, 314n88
Barth, Gustav, 41
Bassett, Edward, 87

Battery Bridge, 174, 192, 202–203, 208, 338n92, 339n2, 342n36
Battery Tunnel, 185, 195–196, 204, 339n2
Bayne, Howard, 292n73
Bayonne, New Jersey, 244; proposed subway route to, 67, 90, 166, 169, 341n21
Bayonne Bridge, 163, 171, 189, 209, *210*, 213–215, 327n29, 336n72, 342n36
Bay Ridge, Brooklyn, 141–142; Hylan/Narrows dual-purpose tunnel, 133–144, *134*, *145*, 146–152; Narrows Bridge opposed by, 219–221, 345n95. *See also* Greenville–Bay Ridge tunnel
Belmont, August, 6–7, 69
Belt Parkway, 164, 184–185, 201
Benedict, Reed, 290n45
Berry, Charles, 136, 165, 171, 331n7
Blair, Charles, 65–68, 71–73, 78, 86, 88, 298n14, 299n31
Bloomberg, Michael, 260, 274
B&O. *See* Baltimore and Ohio Railroad
Board of Aldermen, New York City, 44, 68, 85, 103, 165, 190, 203n12, 308n10, 318n20
Board of Estimate, New York City, 10, 203, 205, 301n10, 302n12, 314n78, 322n69, 340n10, 347n115; appropriations, 193–194, 205, 319n38; Bridge Committee, 162–163, 165, 327n36; conflicts with New York State Transit Commission, 140–143; creation of, 44; Cromwell, 82–85, 88–92, 102–103; on Hylan/Narrows dual-purpose tunnel, 119, 123–129, 137–138, 142, 146–147, 150–151, 314n78, 330n86, 334n49; on Narrows Bridge, 191, 215, 220, 222–223; on Narrows subway tunnel, 161–162, 181–183, 188; on Narrows vehicular tunnel, 155–156, 167–168; power of, 44, 112–114; PSC and, 82–89; on rapid-transit, 304n64, 332n31; RFC loans and, 178–180, 332n31; Smith Act empowering, 112–114; Transit Committee, 91–103, 105. *See also* appropriations, Board of Estimate
Board of Rapid Transit Railroad Commissioners (RTB), 83, 298n18; conflict with PSC, 73–80, 85, 106; creation of, 68–69; Staten Island excluded by, 78–80
Board of Trade, Staten Island, 70, 72, 77, 78–79, 165
Board of Transportation, New York City, 143, 167, 172, 186, 321n52, 330n82, 340n9; creation of, 147; Delaney chairing, 144, 159, 160, 171, 191–192, 203–204, 334n49; on Narrows bridge, 161, 165; on Narrows subway tunnel, 156, 175–176, 182–183, 204, 332n32

Borelli, Joseph, 288n14
Borough Hall, 45, 69–70, 219, 335n61
borough president, Richmond, 205, 268–269, 273; Cahill as, 108, 137, 139, 318n24, 318n25; Cromwell as, 25, 45, 103, 260; Hall as, 176, 203, 205; Lynch as, 139–140, 144, 152, 159, 168, 178; Maniscalco as, 225–226, 267, 272; Palma as, 200–201, 260
boroughs, 3–4, 31, 44, 137, 285n21; population growth across, 17, 227, 228, 229; resource competition between, 5, 52, 54, 140, 152, 156, 176–178, 269. *See also* consolidation, Greater New York (1898); outer boroughs; *specific boroughs*
Bridge Committee, Board of Estimate, 162–163, 165, 327n36
Bridgeman, Edward, 59, 149, 156, 161–162, 290n32, 323n84, 327n33
bridges, 59, 63–64, 265, 273, 297n3, 327n30, 328n48; Moses preferring, 201–203, 206, 208, 339n2; rapid-transit on, 213–219; Staten Island–New Jersey, 143, 158–159, 163–164, 188, 208; suspension, 161–162, 191, 209; tunnels *vs.*, 80, 159–162, 186–187, 191, 202–206, *207*, 208. *See also* vehicular bridges; *specific bridges*
Bronx, 136, 248, 255, *257*, 288n16, 298n19, 298n25; commute for, 233, *234*; employment in, 237–238; housing, 229, *230*, 231; immigrants in, *247*, 249, 250–251, 252, 254; median family income, 245, *246*; population growth in, 17, 79, 226–228, *228*, 229, 298n25, 348n1; pre-consolidation, 14–15
Brooklyn, 44, 213–214, 248, 288n16, 346n104; African Americans in, 255, *255*; Catholics in, 256, *257*; commute for, 233, *234*; employment in, 237–238; housing, 229, *230*, 231; immigrants in, *247*, 250–251, 254; median family income, 245, *246*; opposition to consolidation in, 33–35, 36–37, 58–59; population growth in, 17, 227, *228*, 229, 266, 268; pre-consolidation, 14–15, 20, *20*, 31. *See also* Bay Ridge, Brooklyn; South Brooklyn
Brooklyn Chamber of Commerce, 116, *116*, 161, 163–164, 188, 315n96
Brooklyn Daily Eagle, 42, 47, 75, 87, 93, 127, 169
Brooklyn–Manhattan Transit Corporation (BMT), 143, 321nn52–53
Brooklyn Rapid Transit Company (BRT), 83, 134, 140, 143, 305n89, 310n29, 318n24; in Dual Contracts, 80, *95*, 103–104, 106, *107*, 134; subway expansion plan by, 89, 92–95, 99–101

Brooklyn–Staten Island link, 1, 89, 109, 117, 163–174, *170*, 184, 206, 309n10; Narrows rail tunnel proposals for, *66*, 67–80, *69*, 72–73, *74*, *75*, *76*, 77–80, 101. *See also* Hylan/Narrows dual-purpose tunnel
BRT. *See* Brooklyn Rapid Transit Company
Bruns, Charles A., 304n61
buses, 140, 202, 206, 213, 219, 233, *234*, 346n97; automobiles impacting, 157–158
business leaders, Staten island, 6, 15, 32, 53, 162, 226, 334n54
Buskirk, Dewitt van, 143

Cahill, Matthew, 108, 137, 139, 318nn24–25, 319n27
capacity, 344n80; borrowing/debt, 86, 146, 321n62; of church buildings, *23*, 24; Dual Contracts rider, 106; Fourth Avenue subway line, 213–214, 216, 219, 345n82; Hylan/dual-purpose tunnel, 135, 140, 148–149; Narrows bridge, 216; of schools, 261–262
Caro, Robert, 196, 201–202, 342n37
cars. *See* automobiles
Cashmore, John, 195
Catholics, 24, *24*, 256, 257–258, 259–261, 286n30
Census Bureau, U.S., 8–9, 16, *23*–24, 256, 271, 285n21, 286n26, 286n30, 350nn27–28, 351nn37–38; on agriculture, 232, 233; on housing, 20, *230–231*; on immigration, 22, 247, 250–251, 252, *253–254*, 350n30, 350n33, 350n36; on income, 246, 350n22; on occupations, *19*, 234–235, *236–238*, *240*, *242–243*; on schools, 264, 353n51; urban areas defined by, 16, 227, 228, 229. *See also specific occupation sectors*
Census of Religious Bodies, U.S., 256, 257–258, 351n38, 352nn40–41
Center Street (Staten Island), 74–75, 299n43
Central Park, 13, 31–32, 35, 86, 289n21
Charter Commission, Greater New York, 42–44
Chicago, Illinois, 15, 35, 135–136
cities, 13–15, 31, 34
Citizens Rapid Transit Committee, 86, 302n12
Citizens Tunnel Committee (CTC), 71–75, *74*, 80, 90, 100, 299n27, 300n48
Citizens Union, 87, 108, 138, 164, 308n10, 318n19
City Charter Committee, SICC, 39–40
City Club, 84–85, 86, 91
City Committee on Plan and Survey (Walker administration), 162–163, 327n33

city-owned/independent subway system, 9, 100, 111–112, 140, 159–160
City Planning Commission (CPC), 203, 346n98, 347n111; Moses controlling, 195–196, 205, 217–218, 340n10
civic boosters, 16, 65–66, 110, 123, 136–137; consolidation supported by, 32, 49–51, 226–227, 267–270
Civic League, Staten Island, 121–124, 139, 161, 190, 192, 312n60, 323n83
Civil War, 25, 28
Civil Works Administration, 333n41, 334n57
Clark, Edward D., 290n45
class, social, 4, 244, 271, 308n7; middle, 26, 28, 31, 239, 244–245, 265, 272, 287n35; working, 5–6, 28. *See also* professional class/sector
Clove Lake Expressway, 209, *210*, 222, 342n39, 347n105, 347n111
Cohen, Julius Henry, 112, 121
Coler, Bird S., 46–47, 293n97
Colosi, Natale, 348n126
Commission, Greater New York, 34–39
Committee for the Advancement of a Physical Connection between Richmond and the Other Boroughs, 205, 341n24
Committee of Twelve (Palma administration), 186, 188, 334n54
Committee on the Regional Plan (New York), 135, 162, 165
commuter railroads, 7
commutes, 64, 73, *150*, 346n97; by ferry, 233, *234*, 235
competition, resource, 5, 52, 54, 57, 140, 152, 156, 176–178, 269
Comprehensive Plan, Port Authority, 121, 123–125, 127–130, 135–136, 188, 221, 316n99
Concorde Fallacy, 152, 324n98
congestion. *See* traffic
Congress, U.S., 65, 184–185, 193, 273
Connolly, Maurice, 148, 323n83
Connor, Robert, 273
conservatives/conservatism, 4, 260–262, 270, 273
consolidation, Greater New York (1898), 3–4, 14, 134, 136, 282n10, 288n12, 289n21, 290n34, 291n61; Brooklyn opposing, 33–35, 36–37, 58–59; civic boosters supporting, 32, 49–51, 226–227, 267–270; education and, 45, 261–262, 265; employment impacted by, 235, *236–238*, 237; Green supporting, 29, *30*, 31–37, 267–268, 295n14; municipal incorporation *vs.*, 32–33, 36–37, 39–42, 48, 54; Narrows Freight Tunnel following, 66; population growth

consolidation, Greater
  New York (1898)(*continued*)
  following, 16–18, 227, 228, 229, 267–268;
  rail link failure following, 226;
  referendum, 31–33, 36–39 , *38*, 48, 56–60,
  267–268, 290n41; role of Greenfield in,
  290n32; taxes and, 31, 35, 38, 40–42,
  44–48, 50–51, 58; voting on, 267–268,
  290n41; water supply impacting,
  296n65; Wiman supporting, 32, 35–36,
  38, 41, 43–44, 57–59
constitution, New York State, 144, 146, 156
construction, 64, 106, 141, 330n82; methods
  of tunnel, 142, 146, 152, 172; under New
  Deal programs, 180–187; under RFC,
  177–180; of roads, 157–159; subway, 94,
  97, 111, 143–144, 146, 269. *See also*
  expansion, subway
construction sector, 235, *236–238*, *237*, *239*,
  240, *241*
Contract No. 1, subway, 6–7, 68–69, 79,
  298nn18–19
Contract No. 2, subway, 69, *69*–70, 71–72,
  77, 79, 269, 298n19
Conway, Erik, 284n28
Cornell, D. T., 36, 38, 52–53
Cornell, John B., 324n88
corporate leaders, 5, 109–110, 114–115, 124,
  126–127
corruption, 25–26, 56–58, 84, 109, 139, 162,
  179, 270, 319n27
Cosgrove, Thomas, 209n16
costs, 73, 324n92, 330n83, 335n61, 347n112;
  Hylan/Narrows dual-purpose tunnel,
  117–121, 141–142, 152, 314n78; subway
  construction, 94, 144, 146
costs, projected, 114, 126–127, 130–131, 161,
  314n78, 346n98; of Fourth Avenue
  subway expansion, 213–214, 216–217;
  Hylan/Narrows dual-purpose tunnel,
  117–121, 135, 138, 140, 148–149, 175,
  322n67, 326n14; of Narrows bridge, 209,
  213, 215, 216–217, 346nn97–98; of
  Narrows rail tunnels, 67–68; Narrows
  subway tunnel, 138, 175; Narrows
  vehicular tunnel, 167, 337n85; NYCTA,
  204; of subway expansion, 94–95, 101
Cozzens, Fred, 304n61, 321n55, 327n33
CPC. *See* City Planning Commission
Craig, Charles, 128–130, 138, 314n86, 320n47
Cromwell, George, 65–67, 71, *115*, 138–139,
  292n73, 292n87, 304n58, 327n33; on
  Board of Estimate, 82–85, 88–92,
  102–103; as borough president, 25, 45, 47,
  103, 260; after Dual Contracts, 103–104,
  106; on multipurpose tunnel, 97–98; on
  Staten Island subway, 305n80; on
Transit Committee, 91–98, 100–103,
  106–107, 302n29
CTC. *See* Citizens Tunnel Committee
Cullman, Howard, 221–222
Curry, Edward, 211
Curtis, George William, 13, 35, 54, 57–58,
  289n27
Curtis High School, 45, 262

Dalbey, Matthew, 165
Davis, Pliny E., 304n61
Day and Zimmerman (firm), 163, 172, 216,
  219, 330n83, 346nn97–98
debt ceiling, 86, 96, 144, 146, 149, 156, 171
debts, municipal, 181, 286n26, 321n62,
  341n22; pre-consolidation, 21, 43, 46–47
decline/declining: farm economy, 226–227,
  232, 232–233; population, 229, 248, 252;
  subway ridership, 157–159
deficits, operating, 89–90, 219
deindustrialization, 202, 226–227, 244, 268,
  272
Delaney, John H., 160–161, 182, 330n79;
  chairing Board of Transportation, 144,
  159, 160, 171, 191–192, 203–204, 334n49;
  Narrows subway tunnel opposed by, 171,
  175–176, 191–192, 203–204, 321n55
delays, 161, 195; Board of Transportation,
  171; Dual Contract, 307n119; Hylan/
  Narrows dual-purpose tunnel, 137,
  141–144, *145*, 146–147; Narrows Bridge,
  9, 218–220, 345n95; subway expansion,
  82, 85–86
demand: for a dual purpose tunnel, 117–118;
  for motor vehicle highways, tunnels, or
  bridges, 163, 165, 167, 325n7; for
  rapid-transit, 7, 203–204, 219, 269–270;
  for real estate, 54, 211
Democrats, 84–85, 109, 140–141, 151–152,
  260–262, 273, 276–277, 308n10;
  pre-consolidation, 25–26, 51, 56
demographics, 226, 350nn27–33, 350n36,
  351nn37–41; immigrant, 245, *247*,
  248–249, *250–251*, 252–256, *253–255*;
  outer borough, 268; pre-consolidation,
  14–15; Staten Island, 270. *See also*
  population growth
De Morgan, John, 46, 54, 57
Derrick, Peter, 82, 305n73, 321n52
development, 2, 4, 7, 125–127, 131, 268;
  consolidation as, 14–15; Dual Contracts
  leading to, 158–159; Jamaica Bay, *113*, 116,
  132, 148; of outer boroughs, 136, 212;
  urban, 109, 157, 212, 270
Diamond, Jared, 5
discrimination, 187
diseases, 15–16, 41, 91, 319n41

diversity, 265–266; religious, 258, 259–260. *See also* immigrants/immigration
Doig, Jameson, 112, 202, 309n15, 325n7, 335nn67–68, 336n73, 342n37
domestic sector, 235, *236–238*, 237; pre-consolidation, *19*, 19–20
Doyle, Edward P., 291n53
Dual Contracts (1913), 70, 119, 130–131, 140, 212, 252, 269, 283n27, 305n77, 306n117, 313n63; approval of, 8, 83, 101–103, 107; McAneny responsible for, 92–104, 108, 313nn63–64; population growth following, 227, *228*, 229; Staten Island excluded from, 103–104, *105*, 106–107, 110, 134, 158–159; as subway expansion, 92–103, *95*
dual-purpose tunnels (freight and rapid-transit), 7–9, 110, 130–132, 151; feasibility, 117–125, 138, 147–148, 322n71. *See also* Hylan/Narrows dual-purpose tunnel
Ducklieb, Charles A., 304n61
dump, garbage, 270, 274. *See also* Fresh Kills landfill
Durand, Edward Dana, 46
Dyer, George R., 335n68

East River, 69, 192–193
education. *See* schools
Egbert, Rae, 191, 337n79
Eisenhower, Dwight, 222, 261
elections, 261, 273, 274, 292n87, 319n27, 324nn95–97, 331n116; municipal, 56, 83–85, 205
elevated railways, 6, 348n1
Elizabethport, New Jersey, 63–64, 244
Ellis Island, 21
emancipation, 21
Emergency Relief and Construction Act (ERCA), U.S., 177–180
Emergency Relief Appropriations Act (1935), U.S., 186–187
employment, 233, *234*, 235, *236–238*, 237, 239, *240*, 241, *242–243*, 244–245; on Narrows vehicular tunnel, 194; pre-consolidation, 18–19; through RFC, 177–180; though New Deal programs, 180–187. *See also specific occupations*
engineers, 63, 159–165, 172–173, 175, 187, 193, 313n67; employment for, 194–195; as experts, 5, 114, 125, 128, 313n67, 314n82; on Special Committee, 309n25, 310n26. *See also* railroad engineers
England/English immigrants, 21, 22, 245, 249
enrollment, school, 261, 263–264, 352n49, 353n52

ERCA. *See* Emergency Relief and Construction Act
ethnic makeup, 245, *247*, 248–249, *250–251*, 252–256, *253–255*; pre-consolidation, 21, 22
European immigrants, 249, *250–251*, 252–254, *253–254*, 265, 270, 350n28; pre-consolidation, 21, 22, *22*; World War I impacting, 229, 245
Evening Post (newspaper), 75, 87, 127
exclusion, 28, 103–107, 189; from Dual Contracts, 103–104, *105*, 106–107, 110, 134, 158–159; from subway system, 2, 78–79, 136, 304n63
executives, railroad, 99, 117, 121, 127, 189; committee of, 311n334, 313n75, 315n92. *See also* Rea, Samuel
expansion, subway, 2, 8–9, 78, 143, 269, 326n15, 344n80; Board of Estimate on, 88; BRT plan for, 89, 92–95, 99–101; costs of, 94–95, 101; Delaney opposing Staten Island line, 160; delays for, 82, 85–86; Dual Contracts as, 92–103, *95*; for Fourth Avenue line, 213–214, 216–217; IRT plan for, 89–93, 98–100, 106; population growth and, 227, *228*, 229, 342n28; Transit Commission on, 111, 124–125, 138, 143, 318n26
expectations, 59–60, 64, 73, 271; about consolidation, 48, 50–55, 134, 267–268; about population growth, 2, 52–53, 134, 271–272, 342n28
experts/expertise, technical, 109–110, 132, 152, 156–157, 181, 269, 308n7; engineers as, 5, 114, 125, 128, 313n67, 314n82; public authorities as, 190
expressways, *207, 210*, 215–216, 219–220, 347nn105–106

factories, 18–19, 51–54, 226–227, 268, 340n6
failures, 7, 109, 124, 134, 141, 284n28, 335n66; Battery Bridge, 174, 192, 202–203, 208, 338n92, 339n2, 342n36; consolidation as, 288n14; CPC as, 340n10; exclusion from Dual Contracts as, 103–104, *105*, 106–107, 110, 134, 158–159; Hylan/Narrows dual-purpose tunnel, 134–135, 146–152, *198*; Loop Rapid Transit proposal, 214–215; railroad negotiations as, 114, 126, 129–132, 167, 213; rapid-transit link, 10, 79, 213–219, 224, 226
fares, 77, 206; ferry, 1, 59, 96–97, 274, 337n86; subway, 143, 160, 168–169, 308n10
farms/farmland, 231, 272; decline in, 226–227, 232, *232*–233; pre-consolidation, 18, 20

Fawcett, Lewis, 318n20
feasibility, 106; dual-purpose tunnels, 117–121, 138, 147–148, 322n71; of Fourth Avenue subway line expansion, 213–214; Narrows Bridge, 161, 213–219
federal government, 180–187, 202. *See also specific programs*
federal government, funding by, 7, 9, 188–189, 197, 209, 222–223; PWA, 180–187; RFC, 177–180; WPA, 186–187
Feeny, John L., 292n87
ferries, 67, 77, 150, *150*, 164, 180, 202, 204, 206, 219, 323n84; commute by, 233, *234*, 235; fares, 1, 59, 96–97, 274, 337n86; pre-consolidation, 16–17, 26, 28, 32; St. George, 16–17, 26, 36, 45; Tuttle on, 217
Fetherston, Judge William T., 327n33
Fifth Ward Improvement Association (FWIA), 70, 73, 84, 86, 297n6, 303n41
financial sector, 235, *236–238*, *237*, 239, *240*, 241, 244, 349n17
fire, ferry terminal, 206
firefighters, 25, 28, 59, 236–237, 241, *243*, 244, 287n39
Fitch, Ashbel, 41
Flanagan, Richard, 4, 10, 260–261, 273
Flushing, 290n41
Foord, John, 34
foreign-born residents, 21, 22, 245, *247*, 248–249, *250–251*, 252, *253–254*, 264
"forgotten borough" moniker, 1–3, 226, 270
Fourth Avenue subway line, 65–69, *69*, 72, 73–75, 78, 80, 217; capacity for, 213–214, 216, 219, 345n82; Hylan/Narrows dual-purpose tunnel connecting to, 119–121, *120*, 140; Narrows subway tunnel route along, 85–87, 89, 169, 183
Franklin D. Roosevelt Boardwalk, 1, 185, 335n61
free Black community, 18
free-trade zone/Free Port, 1, 184
free transfers, 96–97, 306n113
freight-and-passenger tunnel. *See* dual-purpose tunnels
freight railroads, 26, *30*, 36, 52, 116, 116–117, *118*, 311n36, 314n78; and Hylan/Narrows dual-purpose tunnel, 119–125, 136–140, 144, 148–149, 313n63, 313n66, 322n71; Narrows freight tunnel, 65, *66*, 188–189; tunnels for, 183–199, 324n92. *See also* dual-purpose tunnels (freight and rapid-transit)
Fresh Kills landfill, 135, 201–202, 205–206, 274, 306n117
Fulton, Thomas A., 304n61
funding/financing, 64, 215, 341n22, 345n95; Dual Contracts, 99–102; Hylan/Narrows dual-purpose tunnel, 137–138, 142–144, 146; Narrows bridge, 344n71; public, 37, 68–69, 96, 171, 177; through special assessments, 86–88, 99, 302n22, 303n31; subway, 304n65. *See also* federal government, funding by
Funk, Isaac K., 290n45
Fusion candidates, 56, 82, 84–85, 103–104, 109, 185, 260, 301n10
FWIA. *See* Fifth Ward Improvement Association

Garbage War of 1916–1918, 8, 104, 130, 291n53
Garrett II, Robert, 297n4
Garribaldi, Giuseppe, 249
gas tax, 222
Gaynor, William, 84–85, 301n10, 302n12; on Board of Estimate, 87–90, 100
gender, *19*, 19–20, 28, 186n22, 262, *263*
General Motors, 158
geography/geographic location, 3, 5–6, 14, 28, 31, 45, 51–55, 283n20
George Washington Bridge, 209, 213, 217, 221–222
Germany/German immigrants, 21, 22, 24, 72, 245, 249, 252, *253*, 350
Giuliani, Rudy, 260, 274
Goethals Bridge, 164, 209, *210*, 330n83
Golden Gate Bridge, 191
Goldman, Albert, 164
Good Government Club, 26, 39–40, 43, 291n48
governance, 44, 51, 55–60, 109, 132, 137, 267–268; pre-consolidation, 14, 25–26, 28
government, 2–3, 31, 137; employment, 235, *236–238*, *237*, 239, *240*, 241; federal, 180–187, 202; localized, 14, 25, 28, 60, 109, 147, 267; municipal, 178, 200–201, 270
governors, of New York: Harriman as, 216–217; Lehman, 184, 190–192; N. Miller as, 110–111, 113, 127–128, 136, 140, 308n10, 309n22; Morton as, 40–42; Rockefeller as, 223, 267; A. Smith as, 135, 140–141
Governor's Island, 169, 191, 329n74, 337n83
graduation rates, 262, 352n49
Graham, James S., 108, 139, 162, 164
Grand Central Station, 6, 114, 164
Great Depression, 156, 176, 189, 229, 239, 255, 272; Narrows vehicular tunnel impacted by, 172–173; New Deal programs addressing, 180–187; unemployment, 173, 177–180
Greater New York/New York City, 6–7, 10, 47–48, 66; African Americans in, 255,

255–256; Charter Commission, 42–44; Commission, 34–39; employment in, 235, 236–238, 237; ethnic makeup of, 245, 247, 248–249, 250–251, 252–256, 253–255; Green on, 29; median family income, 246; population growth, 68, 228; pre-consolidation, 14–15, 23, 33–34; traffic congestion in, 165; vote for Staten Island to join, 267–268; vote for Staten Island to secede, 274. *See also* consolidation movement, Greater New York
Great Migration, 255
Green, Andrew Haswell, 289n19, 289n21; consolidation supported by, 29, *30*, 31–37, 267–268, 295n14
Greenfield, George, 32, 36, 38–41, 43, 52–58, 290n32, 291n52, 292n73
Greenville–Bay Ridge tunnel, 117–121, *122*, 123–130, 136, 188–189, 314n78, 315n90, 315n96, 316n98, 320n49, 335n68
Griffith, Charles E., 304n61
groundbreaking, 172; Hylan/Narrows dual-purpose tunnel, 133–135, *134*, 141–142, 152, 316nn1–2; Verrazzano-Narrows Bridge, 219, 222–224
growth, 15, 51–54, 288n16; projected, 50–55, 183, 217, 224; rapid-transit and, 64–68, *66*, 75; unwanted, 185–186, 218. *See also* population growth

Hall, Cornelius, 203, 205, 341n24, 341n26
Hall, Thomas, 324n88
Hammack, David, 44, 287n35
Hamilton, John, 324n88
Harkness, Leroy, 143, 149, 308n11, 323n83
Harriman, Averill, 216–217, 222–223, 348n124
Harrower, Pascal, 77
Hart, Cornelius A., 290n45
Hearst, William Randolph, 84, 301n10, 324n95
Hedquist, Art, 179, 214–215, 219, 334n54, 343n68, 345n94
Henry Hudson Parkway, 184–185
Hewitt, Abraham, 6, 34, 68
high schools, 45, 185, 193, 261–262, 265, 268, 352n49, 353n51
highways, 157–159, 163, 186–187, 195, 222; in *Joint Study*, 208–213, *210*; Moses plans for, 201–202, 208. *See also* arterial highways
Hofstadter, Samuel, 147–149
Holland Tunnel, 165, 187, 211, 319n41
homeowners, 231, *231*, 273–274; displacement of, 219–221, 346n104, 347n106, 347n112; pre-consolidation, 20, *20*

home-rule, 111–113, 132, 140–141, 144, 147, 149, 191, 221, 289n20, 308n10, 321n52, 347n115
Hood, Clifton, 91, 143, 227
Hoover, Herbert, 177–178
Hopkins, Harry, 186, 333n41
hospital, 42, 47, 79, 180, 185, 220, 292n77
housing, 226, 229, *230–231*, 231–232; displacement of, 219–221, 347n106, 347n112
Housman, Jacob J., 290n45
Hudson and Manhattan Railroad Company, 67, 72, 88, 189
Hughes, James M, 334n54
Hulbert, Murray, 309n25, 323n83
Hylan, John F., 109, 308n10, 321n62, 324n95; city-owned subways supported by, 111, 159–160, 269; on direct subway line, 104, 106; Lynch supported by, 139–141, 144, 146–148, 151–152; as mayor, 8–9, 109, 123, 133–134, *134*, 269; McAneny opposed by, 108, 321n51; Port Authority opposed by, 8–9, 108, 123–129, 314n86, 316n97; Special Committee by, 114, *122*, 309n25, 310n26; Transit Commission opposed by, 108, 114, 124, 127–129, 318n25, 321nn52–53, 322n69
Hylan/Narrows dual-purpose tunnel, *118*, *120*, 156, 167, 188–189, 197, *198*, 205, 213, 313n63, 319n40; Citizens Union against, 138, 164; delays, 137, 141–144, *145*, 146–147; failure of, 134–135, 147–152, *198*; feasibility, 117–125, 138, 147–148; injunction against, 75, 83, 138, 318n20; Narrows subway tunnel reusing right-of-way, 171, 329n63; Port Authority countering, 110, *122*, 123–129, 135–139, 143, 147, 149–150, 313n66, 314n78, 314n88, 320n49; private railroads on, 110, 117–121, 129–130, 138, 148, 323n78; proposed routes, 117–121, *120*, *122*, 208, 318n21, 326n14. *See also* Narrows Tunnel (subway)

Ickes, Harold, 180–181, 184, 186
identity, 4, 57, 225–227, 256, 343n52; middle-class, 26, 272; pre-consolidation, 25–26, 28; rural, 50, 232
immigrants/immigration, 3, 226–227, 248, 255, 255–256; Catholic, 256, 257–258, 259–261; European, 229, 245, 249, 250–251, 252–254, 253–254, 265, 270, 350n28; non-European, 250–251, 253–254, *254*; pre-consolidation, 21, *22*; second-generation, 229, 246, 247, 248–249, 350n25. *See also specific countries of origin*

362 Index

immigration laws, 245
inaccessibility, 15, 41, 235, 248–249, 254–255; of outer boroughs, 248–249
income levels, 244–245, 272–273, 350n22
incorporation, consolidation vs., 32–33, 36–37, 39–42, 48, 54
independent/city-owned subway system, 9, 100, 111–112, 140, 159–160
industrialization, 4, 53, 244
infrastructure, 9, 87, 135, 144, 152, 163, 180–184; pre-consolidation, 14, 25–26, 28, 32
injunction against Hylan/Narrows dual-purpose tunnel, 75, 83, 138, 318n20
inner belt lines, 93, 123, 163
institutions, pre-consolidation, 25–26, 28
Interboro Bridge Company, 162–165, 173, 186
Interborough Rapid Transit Company (IRT), 63, 73, 134, 140, 183, 301n10; Contract No. 2 with, 70, 269, 298n19; Dual Contracts and, 8, 83, 101–103, 106, 304n65, 305n89; subway expansion plan by, 89–101, 106–107; on Triborough plan, 83, 88–89
internal transportation, 26, 64, 75, 77, 202, 206
Interstate Highway Act, U.S., 209
Ireland/Irish immigrants, 21, 22, 25, 245, 249, 252, 253, 254, 350n36
IRT. See Interborough Rapid Transit Company
Irving, Gugy, 304n61
isolation: geographic, 3–4, 189, 226–227, 252–253, 260, 270; political, 59, 181
Italy/Italian immigrants, 24, 28, 249, 252, 253, 253–254, 350nn29–30

Jackson, Kenneth, 158, 202, 284n28, 325n4
Jackson, Tom W., 81–82
Jamaica Bay, 113, 116, 132, 148
Jersey City, New Jersey, 119
Jewish people, 24, 253–254, 256, 258, 259–260
jobs. See employment
Joint Study (TBTA and Port Authority), 208–213, 210, 215, 219–220, 223, 272, 347n105
Jones, Alfred, 195–196

Kaufmann, Herbert, 340n10
Kaufmann, Louis, 182, 334n54
Kay, Jane Holtz, 165
Kill Van Kull, 52, 65, 67, 121, 163, 189, 244, 283n20, 311n59
Kings County, 20, 23, 31, 34, 255, 288n16, 289n21

Klingeibiel, George, 324n88
Knight, John, 323n79
Knight-Adler bill, 111
Kolff, Cornelius, 44, 121, 302n14, 303n41, 304n61, 306n103, 321n56, 323n83, 327n33, 341n20
Kramer, Daniel, 4, 10, 260–261, 273

laborers, 28, 49, 194, 239, 286n22, 319n41, 349n11
La Guardia, Fiorello, 183, 188–192, 331n16, 333nn40–41, 337n84, 337n86; as mayor, 183–187, 200–201, 203–204; on Narrows subway tunnel, 176, 183–187; on Narrows vehicular tunnel, 193, 195–197, 334n49; Palma and, 336n72, 336n78; on subways, 308n10, 333n40
landfill, 4, 201, 274, 283n23
land use, 226, 231, 283n23; farmland as, 232, 232–233; housing as, 229, 230, 231
lawsuits, 138
Lehman, Herbert, 184, 190–192
Leman, Francis, 144, 324n91
Lewis, Nelson, 126
Lexow, Clarence, 40–41
liberals/liberalism, 270
Liberty bridge, 162, 165, 166, 173, 223
Lincoln Tunnel, 178–179, 184–185, 188–189, 211
Lindsay, John, 273
Little, Daniel, 2
loans, federal, 176–184, 187, 193–194
Logan, John, 51
Logue, Ed, 109
Long Island, 29, 54, 65, 224, 273; linking New Jersey to, 100, 159, 164, 205, 211; traffic and, 201–202
Long Island Railroad Company, 67, 117, 320n48
Loop Rapid Transit System proposal, 214–215
Low, Seth, 65, 260
Lutherans, 258, 259
Lynch, John, 165, 178–179, 182–183, 185, 197, 319n27, 323n85, 331n7, 331n92; Hylan supported by, 139–141, 144, 146–148, 151–152; Narrows subway tunnel supported by, 159, 161, 168, 171, 326n13
Lynn, Herbert, 200–201

machine politics, 15, 56; Democrats, 51, 109, 139–140, 276
malaria, 13–14, 16, 18, 44, 75
Maltbie, Milo, 101
Mandelbaum, Michael, 284n30
Manhattan, 1, 6, 29, 244; African Americans in, 255, 255; Catholics in,

256, *257*; commute for, 233, *234*, 270; direct tunnel to, 269; employment in, 237, *237–238*; foreign-born residents in, 248, *250–251*; housing in, 229, *230*; Lower, 67, 72, 117, *118*, 121, 192, 208, 211, 233, 342n39; median family income, *246*; migration from, 229, 248–249, 254; out-migration, 248, 254, 351n37; population growth, *17*, *228*, 229; pre-consolidation, 20, *20*
Manhattan Bridge, 217
Manhattan-Bronx subway, 298n19
Manhattan-Staten Island connection, 6
Maniscalco, Albert, 193, 273, 346n103; on Narrows Bridge, 211, 212–213, 218, 220, 232; as Richmond Borough president, 225–226, 267, 272
manufacturing sector, 235, *236–238*, 237, 239, *240*, 241; pre-consolidation, *19*, 19–20, 32
maps, *30*, *69*, *116*, *118*, 300n46; CTC proposal, *74*; direct Staten Island-Manhattan subway, *105*; Dual Contract proposal, *95*; Hylan/Narrows dual-purpose tunnel, *120*, *122*; Liberty Bridge proposal, *166*; Narrows bridge plan, *207*, *210*; Narrows freight train proposal, *66*; Narrows rail tunnel, *74*, *76*; Narrows vehicular tunnel plan, *194*; Port Authority Greenville proposal, *122*; SPE subway proposal, *170*; SICC proposal, *76*; Staten Island Rapid Transit Railway, *27*
Markham, Edwin, 225–226
mayors, of New York City, 274, 341n21; Gaynor as, 84–85, Hewitt as, 6, 34, 68; Hylan as, 8–9, 109, 123, 133–134, *134*, 269; La Guardia as, 183–187, 200–201, 204; Lindsay as, 273; O'Brien as, 179, 190; O'Dwyer as, 205; Strong as, 291n61; Wagner as, 167, 221–222; J. Walker as, 152, 156, 216
McAdoo, William, 67, 72, 88–89, 297n12
McAneny, George A., 124–125, 130–132, 149, 183, 305n80, 318n21; on Board of Estimate subway committee, 84–87; role in Dual Contracts, 92–104, 108, 313nn63–64; subway to Staten Island supported by, 98–99, 124–125, 318n26, 326nn14–15; Transit Commission chaired by, 111, 138–140, 159–160; on Transit Committee, 91–92, 96–103
McAneny Report, 94–96, 98, 305n89
McAvoy Report, 147–149, 151, 160, 322n71
McCall, Edward, 102, 104
McCormack, Charles, 47, 103–104
McDonald, John B., 69
McGirr, Lisa, 260

McKee, Joseph, 165, 190, 331n16
McLaughlin, Hugh, 37
McMillen, Harlow, 31
median family income, 244–245, 272–273
Melosi, Martin, 4, 10, 283n23
men, 19–20, *20*
mentalité, 2, 281n8
mergers, 32, 58, 77, 196, 203–204, 276–277
Merrill, Bradford, 98, 305n77
Methfessel, Herman, 192, 335n62
Methodists, 258, 259
Metropolitan Police Board, 34, 288n17
Metropolitan Rapid Transit Commission (MRTC): on rapid transit for Narrows Bridge, 215–219, 344n71, 344n80
Metropolitan Transit Authority, 214–216, 345n82
Meyer-Mastick bill, 129–130
middle-class, 26, 28, 31, 239, 244–245, 265, 272, 287n35
Miller, Cyrus, 87; on Transit Committee, 91–92, 96–97, 101
Miller, Nathan, 127–128, 136, 140–141, 308nn10–11; on Knight-Adler bill, 110–111, 113, 309n22
Mills, William Wirt, 103–104, 155, 197, 312n52
Mitchel, John Purroy, 86–87, 103, 146, 260, 302n12, 320n47
Molinari, Guy, 273
Molinari, Robert, 1–3, 191, 331n13, 334n54
Molotch, Harvey, 51
Moravians, 24, 256, *258*, 259
Morris, Ira K., 26, 28, 32, 77, 276
Morrison, Henry, 63–65, 297n1, 297n6
mortgages, 21, 286n26
Morton, Levi, 40–42
Morton, William, 324n88
Moses, Robert, 1, 164, 178, 190, 204, *210*, 267, 341n26, 342n36, 343n68, 346n103; bridges preferred by, 9, 201–203, 206, 208; CPC controlled by, 195, 205, 217–218, 340n10; on Narrows Bridge, 213–223, 341n22, 345n84, 345n94; Narrows subway tunnel opposed by, 176; Narrows vehicular tunnel opposed by, 192–196; on New York Traffic Commission, *207*; on Staten Island, 210, 212; Palma and, 195, 337n86, 339n2
MRTC. *See* Metropolitan Rapid Transit Commission
Mullen, William, 88
Muller, Nicholas, 25, 51
multipurpose tunnels (passenger, freight, and water), 83, 94–95, 101, 107, 130–131
Mulvihill, Frank, 211, 218
municipal: elections, 56, 83–85, 205; government, 178, 200–201, 270

364   Index

Municipal Art Society, 78, 161
Municipal Consolidation Commission, 29
Municipal Engineers of the City of New York, 125, 128, 313n67, 314n82
municipal government, 178, 200–201, 270
Museum of the City of New York, 135

names/naming, 43–44, 223–224, 292n79, 348n124, 348n126
Narrows Bridge, 162–164, 190, *207*; approved by War Department, 161, 208, 210–211, 309n24; Bay Ridge opposing, 219–221, 345n95; Board of Estimate on, 191, 215, 220, 222–223; *Joint Report* for, 208–213, *210*, 272; Maniscalco on, 211, 212–213, 218, 220; Port Authority on, 9, 211, 221, 223, 344n71, 344n75; projected costs of, 209, 213, 215, 216–217, 346nn97–98; rapid transit proposed for, 213–219; SICC on, 165–167, 203, 211, 214–219, 223–224, 345n94; *Staten Island Advance* on, 161, 165, 211–214, 215, 218–219, 223; TBTA on, 208, 214–215, 218, 220–223; as vehicular bridge, 197, 204–205, 208–219, *210*. See also Verrazzano-Narrows Bridge
Narrows crossing, 9, 162–168, 173–174, 201, 203–206, 310n29; automobiles influencing, 157–159; NYCTA controlling, *194*, 195–197, *198*, 199, 203
Narrows dual-purpose/Hylan tunnel, *118*, *120*, *145*, 156, 167, 188–189, 197, *198*, 205, 213, 313n63, 319n40; Citizens Union against, 138, 164; delays, 137, 141–144, 146–147; failure of, 134–135, 147–152, *198*; feasibility, 117–125, 138, 147–148; injunction against, 75, 83, 138, 318n20; Narrows subway tunnel reusing, 171, 329n63; Port Authority countering, 110, *122*, 123–129, 135–139, 143, 147, 149–150, 313n66, 314n78, 314n88, 320n49; private railroads on, 110, 117–121, 129–130, 138, 148, 323n78; proposed routes, 117–121, *120*, *122*, 208, 318n21, 326n14
Narrows freight tunnel, 65, 66, 188–189
Narrows tunnel (rapid transit), 151, 169, *170*, 172–174, *198*, 203, *207*, 329n63; Board of Estimate on, 161–162, 181–183, 188; Board of Transportation on, 156, 175–176, 182–183, 204, 332n32; bridges *vs.*, 159–162; Delaney opposing, 171, 175–176, 191–192, 203–204, 231n55; freight tunnel *vs.*, 183–199; Lynch supporting, 159, 161, 168, 171, 326n13; pre-Dual Contracts, 66, 67–80, *69*, 72–73, *74*, 75, *76*, 77–80, 95–96, 101; RFC funding sought for,

177–180; vehicular tunnel *vs.*, 188–197, *194*, *197*; WPA funding sought for, 180–187. See also Dual Contracts; rapid transit; subways; subway tunnel
Narrows tunnel (vehicular), 155–159, 168–169, 173–174, 190–197, *194*, *198*, 199, 203–204, 216, 312n47, 329n63, 330n83, 337n84; Bridge Committee on, 163–167; Transportation Committee on, 155–156
Nassau county, 253–254, 285n14
nativity/country of birth, 21, 22, 226, *253*, 350n30
neglected, Staten Island as, 2–3, 58, 123, 134–135, 226, 270
New Deal, 7, 9, 176–177, 180–187, 197, 269, 334n57
New Jersey, 26, 36, 52, 65, 67, 117, *122*, 345n95; on Narrows rail tunnel routes, 72–73; Port Authority bridges to Staten Island, 143, 158–159, 161, 163–164, 188, 208; as suburban competition, 54, 173, 273, 316n97
News Letter (newspaper), 53, 276
newspapers, 75, 78, 87–88, 138, 275–277, 302n29, 323n86; on Narrows rail tunnel, 95–96; pre-consolidation, 25–26. See also specific newspapers
New York City. *See* Greater New York/New York City
New York City Tunnel Authority (NYCTA), 193, 203–204; Narrows crossing controlled by, *194*, 195–197, *198*, 199, 203; on Narrows vehicular tunnel, 190–197, *194*, *198*, 199; Port Authority and, 208–213, *210*
New York Harbor, 48, 52, *122*, *145*, 148, 208, 223, 283n20, 298n16; pre-consolidation, 28, 29, *30*, 32
New York–New Jersey Port and Harbor Development Commission, 112–113
New York Times, 78–79, 143, 151, 164, 165, 195, 199, 208, 239, 323n86; on consolidation, 31, 40, 291n58; on Cromwell proposal, 90; on Dual Contracts, 101; on *Joint Study*, 347n105; on Narrows Bridge, 191, 211, 215, 217, 223; on Staten Island, 15, 49
New York Traffic Commission, *207*
New-York Tribune, 127
Nicholson, George, 323n83
Nicoll, Courtland, 147–149
Nicoll-Hofstadter Act, 148–149, 150–151, 160–161, 184, 188, 330n79
non-European immigrants, *250*–251, 253–254, *254*

Norway/Norwegian immigrants, 252, *253*, 259
NYCTA. *See* New York City Tunnel Authority

O'Brien, John, 179, 182–183, 190, 331n16
occupations, 226, 235, *236–238*, 237, 272; pre-consolidation, 19, *19*
O'Dwyer, William, 205
Olmsted, Frederick Law, 13–14, 16, 33–34
Ordeman, Herman W., 175–176, 183, 186, 196, 334n54
other/otherness, 3, 15, 270
outer belt line, 116–117, 119–120, 123, 163, 195
outer boroughs, 3–4, 7–8, 57, 69, 252, 268–269; African Americans in, 255, *255*; development of, 136, 212; immigrants in, 248–249
Outerbridge, Eugenius, 121, 123–124, 127–130, 312n47, 312n60, 315n91, 315n95, 327n33; on Board of Estimate, 314n78; consolidation opposed by, 35
out-migration, Manhattan, 248, 254, 351n37
Oxholm, Theodore, 171, 309n25, 327n33

Palma, Joseph, 185–188, 189–191, 193, 200–201, 203–204, 260, 333n38, 335n60, 337n85; Committee of Twelve formed by, 186–188, 334n54; La Guardia and, 336n72, 336n78; Moses and, 195, 337n86, 339n2
parking lots, 231–232
parks, 59, 164, 185, 201–202, 231, 299n31
parkways, 201–202, *207*, 209
Parsons, William Barclay, 78
"pay-as-you-go" policy, 143, 146, 320n47
Pennsylvania Railroad Company (PRR), 89, 110, 118–119, *122*, 128–132, 189, 269, 309n21, 310n33, 315n92, 320n48; B&O influenced by, 99, 101, 117, 143, 199, 311nn36–37, 314n88; Hylan countering, 8–9, 323n83
people of color, 270–271, 273–274
physical link, Staten Island to Greater New York, 64, *107*, 130, 134, 188–197, *198*, 199, 204, 211, 267–268. *See also* Narrows crossing
Pinney, George M., Jr., 39–40, 42
Platt, Thomas, 31, 40–42, 45
Poland/Polish immigrants, 252, *253*
police, 25, 34, 45, 133, 187, *236–237*, 241, 243, 267, 288n17
political: consolidation, 36–37, 41, 70–71, 227, 260–262; isolation, 59, 181
politics: localized, 14, 25, 28, 60, 77, 109, 147, 267; transportation, 10, 64, 109–110, 132, 157
"polynuclear" pattern, 4, 283n17
population density, 90, 202, 227, 228, 229, 265–266, 297n13; commutes and, 233, 234, 235; Dual Contracts impacting, 158–159; pre-consolidation, 15–16, 28; Staten Island, 4, 9–10, 217–218
population growth, 28, 68, 136, 167–168, 199, 202, 265–266, 346n98, 351n37; Bronx, *17*, 79, 226–228, *228*, 229, 298n25, 348n1; Brooklyn, *17*, 227, *228*, 229, 266, 268; consolidation causing, 16–18, 227, 228, 229, 267–268; expectations about, 2, 52–53, 134, 271–272, 342n28; Manhattan, *17*, 228, 229; projections, 271–272; Queens, 16–17, *17*, 227, *228*, 229, 265–266, 268
Port Authority of New York and New Jersey, 265, 269, 309n15, 335n66, 347nn114–116; Comprehensive Plan, 121, 123–125, 127–130, 135–136, 188, 221, 316n99; formation of, 111–112, 316n97; Hylan/Narrows dual-purpose tunnel countered by, 110, *122*, 123–129, 135–139, 143, 147, 149–150, 313n66, 314n78, 314n88, 320n49; Hylan opposing, 8–9, 108, 123–129, 314n86, 316n97; *Joint Study*, 208–213, *210*, 215, 219–220, 223, 272, 347n105; on Narrows Bridge, 9, 211, 221, 223, 344n71, 344n75; on Narrows subway tunnel, 188–190; NYCTA and, 208–213, *210*; PATH trains, 299n35; power of, 221–222, 309n15, 347n114; Staten Island–New Jersey bridges, 143, 158–159, 163–164, 188, 208; TBTA and, 9, 208–213, *210*; Tribus on, 312n61. *See also* Greenville–Bay Ridge tunnel
postwar, 194, 202, 205, 217, 241, 272–273
Post-War Planning and Capital Reserve Fund, New York State, 193–194
Pouch, Alfred, 204–205, 334n54, 341n20
Pouch, Alonzo, 304n51
Pouch, Oscar, 341n24
poverty, 32, 193, 273
power, 129–132, 134–135, 139, 184, 189; Board of Estimate, 44, 112–114; of Port Authority, 221–222, 309n15, 347n114
Prall, Anning, 178–179, 181–182, 186, 327n33
pre-consolidation, 13; agriculture/agricultural sector, 14, 16, 19, *19*, 28; Brooklyn, 14–15, 20, *20*, 31; debts, 21, 43, 46–47; domestic sector, *19*, 19–20; European immigrants, 21, 22, *22*; ferries, 16–17, 26, 28, 32; infrastructure, 14, 25–26, 28, 32; New York Harbor, 28, 29, *30*, 32; Queens, 16–18, 20, *20*, 23, 28; religion, 23–24, *23–24*
Prendergast, William, 85–86, 87, 302n12
private sector, 5–6, 9–10, 96, 106, 114, 143, 157, 162, 177, 215, 269, 320n47. *See also* railroads, private

professional class/sector, 71, 236–238, 237, 240, *241*, 272, 349n17; pre-consolidation, 19, *19*
profits/profitability, 4–5, 50, 64, 73, 80, 83, 88–89, 92–94, 125–126
projections, 271–272; revenue, 125–126, 148, 175, 180; ridership, 67–69, 175, 269, 332n32. *See also* costs, projected; growth, projected
property owners, 32, 51, 53, 64, 87, 219–221, 295n24
property taxes, 36–37, 45–46, 88, 346n98, 347n112
property values, 1, 36, 60, 104, 197, 286n25, 323n84, 347n112; pre-consolidation, 20–21; rapid-transit impacting, 65–67; Verrazzano-Narrows Bridge impacting, 267–268
Protestants, 21, 24, 256, *258*, 259–260
PRR. *See* Pennsylvania Railroad
PSC. *See* Public Service Commission
public authorities, 45–46, 162–163, 190–191, 208–213, 336n73, 337n79. *See also specific authorities*
public schools, 45, 261–262, *263*–264
public sector, 235, 236–238, *237*, 239, *240*, *241*, 349n11
Public Service Commission (PSC), 63–64, 300n46, 307n119; Board of Estimate and, 82–89; on Dual Contracts subway expansion, 89–103; RTB conflict with, 73–80, 85, 106; SICC and, 86, 88–89, 94, 102–103; Triborough Plan, *69*, 82–92, 96, 106
public works, 176–186, 190, 197, 333n38, 334n57
Public Works Administration (PWA), 176, 180–188, 190, 197, 199, 332n31, 334n57
Puerto Rico/Puerto Ricans, 254
PWA. *See* Public Works Administration

quarantine house, 16, 34, 289n19
Queens, 42, 136, 143, *230*, 248, *257*; African Americans in, *255*, 255–256; commutes to, 233, *234*; on consolidation, 290n41; employment in, 237–238; immigrants in, *247*, 249, *250*–251, 254; median family income, 245, *246*, 273; population grown in, 16–17, *17*, 227, *228*, 229, 265–266, 268; pre-consolidation, 16–18, 20, *20*, 23, 28
Queens Chamber of Commerce, 163, 315n96
Queens–Midtown Tunnel, 164, 172–173, 178, 184–185, 190, 192, 330n82, 330n86
Queens–Midtown Tunnel Authority. *See* New York City Transit Authority

race, 187, 270, 283n21; education and, 262, *264*, 265; pre-consolidation, 21, 22, 23, 28. *See also* ethnic makeup
Radford, Gail, 336n73
Radigan, Edmund P., 205
Rae, Douglas, 284n28
railroad engineers, 142, 147, 151–152, 310n33, 314n82, 315n92; Tuttle and Wilgus consulting with, 114, 116–117, 119–121, 127
railroads, private, 2, 68, 93, *118*, 183–189, 202, 215, 341n21, 342n28; failed negotiations with, 114, 126, 129–132, 167, 213; on Hylan/Narrows dual-purpose tunnel, 110, 117–121, 129–130, 138, 148, 323n78; pre-consolidation, 16–17, 26; roads *vs.*, 157, 162–168; steam, 6, 77, 300n56. *See also* freight railroads; *specific companies*
rallies, 38, 56–57, 93–94, 170–171, 173, 185, 319n33, 322n68, 329n77
Ramsey, John, 169
rapid-transit, 1–6, 70, 158, 167, 311n43, 341n21, 345n96; absence of, 63, 268–269; automobiles impacting, 9, 157–159; Board of Estimate on, 304n64, 332n31; demand for, 203–204, 269–270; failed attempts at, 10, 79, 213–219, 224, 226; growth and, 64–68, *66*, 75; in Hylan/Narrows dual-purpose tunnel plans, 137–139, *145*, 147–148; Narrows rail tunnel as, 67–80, *69*, *74*, *76*; proposed for Narrows Bridge, 213–219; tunnels, 111–112, 159–162, 324n92. *See also* dual-purpose tunnels (freight and rapid-transit); subways
Rapid Transit Act (1894), 68
Rawson, Sidney, 38–39, 57, 291n52
Rea, Samuel, 113–114, *118*, 129, 309n21, 311nn34–35, 315nn90–92, 320n48; B&O influenced by, 99, 101, 117, 143, 199, 311nn36–37, 314n88
real-estate, 1, 20, 51, 64, 167, 211, 324n88; employment in, 235, 236–238, *237*, 239, 349n17; rapid-transit benefiting, 65–67, 70
Real Estate Board, Staten Island, 168, 190, 216, 218, 329n75
Reconstruction Finance Corporation (RFC), 177–181
referendums, 274, 289n27; consolidation, 31–33, 36–39, *38*, 48, 56–60, 267–268, 290n41
reformers, 84–85, 106, 109–111, 192–193, 261, 291n48, 341n36
Regional Plan Association, 163, 214–215, 272, 317n6
regional planning, 135–136, 157–159, 163

Regional Plan of New York and Its Environs, 126, 135
religion, 226, 256, *257–258*, 259–260, 286n30, 351n38, 352nn40–41; preconsolidation, 23–24, *23–24*. See also specific religions
rentals, housing, 231, *231*
Republicans, 110–112, 137, 141, 147–149, 152, 273, 276–277; consolidation and, 25–26, 51. See also Fusion candidates
resignations, 162, 179, 331n16
restaurant/saloon workers, *236–237*, 241, *243*, 244
retail sector, *236–238*, *237*, *239*, *240*
Revell, Keith, 109, 144, 320n47
revenues, 67, 99, 148, 173, 196–197, 202, 208, 332n18; generation of, 160–161, 208; projected, 125–126, 175, 179–180, 332n32, 334n49
Reynaud, George, 209n16
RFC. See Reconstruction Finance Corporation
Richmond Borough Separation League, 46
Richmond County Advance. See *Staten Island Advance/Richmond County Advance* (newspaper)
Richmond County chapter, SPE, 168–169, 174, 214, 329n75, 341n24
Richmond County Democrat (newspaper), 37, 91, 276
Richmond County Herald (newspaper), 276
Richmond County Sentinel (newspaper), 35, 56–57, 276
Richmond County Standard (newspaper), 35, 37, 54, 276
Richmond County/Staten Island. See specific topics
Richmond Light and Railroad Company, 300nn56–57
Richmond Realty Association, 70–71
ridership, 203, 325n2; declining, 157–159; projected, 67–68, 99–100, 175, 269, 332n32; trolley, 17–18
Ridgeway, Robert, 313n67
right-of-way property, 142, 197
roads, 32, 45, 157, 162–168, 211
Robillard, Charles, 337n79
Robinson, Holton D., 162, 327n30
Rockefeller, Nelson, 223, 267
Roosevelt, Franklin D., 179, 189–190, 335n60, 342n36; New Deal programs by, 176, 180–187
routes, *105*, 268–269, 342n37; Fourth Avenue, 85–87, 89, 169, 183; Greenville–Bay Ridge tunnel, 188–189; Hylan/Narrows dual-purpose tunnel, 117–121, *120*, *122*, 208, 318n21, 326n14; Narrows Bridge related, 220–223; Narrows rail tunnel, *66*, 67–75, *69*, 72–73, *74*, *75*, *76*, 77–78; Narrows vehicular tunnel, 159–162, 167; proposed subway to Bayonne, 90, 166, 169, 341n21; Smith and Ninth Street, 169, *170*, 183, 186
RTB. See Board of Rapid Transit Railroad Commissioners
rural: identity, 50, 232; Staten Island as, 14–15, 18, 225, 232–233, 270
Russia/Russian immigrants, 21, 22, 249, 252, *253*
Ruttenau, Max, 303n41, 304n63, 306n103

Sachs, Charles, 4, 18, 340n6
Salmon, Edwin A., 195, 338n101
Sayre, Wallace S., 340n10
Scandinavia/Scandinavian immigrants, 21, 22, 245, 249, 259
schools, 25, 56, 146, 180, 211; attendance, 262, *263–264*, 265; enrollment, 261, *263–264*, 352n49, 353n52; high, 45, 185, 193, 261–262, 265, 268, 352n49, 353n51; public, 45, 261–262, *263–264*
Schwab, A. L., 304n61
Schwartz, Joel, 202
Scientific American, 265
Scotland/Scottish immigrants, 21, 22, 245, 249
Scott, Francis M., 41, 291n58, 291n61
Seaman, Henry, 73, 75
Sea View Hospital, 47, 79, 185
secession movement, 2–3, 47–48, 274
Second Avenue Subway, 215, 345n87
second-generation immigrants, 229, 246, *247*, 248–249, 350n25
self-liquidating mandate, 177, 189; PWA, 181–182, 184–185; RFC, 177–180
Senate, New York state, 149, 273, 289n20
September 11 attacks, 241
sewers systems, 57, 87–88, 144, 187
shafts, Hylan tunnel. See Narrows dual-purpose/Hylan tunnel
shield tunnel method, 142, 146, 152, 172, 337n85
Shonts, T. P., 96–97, 99
Shortt, William A., 292n73
SICC. See Staten Island Chamber of Commerce
Simons, Walter, 324n88
single-family homes, 202, 217–218, 229, *230*, *231*
Singstad, Ole, 164–165, 169, 193–196, 328n48
slavery, 23

Smith, Al, 9, 110–111, 127, 135, 140–141, 144, 146–150, 151–152, 322n69; governor, 135, 140–141; on Hylan, 316n97; on PSC, 307n119; speech by, 129, 315n95
Smith, C. Ernest, 112, 139, 148, 308n11, 309n19, 334n54
Smith, Jason Scott, 181
Smith, Morton W., 82
Smith, R. Penn, 35
Smith Act, 112–114, 117, 123, 125, 137–138, 141, 313n66, 317n14, 318nn19–20
Smith and Ninth Street, 169, *170*, 182–183, 186
Society of Professional Engineers and Land Surveyors (SPE), New York State, 168–169, *170*, 171–174, 203, 214, 329n75, 341n24
South Brooklyn, 8, 69, *69*, 89–90, *170*, 303n31, 304n58; tunnel to, 71, 95, 157, 182, 185
South Richmond Plan, 273–274
Spargo, George, 196, 205
SPE. *See* Society of Professional Engineers and Land Surveyors, New York State
special assessments, 86–88, 302n22, 303n31
special committee (Hylan administration and railroads), 114, *122*, 309n25, *122*, 310n26
Spender, Frederick, 342n28
Spratt, Theodore, 334n54
S. R. Smith Infirmary, 43, 292n71
Stafford, De Witt, 292n73
Stapleton piers, *113*, 114, 119, 125, 184, 217, 312n60, 333n38
State Assembly, New York, 190, 222, 274
State Legislature, New York State, 65, 110–111, 129–130, 134–135, 152, 184, 192, 195, 297n4
Staten Island Advance/Richmond County Advance (newspaper), 2, 4, 168, 200–201, 204, 275–276, 353n1; on Comprehensive Plan, 123–124; on consolidation, 35, 54, 289n30; on Cromwell, 90–91, 96–98; on ferry service, 77, *150*; on Hylan/Narrows dual-purpose tunnel, 144, 148, 151; on Moses, 98, 345n96, 346; on Narrows Bridge, 161, 165, 211–214, 215, 218–219, 223; on Narrows rapid transit tunnel, 85, *145*, 161–162, 171, 178, 182–183, 185–186, 189; on Narrows vehicular tunnel, 165, 192, 195; on subway expansion, 93–94, 102
Staten Island/borough of Richmond. *See specific topics*
Staten Island Chamber of Commerce (SICC), 121, 124, 298n14, 299n31; City Charter Committee, 39–40, 43; Civic League and, 312n60, 324n91; on consolidation, 53–54, 292n73; on Narrows Bridge, 161–162, 165–167, 203, 211, 214–219, 223–224, 345n94, 348n126; on Narrows rapid transit tunnel, 67, 71–73, *74*, 75, *76*, 77–80, 102, 179, 182; on Narrows vehicular tunnel, 165–166, 192; PSC and, 86, 88–89, 94, 102–103; on rapid transit, 298n14, 304n63; Subway and Transit Committee, 86, 212, 304n61; Transportation Committee, 70–71, 155–157, 206, 212
Staten Islander (newspaper), 31, 90, 95–96, 123, 148, 151, 160–161, 276, 312n61; on consolidation, 35–37, 44–45, 51–57, 59
Staten Island Improvement Commission, 16
Staten Island Independent (newspaper), 31, 37, 56, 276
Staten Island Leader (newspaper), 276–277
Staten Island Light (newspaper), 277
Staten Island–Manhattan tunnel, 309n19; direct subway, 104, *105*, 106
Staten Island Midland Railway Company, 300n56
Staten Island–New Jersey bridges, Port Authority, 143, 158–159, 163–164, 188, 208
Staten Island Railway, 2, 202, 235
Staten Island Rapid Transit Railway Company, 26, *27*, 65, 123, 287n34, 300nn56–57, 336n72
Staten Island Times-Transcript (newspaper), 186, 192, 197, 277
Staten Island World (newspaper), 80, 82, 90–91, 277
State Senate, New York, 35, 112, 139–140, 149, 190, 222, 273, 289n20
steam railroads, 6, 77, 300n56
Steinman, David, 162, 184–185, 205, 328n48, 341n20
St. George, ferry service to, 16–17, 26, 36, 45
Strong, William, 41, 45, 291n61
suburbs/suburbanization, 157–159, 202, 226–227, 229, 265, 325n4; pre-consolidation, 13–15, 32; Staten Island as, 51–54
subway, New York City, 157, 213–214, 233, *234*, 268, 333n40; city-owned/independent, 9, 100, 111–112, 140, 159–160; Contract No. 1, 6–7, 68–69, 298nn18–19; Contract No. 2, 69, 69–70, 71–72, 77, 269, 298n19; direct Staten Island-Manhattan line, 104, *105*, 106–107; fares, 143, 160, 168–169, 308n10; free transfers for, 306n113; population growth and, 227, 229. *See also* Dual Contracts (1913); expansion, subway; Fourth Avenue subway line; *specific lines*

Subway and Transit Committee, SICC, 86, 212, 304n61
subway tunnel, Staten Island/Narrows, 8, 115, 188–197, *194*, *198*, 199, 254; absence of, 63–64, 241, 249, 270; Great Depression impacting, 9; Morrison supporting, 63–64; PWA and, 180–187; RFC and, 177–180
Suffolk county, 21, *23*, 216, 253–254
Sunnyside Hospital, 220
suspension bridge, 161–162, 191, 209

Talbot, James, 334n54
Tammany Hall, 25, 35–37, 56–58, 109, 140–141, 147–148, 151, 337n86
taxes, 67, 68, 86–87, 222, 286n26, 293n97, 320n47; consolidation and, 31, 35, 38, 40–42, 44–48, 50–51, 58; property, 36–37, 45–46, 88, 346n98, 347n112
TBTA. *See* Triborough Bridge and Tunnel Authority
TCC. *See* Transit Construction Commission, New York
technologies, 157, 284n28
Temple, E. B., 119, 126–127, 129, 310n33, 311n37, 315n90
Thaten, Max, 123–124, 128, 130, 139, 141, 144, 303n41, 312n52, 327n33
Theodore Roosevelt (ferryboat), 133
Tiernan, Harry, 324n97
Tobin, Austin, 212, 218, 342n37
tolls, 167, 329n63, 330n83, 337n85
Tomkins, Calvin, 100
topography. *See* geography/geographic location
Tottenville High School, 185, 193, 262
towns/townships, 14, 16, 25, 37, 43, 46, 55–56, 77, 265, 275
Tracy, Benjamin F., 42
trade sector, 235, *236–238*, *237*, *240*, 241; pre-consolidation, 19, *19*
traffic, 59, 163; rail, 84, 116, 120–121, 125, 127, 137, 157, 204, 219, 314n88
traffic, vehicular, 159, 164, 165, 192, 271, 274, 330n83, 346nn97–98; arterial highways and, *207*, 208–213, *210*, 342n37; Moses addressing, 201–202; Traffic Commission and, *207*
Transit Commission, New York, 110, 113, 136, 313n66, 319n32, 322n77; Hylan opposing, 108, 114, 127–129, 318n26, 321nn52–53, 322n69; McAneny chairing, 111, 125, 138–140, 159–160; McAvoy Report, 147–149, 160; on subway expansion, 111, 124–125, 138, 143, 318n26
Transit Committee, Board of Estimate, 91–103, *95*

Transit Conference, 169, 171, 175–176, 189, 196–197, 203, 329n75, 332n18; New Deal funding sought by, 180–187; RFC federal funding sought by, 176–180
Transit Construction Commission (TCC), New York, 106, 108, 111, 307nn119–120
transportation. *See specific topics*
Transportation Committee, SICC, 70–71, 155–156, 157, 206, 212
transportation politics, 10, 64, 109–110, 132, 157
transportation sector, 235, *236–238*, *237*, 239, *240*, 241
trench tunnel method, 142, 146, 152, 172
Triborough Bridge, 164, 167, 172, 173, 178–179, 184, 187, 330n83
Triborough Bridge and Tunnel Authority (TBTA), 190, 196, 199, 200–201, 204–206; *Joint Study* by, 272, 347n105; on Narrows Bridge, 208, 214–215, 218, 220–223; Port Authority and, 9, 208–213, *210*
Triborough Bridge Authority, 190, 196, 203–204
Triborough Plan, PSC, 69, 82–92, 96, 106
Tribus, Louis, 94, 102, 128, 139, 161, 212, 304n61, 312n61, 327n33
trolleys, 6, 17–18, 26, *27*, 77, 137, 158, 187, 206
trunk lines. *See* railroads/railroad companies
Tubular Transit Company of Staten Island, 65
tunnels, 32, 269, 297n4, 298n16, 307n120, 319n41, 330n85; bridges *vs.*, 80, 159–162, 186–187, 191, 202–206, *207*, 208; freight, 183–199, 324n92; multipurpose, 83, 94–95, 101, 130–131; shield *vs.* trench method for, 142, 146, 152, 172; subway, 178–179, 185, 188–197, *194*, *198*, 199. *See also* dual-purpose tunnels (freight and rapid-transit); *specific tunnels*
Turner, Daniel, 159, 315n92, 326n15
Tuttle, Arthur, 137–138, 141–142, 310n33, 322n67, 332n32, 344n72; consulting with railroad engineers, 114, 116–117, 119–121, 126–127; dual-purpose tunnel supported by, 125–129, 317n15; on Special Committee, 309n25, 310n26
Tuttle, Charles (on rapid transit for Narrows Bridge), 215–219, 344n72, 345n82
Tysen, David, 52, 71, 77, 89–90, 96–97, 292n73, 295n14, 297n8, 303n41, 304n61

unemployment, 173, 239; New Deal programs addressing, 180–187; RFC addressing, 177–180

Union Free School Act, New York State, 261–262
United Kingdom/British immigrants, 252, 253
United States (U.S.), 157–159, 180–187, 202, 245; agriculture in, 232–233; Army, 181, 218–221; Congress, 65, 184–185, 193, 273; Interstate Highway Act, 209. *See also* Census Bureau, U.S.; War Department, U.S.; *specific programs*
unprofitable, 67, 80, 88–89, 94, 106
urban areas/urban development, 8, 14, 16–17, 109, 157, 270; Staten Island as, 18–21, 23–24
urban-rural dichotomies, 14, 21, 50
U.S. *See* United States

vacation destination, 15
Van Clief, William, 67–68, 86, 88–90, 94, 100, 297n6, 298n14, 302n14, 303n41
Vanderbilt, Cornelius, 26
Van Name, Calvin, 112, 114, *115*, 123, 309n24
vehicular bridges, 9, 186, 202; Narrows bridges as, 197, 204–205, 208–219, *210*
vehicular tunnels, 312n47, 337n85; Narrows rapid transit tunnel *vs.*, 188–197, *194*, *198*, 199. *See also* Narrows Tunnel (vehicular)
Verrazzano-Narrows Bridge, 1–2, 4, 201–202, 219–224, 233, 266, 268, 271–272, 273, 282n10, 347n106, 348n124, 348n126
Verrazzano, Giovanni da, 223
Vigilantes, Staten Island, 193
villages, 14, 16, 25, 37, 43, 55–56, 77, 265, 275
Von Kromer, George, 65–68, 72, 74–75, 85, 90–91, 300n46
voting, 5, 25, 305n80, 314n82, 319n37, 329n75; in consolidation referendum, 31–33, 36–39 , *38*, 48, 267–268, 290n41

Wagner, Robert, 179
Wagner, Robert, Jr., 220–222, 267
Walker, James J., 9, 151–152, 178–179, 216, 324n95; City Committee established by, 162, 327n33; Narrows vehicular tunnel supported by, 156–157, 163–165, 167–168, 171–172; resignation of, 162, 179, 331n16
Wallace, Mike, 237
Walsh, Thomas, 161
war, 193, 298n16

War Department, U.S., 156, 165, 172, 191, 192–193, 328n48, 337n83; Narrows Bridge approved by, 161, 208, 210–211, 309n24
Waring, George, 58–59
water supply/lines, 45, 59, 87, 144, 185, 187, 190, 296n65; in multi-purpose tunnels, 94–95, 97, 101, 107, 109
Weil, François, 45
Welsh, William J., 130, 306n103
Westchester County, 18, 20, 23, 24, 29, 31, 34, 255, 273, 288n16, 289n21
West Side Highway, 184
White, S. V., 291n61
white-collar jobs, 19–20, 239, 272
whiteness, 4, 270
white people, 4, 262, *264*, 265; as homeowners, 273–274; immigrants as, 21, 23, 246, *247*
Whitford, James, 334n54
Wilgus, William, 90, 115, 125–130, 188, 310n27, 310nn29–30, 311n35, 314n78, 317n15; consulting with railroad engineers, 114, 116–117, 119–121, 126–127; on multipurpose tunnel, 94–95
Willard, Daniel, 311n38, 313n75
Willcox, Mary Otis Gay, 149–150
Willcox, William R., 85, 92
Williams, Timothy, 95, 99
Willowbrook Parkway, 209, *210*
Wiman, Erastus, 14, 26, 28, 49, 51–55, 63, 276, 287n34, 292n80, 297nn3–4; consolidation supported by, 32, 35–36, 38, 41, 43–44, 57–59; on Narrows Freight Tunnel, 65, *66*
women, *19*, 19–20, 286n22
work. *See* employment
working-class, 5–6, 28
Works Progress Administration (WPA), 185–188, 199, 333n41, 334n57, 335n61
World War I, 114, 157, 229, 235, 245, 255, 307n119, 310n29
World War II, 4, 200–201, 229, 233, 244, 248, 254, 260–261
Worrell, Judson, 36, 38
WPA. *See* Works Progress Administration

zoning, 217–218, 343n65
Zurmuhlen, Frederick, 136, 168–169, 179, 182, 205, 217

GPSR Authorized Representative: Easy Access System Europe, Mustamäe tee 50, 10621 Tallinn, Estonia, gpsr.requests@easproject.com